Forensic Serology

Forensic Serology

Shanan S. Tobe
Forensic Science
Murdoch University
Australia

ELSEVIER

ACADEMIC PRESS
An imprint of Elsevier

Academic Press is an imprint of Elsevier
125 London Wall, London EC2Y 5AS, United Kingdom
525 B Street, Suite 1650, San Diego, CA 92101, United States
50 Hampshire Street, 5th Floor, Cambridge, MA 02139, United States

ISBN: 978-0-12-812968-5

For Information on all Academic Press publications
visit our website at https://www.elsevier.com/books-and-journals

Publisher: Peter Linsley
Editorial Project Manager: Aleksandra Packowska
Production Project Manager: Prasanna Kalyanaraman
Cover Designer: Christian Bilbow

Typeset by MPS Limited, Chennai, India
Printed in India

Last digit is the print number: 9 8 7 6 5 4 3 2 1

This work is dedicated to my family. None of this would have been possible without you.

Contents

Foreword

The beginnings of this work started over a decade ago, in the form of a chapter on serologic testing that was never published. When I was approached several years later by my editor, Liz Brown, I was still an optimistic young academic and thought the transition to a textbook would be largely straightforward with some minor updates. Instead, it has taken almost a decade to put together in its current form.

Robert E. Gaensslen published *Sourcebook in Forensic Serology, Immunology, and Biochemistry* in 1983, with an update in 1989. Gaensslen's *Sourcebook* is considered a standard reference text and covers much of the field of forensic serology from its inception through to the 1980s. It is an amazing piece of work, and after its publication, serology was generally only featured as a chapter in larger and more general forensic science texts. Gaensslen's work was published before the advancement of DNA profiling in forensic investigations, which has become an important consideration.

Forensic serology continues to be an active and relevant field essential in forensic biology and has uses stretching to medical, and even anthropologic, studies. My goal was therefore to update Gaensslen's work to consider all the numerous improvements and considerations in forensic body fluid identification since 1989. While I have not gone into genetic typing in terms of individual identification, I have included reference to the effect of the different tests on DNA when using serologic techniques in a forensic setting.

First and foremost, this is not a how-to manual for carrying out forensic serologic tests. The field is unregulated. Although certain countries/states/organizations may all use the same tests in the same order, there is no set formula or protocol for many of the tests used. Different formulas for the different types of tests, if available, can be found in the references provided. I have therefore presented the data as they have been published and provided all aspects of both beneficial findings and potential detrimental aspects. Commercial tests have standard protocols and procedures and have been included in the relevant sections, but many laboratories make changes to best suit their needs.

When I started writing, I was conscious of not overlapping too much with Gaensslen as he was extensive and thorough. As I was checking sources, however, I found that with the global push to preserve older texts, I had access to a much wider database of books and papers.

The internet has changed the way we access and do research, and most especially the resources available to us. Although Gaensslen had an incredible reference list, with some references even now I have struggled to find (and some I could not find), he was restricted to what was available in libraries he could access.

Most of the historic literature I have found on forensic serology is in non-English journals, German predominantly, but also French, Italian, Spanish, and Latin. Although the relevance of these historic works may not be immediately apparent, the history of the different tests can be important for their understanding. I have been helped with access to works that were unavailable previously through websites such as Biodiversity Heritage Library (www.biodiversitylibrary.org), Internet Archive (archive.org), Bibliothèque Nationale de France (gallica.bnf.fr), and Google Books. Those resources in combination with online translation tools provided unprecedented access to historic information. I have therefore added to the history of the forensic serologic methods while trying to keep things interesting and to the point.

I hope that you as the reader find the text interesting, useful, and complete. No artificial intelligence was used in the preparation of this text.

A/Prof Shanan (Shane) S. Tobe

Acknowledgments

This text would not have been possible without help from varied directions. First and foremost is my editor, Elizabeth Brown (Elsevier), who approached me for an idea and continued to encourage the completion of the manuscript through multiple setbacks. This included the births of my children, hospitalization, international moves, the global COVID-19 pandemic, and my endless need to procrastinate. Needless to say, this would still be sitting as an unfinished chapter if it were not for Liz.

There have also been a huge number of people who have helped in the preparation of this book, through access to their work, images, and photographs, or through discussion of findings and implications both within and outside of the forensic science field. All relevant credit has been given when images or text has been used.

Special thanks need to be given to Mrs. Amy Brodeur, Boston University, who has provided continued advice and discussion of the work throughout its long preparation, as well as many of the images used in the chapters. I have had wonderful discussions with Pamela Newall and Chantal Brazil, both experts in their respective fields. Discussions also took place with industry experts from Independent Forensics and SERATEC.

Finally, thanks to all who have spoken to me, sometimes at length, about aspects of the writing and serologic testing. My colleagues and managers have also supported me through the writing process.

Author Bio

Shanan (Shane) S. Tobe grew up near Toronto, Ontario, Canada. His original career aspirations were in line with his love of dinosaurs and paleontology, but a last-minute change in focus shifted his university education toward forensic biology with a focus in anthropology. Dr. Tobe completed a BSc Honours from Laurentian University in Canada. His undergraduate research focused on forensic anthropology looking at fresh versus frozen decomposition rates in baby pigs, but he also completed an internship in ancient DNA from Lakehead University. This sparked his interest in genetics and molecular biology. Dr. Tobe subsequently moved to Scotland to study a 1-year MSc at the University of Strathclyde, but ended up staying for almost a decade, completing a MSc, PhD, and Postdoctoral Fellowship and teaching on the university's forensic biology undergraduate program as well as the accredited (Chartered Society of Forensic Sciences) forensic science MSc. His master's research focused on presumptive blood testing in terms of sensitivity and specificity as well as the effect on DNA recovery and profiling. The resulting publication has been widely used in forensic laboratories around the word. His PhD research shifted to genetics and wildlife crime, which continued into his Leverhulme Postdoctoral Fellowship. Dr. Tobe carried out 1 year of teaching forensic science at both undergraduate and postgraduate levels, focusing on serology, DNA, bisphenol A, and other biology related to forensic science.

Dr. Tobe was awarded a Vice Chancellor's Postdoctoral Fellowship at Flinders University in Adelaide, Australia, in 2012, which took him to the opposite side of the world. Here, his research focus remained on wildlife crime and improved sensitivity in genetic testing while he taught forensic biology in the undergraduate program. In 2016, Dr. Tobe moved to the United States to take up a full academic role on the FEPAC-accredited forensic master's program at Arcadia University (near Philadelphia, Pennsylvania). Here, he redesigned and redeveloped a course on forensic serology as part of his wider teaching duties. Dr. Tobe moved back to Australia to take up a position at Murdoch University, in Perth, where he is currently an Associate Professor in Forensic Science. Throughout his academic career, Dr. Tobe has continued to carry out research on forensic serologic testing.

CHAPTER 1

Introduction, History, and Requirements of Presumptive Testing

Introduction

Serology is the detection and identification of serum or serological (biological) fluids usually in terms of detecting antibodies in those fluids and overwhelmingly in relation to health and disease. Forensic serology would therefore be the detection and identification of serum or serological fluids in a legal context. This term is currently not a true reflection of the field, but it has become a common term used to describe the *identification of body fluids in a forensic context.*

In many types of crime, it is common for some form of biological material to be transferred, and this transfer of evidence can be used to support or refute an allegation. For example, blood could be left at a theft involving breaking glass (vehicle or home), blood and saliva could be found at the scene of an assault, or a violent sexual assault case could contain biological fluids in the form of blood, saliva, and semen. This transfer of evidence is referred to as Locard's principle. In 1920, Edmond Locard,[1] considered to be a founding father of forensic science, stated in relation to fingerprints, "It should not be forgotten that the slightest touch of the finger leaves a trace, and that the complainants or neighbours, as well as law enforcement officers, by handling the objects, can overload the traces left by the criminal with their own fingerprints" (p. 106).

This is also a commentary on contamination of evidence and the need for quality assurance (QA) and quality control (QC) measures. Locard[2] developed his theory further by stating, "Any action of an individual, and obviously the violent action constituting a crime, cannot occur without leaving a trace" (p. 8).

Today, Locard's Principle, or Locard's Exchange Principle, is fundamental to forensic investigation and can be found in every criminology textbook and on many popular media shows. It was perhaps best summarized by a modern-day renowned criminalist Paul Kirk:[3]

> *Wherever he steps, whatever he touches, whatever he leaves, even unconsciously, will serve as silent evidence against him. Not only his fingerprints or his footprints, but his hair, the fibers from his clothes, the glass he breaks, the tool mark he leaves, the paint he scratches,*

Forensic Serology. DOI: http://doi.org/10.1016/B978-0-12-812968-5.00001-5

the blood or semen that he deposits or collects—all these and more bear mute witness against him. This is evidence that does not forget. It is not confused by the excitement of the moment. It is not absent because human witnesses are. It is factual evidence. Physical evidence cannot be wrong; it cannot perjure itself; it cannot be wholly absent. Only its interpretation can err. Only human failure to find it, study and understand it, can diminish its value. (p. 4)

In its most simplistic terms, Locard's principle becomes "Every contact leaves a trace," with the implication that in any crime, no matter how careful criminals may be, they will always leave something behind and/or take something away. The onus therefore lies on the investigator to not only find those traces but to recognize their significance.

One of the hurdles in an investigation is therefore not only in the location and classification of biological evidence but also in how it may have gotten there. An extension of Locard's principle involves the subsequent transfer of biologic evidence, over multiple and different levels, to multiple and different items and/or locations. The investigator must therefore consider, based on case scenarios and other experience, the transfer of biological fluids between the different components of an investigation: victim(s), suspect(s), item(s) (weapons, clothes, etc.), and scene(s).

The transfer of biological fluids can be multidirectional and can incorporate primary, secondary, or subsequent levels of transfer (Fig. 1.1). Primary transfer, for example, would include blood

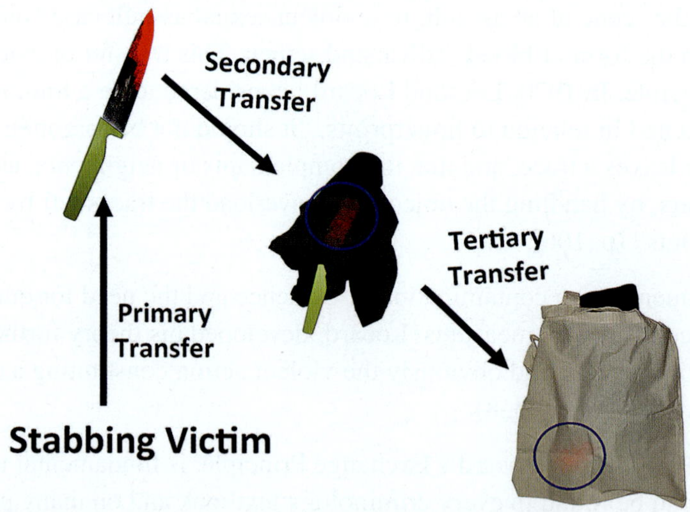

Fig. 1.1 The transfer of biologic fluids using blood as an example.
The deposit of the blood from the source (the stabbing victim wound) to a substrate (the knife) is a primary (first-degree) transfer. Secondary (second-degree) transfer occurs if the blood on the knife transfers to another substrate such as if the knife was wrapped in a shirt. Tertiary (third-degree) transfer can occur if the knife-wrapped shirt is placed into a bag and blood on the shirt subsequently stains the bag. This transfer can go on for many different levels depending on the type of fluid, its state (dry or wet), and the substrates involved in transfers.

to a knife from a stab wound or semen to a vagina after ejaculation. Those fluids can then be further transferred as secondary transfer when, for example, the blood transfers from the knife to a shirt that was subsequently used to wrap it, or the semen flows out of the vagina onto some underwear. Secondary transfer means the fluids in question were not deposited at the point of identification (shirt, underwear) from the source of those fluids (stab wound, ejaculate). These levels of transfer can take many different steps and can be a viable defense if low levels of fluids are found, and they could have plausibly been transferred through multiple levels.

Many studies have looked at the transfer of biologic evidence over several steps using DNA quantity as an indicator of transfer.[4,5] These studies showed that substrate (absorbent vs. nonabsorbent), transfer action (passive vs. active with friction), and biological fluid state (wet or dry) played distinct and important roles in the ability of a fluid to transfer.

It is therefore important to recognize that the transfer of biological evidence is not necessarily a decreasing stepwise mechanism with less and less fluid transferred at each stage, although it can be. Instead, the state of the fluid (wet or dry) and the substrate that is being transferred to, as well as where it was transferred from, all influence ability of a fluid to transfer. For example, a wet bloodstain on a knife, something that is hard and nonabsorbent, would easily be transferred to fabric from clothing (second-degree transfer), something that is soft and absorbent, with the bulk of the blood being transferred. If the bloodstained clothing is then placed in a drawer, little of the blood may be transferred to the drawer from the shirt (third-degree transfer). It is a complicated process, and any scenario provided should be considered carefully to determine where to look for potential biological stains and what to expect from multiple levels of transfer.

The biological material of interest in forensic investigations includes blood, semen, and saliva as the most common body fluids encountered, but it can also include vaginal fluid, vaginal cells, sweat, vomit, menstrual blood, fetal blood, urine, and feces. Each of these fluids will have different strategies of investigation and testing with their own specific considerations. Much of the testing in place today is based on early scientists and practitioners who developed and perfected methods for biological fluid identification hundreds of years ago.

History

The history of legal medicine — and identification of body fluids as part of that overall discipline — began thousands of years ago. By modern standards these ancient techniques may appear unscientific; however, it is important to recognize that the need to identify body fluids was significant enough that tests were developed and deemed important enough to document and record their use. The desire to identify unknown stains as a specific body fluid, particularly blood, or to identify if a body fluid is present has been discussed in the literature since at least the second century.[6] In the *Talmud*, as reported by Rosner,[6] to identify if a stain is blood:

> *Seven substances must be applied to a stain (to ascertain whether it is blood or dye): tasteless spittle, the liquid of crushed beans, urine, natron, lye (borith), Cimolian earth*

(kimonia) and lion's leaf (eshlag). If one immersed (the garment with the suspicious stain) and, ... applied to it the seven substances and the satin did not fade away, it must be a dye ... If the stain faded away or grew fainter (as a result of the application of the seven substances), it must be a bloodstain ...

The principles behind other forensic serology testing were in some cases well established and in use but had not been considered in forensic applications. For example, wet nurses used their saliva by prechewing food to make it more easily consumed and digested by infants,[7] and different cultures have used saliva as part of brewing practices to make beer.[8,9] Both of these applications use the hydrolysis of starch into sugars as their mechanism, but this was not recognized or applied to saliva until 1831.[8,10]

The first known texts relating specifically to forensic medicine originated in China in the 10th century, although these texts have all been lost and are known only from their titles and reference to their content in subsequent texts.[11] The most well-known and relevant text to forensic serology was *The Washing Away of Unjust Imputations, or Wrongs (Hsi Yuan Chi Lu)*, also known as *Instructions to Coroners* by Sung Tzu in 1247.[11,12] The original[12] and translated[13,14] texts provide instructions for identification of latent bloodstains: "Where from lapse of time the knife used shows no stains, heat it red hot in a charcoal fire and pour on it some first-rate vinegar, the marks of blood will then appear."[13]

Another passage,[13,14] recognized as the first recorded use of forensic entomology, describes a different method for latent blood identification:

An instance is given in the notes of a murder being cleared up in the following manner: The coroner who had identified the wounds as inflicted by a sickle, and had found out that a certain man had quarrelled with deceased about a loan of money, went to the village where the suspected man lived and caused every man to produce his sickle laying them on the ground before him. In a little while he turned to the suspected man and accused him of the murder. He denied his guilt with many protestations, but the coroner pointed to the flies which had singled out his sickle among seventy others, attracted by the smell of blood. The murderer confessed.

Not much else in relation to forensic serology was found around this time, but the beginnings of legal medicine took hold in the 13th century, which led to the subsequent need for forensic serology as a discipline itself. Emmert reports that, in the 13th century, state physicians and surgeons were advisers in forensic medicine.[15] He reports that in 1209, Pope Innocent III recommended appointment of physicians in cannon law, and in 1249, Hugo gave a medicolegal opinion (expert witness in today's system), although the exact details are unknown.[15]

In 1532, Holy Roman Emperor Charles V introduced a penal code that included legal medicine and the use of knowledgeable people (the original expert witness) by the courts.[16–18]

About a century later, Paolo (Pauli) Zacchiae (Zacchia) (1584–1659), considered an early father of forensic medicine (and a major influence on contemporary medicine), published *Quaestiones Medico-Legales (Medico-Legal Questions)* in nine volumes between 1621 and 1651, with complete versions published posthumously.[15,17,19,20] Within these volumes were 85 sample consultations used to illustrate his arguments and cover a wide range of medical topics, including murder, rape, postmortem intervals, cause of death, identity, and paternity. He was an expert to the Rota Romana, the highest court of appeals, and was the body physician of Pope Innocentius X. His work, however, was tainted with superstition regarding magic, demons, and witches.[17,21] Other work was published at the same time discussing medicolegal cases with a heavy emphasis on religion, but nonetheless they indicate that the medicolegal investigation of crimes was well established.[22,23]

In 1677, Antoni van Leeuwenhoek[24] published his well-known work describing sperm cells using his custom-designed microscopes, the first in existence. The size and shape of the sperm cells he described were incredibly accurate, and other than the manner in which the sperm cells move, everything else he described remains valid, with the movement of sperm only revised in 2020.[25] His initial observations still reverberate through fields, including forensic science, and the descriptions of sperm cells he offered were used for centuries as a means of identifying semen.

Schurig published a major work on semen and related investigations in 1720.[26] This 700-page work fully referenced other published work between 1535 and 1718; however, it only very loosely touched on what modern forensic serology would consider relevant, with aspects of castration, circumcision, hermaphrodites, and sex changes a focus of the text.[26] In 1751, Deinlein[22] published work on medicolegal opinions, and subsequent work by Alix[27] in 1774 focused on legal surgery. Much of the work around that time focused on medicolegal questions rather than on serological investigations. For example, Ploucquet published a diary of his investigations in 1787 on the criminal process for different types of homicides,[28] and Hunter published a text with a series of his papers in 1786 that covered aspects such as poisoning and smallpox on pregnant women and their fetuses.[29]

The first dedicated research on serological aspects of forensic science started to appear in the early 1800s, with Barruel offering commentary in 1826 on the identification of semen in a legal case.[30] This was followed by another report a year later by Orfila, also investigating semen.[31] At this time, microscopic observation of sperm cells was considered conclusive proof of semen, even at the early stage of forensic serology, but the researchers were also using smell, texture, texture when wet, appearance under candlelight, solubility in different liquids, and other equally subjective methods in their analyses.

In 1829, Barruel[32] put forth research that claimed to distinguish species of origin of blood and determine if a human blood sample was from a male or a female. His method involved subjecting the blood to boiling with sulfuric acid and using the smell emitted from that process to determine the sex and/or species of origin. His evaluation of the smells from different blood follows:

1. That of man gives off a strong smell of sweat of a man that it is impossible to confuse with any other.
2. That of the woman, a similar smell, but much less strong, finally that of woman's sweat.
3. That of a cow a strong smell of Bouverie or that of beef bouze.
4. That of the horse, a strong smell of horse sweat or dung.

Barruel also gave examples for sheep, dog, pig, and rat with equally distinct smells.[32] Other authors also used this technique and found it to be reliable.[33] Around the same time, in 1835, an indication of the awareness of contamination and the need for continuity of evidence was reported as a comment in a larger case report on a homicide: "The integrity of the seals having been noted, the package was opened and the clothes were removed."[33]

Studies in forensic medicine and serology became more widespread, and summaries of previous works began to appear.[34,35] The scope and potential of forensic investigation were also expanding, with scientists looking at new ways to apply the innovative and continually developing tests. For example, Ollivier in 1838 described new ways in which he used the microscope to investigate a multiple homicide, which involved looking at axe heads and differentiating between rust and blood (noting that many other tests of the time could not), and hair. It was around this time that blood crystals were noted and used for identification,[36–41] a form of testing that is still in use today.

Papers on research into different aspects of forensic serology and descriptions of cases became quite regular in the scientific literature around this time. Aspects of blood,[35,39,40,42–46] semen,[35,45,47–53] and other body fluids such as feces[35] and vaginal mucus[45] were being published regularly. Each of these studies confirmed the validity of previous tests and acted as further validation in terms of sensitivity and specificity of the tests. Of particular interest is a paper by Cauvet in 1875,[45] in what appears to be the first to deal with body fluid mixtures (blood and vaginal mucus, and blood and semen) from a sexual assault case. Previous studies focused on identification and potential confusing substances but not as mixtures whose components each needed identification. Other targets were also being investigated that to date were not commonplace. Robin and Tardieu[54] describe testing for meconium and fetal coating in a case of infanticide.

In 1885, Florence[55] published *Blood Stains: Their Meaning, Their Importance in Forensic Medicine*. Despite the title, the text details bloodstains and stains that resemble them; sexual organ fluids (semen and vaginal fluid); amniotic fluid, fetal coating, and milk; saliva, sputum, and nasal mucus; and other tissues. It then goes into plant juices, vegetable and organic colors, mud, colorants, ink, and other things that could make stains and be confused for other body fluids.

A decade later, between 1895 and 1901, a major discovery quickly and significantly influenced not only forensic science but medicine in its entirety. The property of agglutination due to antigen and antibody reactions (both terms undefined at that time) was discovered and applied to cholera and typhus testing.[56–59] Within 5 years, Karl Landsteiner applied them to human blood and made his historic discovery of the ABO blood groups, which thereafter revolutionized medicine and ultimately became the first genetic method to link a sample to a person.[60,61] Studies confirming Landsteiner's work were quick to follow, with some authors offering different names for the groups observed (I, II, III, IV), but the initial observations were confirmed and accepted.[62–65] Over the next 60 years, many further blood group markers were discovered and their inheritance and frequencies in different populations studied. From this point forward, much of the early work in medicolegal serology was heavily focused on these blood grouping tests via ABO and related systems, which is the origin of the term forensic serology. Landsteiner later went on to determine that some of the group specific markers could also be found in semen.[66]

From around 1900 onwards, testing was developed for many different body fluid targets that are still in use today. These tests were either developed or applied to forensic evidence for the first time during this period. In 1919, Wood,[67] looking at alternate light sources (ALS) for communication, made the observation that people also showed reaction to the different wavelengths of light and theorized that this could be used for tissue identification. In 1904, blood testing saw the introduction of benzidine and leucomalachite green,[68] luminol was first synthesized in 1902,[69] orthotolidine was first applied to blood detection in 1912,[70] and phenolphthalein was first reacted with blood in 1903,[71] having previously been used to detect oxidases in potatoes in 1901.[72] Semen identification saw the discovery of acid phosphatase (AP) in 1925,[73] where it was discovered in urine, but 10 years later it was found in much higher concentrations in the prostate[74,75] and used for semen identification. Prostate specific antigen was discovered around 1966.[76]

As forensic serology became more prominent and its significance in terms of body fluid detection and use in criminal investigation was realized, more and more investigations were made into developing standardized and useful assays. One of the first major texts on forensic serology was published in 1907 by Sutherland[77] and covered the identification of blood in detail. Sutherland unsuccessfully attempted to identify the point when the medicolegal importance of bloodstains first came to be recognized. The need and the relevance of forensic serology developed over time and largely through interest and experimentation rather than as a response to a specific legal need. Much of the testing we use as forensic biologists were first applied to other, often completely unrelated things. However, once the potential use in criminal investigations was realized, they were quickly and thoroughly investigated and used in criminal casework.

Need for and Requirements of Presumptive Testing

The nature of an allegation will determine which body fluid(s) will be targeted for search during scene or evidence evaluation. Each body fluid will have its own workflow, and any expectation of finding of mixed fluids must be assessed (Fig. 1.2). Investigations will follow a predictable sequence when determining if there is a potential crime and if an investigation is needed. If biological fluids are expected based on the allegations, then there are several further steps that an investigator would take.

The first question an investigator, either at the crime scene or in the laboratory, must answer is, *Is there a stain*? Although this may seem simple or obvious when considering a recent bloodstain, for example, it can be much more complex. Stains such as saliva, semen, or urine can be hard to see when they are dry, and all biological fluids may not form clear stains if they have been washed, whether through age, weather, or to remove them. Locating areas of potential staining can therefore be a major aspect of an investigation, and prescreening methods such as ALS have been known for over 100 years;[67] even prior to this, scientists used different lighting techniques (e.g., candlelight from behind an item) to identify potential stains for further analysis. Some of the developed testing allows screening of large areas for blood (luminol), semen (acid phosphatase), and saliva (Phadebas paper), each of which will be discussed later.

The two fundamental questions that relate to the location of a stain are as follows: (1) Is the stain biological in nature? and (2) What biologic fluid made the stain (blood, semen, saliva, etc.)?[78,79] These questions are the fundamental goals of forensic serology. There is generally some idea of what to expect based on case allegations or scenarios (e.g., blood in a stabbing or semen in a sexual assault). Therefore investigators rarely enter a scene or examine evidence with no expectations of what they may encounter. The investigator then needs to recognize expected staining and identify any other staining that may be relevant and process those stains in a systematic, logical, and thorough manner.

Further aspects, such as who the body fluid belongs to and any alleged activity that resulted in the deposition of the body fluid, are questions generally beyond the scope of presumptive testing and usually fall to DNA analysis and other specialties in forensic investigations.

A large portion of the work of a forensic biologist is therefore in the examination of scenes or items submitted to the laboratory to search for biological stains and fluids. This is a crucial part of item examination as these stains can play a major role in an investigation and can influence the focus of an investigation, including if it will proceed at all (Fig. 1.3). Based on an allegation, if biological evidence is expected but not identified, the examination may cease, and the case may not progress.

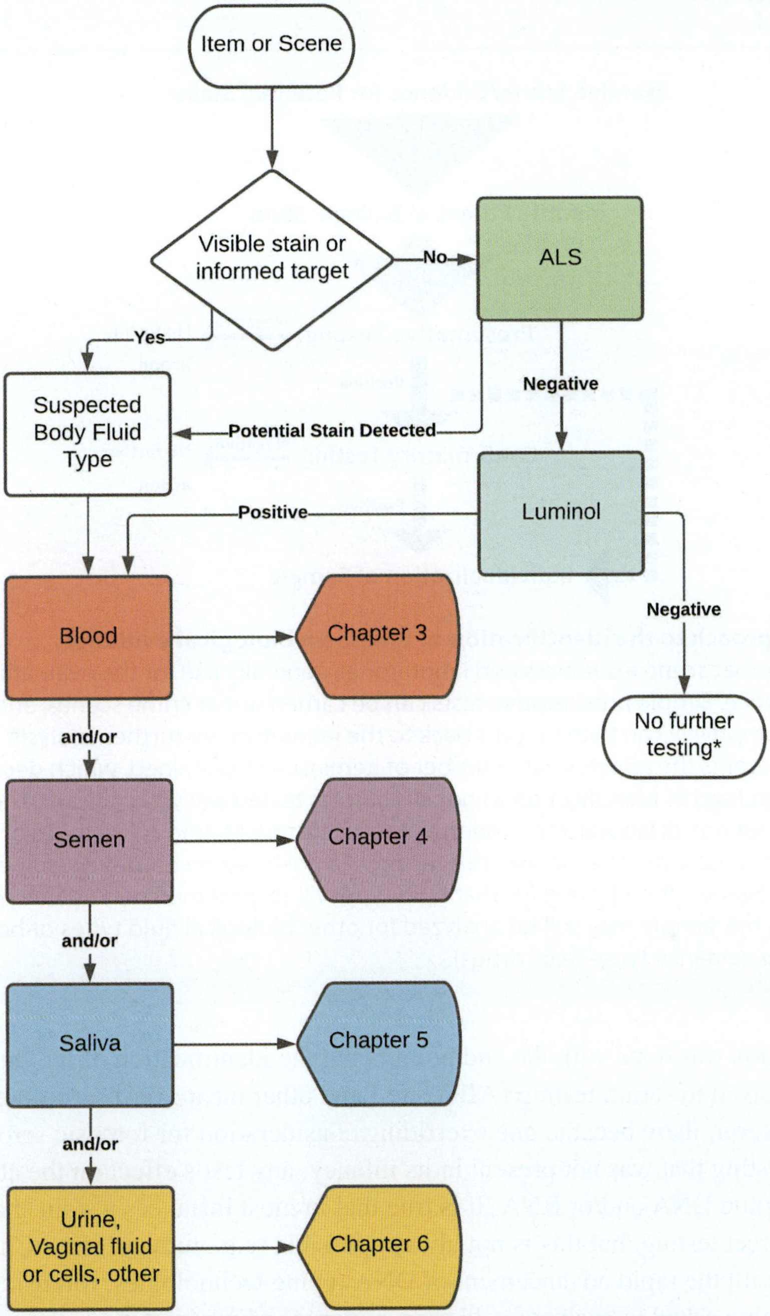

Fig. 1.2 A general schematic of workflow for biological stain identification. If there is a visible stain or a clear indication of where a stain is expected (e.g., the crotch of underwear for semen/vaginal fluid), then testing for the expected body fluid(s) can be attempted. If there is no visible stain, then alternate light sources *(ALS)* can be used to search for stains, and if this does not yield any results then luminol or similar can be used (this is because blood does not react under general ALS). If no stains are identified, then examination will likely cease; if a stain(s) is identified, then testing can proceed depending on the expected fluid type. *, Even if no body fluid is detected, sampling may occur for touch DNA or other nonbiologic testing.

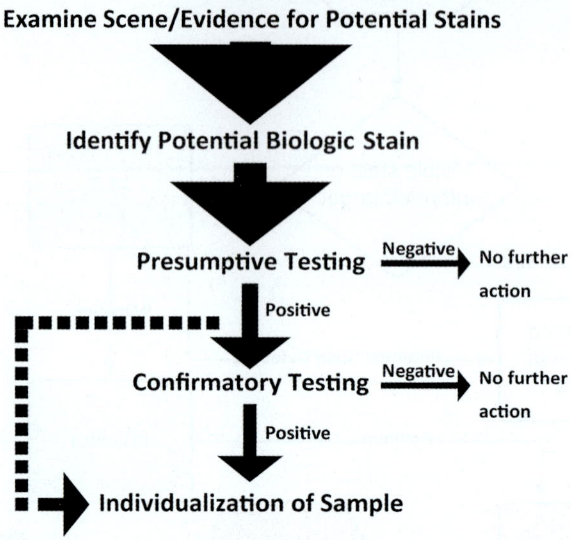

Fig. 1.3 An approach to the identification of unknown biological evidence.
This is the order that scene examiners and laboratories generally use for the evaluation of biological evidence. Simple presumptive tests can be carried out at crime scenes, and evidence identified presumptively can then be sent back to the laboratory for further analysis. The size of the arrows represents the approximate number of items/stains examined, which decreases with each subsequent level of identification as not all samples tested will yield a result. The *dashed line* demonstrates that not all laboratories undertake confirmatory testing on all types of samples and may move right to individualization via DNA testing if a positive presumptive result is obtained. If any result is negative, then testing for that fluid type will stop (semen may still be processed for DNA), although the sample may still be analyzed for other biological fluid types or be examined further for other evidence types (e.g., drugs).

Traditionally, this was done with the end point being the identification of the fluid in question, which later evolved to serum testing (ABO, etc.) and other means of discrimination. Since the 1990s, however, there became one overriding consideration for forensic serology and presumptive testing that was not present in its infancy: any test's effect on the ability to recover and profile DNA and/or RNA. It is true that in most instances a stain should not be subjected to direct testing, but this is not always possible (e.g., luminol) (see Chapter 3). Additionally, with the rapid advancement of DNA typing technologies, forensic scientists are increasingly being asked to evaluate cold case evidence, which in some cases may only be a test result that has been reacted with a presumptive test (e.g., AP filter paper), with no further access to the original evidence.

The ideal presumptive test is therefore one that is specific to the biological target (more particularly specific to the human biological target), has a high sensitivity, will meet the Frye standard (or local equivalent of legal admissibility), and will not damage, interfere with, or remove significant quantities of underlying DNA. Additionally, any test should be quick, simple, and safe so that it can be used in a crime scene setting as well as in the laboratory.

An essential aspect of any presumptive test is to understand its capabilities and its limitations; this is accomplished through the validation of the technique, which includes evaluations of robustness, reliability, and reproducibility, and extends to the evaluation of each test's sensitivity and specificity both analytically and diagnostically.

Validation of a test is required to properly assess the usefulness of the test in particular casework situations. It provides proof that the test is suited for its intended use and that it satisfies any necessary quality requirements. These quality requirements can be assessed and evaluated through detailed knowledge of the test's limits. It is further a requirement of the Frye legislation, which originated in the United States but is used (at least the substance of the ruling) worldwide. Each laboratory will have its own detailed guidelines as to what is needed for validation of any presumptive test. Interestingly, the term validation is not found in published studies until 1987,[80] after which time it becomes more and more frequent in use.

Robustness refers to the ability of a test to work under a wide range of conditions and still provide the same results. This could be in reference to temperature, time of reaction, age of samples (fresh vs. old), concentrations (target and reagents), light conditions (e.g., luminol and ALS), or anything else that may cause discrepancies or departures from the expected normal results.

Reliability of a test refers to its ability to function as intended and is linked to robustness in that it needs to do so under different conditions. Reliability has also been used synonymously with precision, in that the same result should be obtained every time a positive is sampled.

Reproducibility of a test indicates its ability to provide the same result consistently if tested under the same conditions. It is a requirement for any reported results to be trusted. It is qualitative in that the same input should produce the same output if tested under the same conditions. Therefore if the same dilution of blood is repeatedly tested, it should produce the same results in terms of speed of reaction and overall result (color, intensity, etc.) each time.

Sensitivity describes the limits at which the test is effective before false negatives are observed. Because sensitivities can have both maximums and minimums, they could include scenarios where an overload of analyte can cause a false negative as well. An ideal presumptive test will be able to detect highly dilute biologic fluids and not be affected by overabundance of analyte. This is discussed in more detail later.

Specificity refers to the ability of any presumptive test to identify its target — and only its target. It is an assessment of the chance of obtaining a false positive result. The ideal presumptive test is specific only to the human body fluid it is designed for, but this has not been achieved. The ideal test therefore becomes one that cross-reacts with the fewest numbers of other substances (see later).

Other factors that are also considered when selecting a presumptive test are safety, simplicity, ease of use, and cost per test. As the tests will be used frequently in the lab and at crime scenes, the safety to the scientist and any members of the public (if it is used at a scene) needs to be considered. Several presumptive tests have been discontinued due to safety concerns. For example, benzidine was once the most widely used presumptive blood test,[81] but carcinogenic properties were discovered,[82,83] and it was quickly removed from use[84] and replaced by other safer alternatives.

Simplicity refers to the steps taken to use any test, including preparation of the testing reagents, as well as performing the test itself. The preparation of many of the reagents that are used in presumptive testing can be involved and require specialist laboratory equipment. Commercial providers have simplified this aspect of testing, so now most reagents are prepared through the combination of purchased precursors, or many of the reagents can be purchased fully ready to use. Performing the tests also needs to be simple, as does interpretation. Most presumptive tests have a few very simple steps and very clear indication of what constitutes a positive finding. While more complicated testing may offer benefits in terms of sensitivity or specificity, the general requirements of forensic serology in terms of body fluid testing are rapid and clear results.

Ease of use refers to the conditions and steps of any test. Although a test may have simple steps, it would not be easy to use if extra specialist equipment is needed for operation or interpretation. Even common testing such as luminol is not used as often as it might be because of the requirement of near or complete darkness, even though it is a one-step application process and very easy to interpret. Other requirements fall under this category, such as speed of test and reaction, with faster results being preferred, and stability of reagents to avoid special storage requirements.

Cost per test is also a major consideration for laboratories and police forces that use the serological tests. Because these tests can be used hundreds of times per case, they need to be cost effective. Low cost per test also means that more potential stains can be tested. This is reflected in the sequence of testing used by laboratories, with cheaper presumptive testing used to screen evidence first, where many tests may yield a negative, followed by the more specific tests (usually the immunochromatographic tests) being used as confirmatory only on select samples that were positive with the cheaper testing.

Analytical Sensitivity and Specificity

Analytical sensitivity in terms of forensic serology refers more accurately to the limits of detection (LOD) of the tests. This is the point at which a target biological fluid is diluted, usually with water, to where the analytical test cannot detect it. What is both interesting and confusing about this metric when used in body fluid identification is that very few studies agree on the LOD for any of the different tests in terms of manufacturers and published studies. Differences can range by as much as 1,000,000-fold between different studies in the most extreme cases. Luminol has been reported to have a sensitivity ranging from 1:100 to 1:100,000,000.[85–99]

There are many factors that can affect the reported LOD of a test, and these factors can combine to add further error in LOD determination. A knowledge of what these factors are will allow scientists to properly assess the value of their testing and the value of the results, whether they are positive or negative for a particular fluid.

Reagents and how they are applied to a body fluid can have significant influence on the LOD. This is in terms of concentrations of different components, age of those components, and age of the final testing mixture, then compounded to this is how they are applied to the stain/fluid for testing. For example, there have been studies showing that some presumptive tests for blood have an increased sensitivity when applied directly to a stain, compared with subsampling a portion of the stain (which acts to further dilute it).[100] If the tested stain is still wet or dried, this will also affect the LOD of the test. Variations in the concentration of the reagents can affect the sensitivity of the tests and the age of the reagents or final mixture, which may have degraded or converted to nonreactive compounds, which ultimately serves to alter the concentration of the active reagents.

The starting sample itself will affect the LOD. Each body fluid will have a normal range, sometimes quite large, of target analyte. Red blood cells, for example, can range in concentration from 4.7 to 6.1 million/μL for males and 4.2 to 5.4 million/μL for females.[101] Similarly, some of the main targets within semen such as prostate specific antigen range between 0.3 and 4.2 mg/mL,[102,103] and acid phosphatase (AP) ranges between 14,300 and 57,500 units of activity.[104] Saliva has a recorded amylase activity between 72,000 and 1,300,000 IU/L.[105–108] Since almost all studies use volunteer body fluids to determine LOD, the exact concentration of the starting target analyte is unknown; therefore the exact sensitivity cannot be determined, although it is still reported as an exact figure. These ranges pose difficulty for the identification of the limit that the target analyte can be detected, in that samples in one study fail at dilutions where they would be expected to react based on a previous study.

The substrate that the stain is on will also affect the LOD, with more absorbent materials having a lower LOD than less absorbent ones.[99] Samples that are placed on nonabsorbent surfaces will pool on the surface; if they are allowed to dry, the substances in the fluids that are targeted will concentrate on the surface. Conversely, absorbent substrates will spread out the fluids, acting as a further diluting mechanism.

Operator experience also affects outcomes and reported LODs. This can be due to the subjective nature of what is considered a positive result and in the actual physical steps in carrying out the testing. A more experienced scientist may be confident in concluding that a very slight color change is indicative of a dilute positive, but a less experienced scientist may opt that this is negative.

Analytic specificity is more accurately an investigation into cross-reaction and interference, but its determination is crucial for any presumptive test for its implementation and use in forensic investigations. Knowledge of any substances that will cross-react with a test, whether that is through a false positive or through inhibition of the mechanism causing false negative reactions, will in part determine the usefulness of that test for forensic use.

In the literature, specificity is referring to any known cross-reactions that a test is known to have, although this can get confusing. Obvious targets of cross-reaction testing are to other body fluids, which is the base level standard for cross-reactivity testing. This is essential when assessing if more than one body fluid may be present in a tested sample. For example, if a test for semen also reacted with blood if tested on a bloodstain only, it would still show a positive and could be confused as also having semen present.

Additionally, anything else can be tested for cross-reaction, whether it is realistically similar in composition (e.g., the same fluids from different animal species)[109] or could be mistaken for a stain (e.g., tomato ketchup mistaken for blood, mayonnaise mistaken for semen), but also includes various cleaning products,[110,111] fruits, vegetables, and plants,[112–114] and chemical substances.[87] Other aspects that would fall under potential cross-reactants or interference would be aspects such as temperature extremes or age of samples.

Depending on how the results of a specificity study are reported, a substance that causes a cross-reaction in 5% of trials may still be listed as a cross-reacting substance without further qualification. This could act as a misleading metric when assessing the results of a test and even affect how it is received by the courts. The propensity of something to cross-react is also dependent on the state of that substance. For example, bleach is known as a common substance to cause false positives with luminol,[89] but if allowed to dry to its component salts, it has been found to be unreactive with luminol.[87]

How studies report cross-reactions is also a consideration. Some studies will only report those substances that cross-react in the exact same manner as the target analyte, whereas other studies may report any nonnegative reaction as a positive cross-reaction. Some papers find that false positives can be eliminated by the experienced scientist based on speed, exact resulting color, or any other factor that falls under their previous experience with the test. Interference is when a substance is added to a known body fluid, which when tested results in a negative. This is a false negative because the body fluid of interest is present.

There are an unlimited number of possible substances or testing scenarios that could cause cross-reaction or interference with a test. Even if studies contradict cross-reactivity or interference, both studies need to be considered in the evaluation of results. Discrepancies in findings between different studies may be caused by slight variations in the reagents, in the testing parameters, or in the interpretation of what constitutes a positive finding.

All findings in regard to analytic sensitivity and specificity must be considered when choosing what test to use in a particular scenario. Additionally, each batch of reagents should be tested for sensitivity to ensure consistency between preparations. Basic specificity should also be carried out with each new preparation of reagents, with the most common confusing or interfering substances encountered, although the full range of specificity testing carried out in the literature is not needed as standard.

Diagnostic Sensitivity and Specificity

Diagnostic testing is not normally carried out in terms of presumptive testing. Few studies have applied the diagnostic sensitivity and specificity to forensic serology,[115,116] which gives a different analysis of the testing capabilities of the assays relative to analytic sensitivity and specificity. Although common in medical studies, these metrics can easily be applied to forensic serology and could even be used to provide some statistical significance to findings. The state of the unknown sample needs to be known (e.g., Is a sample positive for blood?) to truly assess the value of any test that will be used. This can be accomplished by carrying out high-quality validation studies and using a 2×2 contingency table, which is also called a confusion matrix (Table 1.1).

The contingency table is a summary of all the testing parameters that a particular test has been subjected to, and the results incorporated into this can include both analytic sensitivity and specificity. Cross-reaction would be classified under false positives, and tests below the LOD would be classified under false negatives. What can then be determined from Table 1.1 are the total predicted positive and negative values (n_S and $n_{\acute{S}}$—the results provided by the analytic test), true positive and negative (n_R and $n_{\acute{R}}$—the actual nature of the samples tested), true positives (n_{RS}), true negatives ($n_{\acute{R}\acute{S}}$), false positives ($n_{\acute{R}S}$—type I error), and false negatives ($n_{R\acute{S}}$—type II error).

Other statistical probabilities can be calculated from this table, including positive predictive values (PPV = true positives [n_{RS}]/predicted positive [n_S]), negative predictive values (NPV = true negatives [$n_{\acute{R}\acute{S}}$]/predicted negative [$n_{\acute{S}}$]), diagnostic sensitivity (also called the true positive rate = true positives [n_{RS}]/actual positives [R]), and diagnostic specificity (also called the true negative rate = true negatives [$n_{\acute{R}\acute{S}}$]/actual negatives [Ŕ]). There are further metrics than can be calculated, but those mentioned provide a detailed assessment of any test.

Table 1.1 A 2×2 contingency table for frequencies of samples with or without the target analyte (R or Ŕ) and the analytic test used to detect that analyte, which shows a positive or negative result (S or Ś). True positives (n_{RS}—target analyte present and detected), true negatives ($n_{\acute{R}\acute{S}}$—target analyte is absent and test is negative), as well as false positives ($n_{\acute{R}S}$—target analyte is absent, but test shows it is present), which is a type I error, and false negatives ($n_{R\acute{S}}$—target analyte is present but not detected), which is a type II error, represent the analysis of the test. Total predicted positive (n_S), total predicted negative ($n_{\acute{S}}$), total positive (n_R), and total negative ($n_{\acute{R}}$) are also shown. Using these values, other attributes can be calculated.

		Predicted Condition Based on Test		
		Positive (S)	Negative (Ś)	Total
Actual Condition	Positive (R)	n_{RS}	$n_{R\acute{S}}$	n_R
	Negative (Ŕ)	$n_{\acute{R}S}$	$n_{\acute{R}\acute{S}}$	$n_{\acute{R}}$
	Total	n_S	$n_{\acute{S}}$	

After Aitken C, Taroni F, Bozza S. *Statistics and the Evaluation of Evidence for Forensic Scientists*. Newark, United Kingdom: John Wiley & Sons, Incorporated; 2020. Adapted by author.

Both PPV and NPV are performance measures, and a high result can indicate accuracy; both are derived using Bayes theorem. These measures can be biased in medical diagnostics if there are few true negatives or true positives, but this is unlikely with forensic presumptive tests. Diagnostic sensitivity and specificity are true measures of the accuracy of the test: A positive represents the body fluid being present, and a negative represents the body fluid being absent.

Although use of diagnostic statistics in forensic serology has been limited to a few more recent papers, the potential for informed expectations with different tests could be highly valuable, and the hope is that this usage becomes more commonplace in reporting studies on forensic presumptive tests.

Standards and Quality Controls

There are no current standards for body fluid testing, unlike those available for DNA, arson, and toxicology. This is in reference to a known quantity (concentration) of target molecules for consistent determination of sensitivities. There are similarly no blind trial sample testing scenarios assessed by external organizations in the way that DNA, fire, and toxicology have. While standards have been proposed as a means to help enable laboratories to validate their presumptive tests,[117] there are none readily available, and no oversight organization exists to evaluate results within and between laboratories on a large scale, although organizations such as ANSI/ASB, OSAC, SWGDAM, and ASTM are all actively working on developing some.

Presumptive testing may form part of the competency for other standardized testing (e.g., DNA competency testing) but only if the fluids are identified as biological and DNA profiles are generated, not as a test in their own right. As will be discussed individually for each biological fluid type, all tests used for body fluid identification have varying sensitivities and specificities depending on which study is consulted. This makes the process of informed decision making difficult in regard to a particular case.

It is possible to buy quality-controlled analytes (e.g., hemoglobin) that will have a narrow standardized range, but these introduce their own issues with testing if they are nonhuman in origin or if other components of a fluid are not present, which may influence how a test reacts, as well as its overall sensitivity. Generally, laboratories will have their own standards for each biological fluid type tested for, which they have created from donated fluids from laboratory staff or volunteers. While this provides a suitable quality control sample for the activity of a test, it is not suitable as a standard for LOD. It introduces error simply through the range of target analytes that are expected in normal samples and makes it impossible to compare results confidently between laboratories.

Quality control (QC) samples are essential with any forensic test, and forensic serology is no different. Quality control samples allow assessment of the functionality of a test, and their need has been understood for over a century.[68] Quality control samples take the form of positive and negative controls and are tested before a test is used, after a period of unuse, and can be verified sporadically through extended use. Before a test is used on evidence for the first time, the quality control samples are tested in the same manner as a case sample (noting that sampling and testing strategies are discussed in detail in the sections for each body fluid). This usually involves the subsampling of the control via swab or filter paper, which is then tested with the reagents.

Positive control samples are known stains of the body fluid the test will detect, usually on a neutral substrate such as filter paper or white cotton. A positive reaction in the same color/result and expected time indicates that the test is functioning as expected and that it is valid for use. If the positive control test fails to react, then the reagents cannot be used until the error is identified and rectified. This could be an issue with the positive control sample itself (e.g., old) or could be an issue with the testing reagents.

Negative control samples are simply the testing reagents used on a sample with no analyte. The negative controls are used on the same substrate as the positive controls and are subsampled in the same manner. Note that this also serves as a quality test of the sampling products. The reagents are applied and assessed as if the body fluid was present. A negative reaction should be observed in the normal time frame of the test. If a positive result is observed from the negative control, this indicates contamination at some point in the testing procedure, and materials used for the quality control assessment cannot be used until the cause of the contamination has been identified.

If both positive and negative controls pass by showing a positive and negative result, respectively, then normal evidence testing can take place using the tested reagent. Each laboratory will have its own quality control protocols in place, which is a requirement for accreditation, but it will always involve showing that the testing works as expected.

Theory and Available Tests

This chapter has provided some history and the requirements of forensic serologic testing—or more accurately, forensic body fluid identification—and subsequent sections will provide a detailed account of the common testing methodologies (see Chapter 2) and testing available for different biologic fluids (see Chapters 3–6).

The subsequent chapters will provide a comprehensive review of the different testing methodologies and will limit the detailed analysis to those tests that are still in use or were in regular use over the last 50 years. This will allow the usefulness of the text to include realistic cold case reviews, where older analysis methods may have been used.

Recipes for reagents and tests will not be given, except in the most general way where testing has changed based on new formulations, because the literature contains many different formulations, protocols, and tips of use for the different tests, with no standard recipe or method standing out as being preferred. Further, different laboratories will have different usage standard operating procedures in place depending on their needs and experiences that may not be used by all laboratories. Further, most laboratories no longer make their own testing reagents, and there are many different companies that offer premade reagents under quality-controlled manufacturing scenarios for easy purchase.

References

1. Locard E. *L'enquête Criminelle et les Méthodes Scientifiques*. Ernest Flammarion; 1920.
2. Locard E. *La Police et les Méthodes Scientifiques*. Paris: Rieder; 1934:82.
3. Kirk P. *Crime Investigation; Physical Evidence and the Police Laboratory*. New York-London: Interscience; 1953.
4. Verdon TJ, Mitchell RJ, van Oorschot RAH. The influence of substrate on DNA transfer and extraction efficiency. *Forensic Sci Int Genet*. 2013;7(1):167–175.
5. Goray M, Eken E, Mitchell RJ, et al. Secondary DNA transfer of biological substances under varying test conditions. *Forensic Sci Int Genet*. 2010;4(2):62–67.
6. Rosner F. Blood stain identification as described in the *Talmud*. *Israel J Med Sci*. 1973;9(8):1077–1079.
7. Lyon AB. History of infant feeding. *Am J Dis Child*. 1933;46(2):359–374.
8. Leuchs EF. Wirkung des speichels auf Stärke. *Annalen der Physik*. 1831;98(8): 623-623.
9. Schoch T.J. Starches and amylases. In *Proceedings of the American Society of Brewing Chemists*. San Antonio, Texas; 1961.
10. Leuchs EF. Über die verzuckerung des stärkmehls durch speichel. In: Kastner KWG, ed. *Archiv für die Gesammte Naturlehre*. Berlin: Verlag; 1831:105–107.
11. Lu G-D, Needham J. A history of forensic medicine in China. *Med Hist*. 1988;32(4):357–400.
12. Tzhu S. *Hsi Yuan Chi Lu*. 1247.

13. Giles HA. The Hsi Yüan Lu or Instructions to Coroners. *Sage Publications*. 1924
14. McKnight B. The washing away of wrongs: forensic medicine in thirteenth-century China. In: Sivin N, editor. *Science, Medicine, and Technology in East Asia*. vol. 1. Ann Arbor, MI: Center for Chinese Studies at the University of Michigan; 1981.
15. Emmert JM. State medicine, past, present and future. *JAMA*. 1902;38(21):1568–1578.
16. Wiltenburg J. The Carolina and the culture of the common man: revisiting the imperial penal code of 1532. *Renaiss Q*. 2000;53(3):713–734.
17. Foster B. The history of medicine and of the medical profession. *Northwest Lancet*. 1898;18:261–266.
18. Kornfeld H. In Memoriam. Paul Zacchias. *Med Leg J*. 1885;2:532–534.
19. Zacchiae P. *Quaestiones Medico-Legales, in Three Volumes*. Lyon: Jean Anisson & Jean Posuel; 1701.
20. Zacchia P. Quaestiones Medico-Legales: Qvo Continentvr Consilia et Responsa LXXXV. Ad Materias Medico-legales pertinentia; Nec Non Decisiones S. Rotae Romanae Ad Praedictas Materias Spectantes. Lochner; 1726:vol. 3.
21. De Ceglia FP. The woman who gave birth to a dog. Monstrosity and bestiality in *Quaestiones Medico-Legales* by Paolo Zacchia. *Med Secoli*. 2014;26(1):117–144.
22. Deinlein J.J.F. *Dissertatio Medico Inauguralis de Medico Inter Sententias Medico-Legales Discrepantes Arbitrio Tertio*. Meyer; 1751.
23. Alix M.F. *De Qvaestionibvs Medico Legalibvs Ex Chirvrgia Declarandis / Gratiosi Medicorvm Ordinis Indvltv Pro Svmmis In Arte Medica Honoribvs Impetrandis Die VIII. Febr. MDCCLXXIV. H.L.Q.C. Pvblicae Disqvisitioni Svbmittit Matthaevs Franciscvs Alix Parisinvs Chirvrgicvae Doctor, In Alma Emericiana Eivsdem Et Artis Obstetriciae Demonstrator Pvblicvs*. 1774.
24. Lewenhoeck DA, Observationes D. Anthonii Lewenhoeck, de natis e semine genitali animalculis. *Philos Trans (1665-1678)*. 1677;12(142):1040–1046.
25. Gadêlha H, Hernandez-Herrara P, Montoya F, et al. Human sperm uses asymmetric and anisotropic flagellar controls to regulate swimming symmetry and cell steering. *Sci Adv*. 2020;6(31):eaba5168.
26. Schurig M. *Spermatologia Historico-Medica, hoc est Seminis Humani Consideratio Physico-Medico-Legalis, qua Ejus Natura et Usus, in Simulque Opus Generationis et Varia de Coitu Aliaque huc Pertinentia v.g. Castratione, Herniotomia, Phimosi, Circumcisione, Recutitione, et Infibulation, Item de Hermaphroditis & Sexum Mutantibus, Raris & Selectis Observationibus, Annexo Indice Locupletissimo, Traduntur a D. Martino Schurigio Phyfico Dresdenfi*. Beck; 1720.
27. Alix M.F. *De Quaestionibus Medico Legalibus ex Chirurgia Declarandis... Submittit Matthaeus Franciscus Alix*. Office Nonnii; 1774.
28. Ploucquet W.G. *Guilielmi Godofredi Ploucquet... Commentarius Medicus in Processus Criminales, Super Homicidio, Infanticidio, et Embryoctonia*. A Koenig; 1787.
29. Hunter J. *Observations on Certain Parts of the Animal Oeconomy*. Nicol and Johnson; 1786.
30. Ollivier dA, Barruel M. De taches observées sur un linge dans un cas de médecine légal. *J Chim Méd Parm Toxicol*. 1826;2:565–568.
31. Orfila MJB. Du Sperme, considéré sous le point de vue médico-légal. *J Chim Méd Parm Toxicol*. 1827;3(3):469–480.
32. Barruel M. Mémoire sur l'existence d'un principe propre à caractériser le sang de l'homme et celui des diverses espèces d'animaux. *Ann d'Hygiène Publ Méd Légal*. 1829:267–277.
33. Orfila MJB, Barruel M, Chevallier JB. Taches de sang. *Ann d'Hygiène Publ Méd Légal*. 1835;14:349–370.
34. Briand J., Brosson J.X. *Manuel Complet de Médecine Légale, ou Résumé des Meilleurs Ouvrages Publiés Jusqu'a ce Jour sur Dette Matière*. J. S. Chaudé; 1836.
35. Ritter B. *Ueber die Ermittelung von Blut-, Samen- und Exkrementenflecken in Kriminalfaellen: Ein spezieller Beitrag zur Gerichtlichen Arzneikunde*. Stahel; 1854.
36. Jones CH. Crystals in putrefying blood. *London J Med*. 1852;4(46):956.
37. Parks EA. The formation of crystals in the human blood. *Med Times Gazette*. 1852;26(5):103–104.
38. Teichmann L. Ueber die krystallisation des orpnischen be-standtheile des blutes. *Ration Med*. 1853;3:375–388.

39. Stokes GG. On the reduction and oxidation of the colouring matter of the blood. *Proc Royal Soc London.* 1864;13:355–364.
40. Hoppe-Seyler F. Weitere mittheilungen über die eigenschaften des blutfarbstoffs. *Z Physiol Chem.* 1879;1:121–139.
41. Hoppe-Seyler F. Beiträge zur kenntniss der eigenschaften der blutfarbstoffe. *Z Physiol Chem.* 1889;13: 477–496.
42. Virchow R. Ueber die forensische untersuchung von trockenan blutflecken. *Virchow. Arch Pathol Anat Physiol Klin Med.* 1857;12:334–338.
43. Landerer X. Ueber die teichmann'schen hämatin-krystalle. *Arch Pharm.* 1859;150(3):275–276.
44. Pfaff. Ueber die bestimmung des alters der blutflecke in criminalfällen. *Vierteljahrsschrift Gerichtliche Med Öffent Sanitätswesen.* 1862;26:266–276.
45. Cauvet D. Taches de sperme et taches de sang. *Ann d'Hygiène Pub Méd Légal.* 1875;44:117–126.
46. Tamassia A. Determinazione cronologica delle macchie di sangue. *Atti Regio Istituto Veneto Sci.* 1884;6(2):1–22.
47. Lassaigne JL. Observations sur quelques réactions que présentent les taches spermatiques avec les taches albumineuses et autres taches analogues. *Ann d'Hygiène Pub Méd Légal.* 1858;10:405–408.
48. Longuet M. Recherche medico-legale des spermatozoides. *Ann d'Hygiène Pub Méd Légal.* 1876;2(46): 154–167.
49. Brouardel P. Des taches spermatiques. *Le Procricien.* 1879;2(28):332–336.
50. Hamlin FM. The microscopical examination of seminal stains on cloth. *Proc Am Soc Microscop.* 1883;5: 21–25.
51. Roussin MZ. Examen microscopique des taches de sperme. *Ann d'Hygiène Pub Méd Légal.* 1867;27: 142–164.
52. Laugier M. *Contribution à L'étude Médico-Légale des Taches Spermatiques.* Paris: Martinet; 1877:4.
53. Boutmy MM, Brouardel P. Rapport sur le procédé petel et labiche destiné a faire découvrir les taches de sperme. *Ann d'Hygiène Pub Méd Légal.* 1880;4:224–227.
54. Robin C, Tardieu A. Mémoire sur l'examen microscopique des taches formées par le méconium et l'enduit foetal, pour servir a l'histoire medico-ligale de l'infanticide. *Ann d'Hygiène Pub Méd Légal.* 1857;7:350–374.
55. Florence A. *Les Taches de Sang: Leur Signification, Leur Importance en Médecine Judiciaire.* Doin; 1885.
56. Bordet J. Les leucocytes et les proprietes actives du serum chez les vaccines. *Ann l'Institut Pasteur.* 1895;9(6):462–506.
57. Bordet J. Sur le mode d'action des sérums préventifs. *Ann l'Institut Pasteur.* 1896;10:193–219.
58. Gruber Mv, Durham HE. Eine neue methode zur raschen erkennung des choleravibrio und des typhusbacillus. *Münchener Med Wochenschrift.* 1896;43:285–286.
59. Bordet J. Sur l'agglutination et la dissolution des globules rouges par le serum d'animaux injectes de sang defibrine. *Ann l'institut Pasteur.* 1898
60. Landsteiner K. Zur kenntnis der antifermentativen, lytischen und agglutinierenden wirkungen des blutserums und der lymphe. *Zentralbl Bakteriol.* 1900;27:357–362.
61. Landsteiner K. Agglutination phenomena in normal human blood. *Wien Klin Wochenschr.* 1901;14:1132–1134.
62. Decastello Von, Sturli A. A. Ueber die isoagglutinine im serum gesunder und kranker menschen. *Transfuse Med Rev.* 1902;20:1090–1095.
63. Jansky J. Haematologicke studie u psychotiku. *Sbornik Klinicky.* 1907;8:85.
64. Moss W. Studies on isoagglutinins and isohemolysins. *Tr Assn Am Physicians.* 1909;24:419–437.
65. Moss WL. Studies on isoagglutinins and isohemolysins. *Bull Johns Hopk.* 1910;21:63.
66. Landsteiner K, Levine P. On group specific substances in human spermatozoa. *J Immunol.* 1926;12(5):415–418.
67. Wood R-W. Communications secrètes au moyen de rayons lumineux. *J Phys Théor Appl.* 1919;9(1):77–90.
68. Adler O, Adler R. Über das verhalten gewisser organischer verindungen gegenüber blut mit besonderer berücksichtigung des nachweises von blut. *Hoppe-Seyler's Zeitschrift Physiol Chem.* 1904;41:59–67.

69. Schmitz A. *Uber des Hydrazyde der Trimensinsaure und der Hemimellitsaure* [dissertation]. Heidelberg; 1902.
70. Ruttan RF, Hardisty RHM. A new reagent for detecting occult blood. *Can Med Assoc J*. 1912;2(11):995–998.
71. Meyer E. Beiträge zur leukocytenfrage. *Münchner Med Wochenschrift*. 1903;50(35):1489–1493.
72. Kastle J, Shedd O. Phenolphthalin as a reagent for the oxidizing ferments. *Am Chem J*. 1901;26:526.
73. Demuth F. Über phosphatstoffwechsel. I. Mitteilung: uber hexosephosphatasen in menschlichen organen und korperflussigkeiten. *Biochem Zeitschrift*. 1925;159:415–423.
74. Kutscher W, Wolbergs H. Prostataphosphatase. *Hoppe-Seyler's Zeitschrift für Physiol Chem*. 1935;236 (4-6):237–240.
75. Kutscher W, Wörner A. Prostataphosphatase. 2. Mitteilung. *Hoppe-Seyler's Zeitschrift fur Physiol Chem*. 1936;239(3):109–126.
76. Rao AR, Motiwala HG, Karim OMA. The discovery of prostate-specific antigen. *BJU Int*. 2008;101(1):5–10.
77. Sutherland WD. *Blood-Stains: Their Detection and the Determination of Their Source*. London: Bailliere, Tindall and Cox; 1907.
78. Baxter S, Rees B. The identification of saliva in stains in forensic casework. *Med Sci Law*. 1975;15(1):37–41.
79. De Wolff TR, Kal AJ, Berger CEH, et al. A probabilistic approach to body fluid typing interpretation: an exploratory study on forensic saliva testing. *Law Probabil Risk*. 2015;14(4):323–339.
80. Baechtel FS, Brown J, Terrell LD. Presumptive screening of suspected semen stain in situ using cotton swabs and bromochloroindolyl phosphate to detect prostatic acid-phosphatase-activity. *J Forensic Sci*. 1987;32(4):880–887.
81. Thomas JC. The examination of blood and seminal stains. *Police J*. 1937;10(4):490–503.
82. Holland VR, Saunders BC, Rose FL, et al. A safer substitute for benzidine in the detection of blood. *Tetrahedron*. 1974;30(18):3299–3302.
83. Weisburger JH. Comments on the history and importance of aromatic and heterocyclic amines in public health. *Mutation Res*. 2002:506–507. 9-20.
84. Steinberg H. *The Hazard of Benzidine to Criminal Justice Personnel*. vol. 480. US Department of Commerce, National Bureau of Standards; 1977.
85. Budowle B, Leggitt JL, Defenbaugh DA, et al. The presumptive reagent fluorescein for detection of dilute bloodstains and subsequent STR typing of recovered DNA. *J Forensic Sci*. 2000;45(5):1090–1092.
86. Fregeau CJ, Germain O, Fourney RM. Fingerprint enhancement revisited and the effects of blood enhancement chemicals on subsequent Profiler Plus fluorescent short tandem repeat DNA analysis of fresh and aged bloody fingerprints. *J Forensic Sci*. 2000;45(2):354–380.
87. Tobe SS, Watson N, Nic Daeid N. Evaluation of six presumptive tests for blood, their specificity, sensitivity, and effect on high molecular-weight DNA. *J Forensic Sci*. 2007;52(1):102–109.
88. Germain O., Miller K. *Blood Reagents—Their Use and Their Effect on DNA*. Ottawa (ON) Royal Canadian Mounted Police Forensic Identification Research and Review Section; 1998:no. 42.
89. Lytle LT, Hedgecock DG. Chemiluminescence in visualization of forensic bloodstains. *J Forensic Sci*. 1978;23(3):550–562.
90. Olsen R. Sensitivity comparison of blood enhancement techniques. *Ident News*. 1985:10–14.
91. Grodsky M, Wright K, Kirk PL. Simplified preliminary blood testing—an improved technique and a comparative study of methods. *J Crim Law Criminol Police Sci*. 1951;42(1):95–104.
92. Proescher F, Moody A. Detection of blood by means of chemiluminescence. *J Lab Clin Med*. 1939;24:1183–1189.
93. Webb JL, Creamer JI, Quickenden TI. A comparison of the presumptive luminol test for blood with four non-chemiluminescent forensic techniques. *Luminescence (Chichester)*. 2006;21(4):214–220.
94. Garofano L., Pizzamiglio M., Marino A., et al. *A Comparative Study of the Sensitivity and Specificity of Luminal and Fluorescein on Diluted and Aged Bloodstains and Subsequent STRs Typing. International Congress Series*. Elsevier; 2006.
95. Seashols SJ, Cross HD, Shrader DL, et al. A comparison of chemical enhancements for the detection of latent blood. *J Forensic Sci*. 2013;58(1):130–133.

96. Patel G, Hopwood A. An evaluation of luminol formulations and their effect on DNA profiling. *Int J Legal Med.* 2013;127(4):723–729.
97. Castelló A, Alvarez M, Verdú F. Accuracy, reliability, and safety of luminol in bloodstain investigation. *Can Soc Forensic Sci J.* 2002;35(3):113–121.
98. Grispino RR. The effect of luminol on the serological analysis of dried human bloodstains. *Crime Lab Digest.* 1990;17(1):13–23.
99. Luedeke M, Miller E, Sprague JE. The effects of Bluestar and luminol when used in conjunction with tetramethylbenzidine or phenolphthalein. *Forensic Sci Int.* 2016;262:156–159.
100. Lewis J, Baird A, McAlister C, et al. Improved detection of semen by use of direct acid phosphatase testing. *Sci Justice.* 2013;53(4):385–394.
101. Marieb EN, Hoehn K. *Human Anatomy & Physiology.* 9th ed. London: Benjamin Cummings; 2013:1107.
102. Li R. *Forensic Biology.* 430. London: CRC Press; 2008.
103. Butler J. *Sample collection, storage, and characterization. Fundamentals of Forensic DNA Typing.* Elsevier: London; 2010:79–98.
104. Singer R, Sagiv M, Allalouf D, et al. Acid phosphatase activity in human semen. *Arch Androl.* 1979;3(1): 89–90.
105. Whitehead PH, Kipps AE. A test paper for detecting saliva stains. *J Forensic Sci Soc.* 1975;15(1):39–42.
106. Auvdel MJ. Amylase levels in semen and saliva stains. *J Forensic Sci.* 1986;31(2):426–431.
107. Tsutsumi H, Higashida K, Mizuno Y, et al. Identification of saliva stains by determination of the specific activity of amylase. *Forensic Sci Int.* 1991;50(1):37–42.
108. Kipps AE, Whitehead PH. The significance of amylase in forensic investigations of body fluids. *Forensic Sci.* 1975;6(3):137–144.
109. Human Diagnostics Worldwide. *Design Verification and Product Data for HEXAGON OBTI* [Rev. 0012]. 2018.
110. Castelló A, Frances F, Corella D, et al. Active oxygen doctors the evidence. *Naturwissenschaften.* 2009;96(2):303–307.
111. Castelló A, Francés F, Verdú F. Chemistry in crime investigation: sodium percarbonate effects on bloodstains detection. *J Forensic Sci.* 2012;57(2):500–502.
112. Vennemann M, Scott G, Curran L, et al. Sensitivity and specificity of presumptive tests for blood, saliva and semen. *Forensic Sci Med Pathol.* 2014;10(1):69–75.
113. De Vittori E, Barni F, Lewis SW, et al. Forensic application of a rapid one-step tetramethylbenzidine-based test for the presumptive trace detection of bloodstains at the crime scene and in the laboratory. *Forensic Chem.* 2016;2:63–74.
114. Quickenden TI, Creamer JI. A study of common interferences with the forensic luminol test for blood. *Luminescence (Chichester).* 2001;16(4):295–298.
115. Deshmukh S, Insi F, Goksin Karaaslan M, et al. A confirmatory test for sperm in sexual assault samples using a microfluidic-integrated cell phone imaging system. *Forensic Sci Int Genet.* 2020;48:102313.
116. Butler J, Chaseling J, Wright K. A comparison of four presumptive tests for the detection of blood on dark materials. *J Forensic Sci.* 2019;64(6):1838–1843.
117. Laux DL. Development of biological standards for the quality assurance of presumptive testing reagents. *Sci Justice.* 2011;51(3):143–145.

CHAPTER 2

Selected Common Techniques

Certain aspects of forensic serology and body fluid identification are common among tests, even if the targeted fluid differs. Many of the tests work on the same principles with different targets. It is therefore important to have an understanding of these basic concepts before proceeding with discussion of testing for specific fluids. It is pertinent to discuss some of these techniques here rather than repeating information in each chapter. Therefore this chapter will provide at a base level the foundation for some of the tests that will be described throughout the text. This chapter will not detail aspects of the different foundations but will provide common attributes of the different testing methods.

Readers who are familiar with the concepts described may skip this chapter or review particular techniques under their respective headings.

Lighting and Alternate Light Sources

When examining an item for potential stains, especially a stain that may be difficult to see because it is a clear fluid, or if the stain is the same color as the substrate, consideration of the lighting used to search is essential. Varying the angle at which a light source strikes a stain can make stains and other features stand out, whereas alternate light sources (ALS) can make a stain, or the substrate it is on, fluoresce if the correct wavelength of light is used.

Varying the angle of the lighting used, known as oblique lighting, to search for biological stains is a standard method used at crime scenes and in laboratories. The basis behind the method is that the light will reflect differently between the substrate and the biological stain if it strikes at a specific angle (Fig. 2.1). This is not predetermined, however; the process works by shifting the light around the surface being searched. We have all experienced this in action through looking for a mark or writing on some item (e.g., battery instructions inside the battery compartment of an electronic device) that is not clear, but by shifting or tilting the item back and forth gently under a light source the writing suddenly becomes clear. The same effect can be achieved when looking for biological fluids on different substrates. The result is that a potential stained area can be identified, and further testing can be carried out to determine if the stain is biological in nature and what the fluid might be. The method is only used for initial screening, but it is a good starting point.

Forensic Serology. DOI: http://doi.org/10.1016/B978-0-12-812968-5.00002-7

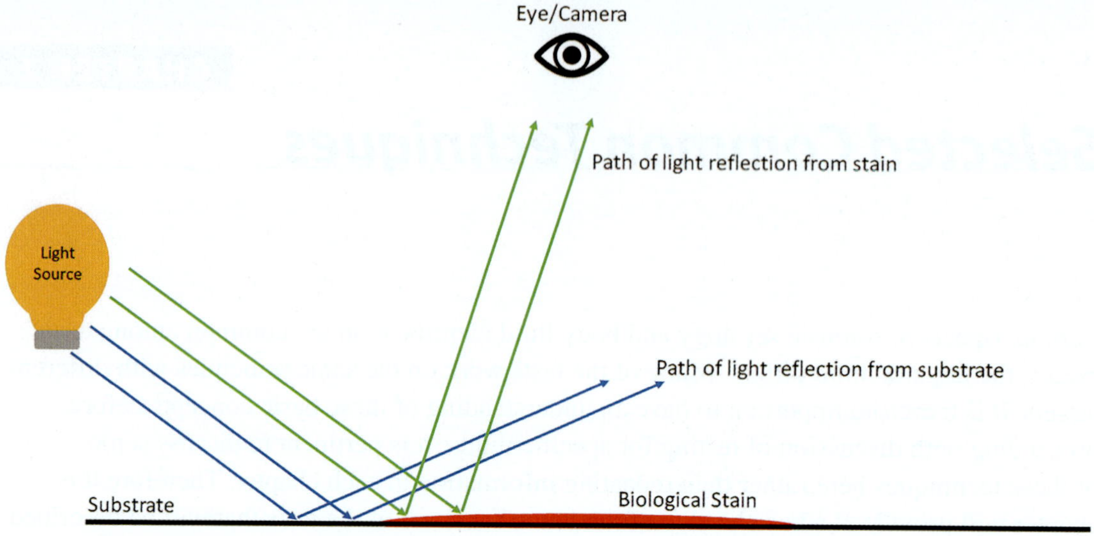

Fig. 2.1 An example of the use of oblique lighting when examining a biological fluid stain on a substrate. The light reflects at different angles from the substrate and the biological fluid. If the light is positioned correctly, then the reflection off the substrate will be diminished while simultaneously enhancing the reflection from the biological stain. In this way, a previously invisible stain can be identified.

The basis behind ALS systems is that certain substances within many biological fluids will fluoresce or absorb light in specific wavelengths. Substances that fluoresce within a fluid are known as fluorophores, and these are usually intrinsic to the fluid, although some chemical treatments can also act as fluorophores (e.g., fluorescein). These chemical treatments are often used in fingerprint examination.

ALS systems use narrow wavelengths of light directed at a stain or evidentiary item with or without an interfering filter (glasses or camera filter). Some substances or substrates will absorb the light energy and reemit the light at a longer wavelength, a process known as fluorescence; others will absorb the light without reemission. Ultraviolet light absorbed can be emitted in the visible spectrum, and visible light in shorter wavelengths (violet and blue) can be emitted at a longer visible wavelength (yellow to red) (Fig. 2.2).

The exact wavelength of light that a fluorophore will absorb and reemit is specific to the fluorophore and can be a means of identifying particular substances. This shift between the maximum absorbance wavelength and maximum emission wavelength, which is always of a lower energy, is known as the Stokes shift (Fig. 2.3). Unfortunately, biological fluids of forensic interest do not have fluorophores that have been extensively classified, despite research to identify them.[1] Most forensic biological fluids of interest likely have several fluorophores that contribute to the intrinsic fluorescence and therefore have multiple different wavelengths that have been suggested as optimal for ALS identification (Table 2.1). A further

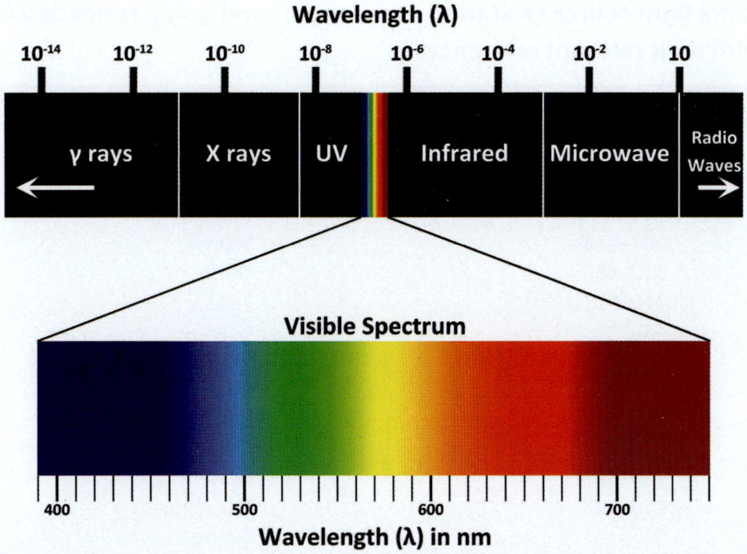

Fig. 2.2 A portion of the spectrum of light, with shorter wavelengths to the left and longer wavelengths to the right. The visible spectrum (approximately 400–750 nm), the colors most people can visualize, is shown. Most forensic alternate light source systems will use wavelengths in the shorter region of the visible spectrum and detect them at longer wavelengths in the visible spectrum. *UV*, Ultraviolet.

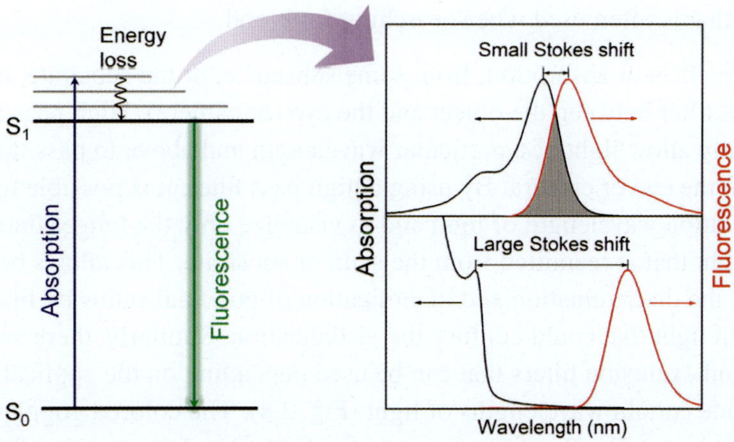

Fig. 2.3 The light energy absorption and fluorescence (emission), and overall energy loss, and how that translates to the Stokes shift. *From Zhou R, Lu X, Yang Q, et al. Nanocrystals for large Stokes shift-based optosensing. Chin Chem Lett. 2019;30:1843–1848.*

Table 2.1 Alternate light source excitation wavelengths and goggles needed for visualization, with their relevant references

Body Fluid	Excitation Wavelength (nm)	Filter/Goggles	Reference
Blood	300–900 broad absorbance	None	2,3
	415 high absorbance	None	2
	900	Wratten 88 A	4
Saliva	300–415	Yellow	5
	320–400	None	6
	415/440	Yellow	7
	450	Orange	8
	460/490	Dark red/orange	7
Semen	400–500	Orange/red	6,9
	570	Dark red	7
Sweat	440/460	Orange/yellow	10
Tears	250–365	None	11
	410–475	Dark blue	11
Urine	415	Orange	7
	440/460	Orange/yellow	7
	490	Dark red	7
Vaginal fluid	450	Orange	8

consideration is the substrate that may have its own florescent properties, which could also be used as a means of locating a stain. For example, if the substrate fluoresces at a certain wavelength of light, but the biological fluid does not, then the stain would show as a dark area, a property that is often used when searching for blood.

If there is fluorescence, or absorption, from some substance, or the substrate, it is visualized using a high pass filter between the object and the eye (or camera). High pass filters, as their name implies, only allow light of a particular wavelength and above to pass through them and ultimately to the eye or camera. By using a high pass filter, it is possible to remove the original excitation wavelength of light and to visualize only the longer fluorescence wavelength of light that is reemitted from the stain or substrate. This allows better visualization for the discrimination and identification of potential stains by filtering out lower wavelength light that could confuse the visualization. Similarly, there are low pass, band pass, or band exclusion filters that can be used depending on the application, each of which will exclude certain wavelengths of light (Fig. 2.4). The colored goggles or filters are recommended for better visualization of the stains. The color designations of these filters are easier to report and understand than providing specific wavelengths.

The main concern when using any ALS system for the screening of body fluids is the large number of false positives that can be obtained. Other biological or nonbiological substances that

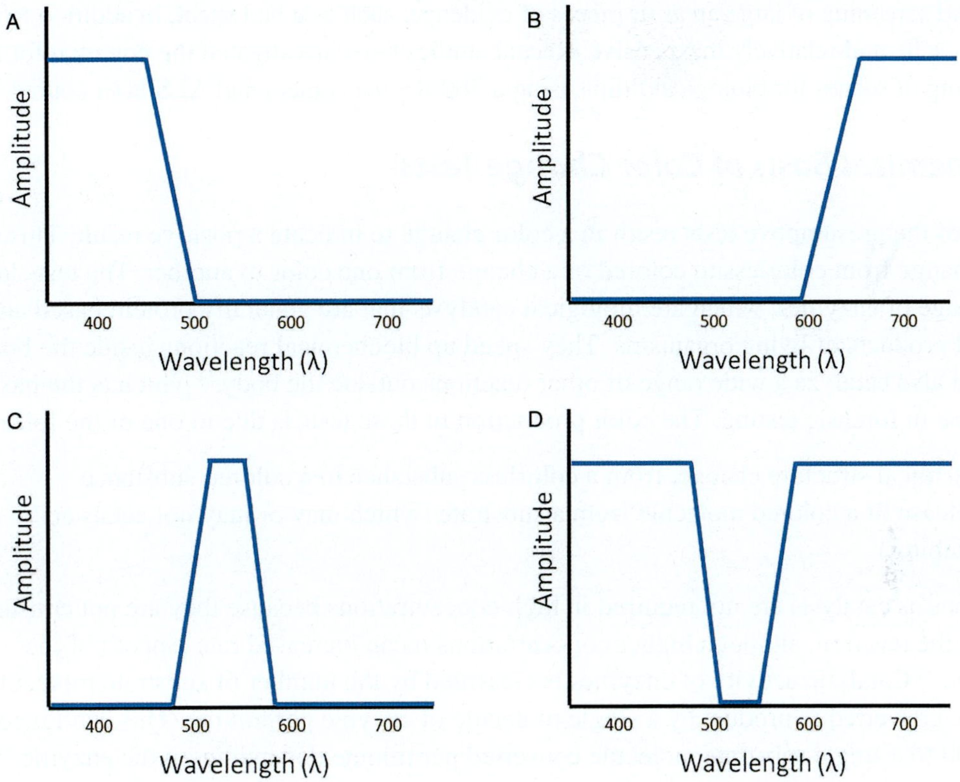

Fig. 2.4 Examples of the different filters that can be used in combination with alternate light sources to allow better visualization of any fluorescence from a stain. The wavelengths of light that can be targeted for inclusion or exclusion are dictated by the filter used. (A) Low pass, which allows only light below a certain wavelength to transmit. (B) High pass, which allows only light above a certain wavelength to transmit. (C) Band pass, which allows only a specific range of light wavelengths to transmit. (D) Band exclude, which allows all light except a specific range of light to transmit.

may not be of interest will also fluoresce using ALS and may be indistinguishable from a fluid of interest. For example, under excitation of 450 nm and viewed through orange goggles, urine will fluoresce in the same manner as semen.[8] Many background materials will also fluoresce, which can sometimes mask fluorescence from a stain. Additionally, ALS systems can produce false negatives, especially when biological fluids have been diluted, as would be expected if clothing was washed prior to examination. If ALS systems are used, they will always be followed by a secondary presumptive test, and if positive, further through confirmatory testing.

There are several commercial companies that produce ALS systems, including Polilight (Rofin, Australia), Orion-Light (Evident, United States), CrimeScope (SPEX, United States), and Crime-Light (Foster+Freeman, United Kingdom). Each company produces several different models depending on the required wavelengths and intended applications. ALS systems allow for rapid screening of large areas or pieces of evidence, such as a bed sheet, in addition to being simple, safe, and relatively inexpensive. Recent studies have investigated the potential for rapid screening of scenes for biological fluids using a 360-degree camera and ALS laser source.[12,13]

Biochemical Basis of Color Change Tests

Many of the presumptive tests result in a color change to indicate a positive result. This could be a change from colorless to colored or a change from one color to another. The tests take advantage of enzymes, which are biological catalysts that are generally protein based and are natural products of living organisms. They speed up biochemical reactions inside the body but can also catalyze a wide range of other reactions outside the body,[14] which is the basis for their use in forensic testing. The color production in these tests is due to one of the following:

- Chemical structure change, from a colorless substance to a colored substance
- Release of a colored molecule from a substrate (which may or may not act as an inhibitor)

Enzymes as catalysts are not required in high concentrations because they are not consumed during the reaction, although higher concentrations mean increased rate (speed) of the reaction.[14] Catalytic activity of enzymes is classified by the number of substrate molecules that are converted to product by a single molecule of enzyme per minute. This can range from 600,000 to a single substrate molecule converted per minute depending on the enzyme.[14]

Enzymes are also highly specific to one conversion (or very narrow range of similar conversions). For example, acid phosphatase (AP) found in seminal fluid cleaves phosphate groups off a number of substrates, which then allows the substrate to react with another substance to form a colored product (full details of this process are provided in the relevant section in Chapter 4). They are named with the suffix -ase and have different classification types depending on the reaction type (e.g., hemoglobin is a peroxidase because it catalyzes oxidative reactions using hydrogen peroxide and other substrates as electron donors).[15]

In simple terms, directly changing the chemical structure occurs through electron transfer. The color production in some chemical tests results from the loss of a hydrogen atom from an indicator (Fig. 2.5), where a colored indicator is suppressed by a hydrogen atom. When

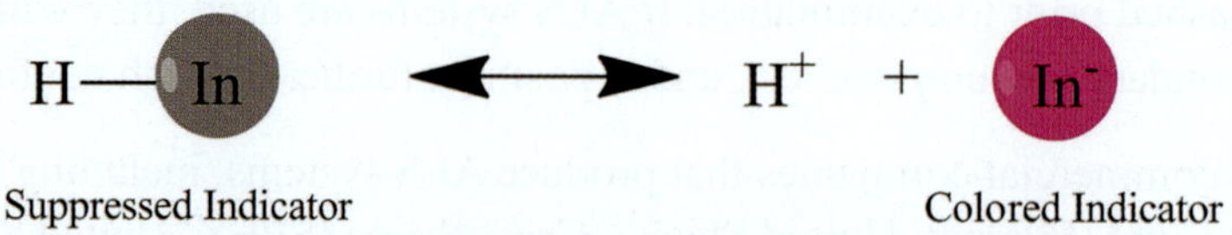

Fig. 2.5 A basic representation of an indicator, suppressed by a hydrogen atom, that when oxidized becomes a colored product that indicates a positive reaction. *Created with Advanced Chemistry Development Inc. ChemSketch. Toronto, Ontario; 2018.* www.acdlabs.com.

the suppressed indicator is oxidized, removing the hydrogen, the colored form remains and indicates a positive reaction. The hydrogen transfer may not cause a color change in itself but may initiate further reactions that change the substrate into a colored product. Note that in the case of chemiluminescent reagents, the resultant indicator is in the form of luminescence and not a color change.

An enzyme in the targeted body fluid will act as the catalyst for the reaction, which will take place with the indicator and another oxidizing substance (hydrogen peroxide is common in the tests for blood). The reaction will generally occur even if the target body fluid is not present but at a much slower rate. For this reason, these tests will have a time limit in which the test must show a reaction to be considered positive. Any color change outside of the time limit will be deemed negative or inconclusive.

The second method of color change relies on fluid-specific enzymes that react in a different way with a substrate. This can be in the separation of one substrate molecule into two parts, allowing one of the parts to interact with an inactive indicator molecule to create a colored indicator complex (Fig. 2.6). Other tests may have an anchored indicator, and the target enzyme will break the bond between the indicator and substrate, allowing the indicator to diffuse or move away from the substrate.

The benefits of these enzymatically driven tests include speed and sensitivity. There are some potential problems with this type of test as the enzymes used are differentially expressed, which means that they may be present in nontarget fluids or may be expressed at different

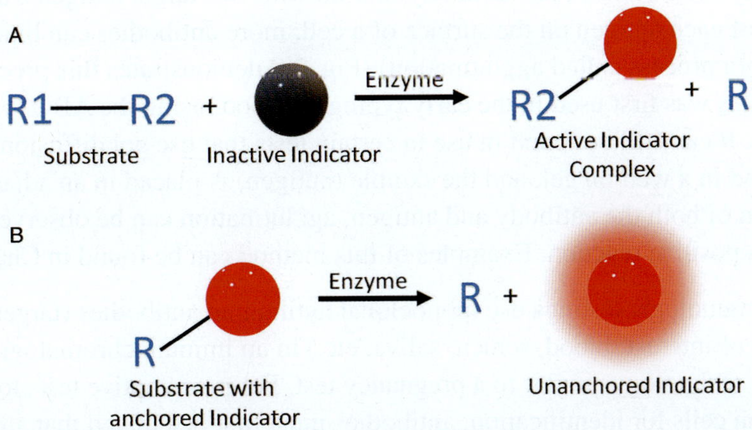

Fig. 2.6 A basic representation of two methods of enzyme activation of an indicator, used in presumptive tests. (A) A substrate molecule is cleaved into two parts by enzymatic action, with one part of the substrate interacting with an inactive indicator molecule and forming a colored active indicator complex. (B) A substrate anchored indicator, where the bond between the substrate and indicator molecule is cleaved via enzyme activity releasing the indicator, which would result in a diffusion of the colored product.

levels between people or even at different times within the same person. Generally, they are expressed at higher levels in the biological fluids of interest than any other fluids, and this only becomes a concern where samples may be diluted, which would show slow or low-level positives that could also be obtained from low-level enzymes in nontarget biological fluids. Each of the tests is discussed in detail in its relevant chapter, including the active molecules and indicators.

Immunologic Testing: Antigen, Antibody, Enzyme-Linked Immunosorbent Assay

Most biological sample types have antigen-antibody testing available through enzyme-linked immunosorbent assay (ELISA) or immunochromatographic test strips. Antigens are chemical structures, usually proteins or polysaccharides, that are found as parts of other cells or as toxins from invading microorganisms. These invading organisms will stimulate the body's defenses, which respond by producing antibodies.[16–18] In addition to foreign substances in the body, each person's own cells will contain antigens that differ for each cell type and can differ between people. For the presumptive identification of body fluids, those antigens that are specific to a particular fluid and are common between different people are targeted.

Each antibody, also called an immunoglobulin, binds to a target antigen tightly and with great specificity.[16] An antibody is a Y-shaped molecule that reacts with a specific antigen, and there is a specific antibody produced for each antigen[16,17] (Fig. 2.7). Each arm of the Y ends in a binding site, which are complimentary to an antigen so that there are two binding sites on every antibody.[16] This allows one antibody to bind with two target antigens; as there are multiple copies of each antigen on the surface of a cell, more antibodies can bind creating a network of cells (a process called agglutination) (Fig. 2.8 demonstrates this process for blood cells). This process was first used in the early typing of blood, using the ABO typing system and similar tests. It can still be found in use in certain tests that use gel diffusion, where the antibody is placed in a well on gel, and the sample (antigen) is placed in an adjacent well; through diffusion of both the antibody and antigen, agglutination can be observed where they meet if there is a positive reaction. Examples of this method can be found in Chapter 6.

Most current immunologic testings use monoclonal antihuman antibodies (targeted to the biological tissue of interest: blood, semen, saliva, etc.) in an immunochromatographic membrane assay technology similar to a pregnancy test. For presumptive tests to target antigens found on cells for identification, antibodies must first be created that are specific to those antigens found on or within those cell types. The process of creating antibodies is complex, but in general terms if an antigen is injected into an animal, usually a rabbit, then the rabbit will produce antibodies to target the invading substance. These can be isolated from the rabbit and are known as polyclonal antibodies because there are several different antigens in the injected substance that the rabbit's immune system will target with antibodies. To

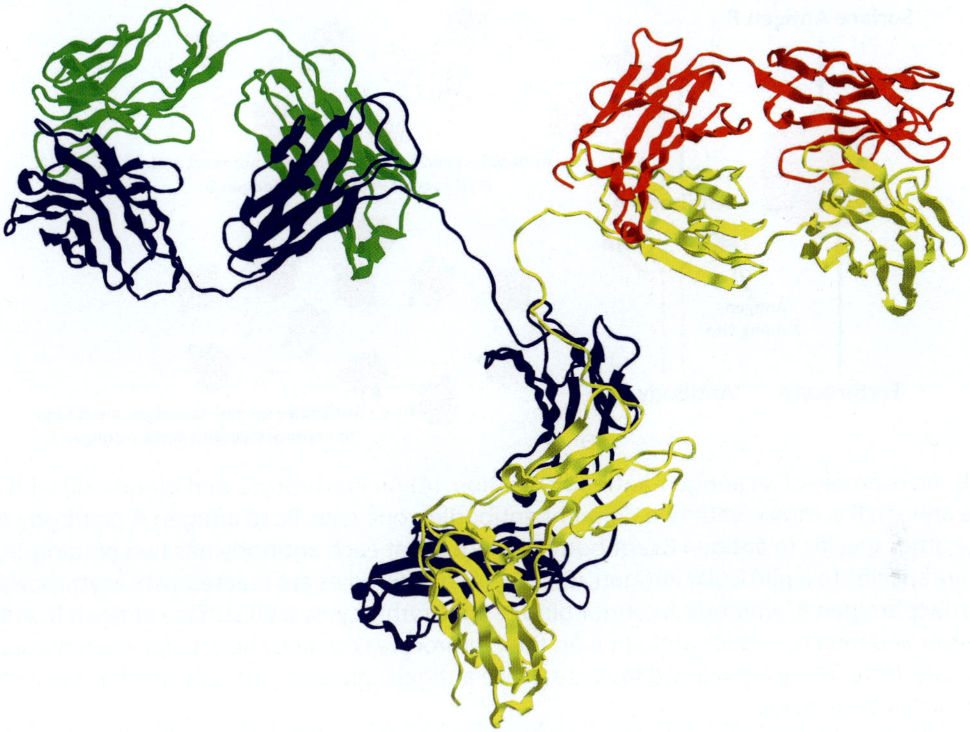

Fig. 2.7 The three-dimensional structure of a typical antibody. Note the Y-shaped structure made up of two heavy chains *(yellow, blue)* and two light chains *(green, red)*. The antigen binding sites, the tips of the Y, contain the variable regions of both the light and heavy chains; these are the regions that vary in their amino acid sequence to give specificity to a particular antigen. This antibody is an IgG2a (PDB:1IGT). Created in Chem3DPro 12.0. *From Harris LJ, Larson SB, Hasel KW, et al. Refined structure of an intact IgG2a monoclonal antibody. J Biochem. 1997;36:1581–1597.*

force a single antibody to be produced, the target antigen, isolated from the fluid of interest, is injected; therefore, only a single type of antibody is produced, known as a monoclonal antibody. To ensure consistency between batches of antibodies, the spleen cells of the rabbit are removed and fused to cancer cells that will produce consistent antibodies.[17]

Due to the nature of the body fluids, despite being human derived and targeted, the protein structure of common antigens will be highly conserved, so there is still the possibility that these tests can cross-react with other species.

ELISA is an assay technique used in many fields to detect low levels of targets (e.g., antigens, antibodies, peptides, proteins, glycoproteins, viruses) in biological samples.[19] ELISA testing has been used for decades for most biological fluids, and it remains in use today.[20–24] The benefits of using ELISA over other immunologic methods is its high sensitivity and specificity. Although this can be beneficial in some circumstances, the level of sensitivity when using ELISA combined with the differential expression of biological targets (antigens) means that

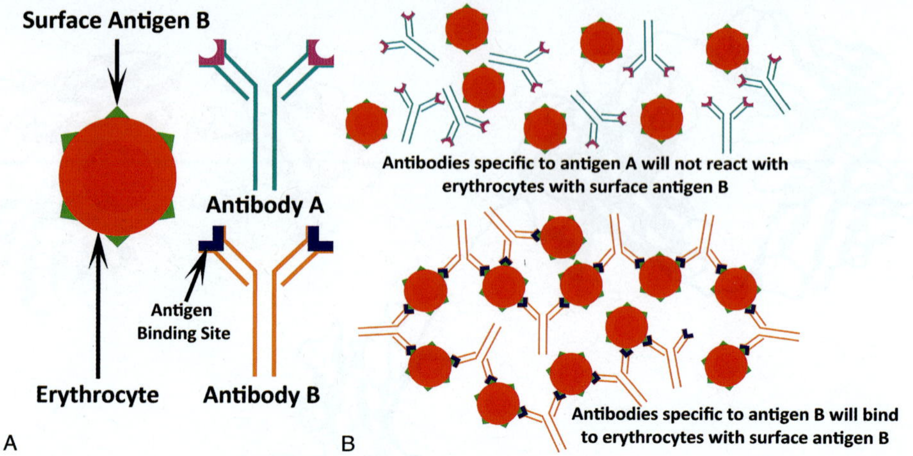

Fig. 2.8 An example of an antigen-antibody reaction. (A) An erythrocyte (red blood cell) with surface antigen B is shown with two different antibodies: one specific to antigen A (antibody A) and the other specific to antigen B (antibody B). Notice that each antibody has two binding sites, which are specific to a particular antigen. (B) If the two antibodies are reacted with erythrocytes with surface antigen B, antibody A cannot bind to the erythrocytes with surface antigen B. Antibody B, however, will bind to surface antigen B on the erythrocytes causing them to form a network, or agglutinate. Note: There are many different surface antigens present, but only one has been shown for simplicity of the image.

cross-reactions with very low levels of antigens in other biological fluids can be observed.[25] There are different types of ELISA (direct, indirect, sandwich, competitive), and each has a different action for detection but the same underlying principle of action (Fig. 2.9). The way an ELISA is assessed is usually based on the intensity of color (or reduced color) as measured using a spectrophotometer or plate reader and can be compared to a series of standards to obtain accurate concentrations of the target.

ELISA testing has several different steps and is susceptible to accurately timing those steps and reading the results at specific times. It is therefore not a method that can be used outside of the laboratory and is restricted for use as a confirmatory assay.

Immunochromatographic test strips function on similar principles as ELISA but are much more portable and less susceptible to variables such as temperature and time that affect ELISA tests. They tend to be less sensitive than ELISA, but this is often beneficial as the differential expression of many biological fluid targets means that cross-reactions are seen less frequently.[25]

The tests are generally contained in a cartridge format, with a well to input the sample; a window contains the anchored antibodies that are used for detection in combination with a secondary reaction site that functions as a control to indicate the test is functioning as expected. The result is often compared to a pregnancy test, with easy-to-determine positive and negative results (Fig. 2.10).

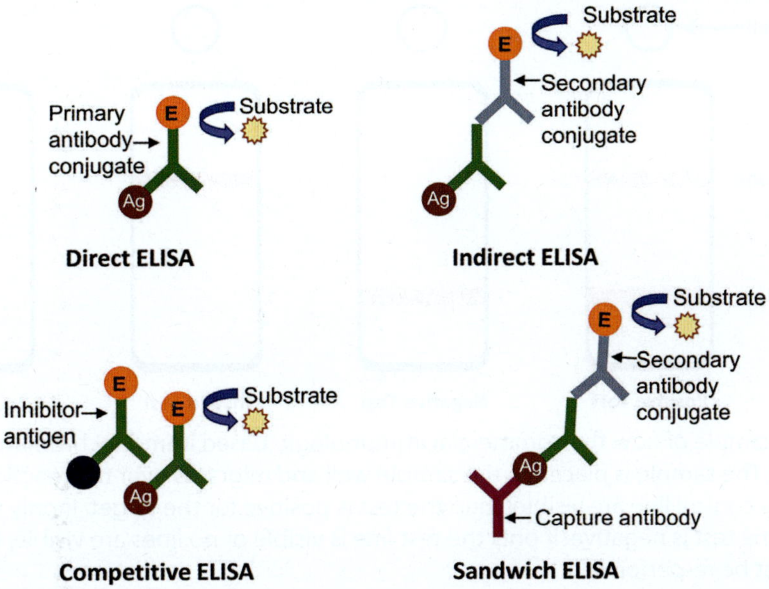

Fig. 2.9 A representation of the methods of action of direct, indirect, competitive, and sandwich enzyme-linked immunosorbent assay *(ELISA)* tests. All methods use an enzyme (*E*, usually horseradish peroxidase [HPA]) that is detected by the application of a substrate resulting in a color change that is proportional to the amount of antigen/antibody complexes present. Direct testing involves the target antigen being immobilized then reacted with an antibody complexed with HPA. Indirect testing involves the target antigen being immobilized then reacted with an antibody, which is then reacted with a secondary antibody conjugate with HPA, which binds to the primary antibody. Competitive ELISA involves the use of an antigen immobilized on a plate, an enzyme conjugated antibody, and a sample. If the sample contains the target antibody, it will be unlabeled and will compete for binding sites on the immobilized antigen, resulting in a reduction in colored product as the sample antibody concentration increases. Sandwich ELISA is the most common method used in forensic testing and involves an anchored antibody that binds with a target antigen, which is then reacted with a secondary antibody, which binds to a different epitope on the antigen; a secondary anti-antibody conjugate with HPA is then reacted, creating a sandwich. *Ag*, Antigen; *E*, enzyme. *From Anagu LO, Andoh NE. In: Ashfield R, Oli AN, Esimone C, et al., eds. Vaccinology and Methods in Vaccine Research. Academic Press; 2022:95–131.*

The lateral flow immunochromatographic tests use multiple antibodies to detect a target antigen. They contain a mobile monoclonal antitarget antibody-dye conjugate that forms a mobile antigen-antibody complex. This complex migrates through the test to an immobilized polyclonal antitarget antibody, which captures the mobile antigen-antibody complex causing a 'sandwich' to be formed. When the concentration of target is above a certain threshold, the dye in the system will be visible and indicate a positive result, which is the test line. All lateral flow immunochromatographic tests also contain an internal control; unbound antitarget antibody-dye conjugate cannot be captured by the immobilized antitarget antibody and instead flow through the strip to a second immobilized antitarget immunoglobulin

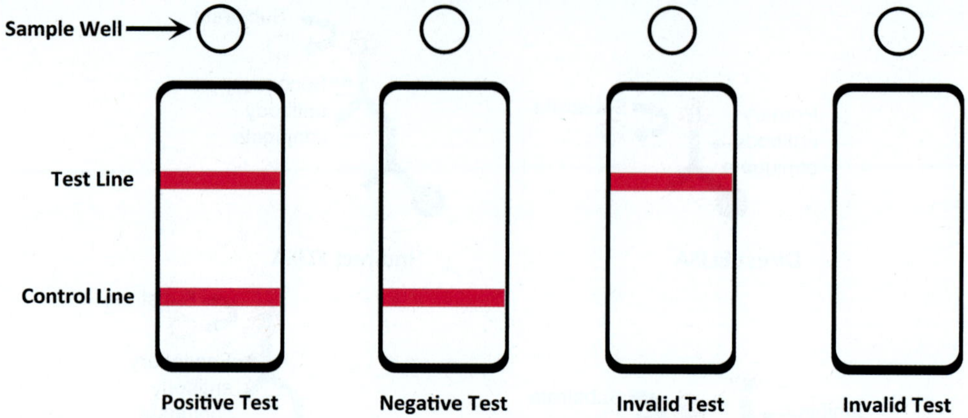

Fig. 2.10 An example of how the commercial immunologic-based immunochromatographic tests are interpreted. The sample is placed in the sample well and migrates over the reaction area. If the test line and the control line are visible, then the test is positive for the target. If only the control line is visible, then the test is negative. If only the test line is visible or no lines are visible, then the test is invalid and must be re-performed.

antibody present and form another product, which is the control line. The sample in fluid form is drawn along the test strip using a wick at the far end of the membrane and all immunochromatographic tests will have a time component after the sample is added to allow the sample and antigen-antibody complex to flow across the entire test strip. An example using erythrocytes as the target is provided in Fig. 2.11.

The lateral flow immunochromatographic tests are available for all major body fluids of interest, and specific considerations of testing for each biological fluid are discussed in relevant chapters. In general, they are more specific to human body fluids than the other methods but are also less sensitive to the fluid of interest. Many laboratories use these lateral flow tests as confirmatory, although cross-reactions are still possible and are discussed with each test individually.

High-Dose Hook Effect

The high-dose hook effect (HDHE), sometimes called the hook effect or prozone phenomenon, is an antigen excess that results in a lowered signal or false negative in two-site immunologic assays. Excessive concentrations of the system by target antigens will inhibit the binding of the mobile monoclonal antitarget antibody-dye conjugate by saturating the immobilized polyclonal antitarget antibody test line with unlabeled/complexed antigens (Fig. 2.12).

This results in what appears to be a negative testing outcome despite huge amounts of target analyte. The phenomenon is well known, and all cartridge-based forensic biological fluid tests incorporate an extraction step. This extraction step is necessary because most samples will

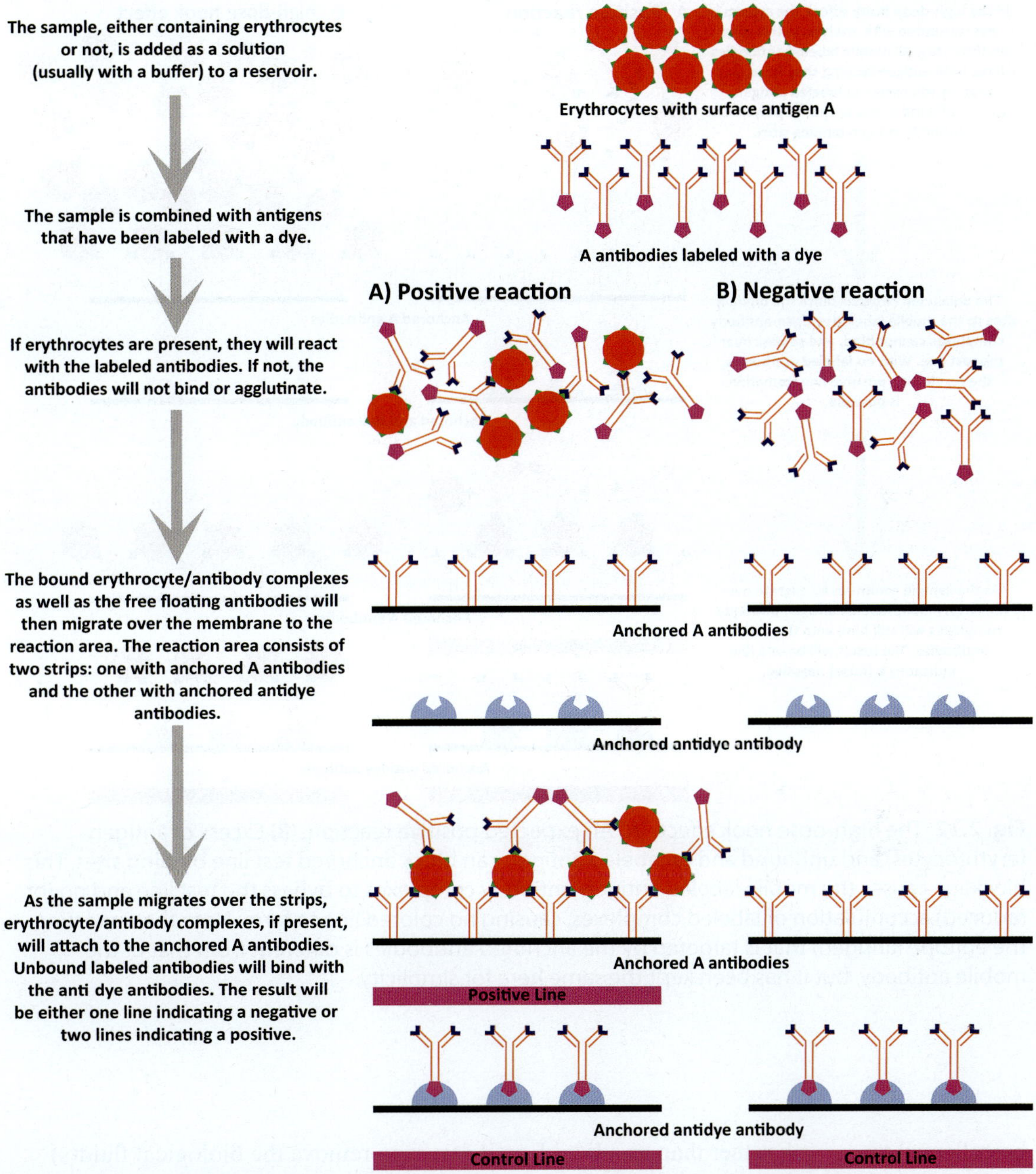

Fig. 2.11 A simplified schematic of an immunologic presumptive blood test. All immunologic presumptive tests function in a similar manner to what is depicted. If no lines are observed or only a positive line is observed, then the test is invalid and must be re-performed. Note that in testing, the epitope (antigen) that is targeted by the anchored antibodies is different from that of the mobile antibody, but it has been kept the same here for simplicity.

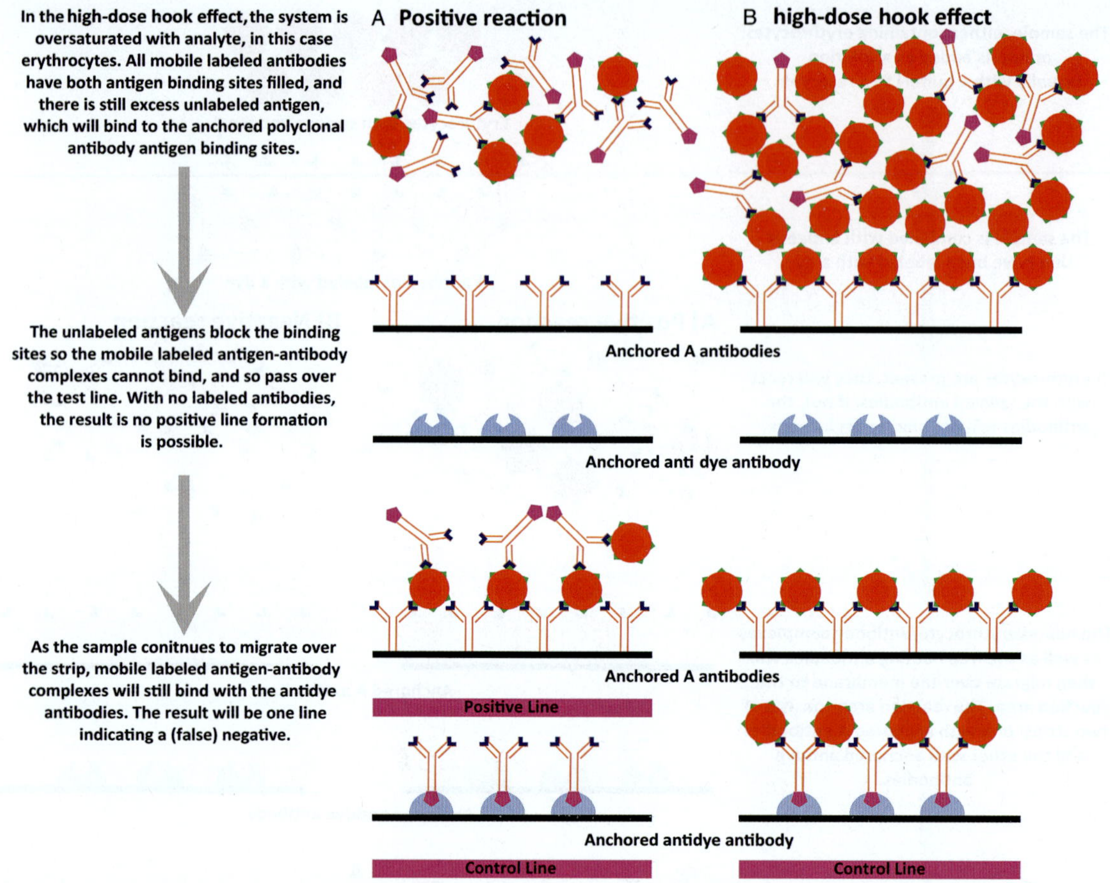

Fig. 2.12 The high-dose hook effect. (A) An expected positive reaction. (B) Excess of antigen (erythrocytes) and unbound and unlabeled antigen can block anchored test line binding sites. This blockage causes the mobile labeled antigen-antibody complexes to bypass the test line and no (or reduced) accumulation of labeled complexes, causing no colored line to form. Note that in testing, the epitope (antigen) that is targeted by the anchored antibodies is different from that of the mobile antibody, but it has been kept the same here for simplicity.

be collected via a swab rather than as a liquid, so it serves to remove the biological fluid(s) from the swab and into a buffered solution that can be added to the cartridge. It also serves to dilute the substance so that HDHE is unlikely to occur. Nevertheless, most modern tests also validate with undiluted fluids to assess the possibility of HDHE.

If there is any suspicion of HDHE, then a portion of the sample can be diluted in water or other suitable buffer and retested on a new cartridge to confirm the results.

References

1. Hensel T. *Identifying the Component Responsible for the Intrinsic Fluorescence of Seminal Fluid*. Adelaide: Flinders University; 2020.
2. Stoilovic M. Detection of semen and blood stains using polilight as a light source. *Forensic Sci Int*. 1991;51:289–296.
3. Gorzkiewicz M, Wozniak M, Grzybowski T, et al. Identification of semen in bloodstains with the use of alternative light source and biochemical screening tests. *Arch Med Sadowej Kryminol*. 2008;58:182–187.
4. Raymond MA, Hall RL. An interesting application of infra-red reflection photography to blood splash pattern interpretation. *Forensic Sci Int*. 1986;31:189–194.
5. Szeremeta M, Pepinski W, Niemcunowicz-Janica A, et al. Evaluation of visualization of biological stains with the use of alternative light source (ALS) for the purpose of genetic identification. Part I. Blood and saliva stains analysis. *Arch Med Sadowej Kryminol*. 2010;60:248–257.
6. Seidl S, Hausmann R, Betz P. Comparison of laser and mercury-arc lamp for the detection of body fluids on different substrates. *Int J Leg Med*. 2008;122:241–244.
7. Sterzik V, Panzer S, Apfelbacher M, et al. Searching for biological traces on different materials using a forensic light source and infrared photography. *Int J Leg Med*. 2016;130:599–605.
8. Vandenberg N, van Oorschot RAH. The use of Polilight in the detection of seminal fluid, saliva, and bloodstains and comparison with conventional chemical-based screening tests. *J Forensic Sci*. 2006;51: 361–370.
9. Karchewski L, Armstrong G, Nicholson ML, et al. Assessment of the Leeds spectral vision system for detecting biological stains on fabrics. *J Can Soc Forensic Sci*. 2014;47:230–243.
10. Sterzik V, Hinderberger P, Panzer S, et al. Visualizing old biological traces on different materials without using chemicals. *Int J Leg Med*. 2018;132:35–41.
11. Aparna R, Iyer RS. Detection and visualization of human tears using alternate light sources for forensic purposes. *Sci Justice*. 2021;61:771–778.
12. Sheppard K, Cassella JP, Fieldhouse S, et al. The adaptation of a 360° camera utilising an alternate light source (ALS) for the detection of biological fluids at crime scenes. *Sci Justice*. 2017;57:239–249.
13. Sheppard K, Fieldhouse SJ, Cassella JP. Simultaneous detection and image capture of biological evidence using a combined 360° camera system with single wavelength laser illumination. *Sci Justice*. 2019;59:75–82.
14. Robinson PK. Enzymes: principles and biotechnological applications. *Essays Biochem*. 2015;59:1.
15. Twala PP, Mitema A, Baburam C, et al. Breakthroughs in the discovery and use of different peroxidase isoforms of microbial origin. *AIMS Microbiol*. 2020;6:330.
16. Alberts B, Johnson A, Lewis J, et al. *Molecular Biology of the Cell*. London: Garland Publishing, Inc; 1994.
17. Saferstein R. *Criminalistics: An Introduction to Forensic Science*. 10th ed. London: Prentice Hall International (UK) Limited; 2011.
18. Voet D, Voet J, Pratt C. *Fundamentals of Biochemistry Upgrade Edition*. Brisbane: John Wiley & Sons, Inc; 1999.
19. Anagu LO, Andoh NE. In: Ashfield R, Oli AN, Esimone C, et al., eds. *Vaccinology and Methods in Vaccine Research*. Academic Press; 2022:95–131.
20. Akutsu T, Saito H, Iwasa H, et al. The applicability of ELISA detection of gastric mucosa-expressing proteins for the identification of vomit. *Int J Leg Med*. 2017;131:359–364.
21. Johnson E, Kotowski T. Detection of prostate specific antigen by ELISA. *J Forensic Sci*. 1993;38:250–258.
22. Newall P. An enzyme linked immunosorbent assay (ELISA) for the identification of Km (3) in dried bloodstains. *J Can Soc Forensic Sci*. 1985;18:78–85.
23. Quarino L, Dang Q, Hartmann J, et al. An ELISA method for the identification of salivary amylase. *J Forensic Sci*. 2005;50:873–876.
24. Sakurada K, Akutsu T, Fukushima H, et al. Detection of dermcidin for sweat identification by real-time RT-PCR and ELISA. *Forensic Sci Int*. 2010;194:80–84.
25. Wing KE. *The Evaluation of Semenogelin Proteins I and II in Semen and Other Body Fluids of Males and Females for Forensic Detection*. Perth, Australia: Murdoch University; 2021.

CHAPTER 3

Blood

Introduction

Testing for blood is the most used scientific test in forensic biology and is a cornerstone of investigation of violent crimes. Blood evidence associated with a crime can provide essential information that may help solve a case, corroborate witness testimony, define a scene of crime, or simply point the investigation in a new direction. Blood can be found in cases of violent crime, where blood from wounds or violent actions can be used to reconstruct a sequence of events through bloodstain pattern analysis.[1,2] It can also be found in many other crime types, including sexual assaults, neglect, vandalism, and other volume crime where small traces of blood may be found. DNA typing from blood has been routine since the 1990s and is used for identification purposes to identify suspects or victims or to link different scenes or crimes. Blood detection is often portrayed in popular media such as film, television, comic books, and both fiction and nonfiction literature, but often with cinematic embellishments to make it simpler and easier for the audience to understand. The reality is the testing methods available are rarely as easy or definitive as depicted in the media.

The result is that the use of blood in reconstruction and identification within a criminal investigation has become common knowledge, and as a result criminals may attempt to subvert the investigative process by cleaning blood from scenes or evidence. This is not true of all cases, but it has put the sensitivity and specificity of the tests used into prominent focus for forensic investigators. Investigators or forensic scientists now need to comment on if a stain is blood, something that is not as simple as it seems. A full understanding is therefore needed of not only the sensitivity and specificity of presumptive blood tests but also the mechanism of those tests so that we can realistically provide opinions on what else might cross-react or what might affect the sensitivity of the tests.

Tests used for the identification of blood fall into two main categories: (1) chemical tests that use the peroxidase activity of heme within hemoglobin (Hb), which are generally sensitive but not specific; and (2) immunological tests that use blood antigens to identify blood, which are generally more specific but less sensitive. There are also crystal tests specific for Hb (not only human), but they are no longer used in all laboratories, and newer methods are being developed that use DNA, RNA, mass spectroscopy, and different forms of microscopy.

Forensic Serology. DOI: http://doi.org/10.1016/B978-0-12-812968-5.00003-9

The purpose of the presumptive blood tests is to detect substances that could be blood, even at low levels that may be invisible to the naked eye. Ideally, they should be specific to human blood, but this is difficult as all vertebrates have blood that is similar in composition to human blood, including containing Hb, and all chemical-based tests cannot distinguish between human and nonhuman blood.[3] Immunological tests are more specific to human blood, but they can still suffer from cross-reactions with other often distantly related species.

Many of the chemical-based tests have been in use for over a century, and newer testing methods that improve sensitivity and specificity are still being developed. Testing will take place at crime scenes, in laboratories, or both, so this needs to be considered when selecting or designing a test. Standard protocols have been developed to ensure the tests are used properly and that evidence remains uncompromised. Each laboratory will have its own practices; however, most will have similar protocols and strategies for testing (Fig. 3.1).

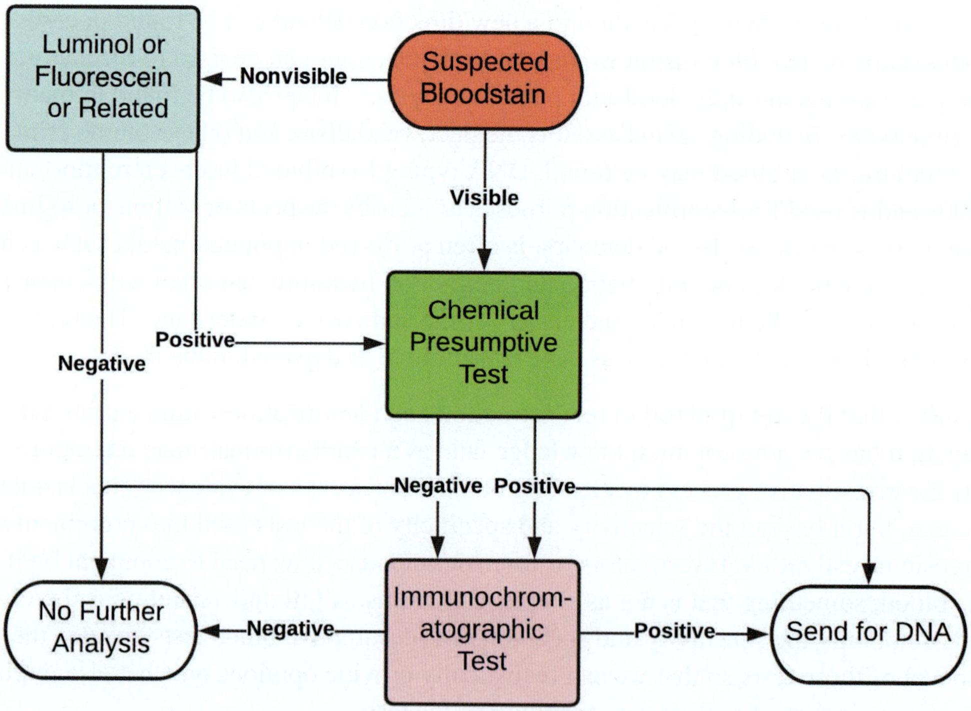

Fig. 3.1 A schematic of the current workflow when testing for a suspected bloodstain. Laboratories have different protocols and procedures, so some laboratories may not use an immunochromatographic test if their chemical test fails or may send the sample directly to DNA if the chemical test is positive. It is usual for chemical tests to be attempted prior to immunochromatographic tests because of their lower cost, speed, and ease of use. Luminol (or similar) may not be used even if a suspected stain is not visible, but chemical testing may still take place (e.g., a knife that may have been cleaned). Circumstances surrounding the alleged crime will dictate the exact workflow. Most laboratories consider the immunochromatographic tests as confirmatory and species specific, so few currently run crystal or species tests.

In addition to forensic science's use of blood identification, there is a large bank of literature relating to the detection of blood in medical samples to diagnose blood in urine and feces for help with disease diagnosis,[4–6] several studies looking at latent blood on medical equipment after hospital sterilization,[7–10] and tests being used in archaeology.[11,12] These studies use many of the same techniques and methods as forensic science, but they are applied to detecting blood in urine, feces, and other medical samples. These medical research papers are useful as they also often carry out validation studies looking at sensitivity and specificity but will not be discussed unless directly relevant to the application of the tests to forensic science.

Our current understanding of testing for blood is based on almost 200 years of worldwide research. Blood was identified through microscopic examination of erythrocytes (red blood cells [RBCs]), microscopic identification of crystals of Hb or derivatives, spectroscopic tests identifying the presence of Hb or derivatives, and tests that reacted based on the peroxidase activity of heme.

History

Blood, of all the body fluids, has the longest history of attempted identification. This is likely due to blood (generally) not being present outside of the body without some sort of trauma, although menstrual blood is an obvious exception. The earliest reference to identify blood comes from the *Talmud*[13] in the second century. The next record comes in the 10th century from China, in the famous text by Sung Tzu,[14] *The Washing Away of Unjust Imputations, or Wrongs*, where two methods of latent blood detection are discussed. The first involves heating a knife and applying vinegar, and the second involves allowing flies to land on a sickle that had been used in a murder.[15] There were probably many other attempts at identifying blood between these two noted events, but they have been lost, much as the original text of Sung Tzu has been lost and is only known from others referencing his work.

Investigations on blood identification specifically in legal medicine were first described in the early 1800s. Rattier[16] used microscopy in 1837 to identify blood and other body fluids on linen by suspending the suspected stain in water to remove cellular material and then examining it microscopically. Crystals from blood were first observed by Parks in 1852,[17] and comments by Jones[18] suggest that these were crystals of haematin. This was further developed by Teichmann in 1853[19] to become the crystal blood test with his name, which was explored by many researchers in the mid-1800s.[20–22]

Other investigators looked at the spectrum produced from blood under various conditions.[23] Further work on microscopic identification of blood was carried out by Ritter[24] in 1854, who published a major text on determining blood, semen, and excrement stains in forensic pharmacology. Barruel[25] put forward research in 1829 claiming he could tell the sex and species of blood by applying sulfuric acid to the stains and assessing the odor to determine if it smelled like an elderly man or an elderly woman.

The same procedure could be used to determine the species by the odor the sample produced with sulfuric acid (if the smell was of a horse, a dog, etc.) provided the sample was processed in the required time frame. In 1907, Sutherland called this Barruel's test, indicating it had been in use for 80 years.[26] In 1860, Robin and Tardieu[27] also looked at microscopy of bloodstains in relation to forensic cases and investigated if the blood came from a male or female using the sulfuric acid test; however, they were unable to determine the sex based on the odor, which they attributed to the stains being too small and old (21 days).[27] They stated conclusively that the stain examined was from a female, but no details are provided given that the odor test failed.

In 1851, Schönbein[28] introduced the guaiac test, and in 1863,[29] he succeeded in using a hydrogen peroxide (H_2O_2) solution to react with blood. A positive result was indicated by foaming, and this formed the beginning of the development of chemical-based blood identification tests. In 1875, Cauvet[30] examined mixed stains of blood and vaginal mucus or semen and was able to identify leukocytes and erythrocytes microscopically. He refers to chemical identification of blood and to heme crystals but provides no details as to what tests or methods he used.

A decade later, Florence[31] published a text exploring a range of questions relating to bloodstain identification, including if a stain is blood, if it is male or female or mammalian, where on the body the blood originated, if it is arterial or venous or menstrual, if it is from rape or childbirth, among other aspects. Most of the details in Florence's text are considered beyond the scope of what we can currently determine, but they aligned with other published claims of the time.[25] Von Baeyer[32] synthesized phenolphthalein in 1880, although its use for blood identification was not realized until 1903.[33]

The turn of the 20th century saw an increase in scientific publications relating to forensic investigations and specifically blood identification. Many of the tests used today were originally developed or applied to forensic science during the early part of the 1900s. The value of blood evidence to forensic investigations also began to be realized more fully, and in 1902, Küster[34] published work on the judicial evidence of blood demonstrating the expanding recognition of its application to criminal investigations. In 1907, Sutherland published a text written for both scientists and laypeople, titled *Bloodstains: Their Detection and the Determination of Their Source. A Manual for the Medical and Legal Professions*.[26] This work was written as a compendium for modern (at that time) detection of blood and determination of its source. Within it, Sutherland details many obsolete methods of blood identification that were used in the 1800s (e.g., solubility of stains, Barruel's test). In subsequent years the testing for blood became more refined, and research into its identification became common. It is also at this point that many of the modern tests for blood were either developed or introduced, or knowledge of them was expanded in terms of sensitivity and specificity. Details of these papers can be found with their respective tests in later sections.

As late as 1933, Medinger[35] was very critical of presumptive blood tests. He referred to them as preliminary, claiming they wreak havoc especially because of their lack of specificity but also lack of understanding and "impermissible generalization of the results obtained." He claimed the tests were in disrepute.

Much of the early work was occult detection of blood mainly in feces.[36,37] In this case, occult refers to undiagnosed or hidden blood within fecal material and was used to diagnose ulcers or carcinomas.[37] Some of the testing used today was originally developed for medical detection of blood, but the levels and possible interfering substances also apply to forensic investigation, so they have been adapted for forensic use. Further details of the early history of each test are provided in this chapter, but know the scientists mentioned in the preceding paragraphs were instrumental in the evolution of presumptive blood identification.

Biology of Blood

Although blood appears as a thick homologous liquid, it consists of a highly complex mixture of cells, enzymes, proteins, and inorganic substances.[38,39] Blood is considered a connective tissue of blood cells surrounded by fluid matrix called blood plasma. If a sample of blood was spun to separate the components, it would form three layers: the heavier hematocrit made up of erythrocytes (red blood cells [RBCs]) at the bottom, a thin middle layer called the buffy coat containing leukocytes (white blood cells [WBCs]) and platelets, and a top layer of plasma. The proportions of each are 45% RBCs, less than 1% WBCs and platelets, and 55% plasma (Fig. 3.2). The cellular components of blood (RBCs, WBCs, platelets) are known as the formed elements.

Blood accounts for roughly 8% of a person's body weight (i.e., 5–6 L for men, 4–5 L for women).[38] The proportion of RBCs can vary and range from 47% $\pm$ 5% to 42% $\pm$ 5% for men and women, respectively (Table 3.1). RBCs are produced in a process called erythropoiesis in red bone marrow, which is found in long bones and flat bones. The process begins with a hematopoietic stem cell, and the process to becoming a RBC (synthesizing Hb, which is what gives the RBC its color, and ejecting the nucleus and organelles) takes about 15 days.[38] At the final stage of development RBCs take on their characteristic biconcave shape. Hematopoietic stem cells, through a different process, also give rise to the different WBCs and platelets. The WBCs are the only cellular components in blood to have normal cell structure and thus a nucleus and DNA.

Blood is pumped by the heart throughout the body and performs essential functions, including transporting oxygen from the lungs, and nutrients from the digestive tract to all areas of the body; transporting hormones to target organs; and transporting metabolic waste products to be expelled from the body. Unlike other body fluids, blood should not naturally be found outside of the body (note this is in reference to venous blood; menstrual blood will

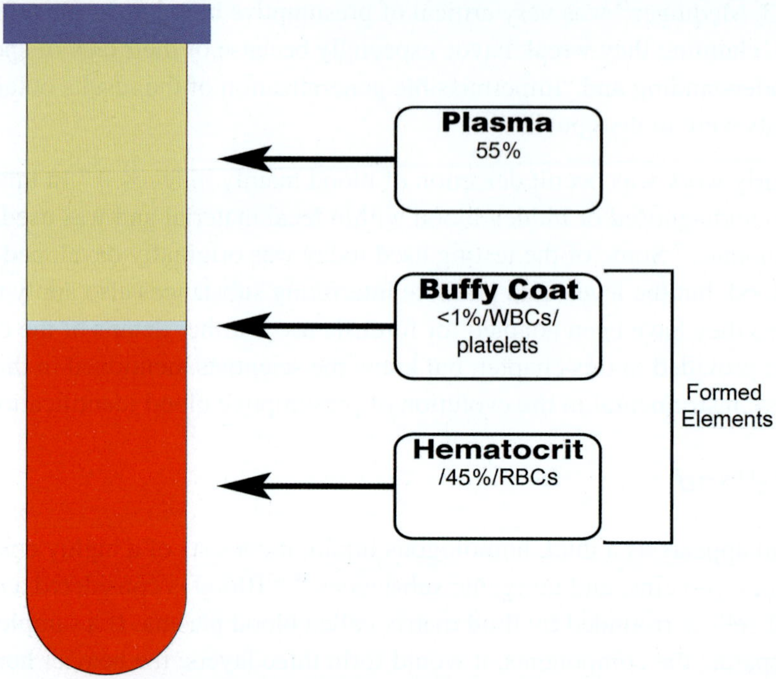

Fig. 3.2 The components of whole blood, showing the proportions of plasma and formed elements. *RBCs*, Red blood cells; *WBCs*, white blood cells.

Table 3.1 The components of blood

Blood Component	Male	Female
Total volume	5–6 L	4–5 L
Formed elements	47% ± 5%	42% ± 5%
Erythrocytes	4.7–6.1 million red blood cells (RBCs)/μL	4.2–5.4 million RBCs/μL
Hemoglobin	250 million/RBC	
Heme	1 billion/RBC	
Platelets	150,000–400,000/μL	
Leukocytes	4800–10,800/μL	

From Marieb EN, Hoehn K. *Human Anatomy & Physiology*. 9th ed. London: Benjamin Cummings; 2013:1107.

be discussed separately). Blood in vertebrates is red, and this can vary from a dark red (low oxygen) to a bright scarlet red (high oxygen) depending on the level of oxygen in the blood (Fig. 3.3).[38] Because of the formation of methemoglobin, however, it becomes brown when dried or stored and can then be confused with other substances.[40]

Unlike most cells in the body, RBCs and platelets do not have a nucleus or mitochondria and so do not hold any DNA. DNA derived from blood comes from WBCs and circulating cell-free DNA (cirDNA).[41] Cell death is the main source of cirDNA, but it can also be released

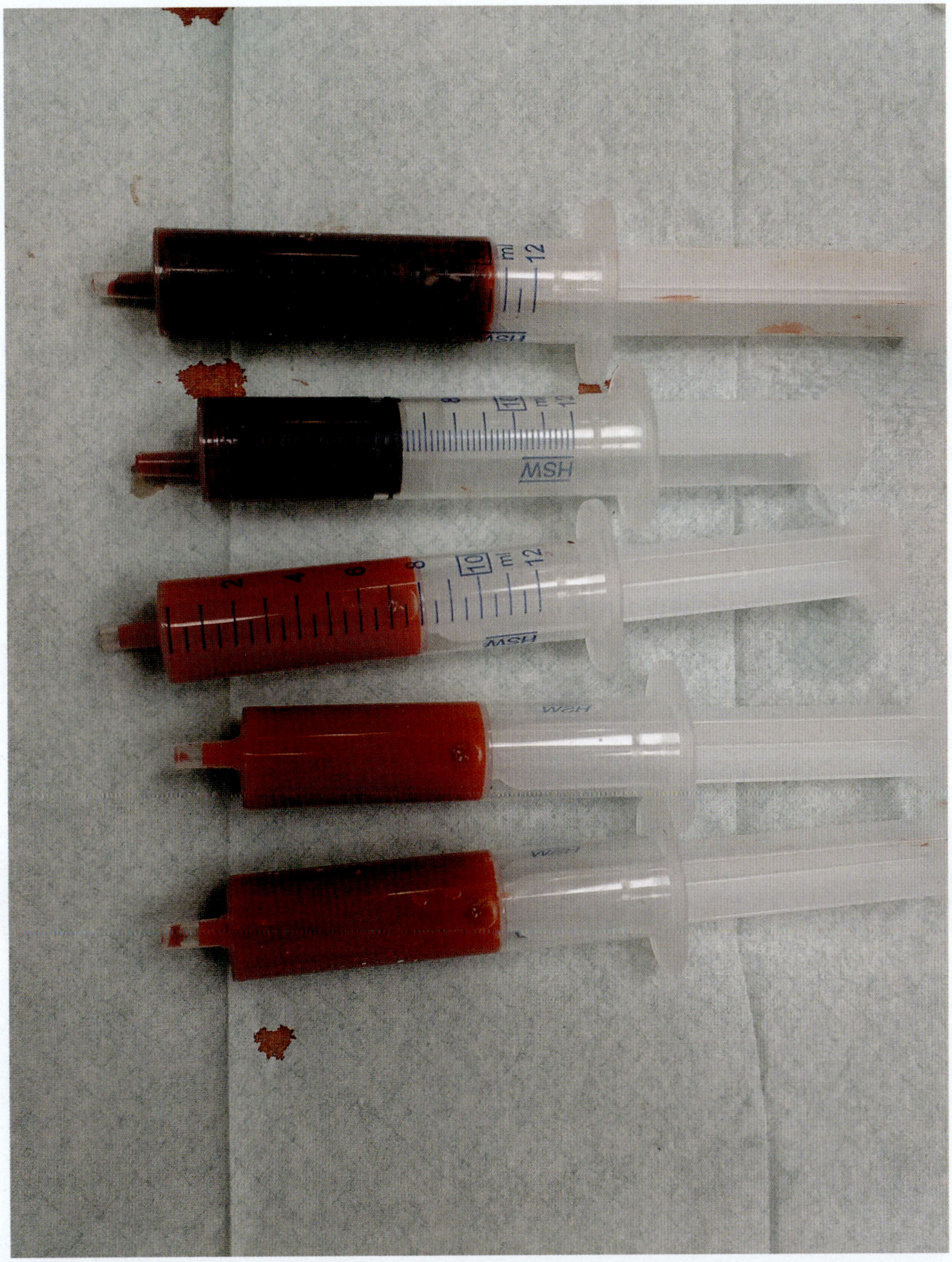

Fig. 3.3 The different colors of blood based on different oxygen levels, from low *(top)* to high *(bottom)*. *From CC BY-SA 3.0 Wesalius.* https://en.wikipedia.org/wiki/Blood#/media/File:Venous_and_arterial_blood.jpg.

by viable cells;[42,43] however, even with few components of blood containing DNA, it is still considered an excellent source of DNA for profiling.

Blood plasma accounts for 55% of blood volume, is composed primarily (~90%) of water, and contains over 100 different dissolved solutes, including nutrients, gases, hormones, waste materials, and proteins (Table 3.2). Plasma proteins account for 8% of plasma weight and serve a variety of functions. Despite the large number of components, the composition of blood plasma remains consistent through several homeostatic processes.

For presumptive testing purposes, the most important component of blood is the RBC because most of these tests react with the Hb found within or with antigens on the surface of RBCs. Erythrocytes are small cells shaped like biconcave disks with an approximate diameter of 7.5 μm.[44] They have a plasma membrane but no nucleus, and they are essentially filled with Hb (Fig. 3.4). Discounting its water content, an erythrocyte is 97% Hb, which is equivalent to approximately 250 million molecules of Hb or 1 billion heme molecules per cell.[38]

Table 3.2 The main components of plasma

Constituent	Components
Electrolytes	Na^+, K^+, Ca^{2+}, Mg^{2+}, Cl^-, PO_4^{3-}, SO_4^{2-}, CHO_3^-
Plasma proteins	Albumin (60%), globulins (α, β, γ; 30%), fibrinogen (4%)
Nonprotein nitrogenous substances	Urea, uric acid, creatinine, ammonium salts, other cellular metabolic byproducts
Nutrients	Glucose, simple carbohydrates, amino acids, fatty acids, glycerol, triglycerides, cholesterol, vitamins
Respiratory gases	O_2, CO_2
Hormones	Steroid and thyroid hormones

From Marieb EN, Hoehn K. *Human Anatomy & Physiology*. 9th ed. London: Benjamin Cummings; 2013:1107.

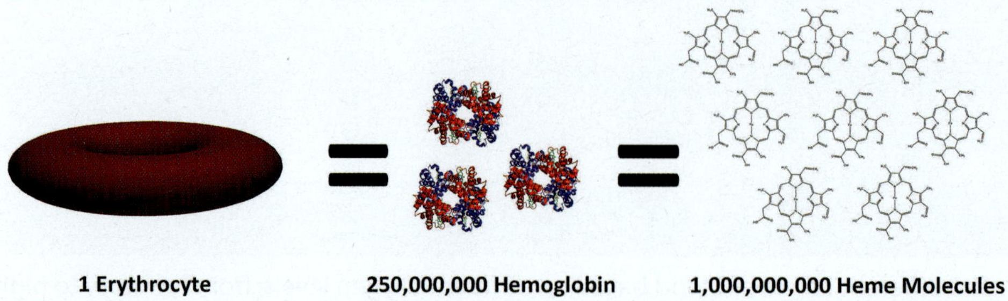

Fig. 3.4 The biconcave nature of red blood cells (RBCs) and the relationship between RBCs and hemoglobin and heme molecules. A single RBC contains in the region of 1 billion heme molecules. *From Wheeler R. Haemoglobin. http://commons.wikimedia.org/wiki/File:1GZX_Haemoglobin.png. 2007 [hemoglobin]; Advanced Chemistry Development Inc. ChemSketch. Toronto, Ontario. www.acdlabs.com. 2018 [heme].*

Hb is the oxygen-transporting molecule found in the RBCs of all vertebrates and some invertebrates.[47] Hb is what gives blood its red color and is a tetrameric hemoprotein composed of four subunits (known as globulins), two α chains and two β chains, each of which is bound to a heme prosthetic group (Fig. 3.5A).[48] Each heme residue contains one central, coordinately bound iron atom that is normally in the Fe^{2+}, or ferrous, oxidation state (see Fig. 3.5B).[47,49] Hb is a peroxidase, and in the presence of H_2O_2 it acts as an electron acceptor and can catalyze a number of oxidative reactions.[50] It is this process that many of the presumptive tests for blood exploit.

Chemical tests for blood use the heme within Hb, which is a protoporphyrin IX coordination complex.[47] The Fe is bound in the middle of the protoporphyrin IX ring by four N atoms;[47] a fifth N atom (from a histidine) is bound above the plane of the heme ring, which serves to stabilize the interaction between the heme and the protein and leaves the remaining position open to bind O_2 (Fig. 3.6). When active in the body, the Fe in heme is kept in the 2+ state through several mechanisms, but once outside an organism the blood undergoes a series of degradation processes.[47] During the degradation process, the histidine is generally lost, and there is rapid spontaneous oxidation of the Fe^{2+} to Fe^{3+}. It is when Hb is in its ferric state (Fe^{3+}) that it is reactive with the chemical tests for blood.

In addition to Hb, blood also contains surface antigens that are targeted by some presumptive tests for blood. Most of these antigens are synthesized by the RBC, but some are adsorbed onto the RBC membrane from the plasma.[52] These antigens can be proteins or sugars, they are attached to various components in the RBC membrane, and they are responsible for a variety

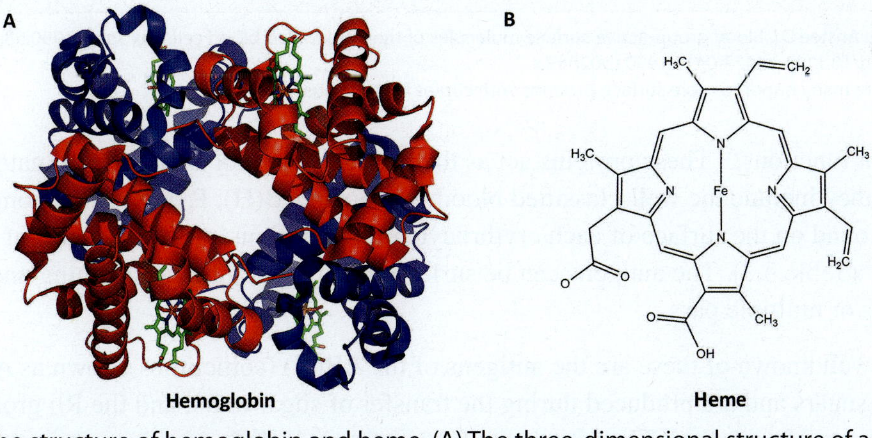

Fig. 3.5 The structure of hemoglobin and heme. (A) The three-dimensional structure of a hemoglobin molecule containing four polypeptide chains: two α chains *(red)* and two β chains *(blue)*. Each chain is complexed with a heme group *(green)* with iron at its center. (B) The structure of a single heme molecule. *(A) From Wheeler R. Haemoglobin. http://commons.wikimedia.org/wiki/File:1GZX_Haemoglobin.png. 2007; (B) from Advanced Chemistry Development Inc. ChemSketch. Toronto, Ontario. www.acdlabs.com. 2018.*

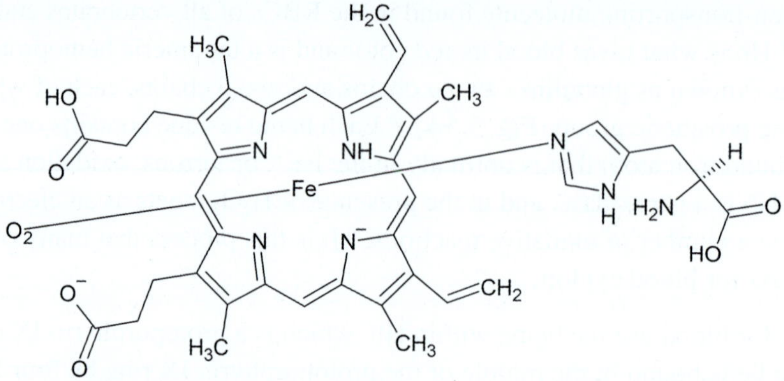

Fig. 3.6 The heme protoporphyrin IX ring bound to a histidine and oxygen. *Image created with Advanced Chemistry Development Inc. From Advanced Chemistry Development Inc. ChemSketch. Toronto, Ontario. www.acdlabs.com. 2018.*

Table 3.3 Some major surface proteins found on red blood cells, their copies per cell, and blood group antigens used to detect them

Protein	Copies per Cell	Blood Group Antigens
Anion transport	1 million	ABH
Glycophorin A	1 million	MN
Glucose transporter	500,000	ABH
Glycophorin B	250,000	N
Rh polypeptides (two types)	200,000–400,000 (combined)	Rh
Glycophorin C	60,000–120,000	Ge
Glycophorin D	15,000–20,000	Ge

Adapted from Anstee DJ. Blood group-active surface molecules of the human Red blood cell. *Vox Sang*. 1990;58(1): 1–20. https://doi.org/10.1111/j.1423-0410.1990.tb02049.x.
Note: There are many hundred more surface proteins with copies in the thousands.

of different functions.[53] These proteins act as the antigen target for immunochromatographic tests, and they include the well-classified blood groupings AB(H), P, MN, Rh, among others. They are found on the surface of each erythrocyte in the millions, with thousands of copies of each[53,54] (Table 3.3). The antigens can be surface based or membrane spanning and either single pass or multiple pass.

The most well known of these are the antigens of the AB(H) (sometimes known as ABO), which are sugars and are produced during the transfer of sugar units, and the Rh group, which consists of proteins.[53] The functions of the antigens include membrane transporters, receptors and adhesion molecules, complement regulatory glycoproteins, enzymes, structural components, and components of the glycocalyx (cell coat).[52] Further details of RBC antigens and blood group markers, which was the main method of genetic profiling prior to DNA, can be found in Appendix I.

Sampling

Since their introduction, presumptive blood reagents have become a standard tool used daily in forensic investigations. Standard operating procedures (SOPs) and protocols have been developed for scene and laboratory use to ensure the tests are properly employed and that evidence integrity is protected. Each laboratory will have its own practices; however, most will have very similar protocols.

It is always advisable that original stains and items be subsampled and not have presumptive reagents applied directly to the suspected bloodstain. This is to maintain sample integrity and allow subsequent resampling as needed (e.g., for DNA or defense scientists). Some tests, such as alternate light sources (ALS), are used to identify potential areas of staining on items or at a scene without any subsampling but do not alter or affect the stain (i.e., destroy DNA) in any way.[55] Other tests (e.g., luminol and derivatives) are almost exclusively applied directly to the stain (e.g., to clothing, walls, other surfaces), but these tests are used only in specific situations and should be used with caution to ensure that stains are not diluted (which would remove some or all DNA) or distorted (which would affect blood pattern analysis interpretation). Luminol and similar chemiluminescent tests need to be carried out in near or complete darkness, which is an important consideration if they will be used.

The presumptive tests for blood are extremely sensitive, so sampling a stain either directly or entirely is almost never required. In most circumstances, a small portion of a suspected bloodstain will be subsampled, and that small section will be tested with presumptive reagents. Even items or scenes where there are no visible stains can be sampled (e.g., a cleaned weapon or a drain) in the same manner because most tests are sensitive to levels beyond where blood would be visible when diluted in water. Sampling can take different methods, including filter paper (wet or dry), swab (wet, dry, or both), cutting or scraping (Fig. 3.7), or in some cases sprayed directly onto a suspected bloodstain. Solutions used for removal of part of a stain (subsampling) can include distilled water or saline.[56]

A recent study by Vandewoestyne et al.[57] used wet filter paper on both sides of an item, which was then pressed between two glass surfaces. Blood, if present, will transfer to the filter paper through capillary forces, which can then be tested using conventional blood tests. They tested this method with multiple different presumptive tests and found sensitivity ranges between 10- and 50-fold dilutions of blood, substrate dependent.

Another method of sampling involves wiping a filter paper across the surface of an item, either in section or entirety, then testing that filter paper. The objective in this sampling method is collecting a latent blood trace where blood may have been cleaned and therefore only present as invisible traces, and there is no prior knowledge of where on the item the blood may have been. Once found, traces could then be tested using standard methods.

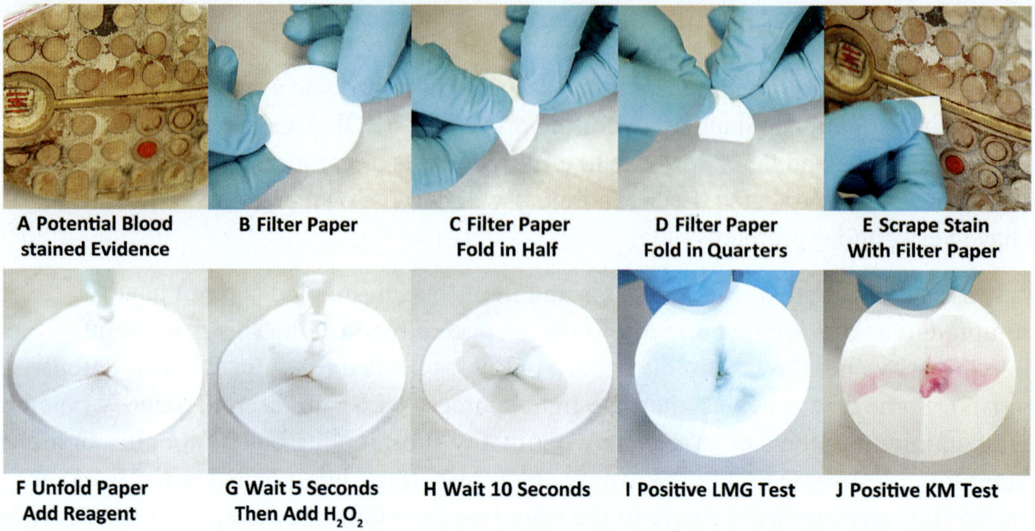

Fig. 3.7 Example of the scraping method of sampling (A) a suspected bloodstain using (B–D) filter paper folded to a point, which is then used to (E) scrape off a small portion of the stain and (F–J) is subjected to testing. Note both leucomalachite green *(LMG)* and phenolphthalein *(KM)* tests are demonstrated.

Sloots et al.[58] describe applying chemical presumptive tests for blood directly to a suspected bloodstain that may have been compromised through washing, detergents, burning, or decomposition. They specify that a small snippet of the stain can be removed with the substrate and then sampled, thereby leaving some of the original stain.

Choosing a Reagent

The subsequent sections detail the presumptive blood tests that are available for use, but a common question is, Which one should be used? This is not a question that can be answered easily or definitively because each test has its own benefits and drawbacks in terms of specificity, sensitivity, time, cost, safety (e.g., toxicity), and ease of use. Each laboratory will have its own policies and procedures, and choice of tests can be based on many different factors, including historic use, SOPs, cost of reagents, mandates by management or other oversight, subsequent testing requirements, or personal preference. Each test will have different sensitivity and specificity factors associated with it, but even these factors can vary between different laboratories and researchers. When using any test, it must be validated prior to use in the laboratory under the conditions it will be used for evidence analysis. Even with validation, controls (both positive and negative) should be run regularly with each use or daily. The following sections detail the range of sensitivities, specificities, and other relevant aspects (e.g., effect on subsequent DNA analysis) for each of the presumptive tests for blood.

Alternate Light Sources

The use of ALS systems for the detection of blood is difficult because there is no substance in blood that will fluoresce in the visible spectrum, and this technique is usually reserved for those fluids that show natural fluorescence. Blood has a broad absorption region from 300 to 900 nm[59,60] (this encompasses the entire visible spectrum). Within that region (at 415 nm) is a band of high absorption that can be targeted.[59] Therefore the general result of the technique is that blood will appear as a dark stain on a substrate that shows some fluorescence (Figs. 3.8 and 3.9). Sterzik et al.[61] found that stains examined using ALS were not any more defined than with the naked eye, although other research has found it useful.

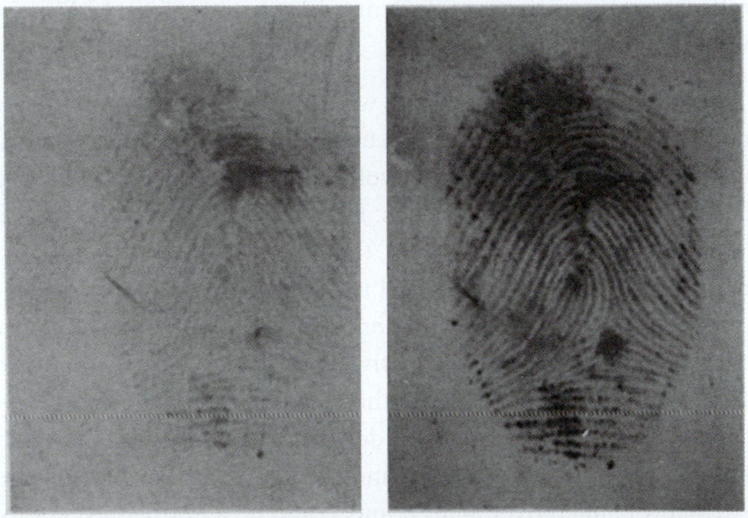

Fig. 3.8 Absorption mode. *(Left)* Bloodied fingerprint under white light. *(Right)* The same fingerprint under violet light. *From Stoilovic M. Detection of semen and blood stains using polilight as a light source. Forensic Sci Int. 1991;51:289–296.*

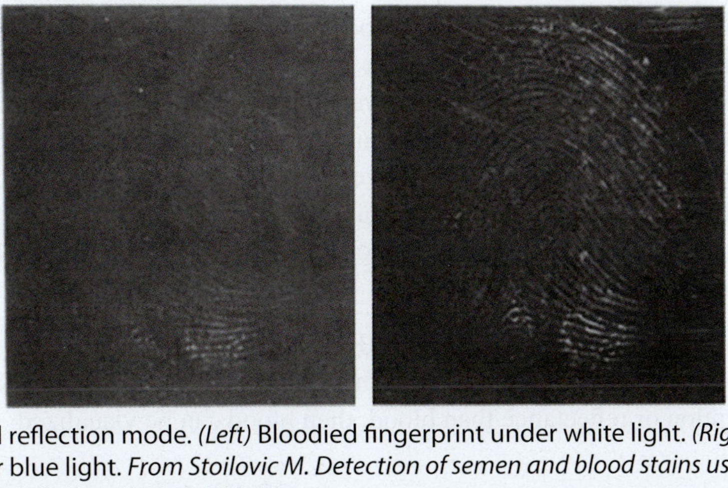

Fig. 3.9 Diffused reflection mode. *(Left)* Bloodied fingerprint under white light. *(Right)* The same fingerprint under blue light. *From Stoilovic M. Detection of semen and blood stains using polilight as a light source. Forensic Sci Int. 1991;51:289–296.*

Benefits of this technique include it is completely nondestructive, it uses no part of any stain, and it does not destroy DNA even when exposed for up to 20 minutes.[55] If the stain is still not visible, then chemical treatments, such as fluorescein, can be used in combination with ALS to better visualize stains, although the effect of those treatments on the stain then needs to be considered. More recently, infrared (IR) thermal imaging has been used to identify potential bloodstains with success, although this is still in the developmental stages and is not yet validated or used in casework.[62]

Other substances that absorb light of the same wavelengths as blood can be mistaken for blood, giving a false positive using this technique. Substrates that absorb light in the same wavelength range as blood may be mistaken for blood or may mask its presence. If there is a difference in reflectance between bloodstaining and substrate, then ALS is possible for the detection of blood.

Ray[63] looked at bloodstains with 530 nm ALS, which were deposited on painted wood that was then repainted, and could detect the blood under three layers of latex paint. Vandenberg and van Oorschot[64] used ALS at 415 nm with yellow filters to examine prepared bloodstains on white cotton cloth under various conditions, including blood mixed with soil, rust, white or black fingerprint powder, semen, and saliva, that was dried and stored at 37°C for 4 weeks and a bloodstain stored for 15 years at ambient temperature. They additionally painted over blood on wood with either white (three coats) or colored (two coats) paint, observing the stains under ALS (Polilight) after each successive coat of paint. Blood on brick, metal, and plasterboard was also painted over with up to three coats of white paint and observed under ALS.[64] They determined black fingerprint powder partially masked the blood, humidity had more of a degrading effect on visualization than time, and mixed stains appeared to be diluted and diffused.[64] All stains painted over at all points could be identified except for the blood on metal under three coats of white water-based paint, although the darker colored paints were better at blocking out the blood.

Adair[65] used drywall (gyprock) that was prepainted with two coats of white primer and then white paint before putting different types of bloodstains on the surface (e.g., drips, spots, shoe marks), which was then painted over with up to four coats of high-gloss acrylic blue paint. Adair[65] used ALS at 445 nm and a deep yellow filter to identify the stains under the paint. Overall, Adair recommends strong oblique lighting in a darkened room as a starting point, followed by ALS at 445 nm and a deep yellow filter, and reports no success from IR methods.[65] Lupica[66] was able to detect bloodstains under three coats of white paint using ALS at 420 nm and an orange filter but was unable to visualize bloodstains using ALS on carpet that had been cleaned.

Other investigations have looked at the use of IR light (between 780 nm and 1 mm) to identify blood, although the same considerations as with other ALS apply.[67] If the background has a different absorption or reflectance than blood, then blood can be visualized. Most light sources, including natural sunlight and flashes (peak 760 nm), emit IR, albeit at different intensities, so an IR filter (high pass) is needed to remove interference from visible light.[68] With modern digital cameras, most IR is removed from reaching the sensor with an inbuilt filter (IR light, because of its different wavelength, can cause images to appear blurry if not filtered), so this needs to be removed from the camera for it to be sensitive to IR. Note that this modification to the digital camera sensor can be done in-house or can be carried out by an outside company, but it is also important to remember that the altered wavelengths of light that will be detected will have a different focal point that needs to be accounted for. Previously, IR film was needed in addition to special light sources and filters.

Raymond and Hall[68] used the technique for a murder case and found it to be powerful in their analysis, where the materials being investigated absorbed the IR so blood could clearly be seen in detail (Fig. 3.10). Finnis et al.[67] found that IR was suitable for large patterns, but fine patterns and small spots may not be seen with IR.

Farrar et al.[69] also investigated the detection of bloodstains that had been painted but used IR (>820 nm) and visible photography for detection using computer image analysis of the photos. They used plasterboard that had been painted white with acrylic primer as the substrate, applied blood, then painted over the stains using white (acrylic, oil, and spray) paint, acrylic colored (black, red, yellow, blue, green, orange, and purple) paint, and several other parameters (e.g., diluted blood). They determined that IR was equal or better than visible light photography for all tested parameters (up to six layers of paint over the blood) except for diluted stains, where visible light gave better identification of the stains.[69] Howard and Nessan[70] found that IR could be used to detect blood only under two layers of white paint but up to four layers of maroon paint, but ALS (multiple wavelengths attempted but 415 nm found to be the best with a yellow filter) could detect blood under four layers of white paint but only two layers of maroon paint.

Barrera et al.[71] found IR to be the best method to identify bloodstains on wallpaper that had been painted over once with any color paint. The traces became undetectable with IR under two layers of black paint, three layers of white paint, and almost invisible under four layers

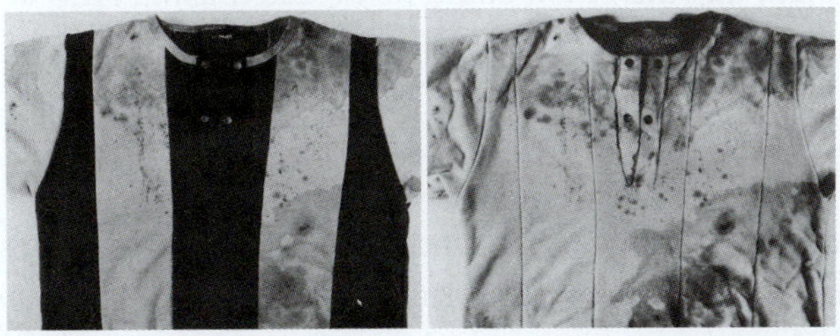

Fig. 3.10 Infrared (IR) photography of blood on a two-toned sweater. Normal lighting *(left)* and IR lighting *(right)*. *From Raymond MA, Hall RL. An interesting application of infra-red reflection photography to blood splash pattern interpretation. Forensic Sci Int. 1986;31:189–194.*

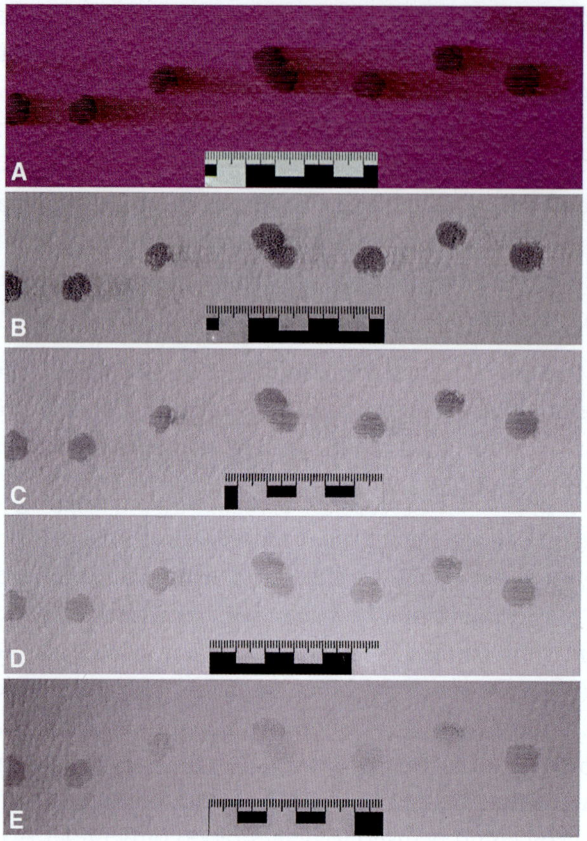

Fig. 3.11 Traces of blood on ground wallpaper, painted over with violet paint. (A) One layer of paint under visible light. (B–E) One, two, three, and four layers of violet paint under infrared, respectively. *From Barrera V, Haas C, Meixner EA, et al. Detection of painted-over traces of blood and seminal fluid. Int J Leg Med. 2018;132:1067–1074.*

of green or blue paint.[71] For orange, red, yellow, and violet paint, IR detected the bloodstains under five layers of paint (Fig. 3.11). They also found that for up to two layers of white or three layers of violet paint that the blood could be detected using ALS at 440 nm and a yellow filter.

Crystal Tests

Crystal testing of blood is a technique that is not in use in all laboratories, although it was common in the past and is considered a confirmatory test for blood. In a survey published in 2010, only 19% of labs were running crystal tests for confirmation of blood.[72] They were standard before the widespread use of immunochromatographic methods, with crystal testing being preferred over even the chemical tests (provided there was enough sample to perform the tests).[56] Part of the reason for their decline is in their difficulty to perform, and they cannot be performed on very small samples.[73] Scheller[74] states that blood crystals often fail with weathered samples, especially if the stain is small. Miller[75] was able to reach sensitivity of 5 μL of 1:1000 dilution of blood (although this involved successive applications of 0.5 μL drops that were allowed to dry between each, in effect concentrating the dilution). Other reasons include the introduction of immunological-based tests, which can offer ease of use, better sensitivity, and better specificity.

Crystal tests use the heme within Hb, which is a porphyrin, and this structure forms the crystals. Human blood crystals were described in 1852 by Parks,[17] who refers to other publications in 1849 and 1851 of researchers finding crystals in other biological fluids. There are two main methods used as crystal tests for blood: the Teichmann (hematin)[19] and the Takayama (hemochromogen)[76] tests.

Teichmann[19] published a study in 1853 on the formation of hematin crystals in blood, which is the basis for the use of crystal tests for blood identification. Since then, the hematin test has been known as the Teichmann test, which detects the crystallization of the hydrochloride of heme, which are brown rhombohedral crystals.[73] It originally involved treatment of the suspected blood with glacial acetic acid and sodium chloride (salt), followed by gentle heating and observation of the crystals (Fig. 3.12) under the microscope (Fig. 3.13).

Modifications of Teichmann's test began to appear quickly and involved variations in the methods[20,22,77] or different (thought to be improved) reagents;[78,79] however, Fiori[80] determined there were no particular advantages to using methods other than the original glacial acetic acid and sodium chloride. Some of the suggested methodological changes have applicability

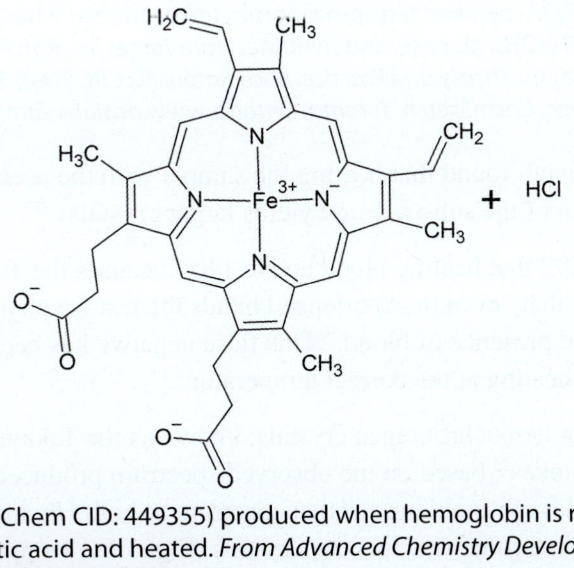

Fig. 3.12 Hematin (PubChem CID: 449355) produced when hemoglobin is reacted with sodium chloride and glacial acetic acid and heated. *From Advanced Chemistry Development Inc. ChemSketch. Toronto, Ontario. www.acdlabs.com. 2018.*

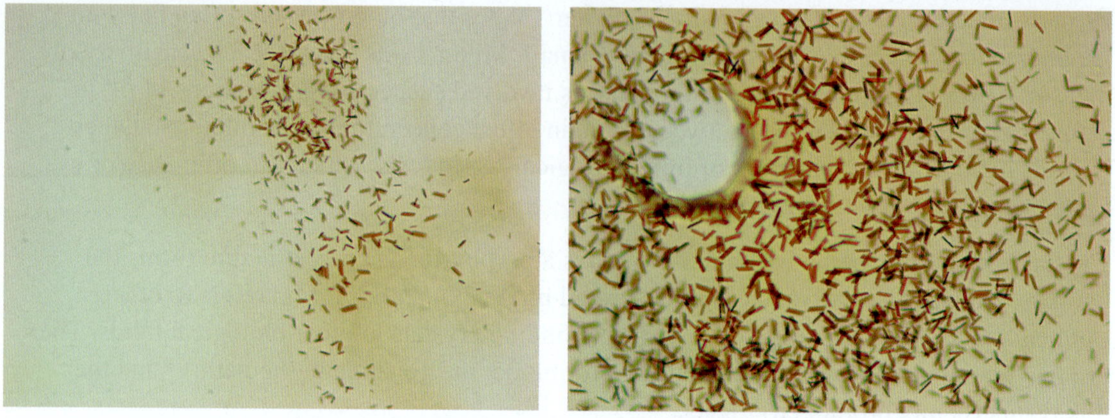

Fig. 3.13 Teichmann test of hematin chloral hydrate crystals indicates the presence of heme, viewed at 100× magnification *(left)* and 400× magnification *(right)*. *From Amy Brodeur, Boston University School of Medicine.*

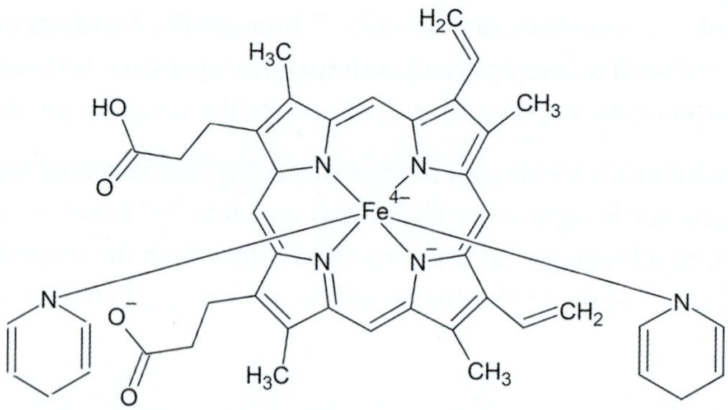

Fig. 3.14 Hemochromogen (pyridine ferroprotoporphyrin) produced when hemoglobin is reacted with sodium hydroxide (NaOH), glucose, and pyridine. *From James SH, Kish PE, Sutton TP. Principles of Bloodstain Pattern Analysis: Theory and Practice. Boca Raton, FL: CRC Press; 2005:576; Advanced Chemistry Development Inc. ChemSketch. Toronto, Ontario. www.acdlabs.com. 2018.*

(e.g., Atkinson and Kendall found that heating the sample with the acetic acid in a sealed test tube removes coloration of the substrate and yields larger crystals).[77]

Hammerl[81] found in 1892 that heating blood above 140°C causes the Teichmann test to fail. Kerr and Mason[82] state that "even in experienced hands the test frequently gives negative results in the undoubted presence of blood." This false negative has been reported to be due to the test's sensitivity to heating at the correct temperature.[1]

An alternative test is for hemochromogen crystals; known as the Takayama test, it was first described in 1864 by Stokes[23] based on the observed spectrum produced. It was Hoppe-Seyler[81] who found a close resemblance of that spectrum to both Hb and hematin and suggested the term hemochromogen,[83] whose crystals (Fig. 3.14) Hoppe-Seyler[84] also

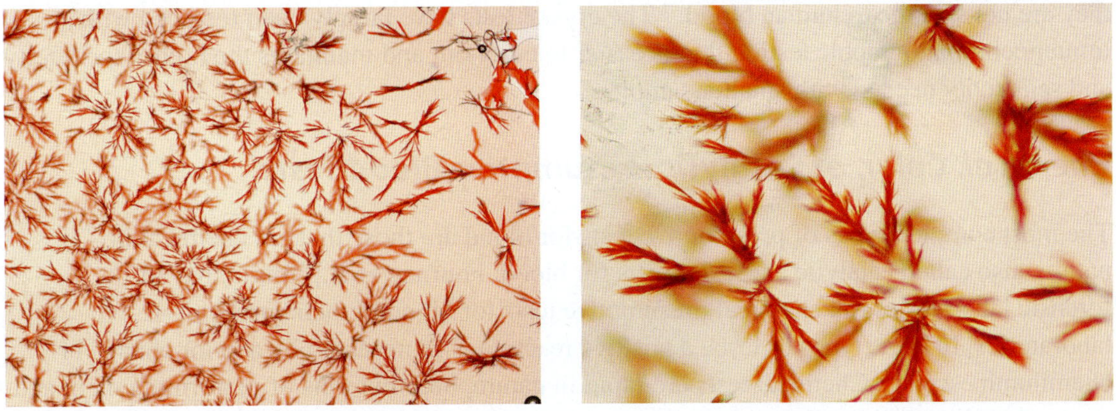

Fig. 3.15 Example of hemochromogen crystals formed with human blood, viewed at 100× magnification *(left)* and 400× magnification *(right)*. *From Amy Brodeur, Boston University School of Medicine.*

first observed in 1889 through heating Hb in a basic solution. Donogany[85] introduced and Dilling[86] confirmed that pyridine and piperidine gave the best crystal formation (these were the now characteristic crystals of pyridine hemochromogen)[73] when doing comprehensive testing with a number of other possible reagents that were suggested or in use at the time. The method became known as the Takayama test because of the study in 1912[76] where Takayama described the recipe for testing that is still used today. The method involves NaOH, pyridine, and glucose and can be carried out at room temperature or heated to expedite crystal formation. The pyridine hemochromogen crystals that form are a characteristic red color, which makes them stand out even when other contaminates may be present (Fig. 3.15).[76]

Hemochromogen crystals are larger and easier to form than hematin crystals.[76] It was found that the Takayama test was more sensitive than the Teichmann test by several orders of magnitude;[82] however, more recent testing found sensitivity to be essentially equal.[73] The Takayama test was also successful in producing crystals in heated samples, in the cold, and contaminated samples, whereas the Teichmann test either failed or required "much care and manipulation."[82] The test was also successful in the identification of blood in a stain that was 166 years old.[87] Platt[88] determined that exposure of a bloodstain to argon laser did not affect the recovery or identification using the Takayama test. False negative results are possible with old blood samples, so a negative crystal test does not preclude blood to be present.[72]

In reference to the spectra produced by hemochromogen, Stokes[23] states that "the blood of animals in general exhibits just the same bands," and Das[89] recently confirmed that hematin from different animals (three of eight tested) could be confused for human hematin (despite very early authors[90] claiming the contrary). Grodsky et al.[56] point out that all Hb-containing bloods react similarly and show the presence of blood only, with no indication of source by species or groups. This indicates that crystal tests may be specific to blood,[72] but they are not specific to human blood.[72] The crystal tests have largely been replaced with immunochromatographic testing that is easier to carry out and maintains the higher specificity and sensitivity needed with smaller samples.

Chemical, Color, or Catalytic Presumptive Blood Tests

The most common types of presumptive tests for blood are those that are chemical in nature, also called catalytic and color tests for blood. Fourney et al.[72] found that all forensic laboratories ran chemical presumptive tests for blood in their survey of 42 laboratories. In these types of tests, a positive reaction is represented by a color change or chemiluminescence. Chemical tests are rapid in nature, both in terms of performing them and in reaction time, making them ideal to use at crime scenes as well as in the laboratory. There are many different types of presumptive chemical tests for blood that are in use, whereas some have been phased out because of safety issues (e.g., cariogenic reagents) or improved testing in terms of sensitivity, specificity, time, or cost.

The basis for the oxidation of the presumptive tests is through a combination of peroxidase and low concentrations of hydrogen peroxide (H_2O_2). All the chemical presumptive tests for blood either contain H_2O_2 as part of their reagent components or H_2O_2 is added as part of the test after the application of the indicator reagent. The H_2O_2 is the oxidizing agent of the reaction and is reduced to water, whereas the peroxidase reverts to its natural state (Figs. 3.16 and 3.17).

Hb is a peroxidase, and along with other heme-containing peroxidases (Enzyme Commission 1.11.1.X), when in the presence of H_2O_2 acts as an electron acceptor and can catalyse a number of oxidative reactions.[50,91–93] Some literature reports Hb as peroxidase like or pseudo-peroxidase, a theory put forward by McFarlane and Hamilton because of Hb's resistance to degradation when heated;[94] however, this designation is not accurate. Hb is able to oxidize organic substrates in the presence of hydrogen peroxide.[95,96] The reaction of H_2O_2 with Hb has been known for over 100 years,[97] and it later became apparent that this was caused by the oxidation of the heme iron from its ferric state (Fe^{3+} or Fe(III)) to the ferryl state forming an oxoferryl ($Fe^{4+}O$ or Fe(IV)O).[92] The catalytic cycle (Fig. 3.17) involves the oxidation of two presumptive test substrate molecules from their uncolored state (RH) to their colored state ($R^{\bullet}$). During this process, the Hb reverts to its resting state, and therefore the cyclic reaction can continue as long as there is H_2O_2 and organic substrate to continue the reaction.

$$H_2O_2 + 2RH + \text{peroxidase} \rightarrow 2H_2O + 2R + \text{peroxidase}$$

Fig. 3.16 The overall stoichiometric equation for one peroxidase cycle involves the basic reaction of hydrogen peroxide *(H_2O_2)* with a peroxidase and an organic substrate *(RH)*.

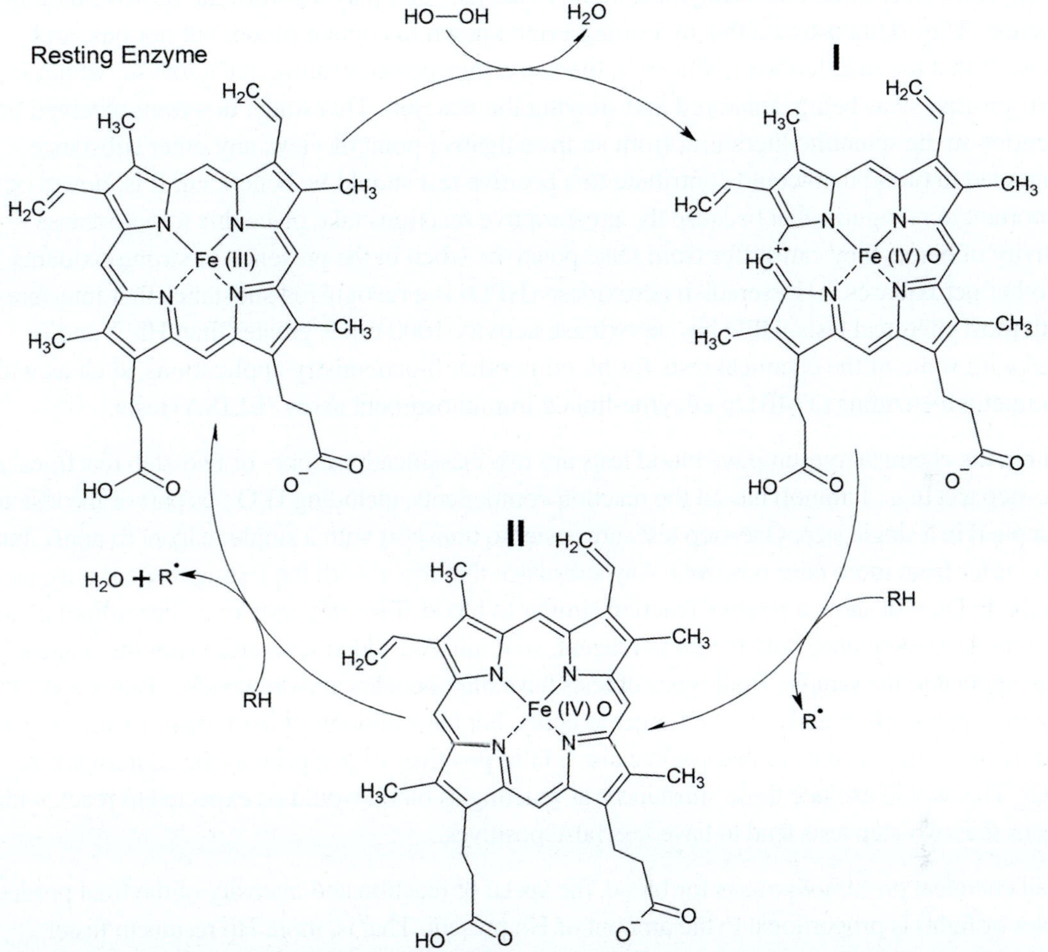

Fig. 3.17 The catalytic cycle of heme peroxidases in the presence of hydrogen peroxide (*H_2O_2 or HO-OH*) and an organic substrate (the presumptive test reagent RH). The resting enzyme *(FeIII)* reacts with one equivalent of H_2O_2 to give compound I, a porphyrin cation radical containing FeIV. It is a two-electron redox reaction where H_2O_2 is reduced to H_2O and the heme is oxidized giving the oxyferryl *(FeIV=O)* intermediate. Compound I then oxidizes an organic substrate (the presumptive blood test RH) to give a substrate radical *(R•)*. It then undergoes a second oxidation reaction yielding compound II, which contains an oxyferryl center coordinated to a normal porphyrin ligand. Compound II is then reduced back to the native resting enzyme ferric state with concomitant one-electron substrate oxidation. Both I and II react with the same organic substrate; therefore once the reaction between I and the substrate starts, II is produced and simultaneously reacts with a second molecule of substrate. As a result, II is reduced back to the native ferric state, the resting enzyme, with concomitant oxidation of a second molecule of substrate and the production of water. *From Torres E, Bustos-Jaimes I, Le Borgne S. Potential use of oxidative enzymes for the detoxification of organic pollutants. Appl Catal B. 2003;46:1–15; Dawson JH. Probing structure-function relations in heme-containing oxygenases and peroxidases. Science. 1988;240:433–439; Advanced Chemistry Development Inc. ChemSketch. Toronto, Ontario. www.acdlabs.com. 2018.*

A study by Anand et al.[98] put forth the idea that, in addition to the peroxidase activity of heme in Hb, there were other RBC enzymes, mainly catalase, that play a part in the positive oxidative reaction. They demonstrated this by boiling urine known to contain blood, but not pus, and showing that the reaction was reduced in intensity, thus demonstrating that catalase, which is heat sensitive, was being denatured and slowing the reaction. This study, however, received little attention in the scientific literature; from an investigative point of view, any other substance contained in blood that would contribute to a positive test should be beneficial. It is, however, important to recognize that because the presumptive reactions take place due to peroxidase activity of heme, they can suffer from false positives when in the presence of strong oxidants or other peroxidases.[99] Horseradish peroxidase (HPD) is a recognized substance that interferes with most chemical tests. HPD has peroxidase activity 1000 times greater than Hb[100] and is used with some of the chemical tests for blood in other biochemistry applications, such as with tetramethylbenzidine (TMB) in enzyme-linked immunosorbent assay (ELISA) tests.

Within the chemical presumptive blood tests are two classifications: one- or two-step reactions. A one-step test (e.g., luminol) has all the reaction components, including H_2O_2, as part of the test and is applied in a single step. One-step tests are easier to transport with a single reagent to apply, but they suffer from more false positives. Any substance that reacts with the testing reagent only, and not the H_2O_2, will show a positive reaction similar to blood. Two-step tests (e.g., benzidine) do not have the H_2O_2 contained with the main reagent, so it must be added separately after the reagent has been applied to the sample. Both types of tests have their benefits and drawbacks. Two-step tests require separate H_2O_2 and can take longer to apply, but the additional step of applying the reagent first allows some substances that could cause a false positive to react prior to the addition of the H_2O_2. This would exclude those substances as reacting as blood would be expected to react, which means that two-step tests tend to have less false positives.

In all chemical presumptive tests for blood, the speed of reaction and intensity of the final product (color or light) is proportional to the amount of Hb present. That is, more Hb results in faster and stronger results than lower levels of Hb, to the point that some positive reactions can appear almost instantaneously. Some of the tests can also oxidize without the presence of Hb (or other peroxidase), either through natural degradation (e.g., phenolphthalein)[56] or with the air (Fig. 3.18), although this reaction is distinguishable from a true positive in that it takes much longer to develop and does not appear at the point where the sample is present. A true positive reaction would occur at the point where Hb (or another peroxidase) is present, and for very strong reactions this could diffuse outward (see Fig. 3.18). Therefore all chemical tests have a recommended reaction time of 30 seconds or less because allowing any more time could result in other substances or natural degradation of the test with the air, showing what could be mistaken for a positive.

All catalytic tests were traditionally prepared for use in lab by the investigators, and recipes can easily be found in the literature, which are often different formulations that authors describe as being better than previous versions. Each laboratory will have its own preferred recipe for different reagents. Each time a new batch of reagents is prepared, it is important

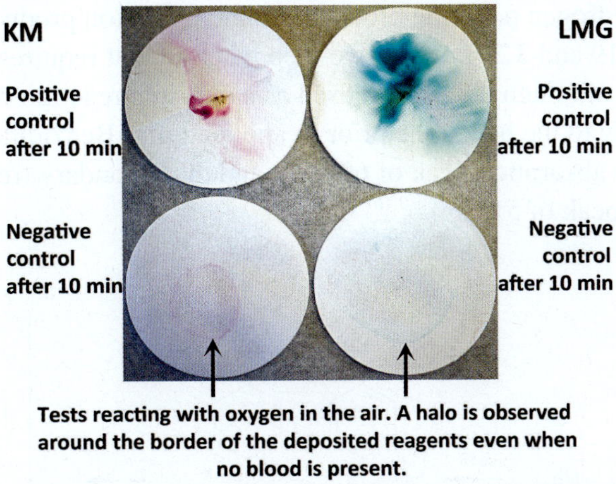

Fig. 3.18 An example of two presumptive blood tests, the phenolphthalein (Kastle-Myer *[KM]*) and the leucomalachite green *(LMG)*, 10 minutes after application for both positive and negative samples. The positive control blood samples show a reaction at the point where hemoglobin is present *(center of filter paper)*, whereas the negative samples show a less intense reaction at the borders of the drying reagent.

that the sensitivity and specificity be revalidated to ensure they are functioning correctly and at the expected levels. Many of these tests are still in use and are available to buy commercially, which offers both benefits and drawbacks. Commercial versions will be more expensive than lab-created stock but will have already had most of the validation testing carried out, and so will save time by requiring minimal lab validation.

Benzidine Test

At one time, the benzidine test was the most widely used test for the presumptive identification of blood. It was recognized as the simplest and safest method.[44] Once its carcinogenic properties were discovered,[101,102] however, it was quickly discontinued from general use.[103] The scale of the cancer in those who worked with benzidine was classified as an epidemic.[104] A modified form of benzidine was developed (i.e., TMB; see later) and was determined not to be carcinogenic or mutagenic and has since largely superseded benzidine. Benzidine can still be found in use in some laboratories, and because of its wide use in previous cases it is still pertinent to describe it here.

Benzidine (4-(4-aminophenyl)aniline ($C_{12}H_{12}N_2$)), an aromatic amine, was first described as a method for detecting blood in 1904.[105] Many different substances were tested, and benzidine along with leucomalachite green (LMG; see later) and leucocrystal violet (LCV; see later) were the final recommendations for the detection of blood. Benzidine can be dissolved for use in glacial acetic acid (standard) or within absolute ethanol (modified but with a final benzidine concentration of 0.14%).[106] Benzidine is a light yellow solution that when in the presence of Hb and hydrogen peroxide produces a blue oxidation product that can progress to red-brown (Figs. 3.19 and 3.20). It is a two-step reaction that requires the separate addition of hydrogen peroxide, although it has been used as a one-step reaction with the hydrogen peroxide added directly to the benzidine prior to application.[44] Benzidine's primary pigment (blue) has a maximum absorption peak of 602 nm, and the secondary (red) pigment has a maximum absorption peak of 515 nm.[101,107]

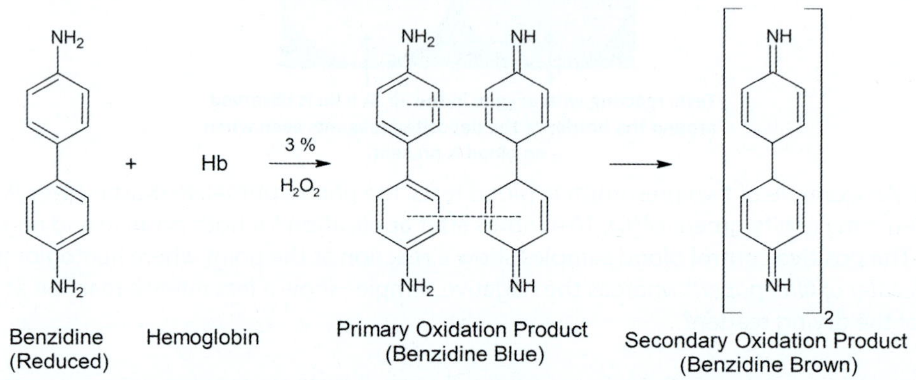

Fig. 3.19 The chemical reaction of the benzidine test for blood. The colorless reduced benzidine (PubChem CID: 7111), which when in the presence of hemoglobin and hydrogen peroxide, converts to the primary oxidation product benzidine blue and then to benzidine brown. A positive reaction will occur rapidly, and the test should be read within 30 seconds. *From Alvarez RS, Wight THT. The Gregersen test. US Vet Bur Med Bull. 1929;5:888–890; Saferstein R. Forensic Science Handbook. Hoboken, NJ: Prentice Hall Inc.; 1982:725; Advanced Chemistry Development Inc. ChemSketch. Toronto, Ontario. www.acdlabs.com. 2018.*

Fig. 3.20 Example of the benzidine test for blood used to detect occult blood in urine. The positive test *(left)* shows a deep blue color, indicating a positive. The negative control can be seen on the right. Note, when testing bloodstains, the negative control is yellowish or clear. *From Alvarez RS, Wight THT. The Gregersen test. US Vet Bur Med Bull. 1929;5:888–890.*

Modified versions of the test have been formulated over the years while benzidine was in use.[56,106,108,109] They had varied names, including Gregersen's test.[110,111]

Benzidine has a reported sensitivity range between 1:48,000 and 1:5 million.[56,105,108,114–116] Grodsky et al.[56] found sensitivity at the lower range, but that sensitivity was tripled (from 1:100,000 to 1:300,000) when prepared in glacial acetic acid. Garner et al.[116] found that the sensitivity changed with the concentration of the reagent from 1:1000 (0.05 M benzidine solution) to 1:1 million (0.20 M benzidine solution). The effect of benzidine on subsequent DNA recovery has generally been negative. Hochmeister et al.[106] found benzidine inhibited DNA analysis when prepared in acidic acid but not when prepared in ethanol. Josephy[104] summarizes a range of research that shows benzidine binds to DNA and transfer RNA (tRNA) at high levels. A more recent study found that it inhibited short tandem repeat (STR) results unless samples were dried, which improved recovery but was still detrimental overall,[117] which was further confirmed.[118]

Early testing found that benzidine could be inhibited by ascorbic acid, and a positive reaction could even be reversed in the presence of ascorbic acid.[119] Castelló et al.[120] investigated the effect of quebracho extract and found significant inhibition of benzidine after 1 day and a 1% quebracho final concentration. Needham and Simpson[4] found that sensitivity was reduced when blood was mixed with feces. They also tested iron and ammonium citrate, ferrous sulfate, and many different foodstuffs, which all tested negative. They found false positive results with various meat products (not considered a true false positive because blood is present), raw turnip, raw potato, boiled green peas, and raw lettuce.[4] Pinker[121] found false positives with ammonium persulfate, calcium hypochlorite, gold chloride, lead peroxide, potassium dichromate, potassium permanganate, sodium chromate, and certain lead oxides. Grodsky et al.[56] found false positives from the white pulp of oranges, lemons, certain melons, and persimmons; the inner part of a tomato skin; flesh of carrot, radish, and turnip; parts of lettuce; and almond when applied directly. They state that most of the false positives obtained with benzidine are "fainter and more fleeting" than with blood and can be distinguished from true blood positives, except for horseradish, which gave a reaction as strong as blood. Culliford and Nickolls[122] carried out further testing and determined that false positives were obtained from chemical oxidants, catalysts, and vegetable peroxidases, but they determined that with some precautions these false positives could be eliminated or explained.

Fluorescein

Fluorescein was described initially in 1871 by von Baeyer,[123] investigated by Kastle[124] at the same time as phenolphthalein in 1901, but it was not proposed as a blood detection method until 1910[125] as a method to detect blood in urine. Fleig[125] was looking for an alternative to phenolphthalein and found fluorescein to be the most suitable, claiming it had better sensitivity.

Fluorescein (3',6'-dihydroxyspiro[2-benzofuran-3,9'-xanthene]-1-one, $C_{20}H_{12}O_5$) is yellow in solution and can be reduced to fluorescin (2-(3,6-dihydroxy-9H-xanthen-9-yl), benzoic acid, $C_{20}H_{14}O_5$, colorless, which then returns to the state of fluorescein by oxidation. For forensic blood detection, this takes place in the presence of Hb and low levels of H_2O_2 (Fig. 3.21). Fluorescein also has the property of fluorescence, which is highly pH dependent.[126,127] This fluorescence means that fluorescein is often compared and classified with luminol; however, unlike luminol, fluorescein is a two-step reaction and therefore requires a separate application of H_2O_2.[128] Cheeseman and DiMeo[128] state that substrate and orientation (vertical vs. horizontal) can affect the use of fluorescein and used a commercial thickener to slow the dispersion/distortion of the blood pattern after application.

Fluorescein has an absorption wavelength of 437 to 490 nm, a maximum emission at 515 nm that can range up to 700 nm,[127] and can be viewed with a yellow or orange barrier filter.[129] The ability to be visible in both normal light and to fluoresce is beneficial, as it can make a positive reaction clearer for stains that may be otherwise difficult to see because of size, substrate interference, or dilution (Fig. 3.22).

Fluorescein has a sensitivity reported of between 1:100 and 1:105,000, which can vary depending on the substrate and level of porosity;[67,128,132,133] however, it has been reported that the sensitivity of fluorescein is as high as 1 part blood to 10 million parts buffer.[134] Fluorescein has been found to react with blood under three layers of white paint but only under two layers of maroon paint.[70] Inherent fluorescence has been reported in coffee, chocolate, cola, strawberry jelly, ketchup, cherry-strawberry juice, cherry-cranberry juice, and specifically at 450 nm with beet juice, horseradish, urine, steel with rust, and copper that may be interpreted as a false positive.[128] It was found that fluorescein produced an immediate bright reaction when applied to a control stain, but it also caused the background substrate (butcher paper) to fluoresce.[135] A study looking at the effect of fluorescein on subsequent

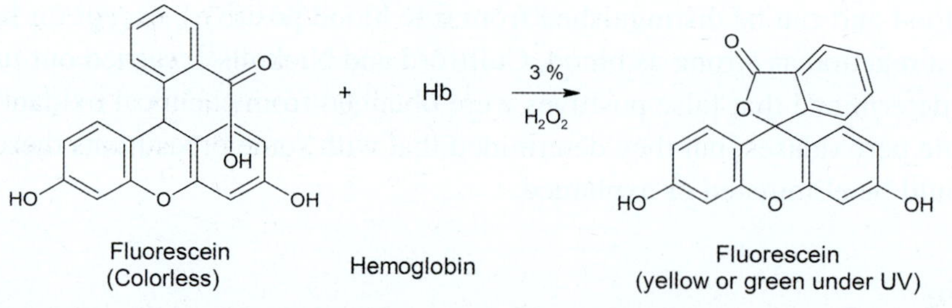

Fig. 3.21 Chemical reaction of the fluorescein test for blood. The colorless fluorescin (PubChem CID: 68205), which when in the presence of hemoglobin *(Hb)* and hydrogen peroxide converts to the colored fluorescein (PubChem CID: 16850), which is yellow under white light and green under ultraviolet *(UV)* light. *From Kratochvil JF, Burris RH, Seikel MK, et al. Isolation and characterization of a-guaiaconic acid and the nature of guaiacum blue. Phytochemistry. 1971;10:2529–2531; Advanced Chemistry Development Inc. ChemSketch. Toronto, Ontario. www.acdlabs.com. 2018.*

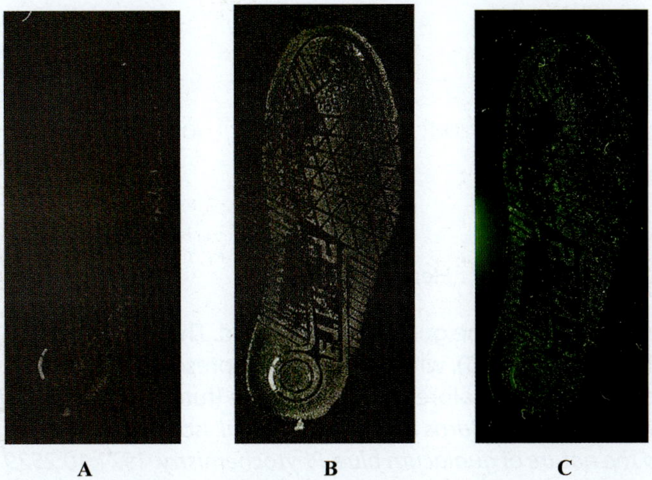

Fig. 3.22 Example of the fluorescein test for blood used on a footwear mark in blood on dark fabric. The untreated stain (A), treated with fluorescein under white light (B) and under ultraviolet light (C). *From Farrugia KJ, Savage KA, Bandey H, et al. Chemical enhancement of footwear impressions in blood on fabric — part 2: peroxidase reagents. Sci Just. 2011;51:110–121.*

spectroscopic methods of identifying Hb found interference, but it was not found to interfere with other serological methods or DNA.[132,136]

Laboratories can make up their own stock of fluorescein, but there is a commercial version available for purchase called Hemascein. In a comparison of methods, Finnis et al.[67] found fluorescein to have the same sensitivity as Bluestar (a commercial luminol) and higher than that of Hemascein with a reported maximum sensitivity of 1:1000 and 1:100, respectively, for blood on cotton.

Guaiac/Guaiacum

The reaction of guaiac resin was first described in 1810 by Planche,[137] who was investigating another resin, jalap, to see if it was genuine, and he observed that the blue color could be produced with horseradish. In 1851, Schönbein[28] also investigated guaiac, or guaiacum, which is a resin obtained from the heartwood of the *Guaiacum officinale* (known as guaiacum or lignum-vitae) and *Guaiacum sanctum* (known as holywood lignum-vitae, holywood, or guaiacum sanctum) trees.[138] The resin, or the wood itself, is used in many medical and pharmacological applications.[130] It turns blue in the presence of many inorganic or organic oxidizing agents for use in detecting oxidative enzymes.[130] The resin was found to fluoresce blue under ultraviolet light and to be a phenol rather than an acid.[130]

It continues to be almost exclusively used for detection of occult blood in feces (e.g., Hemoccult II SENSA, Beckman Coulter), it has been tested as an alternative to the common presumptive blood tests of the past,[105,124] and has recently been proposed as a

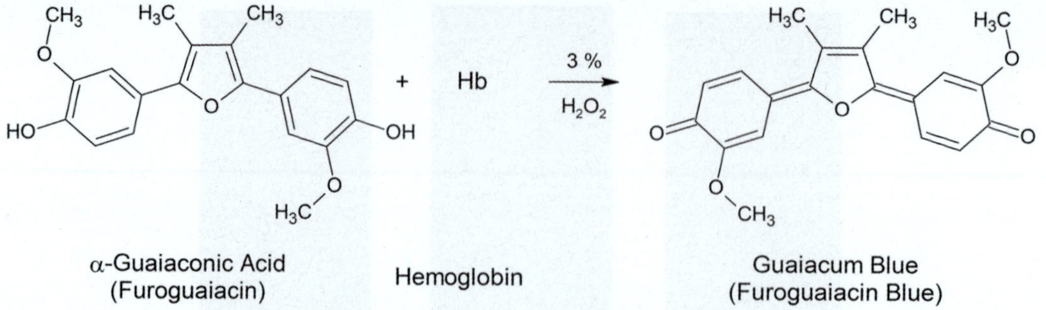

Fig. 3.23 The chemical reaction of the guaiac test for blood. The colorless α-guaiaconic acid (furoguaiacin) (PubChem CID: 165795), which when in the presence of hemoglobin *(Hb)* and hydrogen peroxide, converts to the colored guaiacum blue (furoguaiacin blue) (PubChem CID: 119026203). *From Kratochvil JF, Burris RH, Seikel MK, et al. Isolation and characterization of α-guaiaconic acid and the nature of guaiacum blue. Phytochemistry. 1971;10:2529–2531; Advanced Chemistry Development Inc. ChemSketch. Toronto, Ontario. www.acdlabs.com. 2018.*

presumptive forensic test for blood.[99] It was patented in 1981 as a filter paper bound test for occult blood in feces.[138]

α-Guaiaconic acid (4-[5-(4-hydroxy-3-methoxyphenyl)-3,4-dimethylfuran-2-yl]-2-methoxyphenol, $C_{20}H_{20}O_5$) is colorless and is converted to guaiacum blue ((4*Z*)-2-methoxy-4-[(5*E*)-5-(3-methoxy-4-oxocyclohexa-2,5-dien-1-ylidene)-3,4-dimethylfuran-2-ylidene] cyclohexa-2,5-dien-1-one, $C_{20}H_{18}O_5$) through oxidation. The guaiac test is a two-step test, which for blood detection takes place in the presence of Hb and low levels of H_2O_2 (Fig. 3.23), where a characteristic blue color is formed (Fig. 3.24).

Sensitivity for the guaiac test when used as a fecal test was found to be 1:5000[138] and to be 1:100,000 when tested for forensic use.[99] There are many known false positives that the commercial fecal tests recognize as easy to get and include other peroxidases from plants and from diet (Hb found in meats). A 1951 study[139] found partial inhibition by ascorbic acid and stated the reagent was unstable for periods longer than 1 week. The guaiac test has been found to have no effect on subsequent DNA typing;[99] however, it is rarely used for forensic blood identification currently in the literature and seems to be reserved for detection of blood for medical purposes.

Leucomalachite Green

The use of LMG as a test for blood was first reported in 1904 by Adler and Adler,[105] who were investigating leukabases and found that malachite green proved the most advantageous. LMG and LCV contain a chromophore group that gives them their color (note that Hb contains heme chromophores that give blood its red color).[140] The chromophores are also able to be reduced to a colorless form, which returns to the colored state via oxidation. Early studies placed the sensitivity at 1:20,000[141] or 1:100,000[142] and rated it highly for forensic detection of blood, at dilutions in water beyond the point of

Fig. 3.24 A commercial guaiac test for fecal occult blood showing positive *(blue)* reactions for blood in the two test zones at the top of the image and showing control positive *(blue)* and negative *(clear)* in the red-orange rectangle. *Adapted from James Heilman, MD. Under CC BY-SA 3.0, commons.wikimedia.org/wiki/File:Positive_fecal_occult_blood_test.jpg.*

visibility of blood. Further studies were carried out by Alvarez de Toledo y Valero in 1935,[143] who confirmed the greater sensitivity of 1:100,000, but this was not observed under modern testing conditions.[144] Others did not find LMG as sensitive as benzidine, and it was not widely adopted according to some researchers.[44] Unlike many of the other presumptive blood tests, LMG has not been widely (if at all) used in the detection of blood for medical purposes, which makes it stand out from the other tests described here. LMG has been found to cause cancer in rats,[145] but it can still be found in use.

LMG (4-[[4-(dimethylamino)phenyl]-phenylmethyl]-*N*,*N*-dimethylaniline, $C_{23}H_{26}N_2$) is colorless and when in the presence of Hb and hydrogen peroxide is converted to an oxidized malachite green ([4-[[4-(dimethylamino)phenyl]-phenylmethylidene]cyclohexa-2,5-dien-1-ylidene]-dimethylazanium;chloride, $C_{23}H_{25}ClN_2$), which is blue-green. LMG is a two-step test that, for blood detection, takes place in the presence of Hb and low levels of H_2O_2 (Fig. 3.25), where the characteristic blue-green color is formed (Fig. 3.26).

The sensitivity of LMG has been reported at blood water dilutions between 1:100 and 1:100,000,[56,141–144,146–151] making it one of the least sensitive tests in the literature. Old blood, putrid blood, and blood washed with soap or sulfuric acid (then rinsed with distilled water) react intensely with LMG.[143]

LMG has been proposed as a fingerprint development reagent (for fingerprints in blood), and it performed with good results, showing fingerprint definition on a range of common

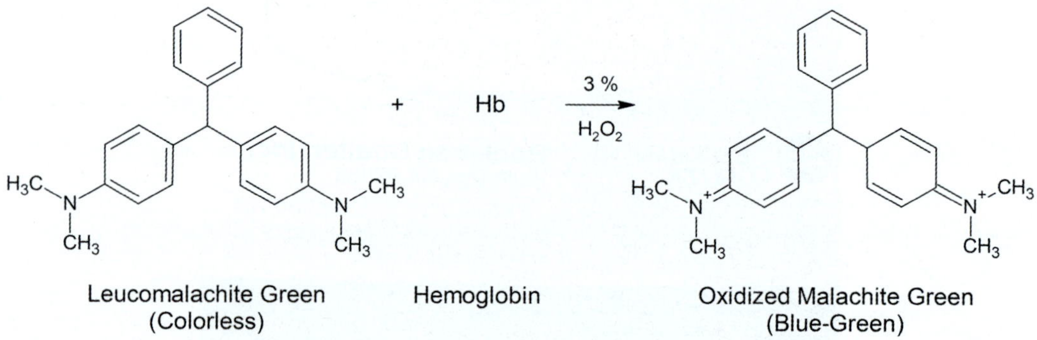

Fig. 3.25 Chemical reaction of the leucomalachite green (LMG) test for blood. The colorless LMG (PubChem CID: 67215), which when in the presence of hemoglobin *(Hb)* and hydrogen peroxide, converts to the blue-green oxidized malachite green (PubChem CID: 11294). *From Advanced Chemistry Development Inc. ChemSketch. Toronto, Ontario. www.acdlabs.com. 2018.*

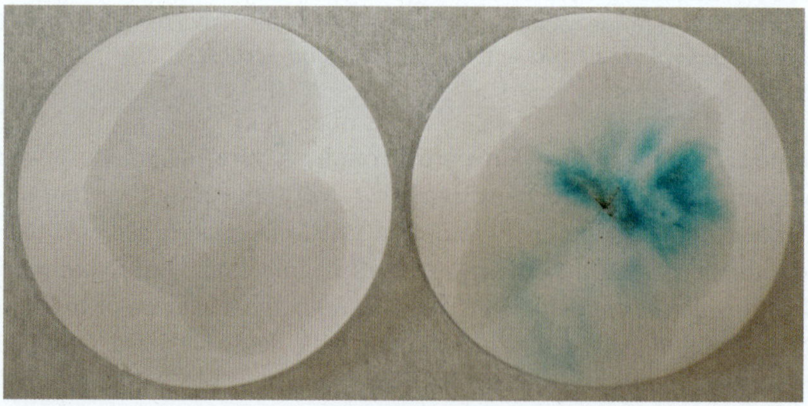

Fig. 3.26 Example of the leucomalachite green test for blood, with a negative control *(left)* and a positive control *(right)*. The blue-green color is indicative of a positive test.

household surfaces.[152] Stow[153] used LMG to impregnate nylon membranes as a means to lift bloody footwear marks and found that it provided excellent lift and enhancement simultaneously from a variety of different substrates.

An early study of specificity found that only pus containing blood would give a positive reaction, but pus itself would not.[35] Other tested substances that were negative include iron rose, copper salts, iron oxide, nitrates, chlorates, iodates, iodine, rhodonites, percarbonates, persulfates, manganese salts, lead chromate, platinum sponge, pumice stone, and fresh fruit juices.[35] Substances that showed a positive reaction prior to the addition of H_2O_2 included bleach, brownstone, lead peroxide, red lead, permanganate, bichromates, and chromates.[35] It was found that many chemical oxidants will give the expected LMG reaction in the absence of H_2O_2, and some catalyze the reaction much the same way as blood.[143] Potato, red onion, cupric sulfate, ferric sulfate, and nickel chloride reacted with LMG, but in a manner that could not be confused with a true positive.[144]

Even after short periods, LMG has been shown to be detrimental to DNA recovery, giving a combination of partial and full profiles over hours and days after testing.[154] This is in contrast to other studies that found full DNA inhibition with LMG.[106,144]

Hemident (McPhail's Reagent) is a commercial LMG solution that comes in two ampules that are combined with a sample swab. The instructions specify that the test reacts with mammalian blood and that the sensitivity is 1 part per 1 million of blood in water; however, literature reports a much lower sensitivity of 1:10,000.[144] Hemident has been shown to cross-react with semen, red onion, 1 M ascorbic acid, 5% bleach, copper, iron, and nickel salts.[144] A positive result is a similar color to LMG, which is a component of the test, but slightly darker (Fig. 3.27).

Leucocrystal Violet

LCV is generally considered a fingerprint reagent for use with bloody fingerprints or other pattern evidence (e.g., footwear), but it has also been used for identification of bloodstains. It was first investigated as a possible presumptive test for blood by Adler and Adler[88] in 1904 at the same time they were investigating LMG. Although first discovered in the early 20th century, few publications related to its use in forensic blood detection were published, with the earliest in 1996 by Bodziak,[155] who cites earlier presentations of LCV use but no publications.

Earlier publications looked at LCV for detecting H_2O_2 and other peroxygen compounds but not for identification of blood.[156,157] Takayanagi and Yashiro[158] used LCV as a colorimetric determination of Hb in plasma; although it detected Hb, it was not used for forensic purposes. Gifford[159] describes the use of LCV in a modified iodine-silver plate method for fingerprints, but it was not used for blood detection.

Fig. 3.27 Example of the Hemident (McPhail's Reagent) test for blood. Note in this example the reagents have been removed from the ampules and tested with a positive control bloodstain.

LCV (4-[bis[4-(dimethylamino)phenyl]methyl]-*N*,*N*-dimethylaniline, $C_{25}H_{31}N_3$) is colorless and is converted through oxidation to crystal violet ([4-[bis[4-(dimethylamino)phenyl] methylidene]cyclohexa-2,5-dien-1-ylidene]-dimethylazanium;chloride, $C_{25}H_{30}N_3.Cl$), which is purple. LCV can be used as either a one-step or two-step test, which for blood detection takes place in the presence of Hb and low levels of H_2O_2 (Fig. 3.28), where the characteristic purple color is formed (Fig. 3.29).

LCV has a reported sensitivity of 1:100, blood in water,[160] and a second study found increased sensitivity to 1:8000,[161] but there are no reports of further testing or specificity studies with blood. White[162] found a sensitivity of 0.01 μg with iron porphyrin, which suggests this makes LCV more sensitive than benzidine.

LCV is used in nonforensic applications, such as iodine concentration in seawater,[163] to detect antimony.[164] Within forensic science, LCV is primarily used as a fingerprint reagent for fingerprints in blood,[165] but it can also be used in standard presumptive blood testing. Bodziak[155] described using LCV as a one-step test with H_2O_2 in the solution that is sprayed onto a surface and claims that this method with the addition of 5-sulfosalicylic acid fixes the stain to the substrate.

Michaud and Brun-Conti[166] used LCV to develop a nylon transfer to lift bloody impressions from crime scenes. They found excellent lift and enhancement of the stains from all nonporous surfaces and most porous surfaces, but stains on carpet were unsuccessful.[166] LCV

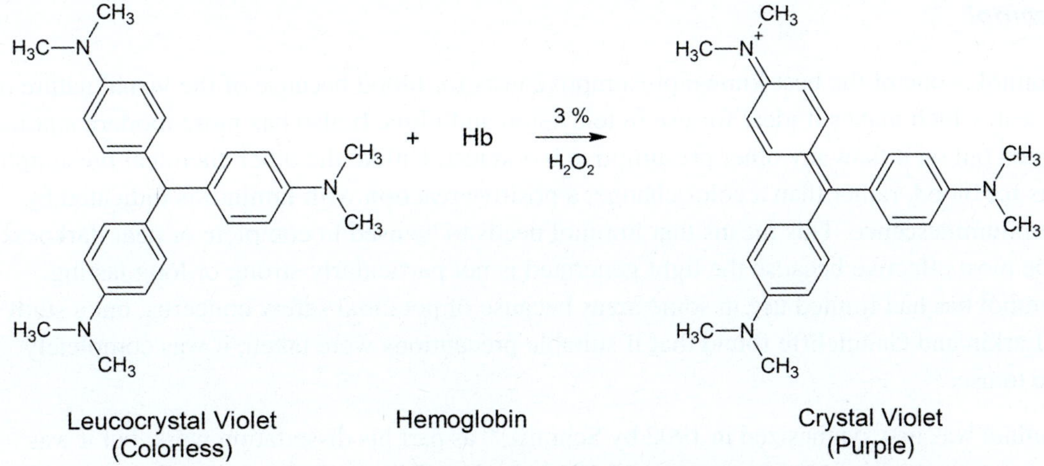

Fig. 3.28 The chemical reaction of the leucocrystal violet (LCV) test for blood. The colorless LCV (PubChem CID: 69048), which when in the presence of hemoglobin *(Hb)* and hydrogen peroxide converts to the purple crystal violet (PubChem CID: 11057). *From Advanced Chemistry Development Inc. ChemSketch. Toronto, Ontario. www.acdlabs.com. 2018.*

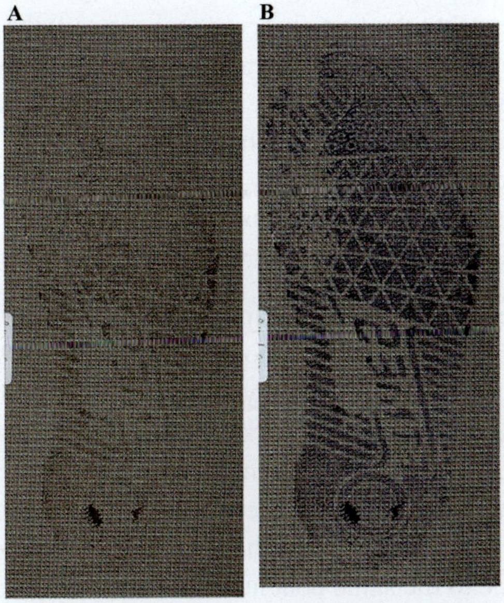

Fig. 3.29 Example of the leucocrystal violet (LCV) test for blood used on a footwear mark in blood on patterned cotton. The untreated stain (A) and treated with LCV (B). *From Farrugia KJ, Savage KA, Bandey H, et al. Chemical enhancement of footwear impressions in blood on fabric — part 2: peroxidase reagents. Sci Just. 2011;51:110–121.*

was deemed the most suitable reagent to detect bloody footwear impressions that had been buried for up to 4 weeks on cotton and paper, but it performed poorly when plastic was used as a substrate.[167]

Luminol

Luminol is one of the best-known presumptive tests for blood because of the visual nature of the test, which makes it ideal for use in television and films. It also has more modern studies carried out on it than any other presumptive blood test. Unlike the other chemical presumptive tests for blood, rather than a color change, a positive reaction with luminol is indicated by chemiluminescence. This means that luminol needs to be used in complete or near darkness to be most effective because the light generated is not particularly strong or long lasting. Luminol has had limited use in some areas because of potential safety concerns, but a study by Larkin and Gannicliffe found that if suitable precautions were taken, it was completely safe to use.[168]

Luminol was first synthesized in 1902 by Schmitz[169] as part his dissertation work, but it was not mentioned again in the literature until 1913,[170] when Schmitz's supervisor, Curtius, further commented on the work, although he did not mention the property of chemiluminescence. According to Albrecht,[171] the chemiluminescence of luminol with lime juice was first observed by Lommel, who shared her observations with Kautsky, who in turn encouraged Albrecht to investigate further. Kautsky was investigating other fluorescing and luminescing compounds around that time. It was Albrecht who first observed (or reported) the property of luminol chemiluminescence in the presence of an oxidizing agent on contact with blood in 1928.[171] Sometimes this discovery is credited to Schmitz's original dissertation, but that work did not detail how he derived the luminol compound in his paper, although it appeared in his thesis work.[172] Further work was carried out by Harvey, who was provided luminol by Albrecht, and determined the reaction was caused by "active oxygen."[173,174] Despite the strong reaction with blood, luminol was not considered for presumptive identification of blood until 1937.[175]

The term luminol was coined in 1934[176] in a paper detailing its preparation, but the authors stated (at that time) that luminol was not well known to most scientists because of the difficulty of accessibility of the necessary reagent. It offered benefits over other chemiluminescent compounds of the time, working at dilute levels and with dilute H_2O_2 of 3% (as opposed to 30% of other tests at that time), and it showed how the reagent could be readily produced with high yields.[177] Huntress et al.[177] further reported that luminol gives a faint glow without another oxidizing agent, although they do not specify if this is constant or immediate (Nickolls[178] came to the same conclusion and did not find luminol satisfactory for use as a presumptive test). They also state that the luminescent intensity and duration can vary with the alkalinity of the luminol solution (Fig. 3.30), and some authors have described the luminescence as short lived.[179,180] Huntress et al.[177] also appear to be the first to detail spraying the reagent for use, although not for blood detection. Gleu and Pfannstiel[181] disagreed in 1936 and stated there is no luminescence with luminol and H_2O_2 alone; they concluded that blood catalyzes the decomposition of H_2O_2 to cause the luminescence, which we now know is a very close approximation of the reaction.

Fig. 3.30 The first image of luminol in use in 1933 described in Huntress et al.[177] using potassium ferricyanide as the oxidant. The image is of Huntress demonstrating the luminol reaction, taken in a completely dark room, and the exposure is entirely due to the light from the luminol. *From Huntress EH, Stanley LN, Parker AS. The oxidation of 3-aminophthalhydrazide ("luminol") as a lecture demonstration of chemiluminescence. J Chem Educ. 1934;11:142.*

The luminol reaction is rapid, although investigations into the reaction mechanisms in 1964[182,183] were unable to determine the intermediate structure of the oxidation step (even in 1977[184] it was confirmed that this intermediate step was unknown). It was also determined the luminescence fell between 350 and 600 nm and had energy of 50 to 80 kcal per mole.[182] That same year, Ponomarenko et al.[185] started looking into organic compounds as inhibitors to the luminol reaction, which were further confirmed.[186] They found that glycol, glycerin, mannitol, mono- and disaccharide, nitrophenols, dinitrophenols, aminophenols, amines, nitroanilines, and naphthols act as inhibitors. Seitz and Neary[184] conversely list a range of other catalysts that can cause a positive reaction with luminol, including Cu(II), Cr(III), Fe(II), VO(II), Mn(II), Ni(II), and Co(II).

There are two common formulations of luminol, sometimes referred to as luminol I and luminol II. Luminol I was described by Grodsky et al. in 1951,[56] which involved the addition of perborate to stabilize the luminol mixture and is the most common formulation in use. This formula is also shown to be more intense than without perborate.[187] Luminol II was described by Weber in 1966,[188] which used sodium hydroxide or potassium hydroxide and hydrogen peroxide, but it had a limited lifespan once prepared.

Luminol (5-amino-2,3-dihydrophthalazine-1,4-dione $C_8H_7O_2N_3$) is colorless and, when in the presence of Hb, is oxidized and emits a blue chemiluminescent light. The light that luminol emits is measured at 438 nm,[189] which is in blue range of visible light. Luminol is a one-step test, which for blood detection reacts with Hb (Fig. 3.31), where a positive reaction is seen as a blue glow (Fig. 3.32).

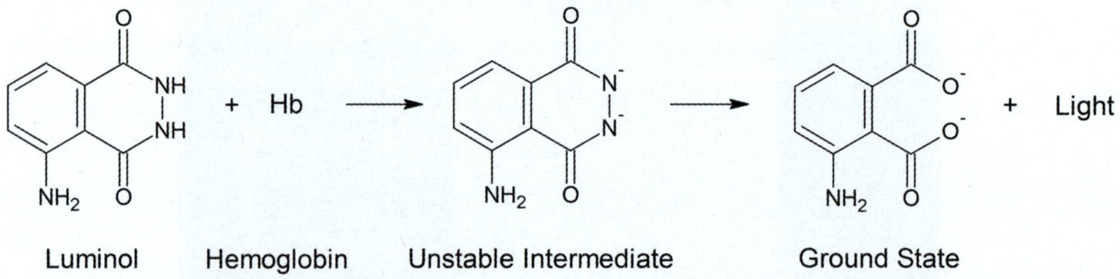

Fig. 3.31 Chemical reaction of the luminol test for blood. The colorless luminol (PubChem CID: 10638), which has hydrogen peroxide as part of the reagent spray, emits luminescence when in the presence of hemoglobin *(Hb). From Advanced Chemistry Development Inc. ChemSketch. Toronto, Ontario. www.acdlabs.com. 2018.*

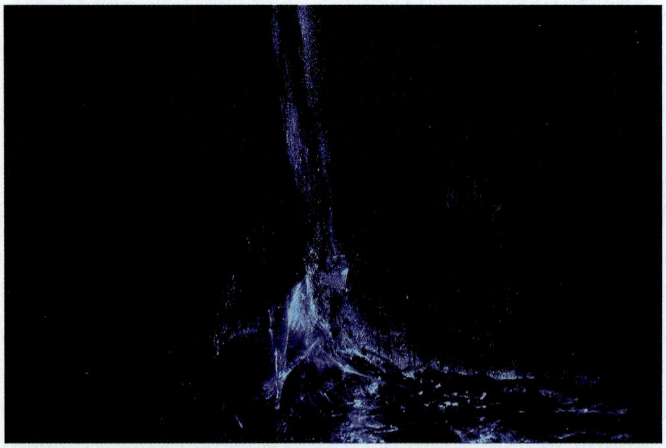

Fig. 3.32 Example of the luminol test for blood. The blue luminescence is indicative of a positive result. Note this image is taken in darkness with a long exposure.

Luminol has been used to treat alopecia,[190] blood clotting, and wound healing.[191–193] Weber[188] described its use to detect neurotoxins (e.g., sarin) and insecticides based on organophosphorus compounds.

Lytle and Hedgecock[194] determined that concentrations of luminol of 1, 2, and 4 g/L did not affect chemiluminescence. They also determined that if luminol was prepared as two solutions (luminol/carbonate/water and sodium perborate/water), then they could be stored separately for at least 8 weeks and retain full activity when combined.[194] Others found that luminol had a faint reaction when first applied, which became brighter with the addition of more reagent and persisted for 3.5 minutes.[135] Luminol can interfere with spectroscopic methods of identifying Hb, but it was not found to interfere with other serological methods or DNA.[136] Other serological testing showed that luminol could affect blood typing results, but minimally with few errors with untreated blood and only in aged samples.[195]

The application of luminol (both formulas) does not affect subsequent presumptive blood testing, crystal tests, ABO typing, or species testing.[196,197] This was not supported by Gross et al.,[198] who found that certain sets of circumstances (e.g., cleaning prior to luminol application) would cause a negative effect on subsequent presumptive testing. It has been found that luminol does not interfere with subsequent blood tests (precipitin or grouping)[56] or DNA analysis;[106,144,197] in contrast, Laux found some negative effect on genetic typing under older profiling systems.[196] Another study found that the Grodsky formulation of luminol reduced the DNA success rate, but no other formulation (including Bluestar) did.[199]

It has been found that luminol has a sensitivity between 1:5 million[56] and 1:10 million.[134] Proescher and Moody also claim sensitivity at 10 million, but they recommend spraying with hydrochloric acid to decompose the Hb and increase sensitivity to that level.[51] Lytle and Hedgecock[162] found the opposite: that hydrochloric acid gave diminished results and increased background fluorescence. The luminol mixture described by Specht[173] was found to have a sensitivity of 1:2000 (blood to water) as a dried spot.[188] Weber[188] claimed his new mixture was sensitive to 1:10 million (blood to water) as either a solution or a dried spot. Other authors report varying maximum sensitivities between 1:100 and 1:100 million.[51,56,132,134,144,146,149–151,194,195,197,200,201]

The substrate on which the stain is located was determined to have a major effect on the sensitivity of luminol, with iron, cotton, rubber, baked clay, and wood having a detrimental impact on the sensitivity.[134] Washing of stains with detergents that contain active oxygen was found to cause false negatives.[202,203] It was found that porous surfaces tended to retain blood detectable by luminol, but smooth surfaces were easy to clean completely.[194]

A wide range of substances has been found that can cause false positive reactions with luminol, including copper, iron and nickel salts, bleach, plant peroxidases, hypochlorites, potassium ferricyanide, ammoniacal copper solution, manganese peroxide, colloidal platinum, potato, turnip, parsnip, horseradish, carrot, onion, pumpkin, tomato, enamel paint, polyurethane paint, jute natural matting, sisal natural matting, terracotta tile, and ceramic tile.[47,51,134,144,175,187,189,194,200] It has been found that many of these substances produce a luminescence that is of a slightly different wavelength than a true blood positive, but the wavelengths were so close that it required specialist spectroscopic equipment to determine the differences.[47,189] For this reason, luminol has been suggested to be excluded from outdoor use because the range of vegetable peroxidases that cross-react is large.[194] According to one study, addition of amines such as 1,2-diaminoethane can eliminate the interference (false positive) that may be caused by hypochlorite (bleach).[204]

An excess of peroxide has been shown to reduce the luminescence output to a glow.[205] Weber[188] states that urine greatly reduces the chemiluminescence of luminol, which may be a reason it is not used for occult blood detection as are most of the other presumptive blood tests. It has been found that ascorbic acid can reduce the sensitivity of luminol.[197] Luminol showed inhibition with stains that had been laundered at high temperature with detergent containing sodium percarbonate, but not with samples laundered with detergent at cold temperatures or laundered samples without detergent.[206,207] Carpet samples washed with detergent containing sodium percarbonate at low and high temperatures showed no inhibition.[207] Samples, carpet and denim, when washed at various temperatures with sodium percarbonate and exposed to different environmental conditions, showed an increasing trend of inhibition first based on temperature and then on time to testing, with samples washed at high temperatures and exposed for 14 days showing the greatest level of inhibition.[207]

Luminol has been found to successfully identify blood on burned wood in some cases, although this was in less than 20% of the samples.[208] It has also identified blood on objects in fire at temperatures as high as 1000°C.[209] One study found bloodstains under paint could not be detected using luminol,[64] but other studies have contradicted this.

In one study, luminol showed chemiluminescence with blood covered in up to four layers of white paint, but only under one layer of maroon paint.[70] Blood was tested on tiles with stains that were wet, semidry, and dry, and then cleaned using one of three methods, then painted over up to seven times before being tested with luminol.[210] Luminol was able to detect blood stains under up to six layers of water-based paint and under up to three layers of solvent-based paint when the stains had been washed prior to painting.[210] Blood on cement, wood, and metal was painted over and tested with luminol after up to 50 days, with blood painted over with distemper paint visible after 50 days under three coats.[211] Similarly, the wood and metal substrates also showed positive chemiluminescence of the stains under three coats of paint after 50 days.[211]

Bluestar, Bluestar Forensic, and Bluestar Magnum are all luminol-based tests, each with modifications that claim to give the test a longer and more intense luminescence with a positive detection. Bluestar was first developed and synthesized by Blum et al.[212] in 2006. Bluestar

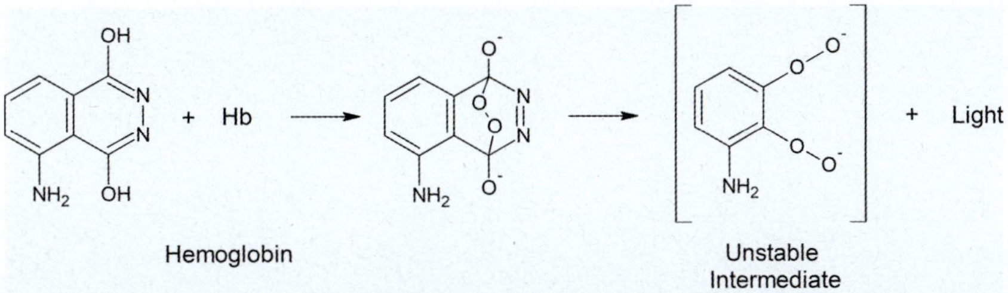

Fig. 3.33 The Bluestar reaction with hemoglobin *(Hb)* to produce luminescence, as described by the manufacturer. *From Advanced Chemistry Development Inc. ChemSketch. Toronto, Ontario. www.acdlabs.com. 2018.*

is a one-step test that comes as two tablets, which are added to water for activation and ease of use.[213] This allows Bluestar to be included in crime scene kits without liquid chemicals, which means it can be made fresh onsite (luminol has a defined shelf life). It is applied in the same manner as luminol in that it is sprayed onto items or scenes with suspected blood staining, although it claims to not need complete darkness because of the more intense chemiluminescence. The forensic and magnum varieties are advertised as being nonharmful to DNA, but studies have shown that even the base version of Bluestar does not affect the recovery or amplification of DNA.[144] The parent company displays a slightly different reaction mechanism to luminol (Fig. 3.33), but the exact variation from standard luminol formulations is not known. The original publication by Blum et al.[212] shows the best reaction with specific concentrations of H_2O_2 and NaOH, which gave the highest light intensity.

Patel and Hopwood confirmed the Bluestar Magnum formulation had the same sensitivity as the base product, but it gave more intense luminescence, and the base version had the same sensitivity and intensity as luminol.[201] In the original paper, Bluestar was, in part, developed to allow subsequent DNA testing,[212] and others have confirmed that DNA could be successfully recovered from Bluestar-treated samples.[201] Nicloux and Bressler[214] found that Bluestar and Bluestar Magnum had a negative impact on DNA recovery with diluted blood. At 1:100 blood to water dilutions and above, DNA artifacts and other profile issues were observed.

It was found that more intense luminescence was achieved with Bluestar, but the reaction persisted for the same length of time as luminol.[135] As with luminol, Bluestar is a one-step test that for blood detection reacts with the Hb where a positive reaction is seen as a blue glow (Fig. 3.34).

Bluestar demonstrated good performance on bloody footwear marks that had been buried for up to 4 weeks, proving to be the most effective on plastic substates, good on cotton, and poor on paper.[167] It was also able to identify bloody footwear marks on carpet that had been cleaned using a commercial cleaner or on walls with three coats of white paint.[66] On samples spanning six substrates (wood, carpet, vinyl, ceramic, cotton, polyester), Bluestar Forensic was found to detect more bloodstains that had been washed off with either bleach

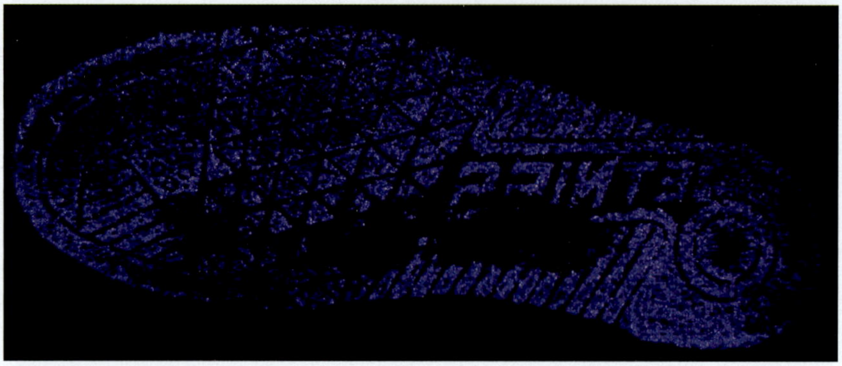

Fig. 3.34 Example of the Bluestar reagent used on a footwear mark in blood on dark fabric. *From Kevin Farrugia.*

or water than did luminol.[213] Washing of stains with active oxygen detergents has been shown to cause false negatives.[203] It has been found to successfully react with blood under four layers of white paint, but it reacted only under three layers of maroon paint for two of four tested bloodstain types.[70] Bluestar Forensic was evaluated using three different substrates (brick, drywall, flakeboard), three different paints (dark purple acrylic, blue-green acrylic, white acrylic), and three different stain types (handprint, drip, swipe). The results found that all patterns on all substrates were detectable under four coats of white paint but only under two coats of colored paint, except for the swipe pattern that was visible under four coats of all colors.[215]

Bluestar has been found to successfully identify blood on burned wood in some cases, although this was in less than 10% of the samples in most treatment sets.[208] Bluestar Magnum showed inhibition with stains that had been laundered with detergent containing sodium percarbonate, but not with laundered samples without detergent.[206] Common household oxidizing cleaners were shown to clean visible blood, but they did not inhibit or cross-react with Bluestar.[216]

Bluestar has been found to be cross-reactive with bleach,[212] although the authors state that bleach reaction can be distinguished from blood reaction by an experienced operator. Castelló et al.[238] found quebracho extract to significantly inhibit Bluestar after 1 day and a 1% quebracho final concentration. A range of other substances has been shown to cross-react with Bluestar, including potato juice, tomato juice, tomato sauce with meat, red onion, red kidney bean, horseradish, 1 M ascorbic acid, bleach, copper and iron salts, household detergents, chlorine, some paints and varnishes, copper, lichen, thyme, some tree mosses, iron-containing soils, banana pulp, turnip pulp, dish detergent, and stain remover; however, some surfaces cleaned with bleach and active oxygen detergent inhibit the reaction.[67,144,200,203,212,213,217]

Orthotolidine

Ruttan was the first to describe orthotolidine (O-Tolidine, O-tol) in detail in 1886,[218] based on an earlier report of its synthesis in 1873.[219] The first reported use of O-tol was to detect free chlorine in water in 1909.[220,221] O-tol was first applied to occult blood detection in 1912 by Ruttan and Hardisty,[222] followed in 1943 by Zwarenstein,[223] who then improved the testing method in 1949.[224] Once the carcinogenic nature of benzidine was determined, O-tol was reinvestigated for detecting blood in urine and feces.[107,225] The primary oxidation product (blue) has a maximum absorption peak of 630 nm, and the secondary oxidation product (yellow) has a maximum absorption peak of 435 nm.[17] O-tol has a similar structure to benzidine, but initially it was not reported as being hazardous,[107] although it was later determined to be possibly carcinogenic in humans,[226] and as such is currently not used widely.

O-tol (4-(4-amino-3-methylphenyl)-2-methylaniline, $C_{14}H_{16}N_2$) is colorless and is converted to a blue primary oxidation product through peroxidation. O-tol is a two-step test, which for blood detection takes place in the presence of Hb and low levels of H_2O_2 (Fig. 3.35), where a characteristic blue color is formed (Fig. 3.36). O-tol's primary oxidation pigment (blue-green) has a maximum absorption peak of 632 nm.[101]

O-tol was originally determined to have a sensitivity of 1:7 million of blood to water and 1:24,000 of blood to urine.[222] Zwarenstein, however, found that a 1:5 million dilution produced negative results in water, but 1:1 million gave a positive result when diluted in urine.[224] Other researchers have found sensitivity ranges between 1:32,000 and 1:10 million.[36,109,114,147,150,222] It was found that bromides and iodides in the urine will give a false

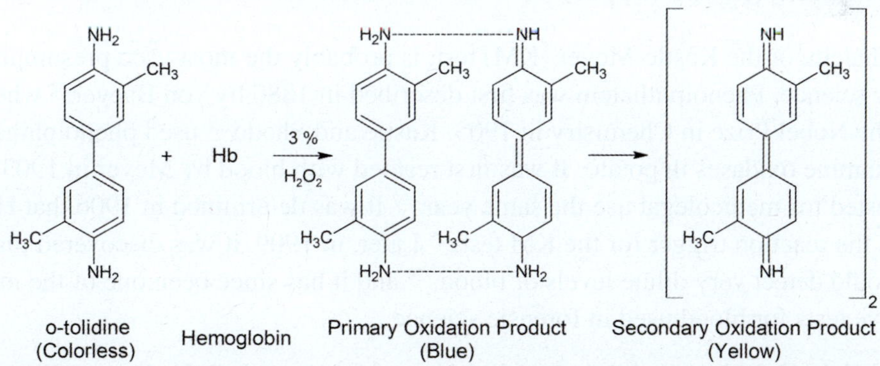

Fig. 3.35 The chemical reaction of the orthotolidine *(O-tol)* test for blood. The colorless O-tol (PubChem CID: 8413), which when in the presence of hemoglobin *(Hb)* and hydrogen peroxide, converts to the blue primary oxidation product. The secondary yellow oxidation product is only formed when the reaction takes place at very low pH. *From Lewis GP. Method using ortho-tolidine for the quantitative determination of haemoglobin in serum and urine. J Clin Pathol. 1965;18:235–239; Advanced Chemistry Development Inc. ChemSketch. Toronto, Ontario. www.acdlabs.com. 2018.*

Fig. 3.36 Example of the Orthotolidine test for blood, with a negative control *(bottom)* and a positive control *(top)*. The blue-green color is indicative of a positive test. *From Amy Brodeur, Boston University School of Medicine.*

positive.[224] Lewis[107] claimed O-tol was better than benzidine and recommended it for use with urinalysis. It was found that treatment with O-tol prior to DNA typing causes the DNA analysis to fail.[106]

Cox[147] found O-tol to have a range of false positives, including asparagus, avocado, green bean, broccoli, Brussel sprout, cabbage, carrot, cauliflower, celery, yellow corn, cucumber, eggplant, garlic, lettuce, mushroom, okra, white onion, green onion, bell pepper, Irish potato, sweet potato, radish, spinach, yellow squash, tomato, turnip root, apricot, banana, cantaloupe, nectarine, peach, pear, pineapple, tangerine, and watermelon. Some, such as mushroom, showed a weak positive in dried form after 60 seconds, so it would be unlikely to be mistaken as blood.

Phenolphthalein (Kastle-Meyer)

Phenolphthalein, or the Kastle-Meyer (KM) test, is probably the most used presumptive test in forensic science. Phenolphthalein was first described in 1880 by von Baeyer,[32] who was awarded the Nobel Prize in Chemistry in 1905. Kastle and Shedd[124] used phenolphthalin in 1901 to examine oxidases in potato. It was first reacted with blood by Meyer in 1903,[33] and was suggested for medicolegal use the same year.[227] It was determined in 1906 that Hb in blood was the reaction trigger for the KM test.[228] Later, in 1909, it was discovered that the KM test could detect very dilute levels of blood,[229] and it has since been one of the main presumptive tests for blood used in forensic science.

Phenolphthalein (3,3-bis(4-hydroxyphenyl)-2-benzofuran-1-one, $C_{20}H_{14}O_4$) can be converted through reduction to phenolphthalin (2-[bis(4-hydroxyphenyl)methyl]benzoic acid, $C_{20}H_{16}O_4$). Phenolphthalin is colorless, and in the presence of Hb and hydrogen peroxide is converted to pink phenolphthalein (Fig. 3.37). KM is a two-step test, which for blood detection takes place in the presence of Hb and low levels of H_2O_2 where the characteristic pink color is formed (Fig. 3.38).

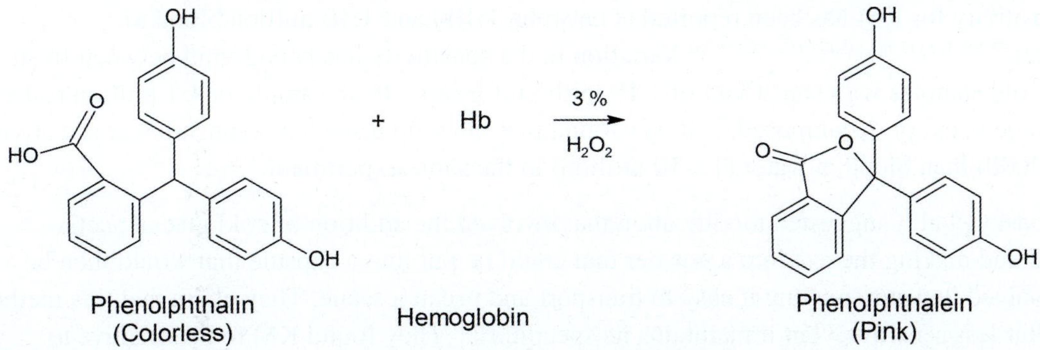

Fig. 3.37 The chemical reaction of the phenolphthalein (Kastle-Meyer) test for blood. The colorless phenolphthalin (PubChem CID: 66494), which when in the presence of hemoglobin *(Hb)* and hydrogen peroxide, converts to the colored phenolphthalein (PubChem CID: 4764). *From Advanced Chemistry Development Inc. ChemSketch. Toronto, Ontario. www.acdlabs.com. 2018.*

Fig. 3.38 Example of the Kastle-Meyer test for blood, with a negative control *(left)* and a positive control *(right)*. The bright pink color is indicative of a positive test.

Originally used as a laxative in 1902,[230] phenolphthalein was common in many over-the-counter laxative products for the better part of a century. A 1950 review found phenolphthalein to be safe,[231] but it was subsequently found to be genotoxic in animal models (although the authors used 10 times the human dose level),[232] to cause oxidative damage (by acting as a peroxidase substrate),[233] and to bind to estrogen receptors.[234] Phenolphthalein was deemed "not generally recognized as safe and effective or misbranded" by the US Food and Drug Administration in 1997[235] and voluntarily removed from over-the-counter purchase.[236] Phenolphthalein has also been used to differentiate between blood from cattle with tuberculosis and those without,[237] to determine alkalinity of stomach contents, and to detect cyanide.[238] It is has also been used to detect latent blood in medical settings, where 20% and 40% of laryngoscope blades and handles, respectively, were found to have latent blood present even after sterilization.[8] Other researchers have also used it to assess blood on medical equipment.[7,9,10]

Sensitivity for KM has been reported at between 1:100 and 1:10 million blood to water.[56,109,114,115,144,147,148,150,151,239–241] Variation in the sensitivity has been found between fresh and old samples with sensitivity of 1:10 million if using a fresh sample or 1:1 million if the sample is old or decomposed.[109] It was found that blood in urine had a much lower sensitivity (1:2000) than blood in water (1:>10 million) in the same experiment.[222]

Grodsky et al.[56] suggested modification that involved the addition of cold glacial acetic acid and making the test into a powder that could be put into a capsule that would then be dissolved in water, making it easy to transport and use at a scene. They claim that this method is "far less sensitive," but it maintains its specificity.[54] They found KM to be sensitive to between 1:100,000 (reaction in 3 seconds) and 1:5 million (reaction in 20 seconds), but the modified version described only 1:10,000 (reaction in 20 seconds).[56]

Research has found that KM has a large range of substances that can produce false positives, including legume root nodules.[242] Blue denim has been found to produce a false positive with KM, and the authors hypothesize that this may be due to peroxidases used during manufacturing, but they were not able to verify this.[243] Signaevsky[244] tested 40 products that could be used to clean bloodstains for their effect on KM testing and found that none interfered and that four showed abnormal results. Pinker[121] found that substances that caused false positives with benzidine and LMG did not do so with KM. Similarly, when compared to benzidine, O-tol, and guaiac, KM showed comparable sensitivity but no adverse effects from ascorbic acid, whereas the other tests did.[139]

Washing of samples with active oxygen detergents was found to produce false negatives, even when the bloodstain was still visible.[202] Some fingerprint enhancement chemicals have also been shown to reduce the speed of, or inhibit, some subsequent KM testing.[245] The effect that quebracho extract (a natural vegetal tannin used in making leather) had on the KM test was investigated. Multiple concentrations of quebracho with multiple dilutions of blood, over multiple days, were used and then tested with KM.[120] Control samples reacted as expected to the 1:10,000 dilution, but after 1 day the sensitivity of KM was reduced to 1:100, and after 240 days it was reduced to 1:10, when in the presence of 1% of quebracho. If the concentration of quebracho was increased to 25%, KM showed false negative results at 80 days, and if placed on actual leather the sensitivity was reduced to 1:10 after 1 day, and only neat blood could be detected at 15 days.[120]

No effects were observed by prior testing with Bluestar or luminol at high blood concentrations, but some effects were seen with very diluted blood that was pretreated.[241] In samples that were exposed to fire, with temperatures ranging between 100°C and 900°C, KM was able to show positive results in most cases, although high temperature appears to cause false negatives.[246] A subsequent study found KM failed in all samples from all burn conditions tested.[208] Stains washed with detergents that have active oxygen fail to produce a result.[203]

Alenazy et al.[154] found that KM has an adverse effect on DNA recovery potentially through degradation of the sample. They found that as much as 95% degradation occurred when samples that were treated with KM were analyzed after 1 week, but they were still able to get full DNA profiles. This reduction in detectable DNA was also observed by other researchers,[106,144] and some have found complete inhibition of subsequent DNA analysis,[58] whereas others have not found any effect.[57]

Tetramethylbenzidine

TMB was originally investigated in 1974 as an alternative to benzidine,[101] which even after being found to be carcinogenic was still in use as a test for blood at that time. Based on the fact that another derivative of benzidine, O-tol, was less hazardous but equally sensitive, it was hypothesized that TMB could also be a viable alternative.[101] Holland et al.[101] determined it was four times as sensitive as benzidine, and did not cause any cancers in rats, whereas both benzidine and O-tol did.

Tetramethylbenzidine (4-(4-amino-3,5-dimethylphenyl)-2,6-dimethylaniline, $C_{16}H_{20}N_2$) is colorless in its reduced form and is converted through oxidation to a blue-green oxidized form. TMB can be used as either a one- or two-step test, which for blood detection takes place in the presence of Hb and low levels of H_2O_2 (Fig. 3.39), where the characteristic blue-green color is formed (Fig. 3.40). TMB's primary pigment (blue-green) has a maximum absorption peak of 655 nm.[101]

TMB is used in many medical tests,[92,247] including for occult blood,[248] having been incorporated because of the adverse health effects of benzidine. The cross-reaction of TMB with HPD is so strong that TMB is used in many ELISA tests and in histochemistry.[249]

Garner et al.[116] investigated TMB in a direct comparison with benzidine, looking at both sensitivity and specificity, and found no difference between the two; however, he did find differences in absolute sensitivity dependent on the concentration of the reagents. The overall range found was between 1:1000 (0.05 M TMB solution) and 1:1 million

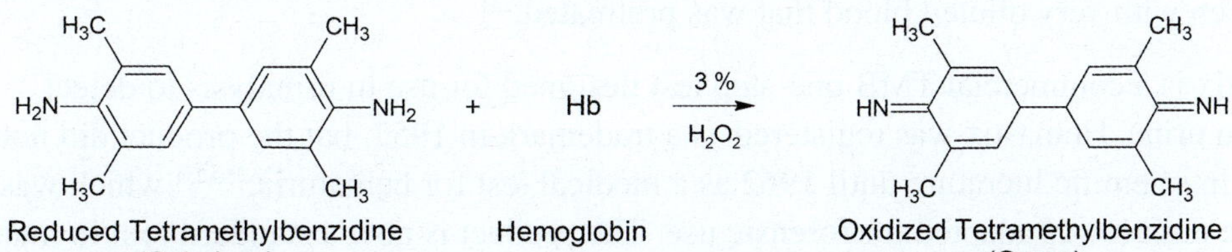

Fig. 3.39 Chemical reaction of the tetramethylbenzidine (TMB) test for blood. The colorless reduced TMB (PubChem CID: 41206), which when in the presence of hemoglobin *(Hb)* and hydrogen peroxide, converts to the blue-green oxidized TMB. *From Advanced Chemistry Development Inc. ChemSketch. Toronto, Ontario. www.acdlabs.com. 2018.*

Fig. 3.40 Example of the tetramethylbenzidine test for blood, with a negative control *(bottom)* and a positive control *(top)*. The blue-green color is indicative of a positive test. *From Amy Brodeur, Boston University School of Medicine.*

(0.20 M TMB solution).[116] Other authors have found sensitivity ranges between 1:16,000 and 1:1 million[147,150,161] (blood to water).

Cox tested a range of fruits and vegetables, both fresh and dried, and found that TMB cross-reacted with most, showing a false positive.[147] False positives have been observed with horseradish, cabbage, lettuce, onion, beet leaf, garlic, tomato, cucumber, nitic acid, potassium permanganate, hydrated sodium hypochlorite, asparagus, avocado, green bean, broccoli, Brussel sprout, carrot, cauliflower, celery, yellow corn, cucumber, eggplant, mushroom, okra, green onion, bell pepper, Irish potato, sweet potato, radish, spinach, yellow squash, turnip root, red apple, apricot, banana, cantaloupe, cherry, grapes, nectarine, peach, pear, pineapple, plum, tangerine, and watermelon; all were all found to cross-react with TMB,[116,147] although some of these could not be confused with the reaction expected with blood.[116]

In samples that were exposed to fire, with temperatures ranging between 100°C and 900°C, TMB was able to show positive results in most cases, although high temperature appears to cause false negatives.[246] Another study found TMB failed in all burned samples tested.[208] TMB showed inhibition with stains that had been laundered with detergent containing sodium percarbonate, but not with laundered samples without detergent.[206] TMB is not affected by prior testing with Bluestar or luminol at high blood concentrations, but some negative effects were seen with very diluted blood that was pretreated.[241]

Hemastix is a commercial TMB one-step test designed for use in urinalysis to detect blood in urine. Hemastix was registered as a trademark in 1957, but the product did not appear in scientific literature until 1962 as a medical test for hematuria,[250,251] which was its purpose until it was adapted for forensic use. The product is now a standard tool in many forensic laboratories. It was first reported in forensic use in 1977,[103] where 8 of 276 forensic laboratories were using the test (one lab had used the test but no longer was).

The test is a short strip with a small square test area at the end for easy sampling of urine, either in a receptacle or while urinating. The exact reaction is proprietary, but TMB is a

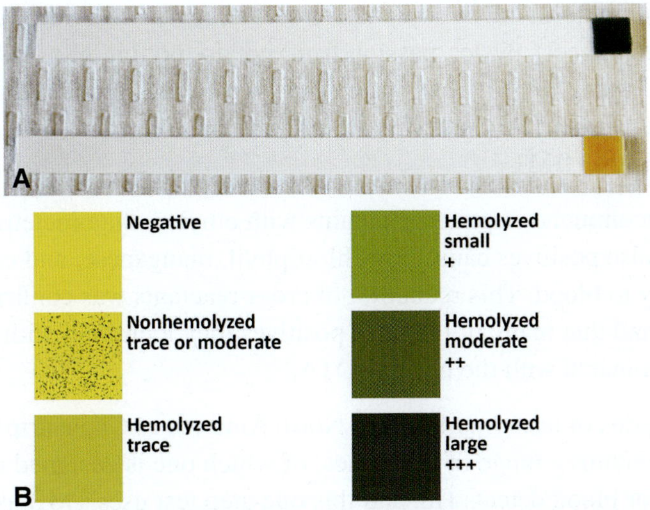

Fig. 3.41 The Hemastix reagent strips for urinalysis that are frequently used by forensic scientists as a presumptive test for blood. (A) One strip *(top)* shows a strong positive reaction, and the other strip *(bottom)* shows a negative reaction. Unlike other chemical presumptive blood tests, Hemastix provides a semiquantitative value of the hemoglobin detected based on the appearance and intensity of the color change. (B) A comparative color chart appears on each bottle so that the level of blood in urine can be estimated. *A, From Amy Brodeur, Boston University School of Medicine; B, from Hemastix packaging.*

component of the test. Unlike the standard TMB reaction, which is a uniform color change, Hemastix reports a gradient of colors depending on the amount of Hb present, regardless if the sample has hemolyzed RBCs (Fig. 3.41). Testing can follow either a direct or indirect test. The direct method involves wetting the test strip with sterile water, then applying it briefly directly to a stain. The indirect method follows the normal testing protocols, where a subsample is taken with a filter paper or swab and then applied to the test strip.

Hemastix was found in one study to inhibit DNA recovery using the Promega DNA IQ system[252] and with other magnetic bead DNA extraction methods,[253] but other studies have found no significant effect on DNA recovery.[144] The reported sensitivity for Hemastix is between 1:100 and 1:100,000 blood to water.[144,151,161] Hemastix has been used to identify blood as old as 166 years.[87]

Hemastix has been reported to show false positives with algae, aloe vera (skin), avocado, baked bean, banana (stalk), bloodworm, capsicum, carrot, celery, chicken egg yolk, chili (hot), Chinese cabbage, cobalt chloride (1.8 M), coconut (flesh), copper sulphate (0.009 M), copper salts, fern, fertilizer, frangipani (trunk), gardenia (shoot), garlic, ginger, grasshopper, hoop pine (branch), hydrogen peroxide (3%), iron oxide (2.0 M), iron sulfate (2.5 M), iron salts, jellyfish, kiwi fruit, magnesium chloride, manganese oxide, mangrove tree, Moreton

Bay chestnut, mud-crab flesh, mushroom, native orchid, nickel chloride (0.09 M), nickel salts, octopus, onion, orange (peel), oyster, passion fruit, potato, potting mix, red onion, saliva, seagrass, sodium polytungstate (1.0 M), strawberry, sugar cane, tomato sauce, tomato sauce with meat, vegemite, vitamin B_{12}, waterlily (root), watermelon (skin), white onion, wild grass, yam, and zinc sulphate (3.0 M).[12,144]

Loy and Dixon[254] recommend treatment of stains with ethylenediaminetetraacetic acid (EDTA) to reduce false positives caused by chlorophyll, manganese, and copper ions with no loss of sensitivity to blood. This reduction of cross-reactants was confirmed by Matheson and Veall,[12] who found that many of the false positives they identified with standard Hemastix testing could be eliminated with the use of EDTA.[12]

The Combur-Test series of tests (marketed in North America as Chemstrip) is designed for urinalysis and contains a range of test zones, of which one is designed to detect blood in urine. The zone for blood detects Hb, and this one-step test uses TMB as the active component.[255,256] There is an iodate impregnated mesh layer, which the test documentation claims reduces false positives for Hb. There is a range of different Combur-Test strips marketed with different numbers of targets, although for forensic science the blood detection is the one used. Combur-Test does not affect DNA typing, except with very low levels of blood.[255] Butler et al.[257] found that the Combur-Test was able to successfully identify 98% of their test bloodstains (out of 500) on different substrates for undiluted samples, but this reduced to 10% success rate for diluted (1 in 100) bloodstains.

De Vittori et al.[255] identified that the Combur3 Test had sensitivity of 1:100,000 blood to a sodium chloride solution (154 mM), but only on glass and painted sheet metal substrates. It showed a maximum sensitivity of 1:10,000 when paper, plywood, or plasterboard was the substrate. The sodium chloride solution was used because it is isotonic to the RBCs and, according to the authors, prevents leakage of Hb outside the cells, which could affect the experimental results. They found a wide range of substances that cause false positives, including ammunitions, apple and banana juices, apple pulp, banana pulp, bird feces, bleach, carrot pulp, $CuSO_4$, dead insects, degreaser, feces, $FeSO_4$, flower, grass, $KMnO_4$, $NaBO_3$, onion pulp, peach juice, pine bark, pineapple juice, potato pulp, red-orange juice, saliva, tomato pulp, tomato sauce, and urine. Interestingly, the bleach and degreaser only cross-reacted with the test when they were diluted.[255] Several substances were found that inhibited the test at diluted levels of blood, with ascorbic acid and aspirin C being the most influential on the test, but bleach, chlorine active gel, neutral detergent, and whitening liquid had some effect.

Other Chemical Tests

There are many different commercial presumptive blood tests available, some of which are commercial offerings of the tests previously described (and are therefore described with their relevant test), others are modified formulations of those previously described and marketed under different names (e.g., Bluestar), and some are entirely new tests that have been developed recently. The last group is primarily in the immunological testing category, which is discussed in the next section.

Commercial versions of the established chemical presumptive tests will generally have similar sensitivities and specificities as described, but those that are modified may have differences due to proprietary modifications of those reagents. There is also one presumptive blood test that falls under the chemical tests that is a combination of two of the previously described methods.

Lumiscene is a combination of luminol and fluorescein; according to the company, it has a sensitivity of 1:50,000 blood in water, luminescence at 525 nm, a more intense reaction, a lower H_2O_2 volume of 0.12% (compared to 3% usually used in other tests, so less damaging on DNA), and it can be visualized using a light source between 415 and 480 nm and an orange filter. It can be seen without any specialized ALS as green light. The combination of luminol and fluorescence was first proposed in 1962 for nonblood detection purposes,[258] and although no increase in output was reported, the shift in color could offer advantages when background interference with luminol is found.[194] Patel and Hopwood[201] found a sensitivity of 1:1 million when carrying out comparison with other luminol mixtures. As with Bluestar, Lumiscene comes as tablets that are dissolved in water prior to use, meaning it has a long shelf life in tablet form. It is used in the same manner as luminol and fluorescein, in that it is sprayed over scenes or items to identify areas of possible latent blood.

Nicloux and Bressler[214] found that Lumiscene had a negative impact on DNA recovery with diluted blood for both the standard and ultra formulations. At 1:100 blood to water dilutions and above, DNA artifacts and other profile issues were observed. Lumiscene was able to successfully identify blood under three coats of paint after 9 days and under four coats of paint after 1 day[259] (Fig. 3.42).

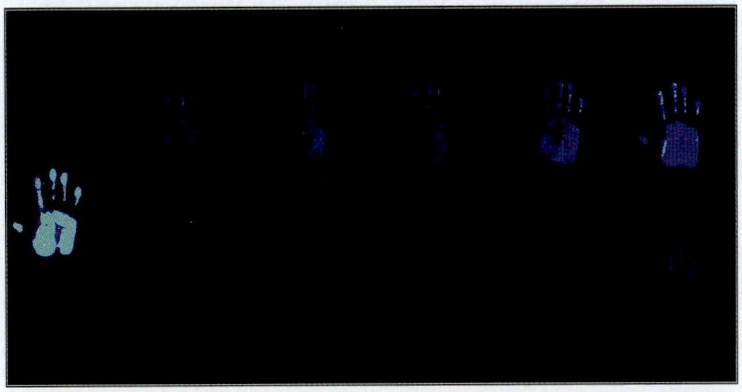

Fig. 3.42 Lumiscene used under painted bloody handprints. *Center left* is the control unpainted print. *Top row, from left to right,* are prints painted over with three coats of paint that are 9, 7, 5, 3, and 1 day old, respectively. The *lower row* shows the same pattern but with four coats of paint. *From Ramsthaler F, Schlote J, Gehl A, et al. Detectability, visualization, and DNA analysis of bloodstains after repainting the walls. Int J Leg Med. 2018;132:1625–1634.*

Other testing methods have been used for blood identification and visualization; however, they are used mainly to visualize bloody fingerprints. These include acid yellow 7, Amido black, Coomassie brilliant blue, Crocein scarlet, or Hungarian red.[152,260] These reagents are not used for typical identification of blood in forensic serology.

Immunological Tests

Landsteiner published a paper in 1900 with a note explaining that mixing serum from human and animal blood caused agglutination, and this sometimes occurred with human sera and different human blood samples.[261] This lead to further work by Landsteiner[262] and into what became the ABO blood grouping system for which he was awarded the Nobel Prize. The first forensic report of an immunological test for blood was reported in 1901,[263] which investigated species identification (see Chapter 6). Blood group typing (see Appendix I), including ABO, became a cornerstone of forensic serology until the introduction of DNA into identity testing, after which time it was superseded by the newer techniques.

Currently, the immunological methods for blood identification are kit based. Some laboratories classify these tests as confirmatory for blood, or for human blood, but most of the tests have some level of known cross-reaction. There are many blood markers available as targets for immunological tests for blood. These tests tend to be more specific to blood, and to human blood, than the chemical tests, but they are less sensitive.

Immunochromatographic tests are generally not used as the main test to screen for blood. Because crime scene or item exam may involve testing multiple stains (potentially hundreds) from the same incident, the speed and cost of the testing therefore become very important. Immunochromatographic testing is more expensive than chemical tests, which are used as a first screen. Final confirmation can be done at a scene using an immunochromatographic test, but this is often left to the forensic laboratory analyzing the evidence to confirm the sample is human blood. Chemical tests take only a few seconds to perform and less than 1 minute for a result, whereas immunochromatographic tests can take hours to prepare and up to 15 minutes or longer for a result.[243,264] Again, with potentially hundreds of stains to be tested, the stains are usually first screened with chemical tests before immunochromatographic tests will be used on a select representative number of samples. All the current immunological tests are lateral flow and have a control zone to show the sample has migrated through the test and components of the test are working correctly.

ABAcard HemaTrace

The ABAcard HemaTrace is a one-step immunochromatographic test that is advertised as being human specific. The test targets human Hb using a mobile monoclonal antihuman antibody in a cartridge test. Samples are placed in a microcentrifuge tube, where buffer is added, and the sample is then vortexed and left to sit at room temperature for up to 5 minutes.

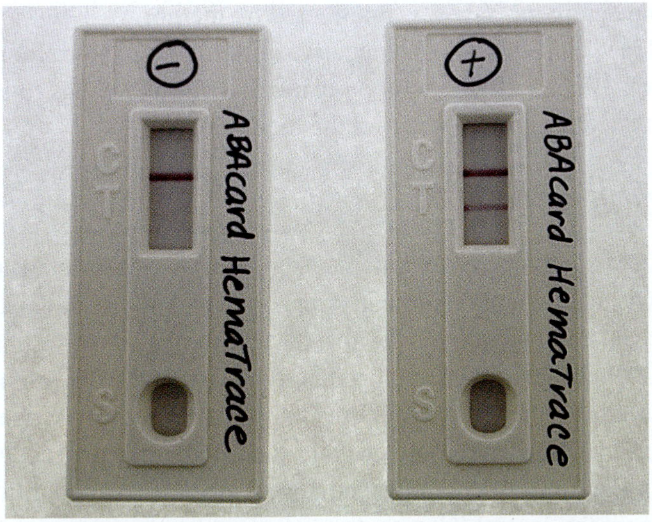

Fig. 3.43 Example of the ABAcard HemaTrace test for blood, with a negative control *(left)* and a positive control *(right)*. Lines at C and T indicate a positive result, whereas a line at C only indicates a negative result. *From Amy Brodeur, Boston University School of Medicine.*

Four drops are then placed into the sample well (labeled S in Fig. 3.43); the sample solution then flows across the test strip for 10 minutes before the test is read, although some authors report positives in as little as 45 seconds.[265] A single line at the control (C) area indicates a negative, whereas an additional line at the test (T) area indicates a positive (see Fig. 3.43). If no line is visible in the C area, then the test is invalid.

Swander and Stites[161] found HemaTrace to have a sensitivity of 1:16.7 million blood to water in one study and 1:32,700 in another, but they were greater than the chemical tests being compared at the same time (Hemastix, TMB, LCV). Johnston et al.[265] found the sensitivity to be 1:500,000 or 1:2 million when liquid blood was diluted in water or buffer, respectively. They found the sensitivity reduced to 1:256 when dried blood was tested in water or buffer.

HemaTrace has been found to show false positives with ferret and primate blood, anal swabs, feces, oral swabs, rectal swabs, semen, and vaginal swabs.[265] Although not all body fluid samples showed cross-reaction, at least 50% of those reported did. Heating blood prior to testing was found to cause a false negative, but pretreatment with the following did not affect the test: luminol; LCV; TMB; bleached samples; samples contaminated with soil or plant material; from leather; from washed jeans; and those 10 years old stored both frozen and at room temperature.[161] Streeting et al.[160] found no inhibition of HemaTrace with stains pretreated with luminol I, but they found minor inhibition with diluted stains pretreated with LCV.

HemaTrace was unable to detect blood from laundered fabric at hot (40°C) conditions with detergent containing sodium percarbonate, but it was able to detect blood on cold

(24°C) wash with the detergent.[206] It was unaffected by the hot wash without the addition of detergent.[206] HemaTrace can show a false negative with high concentrations of blood because of the high-dose hook effect, but whole blood is too viscous and needs to be diluted (1:8) in water or buffer to make it able to flow across the membrane.[265]

Hexagon OBTI and Bluestar OBTI

The Hexagon OBTI test is a precursor to both the HemDirect (Seratec) and Bluestar OBTI tests, and several studies were carried out on this early version, which is also still available. It is a one-step lateral flow immunochromatographic test that detects human Hb and is marketed for detection of blood in feces. OBTI has an antihuman Hb antibody to target Hb. The test has a sample wand, or samples can be placed into the buffer tube provided, which is then shaken and incubated at room temperature for up to 10 minutes; two drops of the solution are then added to the test strip, which is read after 5 minutes. (It is recommended to wait 10 minutes to confirm negative findings). If a single line appears at the control (C) area, then it indicates a negative test; an additional line at the test (T) area indicates a positive. If no lines appear, then the test is invalid.

Hexagon OBTI is advertised with sensitivities ranging between 1:1000 and 1:3.2 million blood to buffer.[266,267] The sensitivity of the test was found to increase with reduction of the sample buffer used from 2 mL to 0.2 mL.[267] Samples that were diluted 1:100 showed a false negative, indicating the high-dose hook effect at this level; samples diluted 1:1,000 reacted as expected.[268] Cross-reactions have been shown with badger, rabbit, weasel, primates, and langur blood; the test has been shown to be resistant to the high-dose hook effect up to 10,000 μg/mL Hb.[266,267,269–272] Cat blood was found to produce a false positive in a batch from 2009, but this was not observed when retested using a 2016 manufactured version.[268] All samples stored for up to 2 years at room temperature and in the fridge tested positive.[266]

Castelló et al.[120] investigated the effect of quebracho extract (a common leather tanning product) on Hexagon OBTI and found significant inhibition of the test after 1 day and a 1% quebracho final concentration. Washing stains with active oxygen products does not remove the visible bloodstain, but it has been shown to cause false negatives. Washing with sodium percarbonate at either high concentrations or high temperatures has been shown to reduce the sensitivity of the test, but washing at high temperature alone did not. It has also been found that pretreatment of stains with luminol (some formulations can fully inhibit the test) and bleach has a negative effect.[269]

HemDirect Hemoglobin Test

The HemDirect Hemoglobin Test from Seratec is based on the Hexagon OBTI test and is a one-step lateral flow immunochromatographic test that detects human Hb with two monoclonal antihuman Hb antibodies as active components.[273] Samples can be collected with the applicator attached to the buffer lid, with a cutting, or a swab and are placed into provided buffer for 10 minutes (recommended), but it is noted that older stains may need a longer incubation. Three drops of the sample solution are added to the HemDirect test, which should fully absorb, and results are recorded after 10 minutes. If a single line appears at the control (C) area, then it indicates a negative test; an additional line at the test (T) area indicates a positive result (Fig. 3.44). If no lines appear, then the test is invalid.

The test can show false negative results with high concentrations of blood because of the high-dose hook effect, and the instructions for use state blood should be diluted to at least 1:500 prior to testing using the kit.[273] It has been found, however, that the kit still displays a positive at a 1:10 dilution of blood to water.[268] The sensitivity is listed as 20 ng/mL Hb, or a range between 1:50 and 1:10 million blood to water, and the test shows the high-dose hook effect with concentrations higher than 1:50.[273]

Misencik and Laux[274] found HemDirect showed positive reactions with higher primates and ferret blood, as well as saliva and semen, although they attribute the later as a true positive with trace Hb in the samples. Stadler et al.[268] found that ferret blood did not cross-react

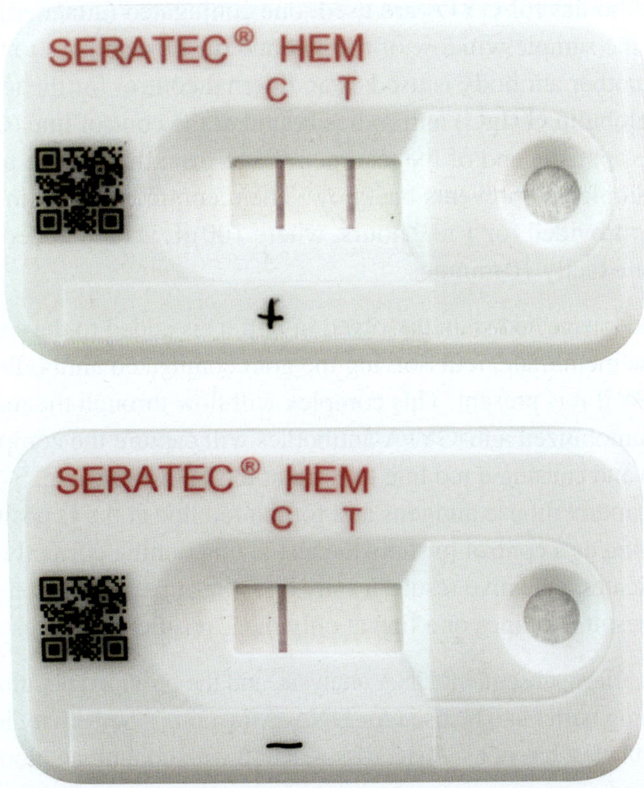

Fig. 3.44 Example of the HemDirect Hemoglobin Test from Seratec for blood, with a negative control *(left)* and a positive control *(right)*. Lines at C and T indicate a positive result, whereas a line at C only indicates a negative result. *From SERATEC Gesellschaft für Biotechnologie mbH.*

with the test when they used a kit manufactured in 2016, but they found that it did with kits manufactured in 2009 and 2015. It was also found that the test was affected by sample degradation in part dependent on the substrate, with some samples 2 weeks old only giving weak positives and subsequently failing, whereas other samples showed positive for the full 4 weeks of tests.[274] Casework samples of 16, 21, and 31 years all tested positive, but they found only a maximum sensitivity of 1:9600 blood to water.[274] False negatives have also been seen with detergents such as sodium dodecyl sulfate, sarcosyl, or bleach mixed with the blood or with pH less than 3 or greater than 12.[268,273,274]

RSID Blood

RSID Blood is a one-step lateral flow immunochromatographic test that detects human glycophorin A (GYPA; PubChem CID: P02724).[264] GYPA is embedded in the lipid bilayer of the RBC and is one of the most abundant RBC proteins. It has MN blood group receptors and was therefore part of the previous blood group type testing (see Appendix I). The RSID Blood test was designed for forensic use and can detect as little as 1 μL of blood.[264]

Two monoclonal antibodies for GYPA are used, one conjugated (attached) to gold nanoparticles under the sample window of the test and the other bound to the test line (T) of the membrane. Another antibody is used as an internal control for the test and consists of antimouse immunoglobulin G (IgG) antibodies bound at the control line (C).[264] There is also a wick located at the opposite end of the test membrane from the sample placement, which absorbs the tested sample and prevents backflow. The recommended protocol is to extract stains into the buffer provided for 1 to 2 hours, where 100 μL is then added to the test. The test is then assessed after exactly 10 minutes.

Once the sample fluid (suspected stain dissolved in buffer) is added to the sample window, it diffuses through the membrane, redissolving the gold conjugated antibodies that will form a complex with GYPA if it is present. This complex will flow through the membrane to the test line where the immobilized anti-GYPA antibodies will capture the complex, forming a sandwich-like image and causing a red line to form at the T position (Fig. 3.45). The antimouse IgG antibodies will capture mouse antigens and form a red line at the C position, regardless if GYPA is present, acting as a control to show the test is functioning correctly.[264] If two lines are observed, then it indicates a positive result; if only one line at the C position is observed, then it indicates a negative result. No lines or a line at only the T position indicates an invalid test.

RSID Blood does not affect subsequent DNA analysis, and the provided documentation specifically states that any remaining buffer can be used for DNA extraction.[264] Sensitivity is reported as 1:2000 to 1:100 million, and the test has not shown cross-reaction with nonhuman blood.[275]

Nicloux and Bressler[214] found that stains tested with RSID Blood and pretreated with Bluestar or Lumiscene had reduced sensitivity to 1:10 blood to water dilutions. They attribute this reduced sensitivity in the presence of other reagents and to the higher

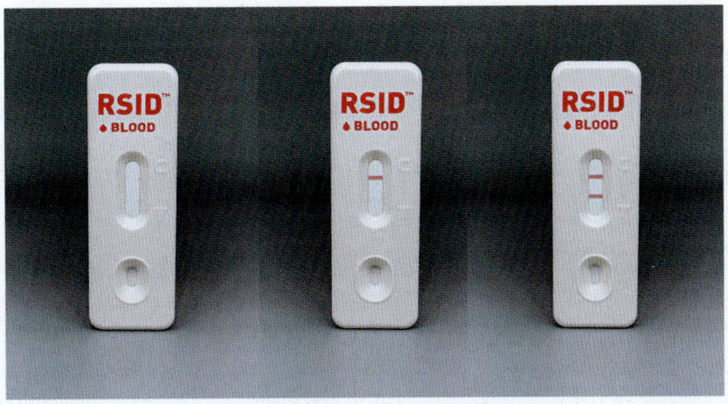

Fig. 3.45 The RSID Blood test showing *(left to right)* a blank cassette, a negative result, and a positive result. The sample window is at the bottom of the test. Lines at C and T indicate a positive result, whereas a line at C only indicates a negative result. *From Dina Mattes, Independent Forensics, Lombard, Illinois.*

specificity of the test.[214] Similarly, Streeting et al.[160] found complete inhibition of RSID Blood with luminol I pretreated stains and partial inhibition of LCV pretreated stains. Some inhibition was found in stains pretreated with fingerprint developing reagents black magnetic powder (BMP), ninhydrin, DFO, and with Bluestar.[245]

RSID Blood was able to detect blood from laundered fabric at both hot (40°C) and cold (24°C) conditions, with and without detergent containing sodium percarbonate.[206] It has been found that laundry detergent applied directly to blood and then tested resulted in a false negative.[275] Other testing showed RSID Blood was able to identify blood in samples that failed (due to the high-dose hook effect or below the limits of sensitivity) in another commercial fecal occult blood lateral flow test.[276]

Summary of Tests

This chapter presents a large amount of information regarding the various tests for blood. The following sections summarize this material for easy comparison and reference.

Effect on Subsequent DNA Analysis

Note that it is not common for samples that have been treated with presumptive testing reagents to undergo direct DNA testing. Because it is normal for a subsample to be taken for presumptive testing, any subsequent DNA analysis samples are usually collected from the original stain and are therefore unadulterated with any testing reagents. There are circumstances (e.g., cold cases, appeals, very small single stains) when a sample that has been tested using presumptive reagents will need to undergo DNA testing, so the effect that the presumptive reagents have on subsequent DNA profiling is relevant. Table 3.4 provides a summary of the different tests and their effects on subsequent DNA typing.

Table 3.4 A sample of color and immunological presumptive blood tests that are currently in use and their effect on DNA

Common Name	Chemical Reagent/Bio Target	Positive Reaction	Effect on Subsequent DNA Analysis
		Color Tests	
Benzidine	Benzidine	Colorless → deep blue precipitate	Negative effect on DNA recovery in glacial acid, but not in ethanol.[106] Detrimental effect[117,118]
Bluestar	Luminol based	Colorless → blue luminescence	No effect;[144,201,212] reduced DNA profiles with diluted blood[214]
Bluestar Forensic	Luminol based	Colorless → blue luminescence	No effect;[144] reduced DNA profiles with diluted blood[214]
Combur-Test	Tetramethylbenzidine	Yellow → blue-green/black	Reduced DNA profiles with diluted blood[255]
Fluorescein	2-(3-hydroxy-6-oxoxanthen-9-yl) benzoic acid	Yellow→ fluorescent under specific lighting	No effect;[57,132] substrate dependent negative effect[134]
Guaiac	α-guaiaconic acid	Clear → blue	No effect[99]
Hemastix	3,3′,5,5′-tetramethylbenzidine	Yellow → blue-green/black	No effect found,[144] but interference with magnetic bead extraction found[252,253]
Hemident (McPhail Reagent)	LMG	Colorless → blue-green	No DNA recovered[144]
Leucomalachite green (LMG)	LMG	Colorless → blue-green	No DNA recovered,[106,144] partial DNA recovered,[154] no effect[149,152]
Leucocrystal violet (LCV)	LCV	Colorless → purple	No reports
Luminol	3-aminophthalhydrazide	Colorless → blue luminescence	No effect;[106, 132, 144, 149, 196] substrate dependent negative effect.[134] Some negative effect both formulas;[196] dependent on recovery swab type[277]
Lumiscene	Fluorescein and luminol	Colorless → green luminescence	No effect;[57] reduced DNA profiles with diluted blood[214]
Orthotolidine (O-tol)	O-tol (3,3′-dimethylbenzidine)	Yellow → blue-green	No DNA recovery[106]
Phenolphthalein (Kastle-Meyer)	Phenolphthalein	Colorless → pink	Reduced DNA recovery.[106,144,154] No effect;[57] no DNA recovered[58]
Tetramethyl-benzidine	Tetramethylbenzidine	Yellow → blue-green/black	No reports; however, Hemastix does not affect DNA recovery
		Immunological Tests	
ABAcard HemaTrace	Hemoglobin	Two lines on test strip	No data
HemDirect (Seratec)	Hemoglobin	Two lines on test strip	No effect[273,278,279]
HemeSelect	Hemoglobin	Agglutination in well	No data
Hexagon OBTI and Bluestar OBTI	Hemoglobin	Two lines on test strip	No effect[280]
RSID Blood	Glycophorin A	Two lines on test strip	No effect[264,275]

Sensitivity

The sensitivity of presumptive blood tests is of primary importance when dealing with minute bloodstains, crime scenes that have been exposed to the elements (e.g., rain or snow), or crime scenes that have been cleaned prior to forensic investigation. It also becomes important when dealing with items such as clothes and weapons that may have been washed after use in a crime and prior to examination. There have been many investigations conducted on the sensitivity of presumptive blood tests, and they are usually not in agreement. The findings of these various studies can be in contradiction with each other, often by several orders of magnitude. Most presumptive blood tests have maximum sensitivities ranging from dilutions of 1:100 (whole blood to water) to greater than 1:100,000. Because of the large variation of reported sensitivities, it is necessary for each laboratory to perform its own sensitivity studies as part of a validation procedure before investigative use of the tests.

The average number of erythrocytes in 1 mL of blood can vary from 4.2 to 5.4 billion for women and 4.7 to 6.1 billion for men (see Table 3.1). Most presumptive blood reagents claim sensitivity to greater than 10^{-4}, which means that they will produce a positive reaction even if blood is diluted to a level where the red color is no longer detectable to the human eye. It has been reported that this occurs between a dilution of blood to water of 1:512[161] and 1:1000.[64] For example, a 1:1000 dilution of blood to water will contain between 4.3 and 5.8 million erythrocytes per mL, depending on sex, and would look colorless to the naked eye. As each erythrocyte contains approximately 250 million Hb, or 1 billion heme, molecules there are at least 10.75×10^{14} molecules of Hb and 43.00×10^{14} molecules of heme per mL. With each test reacting with either a Hb molecule or heme molecule, it is easy to see why most of the presumptive blood tests have maximum reported sensitivities to dilutions of blood greater than 1:100,000. (Note a 10,000 dilution factor is equivalent to 0.10–0.15 μg/mL of Hb.)[255] Within the literature there are a wide range of reported sensitivities for each test (Table 3.5), which can make choosing and interpreting results confusing.

Following are the potential possibilities for the wide range of sensitivities reported by different researchers for each test.

- Differences in maximum dilution. Studies that obtained a positive at their highest dilution will report that result as the maximum sensitivity even if the true sensitivity is much greater (e.g., the limit of detection was not tested). For example, if researchers in a study are looking at a 10-fold serial dilution of blood in water to a maximum of 1:10,000, and the test records a positive at every dilution, they would likely report 1:10,000 as the maximum sensitivity for that test even if the dilution series did not continue to the point a negative was reached.
- Differences in reagent concentrations. Garner et al. found that the concentration of the reagents themselves could significantly affect the sensitivities, with lower concentrations being less sensitive than higher concentrations.[116] The preparation of the reagents can therefore be a factor in the ultimate sensitivity of the tests.

Table 3.5 Reported sensitivities for different presumptive blood tests[a]

Reagent	Type	Maximum Sensitivity Range (1 in X)	Source(s)
ABAcard HemaTrace	Immunological	256–2 million	161,265
Alternative light source systems (various)		100–1000	62,64
Benzidine	Chemical	1000–5 million	56,105,108,109,114–116,141,150
Bluestar (all forms)	Chemical	1000–100,000	144,200,201,212,241
Combur-Test	Chemical	100,000	255
Fluorescein	Chemical	100–10 million	67,128,132–134
Guaiac	Chemical	1000–100,000	36,99,109,115,138
Hemascene	Chemical	100–1 million	200
Hemastix	Chemical	100–1 million	144,151,161
HemDirect	Immunological	10–10 million[b]	268,273,274
HemeSelect	Immunological	100,000	281
Hemident	Chemical	100,000–1 million[b]	144
Hexagon OBTI	Immunological	1000–3.2 million[b]	266–269,280,282
Leucocrystal violet	Chemical	100–8000	161,257
Leucomalachite green	Chemical	100–10 million	56,141–144,146–151,240
Luminol	Chemical	100–100 million	51,56,132,134,144,146,149–151,194,195,197,200,201,241
Lumiscene	Chemical	50,000[b]–1 million	201
Orthotolidine	Chemical	32,000–10 million	36,109,114,147,150,222,224
Phenolphthalein (Kastle-Meyer)	Chemical	100–10 million	56,109,114,115,144,147,148,150,151,239–241
RSID Blood	Immunological	2000–100 million[b]	275
Seratec HemDirect hemoglobin assay	Immunological	1 million[b]	
Tetramethylbenzidine	Chemical	1000–1 million	116,147,150,161,241

[a]The sensitivities shown are the maximums observed in a particular study or are as given by the manufacturer in the case of commercial products. Differing values may be due to several factors, including the maximum dilution tested.
[b]As advertised by the manufacturer.

- Preparation of blood dilutions. Grodsky et al.[56] commented on the fact that when making dilutions, there could be aggregation of clotted blood pigment, which if transferred (or not) would give the test a higher sensitivity (or lower if not transferred).
- Preparation of tested sample. Grodsky et al.[56] point out the difference between testing a diluted dried stain and a solution of diluted blood. If the reagents are added to a solution of diluted blood, this would also serve to dilute the testing reagents (lowering their concentration).
- The substrate that any dilutions are placed on will also affect the sensitivity result.[133] A sample of diluted blood placed on a glass slide will form a drop (due to fluid surface tension), which as it dries will concentrate any RBCs in the sample. The same volume of sample placed on cotton will diffuse in the fabric and either maintain the dilution expected or further dilute as it expands. Luedeke et al.[241] found major differences in sensitivity for four presumptive blood tests dependent on the substrate.

- Substrate type in terms of fabric and fabric weave have also been shown to influence the sensitivity, with natural fabrics having better results for more dilute blood than semi-synthetics.[57] Garofano et al.[134] found a 100,000-fold difference between sensitivities of luminol and fluorescein when analyzed on different substrates, which was also reflected in the DNA recovery.
- Cox[147] showed that both the dilution factor and the substrate combined have an effect in the overall sensitivity and the speed of reaction for several of the chemical tests.
- Garner et al.[113] also found that sensitivity decreased with age of the reagents in their study of time between preparation and final working solutions;[116] therefore, age of the base components of the tests and working reagents may be factors in why such a wide range of sensitivities is recorded.
- Sampling method. It has been shown that testing stains directly provides better sensitivity than subsampling using swabs or filter paper.[151] Subsampling ultimately serves to further dilute a stain by only removing a portion, so calculated dilutions are inaccurate. Subsampling is also a partially random process, so the amount recovered will vary with each testing.
- The way in which the blood for testing is collected is another possible factor in different findings. Sensitivities found for many of the tests in the early periods of their development may be due to the way blood was previously and is currently collected. It was found that when blood was used untreated, or treated with EDTA, that there was a difference in the sensitivity of subsequent testing.
- Operator experience and method. How the tests are carried out and operator experience will also affect outcomes and reported sensitivity. Especially with the extreme lower limits of sensitivity, there is an aspect of subjectivity in what constitutes a positive. These involve the color change (or lack of), the intensity, and the timing of any positive.

Although these factors are all potential causes of variation within sensitivity testing, few if any are accounted for within the literature detailing sensitivity studies. This is the cause of so much and such large variation in reported literature sensitivity studies. It is why each laboratory should perform its own sensitivity validation studies using the tests in the manner that they will perform them for casework.

One final aspect related to sensitivity that must be considered is the effect of washing on bloodstains. Washing can affect all types of bloodstain evidence, and the ultimate dilution factor cannot be known, so studies looking at washing specifically are therefore helpful for evidence evaluation. Jain and Singh[283] immersed bloodstained cloth (natural and synthetic) in water for up to 20 days, and they found that benzidine and KM were still able to identify the stains as blood. Other studies examining washing of cotton garments stained with blood found that even when blood was visibly removed from the garment through washing, if the stain location was known, then a presumptive positive could be obtained using Hemastix and Bluestar[284] or benzidine.[285] This held true for stains sitting up to 30 days and using various washing temperatures and detergents.[284] Cox[286] tested a variety of natural and synthetic fabrics that were stained and washed over 48 hours in a cold wash with chlorine containing bleach. He found that 100% acetate, nylon and polyester failed to yield positive results after being washed, but all other fabric types showed positive results for most of the time periods tested, and retention of blood on washed fabrics was fabric composition dependent.[286] Vaughan[287] prepared a dilution series of blood in duplicate and washed one set, then tested with Bluestar and KM, and found that regardless of the subsequent storage that all the washed samples at all dilutions showed a positive test (unwashed equivalent samples had a maximum sensitivity in per study of 1:4000), indicating that there may have been transfer of blood in the washing cycle. More recently, Mushtaq et al.[288] looked at 12 different fabric types, six different detergents, and four presumptive tests (KM, LMG, TMB, Hemastix) and found that detection after washing was based on a combination of fabric, detergent, total time being washed, and test used. In their study, Hemastix proved the only test to identify blood at all time points, on all fabrics, and using all detergents.[283]

Specificity

The more specific a presumptive test for blood, the less likely a substance other than blood will result in a positive reaction. In the past century, many tests have been conducted on the specificity of presumptive blood tests, although it is important to remember that many of the tests used were originally designed for other purposes and have been adopted by forensic scientists. These tests for specificity include changing substrates and adding materials, detergents, and chemicals to the bloodstains, but many studies disagree as to the effect of particular substances. Some authors report false positive observations with particular substances that, when tested by subsequent researchers, are not found to interfere with the tests. The number of different substances, substrates, and combinations that have been tested is expansive. A list of some substances that have been found to produce or inhibit a reaction with commonly used tests is provided in Table 3.6. Note that tested substances that do not cross-react or interfere with a test have not been listed even if that substance has been previously shown to cross-react. Based on the reaction mechanisms of the different tests, it should also be possible to predict other substances that could cross-react or inhibit those tests.

There are different considerations when investigating specificity for chemical tests as opposed to immunological tests. Because chemical tests are based on the peroxidase action of Hb, there are many more potential cross-reactants due to the wide range of peroxidases in nature and in other forms. Küster[34] discusses the judicial evidence of blood in 1902, and as part of that document details the blood of other nonvertebrate organisms that have red blood (e.g., earthworms, snails). Grodsky et al.[56] point out that all Hb-containing bloods react similarly, and chemical tests show the presence of blood only, with no indication of source by species or groups. Therefore the assumption is all chemical tests will react with red blood in the same way regardless of species, but immunological tests are designed to be human specific. Many of the studies into sensitivity and even specificity (for the chemical tests) use animal blood as a proxy to human blood, so nonhuman blood is not listed as a false positive for the chemical tests because it is expected to cross-react and contains Hb.

Table 3.6 Presumptive blood tests and some substances and substrates that can cause a false-positive or false-negative result[a]

Reagent	Reaction[b]	Substance or Substrate	Source(s)
ABAcard HemaTrace	+	Anal swabs,[c] feces (occasionally), ferret blood, oral swabs,[c] primate blood, rectal swabs,[c] semen (occasionally), vaginal swabs[c]	265
	–	Burned blood, high concentration of blood,[d] increased viscosity, laundered bloodstains, pH >9,[d] soil	
Benzidine	+	Ammonium persulfate, beet, beet leaf, boiled green peas, cabbage, calcium hypochlorite, certain lead oxides, certain melons, copper sulfate, cucumber, flesh of carrot, garlic, gold chloride, horseradish, hydrated sodium hypochlorite,[e] ketchup, lead peroxide, lemons, milk,[e] nitric acid,[e] onion, parts of lettuce, persimmon, potassium dichromate, potassium permanganate, radish, raw lettuce, raw potato, raw turnip, sodium chromate, tomato skin (inner part), when applied directly to an almond, white pulp of oranges	4,56,116,119–121,139
	–	Ascorbic acid, boiled green pea, leather, raw lettuce, raw potato, raw turnip	
Bluestar	+	1 M ascorbic acid, banana pulp, bleach, chlorine,[d] copper and iron salts, copper,[d] dish detergent, horseradish, household detergents,[d] iron-containing soils,[d] lichen,[d] potato juice, red kidney bean, red onion, some paints and varnishes,[d] some tree mosses,[d] stain remover, thyme,[d] tomato juice, tomato sauce with meat, turnip pulp	67,120,144,200,203, 212,213,217
	–	Leather, some surfaces cleaned with bleach, washing with active oxygen detergent	
Combur-Test	+	Ammunitions, apple and banana juice, apple pulp, banana pulp, bird feces, bleach, carrot pulp, $CuSO_4$, dead insects, degreaser, feces, $FeSO_4$, flower, grass, $KMnO_4$, $NaBO_3$, onion pulp, peach juice, pine bark, pineapple juice, potato pulp, red orange juice, saliva, tomato pulp, tomato sauce, urine	255
	–	Ascorbic acid (reduced sensitivity), aspirin C (reduced sensitivity)	
Fluorescein	+	Beet juice, cherry-cranberry juice, cherry-strawberry juice, chocolate, coffee, cola, copper, horseradish, ketchup, steel with rust, strawberry jelly, urine	128,134
	–	Reduced sensitivity with some substrates	
Guaiac	+	Iron-containing substances, soybean (unheated), urease, horseradish	115,137,139
	–	Ascorbic acid	
Hemascene	+	Bleach, carpet cleaner, floor cleaner, kidney bean, red onion, tomato, tomato sauce with meat	200
	–	None reported	
HemDirect	+	Ferret blood, primate blood	268,273,274
	–	Detergents (sodium dodecyl sulfate, sarcosyl, or bleach),[d] high concentration of blood,[d] pH <3 or >12	

Contined

Table 3.6 Presumptive blood tests and some substances and substrates that can cause a false-positive or false-negative result—cont'd

Reagent	Reaction[b]	Substance or Substrate	Source(s)
Hemastix	+	Algae, aloe vera (skin), avocado, baked bean, banana (stalk), bloodworm, capsicum, carrot, celery, chicken egg yolk, chili (hot), Chinese cabbage, cobalt chloride (1.8 M), coconut (flesh), copper sulphate (0.009 M), copper salts, fern, fertilizer, frangipani (trunk), gardenia (shoot), garlic, ginger fresh, ginger 60 days old, ginger 3 years old, grasshopper, hoop pine (branch), hydrogen peroxide (3%), iron oxide (2 M), iron sulfate (2.5 M), iron salts, jellyfish, kiwi fruit, magnesium chloride (0.5 M), manganese chloride (1 M), manganese oxide (0.5 M), manganese oxide (solid), mangrove tree, Moreton Bay chestnut, mud-crab flesh, mushroom fresh, mushroom 30 days old, native orchid, nickel chloride (0.09 M), nickel salts, octopus, onion, orange (peel) fresh, orange (peel) 30 days old, oyster, passion fruit, potato fresh, potato 30 days old, potting mix, red onion, saliva, seagrass, sodium polytungstate (1 M), strawberry, sugar cane, tomato sauce, tomato sauce with meat, vegemite, vitamin B_{12}, waterlily (root), watermelon (skin), white onion, wild grass, yam, zinc sulphate (3 M)	12,144
	–	None reported	
Hemident	+	1 M ascorbic acid, 5% bleach, copper salts,[e] iron salts,[e] nickel salts,[e] red onion,[e] semen[e]	144
	–	None reported	
Hexagon OBTI	+	Badger blood, cat blood, feces, ferret blood,[d] langur blood, primate blood, rabbit blood, saliva, semen, skunk blood,[d] urine, vaginal secretions, weasel blood	120,202,203,266–269, 271,272
	–	Bleach, high concentration of blood,[d] leather, pretreatment of stain with luminol, pH <3 or >12, washing with active oxygen detergent, washing with sodium percarbonate at high concentrations or high temperatures	
Leucomalachite green	+	Bichromates,[e] bleach,[e] brownstone,[e] chemical oxidants,[e] chromates,[e] copper salts,[e] iron salts,[e] lead peroxide,[e] nickel salts,[e] permanganate,[e] potato,[e] red lead,[e] red onion,[e] stain remover	35,139,140,212,235
	–	Ascorbic acid	
Luminol	+	Ammoniacal copper solution, bleach, carrot, ceramic tile, colloidal platinum, copper salts, enamel paint, horseradish, hypochlorites, iron salts, jute natural matting, manganese peroxide, nickel salts, onion, parsnip, plant peroxidases, polyurethane paint, potassium ferricyanide, potato, pumpkin, sisal natural matting, terracotta tile, tomato, turnip	51,134,144,175,184–189, 194,197,200,202,203
	–	Amines, aminophenols, ascorbic acid, dinitrophenols, glycerin, glycol, mannitol, mono- and disaccharide, nitroanilines and naphthols, nitrophenols, reduced sensitivity with some substrates, some surfaces washed with cleaning agents, urine, washing with active oxygen detergent	

Orthotolidine	+	Apricot, asparagus, avocado, banana, bell pepper, Betadine, bleach, broccoli, bromides in urine, Brussel sprout, cabbage, cantaloupe, carrot, cauliflower, celery, cucumber, eggplant, garlic, green bean, green onion, iodides in urine, Irish potato, ketchup, lettuce, mushroom, nail polish, nectarine, okra, peach, pear, pineapple, radish, spinach, sweet potato, tangerine, tomato, turnip root, watermelon, white onion, yellow corn, yellow squash	139,147,217,224
	−	Excess of ascorbic acid	
Phenolphthalein (Kastle-Meyer)	+	1 M ascorbic acid,[e] 5% bleach, alfalfa, bean, chlorine bleach,[e] copper salts,[e] green bean, horseradish, iodine, iron salts,[e] jeans (blue denim), lemon juice,[e] malt extract, nickel salts,[e] other metallic salts, oxygen bleach (Oxiclean),[e] pea, potato, pus and other organic secretions, red clover, red kidney bean, red onion,[e] saliva, semen, sodium nitrate, soil from a sewer, soy bean, soybean, tap water (Dundee supply 1952), tomato sauce, urine, white clover	115,120,144,148,202, 203,239,240,242, 243,245,289–291
	−	Ascorbic acid (at blood dilutions >1:200), leather, some fingerprint development reagents, washing with active oxygen detergent	
RSID Blood	+	None reported[d]	160,214,245,275
	−	Pretreatment of stain with BlueStar, pretreatment of stain with BMP, pretreatment of stain with DFO, pretreatment of stain with leucocrystal violet, pretreatment of stain with luminol I, pretreatment of stain with Lumiscene, pretreatment of stain with ninhydrin, laundry detergent	
Tetramethylbenzidine	+	Apricot, asparagus, avocado, banana, beet leaf, bell pepper, Betadine, bleach, broccoli, Brussel sprout, cabbage, cantaloupe, carrot, cauliflower, celery, cherry, cucumber, dish detergent, eggplant, garlic, grapes, green bean, green onion, horseradish, hydrated sodium hypochlorite,[e] Irish potato, ketchup, lettuce, mushroom, nail polish, nectarine, nitic acid,[e] okra, onion, peach, pear, pineapple, plum, potassium permanganate, radish, red apple, spinach, sweet potato, tangerine, tomato, turnip root, watermelon, wine, yellow corn, yellow squash	116,147,206,217,249
	−	Sodium percarbonate	

[a]False positive reactions with other body fluids may be due to low levels of blood or free hemoglobin within those fluids. This can be a natural phenomenon or can be due to small cuts in the mouth, anus, or vagina, for example. Menstrual bleeding will also be detected. All reported cross-reactions and interferences are included, even if only observed in one of many samples tested.

[b]A positive reaction indicates a false positive, and a negative reaction indicates a false negative.

[c]It is the substance on the swab that is causing a cross-reaction, not the swab itself.

[d]As advertised by the manufacturer.

[e]These substances cause a reaction that cannot be confused with a true positive due to color, the reaction occurring before all reagents are added, or the speed of reaction.

As with issues affecting sensitivity, there are many reasons for disagreement between cross-reactivity, or inhibition, among researchers. It is important to recognize that the following summary is not applicable to all testing methods; some points are universal, but others will relate to only a specific type of testing.

- Nontarget body fluid cross-reaction could be due to blood in those fluids (e.g., bleeding gums) and so would not actually constitute a cross-reaction as blood is being detected. There may be other components of those fluids that are not blood that can cause a cross-reaction. It is still important that these are recognised as cross-reactants and understood for proper interpretation of results.
- One-step versus two-step tests will affect potential false positive results. Two-step tests use a separate presumptive reagent that is applied to the sample before the H_2O_2 catalyst. Any substance that causes a reaction after the addition of the presumptive reagent only can be eliminated as being blood because the reaction with blood requires H_2O_2. One-step tests have a single application step that includes a mixture of the presumptive reagent and H_2O_2; therefore no intermediate reactions can be observed, so anything that cross-reacts can be considered positive.
- Interpretation of a positive can be subjective. Many authors state that false positives can be eliminated by experienced scientists based on speed or reaction, very slight variations in color, and other factors they deem relevant. Several papers use spectrophotometry and find that a very slight variation in wavelength is produced by nonblood reactants, but they also state that these differences in emission are so slight they would not be possible by the naked eye.
- Other peroxidases can be found in normal body fluids at differing concentrations, but unlike Hb these substances tend to be heat sensitive. Anand et al.[98] recommend boiling samples if pus or other substances known to produce false positives are suspected because this will break down the peroxidase enzymes. Matheson and Veall[12] found that treating stains with EDTA would eliminate many of the common false positives with TMB, but this has not been investigated with other tests.
- The method in which samples are tested will have an effect. Garner et al. found that substances showing false positives did not do so under all sampling conditions.[116] For example, some substances only showed a false positive reaction when sampled by rubbing, extract, or directly sampled on cloth. Platt[88] found that exposure to argon laser light for up to 3 minutes did not affect standard testing using KM, TMB, and O-tol, but if a fine mist spray was used, then these tests were negative or had severely reduced reactions.
- The way in which potential cross-reactants are prepared for testing (e.g., using the skin, rind, flesh juice, pulp, stem, leaf, or other part of a plant-based sample) may provide different results. The table 3.6 provides specificity in relation to specific parts of a cross-reactant if provided in the study, but most studies will only state that they tested a substance (e.g., apple) and not anything more specific as to the part of the substance that was tested.

- Horseradish is often listed as a cross-reactant for the chemical presumptive blood tests because peroxidase activity of horseradish is about 1000 times greater than the peroxidase activity of Hb.[100]
- The sample history, if known (e.g., washing, environment, temperature changes), can indicate possible nonstandard results. For example, chemical alteration of Hb can take place as it passes through the gastrointestinal tract and can cause chemical tests to report a false negative.[292] Many studies have investigated heat, time, and other factors on the ability to successfully identify blood.
- The timing of testing from preparing potential false positive samples can have an effect. Vegetable peroxidases are not stable. If they are deposited and tested immediately, then they will likely give a reaction; if left to dry, then over time this reaction will diminish to the point of not reacting.[178] Nickolls[178] suggests that because the peroxidase action of Hb does not degrade in the same way, stains can be left for 1 week before analysis, which would eliminate many vegetable peroxidases that could cause false positives.
- Substances such as surfactants that can denature proteins may interfere with immunological testing, but Hb may still be present and may not interfere with chemical tests.

Pinker[121] did not find a single substance in 1934 that caused a false positive with benzidine, LMG, and KM, but he still stated that getting a positive result with all three was not proof that the sample was blood. It has since been found that there are substances that cause a false positive with all those tests, but using multiple tests would reduce the number of potential false positives.

It has been shown that laundered stains can still be visible, but they test negative with multiple chemical and immunological testing methods, but that other methods continued to report a positive.[206] This incidence of false negative is concerning because if some proteins are still present, then DNA may also be recovered, but multiple negative presumptive tests would render these stains not assessable.

Because of the number of potential cross-reactants and the contradicting nature of some studies, a good understanding of the test being used is essential. If a potential bloodstain is vital to a case, then DNA profiling should still be attempted even if one or more presumptive blood tests fail.

Other Studies

Because blood is such an important target of forensic investigations and therefore testing, other methods of detection have been investigated. These are listed here, separately, because none has been widely adopted, but many show promise and can be beneficial depending on case circumstances.

Applying H_2O_2 directly to items to visualize bloodstains has also been used, where a 6% H_2O_2 solution was used to react with blood, by foaming, and turned the stains white, allowing them to be visualized on dark substrates.[67] This method was shown to have no effect on subsequent DNA typing.[67]

Thorogate et al.[293] developed an immunofluorescent technique to locate bloodstains in situ, including individual leucocytes (Fig. 3.46). They claim ease of use and human specificity by using two antibodies labeled with different fluorophores. They claim to be able to identify bloodstains (cells) on dark fabric, which can then be directly targeted for DNA analysis.

Orphanou[294] used attenuated total reflectance Fourier transform infrared (ATR-FTIR) to identify different body fluids, including blood, and claimed advantages over other techniques due to no reagents, shelf life, or damage to the stains. It was also suggested that potable ultraviolet visible spectroscopy could be used as a nondestructive means to identify if a stain was blood.[295]

Li et al.[296] applied visible wavelength reflectance hyperspectral imaging for both the detection and identification of blood. It was found that blood could be differentiated from 40 other reddish substances and identified at between 1:32 and 1:512 dilution, dependent on the substrate. It could additionally be used to identify bloodstains on interfering substrates (Fig. 3.47).

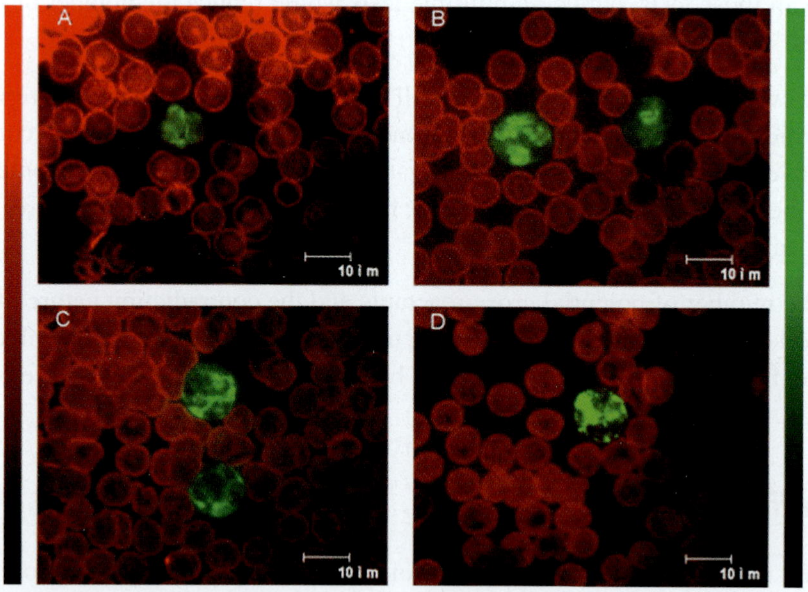

Fig. 3.46 Human blood on glass slides examined with immunofluorescent antibodies. (A) Immediately stained; then at (B) 1 week, (C) 2 weeks, (D) 4 weeks. Red blood cells are *red*, and white blood cells are *green*. *From Thorogate R, Moreira JCS, Jickells S., et al. A novel fluorescence-based method in forensic science for the detection of blood in situ. Forensic Sci Int Genet. 2008;2:363–371.*

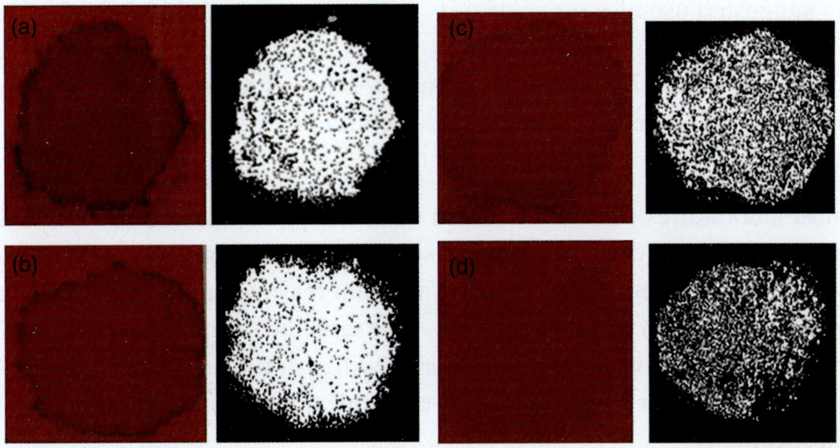

Fig. 3.47 Bloodstains on red tissue paper in different dilutions *(left)* and the processed hyperspectral images *(right)*: (A) 1 in 4 blood to water, (B) 1 in 8 blood to water, (C) 1 in 16 blood to water, (D) 1 in 32 blood to water. *From Li B, Beveridge P, O'Hare WT, et al. The application of visible wavelength reflectance hyperspectral imaging for the detection and identification of blood stains. Sci Just. 2014;54:432–438.*

More recently, surface-enhanced Raman scattering (SERS) has been used for blood identification using a 785 nm SERS spectra.[297] Stains must first be extracted in 1 μL of 50% acetic acid, but spectra could be differentiated from other body fluids, detectable at 1:10,000 blood to water dilution. A proteomic approach has also been proposed.[298] A matrix-assisted laser desorption ionization (MALDI) mass spectrometric method was used to detect protein fragments of blood components. The method requires that the sample be collected and subjected to physical and chemical fragmentation. The method was able to differentiate horse and human blood, and it gave results for blood from a 9-year-old stain that had been pretreated with acid black.[298] The volume of blood needed for this technique is not known.

RNA transcripts that are tissue specific have been used for a range of body fluids, including blood; however, these studies target multiple fluids. Other tests involving multiple fluid identification are covered in Chapter 6.

Interpretation

Interpretation of the presumptive tests for blood is generally straightforward in terms of positive and negative test results. Each test has a known color change or other indication of what constitutes a positive or negative test result, and there is little room for interpretation other than if a color change has been observed. This is in part why it is important to run regular control samples with tests to ensure that any variation (e.g., failure of reagents or contamination of reagents) to expected results can be identified prior to use with evidence. Any result should also be further qualified with knowledge of the sensitivities and specificities of each test that is used.

Early papers suggested use of a range of tests with each suspected bloodstain, with the theory that the tests should not all cross-react with the same substances, so that greater confidence could be placed in the sample being blood if all tests showed a positive. In this way, most if not all potential false positives could be excluded as being the cause the observed results.

Currently, most laboratories will run one main chemical presumptive test for blood for most samples, but luminol (or its derivative) may also be used under specific circumstances. The false positives of the test used should be known within reason, and if there is no reason to suspect a false positive, then some laboratories will send the sample for DNA profiling with a chemical presumptive positive. Many laboratories will also run an immunochromatographic (confirmatory) test to further validate a positive chemical presumptive finding and provide better human specificity.

Usually in reports, stains will be listed as presumptive positive or negative, or confirmatory positive or negative. The test used is specified, and a brief description can be included in the appendix or technical section of the report.

Time Since Deposition

For most other body fluids encountered in forensic science, the persistence of that biological fluid is important, but it is known that blood can persist for thousands of years on stone tools, so this covers all realistic time frames for casework. Instead, what can be important for bloodstains is determining if there are more recent stains, or older stains, that may be relevant to a case. Therefore determining the time since deposition (TSD) of a bloodstain can be highly valuable to scenario reconstructions and in determining which stains may be relevant to a case (e.g., historic vs. current stains, or case related vs. unrelated). However, TSD has been elusive, and some label it as a holy grail of forensic science.[299]

There are no recognized and definitive methods for determining the TSD of blood, although there have been many different attempts for over 150 years (most in the last decade), and research is ongoing. Some methods show promise, but none have been widely accepted for use. Pfaff[300] published work in 1862 on aging of bloodstains, in which he stated that prior to his paper, court doctors would see how long a bloodstain took to dissolve in water to determine its age, which he found unsuitable and irreproducible. Instead, he used an arsenic acid solution because the bloodstains dissolved faster than in water, and his scale went from fresh blood (dissolves at once) to blood 1 year or more old (dissolves in 4–8 hours).[300] Sutherland,[26] in 1907, summarized evaluation of Pfaff's method by Grigorescu[301] and Tamassia,[302] who determined that Pfaff's method was no better than the one he had criticized. A summary of the experiments carried out by Tamassia,[302] and translated by Sutherland,[26] can be seen in Fig. 3.48. This demonstrated that the method was unsuitable for use because of the wide discrepancy between results on different materials.

Source of Blood.	Date of Shedding of Blood.	Kind of Cloth, etc., stained.	First Signs of Solution after— Days.	Hours.	Complete Removal of Stain from Fabric after—
Human ...	May 23, 1875	Thin, coarse	2	10	Many days
Human ...	Jan. 8, 1877	Thin, loosely woven	2	0	Ditto
Human ...	April 30, 1881	Fine, but tough	2	12	Ditto
Human ...	June 28, 1881	Coarse, loosely woven	2	0	Ditto
Human ...	June 28, 1881	Sized paper	0	20	After 6th day the paper had become reddish-yellow
Human ...	May, 1883	Coarse	2	12	8 to 10 days
Domestic fowl	Nov. 1, 1871	Fine	1	8	Ditto
Domestic fowl	Jan. 29, 1883	Closely woven	2 nearly		Ditto
Rabbit ...	Feb. 8, 1883	Tattered rag	1	6	Less than 8 to 10 days
Human ...	4 days old	Loosely woven	0	7	Ditto
Human ...	15 days old	Coarse	0	7	Ditto
Human ...	15 days old	Sized paper	0	2	Ditto

Fig. 3.48 A summary of the findings of time since deposition carried out by Tamassia[297] using Pfaff's[295] method, translated by Sutherland.[26] *From Sutherland WD. Blood-Stains: Their Detection and the Determination of Their Source. London: Bailliere, Tindall and Cox; 1907.*

Scheller[74] used a custom spectroscopic setup in 1937 to identify blood aged in different methods for over 1 year. Also in 1937, Thomas[44] stated that bloodstains vary in color according to their age, with recent stains being reddish and older stains being brown, which he attributes to "a chemical change in the blood pigment, haemoglobin, depending on free access to the air and certain other factors such as temperature." He admits that it is not possible to give an accurate opinion to the age of a stain based on its appearance unless it is very fresh, but he claims that laboratory techniques can give an estimate.[44] No further details were given as to what those laboratory techniques may include.

Laan et al.[303] carried out a detailed study looking at blood drying dynamics, which gives evidence to some claims made in relation to blood color change during drying. They looked at blood pools and took regular photographs during the drying process as well as mass measurements. They concluded there were five drying stages and a predictable (and reproducible) loss of mass (Fig. 3.49).[303] Their study was not focused on TSD, but in short-term time frames it could be adapted for use.

Recently, and primarily in that last decade (2011–2021), there has been a resurgence in the interest in determining the TSD of bloodstains (Table 3.7). With newer and more sensitive techniques, there is a possibility that the ideal method for TSD will be found.

The techniques and methods in Table 3.7 have their own benefits and drawbacks.[299–356] Early studies looked at high-performance liquid chromatography (HPLC) to identify TSD markers, one of which was identified as the X marker, which according to the two studies using HPLC has a retention time of about 5 minutes, is not found in fresh blood, and increases in intensity

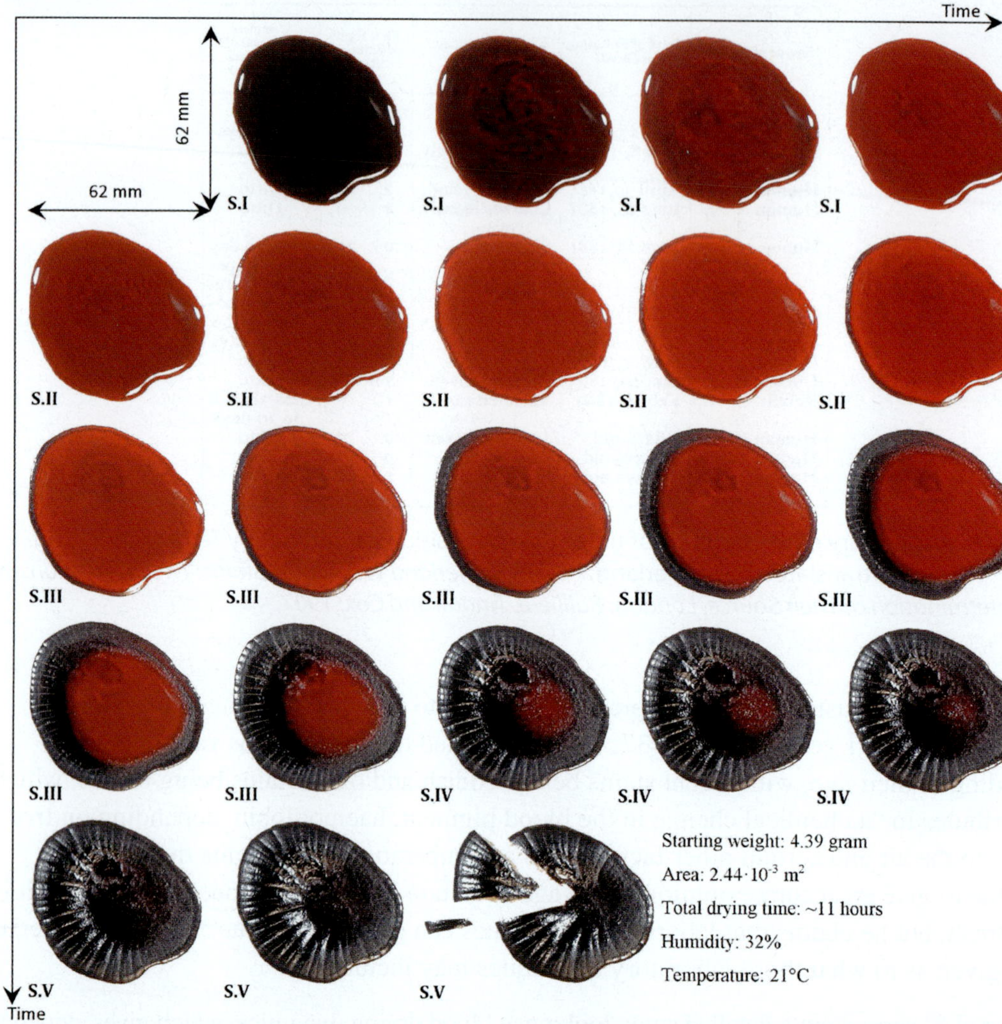

Fig. 3.49 Time lapse of a drying pool of blood from a healthy person showing five stages of drying over 11 hours. This visualization shows a 78% loss of mass from fresh blood to the last image. *From Laan N, Smith F, Nicloux C, et al. Morphology of drying blood pools. Forensic Sci Int. 2016;267:104–109.*

over time (Fig. 3.50).[318,319] Also investigated were peak areas of the α-globin chains and heme, as well as ratios between the two;[320] although trends were observed, there were differences in the different treatment conditions (light vs dark, cold vs hot). Further studies identified two other peaks, Y and Z, which also appeared to increase with TSD.[318]

The next target of investigation for TSD was genetic. Bauer et al.[316] investigated the messenger RNA (mRNA) targets β-actin and cyclophilin, with two amplicons for each. They looked at the ratio of the peak area of each pair for comparison over 59 months, and although an overall trend can be observed in their data, there is a large amount of overlap between time points.

Table 3.7 Recent studies on time since deposition (TSD) and their investigative method

Analytic Method	Technique	Reference(s)	TSD Range
Genetic			
	Bioassay	304–306	0–20 years
	DNA analysis (degradation; non–polymerase chain reaction [PCR])	307,308	1–36 hours
	RNA analysis (PCR)	309–317	0–30 days
High-Performance Liquid Chromatography (HPLC)			
	HPLC	318–320	1–3 weeks
Mass Spectrometry			
	Metabolomics	321,322	0–28 days
	Volatile organic compound analysis	323,324	0–1 year
Optical Spectroscopy			
	Absorbance (ultraviolet visible) spectroscopy	295,307,308,325,326	0–20 days
	Attenuated total reflectance Fourier transform infrared	294,327–330	0–175 days
	Fluorescence spectroscopy	331–334	0–50 days
	Laser-induced breakdown spectroscopy	335	1–9 hours
	Reflectance spectroscopy	336–342	0–60 days
Other			
	Atomic force microscopy	343,344	0–31 days
	Image based; color value	345–348	0–42 days
Review			
	Overview/review	299,349–353	
Vibrational Spectroscopy			
	Near infrared	354	0–77 days
	Raman	355–361	0–2 years

Anderson et al.[309] looked at the ratio of mRNA (β-actin) and tRNA (18S) over 150 days. They found a clear trend with their bloodstains that indicated this could be a useful tool, but their study used only four participants. A follow-up study looking at 30 volunteers and two different size amplicons of each of the same genes was less definitive and was able to differentiate fresh blood from 6-day-old blood, and 6-day-old blood from 30-day-old blood for 28/29 samples, but could not clearly separate blood from 30 and 90 days old.[310] Sirker et al.[313] looked at mRNA recovery over 71 weeks with different storage conditions and volumes, and although not looking specifically at TSD, no trends are observed in their data in relation to time.

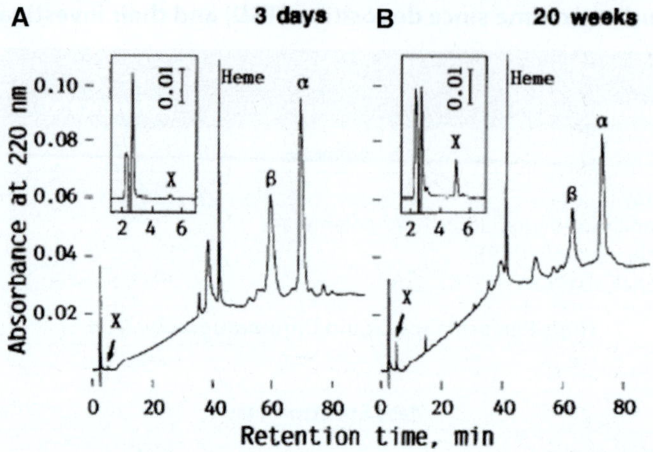

Fig. 3.50 High-performance liquid chromatograms from extracts of human blood stored for different periods of time under fluorescent lighting. Note the X peak that increases with the time since deposition of blood. *From Inoue H, Takabe F, Iwasa M, et al. A new marker for estimation of bloodstain age by high performance liquid chromatography. Forensic Sci Int. 1992;57:17–27.*

Fu and Allen[312] looked at RNA degradation over 1 year from six individuals and four RNA markers and found some trends, but in blind trial testing, comparison to the validation data set showed a wide range of TSDs. Other studies looking at multiple RNA targets also found some overall trends, but a wide range of crossovers as well, making the methods suitable to differentiating fresh vs. older bloodstains but not allowing a narrow TSD range that may be required with some investigations.[311,314,317] To further complicate TSD using RNA, it has been found that the degradation rate (the main factor used for TSD using RNA) is about 5 to 10 times higher for samples in higher temperatures (37°C vs. 20°C) and in higher humidity (75% vs. 35% relative humidity).[315] It was also shown that if the temperature or humidity shifted prior to analysis, then this could affect the results and alter the TSD determination.[315]

Further genetic means to determine TSD were investigated using a bioaffinity-driven cascade of two blood markers, creatine kinase and alanine transaminase,[306] and later looking at alkaline phosphatase.[306] The first study used three volunteers and the change in absorbance corresponding to the consumption of 1,4-dihydronicotinamide adenine dinucleotide (NADH), through the lactate dehydrogenase pathway that both blood markers are part of. The authors found a measurable difference over 5 days for both markers but noted the degradation is affected by temperature.[306] A second study mimicked human blood with different levels of alkaline phosphatase based on literature values for young and old females and males, and analyzed it over 48 hours. The testing method can be used onsite, and the authors were able to determine the age of the person whose blood is found, and for female samples can determine the TSD. They also state that the sex of the person whose blood is present cannot be determined using their method.[304]

Arany and Ohtani[305] applied aspartic acid racemization (AAR), which is used in other areas of forensic science for age estimation of tissues (e.g., teeth). AAR is an estimation of the D/L aspartic acid ratio, usually in slow turnover tissues, that can reflect the age of the individual. They used a single volunteer, whose blood sample was dried, powdered, and subjected to different temperatures to simulate the aging process.[305] Another six bloodstained glass slides ranging in age from 1 month to 20 years were also analyzed, and good correlation was found between the AAR and time, although some samples failed to produce results in the fraction under analysis that the authors determined was optimal (at 1 month and 16 years).[305]

Two papers looked at both DNA degradation and visible absorbance spectroscopy for bloodstains over 15 days and 11 time points.[307,308] In one study, bovine blood samples were taken on FTA cards and into 1.5 mL microcentrifuge tubes with anticoagulant.[307] The second study involved adding an anticoagulant solution to the bovine blood before samples were taken on FTA cards and into 1.5 mL microcentrifuge tubes.[308] The first study stored samples at ambient conditions, and the second at three different temperatures, for 11 time points between 1.5 and 360 hours. DNA was extracted from samples at each time point, and degradation was assessed on a TapeStation, whereas visible absorbance spectroscopy was assessed on a luminometer between 350 and 650 nm, where samples needed to be diluted to avoid oversaturation of the signal. Although overall trends can be seen in the different data, there is a large amount of overlap in the reading for different treatment types.

Bergmann et al.[325] looked at visible absorbance spectroscopy over the entire visible spectrum and determined that there was an overall correlation between the spectra and the TSD, but the error was still high. They determined that a holistic approach is better and that many of their errors may be due to different substrates used. Hanson and Ballantyne[295] looked at the blue spectral shift of blood at various ages up to 1 year, and their study showed a shift in spectra, but this was heavily influenced by both temperature and humidity. They later confirmed the temperature and humidity variations, but found that the shifts observed were unaffected by substrate.[326] Bremmer[353] stated that spectroscopy for TSD is most sensitive for short-term aging (e.g., up to an age of 20 days).

The use of ATR-FTIR was investigated for TSD first by Orphanou in 2015. ATR-FTIR provides more information than FTIR alone and is a nondestructive technique, leaving the underlying bloodstain undisturbed. Orphanou[294] looked at bloodstains of various TSDs, and although they could still be identified as blood, there did not seem to be any correlation with TSD. Lin et al.[328,329] used ATR-FTIR to determine TSD and species. Their TSD examined indoor and outdoor stains and ranged up to 107 days. They analyzed their results using partial least square regression (PLSR) (similar to principal component analysis) and found there was some correlation that could be attributed to TSD (Fig. 3.51). Lin et al. concluded that the method is most useful for stains 7 to 85 days old. The second study found that old human and other mammal blood could not be separated, but recent stains could be classified to

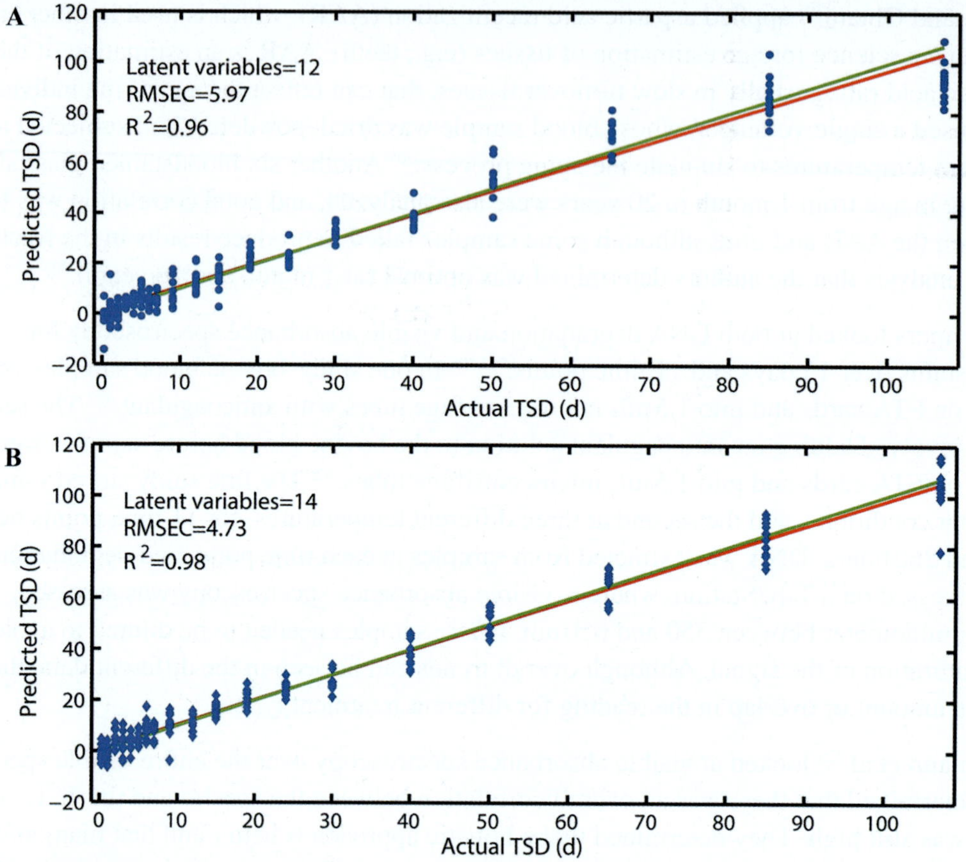

Fig. 3.51 Partial least square regression plots for indoor (A) and outdoor (B) bloodstains between 6 hours and 107 days old and showing the calibrated predictions of time since deposition (TSD) versus the actual TSD. *From Lin H, Zhang Y, Wang Q, et al. Estimation of the age of human bloodstains under the simulated indoor and outdoor crime scene conditions by ATR-FTIR spectroscopy. Sci Rep. 2017;7:1–9.*

species.[328] They also stated that the complexities of real-world crime scene bloodstains pose difficulties based on other factors not investigated, such as substrate and contamination by other substances, and recommended further study.[328]

Zhang et al.[330] looked at ATR-FTIR for TSD but only for short-term differentiation because the bloodstains dried out. They found the absorbance was constant and decreased as the blood dried, which was affected by humidity. Kumar et al.[327] also used ATR-FTIR combined with chemometric methods for determining TSD and claimed they can accurately age blood up to 175 days. Their study incorporated 24 variables to aid with the estimation, and they concluded the method is accurate and can be used in casework for samples that have been exposed to similar conditions as in their study. They were also able to differentiate between human and nonhuman blood.[305]

Guo et al.[331] looked at fluorescence lifetime measurements, which measures the time a fluorophore spends in an excited state before returning to ground state. It is independent of the fluorophore concentration, so the size of the bloodstain is irrelevant. They looked at albumin and γ-globulins in bloodstains that had been dissolved in phosphate-buffered saline, and used a 295 nm (ultraviolet range) pulse of light for excitation. Dog blood from four individual animals was analyzed, and a nonlinear trend was found that plateaued at around 300 hours, and they ultimately recommended that the method is promising for evaluating TSD within the first week.[331] A follow-up study[332] investigated adapting the technique to solid-state stains using a 405 nm (visible range) excitation, but the method involved existent equipment that needed to be adapted for use. No further expansion of the TSD range was given. They also found that different species can be used interchangeably for optical studies as models, which means species testing would need to be carried out on any samples to confirm human origin.

Further work on fluorescence lifetime measurements was carried out by McShine et al.,[333] who looked at blood from six human donors and mixtures with saliva over 1200 hours. They were able to confirm the techniques worked with human blood and found the same nonlinear trend that plateaued as the stains aged. They concluded the technique can be used to differentiate new bloodstains from old ones.[333] Wójtowicz et al.[334] applied the test to TSD of menstrual blood from two individuals, but they had different targets of tryptophan, NADH, and flavins, which were excited at 285 nm, 350 nm, and 465 nm, respectively, over 9 hours as the stains dried. Overall trends were seen of decreasing intensity in tryptophan and increasing intensity in NADH and flavins, but further research was recommended.[334]

Wang et al.[335] used laser-induced breakdown spectroscopy to determine TSD of equine blood between 1 and 9 hours. Spectra were captured between 200 and 1000 nm, and bands relating to Fe, Ca, C, Na, O, N, Si, H, and CN were selected for analysis. They were able to differentiate between substances that could be confused for blood and investigated the effect of substrates to simulate crime scene conditions. Prediction accuracies for different substrates were overall low, but the authors still claim it can be used onsite to identify blood and determine TSD.[335]

Reflectance spectroscopy has also been used to determine TSD of bloodstains since 1960.[342] Patterson,[342] looking at six individuals over 12 days, showed a negative trend in color as blood aged, stating the greatest change can be seen in the first 3 days. Bremmer et al.[336] used the change of color of blood as a guide and targeted oxyhemoglobin (HbO_2) to metHb and hemichrome (HC) between 450 and 800 nm. They looked at different dilutions, temperatures, and effect of light over a maximum of 10 days. Over the 10 days of study, HbO_2 was found to have a nonlinear decreasing trend, whereas metHb had a linear increasing trend, and HC had a nonlinear increasing trend. They concluded the method could be used for TSD. The study was expanded to 60 days[340] using the same targets and found the prediction was accurate within a range (e.g., 14 days), but their final predicted data showed great overlap with other time points. This was also found by Li et al.,[337] who reported large error with data sets when training and test sets of were different stains. A follow-up study by the same authors found that TSD could be accurately determined in fresh stains (hours to 3 days), but error increased with time.[341]

Edelman et al.[354] investigated near IR spectroscopy for TSD of bloodstains on colored backgrounds. They reported a high (>0.94) R^2 for the different colored training sets used; data, however, indicated standard deviation increases with age, as is seen in other techniques. Other TSD has been carried out using Raman spectroscopy; however, there are a variety of complications with this process, including possible damage to the sample from the laser.[359] Work by Menżyk et al.[358] demonstrated that instrumental factors can affect the spectra, including laser power, and if the spectra was generated using a static (single-point) or rotating (multiple-point) sample. In their study, they found high laser power gave overlapping results for stains over 6 hours using the static mode, but laser power did not affect the results when used in rotating mode. Sun et al.[360] used Raman to look at stains from 12 individuals over 80 days and four different storage temperatures, and they recommended the technique as a potential method for TSD. Their results over multiple wavenumbers showed the same nonlinear trend, which plateaued as time increased. Doty et al. carried out two studies: over 1 week[356] and over 2 years.[357] In their first study, Doty et al.[351] identified trends that indicated Hb was denaturing. They stated they were able to differentiate blood from other body fluids, and using PLSR were able to indicate TSD. Two donors were used, and their predictive model showed a range of overlapping times. Their second study[352] consisted of one male and one female donor and analyzed samples over 2 years. They were able to identify prominent changes to the spectra over time (Fig. 3.52), but their predictive model showed more deviation and overlap as time increased. Takamura et al.[361] looked at TSD over 4 months and different temperatures (16°C, 24°C, 30°C), and they found major differences between their results at these varied temperatures. Their displayed aging index also shows greater overlap of times as stains age. Complex statistics and models that are applied to the spectra complicate this method that currently shows promise for recent event bloodstains.

Atomic force microscopy (AFM) has been used for high-resolution imaging of RBCs and to detect elasticity changes. Strasser et al.[344] looked at the same RBCs over 4 weeks in a dried stain and found no microscopic alterations to the morphology. They did find a decrease in the elasticity that they hypothesized was due to the alteration of the blood spot during the drying process. They concluded their preliminary data can be used to create calibration curves for TSD. The second study looking at AFM confirmed the lack of visual change to the RBCs, but found changes quantitatively through their AMF measurements.[343] They found changes in perimeter, height, area, and volume of the RBCs, although there is overlap between TSD points, and height shows an oscillating trend.

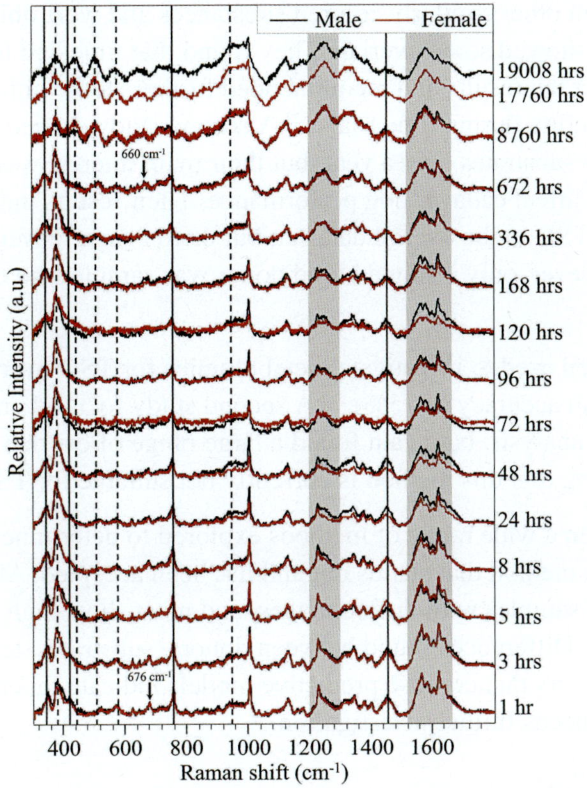

Fig. 3.52 The average preprocessed Raman spectra from male *(black)* and female *(red)* bloodstains aged over 2 years. *Solid lines* show changes that decrease with time, and *dotted lines* show changes that increase with time. *From Doty KC, Muro CK, Lednev IK. Predicting the time of the crime: bloodstain aging estimation for up to two years. Forensic Chem. 2017;5:1–7.*

Color-based image analysis has been used for TSD determination by several groups. The first attempt was made by smartphone using image analysis.[348] They looked at blood from four volunteers over multiple storage temperatures and 42 days. They found that magenta (CMYK) and saturation (HSL) were the best targets, but they also found significant variation between different smart devices and temperature conditions. Their model became highly variable with older stains. Further work was carried out that tried to standardize the light and image, but was unable to provide estimates for stains older than 42 hours.[347] Variation between TSD samples on different substrates and temperatures among multiple other factors showed substrate and temperature are major factors in interpretation of the TSD, and there is overlap between time points within the same sample group.[346]

Volatile organic compound (VOC) analysis for TSD has been investigated and uses a probe that releases a stream of heated N_2 and a second line that will transport the VOCs produced to the mass spectrometry (MS). Rankin-Turner et al.[323] were able to use this method to differentiate blood from other similarly colored substances and were able to differentiate varied TSDs, but they showed some overlap. They found that time and light/dark storage conditions would affect the results and recommended further study with different substrates, temperatures, and humidity during time trials.[323] A second study carried out by Rust et al.[324] looked at two different substrates over a year, but their main interest was how changing VOCs over time could affect cadaver dog performance. Their results indicated a trend that corresponds with TSD in the overall data set, but there is much overlap within short time frames; note, however, only a single blood donor was sampled, so this may not be representative.

HPLC-MS-MS has been used to investigate metabolomics for TSD over 21 days, initially with limited success (an accuracy of 75%).[322] A second study focused on five candidate molecular features for analysis, but again found a large range of overlap between the different time points,[321] indicating that this method is currently not suitable for TSD.

Although there has been a wide range of methods explored to determine TSD of bloodstains, to date there is not one method that stands out and has been accepted. All methods to date have shown overlap of samples with different ages, and most show high variance that increases as stains age. Differences found between donors, substrates, temperature and humidity, and other factors that confuse predictive models indicate this remains an aspect of forensic serology that needs further investigation.

Other Blood Targets

Although not a common target of investigations, it may be important to presumptively identify nonvenous sources of blood. The ability to differentiate menstrual or fetal blood from venous blood is an important consideration in forensic science. These tests are described in Chapter 6.

References

1. James SH, Kish PE, Sutton TP. *Principles of bloodstain pattern analysis: theory and practice*. CRC Press; 2005:576.
2. Bevel T, Gardner RM. *Bloodstain pattern analysis with an introduction to crime scene reconstruction*. 3rd ed. CRC Press; 2008.
3. Casali F, Ciavaglia SA, Gannicliffe C, et al. Validation of presumptive tests for non-human blood using Kastle Meyer and Hemastix reagents. *Science & Justice*. 2020/01/01/2020;60(1):30-35. https://doi.org/10.1016/j.scijus.2019.10.003.
4. Needham C, Simpson R. The benzidine test for occult blood in faeces. *QJM*. 1952;21(2):123-134.
5. Wieten E, Schreuders EH, Grobbee EJ, et al. Incidence of faecal occult blood test interval cancers in population-based colorectal cancer screening: a systematic review and meta-analysis. *Gut*. 2019;68(5):873-881.
6. Clark G, Strachan JA, Carey FA, et al. Transition to quantitative faecal immunochemical testing from guaiac faecal occult blood testing in a fully rolled-out population-based national bowel screening programme. *Gut*. 2021;70(1):106-113.

7. Perry SM, Monaghan W. The prevalence of visible and/or occult blood on anesthesia and monitoring equipment. *AANA*. 2001;69(1):44-48.
8. Phillips R, Patrick Monaghan WP. Incidence of visible and occult blood on laryngoscope blades and handles. *AANA Journal*. 1997;65:241-246.
9. Louie RF, Lau MJ, Lee JH, et al. Multicenter study of the prevalence of blood contamination on point-of-care glucose meters and recommendations for controlling contamination. *Point of Care*. 2005;4(4):158-163.
10. Poonja Z, Uppal J, Netherton SJ, et al. Evaluation of emergency department ultrasound machines for the presence of occult blood. *Canadian Journal of Emergency Medicine*. 2019;21(3):395-398.
11. Gurfinkel D, Franklin U. A study of the feasibility of detecting blood residue on artifacts. *J Archaeol Sci*. 1988;15(1):83-97.
12. Matheson CD, Veall M-A. Presumptive blood test using Hemastix® with EDTA in archaeology. *J Archaeol Sci*. 2014/01/01/2014;41:230-241. doi: https://doi.org/10.1016/j.jas.2013.08.018.
13. Rosner F. Blood stain identification as described in the Talmud. *Isr J Med Sci*. 1973;9(8):1077-1079.
14. Tzhu S. *Hsi Yuan Chi Lu*. 1247.
15. Giles HA. The "Hsi Yüan Lu" or "Instructions to Coroners". *SAGE Publications*. 1924
16. Rattier JJL. Sur Quelque Srecherches Microscopiques Relatives Aux Taches De Linge. *Journal de Chimie Médical de Parmacie et de Toxicologie*. 1837;3:120-122.
17. Parks EA. The formation of crystals in the human blood. *The Medical Times and Gazette*. 1852;26(N.S 5): 103-104.
18. Jones CH. Crystals in Putrefying Blood. *London Journal of Medicine*. 1852;4(46):956.
19. Teichmann L. Ueber die Krystallisation des orpnischen Be-standtheile des Blutes. *Ration Med*. 1853;3: 375-388.
20. Buchner L, Simon G. Untersuchungen uber haminkrystalle und ihre gerichtlichmedicinische bedeutung. *Virchows Archiv fur pathologische Anatomie und Physiologie und fur klinische Medizin*. 1858;15:50-69.
21. Landerer X. Ueber die Teichmann'schen Hämatin-Krystalle. *Archiv der Pharmazie*. 1859;150(3):275-276. doi: https://doi.org/10.1002/ardp.18591500305.
22. Virchow R. Ueber die forensische untersuchung von trockenan Blutflecken. *Virchows Archiv fur pathologische Anatomic und Physiologie und fur klinische Medizin*. 1857;12:334-338.
23. Stokes GG VIII. On the reduction and oxidation of the colouring matter of the blood. *Proc R Soc Lond*. 1864;(13):355-364.
24. Ritter B. *Ueber die Ermittelung von Blut-, Samen- und Exkrementenflecken in Kriminalfaellen: Ein spezieller Beitrag zur gerichtlichen Arzneikunde*. Stahel; 1854.
25. Barruel M. Mémoire sur l'existence d'un principe propre à caractériser le sang de l'homme et celui des diverses espèces d'animaux. *Annales d'hygiène publique et de médecine légale*. 1829:267-277.
26. Sutherland WD. *Blood-stains: their detection and the determination of their source Bailliere*. Tindall and Cox; 1907.
27. Robin C, Tardieu A. Mémoire sur Quelques Applications Nouvelles de L'Examen Microscopique de Diverses Espèces de Tache. *Annales D'hygiène Publique Et De Médecine Légale*. 1860;13:416-442.
28. Schönbein CF. Auszug aus einer der naturforschenden Gesellschaft in Basel am 2. April und 7. Mai 1851 gemachten Mittheilung. *Journal für Praktische Chemie*. 1851;53(1):65-86. https://doi.org/10.1002/prac.18510530111.
29. Schönbein CF. Ueber die katalytische Wirksamkeit organischer Materien und deren Verbreitung in der Pflanzen-und Thierwelt. *Journal für Praktische Chemie*. 1863;89(1):323-344.
30. Cauvet D. Taches de Sperme et Taches de Sang. *Annales D'hygiène Publique Et De Médecine Légale*. 1875;44:117-126.
31. Florence A. *Les taches de sang: leur signification, leur importance en médecine judiciaire*. Doin. 1885
32. Baeyer A. Ueber die Verbindungen der Phtalsäure mit den Phenolen. *Justus Liebigs Annalen der Chemie*. 1880;202(1):36-49. https://doi.org/10.1002/jlac.18802020105.
33. Meyer E. Beiträge zur Leukocytenfrage. *Munch Med Wochenschr*. 1903;50(35):1489-1493.
34. Küster W. Ueber den gerichtlichen Nachweis von Blut. *Angew Chem*. 1902;15(51):1317-1323. https://doi.org/10.1002/ange.19020155104.

35. Medinger P. Zum nachweis minimalster blutspuren. *Dtsch Z Gesamte Gerichtl Med*. 1933;20(1):74-85.
36. Hoerr SO, Bliss WR, Kauffman J. Clinical evaluation of various tests for occult blood in the feces. *Journal of the American Medical Association*. 1949;141(17):1213-1217.
37. Rider JA, Owens FJ. Evaluation of an orthotolidine test (Fecatest) for determination of occult blood. *Journal of the American Medical Association*. 1954;156(1):31-33. https://doi.org/10.1001/jama.1954.02950010033011.
38. Marieb EN, Hoehn K. *Human Anatomy & Physiology*. 9th ed. Benjamin Cummings; 2013:1107.
39. Saferstein R. *Criminalistics: An Introduction to Forensic Science*. 10th ed. Prentice Hall International (UK) Limited; 2011.
40. Patzelt D. History of forensic serology and molecular genetics in the sphere of activity of the German Society for Forensic Medicine. *Forensic Sci Int*. 2004;144(2-3):185-191.
41. Meddeb R, Dache ZAA, Thezenas S, et al. Quantifying circulating cell-free DNA in humans. *Scientific reports*. 2019;9(1):5220.
42. Stroun M, Lyautey J, Lederrey C, et al. About the possible origin and mechanism of circulating DNA: Apoptosis and active DNA release. *Clin Chim Acta*. 2001;313(1-2):139-142.
43. Thierry A, El Messaoudi S, Gahan P, et al. Origins, structures, and functions of circulating DNA in oncology. *Cancer Metastasis Rev*. 2016;35(3):347-376.
44. Thomas JC. The examination of blood and seminal stains. *Police J*. 1937;10(4):490-503.
45. Wheeler R. Haemoglobin. Available from http://commonswikimediaorg/wiki/File:1GZX_Haemoglobinpng Used under GNU Free Documentation License. 2007;
46. *ChemSketch*. Version 2018.2.5. 2018. www.acdlabs.com.
47. Barni F, Lewis SW, Berti A, et al. Forensic application of the luminol reaction as a presumptive test for latent blood detection. *Talanta*. 2007;72(3):896-913.
48. Braunitzer G, Hilschmann N, Rudloff V, et al. The Haemoglobin Particles. *Nature (Lond)*. 1961;190(4775): 480-482. https://doi.org/10.1038/190480a0.
49. Marie C. Presumptive Testing and Enhancement of Blood. In: Bevel T, Gardner RM, eds. *Bloodstain Pattern Analysis with an Introduction to Crime Scene Reconstruction*, 3rd ed. CRC Press; 2008:275-296. chap 12.
50. Kapralov A, Vlasova II, Feng W, et al. Peroxidase activity of hemoglobin·haptoglobin complexes. *J Biol Chem*. 2009;284(44):30395-30407. https://doi.org/10.1074/jbc.M109.045567.
51. Proescher F, Moody A. Detection of blood by means of chemiluminescence. *J Lab Clin Med*. 1939;24: 1183-1189.
52. Daniels G. *Human blood groups*. vol 2. Wiley Online Library; 2013.
53. Dean L. *Blood groups and red cell antigens*. vol 2. NCBI Bethesda; 2005.
54. Anstee DJ. Blood group-active surface molecules of the human Red blood cell. *Vox Sang*. 1990;58(1): 1-20. https://doi.org/10.1111/j.1423-0410.1990.tb02049.x.
55. Shipp E, Roelofs R, Togneri E, et al. Effects of argon-laser light, alternate source light, and cyanoacrylate fuming on DNA typing of human bloodstains. *J Forensic Sci*. 1993;38(1):184-191.
56. Grodsky M, Wright K, Kirk PL. Simplified preliminary blood testing—an improved technique and a comparative study of methods. *The Journal of Criminal Law, Criminology, and Police Science*. 1951;42(1):95-104.
57. Vandewoestyne M, Lepez T, Van Hoofstat D, et al. Evaluation of a visualization assay for blood on forensic evidence. *J Forensic Sci*. 2015;60(3):707-711.
58. Sloots J, Lalonde W, Reid B, et al. Kastle-Meyer blood test reagents are deleterious to DNA. *Forensic Sci Int*. 2017;281:141-146.
59. Stoilovic M. Detection of semen and blood stains using polilight as a light source. *Forensic Sci Int*. 1991;51(2):289-296. https://doi.org/10.1016/0379-0738(91)90194-n.
60. Gorzkiewicz M, Woźniak M, Grzybowski T, et al. Identification of semen in bloodstains with the use of alternative light source and biochemical screening tests. *Archiwum Medycyny Sadowej i Kryminologii*. 2008;58(4):182-187.
61. Sterzik V, Hinderberger P, Panzer S, et al. Visualizing old biological traces on different materials without using chemicals. *Int J Leg Med*. 2018;132(1):35-41. http://doi.org/10.1007/s00414-017-1678-3.

62. Brooke H, Baranowski MR, McCutcheon JN, et al. Multimode imaging in the thermal infrared for chemical contrast enhancement. Part 3: Visualizing blood on fabrics. *Anal Chem.* 2010;82(20):8427-8431. https://doi.org/10.1021/ac101107v.
63. Ray B. Use of alternate light sources for detection of body fluids. *Southwest Assoc Forensic Sci J.* 1992;14(1):30-33.
64. Vandenberg N, van Oorschot RAH. The use of Polilight® in the detection of seminal fluid, saliva, and bloodstains and comparison with conventional chemical-based screening tests. *J Forensic Sci.* 2006;51(2):361-370. https://doi.org/10.1111/j.1556-4029.2006.00065.x.
65. Adair TW. Experimental detection of blood under painted surfaces. *IABPA News.* 2006:12-19.
66. Lupica R. Comparing two alternate light sources with bluestar forensic: locating blood in a manipulated crime scene. *J Forensic Identif.* 2017;67(2):190-204.
67. Finnis J, Lewis J, Davidson A. Comparison of methods for visualizing blood on dark surfaces. *Science & Justice.* 2013;53(2):178-186. https://doi.org/10.1016/j.scijus.2012.09.001.
68. Raymond MA, Hall RL. An interesting application of infra-red reflection photography to blood splash pattern interpretation. *Forensic Sci Int.* 1986;31(3):189-194.
69. Farrar A, Porter G, Renshaw A. Detection of latent bloodstains beneath painted surfaces using reflected infrared photography. *J Forensic Sci.* 2012;57(5):1190-1198.
70. Howard MC, Nessan M. Detecting bloodstains under multiple layers of paint. *J Forensic Identif.* 2010;60(6):682.
71. Barrera V, Haas C, Meixner EA, et al. Detection of painted-over traces of blood and seminal fluid. *journal article. Int J Leg Med.* 2018;132(4):1067-1074. https://doi.org/10.1007/s00414-018-1787-7.
72. Fourney RM, DesRoches AN, Buckle JL. Chapter 14 - Bilogical Evidence and Forensic DNA Profiling. In: Nic Daeid N, Houck MM, eds. *Interpol's Forensic Science Review*, CRC Press; 2007:591-662.
73. Sottolano S, Deforest P. An improved technique for the preparation of Teichmann and Takayama crystals from blood. *Microscope.* 1980;28(2):41-46.
74. Scheller H. Der Einfluß der Witterung auf den Nachweis von Blutspuren. *Dtsch Z Gesamte Gerichtl Med.* 1937;28(1):217-225. https://doi.org/10.1007/BF01750490.
75. Miller LB. Hemochromogen crystal formation with minute amounts of blood. *J Forensic Sci Soc.* 1969;9(1):84-86. https://doi.org/10.1016/S0015-7368(69)70496-0.
76. Takayama M. A method for identifying blood by hemochromogen crystallization. *Kokka Igakkai Zasshi.* 1912;306:15-33.
77. Atkinson JP, Kendall AI. A modification of Teichmann's method for obtaining hemin crystals, with a demonstration of specimens. *Proc Soc Exp Biol Med.* 1907;5(1):22-23. https://doi.org/10.3181/00379727-5-11.
78. Symons CT. A note on a modification of Teichmann's Test for blood. *The Biochemical Journal.* 1913;7(6):596-598. https://doi.org/10.1042/bj0070596.
79. Kirk P.L. Crime investigation; physical evidence and the police laboratory. 1953.
80. Fiori A. Detection and identification of bloodstains. In: Lundquist F, ed. Methods of forensic science. 1962:243-290.
81. Hammerl H. Untersuchung über einige den Blutnachweis störende Einflüsse. *Vjschr f gerichtl Med.* 1892;4:44.
82. Kerr DJ, Mason VH. The haemochromogen crystal test for blood. *Br Med J.* 1926;1(3395):134.
83. Hoppe-Seyler F. Weitere Mittheilungen über die Eigenschaften des Blutfarbstoffs. *Z Physiol Chem.* 1879;1:121-139. https://doi.org/10.1515/bchm1.1879.2.2-3.149.
84. Hoppe-Seyler F. Beiträge zur Kenntniss der Eigenschaften der Blutfarbstoffe. *Z Physiol Chem.* 1889;13: 477-496. https://doi.org/10.1515/bchm1.1889.13.5.477.
85. Donogany Z. Darstellung von Hamochromogenkrystallen. *Cenralblatt fur Physiologie.* 1893;6(21):629-630.
86. Dilling W.J. *Atlas der kristallformen und der absorptionsbander der hamochromogene.* 1910:136.
87. Macey HL. The identification of human blood in a 166 year old stain. *J Can Soc Forensic Sci.* 1979;12(4):191-193. https://doi.org/10.1080/00085030.1979.10757334.
88. Platt SR. The effects of the argon ion laser on subsequent blood examinations. *J Forensic Sci.* 1982;27(3):726-728.

89. Das P. Comparative studies of Haemin crystal of mammals-structural and statistical analysis. *International Journal of Scientific and Research Publications*. 2012:687.
90. Heine. Vergleichende Untersuchungen über den forensischen Wert der Hämin- und Hämochromogenkristalle. *Zeitschrift für analytische Chemie*. 1916;55(4):224-224. doi: https://doi.org/10.1007/BF01393741.
91. Torres E, Bustos-Jaimes I, Le Borgne S. Potential use of oxidative enzymes for the detoxification of organic pollutants. *Applied Catalysis B: Environmental*. 2003;46(1):1-15. doi: https://doi.org/10.1016/S0926-3373(03)00228-5.
92. Reeder BJ, Svistunenko DA, Cooper CE, et al. The radical and redox chemistry of myoglobin and hemoglobin: from in vitro studies to human pathology. *Antioxidants & redox signaling*. 2004;6(6):954-966.
93. Dawson JH. Probing structure-function relations in heme-containing oxygenases and peroxidases. *Science*. 1988;240(4851):433-439.
94. McFarlane WD, Hamilton RCM. On the factors influencing the blood-benzidine reaction as applied to the micro-determination of haemoglobin. *Biochem J*. 1932;26(4):1050.
95. Ortizleon M, Velasco L, Vazquezduhalt R. Biocatalytic oxidation of polycyclic aromatic hydrocarbons by hemoglobin and hydrogen peroxide. *Biochem Biophys Res Commun*. 1995;215(3):968-973.
96. Chapsal J, Bourbigot M, Thomas D. Oxidation of aromatic compounds by haemoglobin. *Water Res*. 1986;20(6):709-713.
97. Kobert R. Beiträge zur Kenntniss der Methämoglobine. *Archiv für die gesamte Physiologie des Menschen und der Tiere*. 1900;82(11):603-630.
98. Anand U, Agarwal R, Anand C. Test for occult blood. The benzidine reaction: A text book error. *Biochemical Education*. 1994;22(4): 212-212.
99. Lim C-W, Kim Y-H, Kim J-G. Preliminary test of forensic identification bloodstain using guaiac mixture and its effect on genetic analysis. *Korean Journal of Clinical Laboratory Science*. 2010;42(1):22-31.
100. Vázquez A, Tudela J, Varón R, et al. Determination of hemoglobin through its peroxidase activity on chlorpromazine. *J Biochem Biophys Methods*. 1991;23(1):45-52. https://doi.org/10.1016/0165-022X(91)90049-3.
101. Holland VR, Saunders BC, Rose FL, et al. A safer substitute for benzidine in the detection of blood. *Tetrahedron*. 1974;30(18):3299-3302. https://doi.org/10.1016/s0040-4020(01)97504-0.
102. Weisburger JH. Comments on the history and importance of aromatic and heterocyclic amines in public health. *Mutat Res*. 2002;506-507:9-20. https://doi.org/10.1016/s0027-5107(02)00147-1.
103. Steinberg H. *The hazard of benzidine to criminal justice personnel*. vol 480. US Department of Commerce, National Bureau of Standards; 1977.
104. Josephy PD. Oxidative activation of benzidine and its derivatives by peroxidases. *Environ Health Perspect*. 1985;64:171-178. https://doi.org/10.2307/3430007.
105. Adler O, Adler R. Über das Verhalten gewisser organischer Verindungen gegenüber Blut mit besonderer Berücksichtigung des Nachweises von Blut. *Hoppe Seyler's Z Physiol Chem*. 1904;41:59-67.
106. Hochmeister MN, Budowle B, Baechtel FS. Effects of presumptive test reagents on the ability to obtain restriction fragment length polymorphism (RFLP) patterns from human blood and semen stains. *J Forensic Sci*. 1991;36(3):656-661.
107. Lewis GP. Method using ortho-tolidine for the quantitative determination of haemoglobin in serum and urine. *Journal of clinical pathology*. 1965;18(2):235-239.
108. Elcaness H. A modification of the benzidine occult blood test. *New York State Journal of Medicine*. 1950;50(3):293.
109. Gradwohl R. *Clinical Laboratory Methods and Diagnosis*. vol 1. St: The CV Mosby Company; 1956: 574-654.
110. Gregersen J. Untersuchungen über okkulte Blutungen. *Digestion*. 1919;25(3):169-195.
111. Alvarez RS, Wight THT. The Gregersen Test. *US Vet Bur Med Bull*. 1929;5(11):888-890.
112. Saferstein R. *Forensic Science Handbook*. Prentice Hall, Inc; 1982:725.
113. Jain A, Jain R, Jain S. *Qualitative Analysis of Urine for Abnormal Constituents. Basic Techniques in Biochemistry, Microbiology and Molecular Biology: Principles and Techniques*. Springer US; 2020: 191-200.

114. Hunt AC, Corby C, Dodd BE, et al. The identification of human blood stains: a critical survey. *J Forensic Med*. 1960;7(2):112-130.
115. Hughes A. A simplified benzidine test. *Br Med J*. 1952;2(4791):970.
116. Garner D, Cano K, Peimer R, et al. An evaluation of tetramethylbenzidine as a presumptive test for blood. *Journal of Forensic Science*. 1976;21(4):816-821.
117. Jin M, Ba H, Zhu A, et al. Effect of benzidine test on DNA analysis of bloodstain. *Fa yi xue za zhi*. 2018;34(2):157-160.
118. Kumar N, Chauhan A, Gupta R, et al. DNA profiling from blood traces present on clothing's and detected by Benzidine test in forensic cases. *Foresic Research & Criminology International Journal*. 2019;7:63-66. https://doi.org/10.15406/frcij.2019.07.00265.
119. Kohn R, Watrous R. Inhibition of the benzidine blood test by ascorbic acid. *J Biol Chem*. 1938;124(1): 163-168.
120. Castelló A, Francès F, Verdú F. Bloodstains on leather: Examination of false negatives in presumptive test and human hemoglobin Test. *J Forensic Sci*. 2017;62(5):1308-1313.
121. Pinker R.H. The preliminary chemical tests for blood. *20th Annual Conference of the International Association of Identification*. 1934:38.
122. Culliford B, Nickolls L. The benzidine test: a critical review. *J Forensic Sci*. 1964;9(1):175-191.
123. von Baeyer A. Uber ein neue Klasse von Farbstoffen. *Berichte der Deutschen chemischen Gesellschaft zu Berlin*. 1871;4:555-558.
124. Kastle J, Shedd O. Phenolphthalin as a reagent for the oxidizing ferments. *Am Chem J*. 1901;26:526.
125. Fleig C. Nouvelle reaction, a la fluorescine, pour la recherche du sang, en particulier dans l'urine. *Comptes rendus des séances de la Société de biologie*. 1910;69:192-194.
126. Sjöback R, Nygren J, Kubista M. Absorption and fluorescence properties of fluorescein. *Spectrochimica Acta Part A: Molecular and Biomolecular Spectroscopy*. 1995;51(6):L7-L21.
127. Martin MM, Lindqvist L. The pH dependence of fluorescein fluorescence. *Journal of Luminescence*. 1975;10(6):381-390.
128. Cheeseman R, DiMeo LA. Fluorescein technique performance study on bloody foot trails. *J Forensic Identif*. 1995;45(6):631-646.
129. Cheeseman R, Tomboc R. Fluorescein Technique Performance Study on Bloody Foot Trails. *J Forensic Identif*. 2001;51(1):16-27.
130. Kratochvil JF, Burris RH, Seikel MK, et al. Isolation and characterization of α-guaiaconic acid and the nature of guaiacum blue. *Phytochemistry*. 1971;10(10):2529-2531.
131. Farrugia KJ, Savage KA, Bandey H, et al. Chemical enhancement of footwear impressions in blood on fabric — Part 2: Peroxidase reagents. *Science & Justice*. 2011;51(3):110-121. https://doi.org/10.1016/j.scijus.2010.11.002.
132. Budowle B, Leggitt JL, Defenbaugh DA, et al. The presumptive reagent fluorescein for detection of dilute bloodstains and subsequent STR typing of recovered DNA. *J Forensic Sci*. 2000;45(5):1090-1092.
133. Cheeseman R. Direct sensitivity comparison of the fluorescein and luminol bloodstain enhancement techniques. *J Forensic Identif*. 1999;49(3):261.
134. Garofano L, Pizzamiglio M, Marino A, et al. A comparative study of the sensitivity and specifity of luminal and fluorescein on diluted and aged bloodstains and subsequent STRs typing. *Elsevier*. 2006:657-659.
135. Young T. A photographic comparison of luminol, fluorescein, and Bluestar. *J Forensic Identif*. 2006;56(6):906.
136. Barbaro A, Cormaci P, Teatino A. Validation of forensic DNA analysis from bloodstains treated by presumptive test reagents. *Elsevier*. 2004:631-633.
137. Planche L. Note sur la sophistication de la résine de jalap et sur les moyens de la reconnaître. *Bulletin de pharmacie*. 1810;2:578-580.
138. Guthlein W, Wielinger H, Rittersdorf W, et al. Guaiaconic acid A from guaiac resin. *Google Patents*. 1981
139. Caplan H, Discombe G. On chemical tests for blood in urine. *Br Med J*. 1951;2(4734):774-775.
140. Gaensslen RE. *Sourcebook in forensic serology, immunology, and biochemistry*. U.S. Government Printing Office; 1983:692.

141. Nicolesco G. Controle Experimental Des Principales Methods D'Identification Du Sang En Medicine Legale. *Annales de médecine légale, de criminologie et de police scientifique*. 1934;14:173-187.
142. von Fürth O. Über eine neue Modifikation des Forensisch-Chemischen Blutnachweises. *Angew Chem*. 1911;24(35):1625-1628.
143. Alvarez de Toledo y Valero R. La reaccion colorante do la sangre con el "leucoverde de malaquita" o tetrametildiaminotrifenilmetano. *Cronica Medica*. 1935;39:39331-39347.
144. Tobe SS, Watson N, Daeid Nic. N. Evaluation of six presumptive tests for blood, their specificity, sensitivity, and effect on high molecular-weight DNA. *J Forensic Sci*. 2007;52(1):102-109. https://doi.org/10.1111/j.1556-4029.2006.00324.x.
145. National Toxicology Program. Toxicology and carcinogenisis studies of malachite green chloride and leucomalachite green (cas nos 569-64-2 and 129-73-7) in F344/N rats and B6C3F1 mice (feed studies). 2005:317.
146. Fregeau CJ, Germain O, Fourney RM. Fingerprint enhancement revisited and the effects of blood enhancement chemicals on subsequent Profiler Plus™ fluorescent short tandem repeat DNA analysis of fresh and aged bloody fingerprints. *J Forensic Sci*. 2000;45(2):354-380.
147. Cox M. A study of the sensitivity and specificity of four presumptive tests for blood. *J Forensic Sci*. 1991;36(5):1503-1511.
148. Ponce AC, Pascual FAV. Critical revision of presumptive tests for bloodstains. *Forensic Sci Comm*. 1999;1(2). http://www.fbi.gov/about-us/lab/forensic-science-communications/?searchterm=Forensic. Science Communications.
149. Germain O., Miller K. Blood reagents - their use and their effect on DNA. *Ottawa (ON) Royal Canadian Mounted Police Forensic Identification Research and Review Section*. 1998:Nov, Bulletin No. 42.
150. Olsen R. Sensitivity comparison of blood enhancement techniques. *Ident News*. 1985;August:10-14.
151. Webb JL, Creamer JI, Quickenden TI. A comparison of the presumptive luminol test for blood with four non-chemiluminescent forensic techniques. *Luminescence (Chichester)*. 2006;21(4):214-220. https://doi.org/10.1002/bio.908.
152. Forsythe-Erman J. A Comparison of blood enhancement techniques. *J Can Soc Forensic Sci*. 2001;34(4): 159-165. https://doi.org/10.1080/00085030.2001.10757525.
153. Stow K. Direct lift-enhancement of blood-contaminated shoe marks by leuco malachite green-impregnated membranes. *Sci Jus*. 1994;34(4):241-244.
154. Alenazy NS, Refaat AM, Babu SR. Comparison of the effects of two presumptive test reagents on the ability to obtain STR profiles from minute bloodstains. *Egyptian Journal of Forensic Sciences*. 2015;5(3):103-108.
155. Bodziak WJ. Use of leuco crystal violet to enhance shoe prints in blood. *Forensic Sci Int*. 1996;82(1):45-52.
156. Draper WM, Crosby DG. Sensitive, enzyme-catalyzed, chromogenic reagent for hydrogen peroxide and other peroxygen compounds on thin-layer chromatographic plates. *J Chromatogr A*. 1981;216:413-416.
157. Feldman MA. *New Applications of Chemistry to Criminalistics: A. Recovering Fingerprints from Skin. B. Evidence in Tire Slashings*. Kansas State University; 1981.
158. Takayanagi M, Yashiro T. Development of a new colorimetric determination of hemoglobin in plasma. *Japanese Journal of Clinical Chemistry*. 1985;14(4):247-252.
159. Gifford RA. *Image enhancement techniques for degraded fingerprints*. Kansas State Univeristy; 1988.
160. Streeting CA, Chaseling J, Krosch MN, et al. A comparison of ABAcard® Hematrace® and RSIDTM-Blood tests on dried, diluted bloodstains treated with leucocrystal violet or luminol. *Australian Journal of Forensic Sciences*. 2020:1-11.
161. Swander CJ, Stites JG. Evaluation of the ABAcard HemaTrace for the forensic identification of human blood. presented at. *Midwest Assoc Forensic Scientists*. 1998
162. White WI. Benzidine substitute visualizing agents for iron porphyrins. *J Chromatogr A*. 1977;138(1):220-222.
163. Agrawal O, Sunita G, Gupta VK. A sensitive colorimetric method for the micro determination of iodine in marine water. *Talanta*. 1999;49(4):923-928. https://doi.org/10.1016/S0039-9140(99)00091-0.
164. Tiwari KK, Mundhara GL, Rai MK, et al. A simple and sensitive analytical method for the determination of antimony in environmental and biological samples. *Analytical sciences*. 2006;22(2):259-262.

165. Rae L, Gentles D, Farrugia KJ. An investigation into the enhancement of fingermarks in blood on fruit and vegetables. *Science & Justice*. 2013;53(3):321-327. https://doi.org/10.1016/j.scijus.2013.05.002.
166. Michaud AL, Brun-Conti L. A method for impregnating nylon transfer membranes with leucocrystal violet for enhancing and lifting bloody impressions. *Journal of Forensic Science*. 2004;49(3):JFS2003195-6.
167. Cullen S, Otto A, Cheetham P. Chemical enhancement of bloody footwear impressions from buried substrates. *J Forensic Identif.* 2010;60(1):45-86.
168. Larkin T, Gannicliffe C. Illuminating the health and safety of luminol. *Science & Justice*. 2008;48(2):71-75.
169. Schmitz A. *Uber des hydrazyde der trimensinsaure und der hemimellitsaure*. Heidelberg: Inaug. Dissert; 1902.
170. Curtius T, Semper A. Verhalten des 1-Äthylesters der 3-Nitro-benzol-1.2-dicarbonsäure gegen Hydrazin. *Berichte der deutschen chemischen Gesellschaft*. 1913;46(1):1162-1171. https://doi.org/10.1002/cber.191304601152.
171. Albrecht HO. Über die Chemiluminescenz des Aminoophthälsaurehydrazids. *Hoppe Seyler's Z Physiol Chem*. 1928;136:312.
172. Albrecht H. *Über die Chemiluminescenz von Aminophthalsäurehydrazid*. Leipzig: Akad. Verlagsges; 1928.
173. Harvey N. Luminescence during electrolysis. *The Journal of Physical Chemistry*. 1929;33(10):1456-1459. https://doi.org/10.1021/j150304a002.
174. Harvey N. Luminescenz während Elektrolyse. *Chemisches Zentralblatt*. 1929;II(25):3107.
175. Specht W. Die Chemiluminescenz des Hämins, ein Hilfsmittel zur Auffindung und Erkennung forensisch wichtiger Blutspuren. *Int J Leg Med*. 1937;28(1):225-234. https://doi.org/10.1007/bf01750491.
176. Huntress E, Stanley L, Parker A. The preparation of 3-Aminophthalhydrazide for use in the demonstration of chemiluminescence. *J Am Chem Soc*. 1934;56(1):241-242. https://doi.org/10.1021/ja01316a077.
177. Huntress EH, Stanley LN, Parker AS. The oxidation of 3-aminophthalhydrazide ("luminol") as a lecture demonstration of chemiluminescence. *Journal of Chemical Education*. 1934;11(3):142. https://doi.org/10.1021/ed011p142.
178. Nickolls LC. *The Scientific Investigation of Crime*. Butterworth; 1956.
179. Everse K, Menzel E. Blood print detection by fluorescence. *International Society for Optics and Photonics*. 1987:184-189.
180. Thornton J, Heye C. Fluorescence detection of bloodstain patterns. *International Society for Optics and Photonics*. 1987 190-190.
181. Gleu K, Pfannstiel K. Über 3-Aminophthalsäure-hydrazid. *Journal für Praktische Chemie*. 1936;146(5-7):137-150.
182. White EH, Bursey MM. Chemiluminescence of luminol and related hydrazides: the light emission step. *J Am Chem Soc*. 1964;86(5):941-942. https://doi.org/10.1021/ja01059a051.
183. White EH, Zafiriou O, Kagi HH, et al. Chemilunimescence of luminol: the chemcial reaction. *J Am Chem Soc*. 1964;86(5):940-941. https://doi.org/10.1021/ja01059a050.
184. Seitz WR, Neary MP. Chemiluminescence and Bioluminescence Analysis. In: Hercules DM, Hieftje GM, Snyder LR, Evenson MA, eds. *Contemporary Topics in Analytical and Clinical Chemistry: Volume 1*. Springer US; 1977:49-125.
185. Ponomarenko A, Popov B, Amelina L, et al. INGIBIROVANIE KHEMILYUMINESTSENTSII LYUMINOLA DOBAVKAMI NEKOTORYKH ORGANICHESKIKH SOEDINENII I ISPOLZOVANIE ETOGO EFFEKTA V ANALITICHESKIKH TSELYAKH. *ZHURNAL OBSHCHEI KHIMII*. 1964;34(12):4118-4118.
186. Gasparič J. Luminol. *Fresenius' Zeitschrift für analytische Chemie*. 1965;214(3): https://doi.org/10.1007/BF00518834. 201-201.
187. Thorpe GH, Kricka LJ, Moseley SB, et al. Phenols as enhancers of the chemiluminescent horseradish peroxidase- luminol-hydrogen peroxide reaction: application in luminescence- monitored enzyme immunoassays. *Clin Chem*. 1985;31(8):1335-1341.
188. Weber K. Die Anwendung der Chemiluminescenz des Luminols in der gerichtlichen Medizin und Toxikologie I. Der Nachweis von Blutspuren. *Dtsch Z Gesamte Gerichtl Med*. 1966;57(3):410-423.

189. Quickenden TI, Creamer JI. A study of common interferences with the forensic luminol test for blood. *Luminescence (Chichester)*. 2001;16(4):295-298. https://doi.org/10.1002/bio.657.
190. Irie S. The treatment of alopecia areata with 3-aminophthal-hydrazide. *Current Therapeutic Research, Clinical and Experimental*. 1960;2:107-110.
191. Irie S. Influence of 3-aminophthalhydrazide on the prothrombin time. *Current Therapeutic Research, Clinical and Experimental*. 1960;2:153-157.
192. Irie S. The treatment of wounds with 3-aminophthalhydrazide. *The American surgeon*. 1961;27:642-645.
193. Irie S. The treatment of wounds with 3-aminophthalhydrazide. *Plastic and Reconstructive Surgery*. 1962;29(1):89.
194. Lytle LT, Hedgecock DG. Chemiluminescence in visualization of forensic bloodstains. *J Forensic Sci*. 1978;23(3):550-562.
195. Grispino RR. The effect of luminol on the serological analysis of dried human bloodstains. *Crime Lab Digest*. 1990;17(1):13-23.
196. Laux DL. Effects of luminol on the subsequent analysis of bloodstains. *J Forensic Sci*. 1991;36(5):1512-1520.
197. Castelló A, Alvarez M, Verdú F. Accuracy, reliability, and safety of luminol in bloodstain investigation. *J Can Soc Forensic Sci*. 2002/01/01/2002;35(3):113-121. doi: https://doi.org/10.1080/00085030.2002.10757540.
198. Gross AM, Harris KA, Kaldun GL. The effect of luminol on presumptive tests and DNA analysis using the polymerase chain reaction. *J Forensic Sci*. 1999;44(4):837-840.
199. Quinones I, Sheppard D, Harbison S, et al. Comparative analysis of luminol formulations. *J Can Soc Forensic Sci*. 2007;40(2):53-63.
200. Seashols SJ, Cross HD, Shrader DL, et al. A comparison of chemical enhancements for the detection of latent blood. *J Forensic Sci*. 2013;58(1):130-133.
201. Patel G, Hopwood A. An evaluation of luminol formulations and their effect on DNA profiling. *Int J Leg Med*. 2013;127(4):723-729.
202. Castelló A, Francès F, Corella D, et al. Active oxygen doctors the evidence. *Naturwissenschaften*. 2009;96(2):303-307.
203. Castelló A, Francés F, Verdú F. Chemistry in crime investigation: sodium percarbonate effects on bloodstains detection. *J Forensic Sci*. 2012;57(2):500-502.
204. Kent EJM, Elliot DA, Miskelly GM. Inhibition of bleach-induced luminol chemiluminescence. *J Forensic Sci*. Jan 2003;48(1):64-67.
205. Plieth C. Peroxide-induced liberation of iron from heme switches catalysis during luminol reaction and causes loss of light and heterodyning of luminescence kinetics. *ACS Omega*. 2019;4(2):3268-3279. https://doi.org/10.1021/acsomega.8b03564.
206. Howard D, Chaseling J, Wright K. Detection of blood on clothing laundered with sodium percarbonate. *Forensic Sci Int*. 2019;302:109885.
207. Oldfield C, Morgan RM, Miles HF, et al. The efficacy of luminol in detecting bloodstains that have been washed with sodium percarbonate and exposed to environmental conditions. *Australian Journal of Forensic Sciences*. 2018;50(4):345-354. https://doi.org/10.1080/00450618.2016.1264478.
208. Vineyard AR, Hazelrigg EJ, Ehrhardt CJ, et al. Evaluation of Bluestar® Forensic Magnum and other traditional blood detection methods on bloodstained wood subjected to a variety of burn conditions. *J Forensic Sci*. 2019;64(3):878-887.
209. Klein A, Krebs O, Gehl A, et al. Detection of blood and DNA traces after thermal exposure. *Int J Leg Med*. 2018;132(4):1025-1033.
210. Brenzini V, Pathak R. A comparison study of the detection of bloodstains on painted and cleaned surfaces with luminol. *Forensic Sci Int*. 2018;289:75-82.
211. Nagesh D, Ghosh S. A time period study on the efficiency of luminol in the detection of bloodstains concealed by paint on different surfaces. *Forensic Sci Int*. 2017;275:1-7.
212. Blum LJ, Esperanca P. Rocquef S. A new high-performance reagent and procedure for latent bloodstain detection based on luminol chemiluminescence. *J Can Soc Forensic Sci*. 2006;39(3):81-100.
213. Dilbeck L. Use of Bluestar forensic in lieu of luminol at crime scenes. *J Forensic Identif*. 2006;56(5): 706-720.

214. Nicloux C, Bressler J. Effect of four latent blood visualization products on DNA. *Forensic Science Seminar*. 2014;4(1):30.
215. Pettolina M, Rainey J, Sanchez R. Using Bluestar forensic to detect latent bloodstains under coats of paint. *J Forensic Identif*. 2017;67(3):341.
216. Adams JL, Rancourt ED, Christensen AM. The effect of household oxidizing cleaners on chemiluminescence of blood using Bluestar®. *J Forensic Sci*. 2019;64(3):869-872.
217. Gomes C, López-Matayoshi C, Palomo-Díez S, et al. Presumptive tests: A substitute for Benzidine in blood samples recognition. *Forensic Sci Int Gen Sup Ser*. 2017;6:e546-e548. https://doi.org/10.1016/j.fsigss.2017.09.213.
218. Ruttan RF. On Derivatives of Tolidin and the Azotolidin Dyes. *Report of the British Association for the Advancement of Science* 1886;56th Meeting 1886:591.
219. Wreden F. Felix Wreden, aus St. Petersburg vom 2./14. und 13./25. April 1873. *Berichte der Deutschen Chemischen Gesellschaft*. 1873;6:556-557.
220. Ellms JW, Hauser SJ. Ortho-Tolidine as a reagent for the colorimetric estimation of small quantities of free chlorine. *Journal of Industrial & Engineering Chemistry*. 1913;5(11):915-917. https://doi.org/10.1021/ie50059a012.
221. Phelps EB, Shoub H. The determination of nitrate in sewage by means of ortho-tolidine. *Industrial & Engineering Chemistry*. 1917;9(8):767-770.
222. Ruttan RF, Hardisty RHM. A new reagent for detecting occult blood. *Can Med Assoc J*. 1912;2(11):995-998.
223. Zwarenstein H. A simple specific test for occult blood in urine. *Clin Proc*. 1943;2:125.
224. Zwarenstein H. Orthotolidine hydrochloride test for blood in urine. *Journal of Clinical Pathology*. 1949;2(2):145.
225. Barsotti M, Vigliani E. Bladder lesions from aromatic amines. Statistical considerations and prevention. *Arch Indust Hyg & Occupational Med*. 1952;5(3):234-241.
226. International Agency for Research on Cancer (IARC). *Agents Classified by the IARC Monographs, Volumes 1–125*. 2020:39.
227. Utz. Beitrag zum forensischen Nachweis von Blut. *Chemiker Zeitung*. 1903;27(94):1151-1152.
228. Kastle JH, Amos HL. *Variations in the Peroxidase Activity of the Blood in Health and Disease*. Vol. 31. 1906.
229. Kastle JH. *Chemical Tests for Blood*. Vol. 51. 1909.
230. Von Vamossy Z. Ueber ein neues Abführmittel (Purgen). *Therap d Gegenw*. 1902;4(May):201.
231. Abramowitz EW. Phenolphthalein today: a critical review. *Am J Dig Dis*. 1950;17(3):79-82.
232. Dunnick JK, Hailey JR. Phenolphthalein exposure causes multiple carcinogenic effects in experimental model systems. *Cancer Res*. 1996;56(21):4922-4926.
233. Sipe HJ, Corbett JT, Mason RP. In vitro free radical metabolism of phenolphthalein by peroxidases. *Drug Metab Dispos*. 1997;25(4):468-480.
234. Ravdin PM, van Beurden M, Jordan VC. Estrogenic effects of phenolphthalein on human breast cancer cells in vitro. *Breast Cancer Res Treat*. 1987;9(2):151-154.
235. Food U, Administration D. Laxative drug products for over-the-counter human use; proposed amendment to the tentative final monograph. *Fed Regist*. 1997 46223-7.
236. Coogan PF, Rosenberg L, Palmer JR, et al. Phenolphthalein laxatives and risk of cancer. *JNCI: Journal of the National Cancer Institute*. 2000;92(23):1943-1944. https://doi.org/10.1093/jnci/92.23.1943.
237. Nuttall GHF, Graham-Smith GS, Strangeways TSP. *Blood immunity and blood relationship; a demonstration of certain blood-relationships amongst animals by means of the precipitin test for blood*. University press; 1904.
238. Smith S, Cook HGH, Stewart CP. *Taylor's Principles And Practice Of Medical Jurisprudence*. vol 2. 10th ed. 104 Gloucester Place: Churchill Ltd; 1948.
239. Higaki R, Philp W. A study of the sensitivity, stability and specificity of phenolphthalein as an indicator test for blood. *J Can Soc Forensic Sci*. 1976;9(3):97-102.
240. Vennemann M, Scott G, Curran L, et al. Sensitivity and specificity of presumptive tests for blood, saliva and semen. *Forensic Sci Med Pathol*. 2014;10(1):69-75. https://doi.org/10.1007/s12024-013-9515-6.

241. Luedeke M, Miller E, Sprague JE. The effects of Bluestar® and luminol when used in conjunction with tetramethylbenzidine or phenolphthalein. *Forensic Sci Int*. 2016;262:156-159.
242. Petersen D, Kovacs F. Phenolphthalein false-positive reactions from legume root nodules. *J Forensic Sci*. 2014;59(2):481-484.
243. Lalonde W, Millman JS. Case study: loss of Kastle-Meyer test specificity on jeans. *Science & Justice*. 2019;59(3):359-361. https://doi.org/10.1016/j.scijus.2018.12.002.
244. Signaevsky M. The effect of household cleaning agents on blood and the suitability for screening using the phenolphthalein test. *J Forensic Identif*. 2019;69(1).
245. Stewart V, Deacon P, Zahra N, et al. The effect of mark enhancement techniques on the presumptive and confirmatory tests for blood. *Science & Justice*. 2018;58(6):386-396. https://doi.org/10.1016/j.scijus.2018.06.007.
246. Tontarski KL, Hoskins KA, Watkins TG, et al. Chemical enhancement techniques of bloodstain patterns and DNA recovery after fire exposure. *J Forensic Sci*. 2009;54(1):37-48.
247. Shibata S, Terao J, Matsushita S. Limitations of the method using peroxidase activity of hemoglobin for detecting lipid hydroperoxides. *Lipids*. 1986;21(12):792-795. https://doi.org/10.1007/bf02535414.
248. Zierdt WS, Zierdt CH. Occult blood testing using tetramethylbenzidine in an extraction procedure for patients on unrestricted diets. *Am J Clin Pathol*. 1985;83(4):486-488. https://doi.org/10.1093/ajcp/83.4.486.
249. Porstmann B, Evers U, Nugel E, et al. Tetramethylbenzidine—a chromogenic substrate for peroxidase in enzyme immunoassay. *Zeitschrift fur medizinische Laboratoriumsdiagnostik*. 1991;32(1):3-8.
250. Adams EC, Fetter MC, Free HM, et al. Hemolysis in hematuria. *The Journal of urology*. 1962;88(3):427-430.
251. Elder TR, Barry JL, Folcik PM, et al. Simplified test for hematuria. *Ann Intern Med*. 1962;56(6):957-959.
252. Poon H, Elliott J, Modler J, et al. The use of Hemastix® and the subsequent lack of DNA recovery using the Promega DNA IQTM system. *J Forensic Sci*. 2009;54(6):1278-1286. https://doi.org/10.1111/j.1556-4029.2009.01173.x.
253. Petersen D, Kaplan M. The use of Hemastix® severely reduces DNA recovery using the BioRobot® EZ1. *J Forensic Sci*. 2011;56(3):733-735.
254. Loy TH, Dixon EJ. Blood residues on fluted points from Eastern Beringia. *American Antiquity*. 1998;63(1):21-46. https://doi.org/10.2307/2694774.
255. De Vittori E, Barni F, Lewis SW, et al. Forensic application of a rapid one-step tetramethylbenzidine-based test for the presumptive trace detection of bloodstains at the crime scene and in the laboratory. *Forensic Chemistry*. 2016;2:63-74. https://doi.org/10.1016/j.forc.2016.10.002.
256. Laberke P, Hausmann R, Wiprächtiger N, et al. Analysis with the Combur Test—special aspects in forensic trace examination. *Archiv fur Kriminologie*. 2012;229(5-6):189-197.
257. Butler J, Chaseling J, Wright K. A comparison of four presumptive tests for the detection of blood on dark materials. *J Forensic Sci*. Nov 2019;64(6):1838-1843. https://doi.org/10.1111/1556-4029.14091.
258. Erdey L, Pickering WF, Wilson CL. Mixed chemiluminescent indicators. *Talanta*. 1962;9(4):371-375.
259. Ramsthaler F, Schlote J, Gehl A, et al. Detectability, visualization, and DNA analysis of bloodstains after repainting the walls. *Int J Leg Med*. 2018;132(6):1625-1634.
260. Mattson P, Bilous P. Coomassie brilliant blue: an excellent reagent for the enhancement of faint bloody fingerprints. *J Can Soc Forensic Sci*. 2014;47(1):20-36. https://doi.org/10.1080/00085030.2014.885728.
261. Landsteiner K. Zur Kenntnis der antifermentativen, lytischen und agglutinierenden Wirkungen des Blutserums und der Lymphe. *Zentralbl Bakteriol*. 1900;27:357-362.
262. Landsteiner K. Agglutination phenomena in normal human blood. *Wien Klin Wochenschr*. 1901;14 1132-4.
263. Uhlenhuth PT. Eine Methode zur Unterscheidung der verschiedenen Blutarten, im besonderen zum differentialdiagnostischen Nachweise des Menschenblutes. *Dtsch Med Wochenschr*. 1901;27(6):82-83.
264. RSID™. Rapid Stain Identification of Human Blood (RSID™-Blood) Technical Information and Protocol Sheet 2016:2.
265. Johnston S, Newman J, Frappier R. Validation study of the abacus diagnostics ABAcard® HemaTrace® membrane test for the forensic identification of human blood. *J Can Soc Forensic Sci*. 2003;36(3).
266. Human Diagnostics Worldwide. Design Verification and Product Data for HEXAGON OBTI. 2018; Rev. 0012

267. Hermon D, Shpitzen M, Oz C, et al. The use of the Hexagon OBTI test for detection of human blood at crime scenes and on items of evidence Part I: validation studies and implementation. *J Forensic Identif.* 2003;53(5):566-575.
268. Stadler C, Dias Filho C, Roca MG. Cross reaction and forensic comparison of blood testing done by private and public sector laboratories. *Rev Bras Crimin.* 2017;6:31-37.
269. Hochmeister MN, Budowle B, Sparkes R, et al. Validation studies of an immunochromatographic 1-step test for the forensic identification of human blood. *J Forensic Sci.* 1999;44(3):597-602.
270. Tobe SS, Daeid Nic. N. Commentary on: Comparison of presumptive blood test kits including Hexagon OBTI. *J Forensic Sci.* 2009;54(1):239.
271. Gascho D, Morf NV, Thali MJ, et al. The use of immunochromatographic rapid test for soft tissue remains identification in order to distinguish between human and non-human origin. *Science & Justice.* 2017;57(3):165-168. https://doi.org/10.1016/j.scijus.2017.02.006.
272. BLUESTAR®. BLUESTAR® OBTI - Verification Report. 2021:5.
273. SERATEC. SERATEC® HemDirect - User Manual. 2019:2.
274. Misencik A, Laux DL. Validation Study of the Seratec HemDirect Hemoglobin Assay for the Forensic Identification of Human Blood. *MAFS Newsletter.* 2007;Spring 2007:18-26.
275. Schweers BA, Old J, Boonlayangoor PW, et al. Developmental validation of a novel lateral flow strip test for rapid identification of human blood (Rapid Stain Identification™-Blood). *Forensic Sci Int Gen.* 2008;2(3):243-247.
276. Dogaroiu C, Diac I, Petca A, et al. A comparison between rapid stain identification-blood (RSID-blood) and faecal occult blood test (FOB) to identify human blood on various suspicious stains. *Rom J Leg Med.* 2019;27:373-378.
277. Della Manna A, Montpetit S. A novel approach to obtaining reliable PCR results from luminol treated bloodstains. *J Forensic Sci.* 2000;45(4):886-890.
278. Holtkötter H, Dias Filho CR, Schwender K, et al. Forensic differentiation between peripheral and menstrual blood in cases of alleged sexual assault—validating an immunochromatographic multiplex assay for simultaneous detection of human hemoglobin and D-dimer. *Int J Leg Med.* 2018;132(3):683-690.
279. Barbaro A, Cormaci P, Votano S, et al. Evaluation study about the SERATEC® rapid tests. *Forensic Sci Int Gen Sup Ser.* 2015;5:e63-e64. https://doi.org/10.1016/j.fsigss.2015.09.025.
280. Johnston E, Ames CE, Dagnall KE, et al. Comparison of presumptive blood test kits including Hexagon OBTI. *J Forensic Sci.* 2008;53(3):687-689.
281. Spear TF, Binkley SA. The HemeSelect™ test: a simple and sensitive forensic species test. *J Forensic Sci Soc.* 1994;34(1):41-46.
282. Andrade AFB, Siqueira MECG, Arantes LC, et al. Forensic identification of human blood: comparison of two one-step presumptive tests for blood screening of crime scene samples. *Revista Brasileira de Criminalística.* 2014;3(1):12-15.
283. Jain P, Singh H. Detection and origin of blood stains on various types of cloth immersed in water for a prolonged period. *J Can Soc Forensic Sci.* 1984;17(2):58-61.
284. Stojanović I. Detection of bloodstains on cotton fabric after washing. *Acta Medica Medianae.* 2019;58(1): 24-27.
285. Spector J, Von Gemmingen D. The effect of washing on the detection of blood and seminal stains. *J Can Soc Forensic Sci.* 1971;4(1):3-9. https://doi.org/10.1080/00085030.1971.10757279.
286. Cox M. Effect of fabric washing on the presumptive identification of bloodstains. *J Forensic Sci.* 1990;35(6):1335-1341.
287. Vaughan J. The effects of Bluestar on the Kastle-Meyer presumptive test for blood. *J Forensic Identif.* 2011;61(1):38.
288. Mushtaq S, Rasool N, Firiyal S. Detection of dry bloodstains on different fabrics after washing with commercially available detergents. *Australian Journal of Forensic Sciences.* 2016;48(1):87-94. https://doi.org/10.1080/00450618.2015.1029971.
289. Glaister J. The Kastle-Meyer test for the detection of blood. *Br Med J.* 1926;1(3406):650-652. https://doi.org/10.1136/bmj.1.3406.650.

290. Pozzi-Escot M. Emploi de la phénolphtaline comme réactif sur sang. *Bull Soc Chim Belg*. 1908;22(11): 415-416.
291. Richard MLL, Harper KA, Craig RL, et al. Evaluation of mRNA marker specificity for the identification of five human body fluids by capillary electrophoresis. *Forensic Sci Int Gen*. 2012;6(4):452-460.
292. Simon JB. Occult blood screening for colorectal carcinoma: a critical review. *Gastroenterology*. 1985;88(3):820-837.
293. Thorogate R, Moreira JCS, Jickells S, et al. A novel fluorescence-based method in forensic science for the detection of blood in situ. *Forensic Sci Int Gen*. 2008;2(4):363-371.
294. Orphanou CMR. *A bioanalytical approach to forensic body fluid identification & age determination*. Staffordshire University; 2015.
295. Hanson EK, Ballantyne J. A blue spectral shift of the hemoglobin soret band correlates with the age (time since deposition) of dried bloodstains. *PLoS One*. 2010;5(9):e12830.
296. Li B, Beveridge P, O'Hare WT, et al. The application of visible wavelength reflectance hyperspectral imaging for the detection and identification of blood stains. *Science & Justice*. 2014;54(6):432-438. https://doi.org/10.1016/j.scijus.2014.05.003.
297. Shaine ML, Premasiri WR, Ingraham HM, et al. Surface enhanced Raman scattering for robust, sensitive detection and confirmatory identification of dried bloodstains. *Analyst*. 2020;145(18):6097-6110. https://doi.org/10.1039/D0AN01132K.
298. Patel E, Cicatiello P, Deininger L, et al. A proteomic approach for the rapid, multi-informative and reliable identification of blood. *Analyst*. 2016;141(1):191-198.
299. Zadora G, Menżyk A. In the pursuit of the holy grail of forensic science–Spectroscopic studies on the estimation of time since deposition of bloodstains. *TrAC Trends in Analytical Chemistry*. 2018;105: 137-165.
300. Pfaff. Ueber die Bestimmung des Alters der Blutflecke in Criminalfällen. *Vierteljahrsschrift Für Gerichtliche Medizin Und Öffentliches Sanitätswesen*. 1862;26:266-276.
301. Grigorescu G. Sur la possibilite de distinguer les hematies de L'homme des hematies des autres mammiferes. *Comptes rendus des séances de la Société de biologie et de ses filiales*. 1892;Ser. 9(T4):325-327.
302. Tamassia A. Determinazione cronologica delle macchie di sangue. *Atti del Regio Istituto veneto di scienze, lettere ed arti*. 1884;Ser. 6 t. 2:1-22.
303. Laan N, Smith F, Nicloux C, et al. Morphology of drying blood pools. *Forensic Sci Int*. 2016/10/01/2016;267:104-109. doi: https://doi.org/10.1016/j.forsciint.2016.08.005
304. Agudelo J, Halámková L, Brunelle E, et al. Ages at a crime scene: simultaneous estimation of the time since deposition and age of its originator. *Anal Chem*. 2016;88(12):6479-6484.
305. Arany S, Ohtani S. Age estimation of bloodstains: a preliminary report based on aspartic acid racemization rate. *Forensic Sci Int*. 2011;212(1-3):e36-e39.
306. Agudelo J, Huynh C, Halámek J. Forensic determination of blood sample age using a bioaffinity-based assay. *Analyst*. 2015;140(5):1411-1415.
307. Stotesbury T, Cossette M-L, Newell-Bell T, et al. An Exploratory Time Since Deposition Analysis of Whole Blood Using Metrics of DNA Degradation and Visible Absorbance Spectroscopy. *Pure & Applied Geophysics*. 2021;178(3).
308. Cossette M-L, Stotesbury T, Shafer AB. Quantifying visible absorbance changes and DNA degradation in aging bloodstains under extreme temperatures. *Forensic Sci Int*. 2021;318:110627.
309. Anderson S, Howard B, Hobbs GR, et al. A method for determining the age of a bloodstain. *Forensic Sci Int*. 2005;148(1):37-45.
310. Anderson SE, Hobbs GR, Bishop CP. Multivariate analysis for estimating the age of a bloodstain. *J Forensic Sci*. 2011;56(1):186-193.
311. Asaghiar F, Williams GA. Evaluating the use of hypoxia sensitive markers for body fluid stain age prediction. *Science & Justice*. 2020;60(6):547-554.
312. Fu J, Allen RW. A method to estimate the age of bloodstains using quantitative PCR. *Forensic Sci Int Gen*. 2019;39:103-108.
313. Sirker M, Schneider PM, Gomes I. A 17-month time course study of human RNA and DNA degradation in body fluids under dry and humid environmental conditions. *Int J Leg Med*. 2016;130(6):1431-1438.

314. Bird TAG, Walton-Williams L, Williams G. Time since deposition of biological fluids using RNA degradation. *Forensic Sci Int Gen Sup Ser*. 2019;7(1):401-402.
315. Heneghan N, Fu J, Pritchard J, et al. The effect of environmental conditions on the rate of RNA degradation in dried blood stains. *Forensic Sci Int Gen*. 2021;51:102456.
316. Bauer M, Polzin S, Patzelt D. Quantification of RNA degradation by semi-quantitative duplex and competitive RT-PCR: a possible indicator of the age of bloodstains? *Forensic Sci Int*. 2003;138(1-3):94-103. doi: https://doi.org/10.1016/j.forsciint.2003.09.008.
317. Alshehhi S, McCallum NA, Haddrill PR. Quantification of RNA degradation of blood-specific markers to indicate the age of bloodstains. *Forensic Sci Int Gen Sup Ser*. 2017;6:e453-e455.
318. Andrasko J. The estimation of age of bloodstains by HPLC analysis. *Journal of Forensic Science*. 1997;42(4):601-607.
319. Inoue H, Takabe F, Iwasa M, et al. A new marker for estimation of bloodstain age by high performance liquid chromatography. *Forensic Sci Int*. 1992;57(1):17-27.
320. Inoue H, Takabe F, Iwasa M, et al. Identification of fetal hemoglobin and simultaneous estimation of bloodstain age by high-performance liquid chromatography. *Int J Leg Med*. 1991;104(3):127-131.
321. Lee Y-R, Lee J, Seok AE, et al. Internal standard metabolites for obtaining absolute quantitative information on the components of bloodstains by standardization of samples. *Forensic Sci Int*. 2019;294:69-75.
322. Seok AE, Lee J, Lee Y-R, et al. Estimation of age of bloodstains by mass-spectrometry: a metabolomic approach. *Anal Chem*. 2018;90(21):12431-12441.
323. Rankin-Turner S, Turner MA, Kelly PF, et al. Transforming presumptive forensic testing: in situ identification and age estimation of human bodily fluids. *Chemical science*. 2019;10(4):1064-1069.
324. Rust L, Nizio KD, Forbes SL. The influence of ageing and surface type on the odour profile of blood-detection dog training aids. *Anal Bioanal Chem*. 2016;408(23):6349-6360.
325. Bergmann T, Heinke F, Labudde D. Towards substrate-independent age estimation of blood stains based on dimensionality reduction and k-nearest neighbor classification of absorbance spectroscopic data. *Forensic Sci Int*. 2017;278:1-8.
326. Hanson E, Albornoz A, Ballantyne J. Validation of the hemoglobin (Hb) hypsochromic shift assay for determination of the time since deposition (TSD) of dried bloodstains. *Forensic Sci Int Gen Sup Ser*. 2011;3(1):e307-e308.
327. Kumar R, Sharma K, Sharma V. Bloodstain age estimation through infrared spectroscopy and Chemometric models. *Science & Justice*. 2020;60(6):538-546.
328. Lin H, Zhang Y, Wang Q, et al. Species identification of bloodstains by ATR-FTIR spectroscopy: the effects of bloodstain age and the deposition environment. *Int J Leg Med*. 2018;132(3):667-674.
329. Lin H, Zhang Y, Wang Q, et al. Estimation of the age of human bloodstains under the simulated indoor and outdoor crime scene conditions by ATR-FTIR spectroscopy. *Scientific Reports*. 2017;7(1):1-9.
330. Zhang Y, Wang Q, Li B, et al. Changes in attenuated total reflection Fourier transform infrared spectra as blood dries out. *J Forensic Sci*. 2017;62(3):761-767.
331. Guo K, Achilefu S, Berezin MY. Dating bloodstains with fluorescence lifetime measurements. *Chemistry (Weinheim an der Bergstrasse, Germany)*. 2012;18(5):1303.
332. Guo K, Zhegalova N, Achilefu S, et al. Bloodstain age analysis: toward solid state fluorescent lifetime measurements. *International Society for Optics and Photonics*. 2013:857214.
333. Mc Shine S, Suhling K, Beavil A, et al. The applicability of fluorescence lifetime to determine the time since the deposition of biological stains. *Analytical Methods*. 2017;9(13):2007-2013.
334. Wójtowicz A, Weber A, Wietecha-Posłuszny R, et al. Probing menstrual bloodstain aging with fluorescence spectroscopy. *Spectrochimica Acta Part A: Molecular and Biomolecular Spectroscopy*. 2021;248:119172.
335. Wang Q, Teng G, Zhao Y, et al. Identification and determination of the bloodstains dry time in the crime scenes using laser-induced breakdown spectroscopy. *IEEE Photonics Journal*. 2019;11(3):1-12.
336. Bremmer RH, De Bruin DM, De Joode M, et al. Biphasic oxidation of oxy-hemoglobin in bloodstains. *PloS one*. 2011;6(7):e21845.
337. Li B, Beveridge P, O'Hare WT, et al. The estimation of the age of a blood stain using reflectance spectroscopy with a microspectrophotometer, spectral pre-processing and linear discriminant analysis. *Forensic Sci Int*. 2011;212(1-3):198-204.

338. Sun H, Dong Y, Zhang P, et al. Accurate age estimation of bloodstains based on visible reflectance spectroscopy and chemometrics methods. *IEEE Photonics Journal*. 2017;9(1):1-14.
339. Wellington E. *Effects of Different Haematocrit Values on Estimation of Time since Deposition of Human Blood Stains Using Diffuse Reflectance Spectroscopy*. Murdoch University; 2017.
340. Bremmer RH, Nadort A, Van Leeuwen TG, et al. Age estimation of blood stains by hemoglobin derivative determination using reflectance spectroscopy. *Forensic Sci Int*. 2011;206(1-3):166-171.
341. Li B, Beveridge P, O'Hare WT, et al. The age estimation of blood stains up to 30 days old using visible wavelength hyperspectral image analysis and linear discriminant analysis. *Science & Justice*. 2013;53(3):270-277. doi: https://doi.org/10.1016/j.scijus.2013.04.004.
342. Patterson D. Use of reflectance measurements in assessing the colour changes of ageing bloodstains. *Nature*. 1960/08/01/1960;187(4738):688-689. doi: https://doi.org/10.1038/187688a0.
343. Cavalcanti D, Silva L. Application of atomic force microscopy in the analysis of time since deposition (TSD) of red blood cells in bloodstains: a forensic analysis. *Forensic Sci Int*. 2019;301:254-262.
344. Strasser S, Zink A, Kada G, et al. Age determination of blood spots in forensic medicine by force spectroscopy. *Forensic Sci Int*. 2007;170(1):8-14.
345. Zheng J, Wen H, Zhang B, et al. Development of integrated device of trace bloodstains imaging and age analysis. *Fa yi xue za zhi*. 2019;35(2):230-233.
346. Choi W, Shin J, Hyun K-A, et al. Highly sensitive and accurate estimation of bloodstain age using smartphone. *Biosensors and Bioelectronics*. 2019;130:414-419.
347. Shin J, Choi S, Yang J-S, et al. Smart forensic phone: colorimetric analysis of a bloodstain for age estimation using a smartphone. *Sensors and Actuators B: Chemical*. 2017;243:221-225.
348. Thanakiatkrai P, Yaodam A, Kitpipit T. Age estimation of bloodstains using smartphones and digital image analysis. *Forensic Sci Int*. 2013;233(1-3):288-297.
349. Aalders M, Wilk L. Investigating the Age of Blood Traces: How Close Are We to Finding the Holy Grail of Forensic Science?. In: Francese S, ed. *Emerging Technologies for the Analysis of Forensic Traces*. Springer International Publishing; 2019:109-128.
350. Weber AR, Lednev IK. Crime clock–Analytical studies for approximating time since deposition of bloodstains. *Forensic Chemistry*. 2020;19:100248.
351. Bremmer RH, de Bruin KG, van Gemert MJ, et al. Forensic quest for age determination of bloodstains. *Forensic Sci Int*. 2012;216(1-3):1-11.
352. Edelman GJ, Aalders MC. Blood degradation and bloodstain age estimation. *Taphonomy of Human Remains: Forensic Analysis of the Dead and the Depositional Environment: Forensic Analysis of the Dead and the Depositional Environment*. 2017:53-64.
353. Bremmer RH. *Non-contact spectroscopic age determination of bloodstains*. Universiteit van Amsterdam [Host]; 2011.
354. Edelman G, Manti V, van Ruth SM, et al. Identification and age estimation of blood stains on colored backgrounds by near infrared spectroscopy. *Forensic Sci Int*. 2012;220(1-3):239-244.
355. Das T, Harshey A, Nigam K, et al. Analytical approaches for bloodstain aging by vibrational spectroscopy: Current trends and future perspectives. *Microchem J*. 2020:105278.
356. Doty KC, McLaughlin G, Lednev IK. A Raman "spectroscopic clock" for bloodstain age determination: the first week after deposition. *Anal Bioanal Chem*. 2016;408(15):3993-4001.
357. Doty KC, Muro CK, Lednev IK. Predicting the time of the crime: bloodstain aging estimation for up to two years. *Forensic Chemistry*. 2017;5:1-7.
358. Menżyk A, Damin A, Martyna A, et al. Toward a novel framework for bloodstains dating by Raman spectroscopy: how to avoid sample photodamage and subsampling errors. *Talanta*. 2020;209:120565.
359. O'Connor M, Jansen K, Hodge J, et al. Shedding new light on forensic timelines. *Article. Spectroscopy*. 2016/09/2016;31(9):40-45.
360. Sun H, Meng Y, Zhang P, et al. Non-invasive prediction of bloodstain age using the principal component and a back propagation artificial neural network. *Laser Physics Letters*. 2017;14(9):095601.
361. Takamura A, Watanabe D, Shimada R, et al. Comprehensive modeling of bloodstain aging by multivariate Raman spectral resolution with kinetics. *Communications Chemistry*. 2019;2(1):1-10.

CHAPTER 4

Semen

Introduction

The requirements for testing for semen arise from sexual assaults, which are usually unwitnessed crimes, and because of the nature of the serological evidence associated with these types of assaults, they can be difficult to investigate. Almost two-thirds of cases submitted for DNA analysis in the United States involve sexual assault evidence.[1] Although sexual assaults without male ejaculation are common, the presence of semen can corroborate victim allegations and indicate if sexual activity has occurred. DNA profiling of the sperm can help to identify unknown perpetrators (if a suspect is known, or a match on a DNA database is found), or it can be used to link different assaults and can indicate that ejaculation has taken place. Studies have also shown that screening evidence for semen is recommended even if victim recollection does not indicate ejaculation because of the trauma surrounding the assault.[2] Therefore the need to locate and characterize semen is important because it may provide strong probative value to a case.

Conversely, although detection of sperm (spermatozoa [pl.], spermatozoon [sing.]) is considered proof of ejaculation, the finding of semen does not in itself indicate a crime. If an accused claims intercourse was consensual, then this can reduce the probative value of seminal evidence if identified. Often other medical, serological, and toxicological tests (e.g., drugs or alcohol) are part of and essential to sexual assault investigations to support or refute allegations, although semen still plays a central role in such cases.

Much of the current forensic knowledge surrounding aspects of semen identification, detection, and persistence is based on either summaries of casework results or has been adapted from fertility studies. Casework-based results[3–8] can pose difficulties in that the actual nature of the samples is usually not known or cannot be confirmed. This means that if semen is not detected in a rape allegation, there may not have been any semen present to begin with (i.e., no ejaculation), but it may be reported as a false negative with testing because semen may have been expected. Fertility studies, conversely, may have abnormal starting sperm concentrations or will have volunteers who are trying to retain semen and sperm for impregnation. The results of these two different types of studies therefore report a wide range of detection limits in terms of sensitivities and persistence.

Forensic Serology. DOI: http://doi.org/10.1016/B978-0-12-812968-5.00004-0

The presence of semen in the vaginal cavity can provide evidence of intercourse, and the quantity and condition of the spermatozoa can give an indication of when intercourse may have occurred.[4] Most forensic laboratories, however, do not evaluate spermatozoa for motility (virtually all samples are on immotile spermatozoa) and are in fact more interested with whether spermatozoon tails are present or the proportion of spermatozoa with tails in a sample. Presumptive tests for semen must detect a component in semen not found in the everyday environment, and this is usually carried out using biochemical tests targeting substances that are found in semen at high levels but are not exclusive to semen.[9] Additionally, they should not rely on the presence or absence of spermatozoa (sperm) to indicate a positive because some males may be azoospermatic (have no measurable or detectable sperm) or oligospermatic (have low sperm counts) for a variety of reasons, including drug use, genetic defects, or through vasectomy. Other sexual dysfunction can also be the cause of lack of findings.[10] Even if an individual is azoospermatic, ejaculation is still possible; if this occurs, then seminal fluid will be released. Analysis of suspected semen stains is therefore generally based on testing for substances found in seminal fluid, but which may also be found at lower levels in other tissue types.

When testing for the presence of semen, there is a standard sequence of testing that is carried out (Fig. 4.1); however, each laboratory will have its own standard operating procedures and protocols in place. The sequence of testing will depend on the item of evidence received by the laboratory, with some tests bypassed for certain evidence types.

Studies into the nature of semen have been ongoing since at least the time of da Vinci (circa 1480), who incorrectly described where semen originated (i.e., partly from the spinal cord).[11] Most of the testing used in forensic science to identify semen and spermatozoa is based on medical investigations into the biological nature of procreation and the detection of cancers. The main presumptive testing used for semen was developed for detection of elevated levels of certain substances in blood, which were indicative of cancer of the prostate.[12–14] Other major research has arisen from the medical need to identify causes and indications of infertility.[15–17] Forensic science has capitalized on those studies to create a series of testing that in combination can conclusively identify if a sample is semen (so long as spermatozoa are present).

History

Theoretical (nonmicroscopic) speculations about the biological properties of sperm were abundant in the 17th century based around disputes between animalculists and ovists (people who believed that embryos are preformed in the sperm or ovum, respectively).[18,19] Sperm cells, however, were first observed by van Lewenhoeck in 1677, using his custom-designed microscope and lenses.[20] He observed both rabbit and canine spermatozoa (Fig. 4.2), and subsequently other animals, and he provided the first details as to the structure of sperm cells. According to translations by Kempers,[21] Lewenhoeck was able to accurately describe

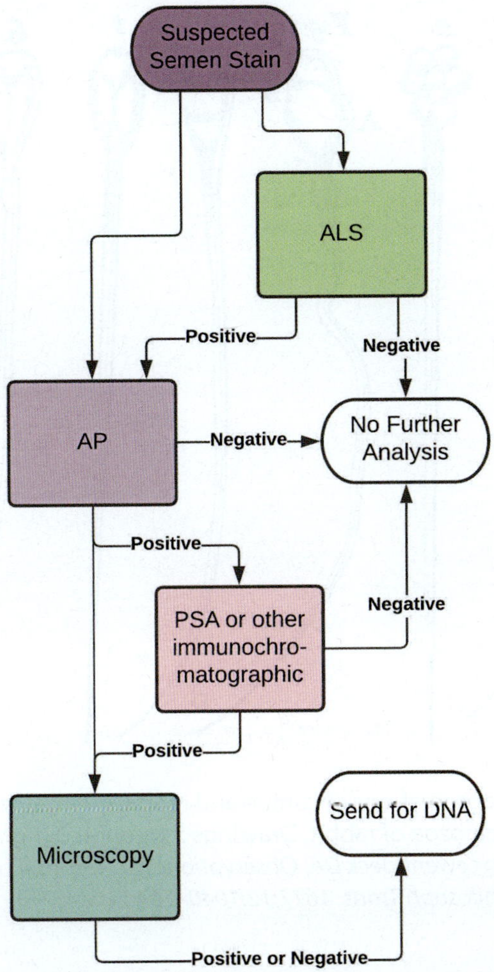

Fig. 4.1 A schematic of the current workflow when testing for suspected semen. Laboratories have different protocols and procedures, and this is not a representation of the process carried out everywhere. It is usual for the Acid Phosphatase *(AP)* test to be attempted prior to immunochromatographic tests because of its lower cost, speed, and ease of use. Alternate light sources *(ALS)* may be used if large areas of an item need to be screened, but this method is generally not used for swabs. Circumstances surrounding the alleged crime will dictate the exact workflow. Most laboratories consider the immunochromatographic tests as confirmatory but will still undertake microscopic examination for spermatozoa. If AP and immunochromatographic tests are positive, but no spermatozoa are identified through microscopy, samples will still usually be sent for DNA because of the possibility of male DNA persisting. *PSA*, Prostate specific antigen.

spermatozoon in terms of number, size, and movement. The accuracy demonstrated by Lewenhoeck over 350 years ago in the measurements and movement of human sperm cells is still valid today, although observed with more modern equipment. The movement of live spermatozoa has only recently been revised,[22] indicating a three-dimensional movement (spinning tail somewhat like a propeller) rather than in two dimensions (back and forth like

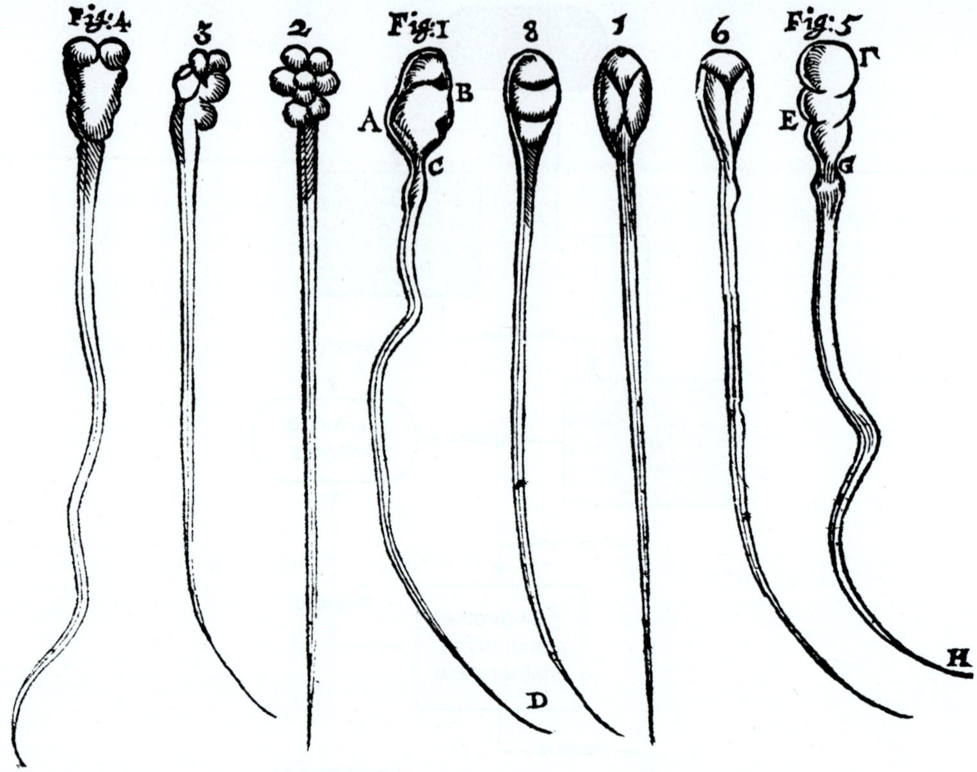

Fig. 4.2 Lewenhoeck's first observations of canine and rabbit spermatozoa. Drawings 1 through 4 (left half of image) are spermatozoa of rabbit. Drawings 5 through 8 (right half of image) are spermatozoa from dog. *From Lewenhoeck DA, Observationes D. Anthonii Lewenhoeck, De Natis E Semine Genitali Aimalculis. Philosoph Trans. 1677;12:1040–1046.*

a fish tail). Further observations of sperm confirming those of Lewenhoeck and identifying sperm cells in other animals were subsequently made by Buffon,[23] Spallanzani,[24] Gleichen,[25] and Prevost and Dumas.[26,27] It was noted that the form of the spermatozoon was "so peculiar that, when once well seen and examined, they cannot be mistaken for any other substance, vegetable or animal, nor, with ordinary care, can any vegetable fibres be mistaken for them."[28]

The earliest record of semen used in a legal framework comes from a Latin text in 1720.[29] The work claims to deal with legal aspects of spermatozoa but focuses on a wide variety of other aspects, including castration, herniotomy, phimosis, circumcision, and hermaphrodites and gender change. Work in 1826 by Ollivier and Barruel[30] describes a case in which, using a complicated system of tests, they concluded that a stain was likely semen. However, the first detailed legal need to identify semen is described by Orfila in 1827,[31] although he indicates the need for semen identification had been required in many cases prior to his report. Orfila described the need to identify semen on linen as opposed to fat or discharge (due to venereal or other disease) and stated that other physicians had also been asked to provide their opinion on similar cases. Examination involved looking at the color, odor, texture when rubbed between fingers, and effect of heating with a candle flame. Orfila claimed that spermatozoa could not be microscopically identified from dried stains (if their tails are removed), only if fresh (moving) or deposited and dried directly on a slide (tails would still be present). He stated he was able to positively observe spermatozoa after 18 years dried on a slide.[31]

In 1837, Rattier[32] described a method to extract spermatozoa from fabric by soaking it in water and scraping the stain. He claimed that at least some of the cells were recovered intact with tails that can be observed microscopically. In the same year, it was reported that spermatozoa could "live very well" in blood, milk, normal state vaginal and uterine mucus, and the purulent matter of gonorrhea.[33] It was determined that they do not survive in saliva, urine, and too acidic vaginal and uterine environments, and that spermatozoa are not found in urine except immediately after ejaculation.

Further research to isolate spermatozoa from fabric without breaking their tails was accomplished by means of a complicated filtrations process using multiple steps and reagents but was able to microscopically observe intact spermatozoa.[34] The advance in recovery of intact spermatozoa from dried stains was by not rubbing or pressing the stain once immersed in water and allowing the cells to break free without force, thereby keeping them intact.

Schmidt[35] described a complicated process of looking at dried seminal stains under various conditions before extracting the stain in water and observing it under a microscope to visualize spermatozoa. A volume was published in 1854 that explored the detailed attributes of semen and spermatozoa at that time, summarizing general characteristics of spermatozoa from different animals; effects of water, acid, and alcohol on semen; microscopic examination; differences in semen at different stages of life; differentiating semen from other stains (e.g., syphilitic vaginal mucus); and many other aspects of semen in legal and medical frameworks.[36]

Most of the work in the following years focused on differentiating seminal stains from other stains of similar appearance (albumin, paste glue, starch, gelatine, or dextrin gum), usually by heating the substrate and stain and observing the results, with microscopic identification of spermatozoa carried out for confirmation.[37] Color, texture, and appearance under different lights (daylight vs. candle) played important investigative roles prior to microscopic examination, always using a soaked stain to rehydrate and remove without damage any spermatozoa that may have been present.[38,39] Also of particular importance was the ability to remove spermatozoa from fabric for microscopic examination, which continued to be problematic and was continually revised in methodology in terms of liquids used, time soaked, and scraping or rubbing the stains, among other things. Even using these basic techniques and early rudimentary microscopes, surprisingly detailed images and descriptions of spermatozoa could be made from evidence (Fig. 4.3).

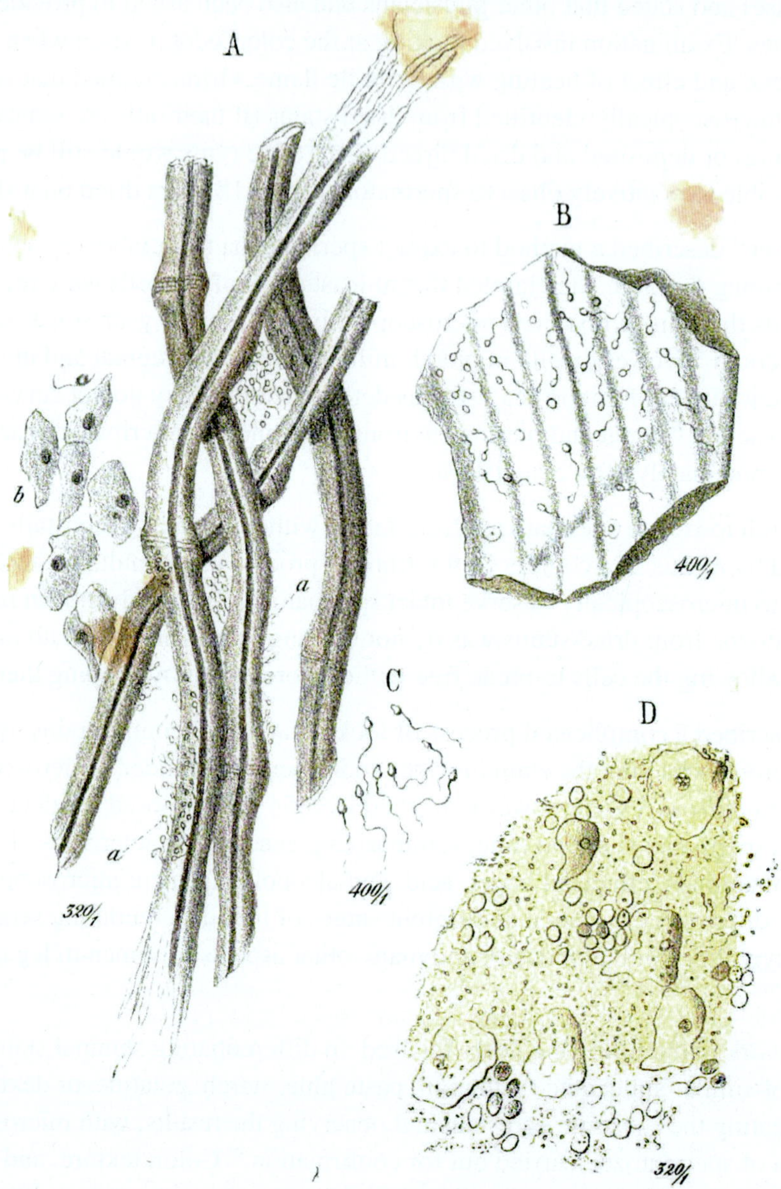

Fig. 4.3 A plate from an 1870 work by Carl Ricker.[40] (A) Linen fibers from a patch on a shirt from a rape case in 1861: (a) spermatozoa adhering to fibers; (b) epithelial cells 320× in water with a drop of ammonia. (B) A semen stain from 1859 spotted on a slide; the dark stripes are imprints of the fibers at 400× moistened with water. (C) Semen from fresh human sperm at 400×. (D) Particles of a spot from a woman's shirt, on which pus, mucus, and epithelial cells were found at 320× in water. *From Ricker C. Anleitung zür Untersuchung Verdächtiger Flecke: Für Artze und Juristen. St. Petersburg: Jahre; 1870:64.*

These methods of separating the spermatozoa from the substrate were considered important because, in part due to the technology at the time, some vegetable fibers (incorporated as part of the fabrics, particularly hemp) could form structures similar to detached spermatozoon head or tail, thus causing confusion.[41] These extraneous objects were similar enough to confuse even those thoroughly experienced in spermatozoa identification.[42]

Around this time, it was also noticed that some men had no spermatozoa in their ejaculate, and they were considered azoospermiatic (see later).[43,44] This was investigated looking at apparently healthy and strong individuals with no spermatozoa who were living, suddenly deceased, or deceased of known conditions; however, no reason could be found to account for the condition. As early as 1867,[45] there was need for a method to identify semen that was independent of spermatozoa, similar to the chemical means of blood identification, and this persisted well into the 20th century[42,46–48] until the first method was developed.

In 1867, it was first reported by Roussin[45] that spermatozoa could be stained for easier identification, which he accomplished using iodine, potassium iodide, and water. He stated that part of the difficulty of identifying spermatozoa was that the bodies were transparent in addition to being very small, and only through trial and error of the lighting could they previously be visualized until the staining was used (Fig. 4.4). Other authors determined that using iodine colored many other plant and cellular substances beyond the spermatozoa, serving only to prevent refringence in examination.[41] Longuet therefore tried all histology stains of the time and found that carmine was the best stain, but he also found that it worked better with older (>5 days) stains.[41,49] A review of work that was claimed to be from Petel and Labiche* indicates that the carmine staining was also suggested as a chemical test to identify semen stains, but the authors found this was not suitable, although its use in staining spermatozoa for microscopic identification was supported.[44]

As staining methods became accepted and recognized, other stains and applications were attempted. Picric acid as a means to identify semen was suggested in the 1880s[50,51] to define seminal stains, although differences between young and older men's semen were noted as a factor affecting the test. Despite Longuet's findings, the iodine test continued to be used,[51] and in 1875, Cauvet[52] investigated a sexual assault and examined mixed stains of what he presumed to be blood mixed with either semen or vaginal mucus using Roussin's staining method. He was able to identify spermatozoa in multiple stains as well as other cellular material from vaginal epithelial cells, blood cells, and mucus. Variations of the method were suggested using, for example, less iodine, and it was noted that crystals also formed that were very similar in appearance to hemin crystals,[42,53] although this was not observed by Roussin. It was determined that these crystals form even if fragments or whole spermatozoa are not

*The first use of carmine for staining spermatozoa is often credited to Petel and Labiche (1877) (by Vogel et al.), but no paper exits by those authors or in the journal or volume that is cited. Longuet published a year prior, in 1876.

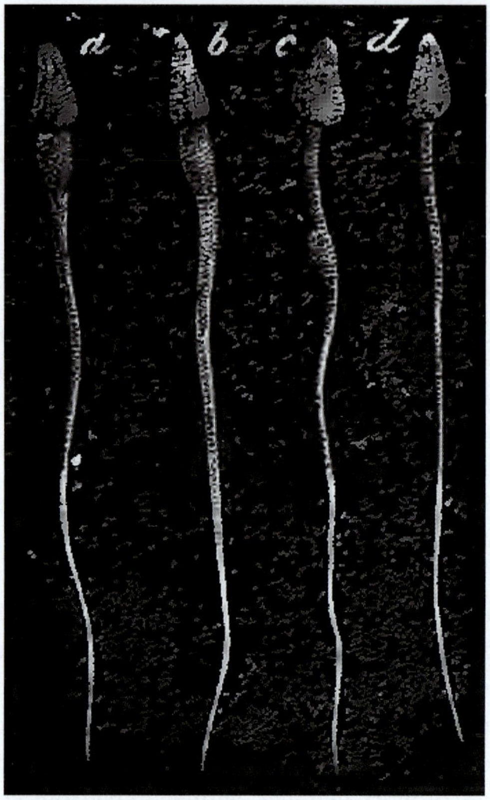

Fig. 4.4 Sperm images by Roussin[45] from different parts of the male reproductive system: (a, b) from the testicles, (c) from the vas deferens, and (d) from the seminal vesicles (as described in the paper).

observed (Fig. 4.5), and at the time this contributed to, but was not indicative of, a positive semen stain determination. This discovery, as the first potential method to identify semen exclusive of spermatozoa, was thoroughly investigated by others,[54–56] but ultimately found that the reaction was also seen with nonhuman semen and other physiological and pathological liquids.[48] False negatives also were found with semen mixed with blood. Further crystal tests using picric acid are described by Barberio[48,57] and targeted spermine to form spermine picrate crystals.[58]

Experts at this time still found identifying disassociated spermatozoon heads and tails difficult and misleading because of other objects in stains that could be confused with spermatozoa parts.[42] Examinations of objects that are not spermatozoa were known to needlessly prolong examination and were cited to have implications for judicial procedure. In 1909, a differential staining method was introduced by Baecchi, which made the microscopic search for, and identification of, spermatozoa much easier and was used extensively for almost a century; in some laboratories, it is still in use today.[59] Additional details of the early history of the

Fig. 4.5 Typical semen crystals as shown by Florence, based on the Roussin iodine staining. *From Florence A. Du Sperme et des Tâches de Sperme en Médecine Légale. Storck; 1897.*

individual tests that are currently in use are further discussed in their relevant sections. The authors and studies described earlier are, however, still instrumental in our understanding of semen and the means to detect it in legal investigations.

Biology of Semen: Anatomy

Male ejaculate, or semen, is a mixture of sperm and seminal fluid (or plasma, but not to be confused with blood plasma) and is the fluid ejaculated during male orgasm. Semen is the body fluid responsible for the delivery of approximately one-half of the genetic material, via the sperm cell, to the ovum via insemination. It is the product of a series of different glands and testicular components that form part of the male reproductive tract. Although forensic science is not generally interested in the anatomy that generates the target body fluid, in the case of semen it is important because of medical conditions or modifications, which may affect the presumptive and confirmatory findings of an investigation.

Several different components combine during ejaculation to form semen originating in different parts of the male reproductive system (Fig. 4.6): the testis, testicular fluid, and accessory gland secretions produced from components from the seminal vesicles, prostate, urethral or periurethral glands (also called Littre glands), and bulbourethral glands (also called Cowper's glands).[60,61] There is no evidence to suggest that ejaculation is a sequentially regulated event; rather, the anatomy of the male reproductive system gives the predictable sequence, which can show differences due to the anatomy of the individual (e.g., amount of smooth muscle, diameter of tubes).[62,63] The components of seminal fluid at the time of ejaculation are therefore not a homogenous mixture and are incompletely mixed from the different glands, combining after ejaculation.[64,65]

Sperm, or spermatozoa (spermatozoon [sing.]), are the end products of meiosis within the testes, a process called spermatogenesis, which takes place in the seminiferous tubules within the testes. Four haploid spermatozoa are created for every mother cell (genetically diploid). Each spermatozoon contains half as many chromosomes as the mother cell and is genetically distinct.

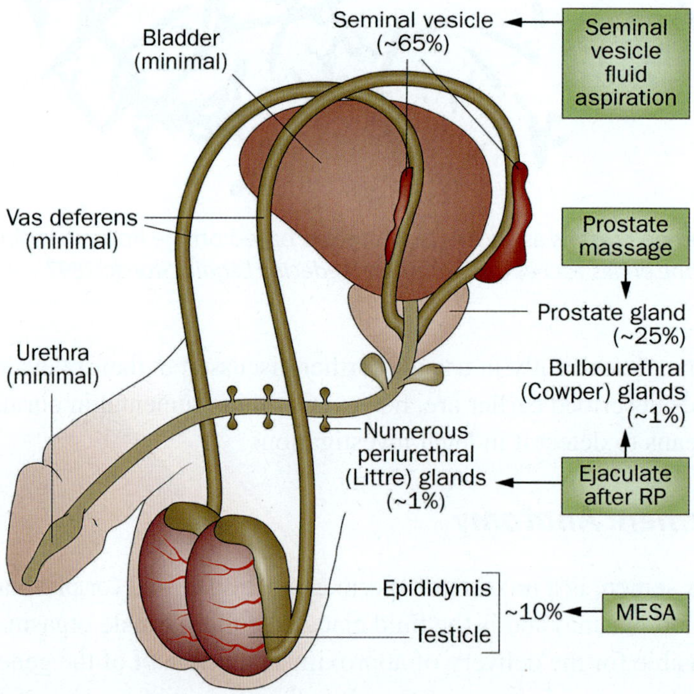

Fig. 4.6 The male reproductive system showing the relevant parts and their contributions to semen. Also depicted (*in green*) are the different techniques to collect tissue-specific proteins. *MESA*, Microsurgical epididymal sperm aspiration; *RP*, radical prostatectomy. *From Drabovich AP, Saraon P, Jarvi K, et al. Seminal plasma as a diagnostic fluid for male reproductive system disorders. Nat Rev Urol. 2014;11:278–288.*

Each spermatozoon is split into two sections, a head and a flagellum, and is attached with a connecting piece (Fig. 4.7).[67] The head contains the nucleus, acrosome, cytoskeleton, and a small amount of cytoplasm[60] and is rich in disulfide bonds.[68] The acrosome tops the head and contains enzymes essential for fertilization.[69] The flagellum is split into three sections: the middle piece containing the mitochondrial sheath, which contains a tightly wrapped helix of mitochondria that provide energy for movement; the principal piece; and the end piece.[60,69]

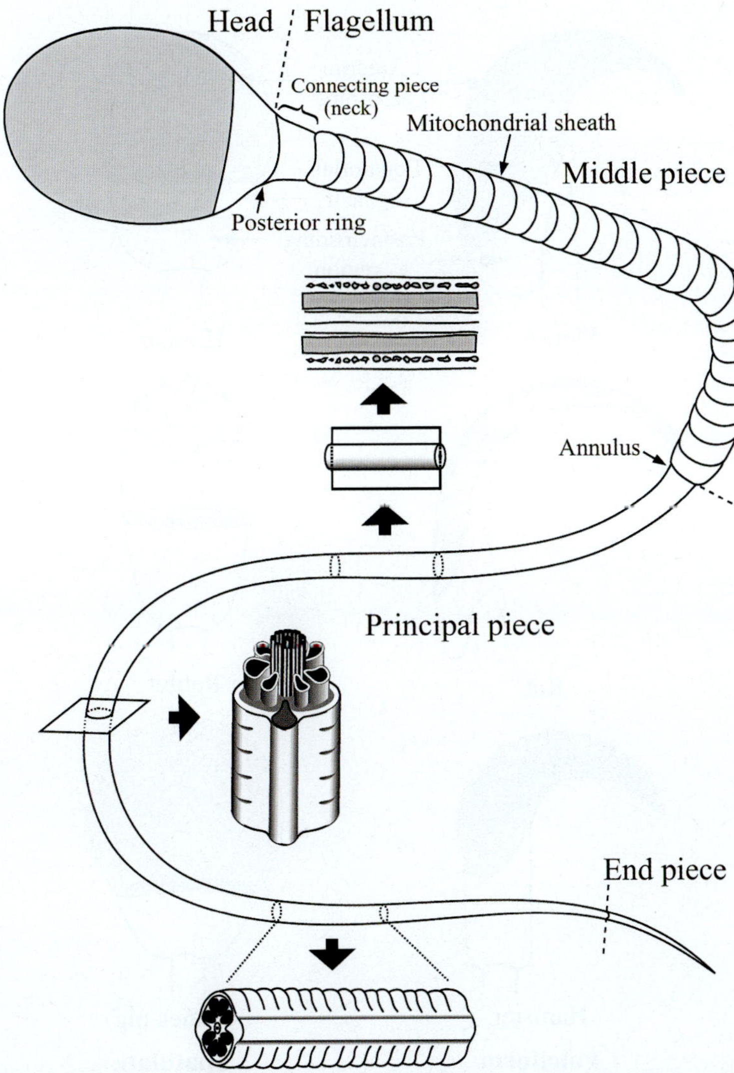

Fig. 4.7 General features of human sperm. The head of the sperm is attached to the flagellum, which consists of three regions: the middle piece, containing the mitochondrial sheath; the principal piece; and the end piece. The acrosome is found at the tip of the head *(gray)* and contains enzymes needed for fertilization. *From Toshimori K, Eddy EM. In: Plant TM, Zeleznik AJ, eds. Knobil and Neill's Physiology of Reproduction. 4th ed. San Diego, CA: Academic Press; 2015:99–148.*

Spermatozoa are between 50 and 70 μm in length with head dimensions of 4.6 × 2.6 × 1.5 μm and a 50-μm tail.[70,71] The head is oval in shape with a length to width ratio of 1.5:1.75, and the acrosome covers between 40% and 70% of the head area.[72] Human spermatozoa heads are classified as ovoid, also called spatulate; however, other animal species can have different shaped spermatozoa heads, such as falciform (curved or sickle shaped) (Fig. 4.8).[9,60] The measurements and overall shape can therefore be important in determining whether a sample is human.

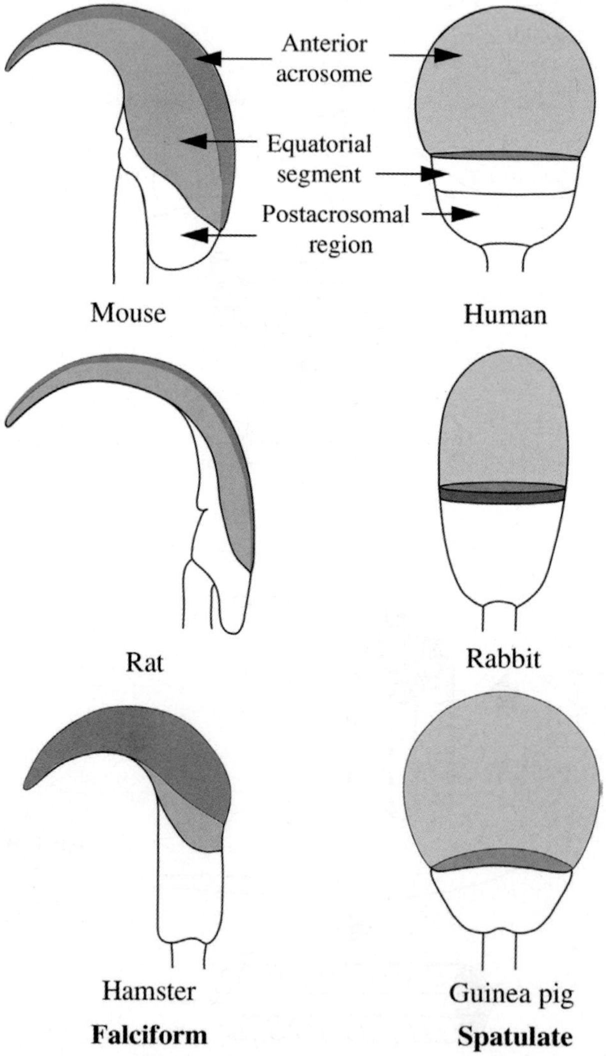

Fig. 4.8 Examples of the differences in sperm head shape of falciform (mouse, rat, and hamster) and spatulate (human, rabbit, and guinea pig). *From Toshimori K, Eddy EM. In: Plant TM, Zeleznik AJ, eds. Knobil and Neill's Physiology of Reproduction. 4th ed. San Diego, CA: Academic Press; 2015:99–148.*

Spermatozoa are produced in the testes, and early development (meiosis) takes place in the seminiferous tubules in the process of spermatogenesis. Both ends of each seminiferous tube drain into the epididymis, where the spermatozoa will mature, after which spermatozoa will pass to the vas deferens. Spermatozoa are released during ejaculation through the ejaculatory ducts, which release them to the urethra in the body of the prostate.[61,73] Severing the vas deferens, as in vasectomy, will prevent the spermatozoa from being released during ejaculation but does not stop their production. Spermatozoa that are released are usually mature, but immature spermatozoon or other common abnormalities can be observed when examining semen microscopically (Fig. 4.9). In a normal ejaculate, there is a high proportion of abnormal spermatozoa, which can be observed during examination. During ejaculation, the spermatozoa are released into fluid derived from the prostate.

The prostate is located anterior to the rectum and is a single, doughnut-shaped gland approximately $3 \times 3 \times 5$ cm, with a volume of 25 mL.[74] It encircles the urethra, and during ejaculation, the prostatic smooth muscles contract and squeeze the alkaline prostatic secretions into the urethra.[61,74] The prostate gland liberates its secretion into the seminal fluid early in the course of ejaculation,[75] and secretions from the prostate gland contain a wide variety of substances necessary for the movement and survival of spermatozoa, including citric acid, fibrinolysin, inositol, calcium, zinc, and magnesium found in the ejaculate.[61,64] It also secretes high concentrations of two useful markers for semen identification: acid phosphatase (AP) and prostate specific antigen (PSA; also called P-30 because of its molecular weight of 30 kDa). Different males vary in the levels of their prostatic components within semen, and even individuals vary between different ejaculates although overall maintain a fairly consistent level.

There are several different conditions that can affect the prostate and subsequently the composition of substances within the fluid. These include prostatitis, an inflammation of the prostate, which can be caused by a number of different factors, usually bacterial;[61] and prostate cancer. Prostate cancer increases the concentrations of AP and PSA, both forensic targets, which are used as a diagnostic measure of the cancer,[76] but it can also eliminate them if the prostate is removed.

The seminal vesicles are a pair of glands found on the posterior bladder surface, and are each about the size of a little finger (5–7 cm in length), but they are double that length when uncoiled.[61] The seminal vesicles secrete fluids during the final stage of ejaculation, and these are alkaline, viscous, and contain fructose, citric acid, prostaglandins, ascorbic acid, and others.[61,64,77] The secretions are highly viscous (gel-like) and are often variable in consistency.[78] Seminal vesicle secretions are high in compounds, such as fructose, which are rapidly (within 5 minutes of mixture) liquified by proteolytic enzymes found in the prostate secretions.[62] The pH is ~8 and is considerably higher than prostatic secretions.[62] Two markers found in the seminal vesicle secretions that are used in forensic identification of semen are

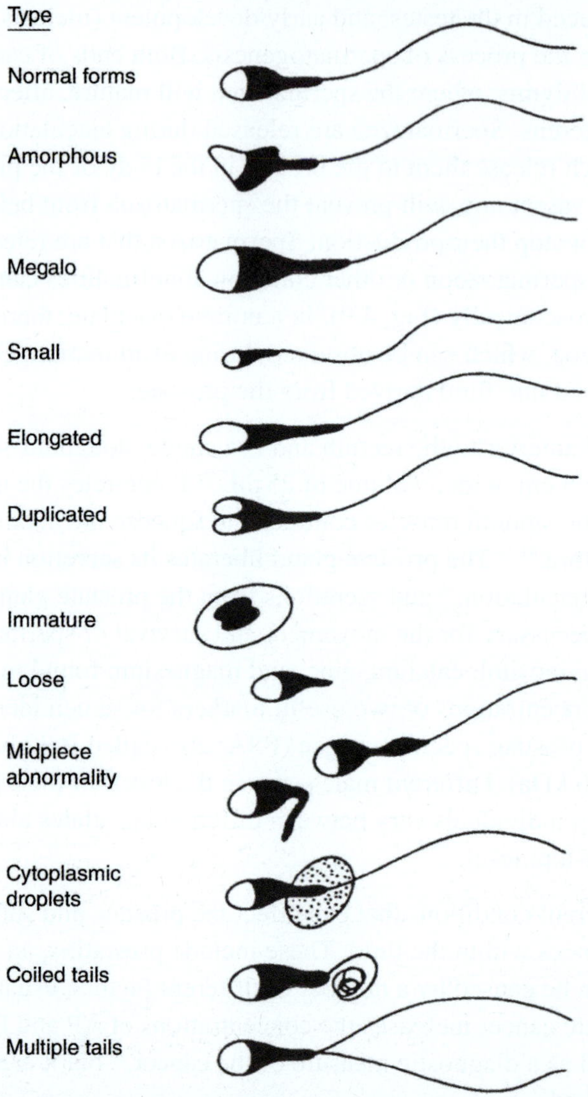

Fig. 4.9 Common abnormalities that can be observed in human spermatozoon morphology. *From Elder K, Dale B. In-Vitro Fertilization. 4th ed. Cambridge University Press; 2020.*

semenogelin (Sg) I and Sg II.[77,79] The Sgs cause the ejaculate to form a coagulum, which is subsequently liquified by PSA.[80,81] The purpose of the seminal vesicle secretions is to enhance motility of the sperm cells. The fluid is yellowish, and it contains a yellow pigment that fluoresces under ultraviolet (UV) light.[77]

Cowper's glands are small glands located inferior to the prostate. They produce a thick, clear mucus, some of which drains into the urethra and lubricates both the urethra and the penis tip when the male becomes aroused. The mucus is alkaline and neutralizes traces of acidic urine in the urethra prior to ejaculation.[61,82]

It is the combination of the anatomic features and the secretions of these different glands that occurs during and after ejaculation into the semen that is usually encountered and examined as evidence in forensic science. A list of the majority of components that are found in semen are in Table 4.1.

Biology of Semen: Ejaculate

Semen is not natively homogenous and only approaches this after ejaculation, although there is a predicable sequence of release of different seminal components that combine after ejaculation.[64,65] The first 5% of the ejaculate is made up of secretions from the bulbourethral and urethral glands, followed by 15% to 30% derived from the prostate. Small contributions follow from the ampulla and epididymis, and the remainder and majority of the ejaculate

Table 4.1 The components of semen, including the different glands contributing to seminal plasma, the proportion of their contribution, and the component(s) contributed

Gland/Site	% Volume	Component
Testicle and epididymis	5%	Spermatozoa (69–647 million per ejaculate)[85]
		Prolactin[86]
		Testosterone[73]
		Albumin, transferrin[87]
		Glycerylphosphorylcholine[88]
		Inositol[88]
		Lactic dehydrogenase C_4[89]
		Transferrin
		Ceruloplasmin
		Glucosidases[90]
		Carnitine and acetylcarnitine[91]
Seminal vesicle	50%–65%	Fructose (1.5–6.5 mg/mL)[64,92]
		Phosphorylcholine[88]
		Ergothioneine[93,94]
		Ascorbic acid[92]
		Flavins[95]
		Prostaglandins (PGs)[61,96]
		Semenogelin I and II[77,79]
		Acetylcarnitine[91]
		Prolactin[86,97]
		Low-molecular-weight proteins (10–20,000)[87]
		β_2-microglobulin[98]
		High-molecular-weight glycoprotein (250,000)[99]
		Glyceride[100]
		PGE, PGF, fructose, lactoferrin[88]
		cAMP[101]
		HMW proteinase inhibitor, α_1-antitrypsin, α_1-X-antichymotrypsin[102]

Continued

Table 4.1 The components of semen, including the different glands contributing to seminal plasma, the proportion of their contribution, and the component(s) contributed—cont'd

Gland/Site	% Volume	Component
Prostate gland	20%–30%	Spermine[103] Citric acid and citrates[64,92] Cholesterol Phospholipids Fibrinolysin Fibrinogenase Vesculate Zinc, calcium, and magnesium[64,83,104] Prostatic acid phosphatase Prostate specific antigen Superoxide dismutase isoenzymes[105] Copper[106] Immunosuppressive factors[107,108] Proteins, prostatein[87] Carcinoembryonic antigen[98] β-inhibin[109] Glucosidases[90] Alkaline phosphatase[110] Lipids, phospholipids, cholesterol[100] Myo-inositol[111] Lysozyme, amylase, neutral proteinase plasminogen activator[112] Immunoglobulin G (IgG), IgA, albumin, transferrin[113] Relaxin[114] Pyruvate kinase[115] Interleukins[116,117]
Bulbourethral glands	<5%	Clear mucus
Buffers		Phosphate Bicarbonate Hyaluronidase
Transudation from blood or no isolated source		Pregnancy-associated plasma protein A[107] Antisperm antibodies[118] Inositol[88] Androgen binding compounds[119] Blood group antigens[120]

From Björndahl L, Kvist U. Sequence of ejaculation affects the spermatozoon as a carrier and its message. *Reprod Biomed Online*. 2003;7:440–448; Barrett KE, Barman SM, Boitano S, et al. *Ganong's Review of Medical Physiology*. 24th ed. Sydney: McGraw-Hill Education; 2012; Jequier AM. *Male Infertility: A Clinical Guide*. 2nd ed. Cambridge University Press; 2011.

come last from the seminal vesicles.[63,64,93,121] After ejaculation, semen first coagulates and then liquefies in a process accompanied by biochemical changes in composition.[64]

Total semen, measured after ejaculation, has specific gravity of 1.028 and an average pH range between 7.35 and 7.5,[84] although the full range of pH has been reported from 7.19[122] to 8.47.[123] It has a high buffering capacity, maintaining its pH near neutral in the acidic vaginal environment.[64] The recognized normal (10th–90th percentile) ejaculate volume is 2 to 6 mL with only 10% (0.2–0.6 mL) being sperm and between 22 and 169 million spermatozoa per mL of semen, or 69 to 647 million spermatozoa per ejaculate.[61,69,85,124,125] Generally, the overall number of spermatozoa per ejaculate does not vary, so lower semen volume would equate to higher concentration, and higher semen volume to lower concentration,[83] although some medical conditions can change this. Classifications and conditions that affect the semen and spermatozoa were initially described in 1970,[126] but they have been through changes, and the currently recognized terms classified by the World Health Organization can be found in Table 4.2. Although most of these terms are in regard to semen quality in relation to fertility, the resultant pathology can be observed in forensic evidence examination and are therefore relevant.

Terms such as aspermia (aspermatic), azoospermia (azoospermatic), and oligozoospermia (oligospermatic) are used in forensic reports and research publications. Interestingly, these conditions are normally diagnosed through detailed medical examination by a medical specialist. Their use in forensic science when classifying observations of casework data are based solely on the observation of the quantity and quality of recovered spermatozoa or lack thereof. Forensic scientists do not generally know the true medical nature of the individual that the semen belongs to or if those conditions are accurate until after a suspect has been identified and tested. Further, there is evidence that features such as oligozoospermia may be a constant feature (every ejaculate) or a periodic feature, and spermatozoa count can vary considerably between ejaculates of one individual.[128] There is some ongoing discussions

Table 4.2 Nomenclature related to medical/fertility semen quality

Term	Definition
Aspermia[a,b]	No semen/ejaculate
Asthenozoospermia[a]	Percentage of motile sperm below the lower reference limit
Asthenoteratozoospermia	A combination of asthenozoospermia and teratozoospermia
Azoospermia[a,b]	No spermatozoa
Cryptozoospermia	Spermatozoa not observed unless pelleted
Hemospermia (hematospermia)	Presence of erythrocytes in ejaculate
Leukospermia (leukocytospermia, pyospermia)	Presence of leukocytes in the ejaculate above the threshold
Necrozoospermia	Low percentage of live, high percentage of immotile spermatozoa
Normozoospermia[a]	Normal ejaculate in reference to number, motility, and morphology
Oligoasthenozoospermia	A combination of oligozoospermia and asthenozoospermia
Oligoasthenoteratozoospermia	A combination of oligozoospermia, asthenozoospermia, and teratozoospermia
Oligoteratozoospermia	A combination of oligozoospermia and teratozoospermia
Oligozoospermia[a,b]	Total number of spermatozoa below the lower reference limit
Teratozoospermia[a]	Low percentage of morphologically normal spermatozoa

[a]Proposed replacements for semen analysis terminology.[127]

[b]Terms used in forensic science.

From World Health Organization. *WHO Laboratory Manual for the Examination and Processing of Human Semen*. Geneva: Author; 2010; Grimes DA, Lopez LM. Elsevier; 2007.

to alter the terms used in semen quality due to overlapping definitions,[127] and this may have implications for reporting sexual assault results. For example, someone who displays aspermia would also be classified as oligozoospermatic (having no ejaculate [semen]) and would be lower than the lower reference limit for sperm count.

Other conditions that relate to seminal volume (e.g., hyperspermia, hypospermia, hematospermia) are also recognized, which can be either congenital or acquired. Hyperspermia is ejaculated semen volume above 6 mL, with a maximum 13 mL being reported.[129,130] Hyperspermia does not affect sperm count per mL;[130] therefore the total number of spermatozoa per ejaculate would be higher. Hypospermia, in contrast, is semen volume lower than 2 mL, but it is not to be confused with aspermia.[131] Hypospermia can be an isolated condition with normal sperm counts, although lower overall sperm numbers due to the lower ejaculate, but the condition can also be in conjunction with other conditions, including oligozoospermia, asthenozoospermia, teratozoospermia, among others.[131] Hematospermia (hemospermia) is a condition that results in blood being found occasionally in the semen, with no apparent injury,[132] although trauma (prostate), infections, and other pathological changes to the prostate have been found as possible causes.[133] Individuals with no spermatozoa in their ejaculate will still have seminal plasma in most instances. The presumptive identification of semen is based on substances found in the seminal plasma and are independent of the presence or absence of spermatozoa, although some levels of these substances may change depending on the concentration of spermatozoa.

Of the fluid portion of semen (seminal plasma), the majority originates from the seminal vesicles, with the prostate providing the next largest component. The seminal fluid protects the spermatozoa from the acidic vaginal environment and provides nourishment for prolonged survival.[61] For many years, it was unknown if the glandular secretions in semen were released at once or if there was a specific order (with purpose) of the release of each component. In 1911, Broesike[65] microscopically examined ejaculate at different points and determined there were four phases, or fractions, of ejaculation with different glands contributing different components at each phase. These consisted of a preejaculation phase, followed by three stages of ejaculation, each with secretions and components from different glands.[65,121] The main ejaculation event has been split into three phases or fractions,[62,65,93,134] and it is known that the various glands contributing to the ejaculate discharge their products in a controlled, successive pattern, with partial mixture between stages.[134] Not all researchers agree that the main ejaculate should be split into three fractions, with studies publishing results with fraction ranges from two to six (or more). Most studies looking at ejaculate fraction are heavily focused on infertility and insemination; however, in general forensic terms, ejaculate would normally be examined after being fully expelled from the penis, so it would be mixed into a largely homogenous fluid.

There are circumstances where this may not be the case (e.g., interrupted intercourse), so the sequence of ejaculation may come into consideration in the expectations of findings, although for forensic science it is easier to consider, in addition to preejaculate fluids, first ejaculate fraction (FEF) and second ejaculate fraction (SEF). In addition, the exact composition of the seminal plasma, even if a single ejaculate is homogenized, is not consistent between men or even between subsequent ejaculates of the same man.[62] The sequence of ejaculation therefore is an important consideration when examining and interpreting findings.

Preejaculate (also known as preejaculatory fluid, preseminal fluid, or Cowper's fluid) is a clear mucoid fluid released during sexual stimulation and erection of the penis prior to ejaculation.[82,135] Broesike[65] describes it as clear, slimy, and alkaline reacting, and he confirms it is a secretion of the Cowper's gland. Further studies found, in addition to the Cowper's gland, the Littre gland also contributed secretions.[135] Generally, preejaculatory volume is between a few drops and 5 mL, although much higher amounts have been reported.[135] It functions as a lubricant and chemical neutralizer to the normal acidity in the urethra and to provide the alkalinity that spermatozoa need for safe passage.[82] Some authors find no spermatozoa in preejaculatory fluid[136]; however, other authors identify that motile spermatozoa can be observed in some cases (<50%).[137,138] Small amounts of PSA have also been identified in preejaculate fluid but not as an abundant source.

The FEF is a "thin and milky" fluid secreted by the prostate and was not found to contain spermatozoa when initially examined in 1911 by Broesike.[65] More recent investigations have confirmed the prostate gland contributes its secretions for this first fraction,[75,134] but they disagree because this phase contains the major proportion of released spermatozoa suspended in the prostatic fluid.[62,139] Spermatozoa preserve their motility and vitality best in prostatic fluid rather than seminal vesicular fluid,[62] which is only important for forensic consideration in the fact that the majority of spermatozoa (if present) will be released in the first part of an ejaculation. Spermatozoa have also been found to be sluggish under acidic pH (<6),[61] which is reflected in the prostatic fluid, which is alkaline, with a mean pH of 7.31.[140] This fraction is found to be high in zinc, required for spermatozoa motility and stabilization of their nuclear chromatin, and a known component of prostate secretions.[139,141]

The SEF is described as a yellowish and clear gel that contains spermatozoa, both motile and immotile, intact and broken. Prostate secretions were noted in this stage of ejaculation, but they were theorized to be remnants of the previous stage,[65] and the majority of the fluids are secreted from the seminal vesicles.[134] In contrast to later studies, the highest portion of spermatozoa has been found in this fraction by some researchers.[134] Although reduced motility and concentration have been observed,[139] this is not at a level that would affect forensic examination. Seminal vesicle secretions have a pH around 8 and high observed concentrations of fructose, glucose, acid soluble phosphate, and reducing substances.[62,142] This fraction has high specific gravity, contains less water (than the FEF), and is rich in proteins.[122] The gel-like nature of the SEF is rapidly liquified by proteolytic enzymes found in the FEF.[62]

Although the ejaculation event takes place as a sequence of different fluids, the fluids combine rapidly after ejaculation to a largely homogenous mixture that is the usual target of forensic testing. The levels of the different seminal plasma components (e.g., AP) are not constant between individuals or consistent between ejaculates of the same individual, but they remain within a nominal range. Investigators have been identifying variation in the levels of seminal plasma constituents for decades and found that many of these components are correlated to the concentrations of spermatozoa.[143] Nun et al.[143] investigated fertile, subfertile, and vasectomized men and found protein, fructose, and alkaline phosphatase concentrations varied between the three groups, but values overlapped significantly. They found significant differences in AP concentrations, which were higher in vasectomized males, and sialic acid, which was reduced in subfertile men.[143]

A consideration should be made to samples that may originate from young males undergoing puberty. A study conducted by Janczewski and Bablok in 1985[144] assessed the semen quality and quantity of Polish boys between 12 and 19 years of age. Their findings indicated the first ejaculation (via masturbation or nocturnal emission) occurred between 3 and 16 months after the first signs of puberty, but on average after around 12 months. They found seminal volume started at less than 0.5 mL and progressed to normal ranges from about 12 months postfirst ejaculation onward. No spermatozoa were observed in the initial ejaculate, and numbers remained low until 6 months after initial ejaculate, but due to the reduced seminal volume, normozoospermia was not recorded until the ninth month after first ejaculate.[144]

Of note is the ability to detect blood group antigens (see Appendix 1) in semen (and saliva), something that was extremely important and used frequently before the now standard use of DNA. Individuals were known as either secretors, in that blood group antigens were detectable in their semen, or nonsecretors, in that there were no detectable blood group antigens in their semen. If the sample was from a secretor, then the blood group antigens present would be the same as those of the blood of the individual, allowing forensic scientists to link semen and blood samples to each other. Early work by Yamakami[145] and Landsteiner and Levine[146] showed that the spermatozoa and seminal fluid could contain blood group antigens, and the relevance and significance to forensic investigations were immediately recognized. Secretor status was found to be determinate on the Lewis blood group factor, with those that were Lewis positive found to be nonsecretors.[147] This can only be determined by testing the Lewis factor in blood, and so for forensic purposes all samples are tested, but a 1:1 correlation was found between ABH antigens in semen and blood if the individual was a secretor.[148] Kerek and Eliasson[120] found within split ejaculates that all fractions contained the same antigen activity, concluding that all glands contributing to the seminal plasma were secreting the antigens. Although this method was widespread and invaluable prior to DNA analysis, it has now been superseded by genetic typing.

Sampling

Because of the various forms that sexual assault can take, and the way evidence can be left behind, the samples submitted for examination in cases of sexual assault can be diverse.

Similar to other presumptive tests, it is always advised that an item be subsampled for testing. Each test will have its own method of testing, which is designed to remove a small portion of the suspected semen stain but leave the majority of the sample in place for further testing while preserving the integrity of the original stain or sample. Standard operating procedures and protocols will be in place and will vary by laboratory.

Most samples from living complainants will be taken by medical practitioners, either nurses or doctors using a sexual assault kit, or from pathologists when the victim is deceased. These kits vary by location and district, but generally will collect samples as indicated by the alleged sequence of events of the assault (if known, in the case of deceased victims, or if remembered, which is not always the case in drug or alcohol facilitated sexual assault). This may include intimate samples of the vagina (external, lower, upper, cervix), rectum and anus, oral (could be via washes), or any other area that may have semen present. Clothing and other items may be collected and analyzed at the laboratory. Other items, such as bed sheets, with suspected or alleged semen on them will be collected by crime scene officers in full and submitted to the laboratory for examination. Finally, other surfaces that may have semen stains (e.g., the floor) can be swabbed or the section removed and submitted for analysis.

Different jurisdictions will offer guidelines on cutoff times for collection on intimate sexual assault samples based on the victim account of time since intercourse (TSI). These cutoff times represent limits after which a laboratory will not analyze sexual assault evidence and are based on empirical research as to persistence or on years of casework reports and victim recollection of time since assault. For example, Forensic Science Ireland collects vaginal swabs for up to 7 days postincident.[149] In New South Wales, Australia, there is a cutoff time of 12 hours, for penile–oral assault, which can be extended to 24 hours in specific circumstances.[3]

Complainants can introduce sampling difficulties through destruction of evidence[150] due to washing (mouth, hands, genitals, anus, body, clothes, sheets, etc.) or even eating and drinking after the incident. There are many papers and textbooks[150–153] that detail the challenges surrounding the recovery and collection of evidence in cases of sexual assault, but these will not be focused on further here.

If items are received or semen is suspected on skin, then an alternate light source (ALS) can be used as a general nondestructive screening method to identify areas of potential interest. As shown with other body fluids, ALS does not affect or destroy DNA.[154] Because of the nonspecific nature of ALS, it is a general screening method only to identify potential areas of interest, although not finding any stains with ALS does not preclude subsequent testing. Following ALS, or directly for areas or samples thought to have semen present, a sequence of increasingly more discriminatory testing is undertaken (see Fig. 4.1).

Alternate Light Sources

The use of ALS for semen screening is a common nondestructive method to identify areas of potential interest, but it is not itself an indication of semen because other body fluids react in the same way. Generally, items of evidence with suspected seminal stains, such as underwear or bed sheets, will be examined with ALS, and areas of fluorescence will be marked for further investigation using other more specific methods of identification. Intimate swabs are assessed without ALS screening because of the small, concentrated area of the sample, which will be tested using subsequent methods.

The potential use of ALS for detecting fluids, including semen, was described first in 1919,[155] and within a few years it was confirmed. Studies indicated that the phenomenon of semen fluorescence was well established, demonstrating the rapid nondestructive screening potential of the method.[156] Further work was carried out in the following decades,[157–159] and since then there have been several studies investigating its potential forensic use.[160–163] The early reports used UV light (<400 nm) and did not describe any filters used to visualize the stains, but were visible without aids beyond the UV light. A more recent study[164] was not able to demonstrate visible semen using UV light, although the authors recognized limitations in their study; Kind[165] stated the value of UV light searching for semen was frequently overestimated in the literature.

Semen, and more specifically seminal fluid, has emission fluorescence at 622 nm when excited by 488 nm of light.[166] It was found that the seminal plasma contained the substances that were responsible for the fluorescence of semen under UV light.[166] More recently, work has indicated that the optimal excitation wavelength is between 440 and 490 nm, which gives the strongest fluorescence, although light from 320 to 550 nm showed detectable fluorescence, with the main consideration being any background fluorescence from the substrate.[160] The phenomena of intrinsic fluorescence of semen is well known, and forensic scientists and crime scene personnel exploit this; however, the exact component(s) within semen that causes this fluorescence has not been identified.[167]

Some authors have suggested that the fluorescence in semen is due to the riboflavin, which has been shown to fluoresce in other (nonforensic, nonsemen) studies;[168] however, the reported fluorescence of flavins does not correspond to the observed wavelengths seen with semen. Further tests were carried out on isolated riboflavin from semen, and it was confirmed to fluoresce at a lower wavelength (~522 nm) compared to semen (~622 nm). Flavins may therefore contribute to the intrinsic semen fluorescence but are not themselves the cause.[95,166]

Current recommendations for visualization of semen stains using ALS are excitation light between 400 and 500 nm and an interference filter for visualization of orange (>500 nm) or red (>590 nm), although variations to this are used depending on the substrate where the stain is located. Karchewski et al.[169] found that the fabric substrate had a significant impact on the ability to visualize a stain using ALS. This phenomenon has been observed in other studies as well.[160] It is therefore advisable to use different combinations of excitation wavelengths and interference filters to maximize the ability to see stains (Fig. 4.10).

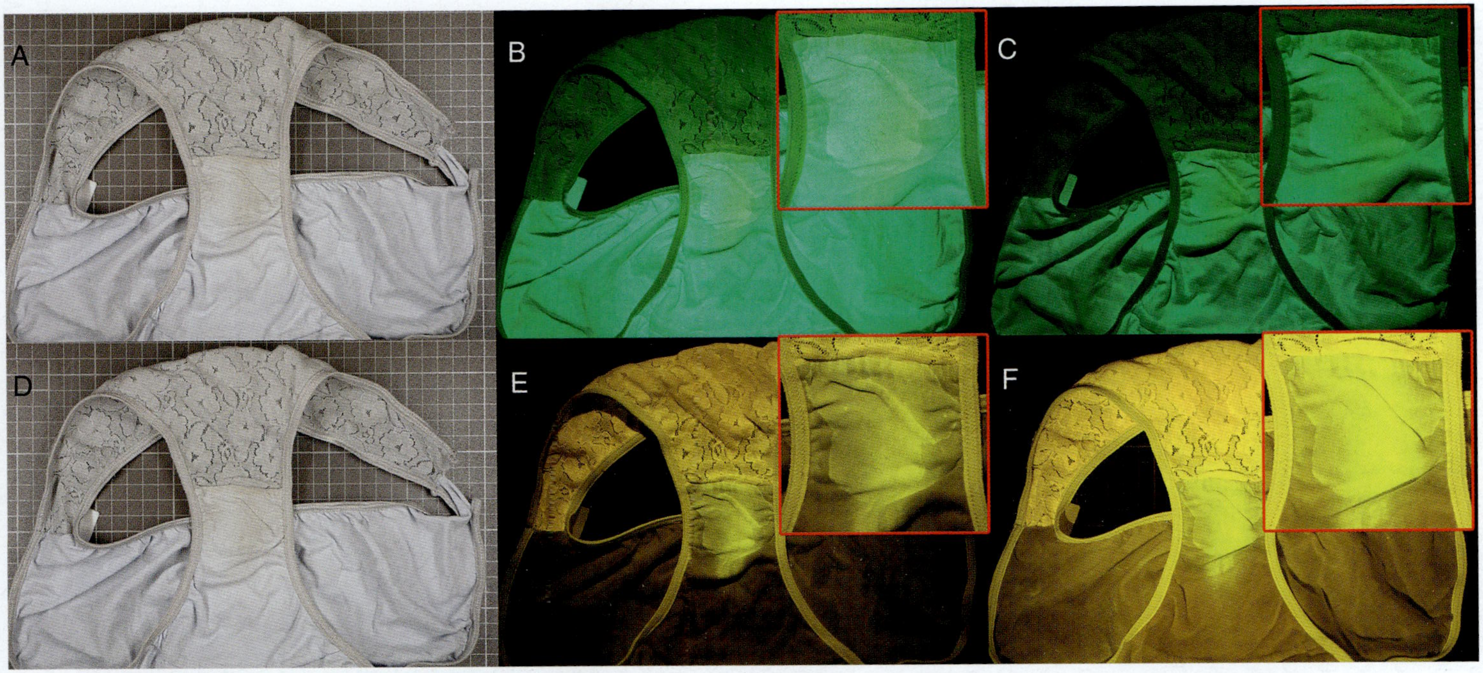

Fig. 4.10 (A, D) A pair of underwear under normal lighting. A stain is slightly visible in the crotch. (B, C) The underwear viewed under a violet Crime-Light (400–430 nm) and yellow filter. The two different images are taken with the light striking the evidence at different angles. Note the background fluorescence from the material. The inlays are a closeup of the crotch area where a stain would be expected. (E, F) The underwear viewed under a blue Crime-Light (420–470 nm) and orange filter. The two different images are taken with the light striking the evidence at different angles. The inlays are closeups of the crotch area where a stain would be expected.

Further examples of ALS of semen stains can be seen in Figs. 4.11 and 4.12. ALS was able to identify semen from a 100-year-old stain.[170] ALS systems were found to be sensitive to semen at a dilution of 1:100, and seminal stains were visible even under three coats of acrylic-based paint.[163,171] Another study was able to detect neat semen on various substrates, but semen diluted to 1:10 was not detectable on bed linen or carpet.[172] Testing various fingerprint development techniques on semen stains showed no effect on ALS results.[173] Beckwith et al.[174] found ALS was able to detect semen stains that had been submerged for up to 24 hours. One study found that diluted semen sensitivity of ALS was different between different semen donors and that the ALS results did not correspond to those of subsequent testing using AP and Sg.[175]

It is important to note that seminal fluid will not always fluoresce or could be masked by other substances. A lack of an ALS result does not preclude the presence of semen or spermatozoa. False positive results may be obtained because other biological fluids, such as urine, can fluoresce in a similar manner to semen.[163] Coffee, onion, and vaginal discharge have also been reported to produce false positives with ALS.[172] Washing may remove detectable traces of the

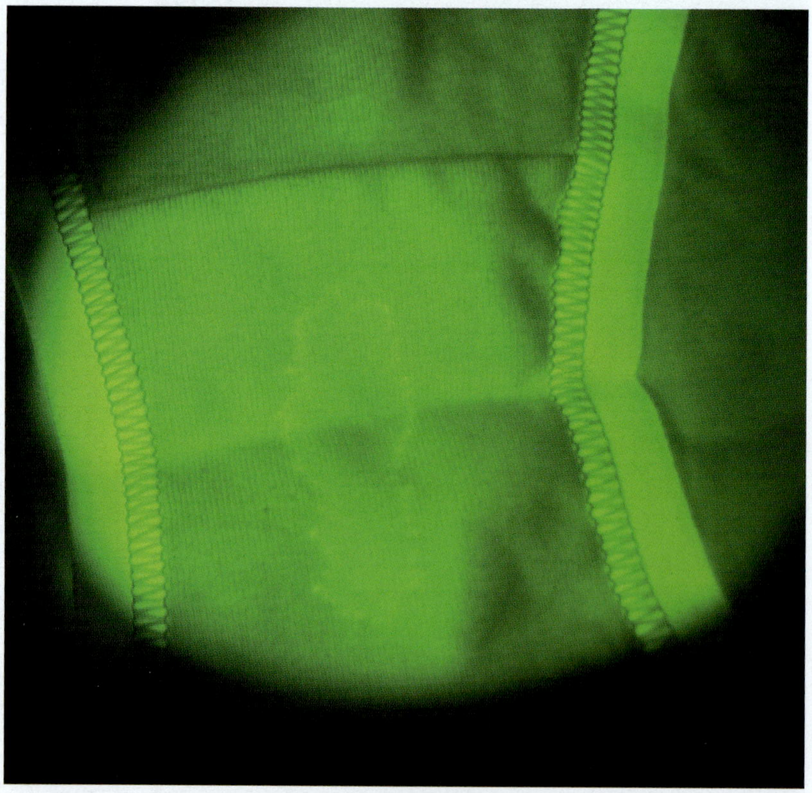

Fig. 4.11 Blue underwear with a semen stain under an alternative light source (ALS). The ALS is 415 nm, and a yellow filter is being used. *From Amy Brodeur, Boston University School of Medicine.*

Fig. 4.12 Pink underwear with a semen stain under an alternative light source (ALS). The ALS is 415 nm, and a yellow filter is being used. *From Amy Brodeur, Boston University School of Medicine.*

seminal stains,[160,176] which was found to be dependent on type of detergent used (biological vs. nonbiological) and temperature of the washing cycle,[176] although spermatozoa may still be present.

Using an ALS can show where potential seminal stains are located for subsequent testing, including AP, PSA, other immunochromatography, sperm visualization, and ultimately DNA profiling. The high number of false positives and false negatives encountered when using ALS for semen means that for most casework examinations in the laboratory it is a preliminary screening method only.

Acid Phosphatase

AP was first described in human tissues in 1925,[177] where it was discovered that urine contained an acidic enzyme that hydrolyzed hexose diphosphate, optimally at pH 5. Subsequent research found that AP was present in the testes, epididymis, seminal vesicles, and spermatic cord, but it was found in much higher concentrations in the prostate.[178,179] AP is found in seminal fluid at concentrations up to 400 times greater than in any other body fluid.[1,71,180,181] This has been reported as 51,525 ± 16,485 units (14,300–57,500 range),[182] or several thousand units per gram of fresh tissue.[183] It is a nonspecific phosphomonoesterase synthesized in prostate epithelial cells, and its level proportionally increases with prostate cancer progression.[76] Further research therefore led to its identification as an indicator in cancer because it was found in higher concentrations in other tissues when certain types of cancer were present.[184–186] Most of the early testing for AP was thus in relation to its ability to detect elevated levels in the blood for cancer diagnosis, and its use for forensic identification of semen in cases of sexual assault was not suggested until 1945.[46,187]

AP (1-prop-2-ynoxypropan-2-ol) (Fig. 4.13) is an enzyme that catalyzes, through hydrolysis, the conversion of a phosphoric monoester and water to an alcohol and phosphate. In semen, the AP breaks down phosphorylcholine (produced in the seminal vesicles) to choline and inorganic phosphate,[188] which is needed for spermatozoa membrane structure and fluidity.[189]

The AP test is one of the best known techniques for semen detection,[191] and most forensic laboratories use AP as an initial semen identification method, which may take place after a general search using ALS. Under acidic conditions (pH 4.9–5.5), AP (a nonspecific orthophosphoric monoester phosphohydrolase) catalyzes the hydrolytic removal of phosphate groups from monophosphate substrates, examples of which can be found in Fig. 4.14.[70,124] One version of the AP reagent contains α-naphthyl acid phosphate monosodium salt, fast blue B salt, maleic acid (PubChem CID: 444266), disodium hydrogen phosphate (PubChem CID: 24203), and water. Note that other dyes can be used, for example, fast black (PubChem CID: 16219369), or ortho-dianisidine (PubChem CID: 8411) that will have similar reaction mechanics (Fig. 4.15). The hydrolyzed substrate yields a product that reacts with the colorless dye to produce a colored product at the site of AP activity[124] (Fig. 4.16).

Previously, AP was measured by activity of the protein in a solution, such as the specific activity of L-tartrate-inhibitable AP, which was assessed using optical densities[181,192,193] or via electrophoresis.[194] Using optical densities, the method of AP detection was more sensitive and specific than the current methods, but it required much longer preparation time and measure units of activity, which was the basis for the specificity. Other methods were proposed, such as electrophoretic techniques,[195,196] and use of different substrates (which led to the current

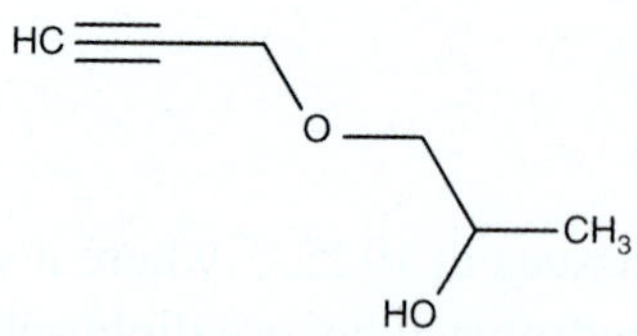

Acid Phosphatase

Fig. 4.13 Acid phosphatase (AP, PubChem CID: 12951370). *From Advanced Chemistry Development Inc. ChemSketch. Toronto, Ontario; 2018. www.acdlabs.com.*

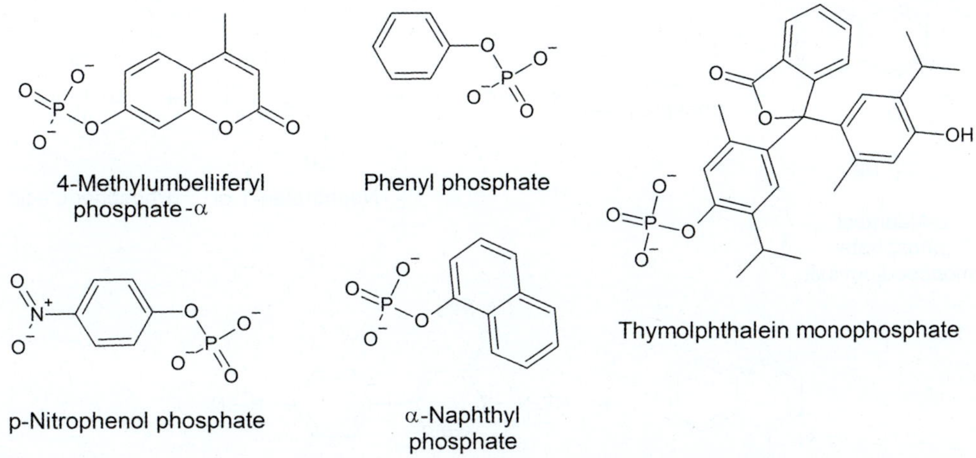

Fig. 4.14 The chemical structure of five AP substrates. 4-Methylumbelliferyl phosphate (MUP) (PubChemID 65118); Phenyl Phosphate (PubChemID 1548902); alpha-Naphthyl phosphate (PubChemID 2115); p-Nitrophenol phosphate (PubChemID 378); and Thymolphthalein monophosphate (PubChemID 86497). *From Advanced Chemistry Development Inc. ChemSketch. Toronto, Ontario; 2018. www.acdlabs.com.*

substrates in use),[197] but they were all based on absorbance and required significant time, equipment, and other chemical reagents. Interestingly, the electrophoretic methods were able to distinguish between seminal AP and those phosphatases found in vaginal fluids, nonhuman semen, other body fluids, and various vegetables.[194] These methods have therefore been phased out for an easier method, despite a reduction in both specificity and sensitivity.

The current general method for AP testing is the spot test. It is important to first prepare the reagent, either from a commercially bought powder or in-house via a pair of solutions that are mixed immediately prior to use. To sample the suspected semen stain, a piece of filter paper is moistened with sterile water and pressed directly onto the stain; alternatively, a moistened swab can be used. If no stain is visible, then a large piece of filter paper can be used to test the whole item. Seminal fluid is highly water soluble, and the test is essentially solubilizing some of the stain and transferring the fluid, including the AP component, to the filter paper. The pressure should be maintained for roughly 1 minute, although each laboratory will have its own recommended timing. The paper is then sprayed with the AP substrate solution containing the colorless dye. If AP is present, then a color change will occur at the site of activity (see Fig. 4.16). Because only a small portion of the stain is removed, the test can be considered nondestructive, and subsequent tests can be performed.

Wetting the item of evidence, in addition to the paper used to test for AP, was suggested, but it was found that doing so would diffuse the AP, which is water soluble, making location of the original stain difficult.[198] They also found a reduction in the number of recovered spermatozoa from samples that had been moistened directly. This was confirmed through

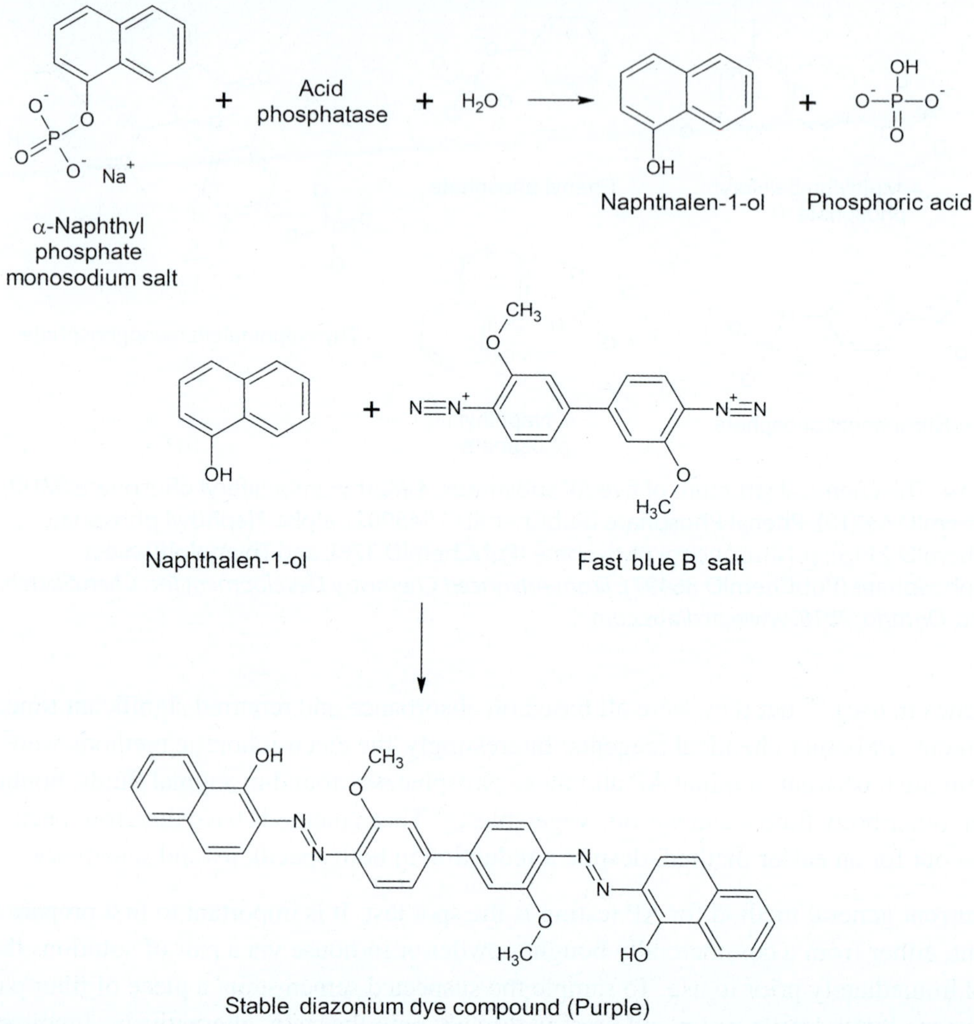

Fig. 4.15 The AP reaction with an alpha-Naphthyl phosphate substrate (PubChem CID: 2114), Fast Blue B Salt (PubChem CID: 84305), and water. The AP cleaves the phosphate from the substrate, naphthalen-1-ol, which reacts with the Fast Blue B Salt to form a stable diazonium dye compound similar to that depicted. *From Advanced Chemistry Development Inc. ChemSketch. Toronto, Ontario; 2018. www.acdlabs.com.*

further research, which found migration of AP by up to 4 cm from the original stain, with some migration of spermatozoa found.[199] Directly wetting the suspected stain is therefore not recommended, and any item that may have been wet prior to examination should be evaluated with the migration of AP in mind.

The timing of the reaction is dependent on the levels of AP present, with a faster reaction (color change) resulting from higher levels of AP. The time after which the test should be read varies between different studies and laboratories, but a color change should usually be

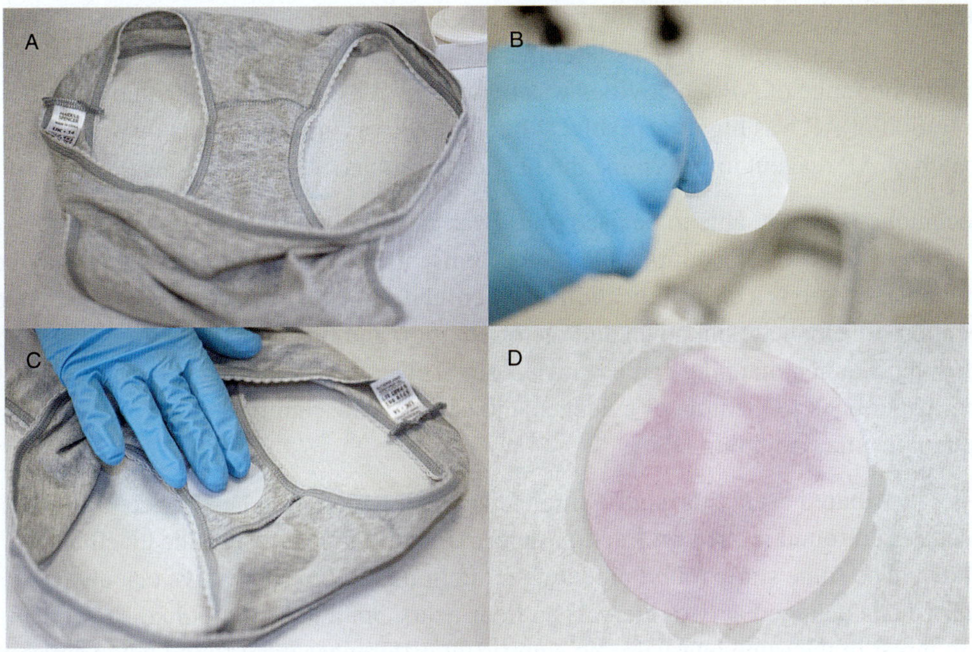

Fig. 4.16 Example of an acid phosphatase spot test being carried out on evidence. (A) The evidence is examined, and a potential stain is identified in the crotch of the underwear. (B) A piece of filter paper is moistened with sterile distilled water. (C) The filter paper is pressed firmly onto the suspected stain for several seconds. (D) The filter paper is then sprayed with acid phosphatase (AP) solution, In this case using α-naphthyl phosphate, and observed after several seconds. The purple color indicates a positive reaction for AP. This example uses ortho-dianisidine (PubChem CID: 8411) as the dye indicator.

observed in less than 1 minute. Shaler[200] stated that a color change within 15 seconds indicates positive for AP, whereas an inconclusive result is observed between 15 and 30 seconds, and a reaction beyond 30 seconds (including no color change) is a negative.

A study carried out over nine laboratories found that under normal caseworking laboratory protocols, AP could be detected to a maximum dilution of 1:200 (in one lab, the test reported 1:40 as the maximum).[201] Conversely, other research argues for longer reaction times for better sensitivity.[202,203] In one study, it was found that increasing the cutoff time to 10 minutes increased the sensitivity of the AP test from 1:200 to 1:1000.[203] One study found an AP reading less than 10 seconds had 0% false positives, but only 5% true positives (meaning that the rate of false negatives was significant), whereas increasing the AP read time to less than 120 seconds resulted in a false positive rate of 32%, but a true positive rate of 78%.[149] Longer reaction times therefore have much greater sensitivity, and it is thought that the risk of false positives (due to, for example, vaginal fluid cross-reaction) is an acceptable risk. One study found a large variation between individuals in the AP development time, although it also stated that no or slow AP did not preclude the identification of spermatozoa.[204] This was confirmed by another study 51 years later that found even when using extended detection time limits the range of AP sensitivities was between 1:2500 and 1:25,000, showing the initial concentration of AP was highly variable.[205] Each laboratory must make its own validation of each batch of AP reagent to determine the best cutoff times.

This technique is robust, able to be used on a swab head (i.e., from a sexual assault kit), or on an entire bed sheet, for example. On larger items, several pieces of filter paper may be required unless there is a clear indication of where the semen is expected. If the presence and location of semen are unknown and the orientation and position of the filter paper are recorded, then semen mapping can be carried out. This involves linking the AP findings on the filter paper back to the item of evidence and can inform scientists of where to sample for subsequent testing, including DNA.

AP is not distributed evenly through a single ejaculate, with the highest concentration of AP having been found in the first fraction (approximately first 1 mL) of the ejaculate in one study.[75] The same study found moderate reduction in AP in successive ejaculates in two individuals obtained at two intervals an hour apart, but a third individual showed an increase in AP in the same intervals. No significant differences were found when subsequent ejaculations were 8 hours apart.[75]

AP is generated in the prostate and is not a product of spermatogenesis, so it is independent of spermatozoa presence; however, the level of AP in semen may be related to the number (if any) of spermatozoa present in the sample, with researchers reporting vastly conflicting results over decades.[75,206] One study found elevated levels of AP in line with ejaculation in victims of alleged vaginal rape in 78% of cases, when spermatozoa were recorded in only 43%.[10] Some researchers[75,207] have found a large difference in AP levels within and between individuals with normal sperm counts, whereas Nun et al.[143] found little difference between AP levels of fertile and subfertile individuals but a significantly increased level in vasectomized individuals. This substantial increase in AP levels of vasectomized individuals was not found when subsequently tested by Saha et al.,[206] where it was measured that azoospermic individuals had less than half the AP activity of the other tested groups (normal, oligospermic, and vasectomized). Further studies found no differences in AP activity between normal and abnormal (including azoospermatic) specimens.[182] Part of the discrepancies reported will be due to the different measures of AP (activity, σ-u/mL, and King-Armstrong units have all been used over the years), but this only explains a small portion of the vast differences reported.

One important point is that AP can be found in vaginal secretions and in lysosomes in addition to seminal fluid.[69] This is especially important because of the nature of many sexual assault samples being intimate in nature and originating from female victims, so vaginal fluid will be present on swabs taken from the vagina and cervix. Goldberg and Jones[208] studied AP levels in different tissues in the vagina and found there was AP activity, but the enzyme, while similar to prostatic AP, has a lower activity per milligram. When compared directly to prostatic tissues, endometrium (tissue from the uterus) showed activity at one-fifth the level of the prostate, and vaginal tissue showed activity at less than half the level of the endometrium,[208] so the AP reaction with vaginal fluid, although expected, occurs at a much slower rate. This was found to be between 40 and 200 seconds in a study by Davies and Wilson,[204] with pregnant women generating faster AP times. This is why the timing of the AP test is so important and why validation must be carried out for each batch of reagent.

The catalytic action of seminal AP can be inhibited by fluoride,[179] anticoagulants,[209] and L-tartrate.[193] Teepol, a strong detergent, was found to inhibit AP, which is theorized to be due to the destruction of proteins.[210] A study by Baechtel et al.[211] found that in 99.4%, a negative AP test was truly negative (i.e., in 1000 samples that showed a negative reaction for AP, semen was subsequently identified in 6 samples), but that in the case of a positive reaction only 69% were found to be true positives. This demonstrates that AP testing is far more sensitive than it is specific, and this fact should be kept in mind when testing using AP. Semen diluted to 1:1000 still reacted with the AP reagent;[210] however, other research has found a maximum sensitivity of 1:200[212] or 1:100[213] unless longer reaction times (>2 minutes) are allowed. Although not generally undertaken, Lewis et al.[213] found that by directly applying AP via an aerosol method, the sensitivity increased to at least 1:3000 (the maximum dilution tested), and that this had no effect on subsequent DNA analysis. Hardinge et al.[214] found direct testing of AP to be sensitive to a maximum of 1:20,000 on liquid semen and 1:2000 when semen was applied to a swab versus 1:50 when the standard method of subsampling was employed. AP has been detected in the postcoital vagina after 14 hours[215] and has been detected in tea leaves; however, the azo dye formation was slow and should not be confused with a positive AP reaction from semen.[216]

AP could be detected in semen and saliva mixtures tested after transfer to, and on, red starch paper[210,217] but not when diluted. AP could also be detected on Phadebas paper in saliva and semen mixtures to a dilution of 1:50[218] (tests for saliva can be found in Chapter 5). Semen and vaginal fluid mixtures showed AP positive for up to 12 hours after intercourse and when in storage for 1 month.[212] Another study found a limit of 24 hours postcoital detection of AP as the limit, but samples were tested immediately.[219] It has been detected in deceased individuals for up to 168 hours (vaginal), 216 hours (rectal), and 120 hours (oral).[220]

The effects of laundering on the ability of AP to detect seminal stains has also been investigated.[221] It has been shown that dry cleaning does not interfere with the ability of AP to detect a seminal stain unless the stain was spot cleaned.[221] However, spot cleaning is done only on visible stains, and seminal stains are often not visible.[221] Washing with and without detergent removed all traces of AP.[221] Beckwith et al.[174] found AP persisted for up to 2 weeks if submerged in tap water, but only 72 hours in pool or ocean water.

AP has been detected in postmortem samples from male individuals without a history of sexual activity prior to death.[222] AP was detected in up to 60% of swabs taken from the glans penis of deceased males; when the urethra was sampled, AP was detected in 70% of samples.[222] It was found that the incidence of positive results increased with the time since death (i.e., as the bodies became more decomposed), so the results may be due to natural leakage from the prostate. Only a single AP result was found when female postmortem samples were assessed, and the authors could not conclude if this was false positive, but they urged caution when collecting postmortem samples.[222]

AP was found to show false positive results with blood (7% of samples tested), saliva, feces contaminated with blood, vaginal discharge, menstrual blood, sweat, tears, cauliflower, chicory, leek, salad, savoy, spinach, sprouts, tea (various varieties), beef, goat, horse, pork, sheep, cheese, chocolate, cinnamon, nutmeg, parsley, polluted canal water, public swimming pool water, apple, oven cleaner, Vanish Oxy Action, and a large range of fruits and vegetables (at 5 minutes read time).[210,212,214,216,223] It is important to note that false positive results may have been recorded after normal AP reactions were expected to occur, and sensitivities will be affected by reagent used, as well as the constituent chemicals of the reagent. Kaye[224] found the AP test to be very specific, although his method was different from the now standard method, and he based his threshold on the number of units of activity in a sample.

Due to the nature of the AP test removing part of the suspected semen stain, the effect on subsequent DNA typing is not generally a consideration because DNA samples would be taken from the parent stain. A study by Reshef et al.[225] demonstrated that DNA profiles could be recovered from AP test strips as old as 2 years, further indicating that the AP reagent does not affect subsequent DNA profiling.

STK Sperm Tracker

STK Sperm Tracker (AXO Science, France) is an alternative method of AP detection that uses ALS and AP specificity for detection of semen stains. It comes in three forms: STK Spray, STK Lab (sheet), and STK Skin, each designed for use in different examination situations. According to the manufacturer, the tests react with AP, and a 365/366 nm UV light is needed to visualize the test and can be combined with an orange filter.

Procedures for the different STK tests vary, but the reagents are directly applied to stains, so their effect on DNA is an important consideration. The spray and skin versions are both mixed and then sprayed onto different surfaces, including skin, and allowed to develop for between 10 seconds and 3 minutes, in line with standard AP testing. The lab version, also known as STK Sperm Tracker Sheet, is a sheet-based detection method for use on absorbent surfaces, with an absorbing side and a laminated reading side. It is cut to the size of the evidence/area to be tested; the absorbent side is moistened, and then the sheet is applied to the evidence and pressed strongly for 3 minutes. Detection is then carried out using a UV ALS at 365/366 nm and appropriate UV blocking goggles, with a positive test showing blue fluorescence.

The STK Lab test showed a sensitivity of 1:25 to 1:1000, and it was not found to cross-react with urine, saliva, blood, vaginal fluid, or feces.[226–228] When tested against nonhuman semen, it showed cross-reaction with pig *(Sus scrofa)*.[227] Mixtures of semen with saliva, blood, vaginal fluid, urine, and feces did not interfere with the test, although fecal mixtures showed a reduced signal.[226] Fabric type showed differences in detection ability of the two tests.[227,228] It was found that the spray test had a sensitivity of 1:100 and did not cross-react with urine, saliva, or vaginal fluid, or react with semen from cattle, chicken, or dog, but reacted with semen from pig.[227] There was no effect on subsequent DNA profiling for either test.[226,227]

Prostate Specific Antigen

There is some debate surrounding the discovery of PSA, with some claiming it was discovered as early as 1966.[229] This was due to some confusion at the time that resulted in the same protein being classified under different names by multiple groups, but all with similar structure to PSA.[229–231] Its use in forensic science was proposed in the 1970s,[232,233] and it is present is seminal fluid at concentrations between 0.3 and 4.2 mg/mL.[1,69]

PSA (P-30) is a nonspecific phosphomonoesterase synthesized in prostate epithelial cells,[76] and it is one of the main proteins found in seminal fluid (Fig. 4.17). There are five known isoforms, of which type B is the most common and the one detected in semen with a weight of 33 kDa.[234] It is a monomeric, sialylated glycoprotein that weighs ~30 kDa (33–34 kDa),

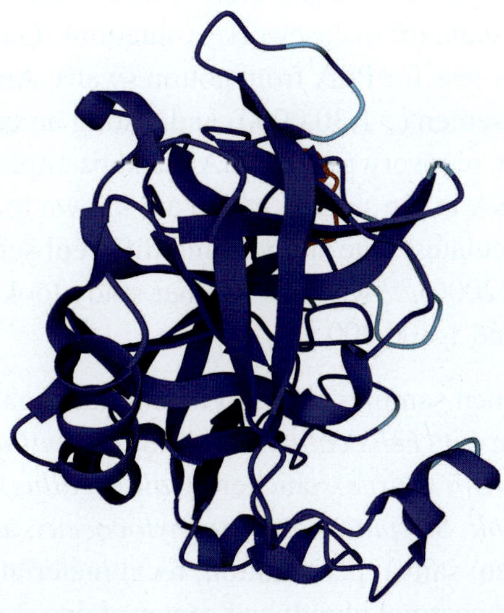

Fig. 4.17 AlphaFold structure prediction of prostate specific antigen protein (PubChem Protein: P07288). *From Jumper J, Evans R, Pritzel A, et al. Highly accurate protein structure prediction with AlphaFold. Nature. 2021;596:583–589; Varadi M, Anyango S, Deshpande M, et al. AlphaFold protein structure database: massively expanding the structural coverage of protein-sequence space with high-accuracy models. Nucl Acid Res. 2021;50:D439–D444.*

hence the synonym of P-30.[232,235] The presence of PSA in seminal fluid is independent of the presence of spermatozoa, and PSA has been demonstrated to originate in the epithelial cells that line the ducts of the prostate.[236] PSA testing is conducted in a similar manner to other immunologic tests. It is an antigen-antibody reaction, with the antigen being PSA and the antibodies specific to PSA. Several commercial kits are available, although most were originally designed for diagnostic use in the detection of prostate cancer and have been subsequently validated for use in forensic science.[237] Commercial kits (e.g., ABAcard p30 [Abacus Diagnostics, United States], IMx PSA assay [Abbot Laboratories, United Kingdom], SERATEC PSA Semiquant [Seratec, Germany]) and other commercial tests are available.

The tests require that some of the stain be removed and soaked in a buffer for an allotted time, usually a few minutes, to allow the PSA to elute from the stain into the buffer. The buffer is then added to the sample well (Fig. 4.18) and will migrate over the reaction area (in the results window). If no PSA is present or it is below the limits of detection of the test, then only the control line and internal standard (if present) will be visible. If PSA is present, then three lines will be visible (control line, internal standard [if present], and test line), which indicates the presence of PSA (see Fig. 4.18). Other tests function in a similar manner.

PSA has been detected at dilutions of 1:50,000 to 1:1 million,[205,214,240,241] but another study found a narrower range of 1:500 to 1:10,000.[201] The method of recovery will significantly affect sensitivity studies, whether samples are diluted from a liquid neat semen sample or subsampled on a swab, as is standard in casework evaluations. Gartside et al.[242] estimated an extraction efficiency of 1% or less for PSA from cotton swabs. Another study found a wide range between testing direct semen (>1:30,0000) and testing an extract of a stain on a swab (1:100),[214] confirming the low recovery rate of PSA via subsample. The range of sensitivity is dependent on the levels of PSA in the semen, which are known to vary between individuals, and even within different ejaculates. One study found different sensitivities of PSA between two volunteers (1:1000 vs. 1:2000),[243] whereas another study looking at five volunteers found a range between 1:100,000 and 1:800,000.[205]

PSA has been detected in semen samples exposed to simulated gastric juices for up to 4 hours.[244] Seminal fluid from cat *(Felis catus)*, dog *(Canis familiaris)*, pig *(Sus scrofa)*, horse *(Equus caballus)*, bull *(Bos taurus)*, chicken *(Gallus gallus)*, *Bacillus*, *Clostridium*, *Pseudomonas*, *Escherichia coli*, *Streptococcus*, *Staphylococcus*, and *Candida albicans*; urine samples from men and women; saliva; perspiration; fecal material; seminal fluid–free vaginal secretions with and without menstrual blood; and semen stains stored for up to 30 years were all tested for PSA.[212,240,241] All semen samples tested positive, as did several male urine samples, but all other samples tested negative.[240] Male urine samples showed PSA positive for up to 24 hours after ejaculation.[245] Another study obtained a PSA positive from a 100-year-old stain.[170]

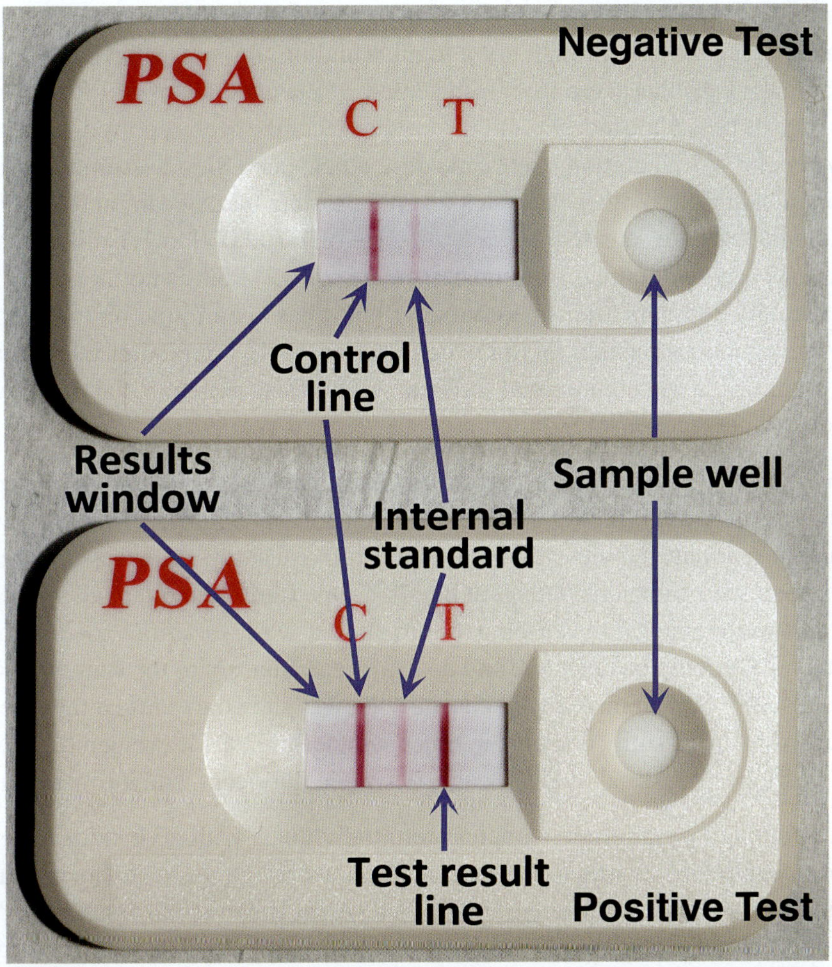

Fig. 4.18 Example of the test for prostate specific antigen *(PSA)* from Seratec showing both a positive *(bottom)* and a negative *(top)* reaction. Any other combination of lines in the results window or absence of lines indicates an invalid test result.

A large study evaluating the PSA test found no cross-reaction with 44 different substances ranging from soda, alcohol, to personal cleaning products, and found none to react when using the supplied buffer, but five cross-reacted when used with Phosphate Buffered Saline (PBS).[246] The same study found a range of other cross-reactions with PSA, but only when using its own in-house PBS buffer. The study found a sensitivity for PSA of 1:100,000 when using the supplied buffer, and this level did not change when the sample had been treated with AP reagent prior to testing.[246]

Conversely, PSA has been found in paraurethral glands, perianal glands, apocrine sweat glands, and mammary glands, meaning that low levels of PSA can be found in urine, feces, sweat, tears, breast milk, breast tissue, cyst fluid, nipple aspirate, and even the bloodstream.[69,214,247,248] Cross-reaction has also been found with apple juice, leek, orange, red wine, and the AP reagent.[214] Although not a regular finding, PSA tests have been shown to react with vaginal swabs that were free from semen.[249] Elevated levels of PSA in the blood are also an indicator of prostate cancer[250] and have more recently been reported in breast, uterine, and lung cancers.[9,70,247] Ejaculation itself can cause an elevated blood serum PSA level for up to 48 hours in addition to other variables (even a prostate biopsy can increase levels for 6 weeks).[251] Some tests are sensitive to PSA at levels of 1:100,000 to 1:1 million, and false positive reactions can be obtained from postejaculate urine.[70] PSA is not normally detected in the vaginal cavity 24 hours after intercourse,[237] but it has been found up to 27 hours[215] and in one study in vaginal and semen mixtures collected up to 48 hours after intercourse[245] and stored for 1 month.[212] Some commercial tests can give a false negative reaction due to the high-dose hook effect (see Chapter 2).

Washing may remove detectable traces of the seminal stains and was found to be dependent on the type of detergent used (biological or non-biological) and temperature of the washing cycle,[176] although spermatozoa may still be present.[252] In one study, PSA was detected after six washes of a semen stain using one detergent brand.[252] One study found that all visible traces of the semen stains were removed by washing, but in all four wash variations tried, if the stain was premarked, then PSA could be detected, and control areas adjacent to the stain did not give a PSA positive result.[245] Semen mixed with caustic soda was shown to cause a false negative PSA result, but PSA was successfully detected in other samples mixed with semen (urine [male and female], saliva, blood, menstrual blood, bleach, detergent, lubricant, and intimate wash).[245]

PSA has been found in postmortem samples from individuals with no history of sexual activity prior to death.[222,253] It was found that male cadavers in a more advanced stage of decomposition had a higher incidence of positive PSA results in rectal swabs than those more recently deceased, but female cadavers did not have any PSA results.[253] Further study found that the highest incidence of PSA positives was from the urethra, with PSA detected also on swabs from the glans penis, perianal region, and rectum.[222] Samples from deceased individuals should therefore be assessed with these findings in mind.

It has been found that PSA can be detected for a maximum 48 to 6 hours after a sexual assault.[243,254] In one study looking at sexual assault cases, sampled within 48 hours of the assault, and the effect of menstrual cycles, they found that 21 of 69 cytologically negative samples showed PSA positivity, but only two of those samples contained enough male DNA for profiling.[255] Menstrual cycle and day of within that cycle did not affect the PSA test. Benschop et al.[254] determined that PSA levels were donor dependent and that different individuals' PSA persisted for longer periods, but that the stability of PSA was low in the vaginal environment.

Several other methods have been investigated to detect PSA beyond the immunologic methods described earlier. Gooch et al.[256] developed a novel forensic use fluorescent substrate that was PSA specific, adapting data from an earlier study in cancer research.[257] The substrate allows the fluorescent emission of PSA positive sample across a range of surfaces and with a sensitivity reported at 1:1000, and no damage to DNA (Fig. 4.19).[256] Similar methods using the same target amino acid sequence have also been investigated.[258] Finally other methods, such as white light reflectance spectroscopy biosensing,[259] electroreduction click chemistry,[260] and quantum dot displacement biosensors,[261] have been investigated. Although these methods all offer benefits in terms of specificity and show promise, none have indicated they are easier or more cost effective than the current PSA membrane-based assays, nor have they become widespread in sexual assault investigations.

Semenogelin

Sg consists of two variants, Sg I and Sg II, both of which have only been recently classified (relative to other forensic serology targets). In 1984, Lilja et al.[262] found three immunologically related proteins at 52, 71, and 76 kDa that were unique to semen and originated from seminal vesicle secretions. Shortly after, monoclonal antibodies were developed, which recognized Sg antigens for forensic identification.[263–265] Subsequent research found that there were only two proteins (Sg I at 52 kDa with 439 amino acids and Sg II with 559 amino acids), but they can be found in both a nonglycosylated and a glycosylated form, accounting for the 71 kDa and 76 kDa, respectively (Fig. 4.20).[266] It was also found that Sg II was primarily produced in the seminal vesicles, but a portion also originated from the epididymis.[267] Subsequent research found that Sg I was also found in the epididymis, and both Sg I and Sg II were found throughout the other parts of the male reproductive tract, in the vas deferens, prostate, and

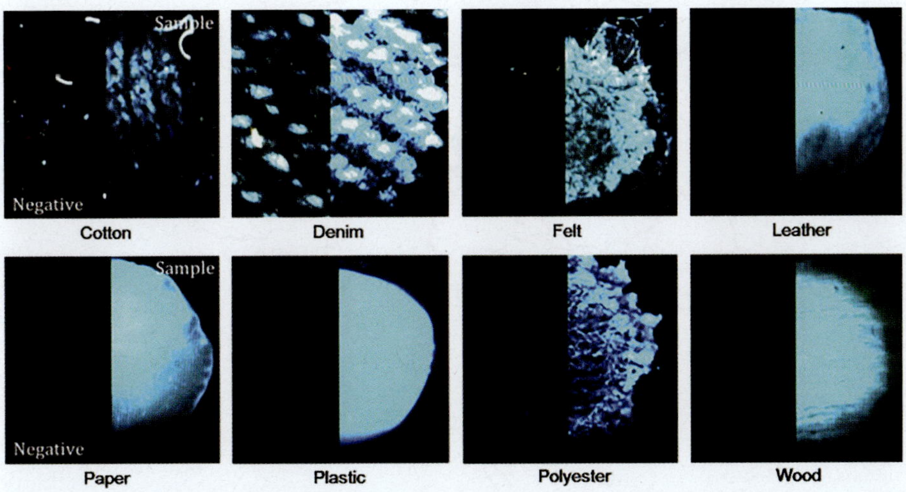

Fig. 4.19 Example of the fluorescent substrate specific to prostate specific antigen reacting with semen on various surfaces relevant to forensic investigations. Negative controls (reagent only) of the various surfaces are shown *(on the right of each image)*, and the *right side* shows semen deposited on those surfaces reacted with the substrate. *From Gooch J, Daniel B, Frascione N. Application of fluorescent substrates to the in situ detection of prostate specific antigen. Talanta. 2014;125:210–214.*

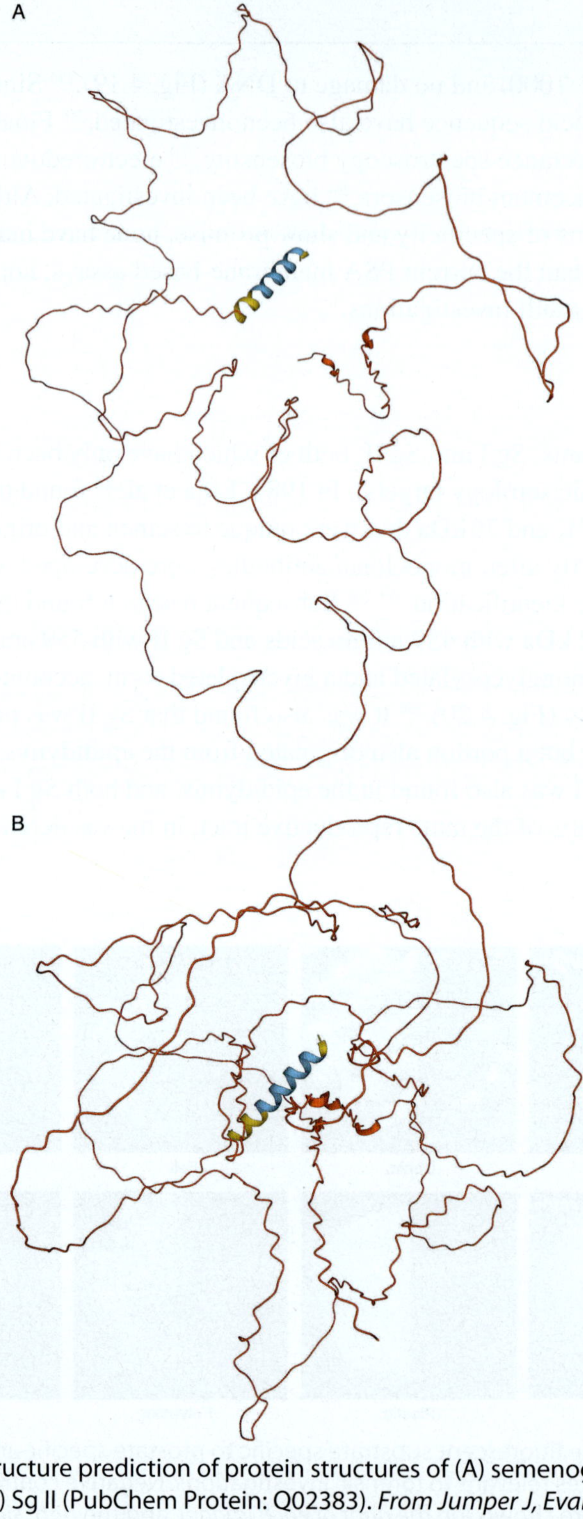

Fig. 4.20 AlphaFold structure prediction of protein structures of (A) semenogelin (Sg) I (PubChem Protein: P04279) and (B) Sg II (PubChem Protein: Q02383). *From Jumper J, Evans R, Pritzel A, et al. Highly accurate protein structure prediction with AlphaFold. Nature. 2021;596:583–589; Varadi M, Anyango S, Deshpande M, et al. AlphaFold protein structure database: massively expanding the structural coverage of protein-sequence space with high-accuracy models. Nucl Acid Res. 2021;50:D439–D444.*

testes.[79] The Sg proteins and fibronectin aggregate into a gelatinous mass that is liquified by PSA after 5 to 20 minutes, which liquifies the Sg.[77,80] Sg is theorized to degrade the ovum envelop to allow spermatozoon penetration of the egg to allow fertilization.[77]

Sg levels in males age 18 to 24 years were found to be 4 to 68 mg/mL,[268] demonstrating the wide starting range. The Sgs, both as intact proteins and fragments, bind zinc (Zn^{2+}), which is found in high levels in seminal plasma.[77] Although originally thought to be highly specific to semen, they have been found in the kidney, skeletal muscles, trachea, and gastrointestinal tract at low levels, but the purpose of Sg in those locations is still unknown.[79] Interestingly, Sg has also been found at differing levels in different parts of the retina[269–271] and in various cancers.[272,273] Using enzyme-linked immunosorbent assay (ELISA)–based testing, Sg has been found in high vaginal fluid (Sg II), saliva (Sg II), blood (Sg II), and urine (male: Sg I).[274] The same study found that levels of Sg differed between individuals and between different ejaculates of the same individual.[274] Medical ELISA-based Sg detection methods assess Sg I and Sg II separately and can detect to dilutions around 1:1 million (Sg I) and 1:10,000 (Sg II) (note that this is variable due to the starting range of Sg that can be found in semen). Sg has been found in other body fluids, including male urine (Sg I), blood (Sg II), and vaginal samples (Sg II), although at levels that do not react with the forensic immunochromatographic test strips.[274]

There are two assays designed for Sg detection in forensic investigations: Rapid Stain Identification (RSID) Semen (Independent Forensics of Illinois [IFI], United States) and Nanotrap Sg (Rohto Pharm, Japan). Both are one-step immunochromatographic tests. There are also other medical Sg tests that are more sensitive, but they are much more expensive and difficult to use (they are ELISA based) and show more cross-reactions.[274]

Nanotrap Sg was developed in 2004 to target Sg II specifically, the seminal plasma motility inhibitor region.[275] Unlike other immunochromatographic tests in forensic serology, Nanotrap Sg has a single test line, but it also has a test completion window that acts as a control for appropriate sample concentration and pH. The mechanism of the test is the reaction of Sg antigens with a mobile mouse monoclonal anti–Sg II antibody and an immobile rabbit polyclonal anti–Sg II antibody on a test cartridge (Fig. 4.21).

Nanotrap Sg was found to have a sensitivity to human semen of 1:400,000 and showed cross-reaction with mandrill *(Mandrillus sphinx)* semen, but to a maximum dilution of 1:2000.[275] It did not cross-react with serum, saliva, breast milk, urine (male or female), vaginal secretions, or semen from bull, horse, pig, or dog.[275] The test was able to successfully detect Sg that had been heated to 150°C for 1 hour.[275] Frozen and refrigerated semen showed weaker signals than did fresh semen, and it was shown to identify semen even when no spermatozoa were observed.[276]

RSID Semen is an immunochromatographic assay that uses two mouse monoclonal antibodies in a lateral flow format in the same manner as those described in RSID Blood, but it targets Sg. It was developed in 2012 by IFI, and it does not disclose the Sg target (i.e., Sg I or Sg II).[277]

The RSID Semen test requires Sg to be extracted from the sample using a provided buffer, by submerging the sample and shaking it for 10 seconds, although extended incubation times can

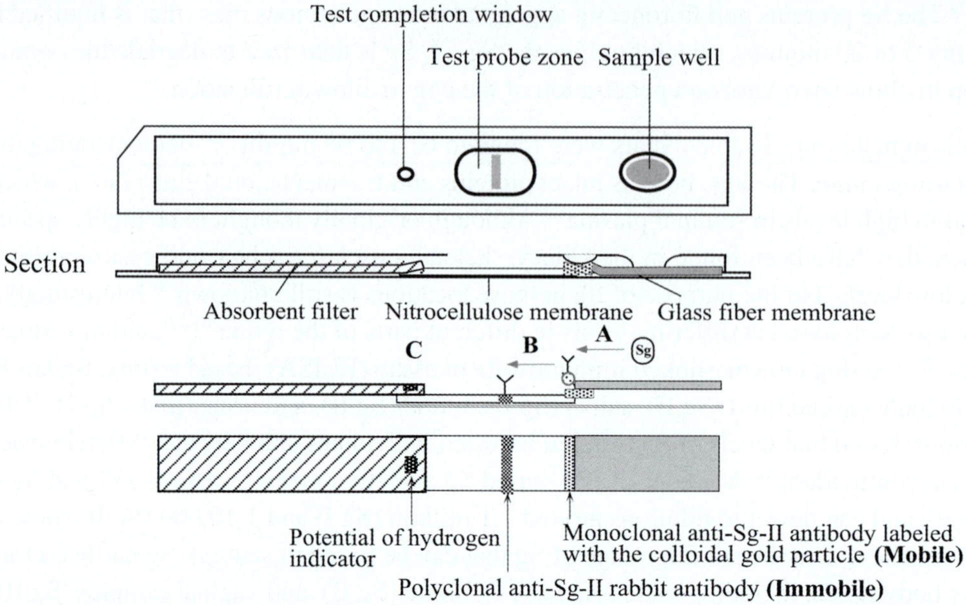

Fig. 4.21 The Nanotrap semenogelin *(Sg)* test schematic. Sg antigens are captured by the monoclonal anti–Sg II antibodies and then migrate to the test probe zone (A); then the mobile antigen-antibody complex is captured with the immobilized polyclonal anti–Sg II rabbit antibody (B), and a positive appears as a red-purple vertical line. The test completion window always contains a red spot when the sample is applied at reasonable volume and pH (C). *From Sato I, Kojima K, Yamasaki T, et al. Rapid detection of semenogelin by one-step immunochromatographic assay for semen identification. J Immunol Method. 2004;287:137–145.*

also be used. Following the extraction, a maximum of 20 μL of extract is further diluted in the provided buffer to a final volume of 100 μL, which is then deposited on the sample window. The test is assessed after 10 minutes.

A positive test is indicated by two lines at the C (control) and T (test) positions (Fig. 4.22), and a negative is indicated by a single line at the C position. If only the T line or no lines are observed, then this indicates an invalid test, and the process needs to be repeated for a result.

RSID Semen shows a range of sensitivities between 1:5000 and 1:1 million when used with the supplied buffer; in contrast, results when using water to elute the Sg showed sporadic positives to a maximum dilution of 1:2500, although most tests were negative.[205,241,245,277] Similarly, when extracted in water, another study found maximum sensitivities of 1:16 when using previously frozen semen and 1:256 when testing with fresh semen.[278] The RSID Semen buffer is designed to dissolve the antibody–colloidal gold conjugate from the conjugate pad, maintain pH, and facilitate the running of the test.[277] The reported use of water for extracting the Sg from samples therefore would affect the assay and may result in not releasing the antibody from the test strip and is the likely cause of the high failure rate when using water for extraction. The provided buffer should therefore be used for maximum sensitivity, which can also be subsequently used for DNA extraction.

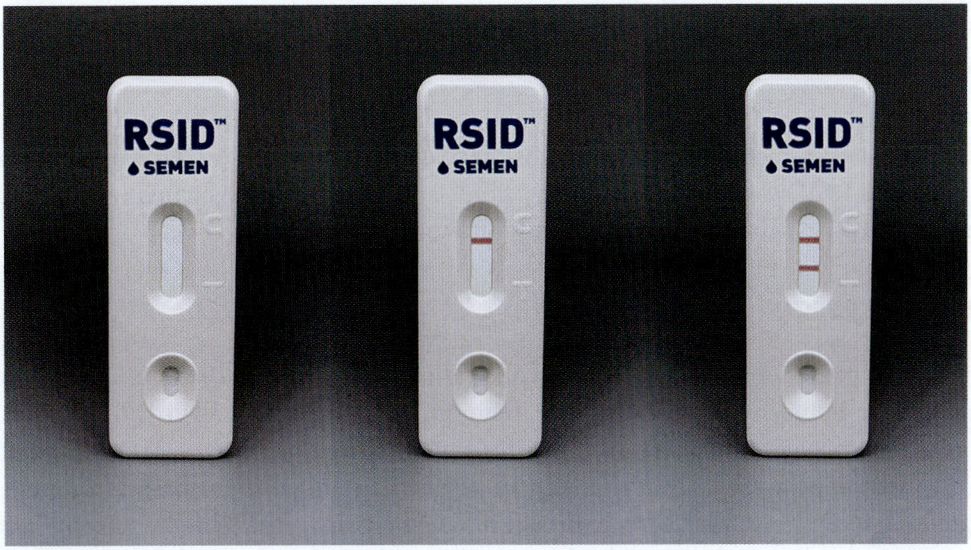

Fig. 4.22 The RSID Semen test showing *(from left to right)* a blank cassette, a negative, and a positive result. The sample window is at the bottom of the test, and lines at C and T indicate a positive result, whereas a line at only C indicates a negative result. *From Dina Mattes, Independent Forensics of Illinois.*

High-dose hook effect was observed when dilutions of semen higher than 1:80 were tested, which showed as a reduction in the intensity of the test line, and complete failure of the test with dilutions of 1:16 or higher.[277] The samples demonstrated a normal positive when further diluted and tested again. It was also found that for some substrates (such as cotton chambray and denim) that taking a cutting of the semen stain was more effective and gave better results than taking a swab of the stain.[277] One study found that Sg could be detected at a 1:200 dilution, and it was effective for up to 72 hours after a sexual assault (this was the time limit of the study, so vaginal persistence of Sg may be longer);[243] however, another study investigating sexual assault found a limit of 48 to 60 hours, with subsequent times (60–84 hours) failing.[254] Benschop et al.[254] determined that Sg levels were donor dependent, although they also theorized that Sg was more stable in the vaginal environment than was PSA.

Caustic soda, urine (male and female), saliva, blood, menstrual blood, bleach, detergent, breast milk, sweat, vaginal secretions, vaginal fluid (high and low swabs), feces, lubricant, and intimate wash did not inhibit or cross-react with RSID Semen.[241,245,274,277] RSID Semen was shown to successfully identify semen even when mixed with four times the volume of blood, urine, saliva, and breast milk.[277] Persistence postejaculation has been found to be up to 72 hours in postcoital vaginal swabs, and up to 48 hours in postejaculate male urine.[245] Washing was not found to affect the ability of RSID Semen to detect Sg, but visible traces of the stain were removed.[245] Another study used RSID Semen to identify semen in feminine hygiene pads up to

48 hours postcoital, up to 3 hours in postcoital vaginal swabs, and in 1:25 mixtures of semen in blood, saliva, or urine.[278] It was able to positively identify semen as old as 56 years.[279]

Species specificity was tested, and it was found that no nonhuman semen sources tested (bull, cat, dog, goat, horse, mouse, pig, sheep) cross-reacted with the test.[241,277] However, another study evaluated RSID Semen with dog body fluids and found a single canine rectal swab showed positive cross-reaction, but a second follow-up test typed negative.[280]

Florence Crystals

First described in 1897 by Florence[53] based on findings using Roussin's staining of spermatozoa (remembering that he was the first to use staining methods in 1867),[45] the test detects the presence of choline, a quaternary saturated amine.[214] The basis of the test is the reaction of iodine within a reagent applied to a suspected seminal stain/sample, with the choline found in semen. Characteristic brown rhombic crystals are formed through a reaction of the choline and iodine to form choline periodide crystals (Figs. 4.23 and 4.24). Although no longer commonplace, it is still used in some laboratories.

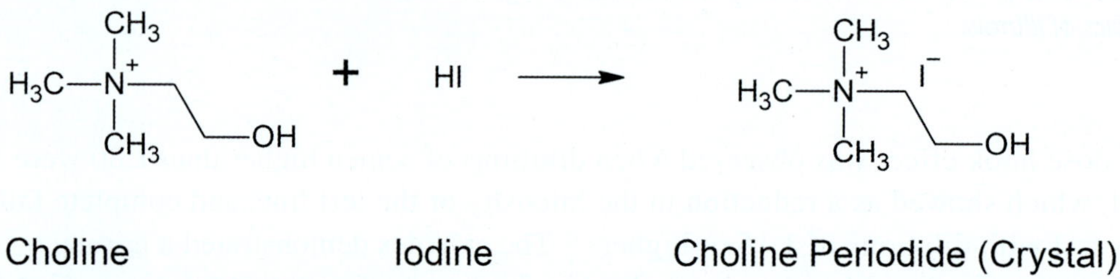

Fig. 4.23 Choline (PubChem CID: 305) reacted with Iodine (I) forms Choline Periodide (PubChem CID: 87300), which forms a crystalline structure (see Fig. 4.23). *From Advanced Chemistry Development Inc. ChemSketch. Toronto, Ontario; 2018. www.acdlabs.com.*

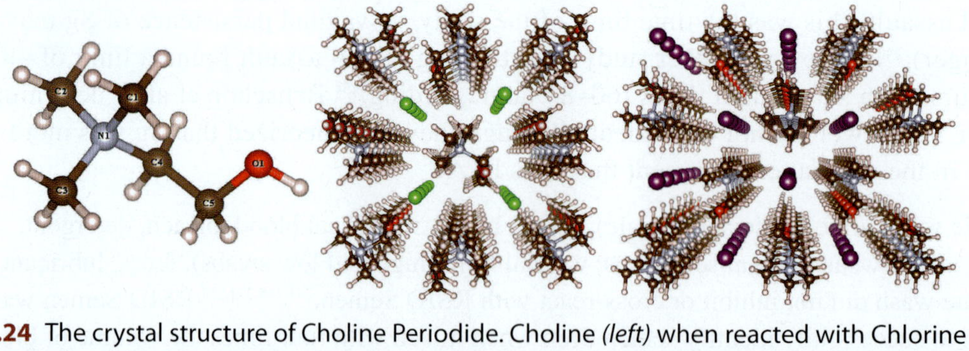

Fig. 4.24 The crystal structure of Choline Periodide. Choline *(left)* when reacted with Chlorine *(C1)* to form Choline Chloride (rhombic structure crystals; *center*), and with Iodine (I) to form Choline Periodide (monoclinic crystal structure; *right*). The synthesis of the choline periodide to determine the structure was by a different synthesis method than Florence's, but the crystals formed are the same shape and chemical makeup. Atoms are colored: carbon *(brown)*, hydrogen *(peach)*, nitrogen *(gray)*, oxygen *(red)*, chlorine *(green)*, iodine *(purple)*. *From Zhuravlev Y, Gordienko K, Dyagilev D, et al. Structural, electronic, and vibrational properties of choline halides. Mater Chem Phys. 2020;246:122787.*

The Florence test is not specific for spermatozoa or for seminal fluid,[282] with choline being found in a range of tissues and plants. It is, however, found in high levels in semen, which is why the test was used extensively, but is now being phased out in most labs.[9] Early results found the test could show false negatives with fresh semen stains and that vaginal secretions would occasionally give false positive reactions.[46] Pollack[158] and Kaye[224] describe many factors that can influence the Florence test, including water, putrefaction, admixture of proteins, and soap, which can cause false negatives; albumin, glycerophosphoric acid, trimethylamine, extracts from mushrooms, corn, blossoms of plants, onions, and many other things can cause false positives. Hardinge et al.[214] also found cross-reaction with urine, banana, blueberry, broccoli, cabbage, cauliflower, cucumber, lager (beer), leek, nectarine, parsnip, pineapple, potato, red wine, swede, and tomato. They also found a cross-reaction with urine, but with a different crystal formation (Fig. 4.25).

Sensitivity has been found up to 1:20,000, making it more sensitive than PSA in one study.[214] Forbes[282] found that even after a fabric was washed with soap and water that the Florence test still produced crystals, but that it took 10 minutes for them to develop. He also found that as a sample was diluted (he found sensitivity varied between individuals and lists negatives observed at between 1:3 and 1:40 dilutions), the size of the crystals reduced until a microscope was needed to see them.[282] A study in 1931, in contrast, found the sensitivity to be 1:70,000.[283]

A

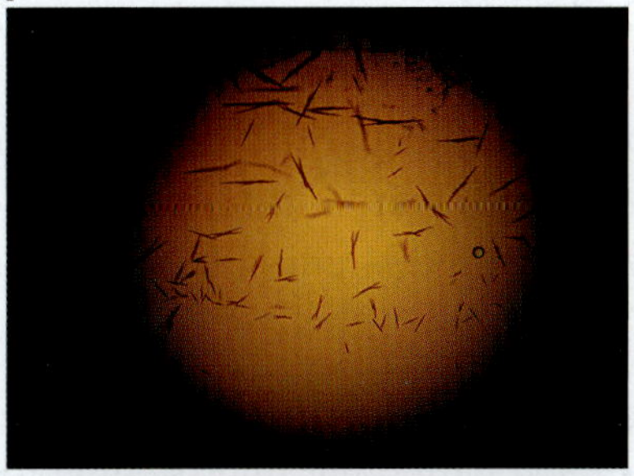

B

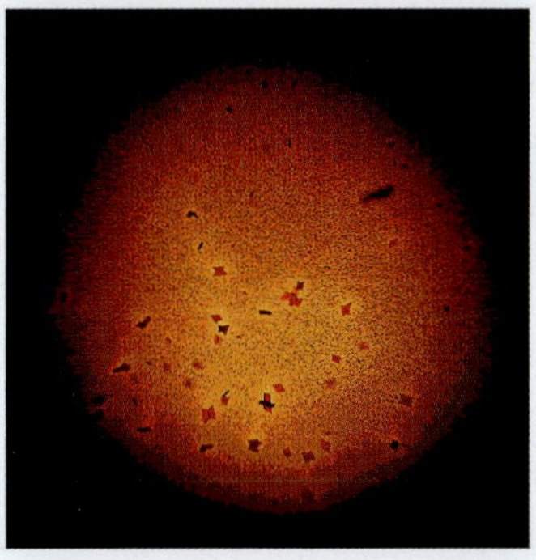

Fig. 4.25 Florence crystals in semen (A) and urine (B). *From Hardinge P, Allard J, Wain A, et al. Optimisation of choline testing using Florence iodine reagent, including comparative sensitivity and specificity with PSA and AP tests. Sci Just. 2013;53:34–40.*

Microscopic Identification of Sperm Cells

Microscopic identification of spermatozoa is the only true nongenetic confirmatory test for any forensic body fluid. Spermatozoa will only be present if ejaculation has occurred, so the finding of even a single spermatozoon can be significant. The circumstances surrounding the ejaculation (e.g., consensual vs. nonconsensual intercourse) cannot be determined by the observation of spermatozoa alone, but it may be useful in confirming or refuting allegations and sequences of events. If spermatozoa are observed microscopically, then male DNA can be obtained from the sample; one study found that if observed, then DNA was recovered 100% of the time.[284]

History surrounding the discovery and identification of spermatozoa has been covered in the first part of the chapter, so it will be discussed only briefly here. The first reported microscopic examination of semen in a legal framework by Orfila[31] found microscopic identification of semen was not possible from dried stains presumably because the recovery and mounting process caused the loss of all tails. A decade later, Rattier[32] developed a recovery method of dried stains that left at least some of the recovered spermatozoa intact with tails. Further research to isolate spermatozoa from fabric without breaking their tails was developed by Bayard in 1839.[12] Current methods are designed to optimize and maximize the recovery of spermatozoa from different substrates, attempting to keep the state of the spermatozoa the same as on the substrate (i.e., with or without tails). Although individualization is now reserved for DNA typing, there were researchers who claimed that individualization of semen could be accomplished based on the morphological abnormalities present in the sample.[285–287] These studies were carried out in a fertility framework, so the levels of spermatozoa recovered in forensic investigation are very low, and the spermatozoa recovered in forensic science are overwhelmingly immotile, which means that this method is unlikely to have any accuracy in a casework setting.

Microscopic search for spermatozoa requires the minimum use of a high-powered microscope, which can be combined with other microscopic features, including fluorescence and phase contrast. Some researchers have even combined microscopic evaluation with laser microdissection to allow excision and capture of individual spermatozoon for DNA typing,[288] as can the use of optical tweezers,[289] both of which can offer insights when mixed samples of ejaculate are analyzed or low levels of spermatozoa are found in excess levels of epithelial cells.

Prior to the microscopic evaluation of evidence for spermatozoa, the samples must first be prepared. In some cases, the samples taken by the forensic medical examiner are slide mounted immediately (or very shortly after) collection during a sexual assault medical examination. Other times, the samples can be slide mounted by forensic laboratory staff later. There are different methods that can also be used to mount slides, with a smear method preferred in some locations,[290] where the swab (e.g., high vaginal) can be smeared immediately onto a slide prior to staining. If the swab is not sampled immediately, then it can be moistened with water or buffer and smeared onto a slide prior to staining.

An alternative method is to extract the spermatozoa from a swab (or substrate) and concentrate it simultaneously to allow for a higher chance of finding spermatozoa. This generally involves soaking part of the stain, or swab, in a liquid (water or buffer) with gentle agitation to physically dislodge the spermatozoa, if present, from the substrate. The volume of liquid and which liquid is used will vary among laboratories. Following the release of any spermatozoa, a small volume of the sample can be removed and placed on a slide. Alternatively, the sample can be centrifuged, allowing the cellular material to pellet at the bottom of the tube, the supernatant can be removed, and the pellet resuspended in a reduced volume of fluid (e.g., 20 μL), which can be fully applied to a slide. Allard et al.[201] found that laboratories that use less aggressive methods (e.g., slower or no centrifugation) resulted in more spermatozoa with tails and theorized that the mechanical nature of the extraction process causes the loss of tails. Nittis et al.[290] found that when smears were used to mount the samples, if done immediately upon collection, there were more spermatozoa, more intact (with tails), and more background material than those smears mounted later at a laboratory.

The slide is then heat fixed by heating the slide to dry off the fluid and to affix the cellular material to the slide. Care must be taken to ensure the samples are not overly heated, and standard operating procedures will detail the correct temperature and time to heat the sample. The sample is then ready to stain using one of the methods described later.

An alteration to the mounting method for semen samples prior to staining is a pretreatment with Proteinase K (Pro K). Pro K is a proteinase, meaning that it breaks down proteins into smaller polypeptides or amino acids (a process called proteolysis), and specifically Pro K hydrolyzes keratin.[291] Chapman et al.[292] investigated whether a method used in DNA extractions could be adapted for use with microscopic spermatozoa searching when spermatozoa may be masked by excesses of epithelial cells (from the vagina or oral cavity). They applied the use of sodium dodecyl sulfate (SDS), a surfactant used in soap, and Pro K to their samples prior to mounting and concluded that, due to the disulfide bonds in the head of the spermatozoa, they would be resistant to the activity of the Pro K, something that had been previously indicated in early DNA typing.[293] They found the epithelial cells and tails of the spermatozoa were digested by the SDS-Pro K lysis, and only the spermatozoan heads remained, which could subsequently be stained for ease of identification (Fig. 4.26). It is not used routinely because of the potential loss of DNA, but it was successful in differentiating spermatozoa from yeast cells of similar appearance and in the isolation of spermatozoa from stomach contents.[292]

A

B

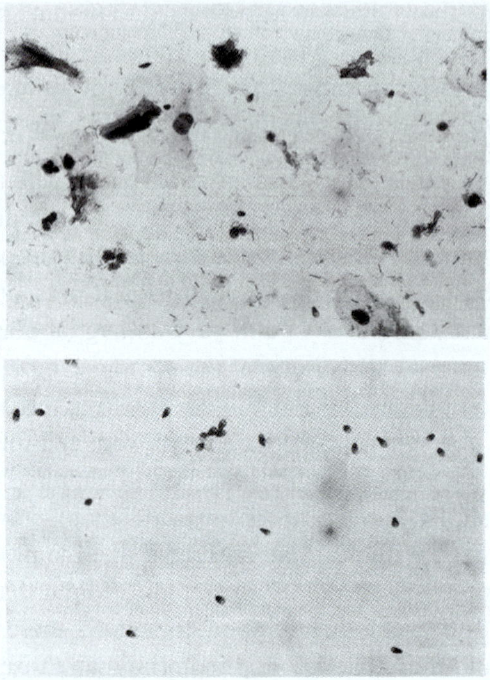

Fig. 4.26 Mixture of spermatozoa and vaginal cells before treatment with Pro K (A) and after treatment with Pro K (B), showing the removal of the vaginal epithelial cells making the identification of the spermatozoa easier. Slides were stained with hematoxylin and eosin, and viewed at 250×. *From Chapman RL, Brown NM, Keating SM. The isolation of spermatozoa from sexual assault swabs using proteinase K. J Forensic Sci Soc. 1989;29:207–212.*

Sensitivity in the visualization of spermatozoa will vary widely and is ultimately dependent on the starting concentration of spermatozoa within the sample. Some research has found identification was possible at semen dilutions up to 1:50,000,[205] but another study found only a single spermatozoon at a dilution of 1:1000.[246] In theory, when considering the minimum normal starting concentration of spermatozoa per milliliter, it should be possible to identify a single spermatozoon at dilutions over 20 million; however, this has not been observed in any study.

More sensitive detection of spermatozoa is possible by extracting the whole swab (in case of uneven collection), use of maceration, filter tubes, concentration columns, repelleting, and Pro K methods.[201] It is important to keep in mind that these more aggressive extraction methods will release more spermatozoa from the substrate but will also affect the proportion of observed intact (with tails) spermatozoa. It has also been observed that the type of swab used for sampling could affect either the recovery or release of spermatozoa, with one study finding a higher (5–10 times) cell yield when using nylon flocked swabs compared with standard cotton swabs.[254] Beckwith et al.[174] found spermatozoa could be recovered for up to 2 weeks if submerged in tap water but only after 1 hour if submerged in ocean water.

Spermatozoa have been found in the postejaculatory urine of men[294,295] and in semen subjected to simulated gastric juice for up to 4 hours.[244] It has also been noted that spermatozoa bind tightly to some fabrics, rendering extraction ineffective.[71] Spermatozoa have been identified in postmortem samples of men with no history of sexual activity prior to death in 21% of cases from smears originating from the glans penis, and in 39% from the urethra.[222] This is likely due to natural leakage of spermatozoa during the decomposition process.

It was found that under high humidity and temperature (37°C) the spermatozoa degraded to the point where they could not be identified after 3 months, but that strong pH (13–1) did not affect the spermatozoa (although time exposed to the pH conditions was not disclosed).[296]

Although spermatozoa can be visualized microscopically without staining, added epithelial cells (usually from the vagina or mouth), fibers from clothing, and low numbers of spermatozoa that may be degraded (no tails) means that samples are now always stained prior to microscopic examination.

Staining

To visualize spermatozoa, if present, on a slide-mounted sample, laboratories will stain the samples prior to microscopic search to better differentiate the biological material from other materials that may be present (e.g., clothing fibers). These stains are cytologic stains used in histology and are therefore not human specific, meaning that caution must be taken when examining some samples with other cellular material. They all require a high-powered microscope to visualize the slides and identify any spermatozoa that may be present. Because the formulation of stains may differ between laboratories, and the staining procedures will differ, only the constituent stains and resulting staining features will be discussed here.

Staining of samples to better visualize spermatozoa was first proposed in 1867[45] using iodine, which was expanded to other cell-staining dyes used at the time.[41,49] Early on, it was found that carmine[41] and picric acid[51] were suitable stains, and both are still currently used. New methods of staining are being investigated,[297] but a few staining methods have become the general standard used in most forensic laboratories. Different laboratories will use different methods to stain the samples suspected of containing spermatozoa, but it is always with a differential staining method, so two stains are used to differentially stain cells—usually the nucleus (DNA) is one color and the cytoplasm is another.

Staining of samples for microscopic identification of spermatozoa has no discrepancies in regard to limits of sensitivity because it is a direct analysis of physical features in the sample. Allery et al.[298] noted that, although the ability to detect and identify spermatozoa at different time points after intercourse did not change between three different staining methods, there was a difference in the number of spermatozoa observed between different staining methods at different time points. This means if there is a spermatozoon on the slide, then it should be detectable through vigorous searching by the analyst. The search can be complicated by other cellular material and other contaminants in the sample (e.g., blood, fibers), which can include masking of the target spermatozoon by other material on top. In other cases, cellular degradation can appear similar in form to spermatozoa.[299,300] This comes down to the unique nature of each sample and is not a feature of any staining technique.

Christmas Tree stain (KPIC or Kernechtrot Picroindigocarmine stain) is a combination of Nuclear Fast Red (PubChem CID: 23677995) and Picroindigocarmine, and it will result in nuclear material staining red and background cellular material staining green-blue[301] (Fig. 4.27). This uses some of the same chemicals as initially investigated in the late 1800s. The method was first proposed to stain and search for spermatozoa in 1969.[302] It has been found to be an effective method for staining and subsequent visualization of spermatozoa in cases of sexual assault, and it was found that 81% of surveyed laboratories used Christmas Tree staining for microscopic examination of sexual assault samples.[9] One study found that with a normozoospermia internal vaginal ejaculate, it would take 700 mL of fluid to dilute the sample to where Christmas Tree staining would be unable to detect them.[303]

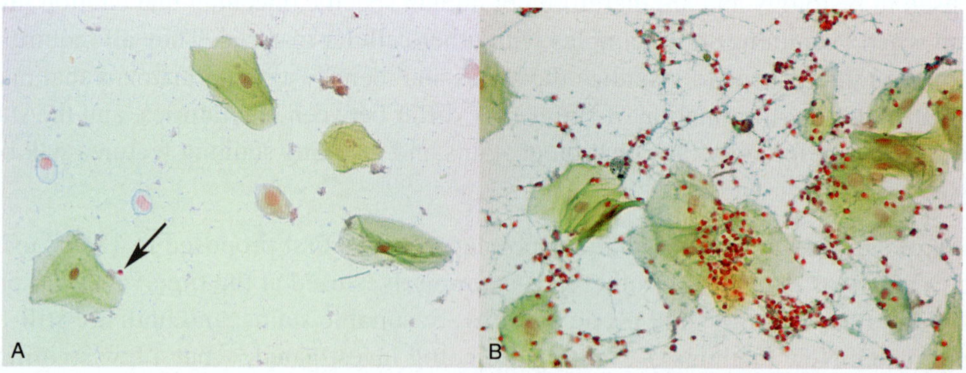

Fig. 4.27 Example of the Christmas Tree staining of two slides with spermatozoa and vaginal epithelial cells. (A) Sample with a single spermatozoon visible *(arrow)*. (B) Sample with several hundred spermatozoa visible. The heads of the spermatozoa and the cell nuclei are stained pink-red with Nuclear Fast Red, and the tails of the spermatozoa and the cellular cytoplasm are stained blue-green with Picroindigocarmine. 400× magnification. *From Amy Brodeur, Boston University School of Medicine.*

This is likely an underestimate because microscopic techniques have advanced since 1983 when that study was undertaken. Allery et al.[298] determined that Christmas Tree staining, along with hematoxylin and eosin (HE), was the gold standard cytologic method of spermatozoa screening, and that Christmas Tree had the added benefit of being easier to read than HE with more spermatozoa being observed than with HE.

HE is a combination of Hematoxylin (PubChem CID: 442514) and Eosin (PubChem CID: 11048), which stains the nucleus purple, and cytoplasm pink, respectively (Fig. 4.28). It was one of the most common staining methods for spermatozoa, being reported as early as 1897,[53] although a different hematoxylin formulation was used that took days to stain the cells. It was found to be the staining method most reported in literature in 2000[298] and still commonly used in other histologic applications. Allery et al.[298] determined that HE was the gold standard cytologic method of spermatozoa screening, although not as easy to read as Christmas Tree staining. It is still used in many laboratories today.

Baecchi testing is a differential staining method using Acid Fuchsin (PubChem CID: 5464362) and Methyl Blue (PubChem CID: 14513727). Baecchi published his method in 1909[59] after testing some of the other common methods of the era, which he found acceptable but "requiring great skill and patience." His method allowed rapid and simple staining that made the spermatozoa stand out for easy identification. Lundquist stated that by 1945, the Baecchi method was the most widespread method for spermatozoa

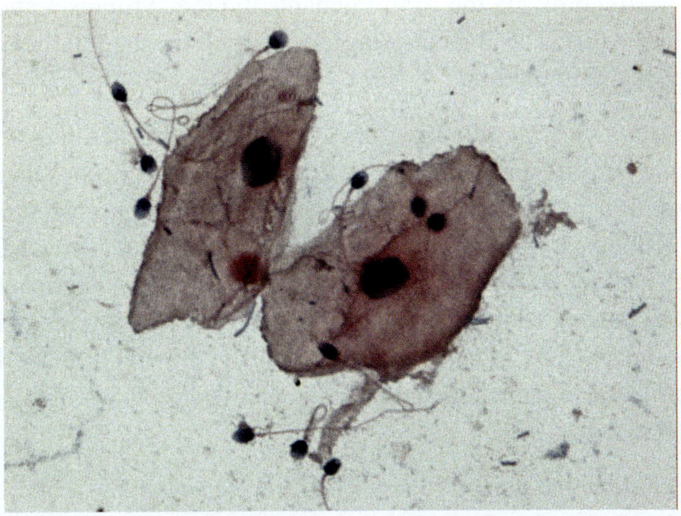

Fig. 4.28 Example of the Hematoxylin and Eosin stain showing two large epithelial cells (buccal) and several spermatozoa with tails. The heads of the spermatozoa and the cell nuclei are stained purple with the Hematoxylin, and the tails of the spermatozoa and the cellular cytoplasm are stained pink with the Eosin. 400× magnification.

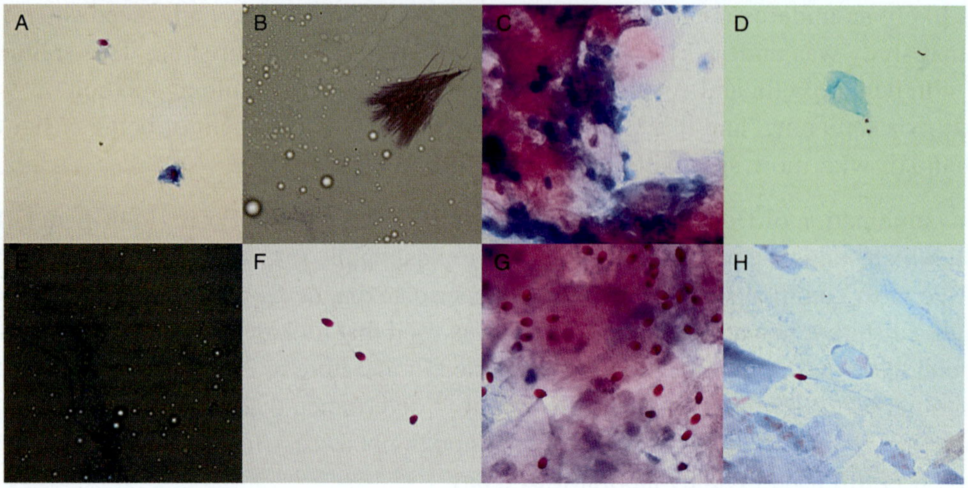

Fig. 4.29 Example of the Baecchi staining method. The heads of the spermatozoa and cell nuclei are stained pink with Acid Fuchsin, and the tails of the spermatozoa and cellular cytoplasm are stained blue with Methylene Blue. (A–D) Panels have no spermatozoa present; (E–H) panels have spermatozoa present. 1000× magnification. *From Golomingi R, Haas C, Dobay A, et al. Sperm hunting on optical microscope slides for forensic analysis with deep convolutional networks—a feasibility study. Forensic Sci Int Gen. 2022;56:102602.*

staining.[46] In 1971, it was suggested that the Methyl Blue be substituted with Methylene Blue (PubChem CID: 6099), which then became the standard; it stained the nuclei (and thus spermatozoa heads) pink via the Acid Fuchsin, and the cytoplasm and tails blue via the Methylene Blue (Fig. 4.29). The Baecchi staining method has largely been replaced by HE and Christmas Tree staining methods.

Sperm HY-Liter is a commercial product from IFI and is another staining method for spermatozoa, although it differs from those previously described because it requires specialist equipment. It is recommended to be visualized with a phase contrast fluorescent microscope, but it requires at minimum a fluorescence microscope for visualization. It uses DAPI (PubChem CID: 18676829) to stain nuclei blue, which must be visualized under fluorescent microscopy using suitable filters. The spermatozoa are stained green with Alexa 488 (flourescein isothiocyanate, PubChem CID: 131730176), which is covalently linked to a targeted derivatized mouse monoclonal antibody against proteins contained in the human sperm heads[305,306] (Fig. 4.30).

There are several different versions of Sperm HY-Liter kits available, but all use the same staining targets and will therefore have the same sensitivities and specificities. The versions are standard, express and SOS (reduced staining time with a different antibody fluorophore [CF 488A]), and PI (designed for sperm isolation techniques, such as laser microdissection

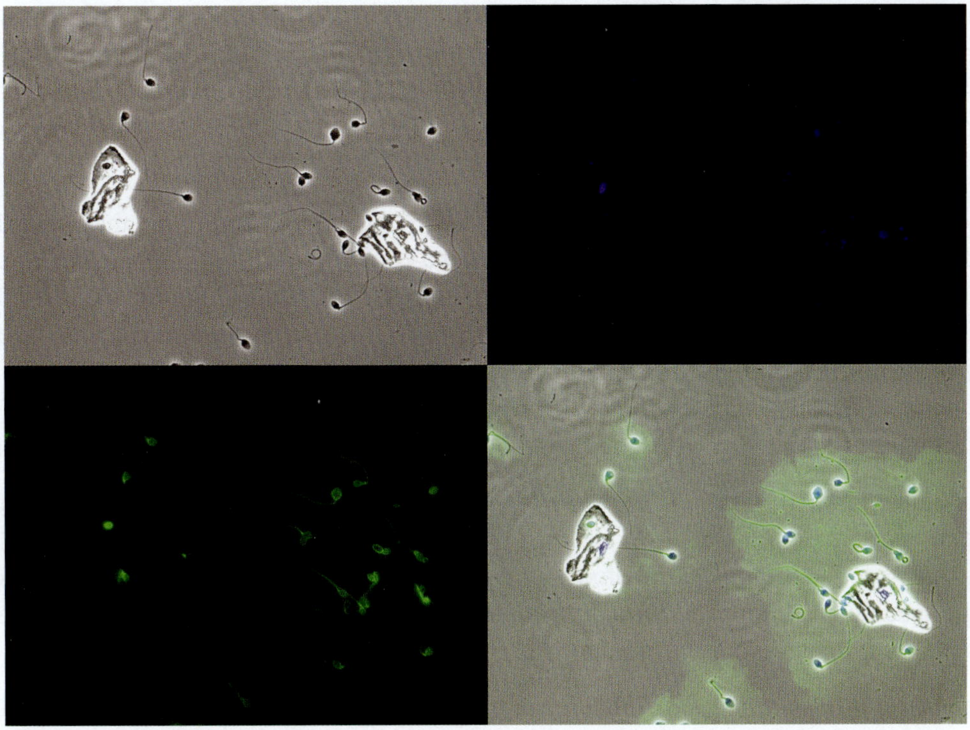

Fig. 4.30 Example of Sperm Hy-Liter used with a mixed semen and vaginal epithelial cell sample. Under phase contrast *(top left)*; Sperm HY-Liter DAPI stained, where all nuclear material is stained blue under the DAPI filter *(top right)*; Sperm HY-Liter Alexa 488 stained, where only the sperm protein is stained and viewed under a fluorescein isothiocyanate (FTIC) filter *(bottom left)*; and combined phase contrast, DAPI, and Alexa 488 *(bottom right)*. This technique is particularly useful for visualization of spermatozoon that are under other cellular material and may therefore be masked. Slides visualized on a Nikon Eclipse C. Pol fluorescence microscope using a FITC (467–556 nm) filter cube at 400×. *From Jasmine Tay and Clare de Sousa.*

or micropicking). There are also custom slides from IFI with designated circular areas that can be used, which can reduce the amount of reagents used and therefore decrease the cost,[300] or a hydrophobic pen is also offered. Spermatozoa examined with Sperm HY-Liter and subsequently removed for DNA profiling indicates that the method has little or no effect on subsequent DNA profiling.[288,300]

Sensitivity was tested with spermatozoa in the presence of excess epithelial cells to a maximum 1:10, and spermatozoa were still readily distinguished due to the differential staining.[307] Another study expanded this to a dilution factor of 1:1000 semen to vaginal swab extract and were still able to identify spermatozoa under both phase contrast microscopy alone, and with Sperm HY-Liter, with the latter providing a significant reduction in the time taken to examine the slides.[300] Ping et al.[288] were able to use Sperm HY-Liter to identify spermatozoa at low levels (1:1000) and mixed with various other body fluids, and in the presence of excess bacterial growth in simulated experiments. Another study, however, found interference with low levels of spermatozoa (i.e., a single spermatozoon) when in the presence of excess epithelial cells, which could sit on top and mask or distort the specific signal generated by the antibody.[300]

Using the express version, Takamura et al.[296] assessed degradation and found that under high humidity and temperature, even though spermatozoa could not be identified microscopically, fragments of the sperm head still remained and could be stained using Sperm Hy-Liter. They also found that strong acids (pH 1) and bases (pH 13) did not affect the spermatozoa or the ability of Sperm HY-Liter to stain them. In a previous study, the same authors identified interference of the specific CF 488 A when samples had been previously stained using Christmas Tree staining (becoming dark and blurred) but not when using Baecchi staining.[308]

When compared to HE staining, Sperm HY-Liter was able to identify spermatozoa on skin from a deceased individual for 110 days, but only 12 days when using HE.[309] It has been successfully used to identify spermatozoa in cases 24 years old.[300] No interference was found with the specificity of Sperm HY-Liter when used with previously stained (via Christmas tree) slides or when subsequent staining was needed.[307]

Sperm HY-Liter has been tested with a range of nonhuman semen, and there was no cross-reaction of the human-specific Alexa 488 antibody when tested with bovine, canine, caprine, equine, feline, murine, ovine, porcine, and simian (*Pan troglodytes, Macaca mulatta*, and *Macaca fascicularis*).[300,307,310] When mixtures of semen from nonhuman and human were tested, only the human spermatozoa showed staining with the specific antibody when tested as directed by the manufacturer.[307]

The test does not generally show cross-reaction with other body fluids even when mixed, and the specific Alexa 488 labeled antibody will only stain spermatozoa. [296,300,307] Sperm HY-Liter showed cross-reaction to nontarget body fluids when the samples were heat fixed using a Bunsen burner, but this was not observed when samples were fixed using a heat plate.[307] Interference was also noted when lubricant (ID Fresh Peach) was present, which was found to retain the antibody dye complex, reducing the staining of the spermatozoa and making visualization difficult.[307]

One study used an additional stain, EnVision+ (DAKO EnVision+ System, HRP), which stains the mouse antibody and allows the Sperm HY-Liter kit to be visualized under normal light microscopy.[5] The Sperm HY-Liter reagents attach the mouse antibodies to the spermatozoa, and subsequently the mouse antibodies (still attached to the spermatozoa) are then stained with the EnVision, which can be visualized under normal light microscopy, adding little time to the staining process. In addition, the study found that crystals were visible when Sperm HY-Liter was viewed under fluorescence; however, under light

SPERMIOGRAM

A. Normal Cells of the Spermatogenesis
- I. Spermatogonia
- 2. Spermatocytes (primary)
- 3. Prespermatids (secondary spcrmatocytes)
- 4. Spermatids
- 5. Metaspermatozoa
- 6. Youthful, immature, unripe, nonmotile spermatozoa
  - (a) Cytoplasm rest at the head
  - (b) Cytoplasm rest at the neck
- 7. Mature, ripe, motile spermatozoa
  - (a) Normal spermatozoa
  - (b) Physiologic variations
    - 1. Round head
    - 2. Narrow head
    - 3. Tapering, piriform, rejuvenated head
    - 4. Small head
    - 5. Large head
- 8. Aged, hypermature, overripe, nonmotile spermatozoa
  - (a) Vacuoles in head
  - (b) Hyperpigmentation or depigmentation of head

B. Abnormal Cells of the Spermatogenesis
- I. Degenerative immature cells
  - (a) Vacuoles (vacuolation)
  - (b) Fatty degeneration
  - (c) Hyaline degeneration
- 2. Degenerative? teratoid? diseased? abnormal spermatozoa
  - (a) Abnormal head
    - I. Asthenic head, pinhead, microspermatozoon
    - 2. Gigantic head, megalospermatozoon, macrospermatozoon
    - 3. Deformed head
    - 4. Abnormities of acrosome, atypical colored head
    - 5. Double head
  - (b) Abnormal neck
    - 1. Thickened center
    - 2. Deformed center
    - 3. Abaxial implantation of the center
  - (c) Abnormal body and tail
    - 1. Displaced centrasome
    - 2. Naked, sheathless center thread
    - 3. Double tail
  - (d) Combined forms and rare forms

Fig. 4.31 Example of the Spermiogram spermiogram as provided by Pollack.[158] Only the first two categories have been reproduced here, with four others forming his analysis report.

microscopy these were not observed, making the background even cleaner.[5] This offers the specificity of the Sperm HY-Liter with a standard high-powered light microscope.

Scoring

Although observation of spermatozoa is significant, the number and quality of the spermatozoa can also provide useful information regarding an alleged incident. Some laboratories use the number of spermatozoa and their quality (intact or with broken tails) to infer a TSI (see later).

Prior to the current method introduced in 1964, there was no reported or standardized method to record spermatozoa found in microscopic examinations. While methods of recording microscopic findings were standard, there was no agreed upon or universal method of recording those findings. In 1943, Pollack[158] indicated the adaptation of a spermiogram, which was used in fertility studies.[311,312] Over 300 cell types were studied as part of semen analysis, and Pollack developed his own, looking at specific cell types that would be counted and, according to studies at the time, would be indicative of an individual based on the distribution of abnormal cells (Fig. 4.31).

In 1964 a simple scoring method was published by Kind,[313] who had used it to record his rough estimates of the number of spermatozoa from vaginal swabs found on slides. This method used five simple classes to assign a series of pluses (+) to indicate the number of spermatozoa observed on a slide.[313] Kind recognized that the boundaries between the classifications were diffuse, but he justified their use as representing real differences because the same operators were carrying out the analysis. The method was cited in use again in 1972,[193] but it was Davies and Wilson in 1974 who[204] popularized the method and to which it is often credited.

In 1997, an additional "T" designation was added to indicate the presence of tails attached to the spermatozoa, and a new classification level, "Few," was proposed by Allard.[4] Sperm scoring is therefore currently accomplished according to the modified method, where the number of spermatozoa observed is recorded by a series of pluses, and the presence or absence of a tail is indicated with a T. The classifications are:[4,193,204,313]

- 0 No spermatozoa present
- Few Less than five spermatozoa
- + Spermatozoa hard to find
- ++ Some spermatozoa in some microscopic fields, easy to find
- +++ Many/some spermatozoa in most fields
- ++++ Many spermatozoa in every field
- T Denotes the presence of tails on some or all spermatozoa

Since the general adoption of the method, laboratories have been attempting to make the method more accurate and reproducible by providing number guidelines (additional classifications) on the number of observed spermatozoa[173,290,300,314] or reducing the number of classifications.[315] Despite attempts to standardize sperm scoring, the method has remained largely unchanged for the 60 years it has been in use, despite the original author recognizing the inexact nature of the assessment. More recent research has confirmed that the method is highly subjective, with differences between observers even with the same training and similar backgrounds.[316] An example of difference concentrations of semen under the microscope can be seen in Fig. 4.32.

The presence of spermatozoa with tails is used by some laboratories as an indicator of TSI,[4,204,317,318] although studies in fertility indicate that there is no link between tail loss and TSI.[319] It has also been suggested that loss of tails could be caused by extraction of the stain.[201] There is some evidence the laboratories with the least aggressive extraction methods could detect intact spermatozoa at lower dilutions than laboratories with more aggressive methods,[201] which further indicates that presence of tails may not be a good method for determining TSI.

Microscopic identification of spermatozoa is not always straightforward, and it has been reported that vaginal swabs from deceased women can contain some forms of cellular degradation that could be mistaken for spermatozoa.[299] Dilution of a sample and time since deposition (TSD) will result in fewer spermatozoa being present and may result in the loss of tails. In studies diluting semen for experimental sensitivity, more spermatozoa are lost than can be explained, and it is thought these losses occur during the slide preparation and staining.[320] In a study involving nine laboratories in the United Kingdom and Ireland, all could detect spermatozoa at a dilution of 1:200 (semen to water), and one laboratory identified a single spermatozoon head at the highest dilution tested (1:10,000).[201] In a study investigating the subjective nature of the score classifications, it was found that in 9.6% of

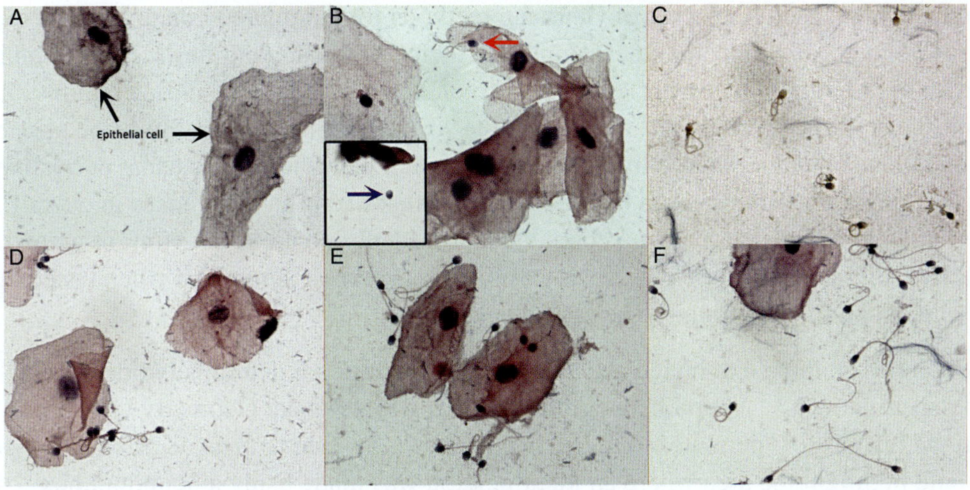

Fig. 4.32 Spermatozoa stained using the hematoxylin and eosin method and viewed at 400×. (A) Example of epithelial cells, which are often present when examining a slide for spermatozoa; no spermatozoa are present. (B) A spermatozoon head without a tail is illustrated in the inlay *(blue arrow)*, and a single spermatozoon can be seen in the field *(red arrow)*. (C–F) Different concentrations of spermatozoa, which would classify as different plus designations.

blind examinations of known positive slides investigators did not identify any spermatozoa.[316] Spermatozoa have been recovered after washing and dry cleaning of garments, and only in the case of spot cleaning by the dry cleaner were spermatozoa not observed;[221] however, DNA profiles were obtained in all cases regardless if spermatozoa were observed.[221]

The absence of detectable spermatozoa does not preclude the presence of semen due to vasectomized, azoospermatic, or oligospermatic men. It may also be casued by the technique used to extract the spermatozoa from the sample. Overall recovery of biological material from swabs is remarkably poor; unpublished work suggests that fewer than 25% of spermatozoa are recovered. Lack of observable spermatozoa does not preclude DNA testing, and it is important that even if no spermatozoa are observed that samples are still considered for DNA analysis based on the case circumstances and requests by the investigators or courts.

There have been attempts to develop methods that would take the subjectivity out of sperm scoring using automated slide scanning and image recognition. One aspect of this type of analysis is that the spermatozoa must be rendered distinct from all other substances on the slide through their shape or other feature (e.g., color via staining). A method was proposed in 2009 by Vandewoestyne et al.,[305] who used a slide scanning tool, image analysis software, laser capture (for subsequent DNA profiling), and Sperm HyLiter, which rendered the spermatozoa distinct via the specific Alex 488–labeled antigen. They determined that the method was fit for purpose and were able to identify and isolate spermatozoon even in the presence of large numbers of excess epithelial cells. This was confirmed in another report using different analysis software, which also concluded that the concordance between manual and automated methods was reliable and reproducible.[306]

Takamura et al.[308] used Laplacian of Gaussian methods for automated image analysis using Sperm HY-Liter. This is a computer vision analysis method that identifies regions in an image that differ in properties, such as brightness or color, compared to surrounding regions, and the size and shape of the spermatozoa along with the specific staining allow this to be possible. For their study, Takamura et al.[308] used an approach that identified edges using derivatives of the fluorescence, and this could be used on slides that had high differences in overall fluorescent signal (low spermatozoa count vs. high). Identified areas 10.3 μm^2 or greater and circularity 0.307 or more were classed as positive as a spermatozoon, and when tested against visual classification were found to be consistent.[308]

More recent work looked at image analysis using convolutional neural networks (CNN) to identify spermatozoa.[304] Neural network architecture of the Visual Geometry Group was used to scan the images for spermatozoa under two frameworks, one with an additional component that would highlight the area where an identification was made using a bounding box.[304] The main issue was the incidence of false negatives, where no spermatozoa were reported when there were some present.[304] Interestingly, the rates of false negatives displayed by the CNN are in line with those reported by Tobe et al.[316] when assessing the subjectivity of the sperm scoring method using investigators to search for spermatozoa.

Other Studies

Several other studies have been put forward recently as a means to identify semen and spermatozoa. A test targeting sperm-specific lactate dehydrogenase[321,322] was developed to detect spermatozoa that had disintegrated over time or because of environmental conditions.[323] This test targeted a spermatozoa-specific product that could be detected even if the spermatozoa were not whole; however, it is no longer used.

Sperm scoring and identification using mobile phone image analysis, using a microfluidic integrated cell phone imaging system, has been investigated.[324] The process is chip based, and the result is a chip that binds spermatozoa to the slide after incubation for 1 hour, with a wash step to remove all unbound (nontarget) cellular material. It also uses a Laplacian of Gaussian blob detection method, with cells stained using DAPI for method development, but it is not needed for the actual use of the device.[324] The novelty of this method is its portability and the ability to access the equipment needed for analysis, which is much cheaper than many of the other confirmatory methods, with researchers finding a 98% concordance with manual scoring in the test slides. Although the use of the mobile phone camera results in lower resolution images, the study still found a 96.5% accuracy with 100% sensitivity (no false negatives) and 93.5% specificity (6.5% false positives).[324]

Proximity ligation real-time polymerase chain reaction (PLiRT-PCR) has been investigated for the confirmatory identification of spermatozoa and PSA was developed.[325] This method uses protein targets for a PSA antigen, chosen for its high concentration in semen and presence even in azoospermatic men, and an acrosomal protein (CRISP-2), which protects it from environmental damage until lysis, allowing for successful detection of even aged samples. The method uses proximity probes (antibodies combined with oligonucleotides) to carry out a real-time reaction, which was shown to detect semen but not cross-react with other bodily fluids. A similar test, with different spermic targets, was developed using aptamers to selectively bind sperm cells through both microscale thermophoresis and enzyme-linked oligonucleotide assays.[326] Both of these testing methods appear promising but have not seen widespread use.

Attenuated total reflection Fourier transform infrared (ATR-FTIR) has been investigated as a means to identify human semen as opposed to semen from other animals.[222] Researchers used semen from human, rabbit, dog, boar, bull, and ram, as well as different substrates (glass slides, tissues, undergarments) over times up to 30 days. Human semen was determined to be distinct from the other species tested using ATR-FTIR and fresh semen.[222] Analyzing semen from a substrate requires removal via saline and centrifugation. The study found that substrate did not influence the results, and human semen could still be distinguished. TSD showed no major change to the ATR-FTIR spectra, and the analysis works with spermatozoa-free extracts and neat semen. Further work was carried out using partial least squares–discriminant analysis and 336 training spectra from the different testings, and was able to successfully establish a classification threshold that differentiates human from the nonhuman semen tested.[222]

Interpretation

Interpretations of the tests for semen and spermatozoa are usually determined in consideration of all testing carried out, rather than each as an individual result. Laboratories will therefore perform multiple tests before making a conclusion as to the presence or absence of semen. ALS positive results are only ever used as an indicator of where a semen sample may be located on items under screening because of the large number of cross-reactants that fluoresce in the same or a similar wavelength. Negative ALS may result in no further analysis.

AP, PSA, and Sg all have different targets, cross-reactions, and sensitivities, and usually two methods are used to indicate a true positive suitable for DNA profiling. Despite a positive in AP/PSA/Sg, all samples are screened for spermatozoa microscopically. The microscopic identification of even a single spermatozoon is definitive proof of ejaculation (bar some exceptions in decomposing males as previously discussed),[222] but the manner of deposit (consensual vs. nonconsensual) cannot be determined. Due to the potential to have low or no spermatozoa in an ejaculate, even if no spermatozoa are observed, samples can still be submitted for genetic profiling if AP and/or PSA and/or Sg are positive.

Usually in reports, stains will be listed as positive or negative, with some further comment made on the speed of reaction (AP) or the number of observed spermatozoa and if tails were present (microscopy). The test used is specified, and a brief description can be included in the appendix or technical section of the report.

Persistence

Persistence of semen after ejaculation is an important consideration as a guide for realistic recovery of evidence. Some laboratories will use the presence, number, and condition (tails or not) to infer a TSI (see later). The nature of semen means it is different than the other biological fluids encountered in forensic casework because it can be found inside the body of a victim or outside the body on any other substrate. Each of these scenarios requires different considerations in terms of sampling and expectations of spermatozoa persistence and recovery.

Persistence of semen and spermatozoa outside the body can be for extended time frames, and one of the more famous cases involving semen persistence is that of Monica Lewinsky. In that case, semen was deposited on Lewinsky's dress in February 1997, and it was handed over for examination at the end of July 1998. The report indicated that the US Federal Bureau of Investigation had confirmed that the stain in question was semen (as opposed to reported spinach dip prior to obtaining DNA), although the exact testing used was not disclosed.[327] Much longer time frames have been reported where spermatozoa have been visually identified from stains as old as 62 years.[279,328,329] In one study looking specifically at recovery from skin (deceased), they found a maximum time frame of 110 days before spermatozoa were no longer identified.[309] Other components, such as ALS, AP, and PSA, have demonstrated positives up to 100 years after deposit.[170,279] Factors, such as washing have an effect on the detection (or recovery) of spermatozoa, with only half of the samples tested showing spermatozoa in one study; because of low sampling numbers, however, the washing factors that affected this recovery could not be determined.[252] Another study found that even if the substrate (cotton) was submerged, spermatozoa and AP could be recovered for up to 2 weeks depending on the water type (tap, pool, river, ocean).[174]

Internal persistence is much shorter and often considered more relevant because some laboratories will use the internal persistence of spermatozoa to infer TSI. One study found that drainage of semen from the vagina was the main cause of loss of seminal constituents, which was enhanced during menstruation (keeping in mind that this only means that the seminal constituents were expelled and could be found externally in underwear, for example). Sleeping (or lying prone) after intercourse reduced the loss due to drainage.[204]

An accurate knowledge of the persistence of semen within the body of victims is also important because many sexual assaults are not immediately reported. Some victims may wash prior to forensic sexual assault examination, and many may not report an assault has taken place for days, weeks, or years.

The persistence of semen and spermatozoa after intercourse is not well understood in a forensic context. What little research has been conducted tends to be based on fertility studies, where couples may be trying to increase the persistence of the semen,[298,319] or through other normal medical examinations.[330] Forensic persistence reports are generally case based,[3–6] and as such the exact conditions surrounding ejaculation, including time, location, semen components (normal range for spermatozoa), and if it occurred at all, may not be known or be clear. Further, most published reports provide only the most extreme limits of persistence of spermatozoa, and these reports will not represent the normal range for recovery, which must be considered when using these limits as a guide for evidence evaluation.

It is common to find no detectable spermatozoa within the vagina, mouth, or anus 1 day after intercourse, although studies have demonstrated that in some instances spermatozoa can be detectable in these orifices for extended periods. Most laboratories will therefore have a cutoff time beyond which they have no expectations of finding semen or spermatozoa on intimate swabs. In the United Kingdom, for example, forensic medical examiners are required to take vaginal swabs up to 7 days after the alleged offense. Similarly, in New South Wales, Australia, there are cutoff limits for oral collection for the detection of spermatozoa depending on the allegation (actual oral ejaculation vs. suspicion of oral ejaculation).[3]

Finding spermatozoa on intimate swabs is dependent, in part, on the initial spermatozoa count of the man, with shorter survival times reported from men with low initial counts.[191] Spermatozoa have been found within the vaginal and higher vaginal cavity (cervix) for up to 408 hours (17 days) after intercourse, although reports vary widely in retention times (Table 4.3). It is therefore important to consider the length of TSI that it would be expected to find spermatozoa in the vagina, mouth, or anus. Dried stains, such as those found on fabrics, will be handled differently and will generally have much longer retention times. Dried stains will differ in their spermatozoa retention, compared to intimate swabs, and will often yield spermatozoa heads without tails (see Fig. 4.32B [inlay]).[70]

It has been found that the recovery of spermatozoa exceeds the detection capabilities of both PSA and Sg testing, whereby PSA and Sg negative tests still had detectable (via microscopy) spermatozoa.[243] This is also found in terms of samples that have undergone washing, which removes the soluble components of semen, but the spermatozoa persist at the site of the original stain.[199] Because the spermatozoa contain the majority of the DNA, this means that DNA can still be recovered from these samples, and even after staining DNA can still be recovered from slides as old as 13 years.[347]

In one study looking at women who presented at a special treatment clinic, coital intervals were known for 178 examinations; of those, 133 had known last menstrual period dates.[330] The overall findings of the study identified spermatozoa in 58.4% of the examinations (either from the cervix, the vagina, or both). Spermatozoa were found more frequently in samples

Table 4.3 Summary of the reported time for spermatozoa recovery and viability after intercourse from living female participants[a]

	Recovery Times in Hours [Source]				
Sperm Viability	**External Vagina**	**Internal Vagina**	**Cervix**	**Mouth**	**Rectum/Anus**
Motile		6[331,332] 8[334] 9[219]	58[333] 72[335] 168[335] fallopian tubes 7–110[331] 120[332] 144[336] 168[337] 25–240[331,338] in uterus and fallopian tubes 600[339]		
Non-motile	16[4,318] with tails 24[340] with tails 62[342] 72–96[149]	14[334] 26[318] with tails 48–72[149] with tails 72–96 (high only)[149]	72–96[149] 179[318] 288[330] 408[331,343]	3[318] 6[318,341] 9[318] from lips 12–15[149]	6[318,340] with tails 20[341] 24[331] 31[340] internal with tails
	120[4,318,340] without tails	48[7]		<24[3] from lips	35[342]
		72[204,219] with tails		24[4] swab without tails	40[4] rectum with tails
		72[219,243,298,342]		28–31[4,340] saliva without tails	46[318] anal without tails
		93[340] with tails		48–96[3] oral swab and oral rinse	52[4,340] anus without tails
		120[318,344] without tails			65[318] rectal without tails
		120[4] with tails			65[340] internal without tails
		144[204] 144[345] in cases of rape 168[4,340] without tails 216[330] 240[319] 240[345] from family planning 384[346]			72–96[149]

[a]These values represent extremes as to the time frames, and the time intervals may not be accurate. Casework samples can be unreliable, and medical studies tend to examine women trying to conceive and maximize semen retention. Time is in hours, and the relevant reference(s) given.

where coitus had taken place after the last menstrual period, but not longer than 12 days after intercourse, and they concluded that the optimal time to recover spermatozoa from intimate swabs was 48 hours or less.[330]

When victims are deceased, the retention times can still be informative, and a spermatozoon head was recovered from a vaginal sample at 1800 hours (2.5 months), but on average this was around 24 hours[220] for postmortem persistence. Similarly, rectal samples had a limit of 48 hours but averaged around 24 hours, but no spermatozoa were observed in postmortem oral samples.[220] It is important to recognize that with postmortem samples, the time since ejaculation is not always known or apparent, nor is the condition of the body controlled, which would add further variables to the retention time in these cases.

One study looking at lab volunteers was unable to detect spermatozoa beyond 3 days postejaculation in lab volunteers.[298] Another study identified spermatozoa in postcoital female urine samples up to 24 hours after intercourse, and even in samples that failed to show spermatozoa, Y chromosome short tandem repeat (Y-STR) profiles were still obtained.[348] Similarly, spermatozoa have been found in the first urination postejaculation in males up to 5 hours after ejaculation.[294]

Time Since Intercourse

TSI refers to the postcoital interval between semen deposition and sample collection.[315] It is related to the persistence of semen components after ejaculation. TSI can also refer to the time between an attack and sample collection. It can be based on the assault timeline as relayed by the victim, the accused, other witnesses (e.g., when others saw the two leave a venue), or closed-circuit television; on detection and levels of AP and PSA; and on microscopic identification and details of spermatozoa (number and presence of tails). All methods of TSI determination rely on the reduction of particular components within semen, but there have been no definitive methods developed because of the wide range of starting concentrations of those targets between different ejaculates.

The presence of motile spermatozoa in the vagina indicates that connection was recent (i.e., usually thought to be within a few hours of the time of examination),[28] although studies in fertility looking at persistence of motile spermatozoa have found extended periods of retention. One study found that under laboratory conditions, spermatozoa were all dead at the 5-hour mark when synthetically stored in ideal conditions at 37°C.[349] Other studies put motile spermatozoa survival at 48 to 72 hours in the vagina,[333,350–352] up to 7 weeks in the cervical mucus,[337] and one study found a motile spermatozoa in the fallopian tubes 25 days after intercourse.[339]

Casey et al.[149] evaluated years of casework data from the analysis of over 5500 sexual assault swabs and offered guidelines for TSI based on AP and spermatozoa (number and condition).

They found a reduction in the proportion of vaginal swabs containing spermatozoa as TSI increased, and in the number containing tails. They did not find a reduction in the proportion of swabs that tested positive for AP up to 48 hours postejaculation.[149]

Findley looked at the activity of AP postcoitus, but the results indicated that despite some correlation there was not a definitive link between AP activity and TSI.[353] Although there was a decrease in AP activity within test samples, it was not predictable (e.g., 8 hours TSI did not result in 50% reduction of AP activity across all volunteers), and there was a marked overlap between samples taken at 8 hours and samples taken immediately after intercourse (different volunteers).[353] A more recent study also concluded that AP cannot be used to predict TSI.[149]

Basing TSI on numbers of spermatozoa observed (sperm density) could be problematic because of the large range of normal spermatozoa content, as recognized by the World Health Organization (69–647 million per ejaculate).[85] One study found the number of spermatozoa identified microscopically changed depending on the staining method used,[298] and there is no standard staining method used for microscopic screening of spermatozoa.[9] One study looking at case data found a reduction in observed spermatozoa as TSI increased, but even in the 0- to 6-hour range there was a maximum of 41% of samples that had spermatozoa observed (external vagina), which dropped to 20% between 72 and 96 hours (endocervical), but 0% at times greater than 96 hours.[149] Hence there was no universal loss of spermatozoa within the case samples examined.

A recent study investigating sexual assault looked at sperm density and condition as an indicator of TSI by trained and experienced forensic staff and found an overestimate of TSI in over 50% of the slides examined.[290] An extensive study by Silverman and Silverman[319] looking at 675 samples found a reduction of recovered spermatozoa as TSI increased, but they reported no increase in tail loss, and tail absence should not be used to determine TSI. They also found that the decline in spermatozoa number was well defined in the first 4 days postejaculation but after that became erratic.[319]

Using tails as a potential indicator of TSI can only be applied to intimate swabs from a victim. Tails remaining intact and recovered from dried stains cannot be used for TSI because the time the stain has been dried for cannot be known, and intact spermatozoa can be observed for extended periods. Because of the fragility of the tail attachment to the spermatozoon, the tails can become unattached with relatively little force. This breaking of the tails has resulted in the plausible theory that a TSI can be determined based on if tails are observed and on the proportion of the spermatozoa that have tails versus those that do not. For example, Davies and Wilson[204] state that "tails are most frequently found attached to spermatozoa on swabs taken within 1 hour of intercourse. They are commonly found up to 16 hours; thereafter spermatozoa with tails occur rarely but have been found as late as 72 hours." In contrast, a fertility study found no correlation between TSI and tail loss, noting there was no apparent increase in the loss of tails as TSI increased with samples taken after 15 days demonstrating over 50% with tails.[319]

The presence or absence of tails on intimate swabs is also influenced by the removal of the spermatozoa from the substrate (e.g., swab), and where and when it is examined. Nittis et al.[290] found that when duplicate swabs were taken from sexual assault cases, the swab extracted at the forensic laboratory contained less spermatozoa with tails than the swab mounted by the examiner at the time of collection. Another multilaboratory study found that the laboratories using the least aggressive methods showed the highest prevalence of spermatozoa with tails.[201]

With all the possible indicators of TSI, it is important to remember that there is variability of the various components in normal and abnormal seminal fluid that could skew any calculated TSI. This precludes the use of hard thresholds to determine TSI because even if there is a predictable and consistent decrease in components (AP, PSA, Sg, or spermatozoa), there will be large overlaps in TSI simply because of the differences in semen component concentrations between individuals, and even between ejaculates. Therefore TSI is at best an estimation. In contrast, other studies found no correlation between TSI, sperm density, or proportion with tails.[314,319]

TSI has been elusive in terms of determining the original time of the ejaculation based on the remaining serological evidence, but it can be used to inform investigators as to the probability of finding evidence of semen in cases of sexual assault based on case information.[342] Although persistence can offer the absolute limits of when spermatozoa were found, TSI can provide more realistic expectations in terms of expected evidence recovery. Casey et al.[149] provide some guidelines as to the expected chance of recovering spermatozoa or returning an AP positive result. These can help inform of cutoff times for the expectation of finding particular substances; it is also important to remember that male DNA has been shown to persist for longer than the serological aspects of semen.[254,284]

Time Since Deposition

Although not as prevalent as determination of the age of bloodstains, there has been some investigations into the age of semen stains, or TSD. Determining the age of seminal stain can be important to determine which stains may be relevant to an allegation, especially when there may be multiple stains present, such as on a bed sheet.

Enzyme activity has been looked at as a method to determine TSD. Jimenez-Verdejo et al.[354] used pooled semen from normozoospermia and vasectomized men. They placed 1 mL of semen onto cotton and stored them at three different temperatures (5°C, room temperature [18–25°C], 38°C), over 6 months. Stains were extracted at various time points ranging from 1 day to 6 months, and eluates were analyzed for γ-glutamyltransferase, lactate dehydrogenase, prostatic AP, and PSA.[354] All enzymes showed loss of activity over the time periods, with the samples stored refrigerated showing the greatest loss of activity. Although not a linear decrease in activity, the combination of multiple targets provides a realistic method to determine recent from older stains.

The loss of PSA as a means to determine TSD was also investigated in a separate study using an ELISA to monitor activity, looking at a similar time frame but a wider range of temperatures.[355] Srettabunjong et al.[355] found that as the temperature decreased, the concentration of PSA over time remained more consistent. At −80°C, they found no loss of PSA, but at 37°C, the other limit of their study, they found complete loss after 5 days, in a nonlinear negative trend.[355]

Achetib et al.[356] developed a noncontact method to determine TSD using fluorescent spectroscopy. They used the intrinsic fluorescent (autofluorescence) properties of semen and examined it over a temporal range. Their signal was measured using excitation and emission maps. Two areas were used: one looking at the protein autofluorescence and the other looking at fluorescent oxidation products (FOX), and these were investigated over 3 months (Fig. 4.33).[356]

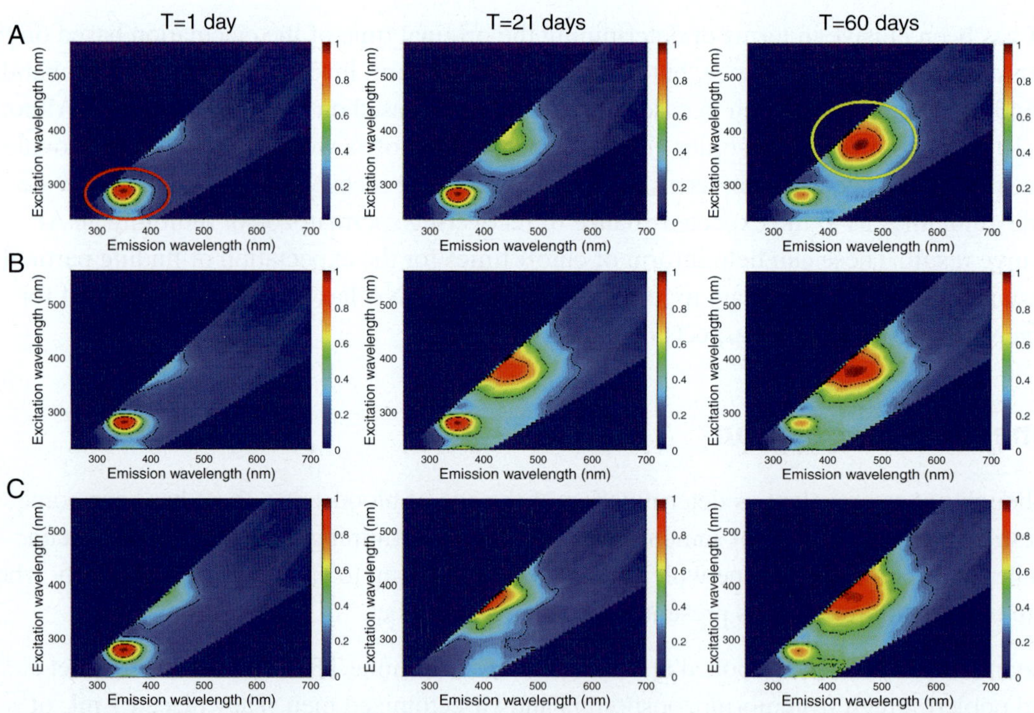

Fig. 4.33 Excitation and emission maps from three different semen donors (A–C) over three different time points. Samples have been normalized, and two different areas were observed, protein fluorescence *(red circle)* and FOX fluorescence *(yellow circle)*. Note that the protein fluorescence decreases over time, whereas the FOX fluorescence increases. *From Achetib N, Wilks LS, Schwartz JCV, et al. Estimating the time of deposition of semen traces using fluorescence protein -lipid oxidation signatures. Anal Chem. 2019;91:3204–3208.*

They found a decrease in the protein autofluorescence over time and an increase in the FOX over time (see Fig. 4.33). From this, they were able to develop an aging curve ratio that acts as an estimate for TSD; when tested, it predicted a stain as being 3 days old (actual 4 days).[356] They further applied the aging curve to semen stains on different substrates, and when tested with a stain on tissue, the curve estimated the TSD as 10 days, when the actual age was 7 days.[356] This method offers the benefits of being noncontact, nondestructive, and a reasonable TSD estimation tool.

Zha et al.[357] used ATR-FTIR coupled with chemometrics to determine the TSD of semen on glass, tissue, and cellulose fabric over 6 days, with testing at 12-hour intervals. They observed that at certain wavenumbers the absorbance changed over six points, either increasing or decreasing, predictably. These points relate to amides, fatty acids, and polysaccharides, as well as sugars and carbohydrates. The results show a predictable trend as TSD increases, but there is significant overlap in the different time point results, which the authors acknowledge, meaning that this method provides an estimate, but it needs further validation before general use.

References

1. J. Butler, in *Fundamentals of Forensic DNA Typing*. (Elsevier, London, 2010), chap. 4, pp. 79-98.
2. Gino S, et al. 58 cases of sexual violence bearing forensic interest: congruence between the victim's report and the data from laboratory analyses. *Int J Leg Med*. 2017;131:1449–1453.
3. Nittis M, Franco M, Cochrane C. New oral cut-off time limits in NSW. *J Forensic Legal Med*. 2016;44:92–97.
4. Allard JE. The collection of data from findings in cases of sexual assault and the significance of spermatozoa on vaginal, anal and oral swabs. *Sci Jus*. 1997;37:99–108.
5. Christoffersen S. Immunohistochemical staining of human sperm cells in smears from sexual assault cases. *Int J Legal Med*. 2011;125:887–890.
6. Collins KA, et al. Identification of sperm and non-sperm male cells in cervicovaginal smears using fluorescence in situ hybridization: Applications in alleged sexual assault cases. *J Forensic Sci*. 1994;39:1347–1355.
7. Dahlke MB, Cooke C, Cunnane M, Chawla J, Lau P. Identification of semen in 500 patients seen because of rape. *Am J Clin Pathol*. 1977;68:740–746.
8. Hooft P, Van De Voorde H. Evaluation of the modified zinc test and the acid phosphatase test as preliminary screening methods in sexual assault case material. *Forensic Sci Int*. 1992;53:135–141.
9. Fourney RM, DesRoches AN, Buckle JL. In: Nic Daeid N, Houck MM, eds. *Interpol's Forensic Science Review*. London: CRC Press; 2007:591–662.
10. Short J, DeLuca M, DiVasto P, Kaufman A. Detection of sperm in victims of rape. *The New England journal of medicine*. 1978;299:424.
11. Noble D, DiFrancesco D, Zancani D. Leonardo da Vinci and the origin of semen. *Notes and Records: the Royal Society Journal of the History of Science*. 2014;68:391–402.
12. Justman S. How did the PSA system arise? *Journal of the Royal Society of Medicine*. 2010;103:309–312.
13. Martin RM, et al. Effect of a low-intensity PSA-based screening intervention on prostate cancer mortality: the CAP randomized clinical trial. *Jama*. 2018;319:883–895.
14. Thompson IM, et al. Prevalence of prostate cancer among men with a prostate-specific antigen level≤ 4.0 ng per milliliter. *N Engl J Med*. 2004;350:2239–2246.
15. Agarwal A, Durairajanayagam D, Halabi J, Peng J, Vazquez-Levin M. Proteomics, oxidative stress and male infertility. *Reproductive BioMedicine Online*. 2014;29:32–58.

16. Mahmoud AM, et al. Seminal plasma alpha-glucosidase activity and male infertility. *Hum Reprod.* 1998;13:591–595.
17. Sills ES, Fryman JT, Perloe M, Michels KB, Tucker M. Chromatin fluorescence characteristics and standard semen analysis parameters: correlations observed in andrology testing among 136 males referred for infertility evaluation. *J Obstet Gynaecol.* 2004;24:74–77.
18. Castellani C. Spermatozoan biology from Leeuwenhoek to Spallanzani. *J Hist Biol.* 1973;6:37–68.
19. de Graaf R.*Regneri de Graaf De mulierum organis generationi inservientibus tractatus novus: demonstrans tam homines & animalia caetera omnia, quae vivipara dicuntur, haud minus quàm ovipara ab ovo originem ducere: ad Cosmum III, magnum Etruriae ducem.* Lugduni Batav: Ex officina Hackiana; 1672:396.
20. Lewenhoeck DA, Observationes D. Anthonii Lewenhoeck, De Natis E Semine Genitali Animalculis. *Philosophical Transactions (1665-1678).* 1677;12:1040–1046.
21. Kempers RD. The tricentennial of the discovery of sperm. *Fertil Steril.* 1976;27:603–605.
22. Gadêlha H, Hernández-Herrera P, Montoya F, Darszon A, Corkidi G. Human sperm uses asymmetric and anisotropic flagellar controls to regulate swimming symmetry and cell steering. *Science Advances.* 2020;6 eaba5168.
23. G.L. L. Buffon, comte de, *L'Histoire Naturelle.* (1786), vol. Tome II.
24. L. Spallanzani, *Experiencias Para Servir a La Historia de La Generación De Animales y Plantas* (1786).
25. W.F. V. Gleichen-Rußwurm, *Abhandlung über die Saamen- und Infusuinsthierchen, und über die Erzeugung.* (1799).
26. Prevost J, Dumas J. Deuxième mémoire sur la génération. Rapports de l'œuf avec la liqueur fécondante. Phénomènes appréciables, résultant de leur action mutuelle. Développement de l'œuf des batraciens. *Annales des Sciences Naturelles.* 1824;2:100–121. 129–149.
27. Prevost J, Dumas J. Nouvelle théorie de la génération. *Annales des Sciences Naturelles.* 1824;1:1–29. 167–187.
28. Smith S, Cook HGH, Stewart CP. *Taylor's Principles and Practice of Medical Jurisprudence.* (Churchill Ltd. 104 Gloucester Place, ed. 10th, 1948), vol. 2.
29. Schurig M. *Spermatologia historico-medica, hoc est seminis humani consideratio physico-medico-legalis, qua ejus natura et usus, in simulque opus generationis et varia de coitu aliaque huc pertinentia v.g. castratione, herniotomia, phimosi, circumcisione, recutitione, et infibulation, item de hermaphroditis & sexum mutantibus, raris & selectis observationibus, annexo indice locupletissimo, traduntur a D. Martino Schurigio Phyfico Dresdenfi.* (Beck, 1720).
30. OIlivier M Barruel. De taches observées sur un linge dans un cas de médecine légal. *Journal de Chimie Médical de Parmacie et de Toxicologie.* 1826;2:565–568.
31. Orfila MJB. Du Sperme, considéré sous le point de vue médico-légal. *Journal de Chimie Médical de Parmacie et de Toxicologie.* 1827;3:469–480.
32. Rattier JJL. Sur Quelque Srecherches Microscopiques Relatives Aux Taches De Linge. *Journal de Chimie Médical de Parmacie et de Toxicologie.* 1837;3:120–122.
33. Donné A.*Nouvelles experiénces sur les animalcules spermatiques, et sur quelques unes des causes de la stérilité chez la femme: suivies de recherches sur les pertes séminales involontaires, et sur la présence du sperme dans l'urine.* Paris: L'auteur; 1837:56.
34. Bayard H. Emploi du microscope en médecine légale. Examen microscopique du sperme désséché sur le linge, sue les tissus de nature et de coloration diverses'. *Annales D'hygiène Publique Et De Médecine Légale.* 1839;22:134–170.
35. Schmidt C.*Die Diagnostik verdächtiger Flecke in Criminalfällen: Ein physiologisch-chemischer Beitrag zur gerichtlichen Medicin.* Mitau, Leipzig: Reyher; 1848.
36. Ritter B.*Ueber die Ermittelung von Blut, Samen- und Exkrementenflecken in Kriminalfaellen: Ein spezieller Beitrag zur gerichtlichen Arzneikunde.* Stahel; 1854.
37. Lassaigne JL. Observations sur quelques réactions que présentent les taches spermatiques avec les taches albumineuses et autres taches analogues. *Annales D'hygiène Publique Et De Médecine Légale.* 1858;10:405–408.
38. Robin C, Tardieu A. Mémoire sur Quelques Applications Nouvelles de L'Examen Microscopique de Diverses Espèces de Tache. *Annales D'hygiène Publique Et De Médecine Légale.* 1860;13:416–442.

39. Brouardel P. Des Taches Spermatiques. *Le Procricien*. 1879;2:332–336.
40. Ricker C. *Anleitung zür untersuchung verdächtiger flecke: für Artze und juristen*. (st Petersbourg in Jahre, 1870), pp. 64.
41. Longuet M. Recherche Medico-Legale des Spermatozoides. *Annales d'hygiène publique et de médecine légale* **s**. 1876;2(46):154–167.
42. Johnston W. On the iodine test for semen. *Boston Med Surg J*. 1897;136:324–327.
43. Schlemmer A. Beitrag zur Histologie des menschlichen Sperma nebst einigen forensischen Bemerkungen über Aspermatozie. *Vierteljahrsschrift Für Gerichtliche Medizin Und Öffentliches Sanitätswesen* **Neue Folge**, 444-463 (1877).
44. Boutmy MM, Brouardel P. Rapport sur le Procédé Petel et Labiche Destiné a Faire Découvrir les Taches de Sperme. *Annales D'hygiène Publique Et De Médecine Légale*. 1880;4:224–227.
45. Roussin MZ. Examen microscopique des taches de sperme. *Annales d'hygiène publique et de médecine légale*. 1867;27:142–164.
46. Lundquist F. Om forensisk paavisning of sperma og spermapletter. *Nordisk Medicin*. 1945;28:2131–2132.
47. Wood ES.Witthaus RA, Becker TC, eds.*in Medical Jurisprudence, Forensic Medicine and Toxicology*. vol. 2. New York: William Wood & Company; 1894:3–82.
48. Barberio M. Nuova, Reaziona microchimica della sperma e sua applicazione nelle ricerche medico-legali. Rendiconti dell'Accademia Scienze Fisiche Mathematiche (Napoli). 1905;(3rd series v. II):156–168.
49. Winkler, Aus Annales d'hygiene publique et de medecine legale des Jahres 1876. *Vierteljahrsschrift Für Gerichtliche Medizin Und Öffentliches Sanitätswesen* **Neue Folge**, 1877;399–402.
50. Hager H.*Hagers Untersuchungen: Ein Handbuch der Untersuchung, Prüfung und Wertbestimmung aller Handelswaren, Natur- und Kunsterzeugnisse, Gifte, Lebensmittel,*. E. Günther: *Geheimmittel etc*; 1888.
51. Vogel H. Untersuchung von Spermaflecken. *Repertorium der analytischen Chemie für Handel, Gewerbe und öffentl. Gesundheitspflege*. 1881;1:327–330.
52. Cauvet D. Taches de Sperme et Taches de Sang. *Annales D'hygiène Publique Et De Médecine Légale*. 1875;44:117–126.
53. Florence A.*Du sperme et des tâches de sperme en médecine légale*. Storck; 1897.
54. Lecco MT, et al. Zur Erkennung von Spermaflecken. *Zeitschrift für analytische Chemie*. 1898;37:341–342.
55. Richter M. Der mikrochemische Nachweis von Sperma. *Wien Klin Wochenschr*. 1897;10:569–572.
56. Lecco MT. Ueber die mikrochemische Erkennung der Spermaflecken in Criminalfällen. *Wien Klin Wochenschr*. 1897;10:820–823.
57. Barberio M. Toxicological-A New Micro-Chemical Reaction of the Sperma and Its Application in Medico-Legal Investigations. *Medico-Legal J*. 1905;23:383.
58. Gamblin AP, Morgan-Smith RK. The characteristics of seminal fluid and the forensic tests available to identify it. *WIREs Forensic Science*. 2020;2:e1363.
59. Baecchi B. Neue methode zum nachweis der spermatozoen in zeugflecken. *DMW-Deutsche Medizinische Wochenschrift*. 1909;35:1105–1106.
60. Eddy EM. In: Neill JD, ed.*Knobil and Neill's Physiology of Reproduction. Third Edition*. St Louis: Academic Press; 2006:3–54.
61. Marieb EN, Hoehn K.*Human Anatomy & Physiology*. ed. 9th. London: Benjamin Cummings; 2013:1107.
62. Björndahl L, Kvist U. Sequence of ejaculation affects the spermatozoon as a carrier and its message. *Reproductive biomedicine online*. 2003;7:440–448.
63. Prins GS. In: Robaire B, Chan P, eds. *Handbook of Andrology,*; 2023122–127.
64. Owen DH, Katz DF. A Review of the Physical and Chemical Properties of Human Semen and the Formulation of a Semen Simulant. *J Androl*. 2005;26:459–469.
65. Broesike G. Ueber die Entleerung und Beschaffenheit der menschlichen Samenflüssigkeit. *Archiv für Mikroskopische Anatomie*. 1911;78:128–150.
66. Drabovich AP, Saraon P, Jarvi K, Diamandis EP. Seminal plasma as a diagnostic fluid for male reproductive system disorders. *Nature Reviews Urology*. 2014;11:278–288.
67. Toshimori K, Eddy EM. In: Plant TM, Zeleznik AJ, eds. *Knobil and Neill's Physiology of Reproduction. (Fourth Edition)*. San Diego: Academic Press; 2015:99–148.

68. Calvin H. Formation of disulphide bonds in the nucleus and accessory structures of mammalian spermatozoa during maturation in the epididymis. *J Reprod Fertil Suppl*. 1971;13:65–75.
69. Li R.*Forensic Biology*. London: CRC Press; 2008:430.
70. Ballantyne J, Lee H, Pagliaro E.Siegel J, Saukko P, Knupfer G, eds.*Encyclopedia of Forensic Sciences*. vol. 3. London: Academic Press; 2000:1322–1338.
71. Saferstein R.*Criminalistics: An Introduction to Forensic Science*. 10th. (UK) Limited, London: Prentice Hall International; 2011.
72. Elder K, Dale B.*In-Vitro Fertilization*. ed. 4. Cambridge: Cambridge University Press; 2020.
73. Barrett KE, Barman SM, Brooks HL, Yuan JX-J.*Ganong's review of medical physiology*. 26th. Sydney: McGraw-Hill Education; 2019.
74. Mitterberger M, et al. Ultrasound of the prostate. *Cancer imaging*. 2010;10:40.
75. Gutman AB, Gutman EB. Quantitative relations of a prostatic component (acid phosphatase) of human seminal fluid. *Endocrinology*. 1941;28:115–118.
76. Kong HY, Byun J. Emerging roles of human prostatic acid phosphatase. *Biomolecules & therapeutics*. 2013;21:10.
77. Jonsson M, Linse S, Frohm B, Lundwall Å, Malm J. Semenogelins I and II bind zinc and regulate the activity of prostate-specific antigen. *Biochem J*. 2005;387:447–453.
78. Robert M, Gagnon C. Purification and characterization of the active precursor of a human sperm motility inhibitor secreted by the seminal vesicles: identity with semenogelin. *Biol Reprod*. 1996;55:813–821.
79. Lundwall Å, Bjartell A, Olsson AY, Malm J. Semenogelin I and II, the predominant human seminal plasma proteins, are also expressed in non-genital tissues. *Mol Hum Reprod*. 2002;8:805–810.
80. Finney A, Fukuda A, Breuel K, Thatcher S. Coagulation and liquefaction of seminal plasma. *Assist Rev Reprod*. 1992;2:164–169.
81. Peter A, Lilja H, Lundwall Å, Malm J. Semenogelin I and semenogelin II, the major gel-forming proteins in human semen, are substrates for transglutaminase. *Eur J Biochem*. 1998;252:216–221.
82. Chughtai B, et al. A neglected gland: a review of Cowper's gland. *Int J Androl*. 2005;28:74–77.
83. Jequier AM.*Male Infertility: A Clinical Guide. Cambridge Clinical Guides*. ed. 2. Cambridge: Cambridge University Press; 2011.
84. Barrett KE, Barman SM, Boitano S, Brooks HL.*Ganong's review of medical physiology*. ed. 24th. Sydney: McGraw-Hill Education; 2012.
85. WHO *laboratory manual for the examination and processing of human semen* (2010).
86. Rui H, Torjesen P, Jacobsen H, Purvis K. Testicular and glandular contributions to the prolactin pool in human semen. *Arch Androl*. 1985;15:129–136.
87. Rui H, Mevåg B, Purvis K. Two-dimensional electrophoresis of proteins in various fractions of the human split ejaculate. *Int J Androl*. 1984;7:509–520.
88. Brown-Woodman P, Marley P, Morris S, Rodger Jt, White I. Origin of glycerylphosphorylcholine, inositol, N-acetylaminosugar, and prostaglandins in human seminal plasma and their effects on sperm metabolism. *Arch Androl*. 1980;4:149–155.
89. Grayhack J, Kropp K. Changes with aging in prostatic fluid: citric acid, acid phosphatase and lactic dehydrogenase concentration in man. *Transactions of the American Association of Genito-Urinary Surgeons*. 1964;56:6–11.
90. Ayedy SB, Gonzales J, Foglietti M, Percheron F, Bernard M. On Some Glycosidases (β-D-Mannosidase, α-L-Fucosidase, N-Acetyl-β-D-Glucosaminidase) of Human Seminal Plasma/Über einige Glykosidase-Aktivitäten (β-D-Mannosidase, α-L-Fukosidase und N-acetyl-β-D-Glukosaminidase) des menschlichen Spermaplasmas. *Andrologia*. 1989;21:432–436.
91. Golan R, et al. Carnitine and short-chain acylcarnitines in the lumen of the human male reproductive tract. *Int J Androl*. 1983;6:349–357.
92. Videla E, Blanco A, Galli M, Fernandez-Collazo E. Human seminal biochemistry: fructose, ascorbic acid, citric acid, acid phosphatase and their relationship with sperm count. *Andrologia*. 1981;13:212–214.
93. Mann T, Lutwak-Mann C.*Male reproductive function and semen: themes and trends in physiology, biochemistry and investigative andrology*. Springer Science & Business Media; 1981.
94. Leone E, Mann T. Ergothioneine in the seminal vesicle secretion. *Nature*. 1951;168:205–206.

95. Tang G, Oka N, Nagamatsu G, Alfano R. Laser fluorescence spectroscopy from human spermatozoa. *Applied optics*. 1993;32:464–467.
96. Gerozissis K, Jouannet P, Soufir J, Dray F. Origin of prostaglandins in human semen. *Reproduction*. 1982;65:401–404.
97. Segal S, Ron M, Laufer N, Ben-David M. Prolactin in seminal plasma of infertile men. *Arch Androl*. 1978;1:49–52.
98. Lizana J, Moberg P, Eneroth P. Beta2-microglobulin, carcinoembryonic antigen and prostatic acid phosphatase in split ejaculates and urine voided before and after massage of the prostate. *Arch Androl*. 1983;11:225–232.
99. Arver S. Studies on zinc and calcium in human seminal plasma. *Acta physiologica Scandinavica. Supplementum*. 1982;507:1–21.
100. Umapathy E, Manimekalai S, Govindarajulu P. Lipid pattern in split ejaculate and Klinefelter's syndrome. *Fertil Steril*. 1980;33:294–296.
101. Stegmayr B, Ronquist G. Distribution of cyclic AMP in human seminal plasma and its relation to sperm progressive motility. *Scand J Urol Nephrol*. 1982;16:91–95.
102. Schumacher G. Components of human split ejaculates II. *Enzymes and proteinaseinhibitors*. 1976
103. Harrison GA. The approximate determination of spermine in single human organs. *Biochem J*. 1933;27:1152.
104. Valsa J, Skandhan KP, Khan PS, Sumangala B, Gondalia M. Split ejaculation study: semen parameters and calcium and magnesium in seminal plasma. *Central European journal of urology*. 2012;65:216.
105. Peeker R, Abramsson L, Marklund S. Superoxide dismutase isoenzymes in human seminal plasma and spermatozoa. *Mol Hum Reprod*. 1997;3:1061–1066.
106. Valsa J, Gusani P, Skandhan K, Modi H. Copper in split and daily ejaculates. *The Journal of Reproductive Medicine*. 1994;39:725–728.
107. Martin-du-Pan R, et al. Pregnancy-associated plasma protein-A (PAPP-A) and immunosuppressive activity in split ejaculates. *Arch Androl*. 1984;12:29–31.
108. Saxena S, Farooq A. Localization of source of immunosuppressive factor in the human male reproductive tract. *J Reprod Immunol*. 1987;12:149–153.
109. Dubé JY, et al. Isolation from human seminal plasma of an abundant 16-kDa protein originating from the prostate, its identification with a 94-residue peptide originally described as β-inhibin. *J Androl*. 1987;8:182–189.
110. Lewin L, et al. Alkaline phosphatase in human semen: an investigation using enzyme inhibitors and gel electrophoresis. *European Journal of Clinical Chemistry and Clinical Biochemistry*. 1993;31:811–814.
111. Lewin L, Beer R, Lunenfeld B. Paper chromatographic estimation of fructose and myo-inositol in human seminal fluid: a method for evaluating seminal vesicle and prostatic function. *Int J Fertil*. 1977;22:48–51.
112. Tauber PF, Zaneveld LJ, Propping D, Schumacher GF. Components of human split ejaculates. II. Enzymes and proteinase inhibitors. *J Reprod Fertil*. 1976;46:165–171.
113. Tauber PF, Zaneveld LJ, Propping D, Schumacher GF. Components of human split ejaculates. I. Spermatozoa, fructose, immunoglobulins, albumin, lactoferrin, transferrin and other plasma proteins. *J Reprod Fertil*. 1975;43:249–267.
114. De Cooman S, Gilliaux P, Thomas K. Immunoreactive relaxin-like substance in human split ejaculates. *Fertil Steril*. 1983;39:111–113.
115. Boonsaeng V, Techa-Udomtaworn W. Prostatic origin of pyruvate kinase activity in human seminal plasma. *Andrologia*. 1980;12:559–563.
116. Matalliotakis I, et al. Cytokine levels in seminal plasma. *Clinical and experimental obstetrics & gynecology*. 1998;25:58–60.
117. Gruschwitz MS, Brezinschek R, Brezinschek HP. Cytokine levels in the seminal plasma of infertile males. *J Androl*. 1996;17:158–163.
118. Meinertz H. Antisperm antibodies in split ejaculates. *Am J Reprod Immunol*. 1991;26:110–113.
119. Iosefi S, Lewin L. Androgen-binding components of human semen. *Andrologia*. 1984;16:509–516.
120. Kerek G, Eliasson R. Absorption activity of the blood group substances in various fractions of split ejaculates from man. *Int J Fertil*. 1975;20:125–127.
121. Polakoski K, Syner F, Zaneveld L.*Biochemistry of human seminal plasma. Human Semen and Fertility Regulation in Men.* St Louis, Mo: *CV Mosby Company*; 1976:133–143.

122. Huggins C, Scott WW, Heinen JH. Chemical composition of human semen and of the secretions of the prostate and seminal vesicles. *American Journal of Physiology-Legacy Content*. 1942;136:467–473.
123. Haugen T, Grotmol T. pH of human semen. *Int J Androl*. 1998;21:105–108.
124. Baechtel FS.Saferstein R, editor.*Forensic Science Handbook Vol. II*. vol. II. London: Prentice Hall; 1988:347–392.
125. Cooper TG, et al. World Health Organization reference values for human semen characteristics. *Hum Reprod Update*. 2010;16:231–245.
126. Eliasson R, et al. Empfehlungen zur Nomenklatur in der Andrologie. *Andrologia*. 1970;2:186–187.
127. D.A. Grimes, L.M. Lopez. (Elsevier, 2007).
128. Zondek B, Bromberg YM, Polishuk Z. Constant oligospermia and periodic oligospermia. *Am J Clin Pathol*. 1948;18:874–878.
129. Cooke S, Tyler J, Driscoll G. Andrology: Hyperspermia: the forgotten condition? *Hum Reprod*. 1995;10:367–368.
130. Zhang Y-j, Zhong J, Zhu W-j. Evaluation on sperm parameters of ejaculates with hyperspermia. *Journal of Reproduction and Contraception*. 2015;26:131–134.
131. Robin G, et al. Pourquoi et comment réaliser un bilan d'hypospermie? *Gynécologie Obstétrique & Fertilité*. 2008;36:1035–1042.
132. Leary F, Aguilo J. in *Mayo Clin Proc*. (1974), vol. 49, pp. 815-817.
133. Mathers MJ, Degener S, Sperling H, Roth S. Hematospermia—a symptom with many possible causes. *Deutsches Ärzteblatt International* **114**, *186*. 2017
134. Eliasson R, Lindholmer C. Distribution and properties of spermatozoa in different fractions of split ejaculates. *Fertil Steril*. 1972;23:252–256.
135. Chudnovsky A, Niederberger CS. Copious pre-ejaculation: small glands—major headaches. *J Androl*. 2007;28:374–375.
136. Zukerman Z, Weiss DB, Orvieto R. Short communication: does preejaculatory penile secretion originating from Cowper's gland contain sperm? *J Assist Reprod Genet*. 2003;20:157–159.
137. Masters WH, Johnson VE.*Human sexual response*. Boston: Little, Brown and Company; 1966:366.
138. Killick SR, Leary C, Trussell J, Guthrie KA. Sperm content of pre-ejaculatory fluid. *Human Fertility*. 2011;14:48–52.
139. Hebles M, Dorado M, Gallardo M, González-Martínez M, Sánchez-Martín P. Seminal quality in the first fraction of ejaculate. *Systems Biology in Reproductive Medicine*. 2015;61:113–116.
140. Fair WR, Cordonnier JJ. The pH of prostatic fluid: a reappraisal and therapeutic implications. *The Journal of Urology*. 1978;120:695–698.
141. Kvist U. Sperm nuclear chromatin decondensation ability. An in vitro study on ejaculated human spermatozoa. *Acta physiologica Scandinavica. Supplementum*. 1980;486:1–24.
142. Huggins CB, Johnson AA. Chemical observations on fluids of the seminal tract: I. Inorganic phosphorus, calcium, non-protein nitrogen and glucose content of semen and of seminal vesicle, prostate and spermatocele fluids in man. *American Journal of Physiology-Legacy Content*. 1933;103:574–581.
143. Nun S, Musacchio I, Epstein JA. Variations in seminal plasma constituents from fertile, subfertile, and vasectomized azoospermic men. *Fertil Steril*. 1972;23:357.
144. Janczewski Z, Bablok L. Semen characteristics in pubertal boys. I. Semen quality after first ejaculation. *Arch Androl*. 1985;15:199–205.
145. Yamakami K. The individuality of semen, with reference to its property of inhibiting specifically isohemoagglutination. *The Journal of Immunology*. 1926;12:185–189.
146. Landsteiner K, Levine P. On group specific substances in human spermatozoa. *The Journal of Immunology*. 1926;12:415–418.
147. Grubb R. Correlation between Lewis blood group and secretor character in man. *Nature*. 1948;162 933-933.
148. Haas GG. Jr, O. J. D'Cruz, ABH blood group antigens in human semen. *American journal of reproductive immunology and microbiology*. 1988;16:28–36.
149. Casey DG, et al. The persistence of sperm and the development of time since intercourse (TSI) guidelines in sexual assault cases at forensic science Ireland, Dublin, Ireland. *J Forensic Sci*. 2017;62:585–592.

150. Magalhães T, Dinis-Oliveira RJ, Silva B, Corte-Real F, Nuno Vieira D. Biological evidence nanagement for DNA analysis in cases of sexual assault. *The Scientific World Journal*. 2015;2015:11.
151. Nittis M. Evidence collection in cases of sexual assault. *Legal and Forensic Medicine*. 2013:1335–1358.
152. Nittis M. In: Stark MM, ed.*Clinical Forensic Medicine: A Physician's Guide*. Cham: Springer International Publishing; 2020:63–141.
153. Lavelle J. Forensic evidence collection. *Child maltreatment: a clinical guide and reference*. 2005: 856–860.
154. Shipp E, et al. Effects of argon-laser light, alternate source light, and cyanoacrylate fuming on DNA typing of human bloodstains. *J Forensic Sci*. 1993;38:184–191.
155. Wood R-W. Communications secrètes au moyen de rayons lumineux. *Journal de Physique Théorique et Appliquée*. 1919;9:77–90.
156. Cordonnier D. Mueller, Étude Sur La Résistance Des Spermatozoïdes Au Lavage Et De Quelques Procédés De Fixation Des Taches De Sperme. *Annales de médecine légale, de criminologie et de police scientifique*. 1922;2:243–252.
157. Thomas JC. The examination of blood and seminal stains. *Police J*. 1937;10:490–503.
158. Pollack OJ. Semen and seminal stains. *Arch Pathol*. 1943;35:140.
159. Ito T. über einige Anwendungen ultravioletter Strahlen zu gerichtlich-medizinischen Zwecken. *Dtsch Z Gesamte Gerichtl Med*. 1927;9:726–727.
160. Fiedler A, et al. Detection of semen (human and boar) and saliva on fabrics by a very high powered UV-/VIS-light source. *The Open Forensic Science Journal*. 2008;1:12–15.
161. Kobus HJ, Silenieks E, Scharnberg J. Improving the effectiveness of fluorescence for the detection of semen stains on fabrics. *J Forensic Sci*. 2002;47:819–823.
162. Nelson DG, Santucci KA. An alternate light source to detect semen. *Acad Emerg Med*. 2002;9: 1045–1048.
163. Vandenberg N, van Oorschot RAH. The use of Polilight® in the detection of seminal fluid, saliva, and bloodstains and comparison with conventional chemical-based screening tests. *J Forensic Sci*. 2006;51: 361–370.
164. Santucci KA, Nelson DG, McQuillen KK, Duffy SJ, Linakis JG. Wood's lamp utility in the identification of semen. *Pediatrics*. 1999;104:1342–1344.
165. Kind SS. Use of the acid phosphatase test in searching for seminal stains, The. *J Crim L Criminology & Police Sci*. 1956;47:597.
166. Amano T, Kunimi K, Ohkawa M. Fluorescence spectra from human semen and their relationship with sperm parameters. *Arch Androl*. 1996;36:9–15.
167. Hensel T. Flinders University, School of Chemical and Physical Sciences. (2020).
168. Kotaki A, YAGI K. Fluorescence properties of flavins in various solvents. *The Journal of Biochemistry*. 1970;68:509–516.
169. Karchewski L, Armstrong G, Nicholson ML, Wilkinson D. Assessment of the Leeds Spectral Vision system for detecting biological stains on fabrics. *J Can Soc Forensic Sci*. 2014;47:230–243.
170. Mameli A, Scudiero CM, Delogu G, Ghiani ME. Successful analysis of a 100 years old semen stain generating a complete DNA STR profile. *J Forensic Legal Med*. 2019;61:78–81.
171. Barrera V, Haas C, Meixner EA, Fliss B. Detection of painted-over traces of blood and seminal fluid. *Int J Leg Med*. 2018;132:1067–1074.
172. Casey DG, Carroll C. An evaluation of the Blue Crime-Lites(tm) for semen detection. *Glob Forensic Sci Today*. 2008;7:26–30.
173. Simmons R, Deacon P, Phillips DJ, Farrugia K. The effect of mark enhancement techniques on the subsequent detection of semen/spermatozoa. *Forensic Sci Int*. 2014;244:231–246.
174. Beckwith S, Murakami J, Chapman B. The persistence of semen on cotton fabric in various water environments. *Australian Journal of Forensic Sciences*. 2018:1–10.
175. Rodriguez JJRB, Calacal GC, Laude RP, De Ungria MCA. Integrating presumptive and confirmatory semen tests into DNA profiling of sexual assault evidence: a Philippine example. *Egyptian Journal of Forensic Sciences*. 2019;9:45.

176. Karadayi S, Moshfeghi E, Arasoglu T, Karadayi B. Evaluating the persistence of laundered semen stains on fabric using a forensic light source system, prostate-specific antigen Semiquant test and DNA recovery-profiling. *Medicine, Science and the Law*. 2020;60:122–130.
177. Demuth F. Über Phosphatstoffwechsel. I. Mitteilung: Über Hexosephosphatasen in menschlichen Organen und Korperflussigkeiten. *Biochemische Zeitschrift*. 1925;159:415–423.
178. Kutscher W, Wolbergs H. Prostataphosphatase. *Hoppe Seyler's Z Physiol Chem*. 1935;236:237–240.
179. Kutscher W, Wörner A. Prostataphosphatase. 2. Mitteilung. *Hoppe Seyler's Z Physiol Chem*. 1936;239:109–126.
180. Fisher RS. Acid phosphatase tests as evidence of rape. *N Engl J Med*. 1949;240:738–739.
181. Poyntz F, Martin P. Comparison of p30 and acid phosphatase levels in post-coital vaginal swabs from donor and casework studies. *Forensic Sci Int*. 1984;24:17.
182. Singer R, et al. Acid phosphatase activity in human semen. *Arch Androl*. 1979;3:89–90.
183. Gomori G. Distribution of acid phosphatase in the tissues under normal and under pathologic conditions. *Arch Pathol*. 1941;32:189–199.
184. Gutman AB, Gutman EB. An "acid" phosphatase occurring in the serum of patients with metastasizing carcinoma of the prostate gland. *J Clin Invest*. 1938;17:473–478.
185. Gutman AB, Gutman EB. "Acid" phosphatase activity of the serum of normal human subjects. *Proc Soc Exp Biol Med*. 1938;38:470–473.
186. Gutman EB, Gutman AB. Estimation of "acid" phosphatase activity of blood serum. *J Biol Chem*. 1940;136:201–209.
187. Babson AL, Read PA. A new assay for prostatic acid phosphatase in serum. *Am J Clin Pathol*. 1959;32:88–91.
188. Lundquist F. Function of prostatic phosphatase. *Nature*. 1946;158:710–711.
189. Lazaros L, et al. Phosphatidylethanolamine N-methyltransferase and choline dehydrogenase gene polymorphisms are associated with human sperm concentration. *Asian journal of andrology*. 2012;14:778.
190. Advanced Chemistry Development Inc. (ACD/Labs) (2018). "ChemSketch." 2018.2.5, Toronto, ON, Canada, www.acdlabs.com.
191. Gaensslen RE.*Sourcebook in forensic serology, immunology, and biochemistry*. Washington, DC: U.S. Government Printing Office; 1983:692.
192. Tamaki K, Fujisawa K, Okajima H, Sato K, Katsumata Y. Identification of semen in stain by determination of the specific activity of L-tartrate-inhibitable acid phosphatase. *Int J Leg Med*. 1989;102:429–436.
193. Willott GM. L-Tartrate inhibitable acid phosphatase in semen and vaginal secretions. *J Forensic Sci Soc*. 1972;12:363–366.
194. Adams EG, Wraxall BG. Phosphatases in body fluids: the differentiation of semen and vaginal secretion. *Forensic Sci*. 1974;3:57–62.
195. Ames PK, Kimes DR, Tahir MA, Stolorow M. Alternative methods for seminal acid phosphatase electrophoresis. *J Can Soc Forensic Sci*. 1983;16:1–5.
196. Adams EG, Wraxall BG. Phosphates in body fluids: the differentiation of semen and vaginal secretion. *Forensic Sci*. 1974;3:57–62.
197. Roy AV, Brower ME, Hayden JE. Sodium thymolphthalein monophosphate: a new acid phosphatase substrate with greater specificity for the prostatic enzyme in serum. *Clin Chem*. 1971;17:1093–1102.
198. Davidson G, Jalowiecki TB. Acid phosphatase screening — Wetting test paper or wetting fabric and test paper? *Science & Justice*. 2012;52:106–111.
199. Brown L. Boston University. (2016).
200. Shaler RC.*Crime Scene Forensics: A Scientific Method Approach*. Washington, UNITED STATES: Taylor & Francis Group; 2011.
201. Allard JE, et al. A comparison of methods used in the UK and Ireland for the extraction and detection of semen on swabs and cloth samples. *Sci Jus*. 2007;47:160–167.
202. Lewis J, Jones S, Baxter F, Siemieniuk A, Talbot R. The fallacy of the two-minute acid phosphatase cut off. *Science & Justice*. 2012;52:76–80.
203. Redhead P, Brown MK. The acid phosphatase test two minute cut-off: An insufficient time to detect some semen stains. *Science & Justice*. 2013;53:187–191.

204. Davies A, Wilson E. The persistence of seminal constituents in the human vagina. *Forensic Sci*. 1974;3:45–55.
205. Martínez P, Santiago B, Alcalá B, Atienza I. Semen searching when sperm is absent. *Science & Justice*. 2015;55:118–123.
206. Saha A, Basu J, Bhattacharyya AK. Seminal acid phosphatase from normal, oligospermic, vasectomized, and azoospermic men. *Int J Fertil*. 1981;26:124–127.
207. Dave B, Rindani T. Acid phosphatase activity in human semen. *Int J Fertil*. 1988;33:45–47.
208. Goldberg B, Jones Jr HW. Acid phosphatase in human female genital tract, a histochemical and biochemical study. *Proc Soc Exp Biol Med*. 1953;83:45–50.
209. Lau J, Frasca J, Nicholson ML, Laurin N. Inhibition of acid phosphatase detection in mixed semen-blood training samples by anti-coagulants present in blood collection tubes. *J Can Soc Forensic Sci*. 2020;53:71–82.
210. Vennemann M, Scott G, Curran L, Bittner F, Tobe SS. Sensitivity and specificity of presumptive tests for blood, saliva and semen. *Forensic Sci Med Pathol*. 2014;10:69–75.
211. Baechtel FS, Brown J, Terrell LD. Presumptive screening of suspected semen stain in situ using cotton swabs and bromochloroindolyl phosphate to detect prostatic acid-phosphatase-activity. *J Forensic Sci*. 1987;32:880–887.
212. Gonçalves ABR, de Oliveira CF, Carvalho EF, Silva DA. Comparison of the sensitivity and specificity of colorimetric and immunochromatographic presumptive methods for forensic semen detection. *Forensic Sci Int Gen Sup Ser*. 2017;6:e481–e483.
213. Lewis J, et al. Improved detection of semen by use of direct acid phosphatase testing. *Science & Justice*. 2013;53:385–394.
214. Hardinge P, Allard J, Wain A, Watson S. Optimisation of choline testing using Florence Iodine reagent, including comparative sensitivity and specificity with PSA and AP tests. *Science & Justice*. 2013;53:34–40.
215. Graves HCB, Sensabaugh GF, Blake ET. Postcoital detection of a male-specific semen protein — application to the investigation of rape. *N Engl J Med*. 1985;312:338–343.
216. Tirimanna ASL. Acid phosphatases in the tea leaf. *Cell Mol Life Sci*. 1972;28 633-633.
217. Martin NC, Clayson NJ, Scrimger DG. The sensitivity and specificity of red-starch paper for the detection of saliva. *Sci Jus*. 2006;46:97–105.
218. Herman Y, Feine I, Gafny R. Acid phosphatase test on Phadebas® sheets — An optimized method for presumptive saliva and semen detection. *Forensic Sci Int*. 2018;288:218–222.
219. Soules MR, Pollard AA, Brown KM, Verma M. The forensic laboratory evaluation of evidence in alleged rape. *Am J Obstet Gynecol*. 1978;130:142–147.
220. Collins KA, Bennett AT. Persistence of spermatozoa and prostatic acid phosphatase in specimens from deceased individuals during varied postmortem intervals. *The American journal of forensic medicine and pathology*. 2001;22:228–232.
221. Crowe G, Moss D, Elliot D. The effect of laundering on the detection of acid phosphatase and spermatozoa on cotton t-shirts. *J Can Soc Forensic Sci*. 2000;33:1–5.
222. Weitzig L, et al. Diagnostic value of PSA and AP tests for the detection of spermatozoa in postmortem swabs from the genital and anal region in males. *J Forensic Sci*. 2015;60:41–44.
223. Hooft PJ, van de Voorde HP. Interference of body products, food and products from daily life with the modified zinc test and the acid phosphatase test. *Forensic Sci Int*. 1994;66:187–196.
224. Kaye S. Acid phosphatase test for identification of seminal stains. *J Lab Clin Med*. 1949;34:728–732.
225. Reshef A, Barash M, Gallili N, Michael A, Brauner P. The use of acid phosphatase test papers for DNA profiling. *Science & Justice*. 2005;45:97–102.
226. Borges É, et al. Evaluation of the SPERM TRACKER™ for Semen Stains Localization on Fabrics. *J. Forensic Res*. 2017;8
227. 綾. 薗田 et al. 新規精液探索法の確立とその実務導入への検討 (Establishment of the new semen identification method and the examination to practical introduction). 日本法科学技術学会誌 (Japanese Journal of Forensic S*cience and Technology*) 27, 85-92 (2022).
228. Margossian RL. Boston University, (2022).

229. Rao AR, Motiwala HG, Karim OMA. The discovery of prostate-specific antigen. *BJU Int*. 2008;101:5–10.
230. Flocks R, Urich VC, Patel CA, Opitz JM. Studies on the antigenic properties of prostatic tissue I. *J Urol*. 1960;84:134–143.
231. Ablin RJ, Soanes W, Bronson P, Witebsky E. Precipitating antigens of the normal human prostate. *Reproduction*. 1970;22:573–574.
232. Sensabaugh GF. Isolation and characterization of a semen-specific protein from human seminal plasma: a potential new marker for semen identification. *J Forensic Sci*. 1978;23:106–115.
233. Hara M, Koyanagi Y, Inoue T, Fukuyama T. [Some physico-chemical characteristics of " -seminoprotein", an antigenic component specific for human seminal plasma. Forensic immunological study of body fluids and secretion. VII]. *Nihon Hoigaku Zasshi*. 1971;25:322–324.
234. Zhang W-M, Leinonen J, Kalkkinen N, Dowell B, Stenman U-H. Purification and characterization of different molecular forms of prostate-specific antigen in human seminal fluid. *Clin Chem*. 1995;41:1567–1573.
235. Wang MC, Loor RM, Li SL, Chu TM. Physico-chemical characterization of prostate antigen purified from human prostate gland and seminal plasma. *IRCS J Med Sci*. 1983;11:327–328.
236. Nadji M, et al. Prostatic-specific antigen: an immunohistologic marker for prostatic neoplasms. *Cancer*. 1981;48:1229–1232.
237. Kearsey J, Louie H, Poon H. Validation study of the "One Step Abacard(R) PSA Test" kit for RCMP casework. *J Can Soc Forensic Sci*. 2001;34:63–72.
238. Jumper J, et al. Highly accurate protein structure prediction with AlphaFold. *Nature*. 2021;596:583–589.
239. Varadi M, et al. AlphaFold Protein Structure Database: massively expanding the structural coverage of protein-sequence space with high-accuracy models. *Nucleic Acids Res*. 2021;50:D439–D444.
240. Hochmeister MN, et al. Evaluation of prostate-specific antigen (PSA) membrane test assays for the forensic identification of seminal fluid. *J Forensic Sci*. 1999;44:1057–1060.
241. Pang B, Cheung B. Identification of human semenogelin in membrane strip test as an alternative method for the detection of semen. *Forensic Sci Int*. 2007;169:27–31.
242. Gartside BO, Brewer KJ, Strong CL. Estimation of prostate-specific antigen (PSA) extraction efficiency from forensic samples using the Seratec(R) PSA semiquant semiquantitative membrane test. *Forensic Sci Comm*. 2003
243. Suttipasit P, Wongwittayapanich S. Detection of prostate specific antigen and semenogelin in specimens from female rape victims. *J Forensic Legal Med*. 2018;54:102–108.
244. McWilliams S, Gartside B. Identification of prostate-specific antigen and spermatozoa from a mixture of semen and simulated gastric juice. *J Forensic Sci*. 2009;54:610–611.
245. Laffan Á, Sawyer I, Quinones I, Daniel B. Evaluation of semen presumptive tests for use at crime scenes. *Medicine, Science and the Law*. 2011;51:11–17.
246. DiFrancesco J, Sutton J. Re-evaluation of the Seratec® PSA Semiquant test: comparison of kit provided buffer with phosphate buffer saline. *J Can Soc Forensic Sci*. 2015;48:137–151.
247. Yu H, Berkel H. Prostate-specific antigen (PSA) in women. *J La State Med Soc: Offic Organ La State Med Soc*. 1999;151:209–213.
248. Breul J, Pickl U, Hartung R. Prostate-specific antigen in urine. *Eur Urol*. 1994;26:18–21.
249. Kishbaugh JM, et al. Detection of prostate specific antigen and salivary amylase in vaginal swabs using SERATEC® immunochromatographic assays. *Forensic Sci Int*. 2019;304:109899.
250. Fall K, et al. Prostate-specific antigen levels as a predictor of lethal prostate cancer. *J Natl Cancer Inst (Bethesda*. 2007;99:526–532.
251. Kashefi C, Partin AW, Parsons JK. In: Su L-M, ed.*Early Diagnosis and Treatment of Cancer Series: Prostate Cancer*. Philadelphia: W.B. Saunders; 2010:1–7.
252. Noël S, et al. Repeatedly washed semen stains: optimal screening and sampling strategies for DNA analysis. *Forensic Sci Int Gen*. 2019;38:9–14.
253. Lunetta P, Sippel H. Positive prostate-specific antigen (PSA) reaction in post-mortem rectal swabs: a cautionary note. *J Forensic Legal Med*. 2009;16:397–399.
254. Benschop CCG, Wiebosch DC, Kloosterman AD, Sijen T. Post-coital vaginal sampling with nylon flocked swabs improves DNA typing. *Forensic Sci Int Gen*. 2010;4:115–121.

255. Cerdas L, et al. Menstrual cycle phase at the time of rape does not affect recovery of semen or amplification of STR profiles of a suspect in vaginal swabs. *Forensic Sci Int*. 2016;259:36–40.
256. Gooch J, Daniel B, Frascione N. Application of fluorescent substrates to the in situ detection of prostate specific antigen. *Talanta*. 2014;125:210–214.
257. Denmeade SR, et al. Specific and efficient peptide substrates for assaying the proteolytic activity of prostate-specific antigen. *Cancer Res*. 1997;57:4924–4930.
258. Gutkin S, Green O, Raviv G, Shabat D, Portnoy O. Powerful chemiluminescence probe for rapid detection of prostate specific antigen proteolytic activity: forensic identification of human semen. *Bioconjug Chem*. 2020;31:2488–2493.
259. Koukouvinos G, et al. White light reflectance spectroscopy biosensing system for fast quantitative prostate specific antigen determination in forensic samples. *Talanta*. 2017;175:443–450.
260. Strzemińska I, et al. Grafting of a peptide probe for prostate-specific antigen detection using diazonium electroreduction and click chemistry. *Biosensors and Bioelectronics*. 2016;81:131–137.
261. Frascione N, Gooch J, Abbate V, Daniel B. Fluorogenic displacement biosensors for PSA detection using antibody-functionalised quantum dot nanoparticles. *RSC Advances*. 2015;5:6595–6598.
262. Lilja H, Laurell CB, Jeppsson JO. Characterization of the predominant basic protein in human seminal plasma, one cleavage product of the major seminal vesicle protein. *Scand J Clin Lab Investig*. 1984;44:439–446.
263. Herr J, Woodward M. An enzyme-linked immunosorbent assay (ELISA) for human semen identification based on a biotinylated monoclonal antibody to a seminal vesicle-specific antigen. *J Forensic Sci*. 1987;32:346–356.
264. Herr JC, Spell DR, Conklin DJ, Flickinger CJ. Electron microscopic immunolocalization of seminal vesicle-specific antigen in human seminal vesicle. *Biol Reprod*. 1989;40:333–342.
265. Herr JC, et al. Characterization of a monoclonal antibody to a conserved epitope on human seminal vesicle-specific peptides: a novel probe/marker system for semen identification. *Biol Reprod*. 1986;35:773–784.
266. Malm J, Hellman J, Magnusson H, Laurell CB, Lilja H. Isolation and characterization of the major gel proteins in human semen, semenogen I and semenogen II. *Eur J Biochem*. 1996;238:48–53.
267. Bjartell A, et al. Distribution and tissue expression of semenogelin I and II in man as demonstrated by in situ hybridization and immunocytochemistry. *J Androl*. 1996;17:17–26.
268. Yoshida K, et al. Quantification of seminal plasma motility inhibitor/semenogelin in human seminal plasma. *J Androl*. 2003;24:878–884.
269. Bonilha VL, et al. Characterization of semenogelin proteins in the human retina. *Exp Eye Res*. 2006;83:120–127.
270. Bonilha VL, et al. Semenogelins in the human retina: differences in distribution and content between AMD and normal donor tissues. *Exp Eye Res*. 2008;86:150–156.
271. Rayborn M, et al. Characterization of semenogelin proteins in the human retina. *Investigative Ophthalmology & Visual Science*. 2004;45 643-643.
272. Shuvalov O, et al. SEMG1/2 augment energy metabolism of tumor cells. *Cell Death & Disease*. 2020;11:1047.
273. Ishiguro H, et al. Semenogelin I promotes prostate cancer cell growth via functioning as an androgen receptor coactivator and protecting against zinc cytotoxicity. *American journal of cancer research*. 2015;5:738.
274. Wing KE. Murdoch University, Perth, Australia (2021).
275. Sato I, et al. Rapid detection of semenogelin by one-step immunochromatographic assay for semen identification. *J Immunol Methods*. 2004;287:137–145.
276. Sato I, et al. Applicability of Nanotrap Sg as a semen detection kit before male-specific DNA profiling in sexual assaults. *Int J Leg Med*. 2007;121:315–319.
277. Old J, et al. Developmental validation of RSID™-Semen: a lateral flow immunochromatographic strip test for the forensic detection of human semen. *J Forensic Sci*. 2012;57:489–499.
278. Boward ES, Wilson SL. A comparison of ABAcard® p30 and RSID™-Semen test kits for forensic semen identification. *J Forensic Legal Med*. 2013;20:1126–1130.

279. Nakanishi H, Hara M, Takahashi S, Takada A, Saito K. Evaluation of forensic examination of extremely aged seminal stains. *Legal medicine*. 2014;16:303–307.
280. Stern AW, Lanka S. Evaluation of human semenogelin membrane strip test for species cross-reactivity in dogs. *Veterinary Pathology*. 2016;53:1095–1098.
281. Zhuravlev Y, et al. Structural, electronic, and vibrational properties of choline halides. *Materials Chemistry and Physics*. 2020;246:122787.
282. Forbes G. The scope and fallacies of the Florence reaction for seminal stains. *The Police Journal*. 1940;13:162–171.
283. Marcille MR. La caracterisation du sperme dans les expertises legales. *Annales De Chimie Analytique Et De Chimie Appliquée Et Revue De Chimie Analytique Réunies*. 1931;13:193–203.
284. Evers H, et al. Investigative strategy for the forensic detection of sperm traces. *Forensic Sci Med Pathol*. 2009;5:182–188.
285. Williams WW. Spermatic abnormalities. *N Engl J Med*. 1937;217:946–951.
286. MacLeod J. Semen quality in one thousand men of known fertility and in eight hundred cases of infertile marriage. *Fertil Steril*. 1951;2:115–139.
287. MacLeod J, Gold RZ. The male factor in fertility and infertility: IV. Sperm morphology in fertile and infertile marriage. *Fertil Steril*. 1951;2:394–414.
288. Ping YS, Chan XLS, Goh SK, Syn CKC. Optimization of spermatozoa detection using immunofluorescent staining and laser micro-dissection. *Forensic Sci Int*. 2015;255:72–79.
289. Auka N, et al. Optical tweezers as an effective tool for spermatozoa isolation from mixed forensic samples. *PloS one*. 2019;14
290. Nittis M, Cochrane C, Hughes R, Franco M. Preparing semen slides in cases of sexual assault: do they who smear first smear best? *J Forensic Legal Med*. 2021;79102130
291. Morihara K, Tsuzuki H. Specificity of proteinase K from Tritirachium album Limber for synthetic peptides. *Agric Biol Chem*. 1975;39:1489–1492.
292. Chapman RL, Brown NM, Keating SM. The isolation of spermatozoa from sexual assault swabs using Proteinase K. *J Forensic Sci Soc*. 1989;29:207–212.
293. Gill P, Jeffreys AJ, Werrett DJ. Forensic application of DNA fingerprints. *Nature*. 1985;318:577–579.
294. Engelbertz F, Korda JB, Engelmann U, Rothschild M, Banaschak S. Longevity of spermatozoa in the post-ejaculatory urine of fertile men. *Forensic Sci Int*. 2010;194:15–19.
295. Lino BF, Braden AWH, Turnbull KE. Fate of unejaculated spermatozoa. *Nature (Lond)*. 1967;213: 594–595.
296. Takamura A, Watanabe K, Akutsu T. Advanced forensic validation for human spermatozoa identification using SPERM HY-LITER™ express with quantitative image analysis. *Int J Leg Med*. 2017;131:933–939.
297. Saenguthai K, Chomean S, Kaset C. The evaluation of Oryza sativa L (Black rice) extracts for detection of spermatozoa on the clothing and vaginal swab samples. *Legal Medicine*. 2018;35:91–97.
298. Allery J, Telmon N, Mieusset R, Blanc A, Rougé D. Cytological detection of spermatozoa: comparison of three staining methods. *J Forensic Sci*. 2001;46:349–351.
299. Dutra FR. Simulated spermatoza. *J Crim Law Criminol Police Sci*. 1957;48:106–107.
300. De Moors A, Georgalis T, Armstrong G, Modler J, Frégeau CJ. Sperm Hy-Liter™: an effective tool for the detection of spermatozoa in sexual assault exhibits. *Forensic Sci Int Gen*. 2013;7:367–379.
301. Jenkinson J. Memoirs: on the relation between the structure and the development of the centrifuged egg of the frog. *J Cell Sci*. 1914;2:61–155.
302. Oppitz E. Eine neue Färbemethode zum Nachweis der Spermien bei Sittlichkeitsdelikten. *Arch Kriminol*. 1969;144:145–148.
303. Leubitz SS, Savage RA. Sensitivity of picroindigocarmine/nuclear fast red (PIC/NF) stain for detection of spermatozoa: a serial dilution study of human ejaculate. *Am J Clin Pathol*. 1984;81:90–93.
304. Golomingi R, Haas C, Dobay A, Kottner S, Ebert L. Sperm hunting on optical microscope slides for forensic analysis with deep convolutional networks – a feasibility study. *Forensic Sci Int Gen*. 2022;56:102602.
305. Vandewoestyne M, Van Hoofstat D, Van Nieuwerburgh F, Deforce D. Automatic detection of spermatozoa for laser capture microdissection. *Int J Leg Med*. 2009;123:169–175.

306. De Moors A, Frégeau CJ. Automated scoring of Sperm Hy-Liter™-stained spermatozoa by the MetaSystems Metafer image analysis software system in sexual assault specimens. *Forensic Sci Int Gen Sup Ser.* 2011;3:e35–e36.
307. Miller KW, et al. Developmental validation of the sperm HY-LITER Kit for the identification of human spermatozoa in forensic samples. *J Forensic Sci.* 2011;56:853–865.
308. Takamura A, Watanabe K, Akutsu T. Development of a quantitative validation method for forensic investigation of human spermatozoa using a commercial fluorescence staining kit (SPERM HY-LITER™ Express). *Int J Leg Med.* 2016;130:1421–1429.
309. Elshama SS, Aly SM, Abdalla ME, Hassan WA. Postmortem identification of spermatozoa on human skin based on fluorescent monoclonal antibody method. *Archiwum Medycyny Sądowej i Kryminologii/Archives of Forensic Medicine and Criminology.* 2017;67:121–133.
310. Anderson JM, Fischer BR, Miller KWP.*International Symposium on Human Identification (ISHI).* USA: Palm Springs; 2019.
311. Moench GL. Sperm morphology and biometrics as a means of identification of the individual. *M. Times.* 1934;62:33.
312. Hotchkiss RS. Methods in sperm analyses and evaluation of therapeutic procedures. *Journal of the American Medical Association.* 1936;107:1849–1851.
313. Kind S. In: Curry AS, ed. Methods of forensic science, 1964;3:267–287.
314. Astrup BS, Thomsen JL, Lauritsen J, Ravn P. Detection of spermatozoa following consensual sexual intercourse. *Forensic Sci Int.* 2012;221:137–141.
315. Dziak R, Parker L, Collins V, Johnston S. Providing evidence based opinions on time since intercourse (TSI) based on body fluid testing results of internal samples. *J Can Soc Forensic Sci.* 2011;44:59–69.
316. Tobe SS, Dennany L, Vennemann M. An assessment of the subjectivity of sperm scoring. *Forensic Sci Int.* 2015;251:83–86.
317. Keating SM, Higgs DF. The detection of amylase on swabs from sexual assault cases. *J Forensic Sci Soc.* 1994;34:89–93.
318. Willott GM, Allard JE. Spermatozoa - their persistence after sexual intercourse. *Forensic Sci Int.* 1982;19:135–154.
319. Silverman EM, Silverman AG. Persistence of spermatozoa in the lower genital tracts of women. *JAMA (J Am Med Assoc).* 1978;240:1875–1877.
320. Taylor D. Probabilistically determining the cellular source of DNA derived from differential extractions in sexual assault scenarios. *Forensic Sci Int Gen.* 2016;21:121–135.
321. Blanco A, Zinkham WH. Lactate dehydrogenases in human testes. *Science.* 1963;139:601–602.
322. Goldberg E. Lactic and malic dehydrogenases in human spermatozoa. *Science.* 1963;139:602–603.
323. Mokashi RH, Madiwale MS. The use of sperm-specific lactate dehydrogenase isoenzyme for the identification of semen in dried stains. *Forensic Sci.* 1976;8:269–275.
324. Deshmukh S, et al. A confirmatory test for sperm in sexual assault samples using a microfluidic-integrated cell phone imaging system. *Forensic Sci Int Gen.* 2020;48:102313.
325. Riman S, et al. Confirmatory detection of sperm and semen via proximity ligation real-time PCR. *Forensic Sci Int Gen Sup Ser.* 2015;5:e109–e111.
326. Gooch J, Tungsirisurp S, Costanzo H, Napier R, Frascione N. Generating aptamers towards human sperm cells using massively parallel sequencing. *Anal Bioanal Chem.* 2021;413:5821–5834.
327. Starr K.Referral from Independent Counsel Kenneth W. Starr in Conformity with the Requirements of Title 28, United States Code, Section 595 (c): Communication from Kenneth W. Starr, Independent Counsel, Transmitting a Referral to the United States House of Representatives Filed in Conformity with the Requirements of Title 28, United States Code, Section 595 (c). vol. 105. Government Printing Office; 1998.
328. Hara M, et al. Relationship between DNA degradation ratios and the number of loci detectable by STR kits in extremely old seminal stain samples. *Legal Medicine.* 2015;17:391–393.
329. Bini C, et al. Analysis of aged seminal stains by current forensic DNA approach. *Forensic Sci Int Gen Sup Ser.* 2015;5:e248–e249.

330. Morrison AI. Persistence of spermatozoa in the vagina and cervix. *British Journal of Venereal Diseases*. 1972;48:141.
331. Sharpe N. The significance of spermatozoa in victims of sexual offences. *Can Med Assoc J*. 1963;89:513–514.
332. Duenhoelter JH, Stone IC, Santosramos R, Scott DE. Detection of seminal fluid constituents after alleged sexual assault. *J Forensic Sci*. 1978;23:824–829.
333. Cohen MR, Stein IF. Sperm survival at estimated ovulation time comparative morphology: relative male infertility. *Obstetrical & Gynecological Survey*. 1951;6:759–760.
334. Rupp JC. Sperm survival and prostatic-acid phosphatase activity in victims of sexual assault. *J Forensic Sci*. 1969;14:177–183.
335. Any Questions? *Br Med J* **1**, 546-547 (1964).
336. Nicholson R. Vitality of spermatozoa in the endocervical canal. *Fertil Steril*. 1965;16:758–764.
337. Perloff WH, Steinberger E. In vivo survival of spermatozoa in cervical mucus. *American Journal of Obstetrics & Gynecology*. 1964;88:439–442.
338. Rubenstein BB, Strauss H, Lazarus ML, Hankin H. Sperm survival in women: motile sperm in the fundus and tubes of surgical cases. *Fertil Steril*. 1951;2:15–19.
339. Mansour RT, et al. In vivo survival of spermatozoa in the human fallopian tube for 25 days: a case report. *J Assist Reprod Genet*. 1993;10:379–380.
340. Keating S, Allard J. What's in a name?—Medical samples and scientific evidence in sexual assaults. *Medicine, Science and the Law*. 1994;34:187–201.
341. Enos WF, Beyer JC. Spermatozoa in anal-canal and rectum and in oral cavity of female rape victims. *J Forensic Sci*. 1978;23:231–233.
342. Fonneløp AE, Johannessen H, Heen G, Molland K, Gill P. A retrospective study on the transfer, persistence and recovery of sperm and epithelial cells in samples collected in sexual assault casework. *Forensic Sci Int Gen*. 2019;43:102153.
343. Taylor AS, Cook WGH, Smith S. *Taylor's Principles and Practice of Medical Jurisprudence*. (J. & A. Churchill, ed. 8th, 1928).
344. Randall B. Persistence of vaginal spermatozoa as assessed by routine cervicovaginal (PAP) smears. Journal of Forensic Science. 1987;32:678–683.
345. Eungprabhanth V. Finding of the spermatozoa in the vagina related to elapsed time of coitus. *Zeitschrift für Rechtsmedizin*. 1974;74:301–304.
346. Wilson E. Sperm's morphologic survival after 16 days in the vagina of a dead body. *Journal of Forensic Science*. 1974;19:561–564.
347. Monaghan B, Newall P. STR results for both epithelial and spermatozoal fractions obtained from 13-year old microscope slides of vaginal swab material. *J Can Soc Forensic Sci*. 1996;29:13–19.
348. Joki-Erkkilä M, et al. Urine specimen collection following consensual intercourse–A forensic evidence collection method for Y-DNA and spermatozoa. *J Forensic Legal Med*. 2016;37:50–54.
349. Ranson R. Rubber and sperm-survival. *The Lancet*. 1937;229:1400–1401.
350. Vander Vliet W, Hafez E. Survival and aging of spermatozoa: A review. *Am J Obstet Gynecol*. 1974;118:1006–1015.
351. Abarbanel A. In: Engle ET, ed.*The Problem of Fertility*. Princeton University Press; 1946:119.
352. Latz LJ, Reiner E. Further studies on the sterile and fertile periods in women. *Am J Obstet Gynecol*. 1942;43:74–79.
353. Findley TP. Quantitation of vaginal acid phosphatase and its relationship to time of coitus. *Am J Clin Pathol*. 1977;68:238–242.
354. Jimenez-Verdejo A, Osuna E, Garcia-Olivares E, Luna A. Study of the enzymatic activity of GGT, LDH, PAP and PSA in semen stains: application to age calculation. *Forensic Sci Int*. 1994;68:7–15.
355. Srettabunjong S, Betset P, Limawongpranee S, Ekpo P. The stability of prostate-specific antigen in semen under various temperatures. *J Forensic Sci*. 2015;60:1577–1581.
356. Achetib N, et al. Estimating the time of deposition of semen traces using fluorescence protein–lipid oxidation signatures. *Anal Chem*. 2019;91:3204–3208.
357. Zha S, et al. Estimation of the age of human semen stains by attenuated total reflection Fourier transform infrared spectroscopy: a preliminary study. *Forensic Sciences Research*. 2020;5:119–125.

CHAPTER 5

Saliva

Introduction

Saliva stains can pose a particular difficulty for forensic scientists because they can be nearly invisible to the forensic examiner. In a survey of 42 global-wide forensic biology laboratories, 17% did not presumptively test for saliva, and 80% did not carry out confirmatory testing for saliva.[1] Saliva stains are only tested if there is some account in the circumstances surrounding a case that saliva might be present, such as in a sexual assault where the victim reports being licked or bitten by the suspect. Other instances when saliva may be encountered as a form of assault or as part of another crime are masks in robberies, stamps and envelopes, drinking vessels, cigarette ends, and spitting. Studies that have examined unstained clothes have reported tiny specs of saliva on pocket flaps and lapels and theorized they originated from talking or sneezing; researchers also investigated the movement of saliva in air, indicating that innocent deposits of saliva on clothing may be more common than expected.[2–4] Comparatively little research, relative to blood and semen identification, has gone into the identification of saliva for forensic purposes, and the frequency with which it is submitted to laboratories is low; however, there are several presumptive tests available, and it is a valuable source of DNA. As with other presumptive tests, it is necessary to target something in saliva that is not found in any other body fluid or any other common substances that can be encountered at a scene.

In forensic toxicology, saliva refers to the pure liquid form recovered directly from the glands in the mouth, and what biologists refer to as saliva is called oral fluid in toxicology. The main difference is the extra components that will be found in addition to pure saliva, which include bacteria, shed buccal cells, food, or other liquid, and this can often be reported as whole saliva.[5] For the purposes of this chapter, the term saliva will refer to whole saliva—the fluid expelled from the mouth in its entirety—because this is what would typically be encountered at a crime scene and examined by forensic biologists.

There are two main types of tests for saliva, those that are based on the enzymatic action of saliva and immunologic tests that use antigens to identify saliva, which are generally more specific but less sensitive. Testing for saliva may be done at a crime scene, but it is usually carried out in the laboratory. Standard protocols have been developed, and each laboratory

Forensic Serology. DOI: http://doi.org/10.1016/B978-0-12-812968-5.00005-2

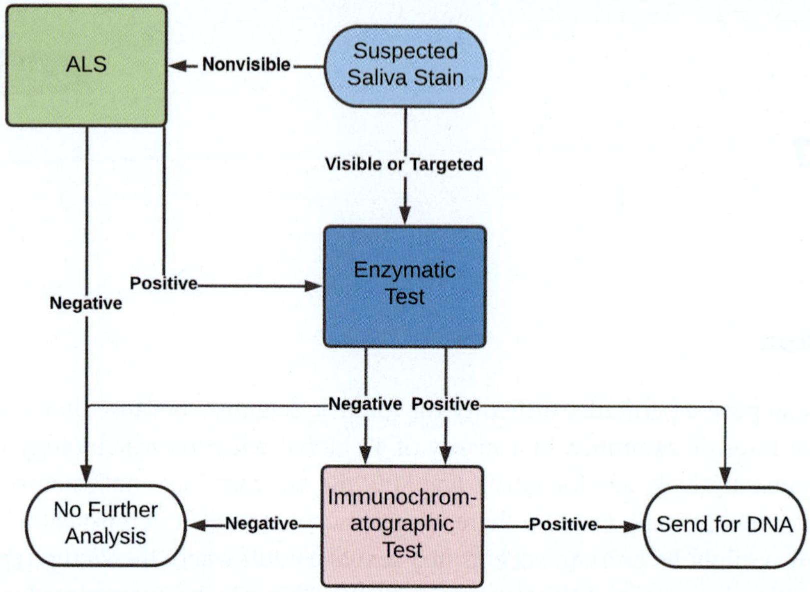

Fig. 5.1 A schematic of the current workflow when testing for a suspected saliva stain. Laboratories have different protocols and procedures, so some laboratories may not use an immunochromatographic test if the enzymatic test fails or may send the sample directly to DNA if the enzymatic test is positive. Circumstances surrounding the alleged crime will dictate the exact workflow. Most laboratories consider the immunochromatographic tests as confirmatory and species specific. *ALS*, Alternate light source.

will have its own practices and workflows; however, most will have very similar protocols and strategies for testing (Fig. 5.1).

The enzymatic aspects of saliva, or at least their results and effects, have been known for over a millennium, but the requirement to identify saliva as a fluid of interest was not considered. Testing for saliva has been sporadic and usually as a side note in the testing of other fluids, mainly blood and semen. Therefore, the history of saliva identification in forensic science is much shorter than other body fluids.

History

The history surrounding identification of saliva in a forensic context is largely based on how it reacted differently to other body fluids of interest, usually semen. This does not indicate the experiments are not valuable, however, because the different ways in which saliva reacts could also be used to identify it. In fact, some of the principles discovered centuries ago are still the basis of testing today. The number of publications is low, especially when compared against body fluids that are more obviously seen as relevant to forensic science.

In ancient Greece, there are records that wet nurses chewed the food of their charges to make it more easily digestible, and similarly different cultures have used saliva as part of brewing practices to make beer.[6] Converting starch into sugars for fermentation has been featured in many cultures and is still required today, although saliva is not the mechanism of the hydrolysis.[7] Although the mechanism of the reaction of saliva with food was not known, the results were well understood and exploited.

In 1827, Orfila[8] carried out a study of saliva as part of semen identification testing. His experiments were different in that they involved repeated applications of saliva to linen, although the exact number of applications was not reported. He found three different types of saliva. The first type was coarse to the touch, yellowish, and had a disagreeable odor. Upon application of heat, the yellowing intensified and mimicked the reaction of semen; when placed in cold water, it had an odor of semen and separated into two parts.[8] The second saliva type did not yellow on heating or emit a semenlike odor; the third type caused the linen to yellow but not stain, again unlike semen.[8] Orfila's overall conclusion was that saliva could be mistaken for semen, but that it was unlikely given the repeated nature of the application and the requirement that it dry between applications.[8]

A substance called thiocyanate, found in saliva, was first described in 1814 by Treviranus,[9] who called it "blood acid," but it was officially identified as thiocyanate in 1926.[10] It was later determined that saliva has a high concentration of thiocyanate,[11] and smokers have even higher levels.[12] The method to detect thiocyanate involves adding $FeCl_3$ to the sample, and a positive is indicated by a pink color change.[13] This was further investigated by Nelson and Kirk,[14] who also looked at identification of saliva through the presence of nitrite. Nitrite was found in saliva in 1937,[15] and is in part derived from nitrates ingested,[16] but is found at around 4.6 μg/mL in saliva.[14] It can be detected by the Griess test, developed in 1858,[17] and used in chemistry to detect nitrite ions in solutions, usually drinking water. The test involves application of the Griess reagent, an acidic solution, and a positive is indicated by a pink color.

The ability of saliva to cause a chemical change as an indication of its activity, its ability to digest starch, was first described in 1831 by Leuchs,[6,18] and this feature of saliva remains the target of current presumptive testing. Although Leuchs did not use the discovery of the hydrolysis of starch by saliva forensically, it did form the basis of subsequent forensic testing. He used boiled potato starch to form a paste into which he added saliva, and he noted within 2 hours that the paste was completely dissolved, although volumes were not disclosed in the work.[18] His second work[6] cited earlier research by Tiedemann and Gmelin[10] looking at overall digestion; found that some substances in a dog's stomach could be stained with iodine and others could not. It was not until 1928 that Mueller[19] first suggested the activity of amylase as an indicator of saliva.

Historically, the starch iodine test was used to detect amylase and was first described in 1881.[20,21] Iodine, when reacted with starch, turns a deep blue, and a decrease in the color can be used as an indication of amylase activity. This method has been superseded by easier and more sensitive techniques. Several of these newer techniques, however, continue to rely on the digestion of starch by amylase.

Biology of Saliva

Between 0.5 and 1.5 L of saliva are produced per day by the average person, and most saliva is produced by three major salivary glands: 65% originates from the submandibular salivary glands (found below the jawbone), 20% from the parotid salivary glands (found in the cheeks), and 5% from the sublingual salivary glands (under the tongue) (Fig. 5.2).

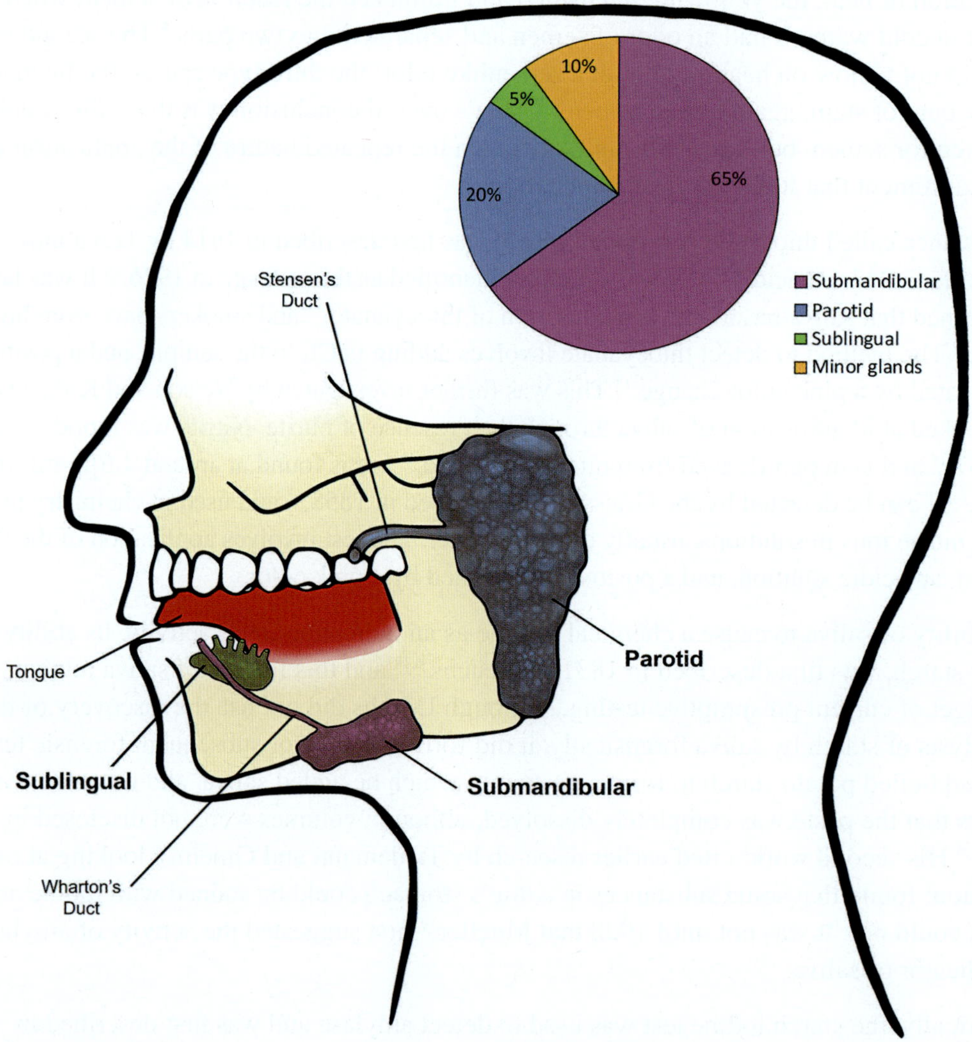

Fig. 5.2 Anatomic location of the major salivary glands and their contribution to saliva in the resting state. Minor glands are not shown. *From Vila T, Rizk AM, Sultan AS, et al. The power of saliva: antimicrobial and beyond. PLOS Path. 2019;15:e1008058.*

Additional minor salivary glands contribute the remaining 10%.[5,22] In the resting state (i.e., nonstimulated), approximately 66% of the saliva is produced from the submandibular glands; however, upon stimulation, the parotoid glands contribute at least 50%.[5] Certain medical conditions (e.g., hyposalivation, xerostomia) result in reduced salivary flow.[23]

Saliva is 97% to 99.5% water and has a pH of 6 to 7.5. It contains solutes in the form of electrolytes (Na^+, K^+, Cl^-,PO_4^{3-},HCO_3^-), digestive enzymes, salivary amylase, and lingual lipase. Saliva contains the proteins mucin, lysozyme, and immunoglobulin A, and it contains metabolic wastes (urea, uric acid).[5,24] The purpose of saliva is its defense or buffering capacity, remineralization of teeth, restoration of soft tissues, lubrication, digestion, and antimicrobial capacity.[5,23] A major component of saliva, and of particular interest for its identification, is the enzyme amylase.

Amylases break down starch into sugar through the process of hydrolysis. Amylase (Enzyme Commission 3.2.1.1) is found in high concentrations in saliva, where it begins the process of digestion, but it is also involved in lubrication and has antibacterial properties.[22] There are three classes of amylases: α-amylase (found in humans, animals, plants, and bacteria), β-amylase (found in plants and bacteria), and γ-amylase (most efficient in acidic environments with an optimum pH of 3). α-Amylases are endoglucanases and calcium metalloenzymes, which are completely unable to function in the absence of calcium[25] (Fig. 5.3).

Human α-amylases are found as two major isoenzymes: human salivary α-amylase (HSA) and human pancreatic α-amylase (HPA). Both HSA and HPA have similar amino acid sequences, although they are coded for by two different genes, *AMY1* and *AMY2*, respectively.[26] For the identification of saliva, the HSA hydrolysis of starch is detected for the enzymatic test, although HPA can also react. HSA is found in saliva at much higher concentrations than any other body fluid (Table 5.1), making it an ideal target as a presumptive marker.

Amylase is found within the vaginal cavity, where it is used to break down sugars to carbohydrates for *Lactobacillus*, a major part of the vaginal microbiome,[27] and it was found to fluctuate during the menstrual cycle.[28] Previously, the differentiation between HPA and HSA was taken into consideration[29,30] because the source of the amylase activity is important. However, since the wider adoption of DNA typing, it is now more efficient and informative to use the DNA profile to determine the source of the amylase found (e.g., HSA on genitalia is from a suspect, and HPA is from the victim, with obvious exceptions that would be case specific).

Alternate Light Sources

The use of alternate light source (ALS) systems for the presumptive identification of saliva has been investigated,[31–33] although the resulting fluorescence is less intense than that of semen and can be hard to identify (Fig. 5.4). The optimum wavelengths for the detection of saliva are the same as for semen (between 415 and 490 nm with a yellow filter),[33,34] although

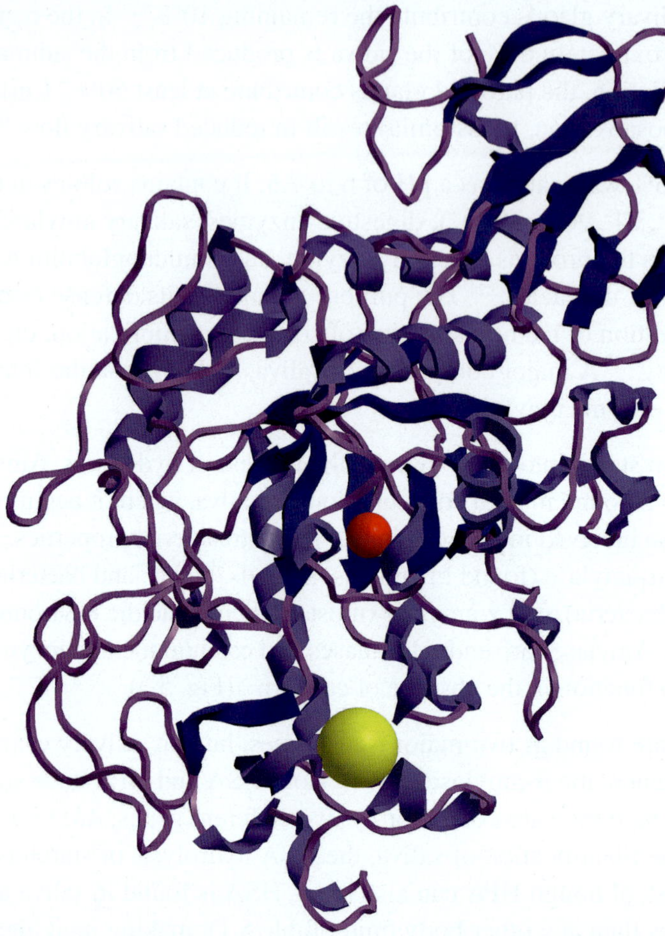

Fig. 5.3 Three-dimensional structure of human salivary α-amylase (PDB:1SMD). The *yellow* molecule represents calcium, and the *red* molecule represents chloride. *Structure determined by Ramasubbu N, Paloth V, Luo Y, et al. Structure of human salivary α-amylase at 1.6 Å resolution: implications for its role in the oral cavity. Acta Crystallogr Sect D Biol Crystallogr. 1996;52(pt 3): 435–446. Created in Chem3DPro 12.0.*

using the Polilight it was found that 450 nm with orange goggles gave better signal in one study.[31] As with other biologic fluids, ALS is mainly used to locate possible stains and is not a presumptive identification of saliva in itself because other body fluids fluoresce under the same conditions.

Vandenberg and van Oorschot,[31] in their evaluation of the Polilight, found that a 450 nm light source with orange goggles provided the best resulting fluorescence with saliva stains. They also found that, depending on the substrate and pattern, saliva was not always observed despite being present. They concluded that the absorbency of the material may be a factor. It was also found that saliva could only be detected to a dilution of 1:10 and that the edges of the stains

Table 5.1 Amylase levels found in other body fluids

Body Fluid	Amylase (IU/L)
Saliva	72,000–1.3 million
Semen	1–6820
Urine	84–3500
Lip mucus	170–2900
Tears	870–2150
Meconium	52–1400
Sweat	45–895
Breast milk	425–810
Nasal secretions	56–536
Serum	84–300
Blood	110
Vaginal secretions	45–60

From Whitehead PH, Kipps AE. A test paper for detecting saliva stains. *J Forensic Sci Soc*. 1975;15:39-42; Auvdel MJ. Amylase levels in semen and saliva stains. *J Forensic Sci*. 1986;31:426-431; Tsutsumi H, Higashide K, Mizuno Y, et al. Identification of saliva stains by determination of the specific activity of amylase. *Forensic Sci Int*. 1991;50:37-42; Kipps AE, Whitehead PH. The significance of amylase in forensic investigations of body fluids. *Forensic Sci*. 1975;6:137-144; Ceska M, Brown B, Birath K. Ranges of α-amylase activities in human serum and urine and correlations with some other α-amylase methods. *Clin Chim Acta*. 1969;26:445-453.

showed the brightest fluorescence (as can be seen in Fig. 5.4).[31] In simulated casework, saliva could be detected on all items that had direct transfer, but it was not detected in secondary transfer using ALS, and the sensitivity was found to be the same as Phadebas testing (see later).

A subsequent study found the optimal wavelength for saliva detection to be between 440 and 490 nm using either orange or red goggles.[33] In their experimental results, however, Fiedler et al.[33] were only able to detect 60% of the saliva samples (compared to 100% of the semen stains tested under the same conditions). They did not identify substrate type as affecting the ability to detect a stain, but they noted the pattern had an effect.

Karchewski et al.[35] evaluated several different ALS systems, and of the various fluids examined, saliva showed the lowest identifications using various volumes and substrates. They found that infrared wavelengths (850 nm) allowed greater identification of saliva at the lowest volume (3 μL) tested.[35] In an attempt to standardize ALS detection of saliva, Miranda et al.[36] used Photoshop to differentiate between the stain and the background. They found that saliva showed low fluorescence compared to other body fluids, and the fluorescence was concentrated at the edges of the stain. They also showed persistence over 60 days without loss after the saliva stain dried.[36]

Sterzik et al.[37] investigated this further and found that saliva stain fluorescence increased over the 2 years of their study. They found that only three saliva samples could be detected in their recent stain tests, but a further eight that were previously undetected were observed after 2 years.[37]

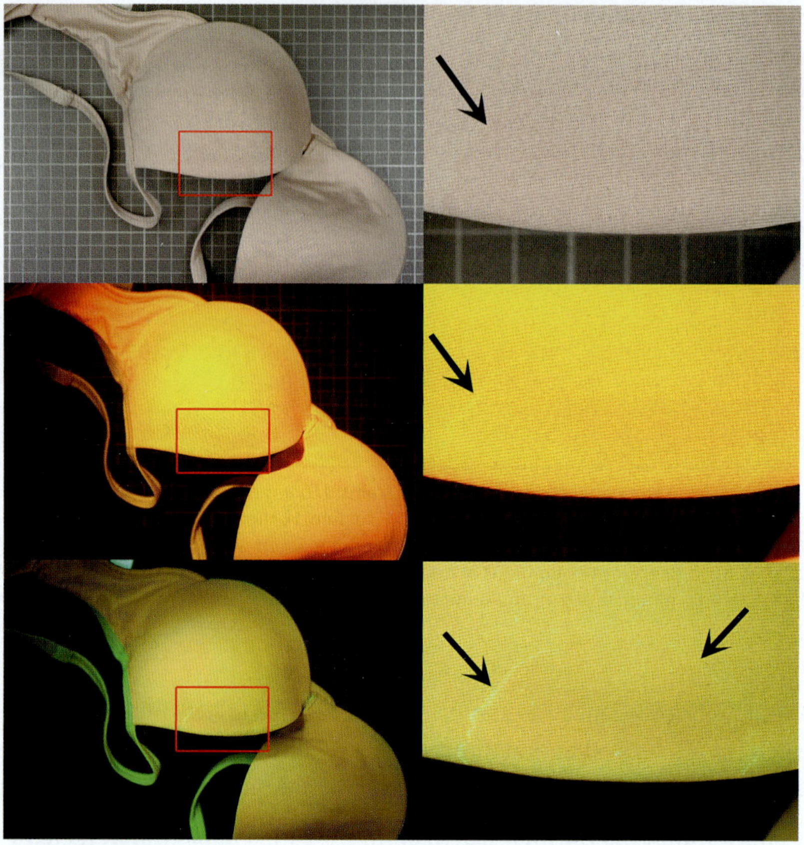

Fig. 5.4 A bra with a saliva stain. The images on the *left* show the overall bra, and the images on the *right* show the highlighted section magnified. Note the background fluorescence from the different materials of the straps and the cups. *Arrows* indicate the presence of a slight discoloration that could be indicative of a saliva stain. *(Top row)* The bra under normal lighting, showing a slightly visible stain. *(Middle row)* The bra viewed under a blue Crime-Light (420–470 nm) and orange filter. *(Bottom row)* The bra viewed under a violet Crime-Light (400–430 nm) and yellow filter.

The use of ALS systems for saliva detection suffers from confusing results because many other substances or substrates also fluoresce under the same wavelengths as saliva. ALS has been able to identify saliva stains stored between 3 and 5 weeks with similar intensity.[33] One ALS system (Polilight) was found to be sensitive to saliva at a dilution of 1:10.[31,32] Certain laundry detergents have been found to fluoresce under some commercial ALS systems, both before and after washing,[31] and washing of garments often removes biologic stains.[33] A study by Feia and Novroski[38] found that saliva laundered with Era detergent (Procter & Gamble) could still be visualized using ALS, but that all other detergents tested removed saliva traces entirely. Additionally, it has been found that the absorbency of the substrate has an effect on the detection of saliva with ALS.[31] Saliva stains on the top of unabsorbent materials is more

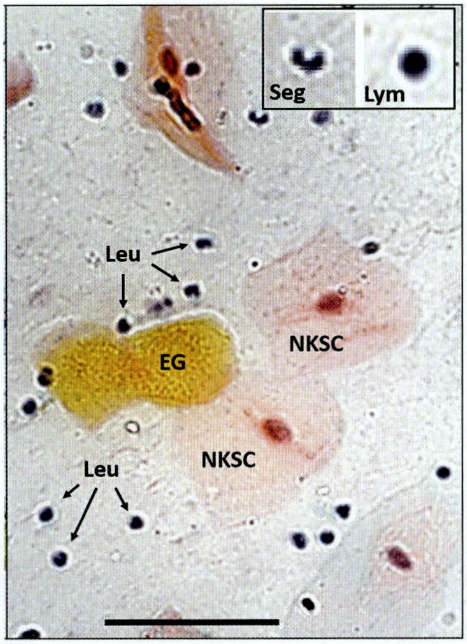

Fig. 5.5 Representative fields of view (200× magnification) of Pap staining of an adult's saliva sample. Visible features are pink nonkeratinized superficial squamous cells *(NKSC)*, enucleated orange ghost cells *(EG)*, and a large number of leukocytes *(Leu)* with the *insert* showing a segmented cell *(Seg)* and a lymphocyte *(Lym)*. The scale bar is 50 μm. *From Theda C, Hwang SH, Czajko A, et al. Quantitation of the cellular content of saliva and buccal swab samples. Sci Rep. 2018;8:6944.*

easily detected than stains on absorbent materials.[31] In one study, saliva was only detected in 60% of test cases.[33] ALS is therefore only used as a general search tool to locate potential areas to test, although even with ALS saliva stains can be almost invisible.

Microscopic Examination

According to a survey by Fourney et al.,[1] 26% of laboratories use microscopic identification of epithelial cells as a means to identify saliva. Interestingly, there are very few publications that investigate or validate this method of saliva identification. Despite wide use, texts limit descriptions of this form of analysis to a few sentences.

Within the mouth, and contained within saliva, are cellular components that are primarily leukocytes and squamous epithelial cells from the surface of the oral cavity (Fig. 5.5).[39]

The morphology of squamous epithelial cells are flattened and described as scale like, which derives from its name,[24] but they have also been said to resemble a fried egg. Squamous epithelial cells line the inner and outer surfaces of the body and are flattened laterally with

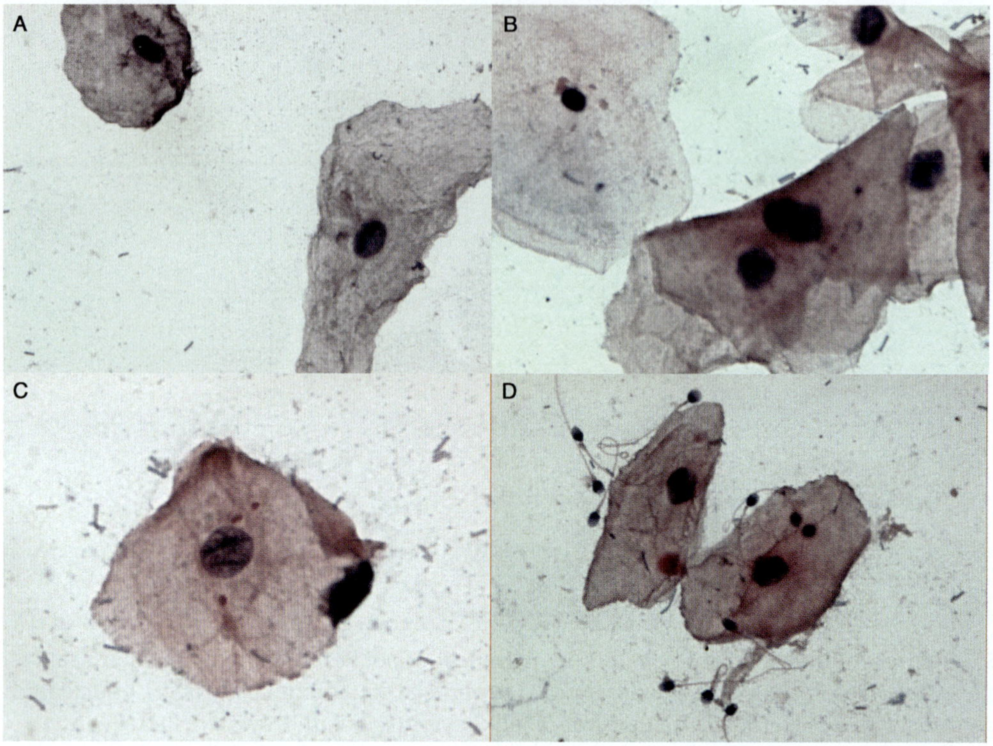

Fig. 5.6 Buccal cells from saliva stained with hematoxylin and eosin from a study looking at cells and spermatozoa. (A–C) Various levels of buccal squamous epithelial cells. (D) A mixture of buccal cells and spermatozoa. Magnification 400×.

little cytoplasm. More specifically, these cells are stratified squamous epithelial cells, which are classified by being several layers thick, well suited to protection of the body, and found in areas of wear and tear (e.g., the mouth). The surface areas with stratified squamous epithelial cells are constantly being rubbed away, and the cells are replaced from division of the cells beneath (basal cells). For this reason, these distinctive cells can be found in large numbers in saliva and are used as an identifying feature.

The cells are nucleated and can be stained with various histologic stains, although recent publications suggest that staining with Lugol iodine or with methylene blue and eosin is current.[40] However, any set of differential stains (e.g., hematoxylin and eosin, HE) would also be suitable because cell morphology is the important factor (Fig. 5.6).

Enzyme-Based Saliva Identification

The enzymatic identification of saliva is achieved through the hydrolysis of starch by HSA. Starch is tasteless, odorless, and cannot be dissolved in water or alcohol. It is found in many foods, including flour (from wheats and other grains used in breads and other baked

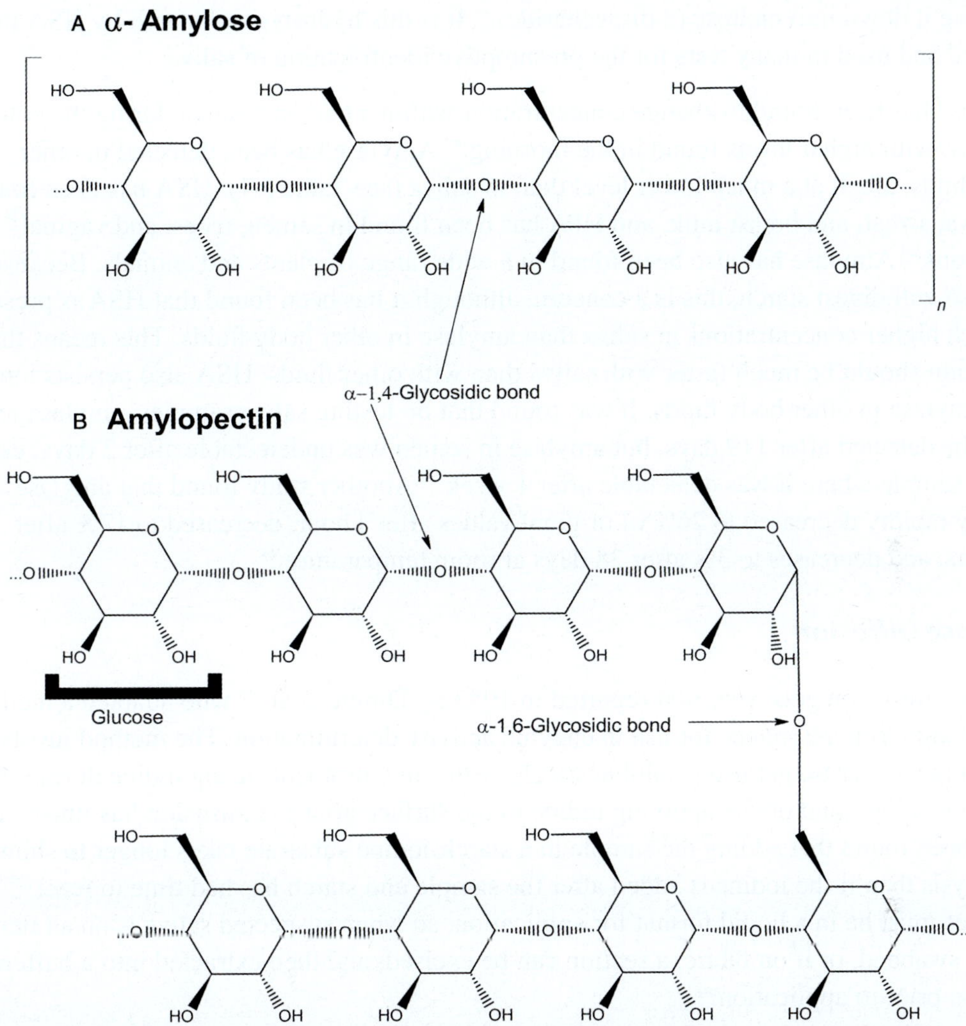

Fig. 5.7 Chemical structures of the polysaccharides found in starch: (A) α-amylose and (B) amylopectin. 1,4-glycosidic bonds and 1,6-glycosidic bonds are shown. Note the chains of glucose residues stretch for thousands of glucose repeats. *Image created with Advanced Chemistry Development Inc. ChemSketch. Toronto, Ontario; 2018.* www.acdlabs.com.

products), rice, oats, and potatoes. Starch is a polysaccharide composed of α-amylose and amylopectin (Fig. 5.7). α-Amylose is composed of several thousand glucose residues linked by α-1,4-glycosidic bonds. Amylopectin, like α-amylose, is composed mainly of glucose residues (up to 10^6) linked by 1,4-glycosidic bonds but also contains branches with 1,6-glycosidic bonds every 24 to 30 glucose residues.[41] Its counterpart in animals is glycogen, which has the same composition and structure, but with more extensive branching that occurs every 8 to 12 glucose units. The hydrolysis of starch by saliva was first described in 1831 by Leuchs.[6,18] In the mouth, HSA serves to hydrolyse starch at random α-1,4-glycosidic bonds breaking it down into maltose (a disaccharide).[41] It is this hydrolysis of starch by HSA that is targeted and used in many tests for the presumptive identification of saliva.

Amylase has been found to change concentration within a person's saliva during the course of a day, with higher levels found in the morning.[42] Amylase has been detected in other body fluids, albeit at a much lower level than in saliva (see Table 5.1). HSA has been found in saliva, sweat, and breast milk, and HPA has been found in semen, feces, and vaginal secretions.[43] Amylase has also been found in a wide range of plants and animals. Because all amylase will digest starch, this is a concern, although it has been found that HSA is present in much higher concentrations in saliva than amylase in other body fluids. This means that a reaction should be much faster with saliva than with other fluids. HSA also persists longer than amylase in other body fluids. It was found that on testing saliva samples, amylase levels could be detected after 119 days, but amylase in semen was undetectable after 2 days, except in one sample where it was detectable after 1 week.[44] Another study found that amylase activity rapidly decreased to 26% of original values after 1 hour, decreased to 17% after 24 hours, and decreases to 3% after 28 days at room temperature.[45]

Amylase Diffusion

Amylase diffusion gels were first reported in 1953 by Dingle et al.,[46] who adapted a method used in antibiotic resistance for use in enzyme activity determination. The method involves preparing an agarose gel using soluble starch, with some protocols using iodine during the gel preparation[46] and others applying iodine to the surface after the diffusion has finished.[47,48] It has been found that adding the sample to a starch-iodine substrate takes longer to show hydrolysis than if the iodine is added after the sample and starch has had time to react.[20] Samples must be in a liquid format for application, so when suspected saliva is on an item, it can be swabbed, or if on fabric, a section can be excised, and then extracted into a buffered solution prior to application.[48]

Once the gel has set, small divots or cups are cut into it, and the sample is placed in the cups and allowed to incubate at 37°C for 18 to 24 hours. After incubation, the gel is assessed directly if iodine was part of the gel; if not, then iodine is applied to the gel and allowed to saturate the remaining starch. Unstained or clear areas indicated amylase activity and are considered positive for saliva (Fig. 5.8).

The size of the zone of amylase activity (i.e., clear zone) is proportional to the logarithm of enzyme concentration.[49] Therefore the larger the clear area, the more amylase is present in the sample. It has been found that pH has a significant effect on the diameter for the activity zone, with the optimal pH 4.5 noted, and pHs approaching 3 and 6.5 reduce the activity zone by as much as 30%.[46] Maidment and Ringham,[47] in a comparison test between Phadebas and iodine methods, found that the gel diffusion relationship with increased amylase was curvilinear.

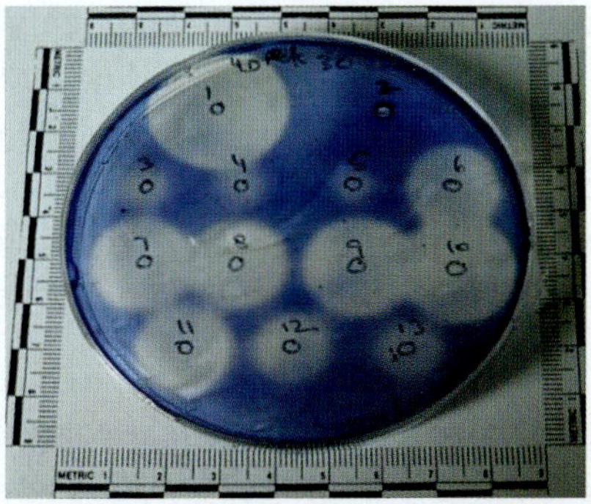

Fig. 5.8 Example of a starch gel amylase diffusion test with iodine solution applied after development. *Clear areas* indicate amylase activity, which has digested the starch in the gel and therefore does not stain with iodine. The size of the clear zones indicates different levels of amylase activity, with larger clear zones indicating higher amylase activity. *From Draz U, Ali S, Firyal S, et al. Detection of human salivary amylase level deposited on fruits with first bite mark. Adv Life Sci. 2019;6:176-181.*

Despite approximately 30% of laboratories using amylase diffusion gels,[1] there are few publications on the technique in forensic science. A study by Lim et al.[50] found a sensitivity of greater than 1:15,000 saliva to water. A study by Park et al.,[51] however, found the maximum method sensitivity at only 1:250.

Another study investigated the method used on bitemarks on fruit over a period of 48 hours.[48] They found that males and females had different levels of amylase activity, with males being higher. It was also found that recovery of saliva samples from bite marks in apples and apricots over 48 hours was successful, with a reduction in amylase activity as time increased.[48] Bite marks on peaches failed to show any amylase activity from 24 hours onward after biting the fruit, regardless of biological sex.[48]

The assay is not specific for HSA and has been shown to react with other sources of amylase, including pig (*Sus scrofa*) pancreatic α-amylase,[52] and the Enzyme Commission lists 17 other organisms that have the same class of amylase as humans and include different strains of bacteria (https://www.brenda-enzymes.org/enzyme.php?ecno=3.2.1.1#SYNONYM). Other than the initial testing, there have been no dedicated studies identified that deal with the sensitivity of the test, and instead all samples with amylase tested show diffusion and negative controls show none.

Iodine or Soluble Starch Test

The iodine (soluble starch test) method of amylase activity detection involves the preparation of a buffered starch substrate and separate iodine solution. These solutions are combined with the unknown sample and color is assessed, either by visual observation or with a spectrophotometer. The basis is the loss of color indicating amylase activity: Amylose and iodine produce a blue color and amylopectin and iodine a reddish color,[53] but as these products hydrolyse via the amylase activity, the color is lost. Maximal absorbance of iodine bound to amylopectin is between 500 and 560 nm, and that for iodine bound to amylose is above 580 nm.[54,55] When assessing the sample using spectrophotometric methods, the exact activity (i.e., amount of amylase present) can be determined when a time series is carried out and compared to a standard series.

Sensitivity studies show that lower levels of amylase take longer to record a color loss,[47] but it was found that the iodine method had a lower reported amylase activity than the same sample test using Phadebas isoamylase.[47] The method has been largely phased out for easier to operate methods of amylase detection.

AmylasePaper (SERATEC) is a modern application of the iodine method based on starch-imbedded paper. The paper is moistened, then placed on a suspected saliva stain (or an entire garment if a stain is suspected but the location is unknown). If present, the amylase will digest the starch in the paper. After a short incubation time, an iodine solution is applied to the paper, and areas of white indicate areas of amylase activity. Using AmylasePaper, one study found the substrate played a major factor in the sensitivity of the test, with polyester successfully detecting amylase activity at all dilutions for 3 weeks.[56] Denim and cotton samples showed much lower sensitivity, and sensitivity reduced with time over the study period.[56]

Phadebas

The Phadebas test is probably the most used saliva presumptive test currently. It uses starch microspheres linked to blue dye (Fig. 5.9), which can be in solution or immobilized on filter paper sheets for this purpose. The starch-dye complex is insoluble in water; however, in the presence of HSA, the starch is digested and releases the blue dye, which is then released into the solution or diffuses across the filter paper. Water will not cause the starch spheres to digest, and they will therefore not release the blue dye or diffuse. The methodology behind Phadebas was first described in 1967 by Rinderknecht et al.[57] for use in clinical detection of amylase activity in serum for medical purposes.[57–60] It was later adapted for use in forensic science.[61,62] Originally referred to as Amylose Azure,[63–65] this test can still be found under that name in other fields.[66]

The original Phadebas test was an isoamylase test tablet that was added to a sample and incubated, then time to optical density (OD) would be measured.[67] The solution-based method using OD allows the specific activity of amylase to be determined when compared with the supplied standard curve. It remains in use today mainly in clinical applications; however, it is also used in forensic casework because it is more sensitive than the paper-based test. The use of Phadebas in forensic science nonetheless has shifted toward the filter paper method, currently marketed as Phadebas Forensic Press Test, because of its ease of use, ability to search large areas/items, and speed of results.

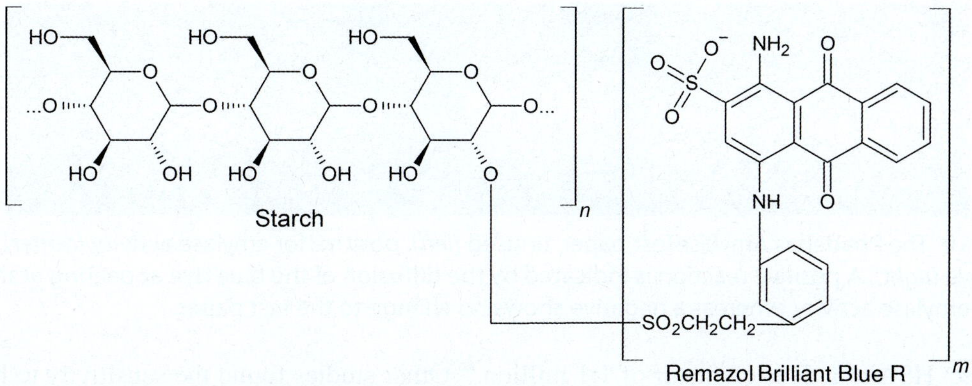

Fig. 5.9 Example of how a dye, in this case Remazol Brilliant Blue (PubChem CID: 17409), attaches to the starch molecule. Different dye molecules can be attached, and this example shows the first reported instance of this technique. m<<<n. A later study suggested using Procion Blue HB (Cibacron Blue F.3GA; PubChem CID: 656725) as the dye. *After Ceska M, Hultman E, Ingelman BGA. A new method for determination of α-amylase. Cell Mol Life Sci. 1969;25:555-556; Image created with Advanced Chemistry Development Inc. ChemSketch. Toronto, Ontario; 2018.* www.acdlabs.com.

The tablet-based Phadebas test (OD) requires the sample to be in solution and heated to 37°C, after which the Phadebas tablet is added, the sample is vortexed, then heated at 37°C for a further 15 minutes. The reaction is terminated using 0.5 M NaOH, centrifuged, and the OD of the supernatant is determined in a photometer at 620 nm with the reading being compared to the standard curve provided to determine the amylase activity.

The Phadebas Forensic Press Test is marketed to detect and search for saliva on fabrics, although it also can be used with swabs. It requires a flat surface, and the item must be moistened with sterile water, then Phadebas paper is placed on top of the item, and is also moistened. A glass plate is then overlayed, and a weight of at least 4 kg is applied. The paper is observed over this time, with a positive result indicated by the blue color appearing on the back of the test paper, and diffusion of the dye on the front, at the site(s) of amylase activity (Fig. 5.10). When using this method with a swab, the swab is moistened, then the paper is wrapped around it and pressure is applied; or the swab can be extracted into solution, and the solution can be applied directly to the Phadebas paper. It has been found that positive results can be obtained in as little as 2 minutes after starting the test and that the speed of reaction is directly proportional to the amylase activity of the saliva.[68]

The Phadebas OD tested on stamps was found to produce a positive reaction from stamps as old as 16 years.[69] In another study, it was found that amylase activity decreased with time (up to 49 days), but it was still detectible using the Phadebas reagent.[67] When assessing casework samples, it was found that amylase activity could be detected for 16, 55, and 30 hours on penile, vaginal, and breast swabs, respectively.[70] Using serial dilutions, this method was able

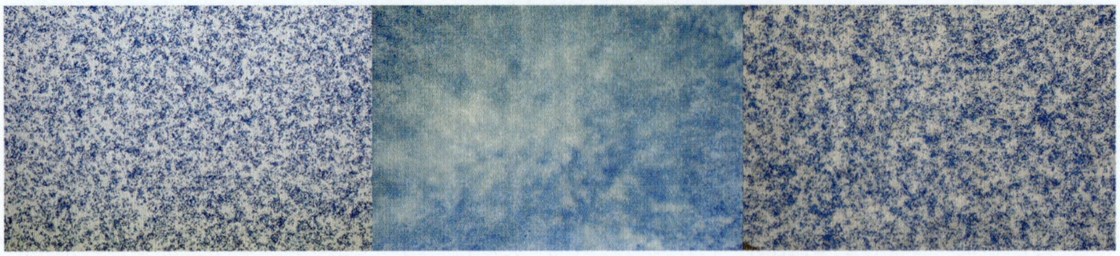

Fig. 5.10 The Phadebas AmylaseTest paper, unused *(left)*, positive for amylase activity *(center)*, and negative *(right)*. A positive reaction is indicated by the diffusion of the blue dye appearing at the site of amylase activity, whereas a negative shows no change to the test paper.

to detect HSA to a dilution factor of 1:1 million.[69] Other studies found the sensitivity to be no greater than 1:100.[71,72] In an analysis of 400 casework samples, amylase activity was detected in 25% of penile swabs tested, 32% of vaginal swabs, and 50% of breast swabs.[70] The longest time interval between the alleged offense and sampling in which a positive reaction was observed was 16 hours, 55 hours, and 30 hours for penile, vaginal, and breast swabs, respectively.[70]

The Phadebas Forensic Press Test was found to have a maximum sensitivity of 1:50[51] and was able to identify amylase activity in mixed fluids to the maximum ratio tested of 90:10 blood to saliva, although the results were made more difficult to interpret due to the masking of the diffusion by the amount of blood.[51]

The Phadebas test failed to identify saliva on fabrics that had been laundered using various detergents; however, five of the detergents tested directly (e.g., Tide Liquid, Kirkland Signature, OxiClean Gel, Gain, and Era) showed a false positive reaction with the test.[38] A study found no difference in reaction between room temperature use of the Phadebas test, but did find that saliva could be identified to a 1:500 dilution if a longer reaction time of up to 40 minutes was used.[73] This was confirmed in a study by Woodford et al.,[74] who found no benefit to conducting the test at 37°C compared with room temperature, but they did find a decrease in reaction when used with dilute aged stains. Longer reaction times were found to increase cross-reactions with nontarget body fluids, including feces, nasal secretions, perspiration, semen, vaginal secretions, used underwear, and urine.[68,73] Other cross-reactions observed under standard testing include blood, semen, sweat, and urine, although not all samples for each fluid produced a cross-reaction.[75] Phadebas can be inhibited by some fingerprint developing techniques, with acid violet 17 completely inhibiting the reaction, and black magnetic powder, ninhydrin, DFO, cyanoacrylate/BY40, Bluestar Magnum, and black iron oxide powder causing a decrease in the reaction strength.[34]

The Phadebas test has been found to cross-react with saliva stains and whole saliva from pig, rat, mouse, rabbit, guinea pig, and hamster.[72] A reaction was also observed with HPA, porcine pancreatic α-amylase, bacillus α-amylase, barley α-amylase, sweet potato α-amylase, apple extract, sweet corn extract, red carrot extract, green radish extract, and cabbage extract.[72] The

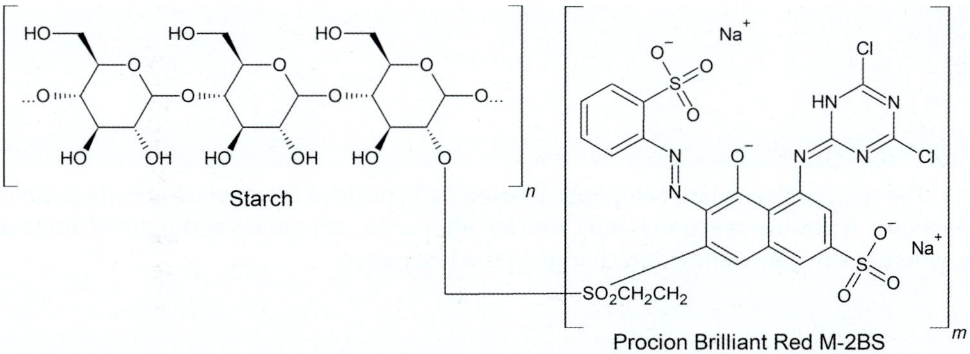

Fig. 5.11 Example starch bound to Procion Brilliant Red M-2BS (PubChem CID: 87291), which is then applied to a filter paper to make red starch paper. m<<<n. *After Sax SM, Bridgwater AB, Moore JJ. Determination of serum and urine amylase with use of Procion Brilliant Red M-2BS-Amylopectin. Clin Chem. 1971;17:311-315; Image created with Advanced Chemistry Development Inc. ChemSketch. Toronto, Ontario; 2018.* www.acdlabs.com.

Phadebas test paper is suitable for subsequent testing of acid phosphatase,[76] and it can be used in DNA extraction without issue.[77]

Red Starch

Another test called red starch paper functions in a similar manner to Phadebas but with a different dye. Red starch paper uses Procion Brilliant Red M-2BS-Amylopectin (Fig. 5.11) and was initially used to detect HPA,[78] but it was later applied for forensic detection of HSA.[2] The first publication by Sax et al.[79] used the method in solution, with detection at 517 nm taking place in a photometer. It was later applied to a paper-based format in 1975.[2] In this method, filter paper is dipped into a solution of Procion Red dissolved in phosphate buffer and allowed to dry.[80] Previously, the saturated filter paper would be subsequently sprayed with ethylene glycol monomethyl ether (EGME or 2-methoxyethanol) and zinc sulfate,[2] but because of health concerns this is no longer standard practice. Unlike with Phadebas paper, amylase reacted with red starch paper will cause a loss of color (Fig. 5.12), which can be enhanced by rinsing the paper with water after analysis to remove any remaining unlinked dye.

The procedure for the red starch test is similar to the Phadebas test in that the sample must be moistened along with the paper, and the paper pressed down on the fabric. The sample and paper are then incubated in a moist cabinet at room temperature for 15 to 30 minutes before being assessed.[2]

It was found that allowing the test to incubate for increased periods of time did not increase the effectiveness or sensitivity of the test.[78] Red starch paper has been tested for sensitivity and specificity with many commercial products. Sensitivity was tested and found to be between 1:10 in one study[2] and 1:64 and 1:640 for liquid samples, but it was found to be only 1:2 for dried stains in another.[80] Even with known stains, it was found that red starch

Fig. 5.12 The red starch amylase test paper, unused *(left)*, positive for amylase activity *(center)*, and negative *(right)*. A positive reaction is indicated by white areas appearing at the site of amylase activity, whereas a negative shows no change to the test paper.

paper had a 91% to 97% efficiency (3%–9% false negatives).[78] Red starch paper produced a positive reaction with Persil biologic and nonbiological powders, Tesco nonbiologic powder, Vaseline Intensive Care dry skin hand and body lotion, and Garnier Pure antiblemish pen.[80] It has also been shown to produce false positives with blood and semen, although not in all cases.[78]

The following tested negative: fabric conditioner, two other types of washing powder, five types of soap, five types of liquid dish soap, five types of shampoo, five types of hair conditioner, five types of shower gel, bath lotion, face wash, five types of face cream, face and hand cream, four types of hand cream, foundation, four types of toothpaste, lip cream, shaving cream, baby wipes, absorbent diaper crystals, lubricant, and four types of condoms.[80] Plant amylases from potato and broccoli did not cause a reaction with the test.[2] Whitehead and Kipps[2] caution that all body fluids contain some levels of amylase, so extending the incubation beyond 15 to 30 minutes may lead to false positives. Substate type did not have an effect, although only printed cotton, printed Tricel, polyester crepe, satin, polyester curtaining, bonded crimplene, thick woven wool, cavalry twill, and thick wool boucle were tested.[2] Amylase was detected in fecal samples to a dilution of 1:1000, in five urine samples with no dilution, and with one urine sample to a dilution of 1:10.[80]

SALIgAE

SALIgAE (Abacus Diagnostics, United States), a commercial test for saliva, results in a color change of a solution in the presence of amylase. This test requires the suspected stain to be added to a solution, which will change from clear to yellow if saliva is present (Fig. 5.13). The mechanism for this reaction is unknown due to the commercial nature of the test.

The test requires that a suspected sample, either swab or fabric cutting, is incubated at room temperature in sterile water. A small amount of the sample solution is added to a SALIgAE test vile and is gently mixed and allowed to incubate at room temperature for 10 minutes before it is assessed. A yellow color change is indicative of amylase activity, with no color change indicating a negative sample or a sample below the detection limits.

Fig. 5.13 The SALIgAE test for saliva. A negative *(left)* and positive *(right)* are shown, with the positive indicated by a color change to yellow. *From Amy Brodeur, Boston University School of Medicine.*

SALIgAE has been shown to detect saliva to dilutions of 1:2000 and does not react with cat saliva, dog saliva, semen, vaginal secretions, sweat, or blood.[72,81] It was found to react with pig saliva to a dilution of 1:100[72] and additionally to saliva stains and whole saliva from rat, mouse, rabbit, guinea pig, and hamster.[50,72] SALIgAE also shows cross-reaction with HPA, porcine pancreatic α-amylase, breast milk, urine, and feces.[72] Further cross-reactivity has been observed if the test was left longer than the indicated reaction time, and nasal discharge, sweat, urine, semen, and vaginal fluids all could be considered positive if left for extended times.[50]

Another study found the limit of detection to be 1:500, with a modified version detecting 1:600.[50] The modified version involved placing a small amount of the SALIgAE reagent in a PCR (0.2 mL) tube, which also served to reduce the time to result from 30 minutes to 5 minutes.[50] A subsequent study using the modified version found the sensitivity to be 1:1250.[51] Still another study determined the sensitivity to be at least 1:1000, the highest dilution tested.[81] It was further used on mock case items, successfully indicating the presence of saliva on envelopes, drinking cans, face masks, and cigarettes.[81] When testing samples of mixed body fluids, SALIgAE was able to positively identify saliva at a maximum ratio of 20:80 (blood to saliva), and even at this ratio the result was difficult to interpret because the blood masked the color change.[51]

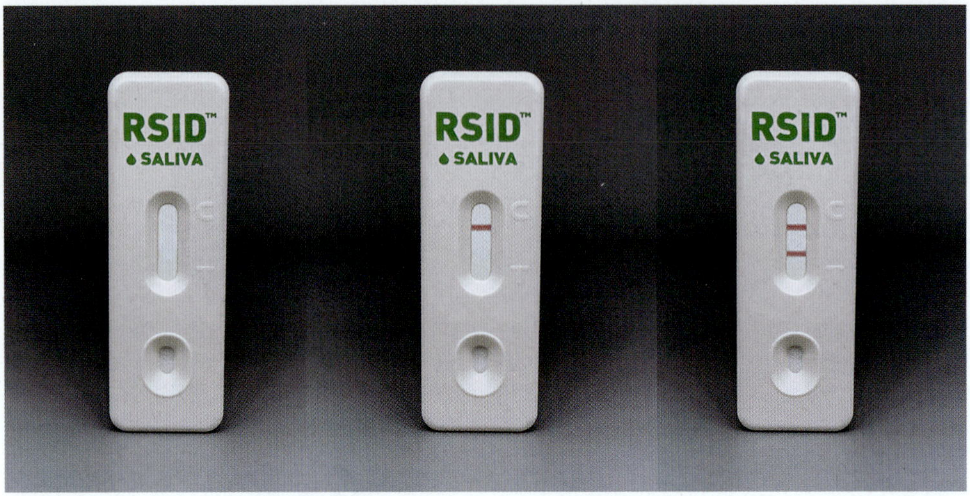

Fig. 5.14 The RSID Saliva test showing a blank cassette *(left)*, a negative result *(middle)*, and a positive result *(right)*. The sample window is at the bottom of the test, and lines at C and T indicate a positive result; a line at C only indicates a negative result. *From Dina Mattes, Independent Forensics, Lombard, Illinois.*

Immunologic Tests

As with other biologic fluids, there are commercial immunological tests available for the detection of saliva; these include RSID Saliva (Independent Forensics of Illinois - IFI) and AmylaseTest (SERATEC). Both of these use α-amylase as the target, although the mechanism is not the activity of the enzyme as with the previously described tests, but rather is an antigen-antibody reaction. Other tests have been developed for other medical purposes for detection of amylase activity, such as Rapignost-Amylase (Behring), which was designed for the rapid determination of α-amylase in urine, and was investigated for forensic use in the 1980s.[82,83]

RSID Saliva

RSID Saliva was developed in 2009 by IFI, and it uses two monoclonal antibodies specific for human salivary α-amylase in a lateral flow format.[84] The RSID Saliva test requires samples to be swabbed and extracted using a provided extraction buffer by submerging the sample and incubating at room temperature for 1 hour. Following the extraction, a portion of the extract (25 μL in the validation paper)[84] is mixed with running buffer to a final volume of 100 μL, which is then deposited to the sample window. The wicking action of the test strip will allow the solution to travel across the strip. The test is assessed 10 minutes after sample is added.

A positive test is indicated by two lines at the control (C) and test (T) positions (Fig. 5.14), and a negative is indicated by a single line at the C position. If only the T line or no lines are observed, then this indicates an invalid test, and the process needs to be repeated.

RSID Saliva can detect saliva to a dilution of 1:100 and does not suffer from the high-dose hook effect.[84] Other studies found the limit of sensitivity to be 1:500,[71] 1:10,000,[72,81] and 1:31,250.[51] Time and dilution have both been shown to have an effect with RSID Saliva, with increasing time and dilution both contributing to earlier failure of the tests to detect saliva (between 3 and 50 days).[85]

RSID Saliva was initially not found to cross-react with blood, semen, or urine, and it could identify saliva even if mixed with those fluids, demonstrating that they do not interfere with the test either.[84] One study was able to identify saliva in mixtures with blood at all dilution levels to the maximum ratio of 90:10 (blood to saliva).[51] Another study found it was able to detect saliva mixed with blood to a dilution of 1:1000.[71] It was found not to cross-react with postcoital vaginal swabs, but did show a reaction 1 day after oral-vaginal contact.[84]

In other studies, RSID Saliva has been found to cross-react with HPA, at low levels with breast milk, pancreatin, and occasionally with semen, sweat, fecal swabs, and urine;[51,71,72,84] cross-reaction with labia wipes and vaginal swabs has also been observed.[86] When tested on fabric from underwear worn for 12 hours by different age groups of females with no saliva present or applied, cross-reaction with RSID Saliva was found in 25% (prepubescent), 55% (postpubescent), and 20% (postmenopausal) of the samples.[87] Fecal material from diapers showed a positive reaction in four of five samples tested,[71] as did rat saliva.[72] Conversely, another study found no cross-reaction with urine, sweat, vaginal swabs, penile swabs, used underwear, or anal swabs.[71]

RSID Saliva was found to be highly specific to human α-amylase, but it was not found to react with saliva from donkey, opossum, cat, mouse, pig, sheep, rabbit, guinea pig, hamster, dog, woodchuck, cow, tokay gecko, cuckoo, mongoose, chameleon, llama, horse, goat, grey gull, ferret, hedgehog, skunk, lion, tiger, rhinoceros, marsh snake, Sykes monkey, Capuchin monkey, tamarin, and marmoset.[71,72,84] It did show cross-reaction with saliva from a gorilla.[84]

RSID Saliva showed inhibition after stains were exposed to some fingerprint development methods, with acid violet 17 and black iron oxide powder completely inhibiting the test, and black magnetic powder, ninhydrin, DFO, cyanoacrylate/BY40, and Bluestar Magnum causing partial inhibition, which produced false negatives at lower dilutions.[34] RSID Saliva was unable to detect saliva from stains that had been laundered using a variety of different detergents.[38]

RSID Saliva was able to positively identify saliva on 40-year-old stamps, 26-year-old envelopes, and 10-year-old cigarette butts.[88] It has been shown to positively identify saliva in expirated bloodstains in all cases, although in 7% of cases a longer time was needed to show a positive.[89] It was able to identify saliva stains over a variety of substrate surfaces, over a time series of 40 days.[90]

The test was designed with the ability to subsequently test for DNA in mind, and the extraction buffer also acts as a buffer for DNA that can be carried forward into a standard DNA workflow. Only 25 μL of the extraction buffer is used in the RSID Saliva test, but up to 1 mL can be used during the extraction of the sample to allow subsequent DNA profiling.[84]

SERATEC AmylaseTest

The SERATEC AmylaseTest is an immunochromatographic assay with two monoclonal anti-α-amylase antibodies on a lateral flow test strip. According to manufacturer information, it has a sensitivity equivalent to 1 μL of saliva. There is also a SERATEC Saliva Crime Scene version for use in the field.

Liquid samples of suspected saliva are diluted at least 1:100 with buffer because of the high viscosity of pure saliva. Swabs or stains on fabrics or condoms, up to 1 cm^2, can be extracted in buffer sufficient to cover the sample, generally between 0.5 and 1 mL. Samples are then incubated at room temperature for 10 minutes, with the recommendation that older stains may need a longer incubation. Three drops of the sample extract solution are added to the AmylaseTest sample well, which should be fully absorbed, and results are recorded after 10 minutes. If a single line appears at the control (C) area, then it indicates a negative test; an additional line at the test (T) area indicates a positive (Fig. 5.15). If no lines appear, then the test is invalid.

Both the AmylaseTest and the Saliva Crime Scene version were able to positively detect saliva stains on denim, cotton, and polyester over a 6-month time series.[91] Both gave similar band intensities over all fabrics and times, but the AmylaseTest buffer had a better recovery of DNA based on quantification results.[91,92]

One study found that false positives were generated with the AmylaseTest when tested with citric acid and lactic acid (between pH 1.74 and 12),[93] although these results are with direct application to the test strip; when the kit-supplied buffer was used, negative results were obtained (for the one acid tested). The user information states that pH below 3 or above 11 causes invalid results. Orange juice, white vinegar, and Pine-Sol all caused false positives with the test.[93] The AmylaseTest showed positive results with vaginal swabs in 8% of samples tested,[94] but it could not be attributed to menstrual cycle phase.[28]

The remaining extraction buffer is suitable for DNA profiling,[95] with a manufacturer recommendation that the extraction buffer is stable for 2 days; if longer times are expected, then the extract should be refrigerated. It has also been demonstrated that DNA can be recovered from the AmylaseTest test strip itself, with the entire test strip or just the area under the sample well suitable for a DNA profile, DNA kit dependant.[96]

Other Studies

More recently, there have been several other attempts to develop presumptive tests for the identification of saliva that do not rely on HSA, such as Raman spectroscopy,[97] enzyme-linked

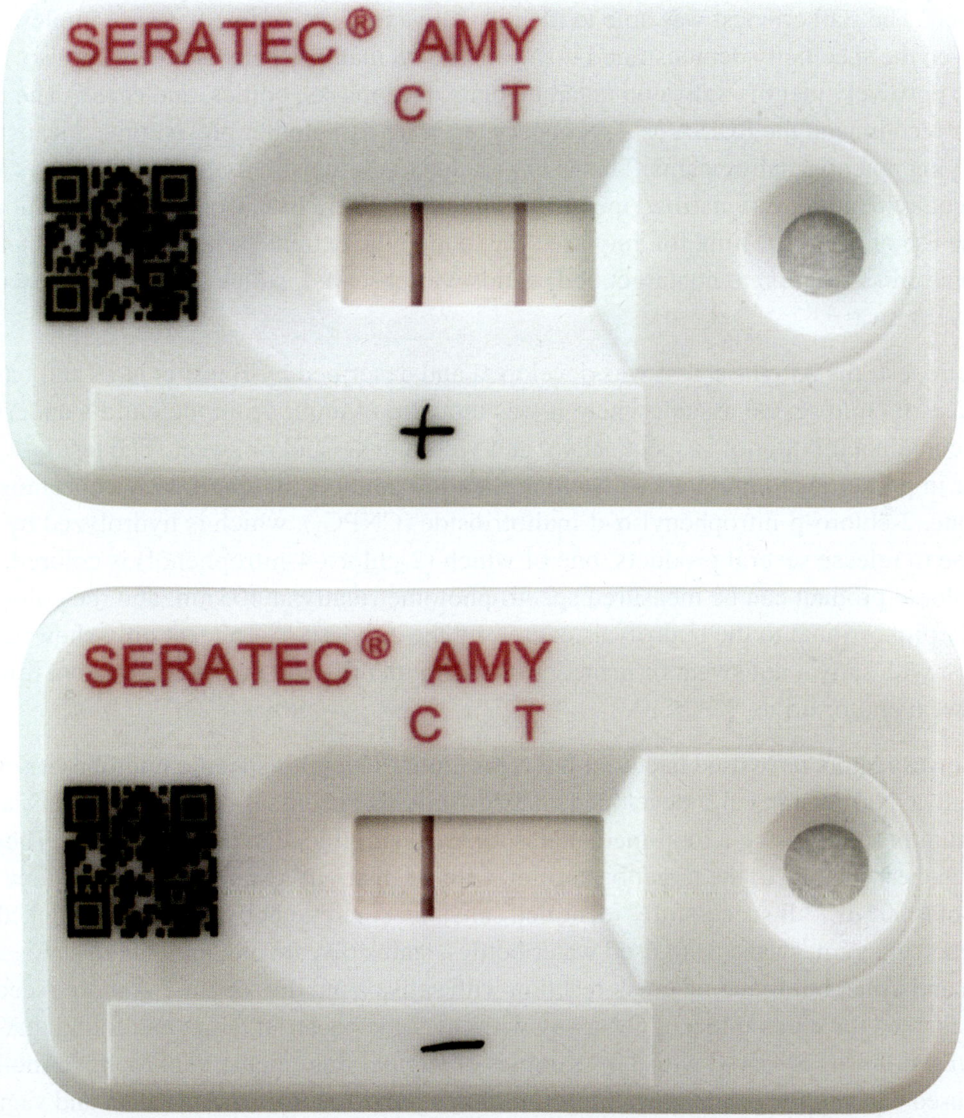

Fig. 5.15 An example of the SERATEC AmylaseTest for saliva, with a negative control *(bottom)* and a positive control *(top)*. Lines at C and T indicate a positive result, whereas a line at C only indicates a negative result. *From SERATEC Gesellschaft für Biotechnologie mbH.*

immunosorbent assay (ELISA) testing for statherin (another salivary protein),[75] and the detection of a bacteria found in saliva (*Streptococcus salivarius*).[98] Although these methods show benefits and drawbacks, none have been adopted for widespread use at this time.

An ELISA test for statherin has been proposed as a saliva identification method.[75] Statherin is a protein secreted from the parotid and submandibular glands. The test was found to be specific to saliva, showing no cross-reaction with blood, semen, vaginal fluid, sweat, or urine.[75] The statherin test was able to identify saliva in all mixed body fluid samples, and given the specificity demonstrated it was the saliva that was detected.[75] It was also used to positively identify saliva on cigarette butts, face masks, bottles, and cans.[75] The authors recommend the ELISA as a secondary test after using other presumptive means for identifying potential saliva stains. This is in part due to the sensitivity of ELISA assays and their requirement for very narrow operating conditions. There has also been investigation into the use of ELISA testing for amylase,[99] but due to the extreme sensitivity of the method, extensive cross-reaction to nontarget body fluids was observed, which could be confused for low-level saliva.

A kinetic test, the Amylase Test was developed and described by Barni et al.[100] and based on a case of child sexual assault where it was thought a sample from the child's underwear could contain a mixture of suspect saliva, and victim urine and/or sweat. The test is similar in properties to previous saliva identification methods in that it uses a chromogenic substrate, 2-chloro-p-nitrophenyl-α-d-maltotrioside ($CNPG_3$), which is hydrolyzed by amylase to release several products, one of which (2-chloro-4-nitrophenol) is colored.[100] The colored product can be measured spectrophotometrically at 405 nm, and the color is directly proportional to the hydrolysis caused by the amylase.[100] The test only showed a reaction with saliva, not sweat or urine, but it could identify the presence of saliva if mixed with sweat and/or urine.[100]

Some investigators have used bacterial DNA profiling to identify specific microbes associated with saliva. Nakanishi et al.[98] developed an assay looking specifically for *S. salivarius*, a bacterium in saliva, using a loop-mediated isothermal amplification assay (LAMP). They found the test specific to the target bacterium, with a sensitivity to an equivalent volume of saliva of 0.005 μL.[98] It successfully identified saliva on cigarette butts, swabs from licked skin, chewing gum, swabs from used water bottles, stains 6 years old, and mixed stains with semen and urine, but found no cross-reaction with saliva from dog or cat.[98] A more recent paper adapted the method to a qPCR assay with the same bacterial target and found that a cross-reaction was observed with 1/17 samples of vaginal fluid/menstrual blood.[101] Another study used 16S profiling in females from Guangdong Han and found that saliva and vaginal fluid could be differentiated based on the microbial profile, and there were significant different bacterial types in saliva.[102] The study indicates that 16S is a possible tool for saliva identification, but population-specific studies would need to be carried out because of the expected variation of bacterial types in different cultures.

Several studies have investigated RNA as a means of saliva identification.[103–105] Zubakov et al.[104,105] were able to identify stable tissue-specific mRNA markers from five genes for saliva (*SPRR3*, *SPRR1A*, *KRT4*, *KRT6A*, *KRT13*) and to recover and profile RNA from saliva stains

2 to 6 years old. They demonstrated that the RNA was sufficiently stable and sensitive to enable the detection of saliva for extended periods up to 6 years. More recently, Watanabe et al.[103] used RNA analysis of *Statherin* (*STATH*) and *Histatin 3* (*HTN3*), two markers that have higher saliva specificity than α-amylase. Although these genes may be more specific to saliva, they did not show the same persistence when tested against RSID Saliva and blue starch gels.[103] Other RNA-based assays have been used, but these will be discussed in Chapter 6 in multifluid tests.

Raman spectroscopy has been used as a means of saliva identification.[97,106] Raman spectroscopy uses the scattering of low-intensity laser light to generate a spectrum that can be specific. It was found that specific chemical properties within saliva could be detected as a means of identification, providing a spectrum different from semen, vaginal fluid, sweat, and blood, although only a single sample per fluid was used in this study.[106] Subsequent investigations found variation in the spectra when different donors' saliva samples were used, but the spectra fit the saliva samples using goodness of fit statistics.[97]

Interpretation

The interpretation of the presumptive tests for saliva are less clear than with other body fluids. There are many other amylases and enzymes that cause the same reaction in the enzyme-based tests, and although the immunological tests are more specific, the actual activity surrounding the saliva transfer can in certain cases be difficult to determine. If saliva is found on a penis or other intimate area, then this can be probative depending on the allegation. It is important to remember that in more open or exposed areas, there are other means of saliva transfer that can occur without being related to a case or criminal activity. Advantageous transfer through talking, coughing, and sneezing has been observed and is an accepted means of noncontact and potentially innocent transfer of saliva.[3,4,107] One study investigating the distribution of amylase on worn clothes found significant advantageous staining on clothing front and back, both tops and trousers (Fig. 5.16).[107] In one retrospective casework study, it was found that only 64% of positive saliva samples matched the person of interest, with the assumption that the remaining 36% were not case related and were therefore advantageous.[108]

The persistence of saliva has been evaluated by detecting salivary DNA.[109–111] The longest length of time that DNA was recovered was 96 hours after deposition of saliva.[109] Eight of nine samples showed full DNA profiles after 96 hours, which was the longest length of time allowed to pass before testing.[109] This indicates the potential to recover salivary DNA for longer lengths of time than what was tested, which could be extended further for partial DNA profiles.

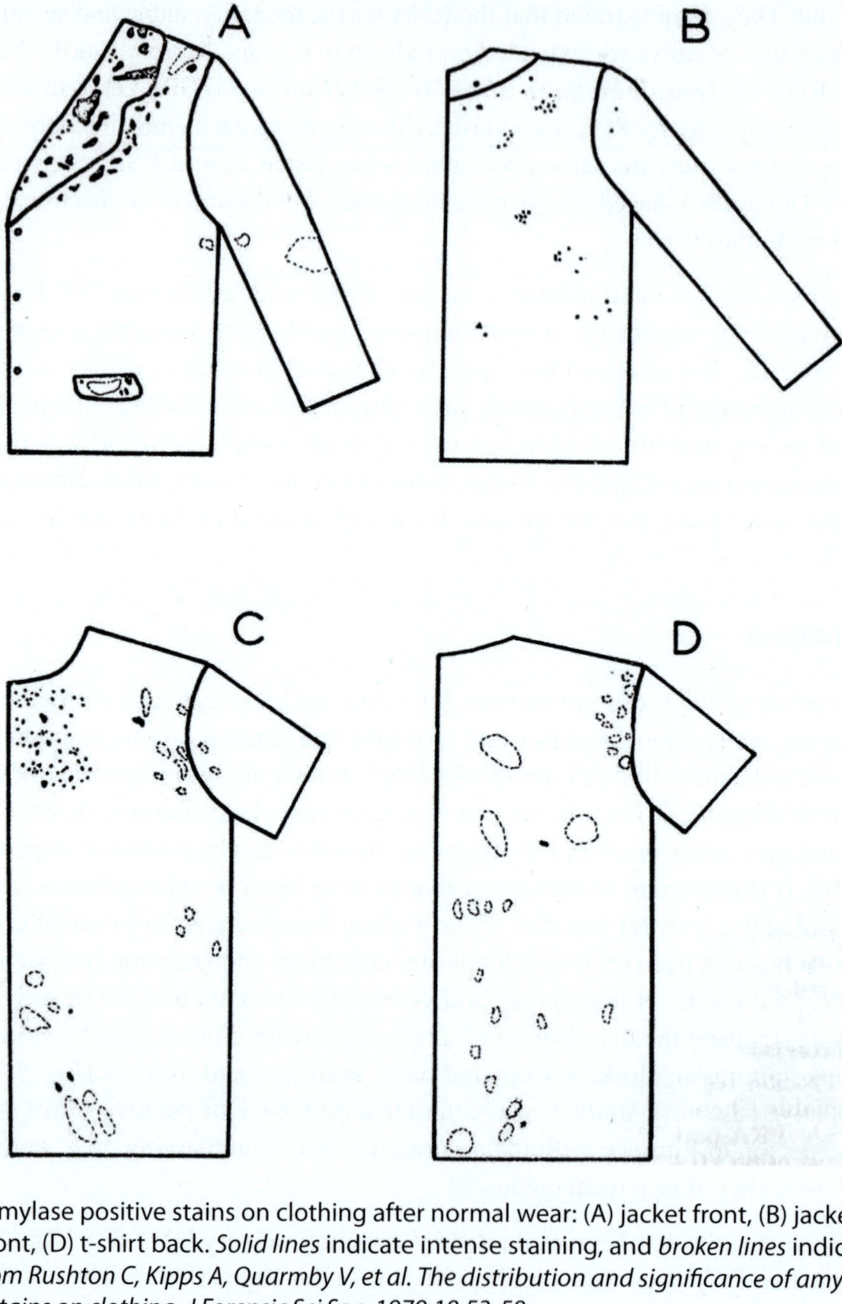

Fig. 5.16 Amylase positive stains on clothing after normal wear: (A) jacket front, (B) jacket back, (C) t-shirt front, (D) t-shirt back. *Solid lines* indicate intense staining, and *broken lines* indicate diffuse staining. *From Rushton C, Kipps A, Quarmby V, et al. The distribution and significance of amylase-containing stains on clothing. J Forensic Sci Soc. 1979;19:53-58.*

References

1. Fourney RM, DesRoches AN, Buckle JL. In: Nic Daeid N, Houck MM, eds. *Interpol's Forensic Science Review*. London: CRC Press; 2007:591–662.
2. Whitehead PH, Kipps AE. A test paper for detecting saliva stains. *J Forensic Sci Soc*. 1975;15:39–42.
3. Zhu S, Kato S, Yang J-H. Study on transport characteristics of saliva droplets produced by coughing in a calm indoor environment. *Build Environ*. 2006;41:1691–1702.
4. Duguid J. The size and the duration of air-carriage of respiratory droplets and droplet-nuclei. *Epidemiol Infect*. 1946;44:471–479.
5. Iorgulescu G. Saliva between normal and pathological. Important factors in determining systemic and oral health. *J Med Life*. 2009;2:303.
6. Leuchs EF. Wirkung des speichels auf stärke. *Ann Phys*. 1831;98 623-623.
7. Schoch TJ. *Proceedings of the American Society of Brewing Chemists*. San Antonio, TX: American Society of Brewing Chemists; 1961:83–92.
8. Orfila MJB. Du sperme, considéré sous le point de vue médico-légal. *J Chim Méd Parm Toxicol*. 1827;3:469–480.
9. Treviranus GR. Drittes kapitel, speise und trank, aufnahme, verahnlichung und aaeignung derselben. *Biol Philosoph Lebenden Nat Naturforscher Aerzte*. 1814:686.
10. Tiedemann F., Gmelin L. Recherches Expérimentales, Physiologiques et Chimiques sur la Digestion. Baillière; 1826: vol. 1.
11. Fischmann EJ, Fischman A. The thiocyanate content of saliva in normal and hypertensive subjects before and after ingestion of the drug. *J Lab Clin Med*. 1948;33:772–776.
12. Ruddell W, Blendis L, Walters C. Nitrite and thiocyanate in the fasting and secreting stomach and in saliva. *Gut*. 1977;18:73–77.
13. Kirk PL. *Crime Investigation; Physical Evidence and the Police Laboratory*. Interscience Publishers; 1953.
14. Nelson DF, Kirk P. The identification of saliva. *J Forensic Med*. 1963;10:14–21.
15. Savostianov G. On the question of nitrites in saliva. *Fiziol Zh*. 1937;23:159–164.
16. Spiegelhalder B, Eisenbrand G, Preussmann R. Influence of dietary nitrate on nitrite content of human saliva: possible relevance to in vivo formation of N-nitroso compounds. *Food Cosmetic Toxicol*. 1976;14:545–548.
17. Griefs P. Vorläufige notiz über die einwirkung von salpetriger säure auf amidinitro- und aminitrophenylsäure. *J Liebigs Ann Chem*. 1858;106:123–125.
18. Leuchs EF. In: Kastner KWG, ed. *Archiv für die Gesammte Naturlehre*. Nürnberg: Johann Leonhard Schrag; 1831:105–107.
19. Mueller B. Über den nachweis eingetrockneten speichels in tüchern. *Dtsch Z Gesamte Gerichtl Med*. 1928;11:211–224.
20. Searcy RL, Hayashi S, Hardy EM, et al. The interaction of human serum protein fractions with the starch-iodine complex. *Clin Chim Acta*. 1965;12:631–638.
21. Roberts W. On the estimation of the amylolytic and proteolytic activity of pancreatic extracts. *Proc R Soc Lond*. 1881;32:145–161.
22. Vila T, Rizk AM, Sultan AS, et al. The power of saliva: antimicrobial and beyond. *PLOS Path*. 2019;15:e1008058.
23. Schenkels LCPM, Veerman ECI, Nieuw Amerongen AV. Biochemical composition of human saliva in relation to other mucosal fluids. *Crit Rev Oral Biol Med*. 1995;6:161–175.
24. Marieb EN, Hoehn K. *Human Anatomy & Physiology*. 9th ed. London: Benjamin Cummings; 2013:1107.
25. Yu-Feng H, Chia-Jui Y, Yi-Wei Y, et al. Bioinformatics and biomedicine workshops, 2008. *IEEE Int Conf*. 2008:9–16.
26. Ramasubbu N, Paloth V, Luo Y, et al. Structure of human salivary α-amylase at 1.6 Å resolution: implications for its role in the oral cavity. *Acta Crystallogr Sect D Biol Crystallogr*. 1996;52:435–446.
27. Spear GT, French AL, Gilbert D, et al. Human α-amylase present in lower-genital-tract mucosal fluid processes glycogen to support vaginal colonization by Lactobacillus. *J Infect Dis*. 2014;210:1019–1028.

28. Skerlavay M, Epstein JA, Sobrero AJ. Cervical mucus amylase levels in normal menstrual cycles. *Fertil Steril*. 1968;19:726–730.
29. Quarino L, Hess J, Shenouda M, et al. Differentiation of alpha-amylase from various sources: an approach using selective inhibitors. *J Forensic Sci Soc*. 1993;33:87–94.
30. Keating S. Oral sex—a review of its prevalence and proof. *J Forensic Sci Soc*. 1988;28:341–355.
31. Vandenberg N, van Oorschot RAH. The use of Polilight in the detection of seminal fluid, saliva, and bloodstains and comparison with conventional chemical-based screening tests. *J Forensic Sci*. 2006;51: 361–370.
32. Ray B. Use of alternate light sources for detection of body fluids. *Southwest Assoc Forensic Sci J*. 1992;14:30–33.
33. Fiedler A, Rehdorf J, Hilbers F, et al. Detection of semen (human and boar) and saliva on fabrics by a very high powered UV-/VIS-light source. *Open Forensic Sci J*. 2008;1:12–15.
34. McAllister P, Graham E, Deacon P, et al. The effect of mark enhancement techniques on the subsequent detection of saliva. *Sci Just*. 2016;56:305–320.
35. Karchewski L, Armstrong G, Nicholson ML, et al. Assessment of the Leeds spectral vision system for detecting biological stains on fabrics. *J Can Soc Forensic Sci*. 2014;47:230–243.
36. Miranda GE, Prado FB, Delwing F, et al. Analysis of the fluorescence of body fluids on different surfaces and times. *Sci Jus*. 2014;54:427–431.
37. Sterzik V, Hinderberger P, Panzer S, et al. Visualizing old biological traces on different materials without using chemicals. *Int J Leg Med*. 2018;132:35–41.
38. Feia A, Novroski N. The evaluation of possible false positives with detergents when performing amylase serological testing on clothing. *J Forensic Sci*. 2013;58:S183–S185.
39. Theda C, Hwang SH, Czajko A, et al. Quantitation of the cellular content of saliva and buccal swab samples. *Sci Rep*. 2018;8:6944.
40. Shukla RK, Biswas P, Yadav RS. *Forensic applications of compound microscope. Forensic Microscopy: Truth Under the Lenses*. Boca Raton, FL: CRC Press; 2022.
41. Voet D, Voet J, Pratt C. *Fundamentals of Biochemistry Upgrade Edition*. Brisbane: John Wiley & Sons; 1999.
42. Bhoola K, Matthews R, Roberts F. A survey of salivary kallikrein and amylase in a population of schoolgirls, throughout the menstrual cycle. *Clin Sci Molec Med*. 1978;55:S561–S566.
43. Merritt AD, Rivas ML, Bixler D, et al. Salivary and pancreatic amylase: electrophoretic characterizations and genetic studies. *Am J Hum Genet*. 1973;25:510–522.
44. Auvdel MJ. Amylase levels in semen and saliva stains. *J Forensic Sci*. 1986;31:426–431.
45. Tsutsumi H, Higashide K, Mizuno Y, et al. Identification of saliva stains by determination of the specific activity of amylase. *Forensic Sci Int*. 1991;50:37–42.
46. Dingle J, Reid W, Solomons G. The enzymic degradation of pectin and other polysaccharides. II—application of the "cu-plate" assay to the estimation of enzymes. *J Sci Food Agric*. 1953;4:149–155.
47. Maidment DCJ, Ringham JM. A study into the measurement of α-amylase activity using Phadebas, iodine and gel-diffusion procedures. *Nutr Food Sci*. 2001;31:141–146.
48. Draz U, Ali S, Firyal S, et al. Detection of human salivary amylase level deposited on fruits with first bite mark. *Adv Life Sci*. 2019;6:176–181.
49. Briggs D. Gel-diffusion method for the assay of α-amylase. *J Inst Brew*. 1962;68:27–32.
50. Lim S-K, Kwak K-D, Choi D-H, et al. Validation of new saliva test using SALIgAE. *Anal Sci Technol*. 2008;21:48–52.
51. Park HY, Son BN, Seo YI, et al. Comparison of four saliva detection methods to identify expectorated blood spatter. *J Forensic Sci*. 2015;60:1571–1576.
52. Schill W-B, Schumacher GFB. Radial diffusion in gel for micro determination of enzymes. *Anal Biochem*. 1972;46:502–533.
53. Brust H, Orzechowski S, Fettke J. Starch and glycogen analyses: methods and techniques. *Biomolecules*. 2020;10:1020.

54. Carciofi M, Blennow A, Jensen SL, et al. Concerted suppression of all starch branching enzyme genes in barley produces amylose-only starch granules. *BMC Plant Biol*. 2012;12:1–16.
55. Hovenkamp-Hermelink J, et al. Rapid estimation of the amylose/amylopectin ratio in small amounts of tuber and leaf tissue of the potato. *Potato Res*. 1988;31:241–246.
56. Lotozynski A. Sensitivity and intertextile variance of amylase paper for saliva detection. *J Forensic Sci Res*. 2020;4:1–3.
57. Rinderknecht H, Wilding P, Haverback B. A new method for the determination of a-amylase. *Cell Mol Life Sci*. 1967;23 805–805.
58. Ceska M, Brown B, Birath K. Ranges of α-amylase activities in human serum and urine and correlations with some other α-amylase methods. *Clin Chim Acta*. 1969;26:445–453.
59. Ceska M, Birath K, Brown B. A new and rapid method for the clinical determination of α-amylase activities in human serum and urine. optimal conditions. *Clin Chim Acta*. 1969;26:437–444.
60. Ceska M, Hultman E, Ingelman BGA. A new method for determination of α-amylase. *Cell Mol Life Sci*. 1969;25:555–556.
61. Willott GM. An improved test for the detection of salivary amylase in stains. *J Forensic Sci Soc*. 1974;14:341–344.
62. Baxter S, Rees B. The identification of saliva in stains in forensic casework. *Med Sci Law*. 1975;15:37–41.
63. Hall F, Ratliff C, Hayakawa T, et al. Substrate differentiation of human pancreatic and salivary alpha-amylases. *Am J Digest Dis*. 1970;15:1031–1038.
64. Rosalki S. A direct staining technique for amylase isoenzyme demonstration. *J Clin Pathol*. 1970;23:373.
65. Warshaw AL. Studies on isoenzymes of human amylase: evidence for a circulating amylase not of pancreatic or salivary origin. *J Surg Res*. 1974;16:360–365.
66. Lehoczki G, Kandra L, Gyémánt G. The use of starch azure for measurement of alpha-amylase activity. *Carbohydr Polym*. 2018;183:263–266.
67. Gutowski SJ, Henthorn PL. The preliminary evaluation of a commercial test kit in the identification of saliva. *J Forensic Sci Soc*. 1983;23:135–137.
68. Olsén E-L, Edenberger E, Mattsson M, et al. Phadebas Forensic Press Test and the presence of amylases in body fluids naturally deposited on textile. *Forensic Sci Int Gen Sup Ser*. 2011;3:e155–e156.
69. Leo D, Tagliaro F, Maschio S, et al. A sensitive and simple assay of saliva on stamps. *Int J Leg Med*. 1985;95:27–33.
70. Keating SM, Higgs DF. The detection of amylase on swabs from sexual assault cases. *J Forensic Sci Soc*. 1994;34:89–93.
71. Casey DG, Price J. The sensitivity and specificity of the RSID Saliva kit for the detection of human salivary amylase in the Forensic Science Laboratory, Dublin, Ireland. *Forensic Sci Int*. 2010;194:67–71.
72. Pang BCM, Cheung BKK. Applicability of two commercially available kits for forensic identification of saliva stains. *J Forensic Sci*. 2008;53:1117–1122.
73. Wornes DJ, Speers SJ, Murakami JA. The evaluation and validation of Phadebas paper as a presumptive screening tool for saliva on forensic exhibits. *Forensic Sci Int*. 2018;288:81–88.
74. Woodford H, Mitchell N, Henry J. Comparative performance of the Phadebas Forensic Press Test at room temperature and 37°C for the detection of saliva stains on fabric exhibits. *Sci Just*. 2021;61:170–174.
75. Akutsu T, Watanabe K, Fujinami Y, et al. Applicability of ELISA detection of statherin for forensic identification of saliva. *Int J Leg Med*. 2010;124:493–498.
76. Herman Y, Feine I, Gafny R. Acid phosphatase test on Phadebas sheets—an optimized method for presumptive saliva and semen detection. *Forensic Sci Int*. 2018;288:218–222.
77. Hedman J, Gustavsson K, Ansell R. Using the new Phadebas Forensic Press Test to find crime scene saliva stains suitable for DNA analysis. *Forensic Sci Int Gen Sup Ser*. 2008;1:430–432.
78. Vennemann M, Scott G, Curran L, et al. Sensitivity and specificity of presumptive tests for blood, saliva and semen. *Forensic Sci Med Pathol*. 2014;10:69–75.
79. Sax SM, Bridgwater AB, Moore JJ. Determination of serum and urine amylase with use of Procion Brilliant Red M-2BS-Amylopectin. *Clin Chem*. 1971;17:311–315.

80. Martin NC, Clayson NJ, Scrimger DG. The sensitivity and specificity of red-starch paper for the detection of saliva. *Sci Just.* 2006;46:97–105.
81. Miller DW, Hodges JC. *Validation of Abacus SALIgAE Test for the Forensic Identification of Saliva.* West Virginia State Police Forensic Laboratory; 2005.
82. Troeger H, Schuck M, Tutsch-Bauer E. Detection of saliva traces using test strips. *Forensic Sci Int.* 1984;25:143–146.
83. Brettell TA, Saferstein R. Forensic science. *Anal Chem.* 1985;57:R175–R187.
84. Old JB, Schweers BA, Boonlayangoor PW, et al. Developmental validation of RSID Saliva: a lateral flow immunochromatographic strip test for the forensic detection of saliva. *J Forensic Sci.* 2009;54:866–873.
85. Castelló A, Francès F, Verdú F. The effectiveness of the RSID confirmatory test kit for human alpha amylase: the effects of environmental factors and substrate materials. *Aus J Forensic Sci.* 2017;49:217–224.
86. Pham-Nguyen V, Mitchell N, Absolom J, et al. Reactivity of the RSID Saliva test to α-amylase present in vaginal secretions. *Aus J Forensic Sci.* 2021:1–9.
87. Sari D, Hitchcock C, Collins S, et al. Amylase testing on intimate samples from pre-pubescent, post-pubescent and post-menopausal females: implications for forensic casework in sexual assault allegations. *Aus J Forensic Sci.* 2019:1–8.
88. Carboni I, Rapi S, Ricci U. Stability of human α-salivary amylase in aged forensic samples. *Legal Med.* 2014;16:214–217.
89. Thompson C, Bennett R, Krosch MN, et al. Evaluation of the RSID Saliva test to detect saliva in expirated bloodstains and development of an "in-scene" protocol. *Aus J Forensic Sci.* 2022;54:438–449.
90. Valls Trepat E, Castelló A. More about RSID-saliva: the effect of sample age and the environment on the test's efficacy. *Aus J Forensic Sci.* 2015;47:450–455.
91. Zapico SC, Lascano V, Sadik T, et al. The killer outfit and timing: impact of the fabric and time in body fluid identification and DNA profiling. *Forensic Sci Int Gen Sup Ser.* 2022;8:248–250.
92. Zapico SC, Roca G. A spit in time: identification of saliva stains and assessment of total DNA recovery up to 180 days after deposition. *Forensic Sci Med Pathol.* 2023:1–8.
93. Foley MM, Brown CO, Westring CG, et al. Effects of organic acids and common household products on the occurrence of false positive test results using immunochromatographic assays. *Forensic Sci Int.* 2020;308 110165.
94. Kishbaugh JM, Cielski S, Fotusky A, et al. Detection of prostate specific antigen and salivary amylase in vaginal swabs using SERATEC immunochromatographic assays. *Forensic Sci Int.* 2019;304 109899.
95. Barbaro A, Cormaci P, Votano S, et al. Evaluation study about the SERATEC rapid tests. *Forensic Sci Int Gen Sup Ser.* 2015;5:e63–e64.
96. Conte J, Ruddy A, Domonoski L, et al. Recovery of DNA from SERATEC immunochromatographic PSA and saliva test strips. *J Forensic Sci.* 2022;67:1176–1183.
97. Virkler K, Lednev IK. Forensic body fluid identification: the Raman spectroscopic signature of saliva. *Analyst.* 2010;135:512–517.
98. Nakanishi H, Ohmori T, Hara M, et al. A simple identification method of saliva by detecting *Streptococcus salivarius* using loop-mediated isothermal amplification. *J Forensic Sci.* 2011;56:S158–S161.
99. Quarino L, Dang Q, Hartmann J, et al. An ELISA method for the identification of salivary amylase. *J Forensic Sci.* 2005;50:873–876.
100. Barni F, Berti A, Rapone C, et al. α-amylase kinetic test in bodily single and mixed stains. *J Forensic Sci.* 2006;51:1389–1396.
101. Lewis C, Seashols-Williams SJ. Design and optimization of a 16S microbial qPCR multiplex for the presumptive identification of feces, saliva, vaginal and menstrual secretions. *J Forensic Sci.* 2022;67:1660–1667.
102. Huang H, Yao T, Wu W, et al. Specific microbes of saliva and vaginal fluid of Guangdong Han females based on 16S rDNA high-throughput sequencing. *Int J Leg Med.* 2019;133:699–710.
103. Watanabe K, Akutsu T, Takamura A, et al. Practical evaluation of an RNA-based saliva identification method. *Sci Just.* 2017;57:404–408.

104. Zubakov D, Hanekamp E, Kokshoorn M, et al. Stable RNA markers for identification of blood and saliva stains revealed from whole genome expression analysis of time-wise degraded samples. *Int J Leg Med.* 2008;122:135–142.
105. Zubakov D, Kokshoorn M, Kloosterman A, et al. New markers for old stains: stable mRNA markers for blood and saliva identification from up to 16-year-old stains. *Int J Leg Med.* 2009;123:71–74.
106. Virkler K, Lednev IK. Raman spectroscopy offers great potential for the nondestructive confirmatory identification of body fluids. *Forensic Sci Int.* 2008;181:e1–e5.
107. Rushton C, Kipps A, Quarmby V, et al. The distribution and significance of amylase-containing stains on clothing. *J Forensic Sci Soc.* 1979;19:53–58.
108. Fonneløp AE, Johannessen H, Heen G, et al. A retrospective study on the transfer, persistence and recovery of sperm and epithelial cells in samples collected in sexual assault casework. *Forensic Sci Int Gen.* 2019;43 102153.
109. Kenna J, Smyth M, McKenna L, et al. The recovery and persistence of salivary DNA on human skin. *J Forensic Sci.* 2011;56:170–175.
110. Sweet D, Lorente JA, Valenzuela A, et al. PCR-based DNA typing of saliva stains recovered from human skin. *J Forensic Sci.* 1997;42:447–451.
111. Sweet D, Lorente M, Valenzuela A, et al. Increasing DNA extraction yield from saliva stains with a modified chelex method. *Forensic Sci Int.* 1996;83:167–177.

CHAPTER 6

Other Body Fluids and Future Directions

Introduction

Blood, semen, and saliva are the most common biologic fluids encountered during investigations, and all have extensive tests available, but other fluids may also be encountered, and their identification can also form an important part of investigations. Many other fluids can be relevant to an investigation, and many have had testing developed, although the scope and number of publications are low relative to the more common body fluids of forensic interest. Most forensic biology laboratories will not test for fluids beyond the most common, although urine is usually included in those tested. Other relevant fluids, such as feces and sweat, are generally not assessed in a serology manner but may still be processed for DNA. Additionally, forensic serologic testing is still of major interest, and new techniques and applications are being applied to forensic body fluid identification.

Historically, the need to identify other body fluids included mucus and pus,[1] mucus,[2,3] gonorrheal discharge, and other venereal discharges.[3] Many other odd body fluids were used as validation fluids for other tests. Here we will deal only with the fluids that are still occasionally investigated. Because of the low number of publications for each, this section will be split by body fluid and describe the testing available for each.

Other body fluids that are encountered and have tests available for identification include feces, fetal blood, menstrual blood, sweat, tears, urine, vaginal epithelial cells, vaginal fluid and secretions, and vomit or gastric juice. In addition, species testing and multifluid testing will be discussed in this section.

Feces

Feces is the undigested residues of ingested food, water, and microbes, usually from the preceding 12 to 24 hours. The main means of identification until recently was microscopy, with Gaensslen[4] stating that an experienced operator should be able to easily identify all the expected features within fecal material. This includes substances from food that were mainly undigested, undissolved, and insoluble; fibrous materials from meats, fish, vegetables, fruits,

Forensic Serology. DOI: http://doi.org/10.1016/B978-0-12-812968-5.00006-4

seeds, and pits; precipitation of decomposed bile; intestinal canal mucus; and the residues of substances whose absorption was not completed.[4,5]

Although fecal material was something that was often encountered historically during investigations, it was usually not a focus of investigations that were part of a crime. In 1854, Ritter[5] reported the need to identify fecal material from cases of sodomy and infanticide (presumably meconium); to identify fecal material, it needed to be distinguished from spots of similar nature, but the excrement stains of people are particularly different from those of animals. At that time, the physiologic examination (via microscopy) was the main means of identification. Ritter[5] noted that cellular structures from ingested food were intact, but many were robbed of their content (i.e., their internal organelles). Earlier, in 1831, Berzelius[6] examined in detail the excrement from various different animals with a full microscopic and chemical analysis, which is how Ritter[5] was able to say that human fecal material was different from animals.

Thereafter, several studies based on microscopic examination of feces were released sporadically.[2,7–11] In 1869, Jaffe[12] published a paper that identified urobilin in both urine and feces, which was further confirmed by several other authors.[13,14] This provided for the first time something that was found in fecal material that could be targeted for identification, but it was still almost a half century until something suitable was developed.

Besides microscopy, there is only one chemical test available for the presumptive identification of fecal material, originally described by Schlesinger,[15] but modified and currently called the Edelman test. The Edelman test, described by Edelman in 1915,[16] relies on the identification of urobilinogen ($C_{33}H_{44}N_4O_6$). Bilirubin ($C_{33}H_{36}N_4O_6$) is created during the natural breakdown of red blood cells (RBCs, the end product of heme metabolism), and this is further broken down to urobilinogen by gut bacteria and released in fecal material.[17] This can be suspended in water, where if mercuric chloride and alcohol are added, it is converted to urobilin ($C_{33}H_{42}N_4O_6$), which is red. If that is further reacted with chlorinated zinc and amyl alcohol, then a "magnificent green fluorescence unlike any other sample" is produced[16] (Fig. 6.1).

The Edelman test was further described by Nickolls in 1956,[18] and it remains in use today. Other attempts were made for different forms of identification. Vanni[19] attempted to use parasitology to link fecal samples to an individual. Kraft[20] attempted to use chlorophyll content based on plant material consumed. Neither of these testing strategies have been adopted.

Despite these other attempts, the Edelman test has remained the method of choice. Lloyd and Weston[17] carried out an extensive validation study on the method using exact wavelengths measured using a fluorescent spectrometer. They found that they could predictably identify the urobilin peak, and even when nonhuman feces was tested, it gave the expected urobilin peak but also other peaks that were not present in human feces, so they claimed better specificity than the visual method and a 1000-fold increase in the detection limits.[17]

Microscopy is still also used in laboratories for fecal identification. A case in 1948 went before the New Hampshire Supreme Court, involving fecal material on a suspect's shoe,

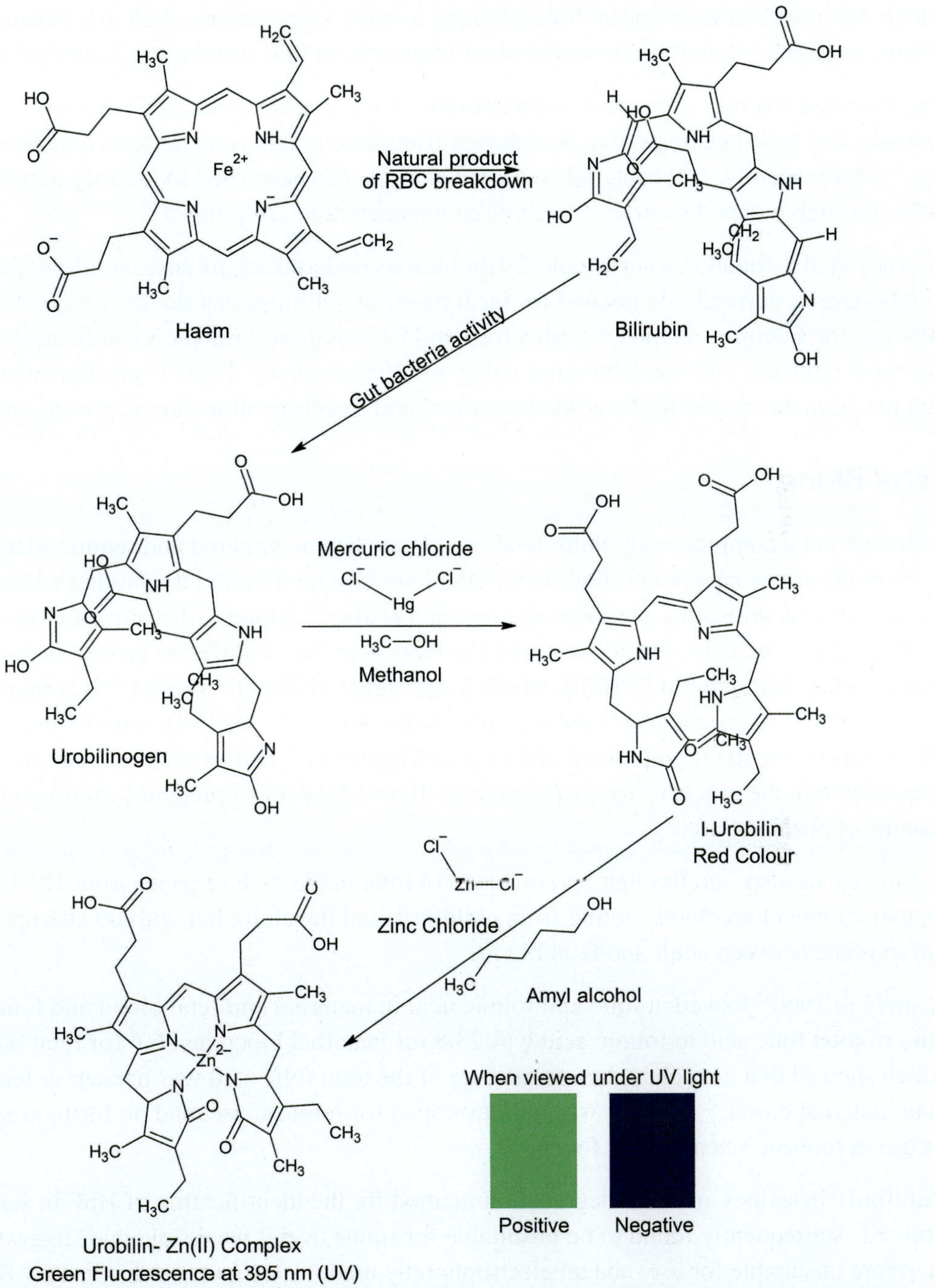

Fig. 6.1 The Edelman test for feces. Heme is broken down through the natural red blood cell *(RBC)* breakdown process to bilirubin, which is further broken down via gut bacteria to urobilinogen. When urobilinogen is reacted with alcoholic mercuric chloride, it forms urobilin, which is red. If it is further reacted with alcoholic zinc chloride, then it forms a urobilin–zinc *(Zn)* complex that shows intense green fluorescence under ultraviolet *(UV)* excitation. *Created using Advanced Chemistry Development Inc. ChemSketch. Toronto, Ontario; 2018.* www.acdlabs.com.

which was matched with smears found around a crime scene and resulted in a conviction.[21] Norris and Bock[22,23] used microscopic plant fragments to link suspects to crimes successfully.

The Edelman test may cross-react with substances (e.g., urine, vomit, feces) from various animals, and false negatives may be reported from individuals younger than 6 months of age.[24] More recently, 16S bacterial sequence analysis has been used to identify fecal material either through targeted strains[25,26] or through metagenomic sampling.[27]

Fourney et al.[24] found in a survey of 42 laboratories undertaking forensic serology that 52% of laboratories currently do not test for fecal material. Of those that do test for fecal material, 80% use the Edelman method,[24] with a further 45% using microscopic identification of digestive remnants and one laboratory using an olfactory test.[24] There is no confirmatory test that has been developed for fecal identification, and therefore all testing is presumptive.

Fetal Blood

Although not a common body fluid, fetal blood may be encountered and require identification in cases of miscarriage or abortion. Fetal DNA can also be found in the mother's blood and used for identification purposes and parental testing.[28] Blood cells form early during fetal development, over several sites, and the fetus generates a different type of hemoglobin than an adult, hemoglobin F (HbF), which has a higher affinity to oxygen.[29] It contains two α-polypeptide chains and two γ-polypeptide chains (Fig. 6.2), whereas adult hemoglobin (HbA) has two α-chains and two β-chains (see Chapter 3).[29] HbF is the dominant form of hemoglobin in the fetus during gestation from 10 to 12 weeks of pregnancy through the first 6 months of postnatal life.[30]

Robin and Tardieu[31] go through several cases of infanticide in their paper from 1857, with regular comment on blood coming from childbirth and the child, but with no attempt to differentiate between adult and fetal blood.

A study in 1960[32] looked at folic and folinic acid in maternal and fetal blood and found the ratio of total folic acid to folinic acid was 23.8 for maternal blood and 6.6 for fetal blood, which showed that a much higher percentage of the total folic acid was present in fetal rather than maternal blood.[32] This test was not developed for forensic use, and no further records of its use in forensic science were found.

Culliford[33] describes an alkali degradation method for the identification of HbF in stains. This was subsequently found to be unsuitable for stains over 2 weeks old and suggested as therefore unsuitable for use, and an electrophoretic method was proposed instead.[34] Both methods, however, require significant amounts of blood and are therefore not suitable for trace analysis.

Weber et al.[35] investigated the use of luminol with adult and fetal blood and found the fetal blood reacted more slowly and less intensely than the adult blood. They altered the method

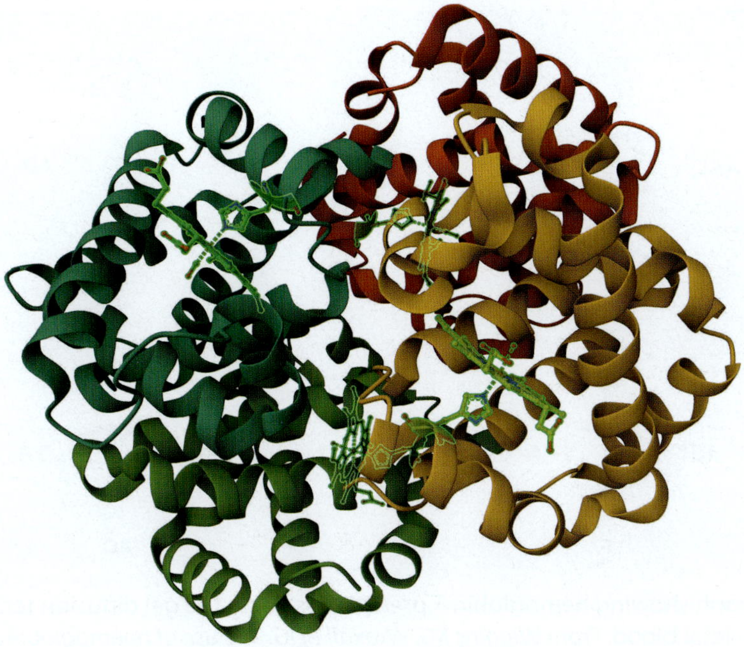

Fig. 6.2 The structure of fetal hemoglobin F. α-Chains are in the two *uppermost chains*, and γ-chains are the two *lower chains*. Heme is highlighted in *bright green*. *From Soman J, Olson JS. Structure of wild-type fetal human hemoglobin HbF. RSCB Protein Data Bank; 2013; Drew HR, Wing RM, Takano T, et al. Structure of a B-DNA dodecamer: conformation and dynamics. Proc Nat Acad Sci. 1981;78(4):2179–2183.*

of luminol to allow for sensitive detection and light assessment using photoelectric recording. They attributed the slower speed of fetal blood reaction as being caused by the influence of alkalis in the fetal blood.[35] How this compares to dilute HbA is not discussed. This method, however, has received little further investigation, with only two registered citations in the last 56 years.

Fiori[36] described the preparation of antihuman HbA and HbF antisera, and there was a commercial HbF immunologic test evaluated a decade later, which showed many of the characteristics needed for a forensic test but was for clinical applications.[37] Baxter and Rees[38] retested the antihuman HbA and HbF antisera and found them to be sensitive to 1:6400 dilutions, and specific for adult blood and cord (fetal) blood, respectively, although the HbF showed indication of the high-dose hook effect. Their testing also showed interference with excess liver and serum but not from mixtures of fetal and adult blood.[38]

Wiggins and Wraxall[39] tested the HbF antiserum with crossover electrophoresis and gel diffusion methods. They found the precipitate test gave positive to only fetal blood up to 1:5000 dilution (Fig. 6.3). They concluded that the crossover electrophoretic method was suitable, but it needed extra care to use, whereas the precipitate method was equally as good, but a larger area of the stain was needed to get results. The anti-HbF antiserum was further

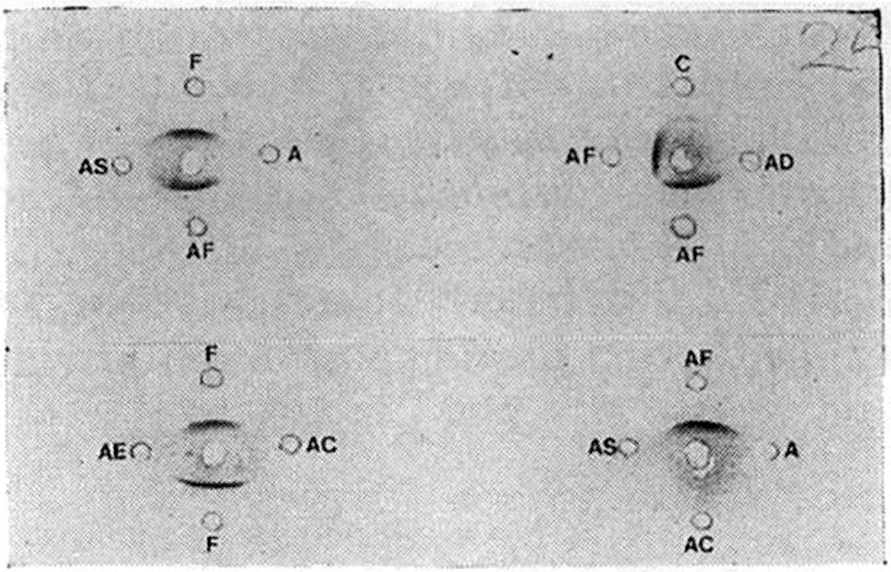

Fig. 6.3 Photograph showing hemoglobin F precipitates using the gel diffusion technique. AF and F both react with fetal blood. *From Wiggins KG, Wraxall BDG. The use of haemoglobin F antiserum for the detection of foetal haemoglobin (HbF). J Forensic Sci Soc. 1979;19(1):49–52.*

tested in a thin-layer immunoassay,[40] which found that blood containing 0.18 to 0.24 μg of HbF could be detected, and stains up to 2 years old as well as blind trials demonstrated the test to be sensitive and specific, and therefore suitable for forensic serology use.

The identification of fetal blood through reverse-phase high-performance liquid chromatography (HPLC) has also been attempted. Inoue et al.[41] found distinct chromatogram peaks for α, β, γA, and γB chains when looking at adult and umbilical cord blood. They found that γ peaks were found infrequently and at a lower level in adult blood, and cord blood was stable for up to 12 weeks.[41] In a follow-up study, they further tested the stability and found the HbF levels were stable up to 20 weeks and confirmed the chromatograms were the same if neonatal blood was used.[42]

A related paper looked at determining if a bloodstain came from a pregnant or recently postpartum woman.[43] A pregnancy protein (SP_1) was identified, and it can be found in the mother's blood. SP_1 is a β-glycoprotein that is synthesized by the placental cells and can be found as early as 7 days postovulation, after which time it increases in concentration in the circulatory blood until a plateau at 34 weeks.[43] It was detected using an enzyme-linked immunosorbent assay (ELISA)–based test, and the protein was shown to be stable for up to a year and up to 37°C, unless high levels of humidity were present when it showed stability to 7 days.

Menstrual Blood

The identification and the differentiation of menstrual blood from venous blood are important steps primarily in cases of sexual assault. Blood in a sexual assault case can be indicative of physical trauma through abrasions and tears, but if the origin of the blood is from menstrual discharge, which is a natural (nontraumatic) discharge, this may alter the probative nature of the findings. Similarly, menstrual blood may offer cross-transfer to an assailant from a victim and could form another link. Davies[44] found approximately one-third of casework penile swabs examined showed positive for presumptive blood tests. A later study by Keating[45] looking at 600 penile swabs (primarily from sexual assault cases) found few (~10%) that had blood of any kind on them.

Although sexual assault cases account for the main need for menstrual blood identification, there are other cases that may require a differentiation between venous and menstrual blood. For example, there was a woman who was jailed for mixing, among other fluids, her menstrual blood with a family's drinking water.[46] A second recent case involves a protestor throwing her menstrual blood onto politicians.[47]

Menstrual blood is a product of the menstrual cycle, which has an average figure of 28 days from the start of one menstrual period to the start of the next.[48] If fertilization does not occur, or if it fails, then the endometrium is shed and expelled as the menstrual period. Menstrual blood is predominantly arterial blood, but it also contains tissue debris, prostaglandins, and large amounts of fibrinolysin from the endometrial tissues.[48] The volume of menstruation is on average 30 mL, but it can range from a slight spotting to 80 mL, with more than that being abnormal.[48] The difficulty with the identification of menstrual blood is that it is peripheral blood at its base, so other components that are part of it must be the target for any test. As early as 1794,[49] it was understood that menstrual blood does not coagulate: "In healthy menstruation, the blood which is discharged does not coagulate; in the irregular or unhealthy it does."

According to Gaensslen,[4] the earliest report of identification of menstrual blood was from an 1848 paper that was primarily concerned with species identification of blood.[50] Ten years later, Robin,[51] in consideration of earlier work on the stages of menstruation analyzed microscopically by Pouchet,[52] used the microscopic features of menstrual blood: primarily that they contain epithelial cells identical to those found in the uterus and vagina (mainly squamous epithelial cells, some without nuclei). Further casework was reported by Ricker[53] in 1870, who had a case where he had to determine if the bloodstain was due to "defloration" (venous) or from menstruation. Using microscopic evaluation, he claimed that menstrual blood spots are "missing morphological elements found in venous blood, but do have fine grain components and fibrous formations allowing them to be differentiated" (Fig. 6.4).

The use of microscopy to identify menstrual blood through identification of mainly squamous epithelial cells was discussed through this time, with additional research finding that

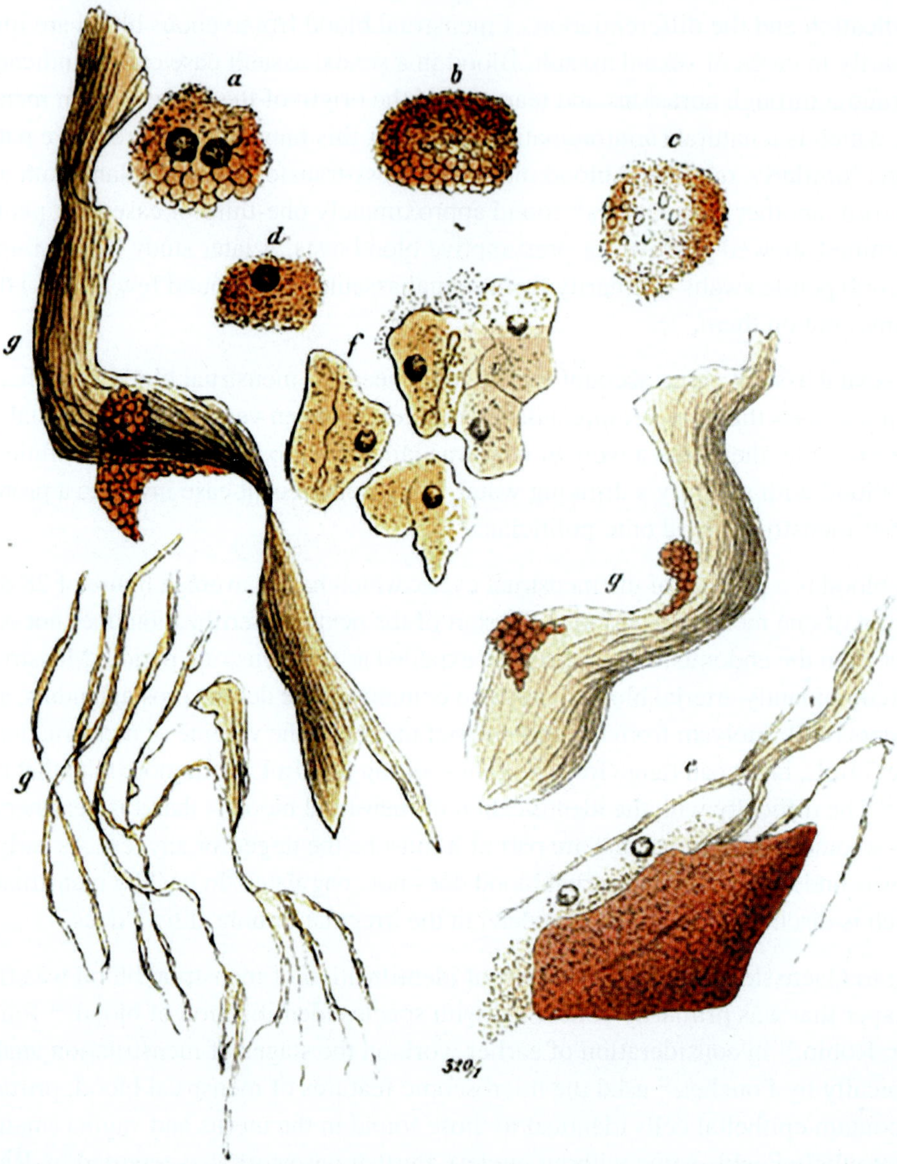

Fig. 6.4 Ricker's depiction of what he observed looking at menstrual blood in 1870. *(a–e)* Small spots caused by menstrual blood, in water. *(f)* Patch epithelial cells, which were found in large quantities in the menstrual blood. The nuclei in these cells always appear very clear. *(g)* Clots of fibrous material, which are isolated in the solution of the bloodstain, swim around, and individual undissolved blood particles still cling to them. 320× magnification. *From Ricker C. Anleitung zür Untersuchung Verdächtiger Flecke: Für Artze und Juristen. St. Petersburg: Jahre; 1870:64.*

characteristic bacteria from the vagina could also be found in menstrual blood.[54] Wood[55] also described menstrual blood in 1894, stating that the composition changes between different women or even in the same individual over time. Wood[55] also stated that apart from identification of menstrual blood, the peculiarities of the individual must be considered, including cleanliness, mode of living, health, the exact period of menstruation, and abundance of menstrual flow. He also stated that with microscopic examination, he would see squamous epithelial cells (noting that these were very similar to those from the mouth) and on occasion ciliated epithelium from the uterine membrane.[55]

Microscopy was the main method of identification until the significant discovery that vaginal epithelial cells contain glycogen,[56] and it was subsequently used to stain the cells for identification using Lugol's iodine[57,58] (see discussion on vaginal epithelial cells, later).

In 1972, Asano et al.[59] tried to use isoenzymes of lactate dehydrogenase present in higher levels due to the bacteria in the vaginal environment. This was followed up by an electrophoretic method in 1974,[60] but a follow-up study in 1983 by Divall and Ismail[61] found there was no difference in profile between menstrual blood and peripheral blood contaminated with vaginal fluid. This indicated the method was not suitable for menstrual blood identification.

Other researchers started to investigate the anticoagulation factors in blood (the fibrinolytic properties) and their potential to identify menstrual blood. Culliford,[62] finding microscopic methods unsuitable, investigated electrophoretic properties of fibrin and menstrual blood. This was followed by other studies by Whitehead and Divall,[63,64] investigating its use further; however, in 1972, Gaffney[65] identified a particular fibrin breakdown product that cross-linked two D domains (covalent links between the two chains) that he designated D-dimer. The D-dimer was then used in medical diagnosis for thrombosis,[66] ovarian carcinoma,[67] and other thrombotic disorders.[68–70] Several commercial methods for D-dimer detection have been developed for medical use, and several have been assessed for use in forensic science as an indicator of menstrual blood.

In 1996, Miyaishi et al.[71] determined that menstrual blood had 200 times more D-dimer than peripheral blood (without thrombosis) and had around 1/4000 the amount of myoglobin (protein located mainly in muscles). They proposed a combination test that looked for high levels of D-dimer and low levels of myoglobin as being indicative of menstrual blood. Further work followed in 2011 by Baker et al.,[72] who looked at several commercial products for D-dimer detection and different factors that may affect the readings, including sensitivity, specificity, mixtures of different body fluids, and other factors that could cause an increase in D-dimer formation in peripheral blood (e.g., exercise). The most sensitive of the kits tested was able to identify D-dimer at 1:64 dilution, and D-dimer could be detected up to 2 weeks after deposit.[72] Their study found that peripheral blood and vaginal secretions mixed together did not produce a false positive, whereas menstrual and peripheral blood mixed together showed a positive result.[72]

Akutsu et al.[73] investigated a latex agglutination test (FDPL Test) for the detection of menstrual blood and found that it was capable of identifying D-dimer at dilutions of at least 1/320, but the test showed false positives with postmortem blood 100% of the time. It was also able to detect menstrual blood after 90 days in dry storage at 37°C (only to 7 days if stored wet). Holtkötter et al.[74] investigated an immunochromatographic D-dimer test (Clearview Simplify D-dimer Kit [Alere, Cheshire, UK]) and found it sensitive to 1:50 if liquid sample was used, but less if dried, but it did not cross-react with semen, saliva, urine, vaginal secretions, or peripheral blood; however, it cross-reacted with most postmortem peripheral blood samples tested.

Holtkötter et al.[75] carried out further work on the Seratec PMB Test, the only commercial forensic targeted D-dimer test (Fig. 6.5). Seratec PMB Test is a dual lateral flow test strip, which is capable of identifying both human peripheral (venous) blood via a hemoglobin marker and human menstrual blood via a D-dimer marker. It contains four monoclonal antihuman antibodies on a lateral flow test strip. It was found that the sensitivity of the test was to 120 nL of menstrual blood (1:1000 equivalent dilution) and that incubation could be as short as 5 minutes with a liquid sample or as high as 90 minutes if an older or diluted sample was used.[75] They found no cross-reaction with peripheral blood, vaginal fluid, semen, saliva, and urine, or with nonhuman blood from dog, cat, horse, sheep, and goat, but they did find a weak false positive with rabbit blood.[75] It was determined that the Seratec PMB Test cross-reacted with 70% of the postmortem peripheral blood samples tested,[75] and peripheral blood

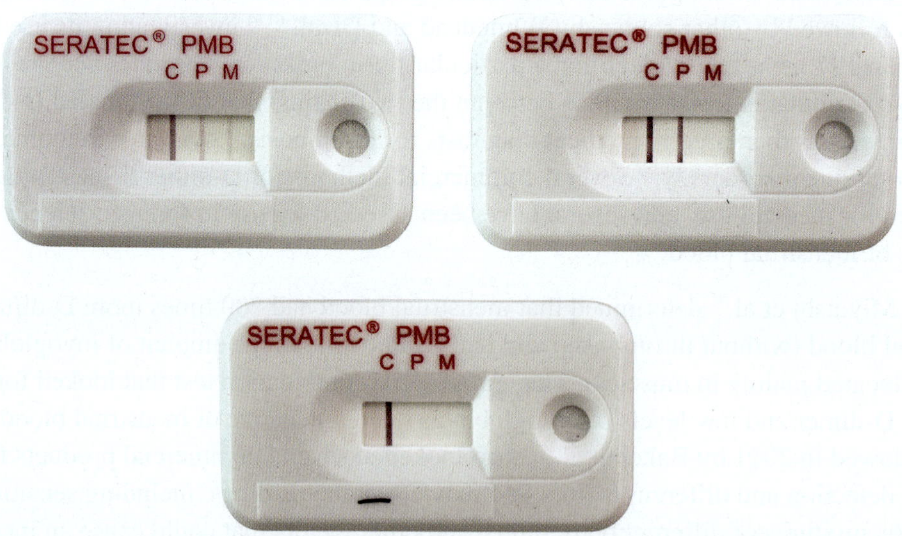

Fig. 6.5 Example of the PMB Test from Seratec for blood and menstrual blood, with a negative control *(bottom)*, positive for blood *(top right)*, and positive for menstrual blood *(top left)*. Lines at C, P, and M indicate a positive result for menstrual blood, whereas a line at C and P only indicates a positive for peripheral blood, and a line at C only is a negative. *From Seratec Gesellschaft für Biotechnologie mbH.*

from injury, nasal blood, postmortem blood, and wound crust (scab) also demonstrated false positive results for D-dimer.[76]

Gray et al.[77] developed an immunoassay for the identification of menstrual blood. They developed antibodies to estrogen receptor-α and matrix metalloproteinase 14 (MMP-14), cells found only in the endometrium, for use in a fluorescent detection test, but found that there were few cells on typical simulated menstrual blood samples; therefore the method may not be suitable for casework use. A second assay assessed used a fibrinogen target in an ELISA test, and it was found to be a suitable menstrual blood test for forensic science.

Attenuated total reflection Fourier transform infrared (ATR-FTIR) has been used as a means of identification of menstrual blood. Quinn and Elkins[78] identified a menstrual blood–specific peak in the spectra at 1039 cm^{-1} that was different from venous blood and which they identified as originating from phosphoric acid. It was not found in spectra from semen, saliva, and breast milk, but it was reduced in mixtures of menstrual and peripheral blood. Sharma et al.[79] found discrimination with spectra alone problematic, and even with principle component analysis (PCA) only found a 93% correct identification for menstrual blood; however, when combined with chemometrics, that accuracy improved to 100% discrimination and identification of menstrual blood. Mistek-Morabito and Lednev[80] used partial least squares discriminant analysis with their spectra, and both internal and external validation of the method showed 100% concordance in differentiation of menstrual and peripheral blood.

Messenger RNA (mRNA) and micro-RNA (miRNA) have also been used for menstrual blood identification,[81–85] although this will be dealt with further in the multifluid testing section. Menstrual blood poses difficulty for RNA-based tests because of the potential for cross-reactivity of markers in both peripheral blood and vaginal secretions. Bauer and Patzelt[81] assessed a variety of female reproductive tissues for mRNA linked to hormone receptors, intermediate filaments, MMP, heat shock proteins, cytokines, and growth factors. They found several that showed cross-reaction with other body fluids, but MMP mRNA is preferentially expressed in endometrium (not in blood or vaginal mucus), and MMP-11 (stromelysin 3) specifically showed the best marker for endometrial cells (and therefore menstrual blood).[81] They carried out further validation using MMP-7 (a marker set could not be developed for MMP-11) and quantitative polymerase chain reaction (QPCR) to generate a test that was able to identify 54/60 menstrual blood samples. If the reaction was not allowed to proceed beyond 40 cycles, then there were no false positive results with other body fluids, including peripheral blood or vaginal fluid.[82] Further work was done on MMP-7 using capillary electrophoresis, which found MMP-7 signal still detectible in postmenstruation vaginal fluid, in one donor at higher levels than during menstruation.[83] This makes the MMP-7 marker unsuitable on its own, but in combination with a blood marker the pair provides discrimination for menstrual blood (note that no mixture of peripheral blood and vaginal fluid was tested). MMP-7 has been found in vaginal fluid outside of menstruation,[86] and oral contraceptives may interfere with its detection.[87]

Hanson et al.[85] used three miRNA markers that they had previously identified as being specific to menstrual blood.[88] Their markers (hs-miR144-3p, hs-miR144-5p, hs-miR185-5p) were found to not cross-react with peripheral blood, although they did show one false negative with a menstrual blood sample. Using two donors, they determined the limit of detection at 50 pg of input, and it could detect menstrual blood in mixed samples with semen and saliva, but it did not cross-react with these fluids.[85] They did further validation work and demonstrated the test would only work on samples during menstruation (days 1–3 and 1–4 in two donors, respectively) and recommended further testing to allow general use of the test.[85]

Sweat

Sweat (perspiration) originates from sweat glands that are found over the entire surface of the body, except the nipples and some parts of the external genitals.[29] There are two different types of sweat glands: eccrine and apocrine.

Eccrine sweat glands are more numerous and are found over the entire body, with high concentrations on the hands, feet, and forehead. The secretion, sweat, is a hypotonic solution that originates in the blood and is 99% water, with other minor components (Table 6.1). The exact composition is in part based on heredity and diet.[29,89] It is a sympathetic part of the nervous system, meaning there is little control over the release of sweat, which is largely for heat regulation, where it will begin on the forehead and spread over the remainder of the body. Emotionally induced sweating (due to fear or nervousness) begins on the palms, soles, and armpits, before spreading to other bodily areas.[29]

Table 6.1 The makeup of sweat from the different sweat glands: eccrine and apocrine

Eccrine Sweat	Apocrine Sweat
• 99% water	• Oily and odorless
• Sodium chloride	• Proteins
• Potassium	• Lipids
• Calcium	• Steroids
• Magnesium	• Sodium
• Lactate	• Potassium
• Ammonia	• Calcium
• Urea	• Magnesium
• Vitamin C	• Lactate
• Antibodies	• Ammonia
• Dermcidin (antimicrobial)	• Urea

From Marieb EN, Hoehn K. *Human Anatomy & Physiology*. 9th ed. London: Benjamin Cummings; 2013:1107; Chen YL, Kuan WH, Liu CL. Comparative study of the composition of sweat from eccrine and apocrine sweat glands during exercise and in heat. *Int J Environ Res Publ Health*. 2020;17(10):3377.

Apocrine sweat glands are largely confined to the armpits and anogenital areas, and they secrete the same basic components, plus fatty substances and proteins (see Table 6.1). It is milky in color and is naturally odorless; when skin surface bacteria decompose the organics in it, however, it takes on an unpleasant odor (i.e., body odor).[29]

Odor upon heating has been used to differentiate between urine and sweat.[90] Giusti and Panari[91] used thin-layer chromatography (TLC) to differentiate urine and sweat. Yasuda et al.[92] used a DNase I polymorphism found in sweat as a means to identify individuals because the DNase I type was also found in semen, serum, and urine, but it was not a sweat identification method in itself.

Sagawa et al.[93] developed a monoclonal antibody to a sweat-specific protein (dermcidin) for identification, one they found to have unique specificity, which they called G-81. They analyzed the protein using ELISA, where they found G-81 to have a sensitivity of 1:200 dilution, and it was stable up to 11 weeks in storage. Sakurada et al.[94] further validated dermcidin found in sweat as a means of identification using quantitative PCR (QPCR) and ELISA using mRNA. They found that dermcidin was only found in sweat and was detectable, using ELISA, to a dilution of 1:10,000. They also found that the ELISA assay was more sensitive than the QPCR, and they were able to detect sweat in more simulated case samples.[94] Although the dermcidin exon was found only in sweat in the samples that they tested, the authors acknowledged that it could be found in other body fluids, but they still recommended it as a suitable marker for sweat identification.

Huynh et al.[95] developed a cascade-based bioassay immobilized onto a portable strip, based on lactate found in sweat. They found that the test was sensitive to the equivalent of 100 nL of sweat and could detect sweat up to 2 weeks old[96] (Fig. 6.6).

Raman spectroscopy has been used to identify sweat.[97,98] When used in comparison with other body fluids, there was a distinction between sweat and other fluids,[97] but when multiple

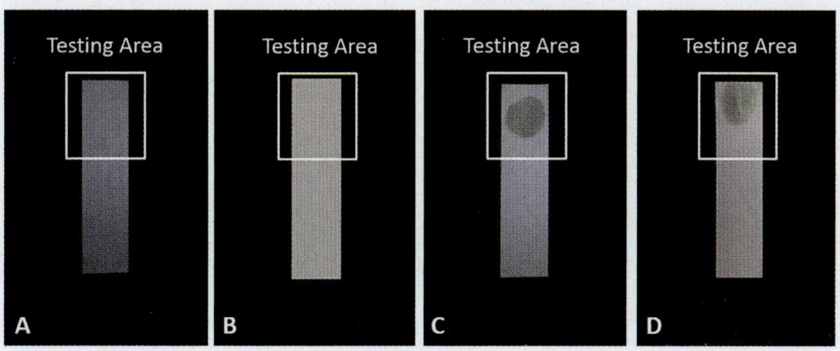

Fig. 6.6 Bioaffinity assay for sweat. (A) Blank strip, (B) saliva control, (C) positive control using resuspended sweat, and (D) positive control using lactate sample for activation. *From Huynh C, Brunelle E, Agudelo J, et al. Bioaffinity-based assay for the sensitive detection and discrimination of sweat aimed at forensic applications. Talanta. 2017;170:210-214.*

individuals' sweat was analyzed, there was variation between the spectra for sweat.[98] It was determined that three components of sweat (lactate, lactic acid, urea) could be used to distinguish sweat, and despite the interindividual variation, the spectra was still distinct from other body fluids (blood, semen, saliva).[98]

In an analysis of 20 sweat stains using an alternate light source (ALS), Sterzik et al.[96] found that wavelengths of 440/460 nm and an orange or yellow filter were optimal. They assessed the luminance of the stains based on photographs and Photoshop (Adobe). They found that only 1 stain was visible (at 490 nm) when tested after recent deposit, 9 stains were undetectable, and 10 stains that were initially undetectable became detectable with increased fluorescence after 2 years in storage[96] (Fig. 6.7).

Metabolite biometrics from sweat samples have been used to individualize samples, rather than identify if they are sweat.[99] Overall, sweat is a relatively understudied body fluid despite it being abundant in fabric evidence and a potential source of DNA.[100]

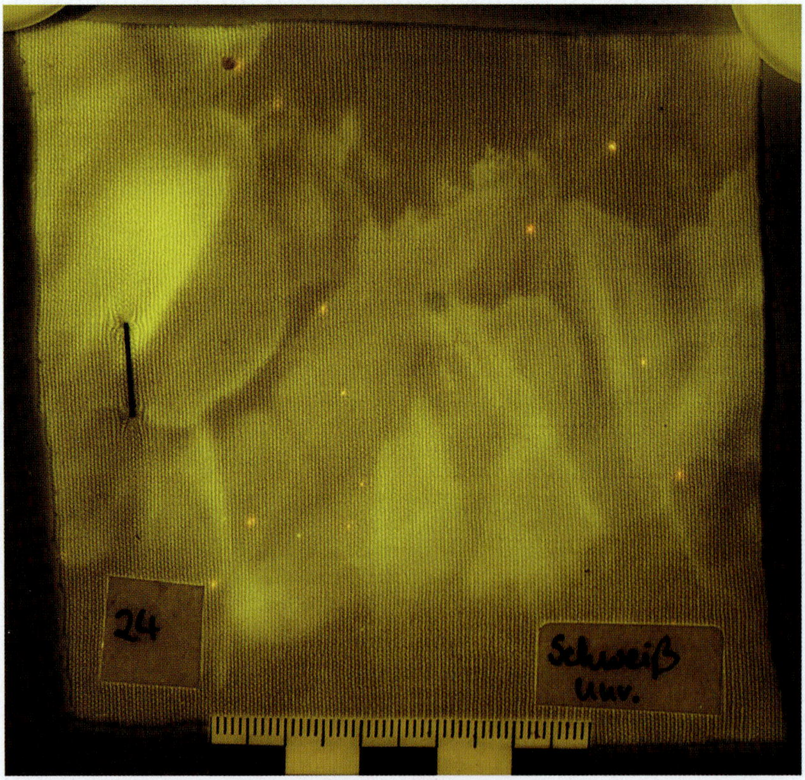

Fig. 6.7 Sweat trace on a t-shirt, 2 years after deposit. Alternate light source of 440/460 nm and an orange or yellow filter was used. *From Sterzik V, Hinderberger P, Panzer S, et al. Visualizing old biological traces on different materials without using chemicals. Int J Legal Med. 2018;132(1):35-41.*

Tears

Tears are a protection mechanism of the eyes that keeps them moistened and clear of debris. Tears come from the lacrimal gland in the upper portion of each eye and travel across the surface of the eye, then empty into the lacrimal duct and into the nose.[48] Tears contain salts (NaCL), potassium (K), bicarbonate (HCO_3^-), and proteins, including albumin and globulin (noting that these are all also found in blood serum).[101]

Very few studies have looked at tears as a fluid needed for identification. A study in 1964 identified several different proteins for which antisera were developed.[102] They found several proteins that occurred in natural tears, and they found that other proteins appeared with mild trauma (such as rubbing the eyes).[102] This was followed up by several studies looking at other proteins,[103,104] but they were also found in some animal tears.[104] This testing has not been reported in use for some time.

A study by Aparna and Iyer[105] highlights the possible evidence that could have tears associated with it, but which is often overlooked, including tissues, pillows, bedding, or any other surface that could absorb the small volume of tears. They also list three types of tears (basal, reflex, psychic), each of which has a different cause.

In a subsequent paper,[106] they investigated the use of ALS for identification of tears and found that tears fluoresce under various wavelengths (Fig. 6.8). They were able to show that even after 3 months postdeposition, tear stains could be clearly visualized on both tissues and fabric.

Aparna et al.[107,108] have also shown that it may be possible to determine the age of tears using ATR-FTIR and that it is possible to retrieve DNA from shed tears.

Urine

Urine is a liquid metabolic byproduct, which is continually filtered from the blood in the kidneys and travels to the bladder through the ureter.[29] Urine is 95% water, with the remaining 5% being primarily urea, but uric acid, creatine, creatinine, Na^+, K^+, PO_4^{3-}, SO_4^{3-}, CA^{2+}, Mg^{2+}, and HCO_3^- are also present.[29] Other abnormal constituents of urine are glucose, proteins, ketone bodies, hemoglobin, bile pigments, erythrocytes, and leukocytes, which all represent different pathologic conditions, but which may also cause cross-reactions with other serologic tests.[29]

Forensic identification of urine has historically focused on organic compounds found within urine, although some inorganic compounds have also been historically investigated. Gee[109] states that some of the methods used for urine stain identification were odor, appearance and deposition, reaction to ultraviolet rays, and the presence of sodium chloride. Repeatedly

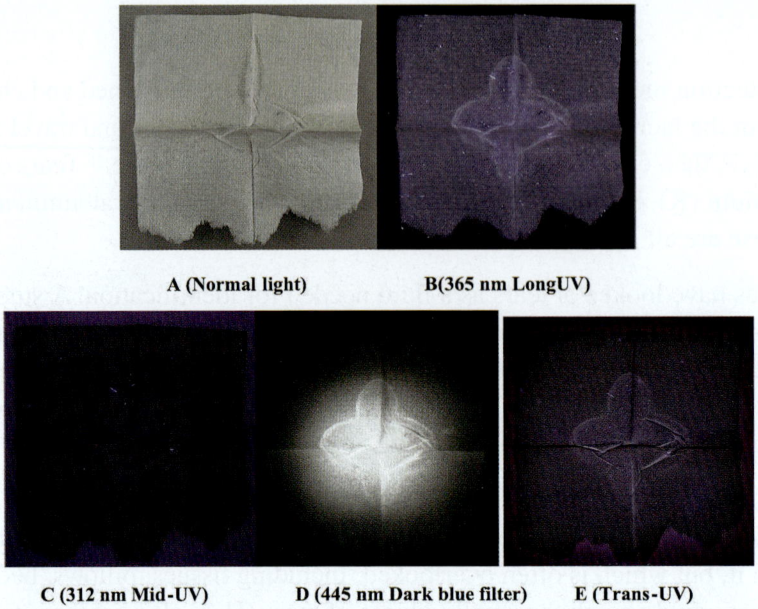

Fig. 6.8 Tears under various alternate light source (ALS) wavelengths. (A) Normal light; (B–E) different ALS wavelengths. *UV*, Ultraviolet. *From Aparna R, Iyer RS. Detection and visualization of human tears using alternate light sources for forensic purposes. Sci Just. 2021;61(6):771-778.*

mentioned in the literature is a heat and sniff test for urine, which states that heating part of a stain will give off a characteristic odor.[90]

ALS has been used for urine identification, with urine having very strong fluorescence, being the brightest of all the fluids tested in one study,[110] but with 40% failing to show any fluorescent signal in another.[96] ALS was used for urine identification as early as 1927.[111] A study by Miranda et al.[112] found that fluorescence was lower when the samples were moist, but remained constant when samples were dry for up to 60 days, and were independent of the substrate on which they were found (fabric, paper, wood, tiling). Because the concentration of urine changes depending on water intake, failed samples may be due to a dilute urine sample and too low a concentration of fluorophores to register with ALS.

Urea is a major component of urine and has been a target for identification for several centuries, although not in a forensic sense but in medical research and diseases. In 1773, Rouelle[113] isolated a "soapy extract of urine" *(matière savonneuse)*, which was an impure form of urea from the alcohol extract of evaporated urine residue. Even earlier, it was reported that in 1709, Scheele found (in another named study) a nitrogenous substance particular to urine.[114] It was not purified and designated as urea until 1799,[115] with further details of its chemical composition determined in 1819.[116] In 1907, Fosse[117] found that a reaction with xanthydrol would produce crystals of xanthyl amide that "crystallizes into silky needles, very lightly tinted pink" (Fig. 6.9).

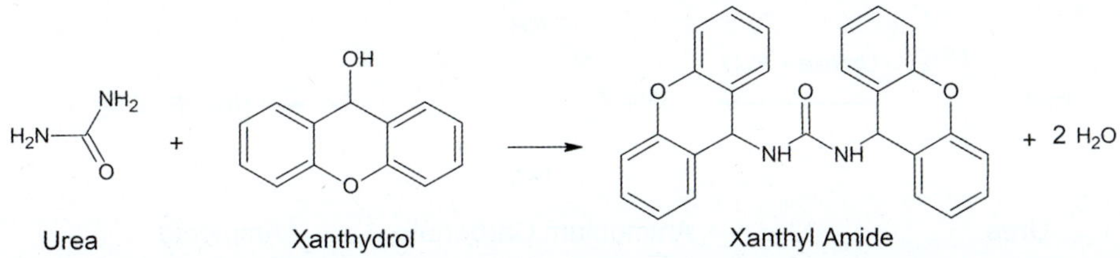

Fig. 6.9 The reaction of urea and xanthydrol (9H-xanthen-9-ol) to create xanthyl amide crystals, which are needlelike and pink. *From Fose MR. Action de l'urée, de la thiourée, de l'uréthane et de quelques amiedes sur le xanthydrol. Comp Rendus Hebdomadaires Séances Acad Sci. 1907;145:813-815; Created using Advanced Chemistry Development Inc. ChemSketch. Toronto, Ontario; 2018.* www.acdlabs.com.

Studies shortly after its description reported that positive results could also be obtained from serum, saliva, and tears,[4,118] but with no reaction found with semen, blood, egg white, milk, or fecal material.[119] Urea has also been shown to present in many different plants.[114] The test has been reported as being effective on as little as a few fibers of urine-stained cloth, but reports of false positives were also common.

In 1940, Gee[109] suggested another method to identify urea in urine stains, by boiling stained tufts of carpet with methylated spirits three times and then evaporating the alcohol. The dry remains are then reextracted three times using acetone, then placed drop by drop onto a microscope slide. This serves to concentrate the residue, which will form into characteristic urea crystals and could be further processed with concentrated nitric acid to form urea nitrate crystals (small, separate diamond-shaped plates or elongated hexagons).[109]

In 1913, Marshall[120] used the well-known (since at least 1876) conversion of urea into ammonium carbonate via an enzyme (urease) that was found in bacteria, fungi, and higher plants. He was able to purify urease from soybeans, and using a method involving acid-base detection (due to the degradation of the ammonium carbonate into ammonia), he was able to identify urea; the method was also quantitative. Marshall's[120] test could take up to 24 hours to complete and had modifications that allowed many of the interfering substances to be removed, but it extended the time taken for analysis.[121] The method was developed into a test paper in the late 1930s,[122,123] and in 1948, Cook[124] further developed the method using bromothymol blue and incorporating it into both test strips and an agar diffusion gel (Fig. 6.10). In the mid-1960s, Cook's test was commercially developed as Azostix (currently from Siemens Healthineers), which was introduced for the medical diagnosis of urea in whole blood.[125,126] It detects a pH change when urea is catalyzed to CO_2 and ammonia.[127] The test is sensitive to alkaline substances that can cause a false negative reaction by keeping the sample acidic and not allowing the bromothymol blue to react to its alkaline form. It was used for the detection of urea in the urine of dogs and rabbits, showing the nonspecificity of the test.[128] The first indication it was being used for forensic urine detection came in 1984, from Poon,[129] who mentioned it in passing, but a survey in 2009 indicated that 45% of laboratories that test for urine use Azostix.[130]

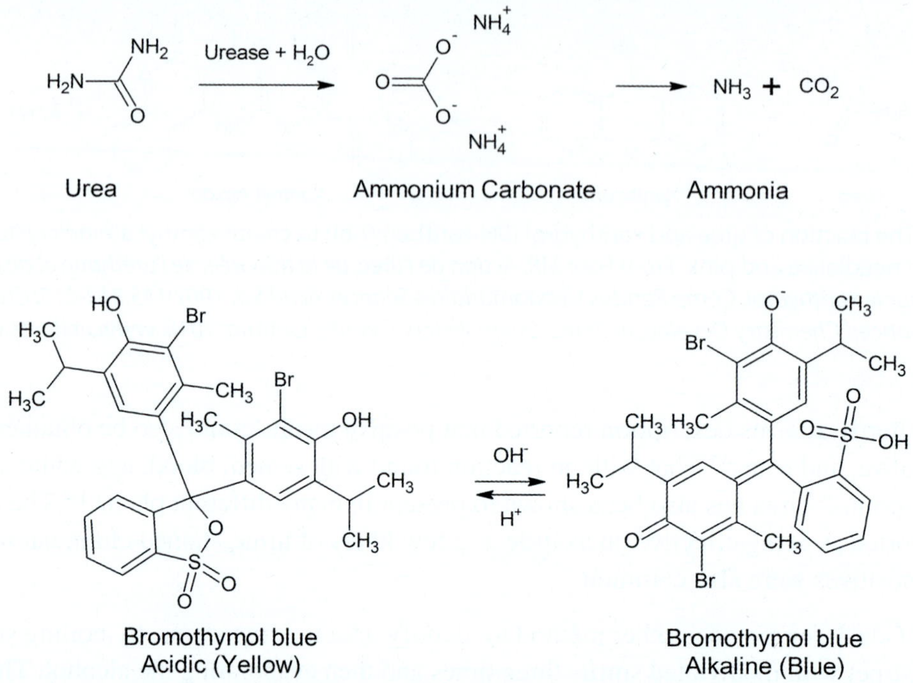

Fig. 6.10 The detection of urea via urease and bromothymol blue. The urease forms ammonium carbonate, which is degraded to ammonia, that will react with the bromothymol blue, converting it to its alkaline form, which is blue. *Created using Advanced Chemistry Development Inc. ChemSketch. Toronto, Ontario; 2018.* www.acdlabs.com.

Kozu et al.,[131] in 1977, describe developing a urease spray test, and the use of the test with radial diffusion gels was also suggested.[132] The reaction of urea with urease to form ammonia can also be detected using Nessler reagent, a solution containing K_2HgI_4 and KOH, which when under alkaline conditions will react with ammonia to produce a red-brown complex, which absorbs strongly at 420 nm.[133] In 1933, Feigl[134] used manganese nitrates and silver nitrates to detect free ammonia product, which were adapted for urine detection using the urease reaction; these turn black in the presence of urine[135,136] and were adapted for spectrophotometric detection.[137] The process was found to be more sensitive than Nessler reagent but is no longer used.

In 1976, Rhodes and Thornton[138] investigated the use of the paradimethylaminocinnamaldehyde (DMAC) test for urine detection, which had been investigated a few years earlier as an alternate fingerprint development technique, and which is used in the detection of urea used in explosives.[139] DMAC is highly sensitive to urea, turning a pink-red color when urea is present (Fig. 6.11), which is why Rhodes and Thornton[138] investigated its use for urine detection, as urea is found in the highest concentration in urine, with the next highest level being in semen (10–30 times less than urine). The DMAC reagent used for fingerprinting was so sensitive

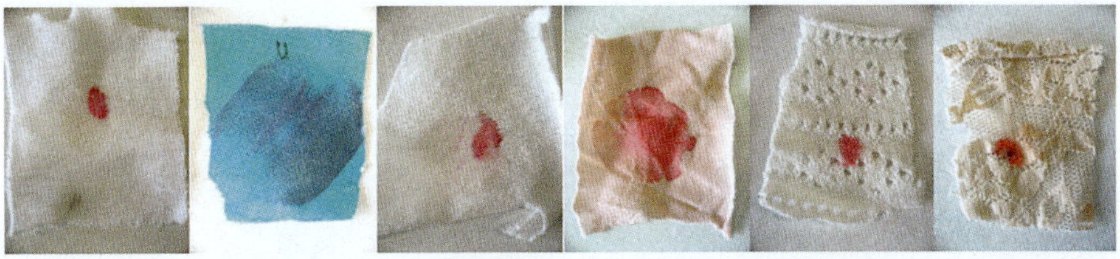

Fig. 6.11 The paradimethylaminocinnamaldehyde (DMAC) test used on urine stains on different fabrics: 0.1% DMAC was used, but similar color and intensity were observed with DMAC concentrations of 0.05% and 0.025%. *From Ong S, Wain A, Groombridge L, et al. Forensic identification of urine using the DMAC test: a method validation study. Sci Just. 2012;52(2):90-95.*

to urea, however, that it reacted with all physiologic fluids, with semen and sweat reacting strongly.[138] They deduced that a lower concentration, however, might reduce the sensitivity of the test enough to react with concentrations of urea only found in urine. They found that a 0.005% solution of DMAC (0.1% is used in fingerprinting) would give a strong reaction with urine but virtually no reaction with semen.[138]

It has been shown to be specific to urea but not react with creatinine, ammonia, or uric acid, although at high DMAC concentrations there is observed cross-reactions with blood, saliva, semen, sweat, and vaginal fluid.[140] Other cross-reactions have been observed with apple juice, banana, broccoli, butter, egg yolk, foot cream, hair removal cream, milk, orange juice, tea, and washing detergent.[140] Later studies indicated that the DMAC concentration used for urine was reverted to 0.1% due to increased sensitivity required for aged or dilute stains, but the same study carried out found that lower concentrations were just as effective.[140] DMAC was found to fail to identify urine on some substrates, with black cotton, black polyester, black nylon, leather, and blue denim all failing to show footwear marks in urine.[141] DMAC can also be enhanced using ALS with excitation in the blue-green wavelengths (473–548 nm) and emission in yellow, which can be enhanced with orange goggles.[141]

The most used test to identify urine is one for the identification of creatinine, with 52% of surveyed laboratories that test for urine using it.[130] It is often called the Jaffe color test after a paper from 1886 in which Jaffe[142] describes the process of identification of creatinine in urine through the addition of picric acid in an alkaline environment to create creatinine picrate (Fig. 6.12), which turns red-orange if positive and yellow if negative (Fig. 6.13). In fact, the discovery came earlier with one book in 1879 by Hofmann,[143] and another by Beaunis[144] in 1881, both describing the process as forming crystals (in a nonalkaline medium), but without referencing earlier work, and with Beaunis stating the crystals formed were due to uric acid.

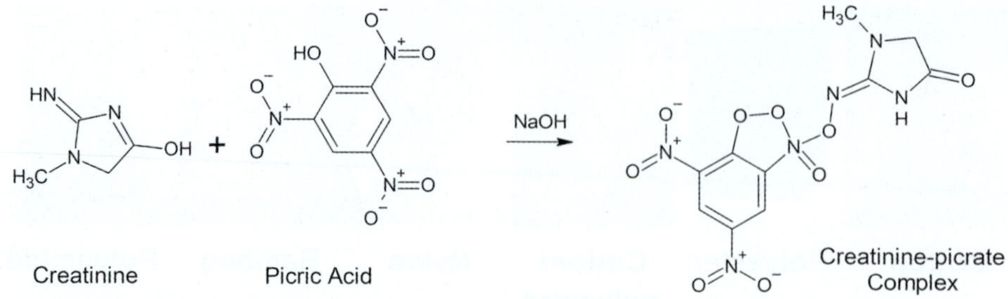

Fig. 6.12 The Jaffe test for creatinine, which is reacted with picric acid in an alkaline medium to form the chromogen creatinine-picrate. *From de Morais CLM, de Lima KMG. Determination and analytical validation of creatinine content in serum using image analysis by multivariate transfer calibration procedures. Analyt Meth. 2015;7(16):6904-6910; Created using Advanced Chemistry Development Inc. ChemSketch. Toronto, Ontario; 2018.* www.acdlabs.com.

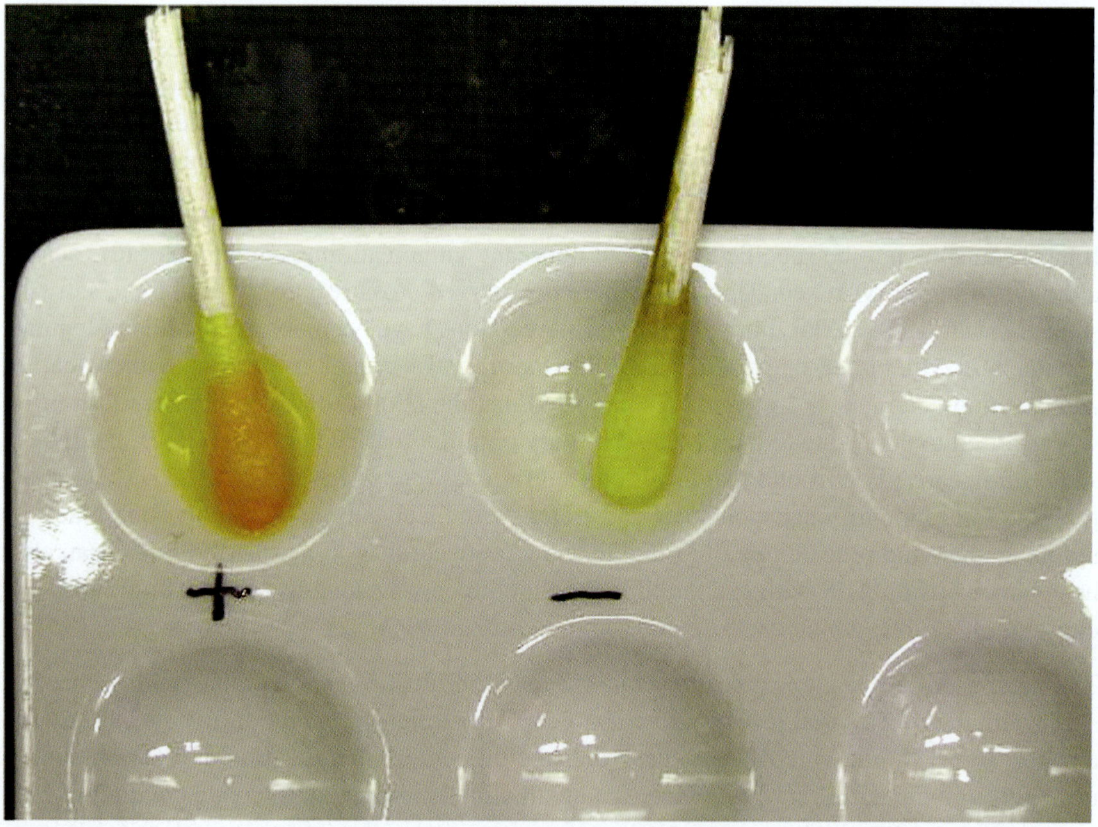

Fig. 6.13 The Jaffe test for creatinine. A positive *(left)* is indicated by a color change to orange-red with the exact color dependent on the concentration of creatinine in the sample. A negative *(right)* is indicated by the solution remaining yellow. *From Amy Brodeur, Boston University School of Medicine.*

Creatinine (α-methyl-guanidinoacetic acid) is synthesized from various amino acids and is a waste product of creatine that forms in the muscles, enters the blood, and is removed through the kidneys into urine.[145] This shows that creatinine is not specific for urine and is found innately in blood, and in fact most of the uses of creatinine detection are based on serum analysis and not urine. The color is proportional to the concentration of creatinine (Fig. 6.14), which is higher in urine, so it can be measured against a standard curve. Because creatinine is produced in the muscles, the amount excreted is relative to the muscle mass of the individual, which will affect the color results. This has been demonstrated in a paper by Barr et al.[146] They carried out a large-scale study in the United States and found that urinary creatinine concentrations differ considerably between demographic groups and can range as high as 17,680 μM in non-Hispanic Black 20- to 29-year-olds, to as low as 7500 μM in women over age 70 years (note, a full range of age groups and other demographics can be found in their paper).[146]

Recognized criticisms of the test include the nonspecific nature of the reactions with ketones and amines causing interference with the test.[147,148] It has been demonstrated that taking creatinine oral supplements will increase the levels detected in urine.[149] Jaffe[142] reported that acetone or glucose reacted with picric acid to give similar colors. Cook[150] summarized different variations on Jaffe's method that had been suggested to overcome interference;

Fig. 6.14 The color range of the Jaffe test relative to the concentration of creatinine. From *left to right*, 0, 20, 40, 60, 80, and 100 μM creatinine detected using the Jaffe test at room temperature (22°C) and 20-minute reaction time. *From D. Rovnyak.*

however, he concluded that none of those methods appeared to be better or more specific than Jaffe's original method.

Other methods for creatinine detection include the historic Neubauer test[151] and the Weyl test,[152] which involves adding a solution of sodium nitroprusside and sodium hydroxide that turns ruby red in the presence of creatinine, and will further change to blue on warming with acetic acid (which has been referred to as the Salkowski test or the Weyl-Salkowski test[153] because the two published reports occurred around the same time on the same reaction). There is also a commercial creatinine test called Uritrace (Abacus Diagnostics) that has similar coloration to the Jaffe test, but no details as to the reaction mechanism are provided (Fig. 6.15).

In 1950, Tamm and Horsfall[154,155] characterized a glycoprotein found in urine that had a high molecular weight, which they first identified as an unknown substance that inhibited the hemagglutination of various viruses. They identified that the protein was also found in cat, rabbit, and guinea pig urine. They determined that the activity of the protein was inversely related to the salt concentration in urine, and that it precipitated in moderate-concentration NaCl solutions.[154] It thereafter became known as the Tamm-Horsfall protein (THP, also sometimes referred to as uromucoid or uromodulin) and spent years of analysis by various scientists to determine its exact properties.[156]

It was not until 1983 that Taylor and Hunt[157] developed a radioimmunoassay for the forensic detection of urine using THP. They developed antihuman THP antigens from rabbit, and labeled it with a radioisotope of iodine for use in a sandwich assay. Their study found that the detection limit was reliable to 1:100 and that cross-reaction at allowable levels was seen in the negative phosphate buffered saline (PBS), and all other substances tested, but well below the 1:100 limit. They found stability over several weeks of THP but found no cross-reaction at high levels with urine from horse, sheep, cat, bobcat, pig-tailed monkey, and crab-eater monkey.[157] THP became a common target for urine identification, and different techniques were investigated for its identification, including crossover electrophoresis and gel diffusion[129] and ELISA.[158,159]

THP is incorporated into the commercial test RSID Urine, which is a cartridge-based assay that was developed by Independent Forensics of Illinois, and it uses polyclonal rabbit antibodies specific for THP in a lateral flow format.[160] The RSID Urine test requires samples to be swabbed and extracted using a provided extraction buffer by submerging the sample and incubating at room temperature for 1 hour. Following the extraction, 100 μL is then deposited to the RSID Urine sample window. The wicking action of the test strip will allow the solution to travel across the strip. The test is assessed 15 minutes after sample is added. A positive test is indicated by two lines at the control (C) and test (T) positions (Fig. 6.16), and a negative is indicated by a single line at the C position. If only the T line or no lines are observed, then this indicates an invalid test, and the process needs to be repeated.

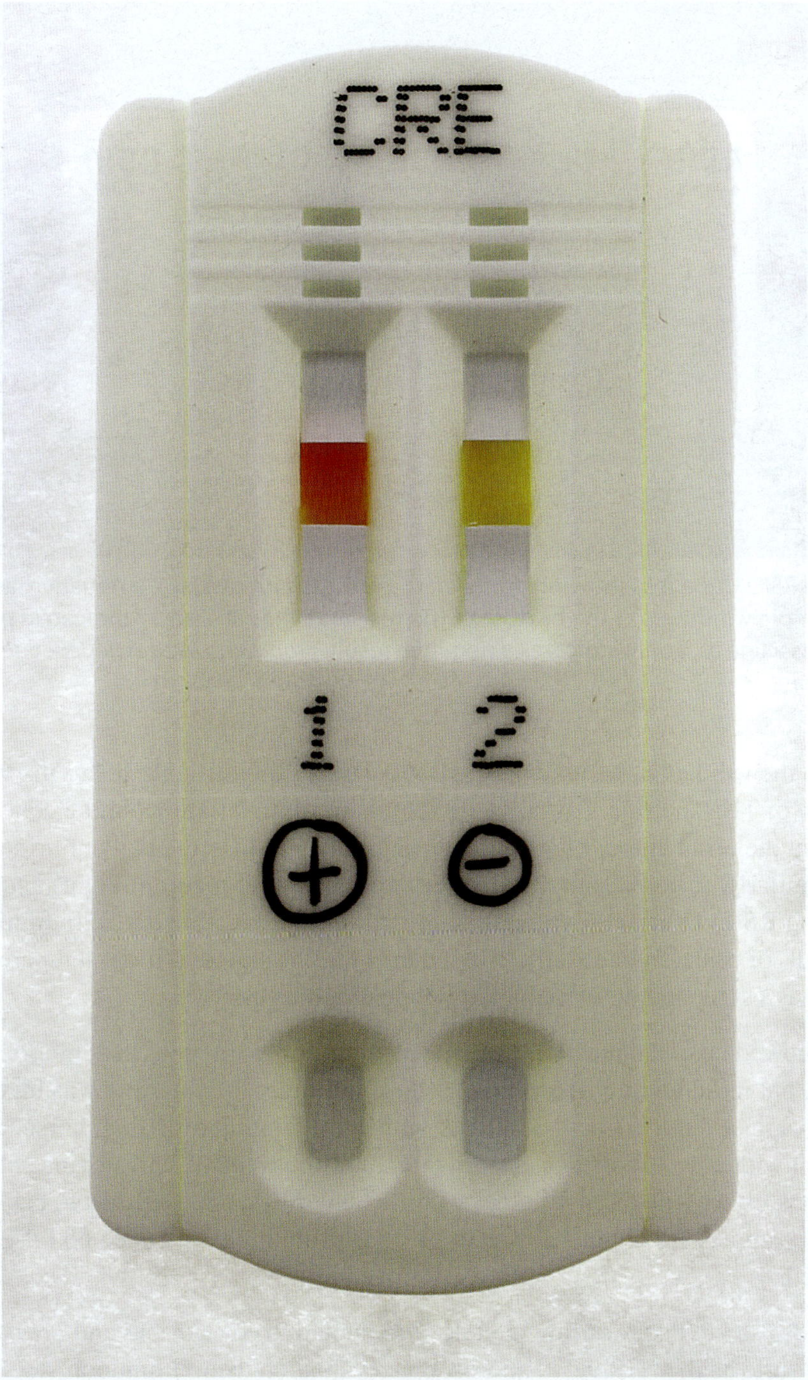

Fig. 6.15 Example of a Uritrace (Abacus Diagnostics) cartridge for the identification of urine showing a positive reaction *(left)* and negative control *(right)*. *From Amy Brodeur, Boston University School of Medicine.*

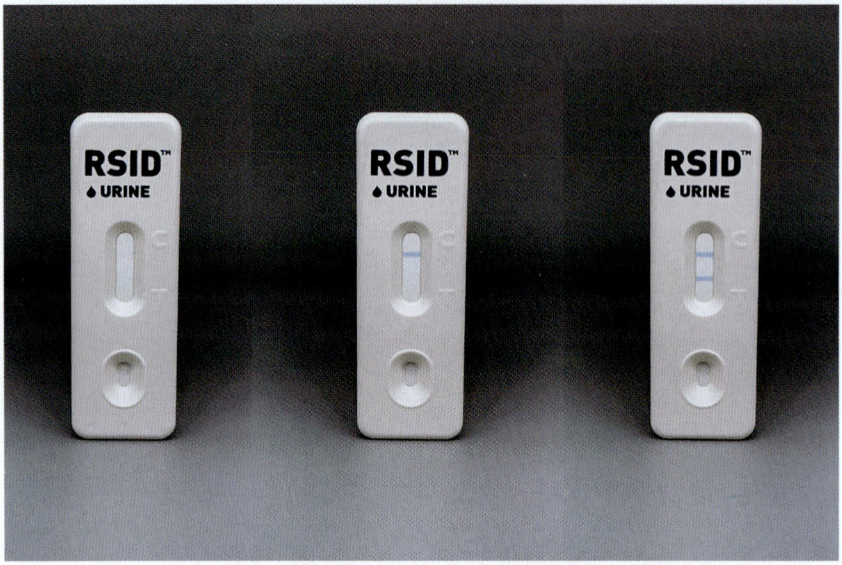

Fig. 6.16 The RSID Urine test showing, from *left to right*, a blank cassette, a negative, and a positive result. The sample window is at the bottom of the test, and lines at C and T indicate a positive result, whereas a line at C only indicates a negative result. *From Dina Mattes, Independent Forensics, Lombard, Illinois.*

According to the validation document, sensitivity studies are difficult due to the variable concentration of THP in urine. It was found that there were variations in the concentration of THP within the urine output of individuals and between different days of urine output.[161] There was similarly no correlation between urine color (dark, medium, light) and the results obtained using RSID Urine. It was found that the limit approximated a 1:20 dilution of urine, or about 0.5 μL of urine, in one study.[162] Aged urine stains stored at room temperature for 5 years were assessed, and 66% could still be identified as urine.[162]

Specificity showed no cross-reaction with saliva, semen, blood, menstrual blood, sweat, or vaginal fluid, but it did identify interference (false negatives) when urine was mixed with blood[160] and vaginal fluid.[162] Cross-reactions with urine from gorilla, dog, horse, and rat were found, but not with cow, cat, alpaca, sheep, rabbit, or opossum.[160] RSID Urine showed mild high-dose hook effect with large volumes of urine, but this is not expected to cause issues because most samples are diluted as part of the extraction process; hence no false negatives were observed.

Other methods used to test for urine include a combination of uric acid and urea nitrogen,[159,163] uric acid,[164] HPLC,[165] microscopic evaluation using immunohistochemical staining targeting uroplakin III,[166] and multicomponent (urea, uric acid, creatinine) detection using liquid chromatography/mass spectrometry.[167]

Vaginal Secretions and Vaginal Epithelial Cells

Identification of components from the vagina, including epithelial cells and secretions, or fluid, is important in cases of sexual assault, especially where there is no semen present. Identification of these cells and fluids can show cross-transfer when no ejaculation takes place or when objects are used for penetration. A recent survey of forensic biology laboratories has shown that only 50% of laboratories carry out testing for vaginal secretions or cells.[24]

The vagina is a thin-walled tube 8 to 10 cm long, which lies between the bladder and rectum, from which infants pass during birth. It is distensible (stretches) and is made of three layers: an outer fibroelastic adventitia, a middle smooth muscle muscularis, and an inner mucosa.[29] Its outer opening (the vulva) consists of the mons pubis, labia majora, labia minora, clitoris, vestibular bulbs, vulva vestibule, Bartholin glands, Skene glands, and urethra[168] (Fig. 6.17).

The inner mucosa of the vagina is a modified stratified squamous epithelium adapted to withstand friction (due to intercourse).[29] The desquamate, or cells that flake off, have large amounts of cytoplasm and shrunken nuclei.[169] The vaginal secretions are composed of components from the vagina originating from sebaceous, sweat, and Bartholin and Skene glands; transudate; exfoliated cells; cervical mucus; and endometrial fluids; and the composition changes during the menstrual cycle.[169,170] There are no glands within the vagina, but it is lubricated by the cervical mucous glands and mucosal transudate that is released from the vaginal walls.[29] The transudate is a protein-poor plasma ultrafiltrate coming from the capillaries, which in the vagina percolates through the epithelium to the vaginal surface.[171] This baseline fluid is not enough to allow for painless intercourse, and the fluids are increased by activation of vasoactive intestinal peptide through sexual stimulation.[171] The vaginal epithelial cells also

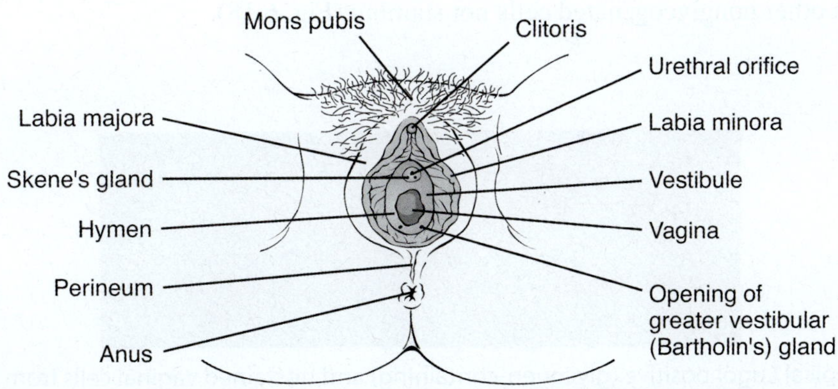

Fig. 6.17 The external female anatomy. *From Curtis LG. The pelvic examination and obtaining a routine Papanicolaou smear. In: Dehn RW, Asprey DP, eds. Essential Clinical Procedures. 2nd ed. Philadelphia: WB Saunders; 2007:229-249.*

release large amounts of glycogen,[172] which is metabolized by resident bacteria to lactic acid, making the vaginal environment acidic and contributing to the composition of secretions.[29]

Bartholin glands, first described in 1677,[173] are homologous to the bulbourethral glands in males and are located slightly below the external vaginal opening on either side.[174] The glands produce a mucoid secretion into the vagina and within the borders of the labia minora, which is believed to provide lubrication during intercourse and maintain the moist surface of the vulva.[174]

Skene glands are paraurethral glands localized on the upper wall of the vagina, to either side of the urethra,[175] and are also known as the female prostate.[176] They were described by Skene in 1880,[177] although they had been known since 1672 and were described by Graaf[178] in his details of gonorrheal infection with an illustrated set of glands and ducts surrounding the female urethra. The glands secrete a fluid that helps lubricate the urethral opening during intercourse.[179] They contain both prostate specific antigen and acid phosphatase,[180] but are not present in all women, with one-third of women in one study lacking them.[181]

The history of the identification of vaginal epithelial cells and secretions is sparse, with Gaensslen[4] only providing a single short section that focused almost entirely on the known composition of vaginal secretions. The earliest reference found is from Cauvet,[182] in 1875, who claimed to be able to identify vaginal mucus through microscopy by "colour or special shape" which "allowed easy determination."

Lugol[183] published work in 1829 in which he introduced an iodine staining method for cellular material, and this would become a major staining technique for the identification of vaginal epithelial cells. Lugol's iodine is an iodine-potassium iodide solution, which can be used as medication, disinfectant, and cellular stain, most commonly in the Gram staining technique. Iodine is glycophilic and is taken up by the squamous epithelium, staining the cells brown, with other nonglycogenated cells not staining (Fig. 6.18).

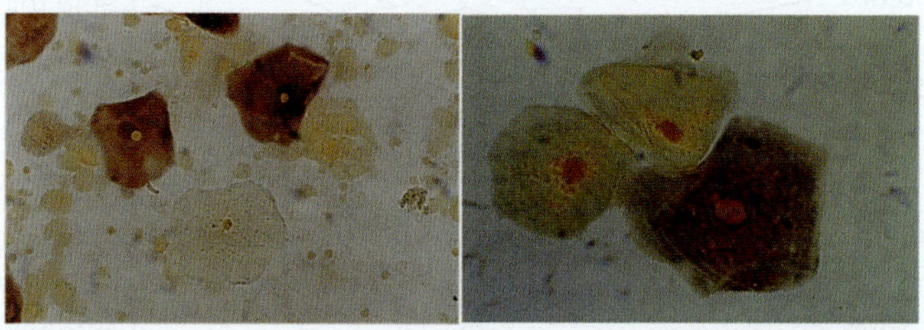

Fig. 6.18 Typical Lugol positive (glycogen-containing) and unstained vaginal cells from a smear from a healthy adult (200×) *(left)*, and glycogen-containing cells from an oral swab from a healthy adult stained with Lugol's iodine (400×) *(right)*. Note the shape and shrunken nuclei in the vaginal cells. *From Hausmann R, Pregler C, Schellmann B. The value of the Lugol's iodine staining technique for the identification of vaginal epithelial cells. Int J Legal Med. 1994;106:298–301 [figs. 1 and 5].*

Glycogen in the vaginal epithelial cells was known from at least 1890,[56,57] and staining samples with Lugol's iodine with microscopy became the most common means of identifying vaginal cells,[57] and is still used in about 14% of laboratories.[24] It is also a recognized medical diagnosis method.[184] It is known that it is not specific for vaginal cells, and other common cells from the lining of the anus, pharynx, esophagus, urethra, and glans penis also continue glycogenated cells. In a study by Jones and Leon,[185] it was found that if more than 1% of the observed cells stain with Lugol's iodine, then the sample is likely from the vagina and not oral cavity.

It was proposed that by detection of glycogenated stratified squamous epithelial cells on the surface of a penis, recent intercourse could be determined.[186] However, later studies identified the same cellular types at the tip of the male urethra without recent intercourse[187] in as many as 50% of samples.[188] It should be noted that even in the papers finding penile glycogenated cells, they appear more like buccal examples than vaginal ones with a larger nucleus (Fig. 6.19). Other staining methods have been proposed, including Dane, Csaba, and Ayoub-Shklar,[189] or immunohistochemical methods.[190] It was found that only the Dane method could differentiate between skin, buccal, and vaginal cells[189] (see Fig. 6.19).

It should be noted that despite microscopic identification methods falling into and out of favor frequently in the literature, it has been largely superseded by DNA analysis, which if necessary could also be used to type individual Lugol, or other staining method, positive cells for individual identification.

ALS has been shown to be used for vaginal fluid screening in 76% of the labs that test for vaginal fluid.[24] One paper described the detection of vaginal fluid using ALS, in which it appears in a similar manner as saliva, as a low-intensity stain identified mainly by the ring along the outer edge.[110] In that study, vaginal fluid could not be distinguished from tea, saliva, or nasal secretions.[110] De Vos et al.[191] looked at the fluorescent properties of vaginal fluid over time but used a spectrometer and very specific wavelengths. They focused on proteins and FOX and found the same pattern of decreased protein and increased FOX signals as time since deposition increased, in the same manner as semen (see Chapter 4), but it is not specific for vaginal fluid. Despite the high use of ALS for vaginal fluid screening, it has not been investigated to a large extent.

Other methods for vaginal secretion identification rely on the bacteria that are present in the vaginal environment, or vaginal-specific mRNA. Bacterial identification has focused on *Lactobacillus* spp.[25,103,192] Fleming and Harbison[192] demonstrated that *L. crispatus* and *L. gasseri* could be found in vaginal swabs from women who were pregnant, pre- and postmenopausal, and who have had a hysterectomy, demonstrating the wide applicability. They did identify those species in some menstrual blood samples, but not in blood, semen, or saliva. In another study looking at six different bacterial strains, it was found that *Atopobium vaginae* was the only species present in only vaginal samples, with all others tested being also found in female urine.[193]

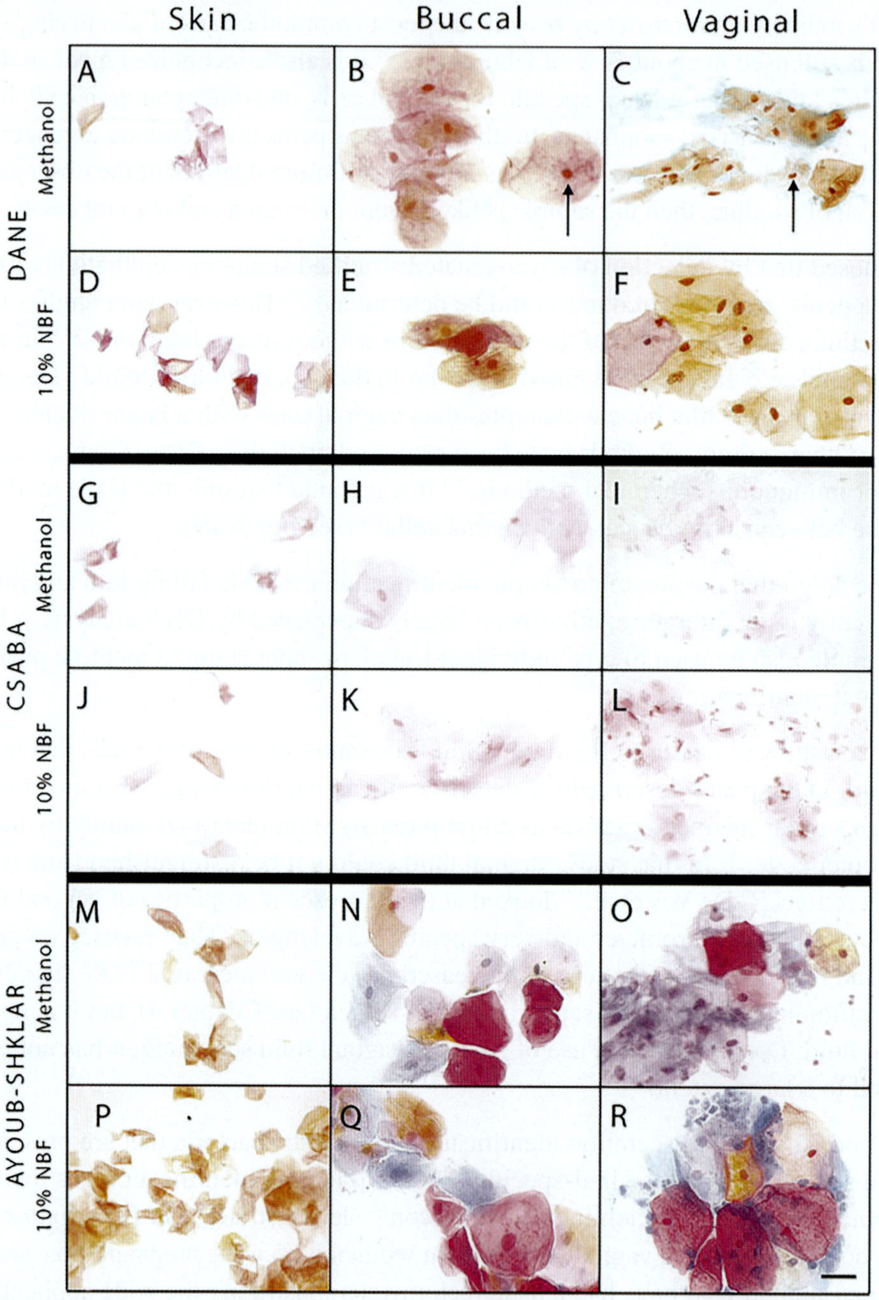

Fig. 6.19 Staining of epithelial cell smears with Dane, Csaba, and Ayoub-Shklar staining methods under different fixations, methanol (A-C, G-I, M-O) or 10% neutral buffered formalin (D-F, J-L, P-R). *Arrows* in (B) and (C) indicate magenta-red nuclei in buccal and orange nuclei in vaginal cells. Scale bar = 20 μm. *From French CEV, Jensen CG, Vintiner SK, et al. A novel histological technique for distinguishing between epithelial cells in forensic casework. Forensic Sci Int. 2008;178(1):1-6.*

A series of QPCR tests for different bacterial species was developed by Giampaoli et al.[194] They designed markers for bacterial species expected in the vagina (using the same species as Fleming and Harbison),[192] oral cavity, and fecal samples. In control samples, they found that each of their target tests was mostly specific to the body fluids they were designed for, but there was fecal bacteria found in over half of the vaginal samples, and vaginal bacteria was found in one fecal sample, but results grew more confusing with casework samples showing signal from most of the targets.[194] More recent research has looked at high throughput sequencing of 16S ribosomal RNA (rRNA) as a means of identifying all bacteria present in a sample. Huang et al.[195] did this for vaginal secretions from Guangdong Han females, but the results are likely to be population specific.

mRNA testing has also been carried out in vaginal samples, with human β-defensin 1 (HBD1) and mucin 4 (MUC4) being identified as targets.[83,196] MUC4 was shown as having a greater sensitivity and was used in subsequent studies.[83] In the initial study, both HBD1 and MUC4 also cross-reacted with menstrual blood, but not with blood, semen, or saliva, and could also be identified in mixtures.[196] Further studies confirmed cross-reaction with menstrual blood and showed stability over 1 week.[83] Further markers were developed by Hanson and Ballantyne[197] that identified six new mRNA markers for vaginal secretions, which were evaluated with blood, semen, saliva, and menstrual blood. Some cross-reaction was observed with menstrual blood and saliva, but not with semen or blood.[197] Other tests to identify vaginal secretions include Raman,[97] 17β-estradiol,[198] and vaginal peptidase.[199]

Vomit or Gastric Juice

Vomiting, or emesis, is the emptying of the stomach via the mouth. The process of vomiting is accompanied by excess saliva and is generally caused by overeating (stretching of the stomach) or irritants from bacterial toxins, excess alcohol, spicy foods, motion sickness, traumatic brain injury, emotionally charged stimuli, and certain drugs.[29,48] It is a protective response to central regulation of gut function.[48] Large amounts of hydrochloric acid, from stomach acid, are lost during vomiting, and the blood becomes alkaline to replace it.[29]

Few if any labs carry out testing for vomitus or gastric fluid. There are few studies that deal with the identification of vomitus, and the general method was microscopical examination searching for various cells, fat globules, and food materials identified microscopically to provide an indication that the sample may consist of stomach contents; however, a positive identification of gastric fluid cannot be made in this way.[200]

The first scientific published assay for the forensic identification of vomit was released in 1985.[200] The study looked at pepsin and renninlike enzyme activities as an indicator of gastric juice. Pepsin acts on denatured proteins to produce low-molecular-weight peptides, and rennin coagulates milk, and both are part of the digestion process in the low pH of the stomach. It was found that gastric fluid contained high activity of both rennin and pepsin activity, and in a sample of 10 individuals, all showed high activity for both enzymes, although one sample had low pepsin activity, but still hundreds of times more than nongastric samples.[200] Activity for both enzymes decreased linearly over 12 weeks of study.

The next study appeared in 1992, where Yamada et al.[201] adapted earlier nonforensic work on proteolytic enzymes[202] to use with a fibrin blue agarose gel diffusion method. Only pepsin showed a reaction, and the test cross-reacted with blood and nonhuman gastric fluid, and not all known gastric samples showed a definitive positive.[201]

An ELISA method was suggested in 2017,[203] which targeted precursors pepsinogen I (PGA), pepsinogen II (PGC), and MUC5AC, all of which can be found in vomit; however, cross-reactions with urine and semen and the nonspecific mucous marker mean that this test has limited use. A liquid chromatography coupled to tandem mass spectrometry (LC-MS/MS) proteomic analysis was used to identify vomit in a case in Italy by Pieri et al.,[204] but this relied on the identification of food-derived proteins, matching what the victim had last eaten, as well as some enzymes coming from the human small intestine as the means of vomit identification. Because the last meal may not be known, and not all vomit has food matter in it, this method is limited to cases where there is food matter present and the last meal is known.

Most recently, a test targeting PGA and PGC was published based on latex agglutination turbidimetric immunoassay for clinical examinations.[205] Despite good sensitivity and the successful identification of samples as old as 12 months, the test still suffers from the same cross-reactions as previously determined. Therefore there is currently no generally accepted method for vomit identification.

Species Identification

Presumptive tests are generally not human specific, although some of the immunologic tests have few if any cross-reactions verified, but it can be important to confirm that a presumptive positive stain is human in origin, especially if a negative DNA test is obtained. Blood presumptive positive results on a kitchen knife, for example, can be obtained due to blood from meat, or even some vegetables, that may have been cut previously and cross-react with the test used.

The earliest reported species test is from 1829, when Barruel[206] used boiling sulfuric acid to determine sex and species of origin of blood based on the odor emitted. Casanti[50] attempted a similar test in 1848 using phosphoric acid, finding that human blood reacted differently than other animals. The test was reported sporadically for about 30 years before multiple reports found it unreliable.[207,208]

Another method to determine species historically was in the size of RBCs. This was first proposed in 1821[209] and is based on the differences in size between the RBCs of different species. There was disagreement in the literature as to the validity and usefulness of this method with studies in support[210] and against[211] being common. Gaensslen[4] points out that many mammals can have RBCs that are the same or similar size, and states that this method of species identification was quite controversial at the time, but it was never resolved because of the discovery of immunologic techniques. Gulliver[212] provides a detailed overview of the different sizes of RBCs (Fig. 6.20).

The immunologic test that developed into the main method of species determination in the 20th century was the precipitin (precipitation) test. It is the next stage in an antigen–antibody reaction, when the agglutination of the antigen–antibody complex reaches a certain level and precipitates out of the solution. This can be measured as a solid mass visible to the naked eye that drops out of the solution or it can be measured as turbidity (making the solution cloudy and opaque).

VERTEBRATA APYRENÆMATA.

Homo.
1. Corpuscle lying flat.
2. The same on edge.
3. Membranous base of the same, after removal by water of the colouring-matter.

Quadrumana.
4. Simia troglodytes.
5. Ateles ater.
6. Lemur anguanensis.

Cheiroptera.
7. Cynonycteris collaris.
8. Vespertilio noctula.
9. Vespertilio pipistrellus.

Feræ.
10. Sorex tetragonurus.
11. Ursus labiatus.
12. Bassaris astuta.
13. Cercoleptes caudivolvulus.
14. Trichechus rosmarus.
15. Canis dingo.
16. Mustela zorilla.
17. Felis tigris.
18. Paradoxurus pallasii.
19. Paradoxurus bondar.

Cetacea.
20. Balæna boops.
21. Delphinus globiceps.
22. Delphinus phocæna.

Pachydermata.
23. Elephas indicus.
24. Rhinoceros indicus.
25. Tapirus indicus.
26. Equus caballus.
27. Dicotyles torquatus.
28. Hyrax capensis.

Ruminantia.
29. Tragulus javanicus.
30. Tragulus meminna.
31. Tragulus stanleyanus.
32. Cervus nemorivagus.
33. Capra caucasica.
34. Capra hircus.
35. Bos urus.
36. Camelopardalis giraffa.
37. Auchenia vicugna.
38. Auchenia paco.
39. Auchenia glama.
40. Camelus dromedarius.
41. Camelus bactrianus.
42. Cervus mexicanus

Rodentia.
43. Hydrochœrus capybara.
44. Castor fiber.
45. Sciurus cinereus.
46. Mus messorius.

Edentata.
47. Myrmecophaga jubata.
48. Bradypus didactylus.
49. Dasypus villosus.

Marsupialia.
50. Phascolomys wombat.
51. Hypsiprymnus setosus.

Monotremata.
52. Echidna hystrix.

VERTEBRATA PYRENÆMATA.

Aves.
53. Struthio camelus.
54. The same, made round and deprived of colour by water.
55. Vanga destructor.
56. Lanius excubitor.
57. Bubo virginianus.
58. Syrnea nyctea.
59. Columba rufina.
60. Columba migratoria.
61. Dolichonyx oryzivorus.
62. Buceros rhinoceros.
63. Psittacus augustus.
64. Phasianus superbus.
65. Pelecanus onocrotalus.
66. Trochilus, sp.

Fig. 6.20 The size of red blood cells (RBCs) according to Gulliver *(right)* showing human and various other species' RBC sizes. It can be seen that human is similar in size to several other species. The legend to the *left* describes the different species. *From Gulliver G. Observations on the sizes and shapes of the red corpuscles of the blood of vertebrates, with drawings of them to a uniform scale, and extended and revised tables of measurements. Proc Zool Soc London. 1875:474-495.*

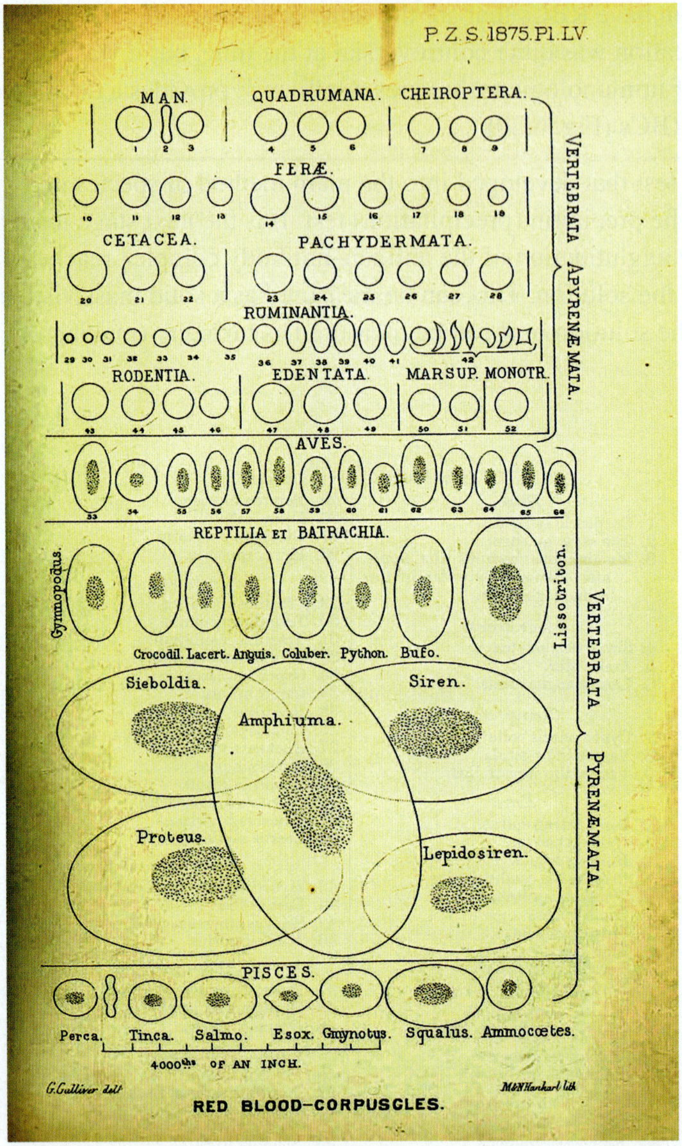

Fig. 6.20, cont'd

The precipitin test was first officially described in 1897 by Kraus,[213] based on earlier work,[214,215] who at that time thought it applied only to bacteria. This was further supported by several studies confirming the findings, but still in bacteria and viruses;[216,217] however, the theory at the time was: "These reactions are specific; no serum other than the homologous serum gives them."[217]

We now know that this is not the case, and the precipitin test is still used in systematics because it is not specific to one organism.[218] Bordet[219] first described cross-reactions between different closely related species (fowl/pigeon) shortly after the initial publication describing the method in 1899. The applications of the precipitin test were quickly explored and refined, with Wood[220] offering an excellent explanation of the process:

> *It has been found that rabbits are the animals which are best suited for this kind of experimentation. If a rabbit is prepared by injecting into the peritoneal cavity, several times, at intervals of a few days, about 10 cc. of any kind of blood or blood serum, there will be formed in the blood of that rabbit a peculiar body, called by Myers and Nuttall[221,222] a specific precipitin, which will produce a precipitate, called by them the precipitum, in the diluted blood or blood serum of an animal of the same kind as the one with which the rabbit was prepared. It will not produce a precipitum in the diluted blood or blood serum of an animal of any other kind unless it be very closely allied generically, nor will it produce a precipitate with the dilute blood or blood serum of a normal rabbit.*[220]

Uhlenhuth[223] was the first researcher to use the method to identify human blood, and even other animal blood, and was able to do so from a bloodstain that was 1 month old. He tested his method on bloodstained articles, such as sticks, sand, cotton, trousers, and even a hatchet.[223] He was further able to increase species specificity of the precipitin test by reacting human serum, for example, with primates to develop the antisera.[224] Whereas previously there may have been cross-reactions observed between a human antisera and other higher primates,[225] this was not observed under Uhlenhuth's new method.

This was the beginning of a huge expansion of the use of the precipitin test in forensic investigations. There were many different studies that developed, tested, validated, and applied the precipitin test to forensic investigations.[220,225–227] The main target for species identification was blood, but the test can be applied to other body fluids, including semen[228,229] and saliva.[230] Wolfe[231] determined that through repeated injections the titer of the antisera could be increased.

The typical method was to react the sample with the antisera and observe any precipitate that formed. It was typically accomplished in a test tube, which was suitable for many biological applications, but it was found that in forensic investigations the method was too sample intensive (i.e., it used too much of the sample for the precipitin test). Culliford[232] described reducing the volume of the tube to 2 mm diameter to reduce the volume of starting sample needed, but conceded that this was time consuming and expensive in terms of carrying out the tests and in the manufacture of the specialist tubes.

Ouchterlony[233,234] further developed the technique into what is generally known today, which also bears his name. He used a thin layer of agar gel and placed the sample and antisera in divots/rosettes in the gel and then allowed them to diffuse. If there is a reaction, this appears as a white precipitate line between the two divots, and multiple samples, or multiple antisera, can be tested simultaneously (Fig. 6.21).

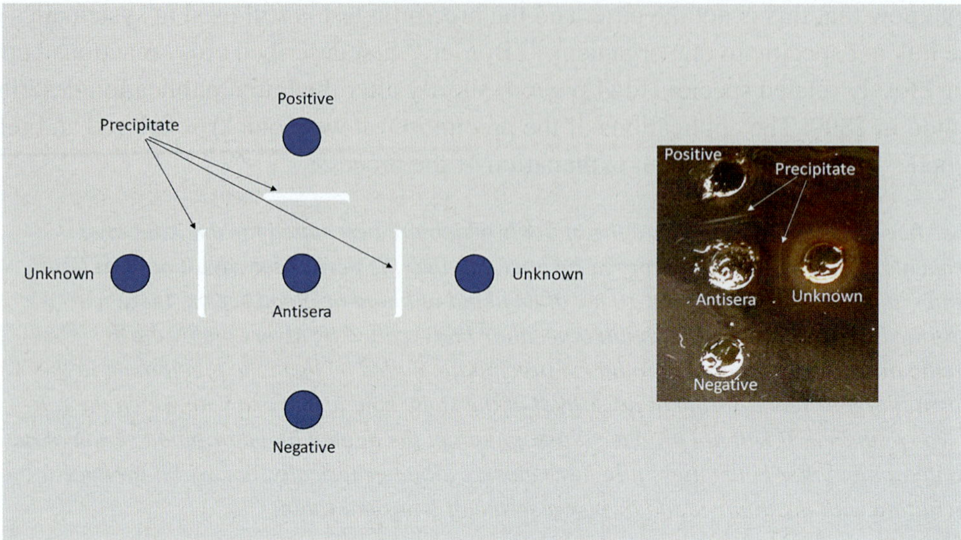

Fig. 6.21 An example of the Ouchterlony assay. Divots are punched into the agar gel. In the example to the *left*, the antisera are placed in the middle divot, with a positive control antigen at the top, a negative control at the bottom, and two unknown samples to either side. A positive reaction is indicated by a white precipitate line forming between the sample and the antisera, seen here for the positive, and both unknowns, but not for the negative. In the second example to the *right*, the antisera are placed in the middle divot, with a positive control antigen at the top, a negative control at the bottom, and an unknown blood sample to the right. Two white precipitate lines can be seen indicating that the positive and unknown both reacted with the antisera. *From Amy Brodeur, Boston University School of Medicine (right image).*

The Ouchterlony test has been shown to be robust; prior exposure to argon laser does not affect the test,[235] and it has been used on a 166-year-old stain.[236] It has also been shown to have sensitivity to bloodstains diluted to 1:1000.[237] There are issues, however, which means it is generally used only to identify if a sample is human or nonhuman and will rarely identify an exact species.

There are several problems with this method of testing. One problem is that an antibody/antisera must first be produced and isolated depending on the species that needs to be identified, which is not generally an issue if only trying to determine if a sample is human.[238–240] Enough material must be present to extract proteins for identification, which may be too much even when using the reduced volume needed for the Ouchterlony test. Some antiserum work only in a narrow range of concentrations, and under unstable conditions can give rise to multiple precipitates.[240] Other commercial antisera often suffer from low titer and cross-reactivity, and each batch must be independently validated. Gradwohl[229] therefore suggests that the antisera be made in the laboratory that will do the testing if done regularly, and should only be purchased from reputable biologic companies because of short shelf life of the sera.

One commercial human-specific test for blood was developed, called HemeSelect. HemeSelect was designed to be specific for human hemoglobin based on the principle of reverse passive hemagglutination.[241] It was overwhelmingly used in fecal blood testing. Although it was developed for use with blood, Spear and Binkley[242] demonstrated that it worked occasionally with saliva, semen, and vaginal fluid. They also showed that it was not human specific and that blood from all primate species tested showed cross-reaction. ATR-FTIR spectroscopy and advanced chemometric methods have also been used for bloodstain species identification.[243] It was able to correctly classify samples as blood and indicate if it was human in origin in the validation study looking at over 52 different samples.

Currently for definitive species identification, DNA is the easiest way and can give high confidence in the species determination. These tests are usually based on mitochondrial DNA and are able to confidently determine the species of origin of a sample. Because the main question is if the sample is human, this can be answered easily and quickly using methods, such as QPCR, while simultaneously providing details of DNA quality and quantity.[244] If the identification of the exact species is required, there are two available options depending on the state of the sample (single source or mixture), the speed of results, and if there is a presupposition of a particular species being the contributor of the fluid (e.g., from a cat or a dog). If it is a single source sample and is not time sensitive, then a universal test and sequencing can identify the source of the fluid.[245] If a mixture is suspected or expected, or there is an idea of the species that may be present, then target testing can be used.[246]

Although species testing still plays a role in investigations, it is no longer as significant a test as it was. This is largely because the specificity of the immunologic assays for the different body fluids is so high that they can act as species tests as well. As an example, it is unlikely that primate, ferret, or skunk blood would be encountered at a general crime scene, all of which are known cross-reactants of Hexagon OBTI,[247] so a positive reaction with that test is most likely to be human, with other immunologic tests having similar specificity.

Multifluid Assays

As technology has advanced and the detection methods for different substances have improved, science has been able to develop equipment and testing that can simultaneously identify multiple different targets. Although these methods offer enormous advantages in terms of sensitivity and specificity, they are not used extensively or universally. This is in part because the testing is not quick, simple, or cheap, which at present are all requirements for the mass testing of samples at crime scenes and in the laboratory. Despite this, these newer methods offer advantages and are used in specific case scenarios, but not on all biologic stains.

There is one test that has been developed based on established forensic serology testing for various body fluids in a single microfluidic device. Cromartie et al.[248] developed a microfluidic device that is able to identify four relevant forensic body fluids from a single sample at the same time (blood, semen, saliva, urine). It uses already established serologic testing methods for each of these fluids: urine—urea detection using Nessler reagent; blood—Kastle-Meyer test; saliva—α-amylase; semen—acid phosphatase.[248] The benefit to using established testing is that the abilities to detect and the limitations of the tests are known, and standard operating procedures are already in place. The sensitivity of the test is in line with the individual tests used, and the benefit is being able to test for all four fluids from a single sample extract. Currently the shelf life for the tests is 2 weeks.

Other methods for multifluid testing tend to look at the overall components of a sample rather than targeting a single analyte. Some of these methods have been in the scientific literature for over a decade, but none have yet to become standard or common in the forensic community. All these techniques are well developed, and most have entire textbooks written regarding their use and scientific foundations.[249] The tests are based on more advanced scientific methods and therefore require different and generally more expensive infrastructure. In this section, we will therefore only deal with their direct application to body fluid identification.

Raman Spectroscopy

There are many different spectroscopic techniques that have been used to identify different body fluids, and they have been detailed in their relevant sections. Raman spectroscopy, however, has been put forward as a means to identify multiple fluids. Research generally states that the Raman spectra of different fluids are a confirmatory rather than presumptive indication of a particular fluid.

Raman spectroscopy is a technique described in 1928 by Raman and Krishnan,[250] where scattered light is used to measure energy modes in a sample. It can provide details on the chemical structure of a substance and offer a Raman fingerprint that is characteristic of a substance. The basis of the technique is excitation of molecules by photons of light, which interact with the molecule by exciting the electron cloud, and the photon is reemitted almost immediately as scattered light. This scattered light is generally at the same wavelength as the excitation photon, known as Rayleigh scattering, but in rare instances it can gain energy (Raman or Stokes-Raman) or lose energy (anti–Stokes-Raman) (Fig. 6.22). These different scattering events are detected by specialist sensitive microscopes.

Raman detection has been used for multiple fluid types,[98,251,252] identification of human fluids versus. nonhuman,[253] and as a potential means of determining the age of bloodstains[254–256] (each discussed in its relevant sections). Each forensic body fluid has its own Raman fingerprint (Fig. 6.23), and because it was first proposed as a means of identifying body fluids, many papers have been published on validating the method by testing multiple different samples of the same body fluid to establish baseline natural variation in the spectra. At this point, there is no indication that Raman spectra for different body fluids are individual in nature, but there is a variation found likely based on the concentration of different components in those fluids.

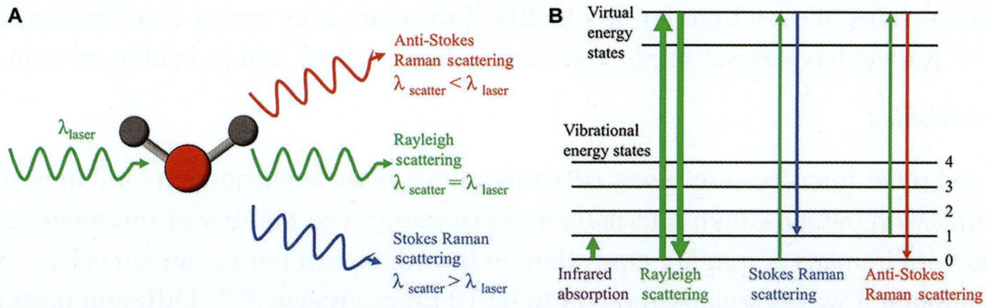

Fig. 6.22 The principle of Raman scattering showing the three types of scattering that can happen when light interacts with a molecule (A), and the energy level diagrams of different scattering and absorption (B). *From Liu K, Zhao Q, Li B, et al. Raman spectroscopy: a novel technology for gastric cancer diagnosis. Front Bioeng Biotech. 2022;10:856591.*

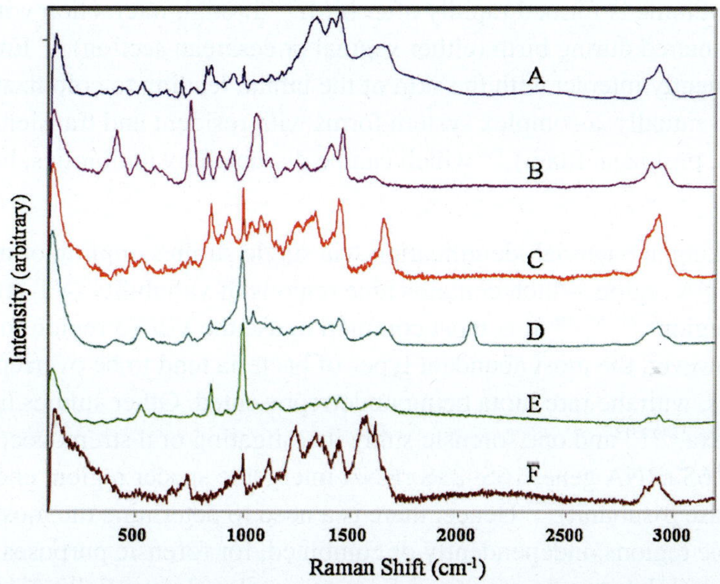

Fig. 6.23 Example of the different Raman fingerprints from different serologic fluids: (A) human semen, (B) canine semen, (C) vaginal fluid, (D) saliva, (E) sweat, and (F) blood. *From Virkler K, Lednev IK. Analysis of body fluids for forensic purposes: from laboratory testing to non-destructive rapid confirmatory identification at a crime scene. Forensic Sci Int. 2009;188(1-3):1-17.*

Currently, the method has been shown to be effective on single fluid (and source) samples, meaning that the validation to date has focused on intrafluid variation from different donors. There has recently been a paper that investigated mixtures of semen and saliva using Raman, and the authors concluded that even with the heterogeneity within the Raman signals of the same fluid, when using multiple linear regression, they found a smooth linear transition from pure semen to pure vaginal fluid.[257] The authors state that the goal was not to identify the relative proportions of each fluid but to identify if there are even minor contributions of one in the other.[257] Raman has the potential to be used at crime scenes and in evidence evaluation.

Microbial Profiles

Bacteria and other microbes are essentially ubiquitous in the environment, and they share an intimate link with humans, both internally and externally. The number of microbes directly associated with humans is roughly equivalent to the number of native human cells ($\sim 3 \times 10^{13}$),[258] although it was originally thought to be 10 times greater.[259,260] Different parts of the body will have different types of bacteria associated with it, and these bacteria are present in a symbiotic relationship. The differences between the types of bacteria associated with different body fluids, or body parts, have been proposed as a means to identify the source of biologic stains.

The human microbiome is formed rapidly after birth[261] through interaction with the mother's microbiota encountered during birth (either vaginal or cesarean section).[262] Environmental microbes subsequently interact with the skin of the infant, leading to colonization and coexistence.[263] Eventually, a complex system forms with resident and transient microbes (bacteria, viruses, protozoa, fungi),[264] which can be disrupted by antibiotics, hand washing, or lotions.[263]

Most studies looking at bacterial identification, via single strain sampling or metagenomics, target the 16S rRNA region, which contains nine regions of variability (V1–9) interspaced with conserved regions.[263,265–269] It is most common to use the V2/V3 region for bacterial identification; however, the most abundant types of bacteria tend to be overrepresented in the sequence samples, with the rare biota being underrepresented. Other studies have used the V6 to identify rare taxa,[270,271] and one forensic study investigating oral streptococcus (saliva) used multiple genes (16S rRNA gene, 16S–23S rRNA intergenic spacer region, endoribonuclease P, RNA polymerase β-subunit).[272] Hence, there is a need to determine the most discriminating region, or multiple regions, independently or combined, for forensic purposes to ensure the maximum amount of data can be recovered from minimal and potentially degraded samples.

Microbes have been previously used in forensic science in the field of microbial forensics,[273,274] but in the context of bioterrorism,[275] identification of bacterial strains and sources in cases of disease,[276] poisoning,[277] and drug use.[278] Some studies have attempted to use one strain or species of bacteria as indicative of a body fluid,[25,193,194] with one finding only a single species present in vaginal samples. Other studies have looked at total bacteria contained in a sample, indicative signals, which is likely to be population specific and unlikely to be applicable to the wider forensic community.[195]

A study looking at saliva on skin found different dominant bacterial species in the different sample types and overall good discrimination, but there was still a 6.25% error rate.[279] A follow-up study investigated additional fluid types and found different dominant species

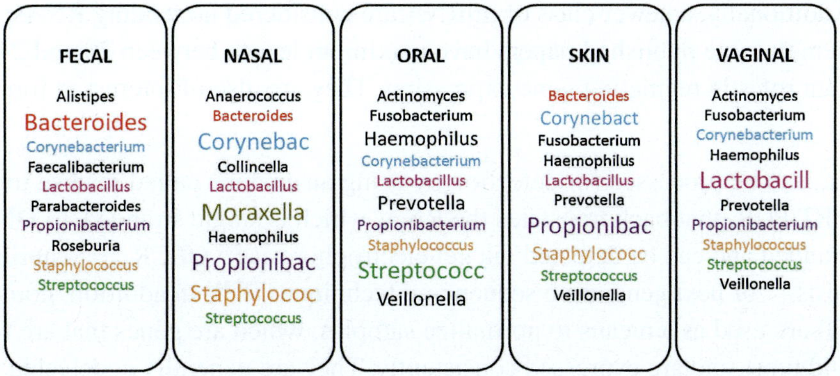

Fig. 6.24 The 10 most frequent bacterial genera for five different body fluids. Text size is proportional to the abundance of different genera, with the larger text indicating higher abundance, and colors indicate the same species found in all fluids. *Black* text indicates the species is not found in all fluid samples. *From Hanssen EN, Liland KH, Gill P, et al. Optimizing body fluid recognition from microbial taxonomic profiles. Forensic Sci Int Genet. 2018;37:13-20.*

across the different fluids, but still found common strains between all sample types[280] (Fig. 6.24). The authors found that inputting their data into a model composed of partial least squares in combination with linear discriminant analysis provided good discrimination of the body fluids.[280]

Because the same species of bacteria may be found in multiple fluids, mixtures may therefore pose a problem with this method, which is a recognized fact.[280] Other issues relate to the persistence of bacteria after a fluid is deposited, as living bacteria will die, and other surface bacteria will colonize the fluid over time. The use of microbes may therefore only be suitable for recently deposited fluids. This method is not suitable for rapid use or use at a crime scene because of the need for molecular genetic testing.

Ribonucleic Acid

RNA is the link between DNA and expressed proteins in cells and tissues, which can therefore be detected in associated fluids. It has gained significant interest for forensic body fluid identification in recent years as a potential new method that can act as a confirmatory test for multiple fluids simultaneously. The ability to coextract RNA and DNA from a single sample also means that it can fit into already established workflows, although it requires specialist laboratories and equipment and cannot be used at a scene. The time needed for testing also rules it out as a rapid screening test.

RNA is part of the protein synthesis process, with mRNA carrying the coding sequence transcripts to rRNA, where protein synthesis takes place though the aid of transfer RNA, which carries the amino acids to the ribosomes during synthesis to make the protein sequence. Additionally, a newer class of miRNA are considered noncoding RNAs; they are 18 to 24 bp in length (note published papers have maximum length between 20 and 24 bp) and play important roles in regulating gene expression. They are also of interest in forensic body fluid typing.

All RNAs have to be processed for detection by using an enzyme called reverse transcriptase (RT), using RT-PCR, that back translates the RNA, which is single stranded, to DNA, which is double stranded and can be detected via gel electrophoresis,[281] QPCR,[86,282] capillary electrophoresis,[196] or next generation sequencing techniques.[283,284] In addition, housekeeping genes (HKG) are used as a means to normalize samples, which are genes that are found in all tissue/fluid types and are expressed consistently. They are generally codetected with any RNA, or panel of RNA, markers. An alternative to HKG has been suggested as a positive control sample with all possible markers present,[285] similar to positive controls and ladders used in DNA typing.

As with other presumptive tests, many RNA markers have been classified as part of medical diagnoses[286,287] that have then been tested for use in forensic body fluid identification. In addition, there has been dedicated discovery of different RNA markers for forensic use. Most studies have small cohorts of reference samples for testing, and the suitability of the different RNAs for different body fluids has changed over time as other studies have identified potential cross-reactions. Table 6.2 lists some RNA markers that have been used for different body fluids.

Once RNA markers are established and primers developed, they can be multiplexed into a test to detect multiple fluids in one reaction. This also allows them to identify mixtures. Juusola and Ballantyne[196] created a multiplex to identify blood, saliva, semen, and vaginal secretions in one test, which also worked with mixtures of body fluids. Nussbaumer et al.[288] multiplexed four RNA markers in a QPCR probe-based assay for the identification of blood, semen, and vaginal fluid, plus a housekeeping control. They found stability in the markers over 10 days of storage at room temperature. Patel and Peel[293] multiplexed nine markers for detection using capillary electrophoresis (Fig. 6.25), but found that the marker for menstrual blood was not detected in donors taking hormonal contraceptives, and one vaginal fluid marker was not detected in all donors throughout a menstrual cycle.

As with other body fluid testing, there is disagreement in the capabilities of some RNA markers used. It was found that statherin and histatin 3, the two markers generally used for saliva, were not detected in one study.[284] According to the authors, this was because those markers derive from secreted saliva and were therefore not detected using the lower sensitivity hybridization method of their study, and they opted for markers expressed in epithelial cells of the mouth and pharynx. A study specifically looking at stability, however, found that statherin and histatin 3 could be stable for extended periods, up to at least 547 days; however, statherin showed faster degradation.[294]

Table 6.2 RNA markers[a] used for identification of different body fluids

Body Fluid	Marker	Reference(s)	Notes
Housekeeping genes	18S rRNA	(86,288)	
	β-actin	(81,289)	
	Glucose 6-phosphate dehydrogenase	(86,289,290)	
	Ribosomal protein S15	(289)	
	Transcription elongation factor-1α	(291)	
	Ubiquitin conjugating enzyme	(291)	
Peripheral blood (Pb)	Hemoglobin-δ	(292)	Cross-reacts with menstrual blood
	Solute carrier (SLC4A1)	(292)	Cross-reacts with menstrual blood
	β-spectrin	(196,290)	
	Porphobilinogen deaminase	(196,293)	
	Hemoglobin-α locus 1	(288)	
	Erythroid δ-aminolevulinate synthase	(290)	
	Hemoglobin-β	(86)	
	Glycophorin A	(291)	
Menstrual blood	Matrix metallopeptidase 3	(292)	
	Stanniocalcin 1	(292)	
	Matrix metalloproteinase (MMP) 7	(290)	
	MMP 10	(290)	
	MMP 11	(86,291)	
Vaginal fluid	Human β-defensin 1	(196)	Not detected consistently in all donors[293]
	Mucin 4	(196,288)	
Semen	Protamine 1	(196,281)	
	Protamine 2	(196,281)	Used for sperm only[291]
	Transition protein 1	(292)	If sperm are present
	Kallikrein-related peptidase 2	(292)	
	Kallikrein 3	(288)	
	Transglutaminase 4	(291)	For seminal fluid
Saliva	Statherin	(196,289)	
	Histatin 3	(196,289)	

[a]Not all markers have been included that can be found in the literature as some have been found less suitable due to cross-reaction, and more suitable markers being determined. Relevant references are provided where further details, including experimental design and primers used, can be found.

Despite the RNA markers being tissue specific for different fluids, cross-reactions are still a major concern. Hass et al.[86] found cross-reaction with peripheral blood and one of their menstrual blood markers, although not when detected via QPCR. Similarly, cross-reaction was seen with vaginal secretions and menstrual blood markers even when detected using QPCR, which for other markers had increased the specificity. They did find that when using

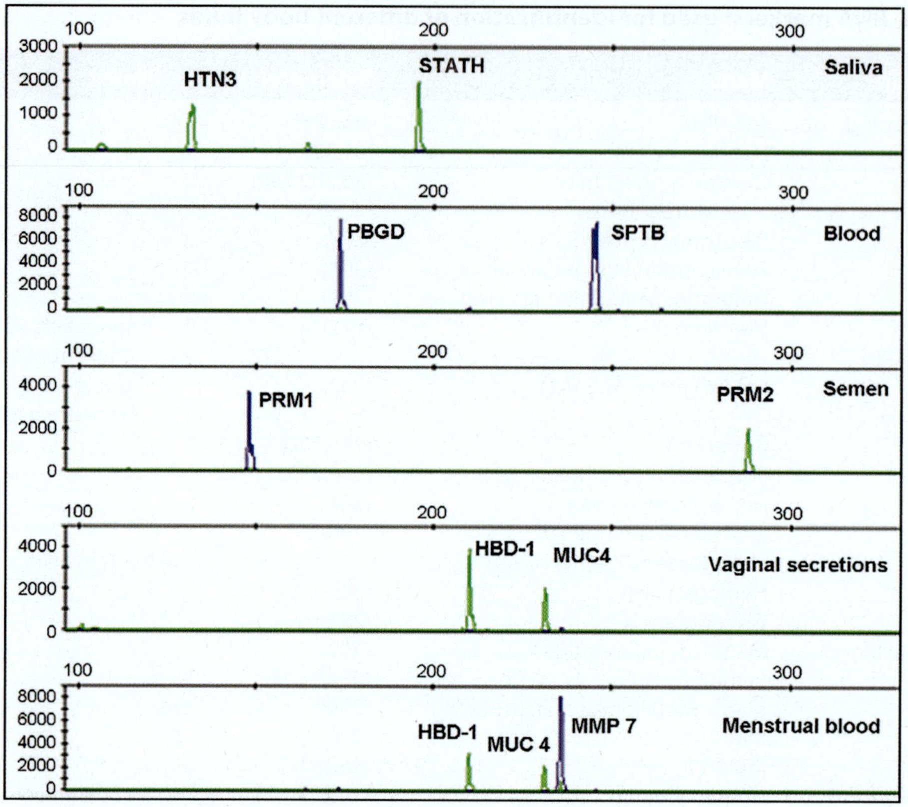

Fig. 6.25 An example of an electropherogram of RNA markers for saliva, blood, semen, vaginal secretions, and menstrual blood. *From Patel G, Peel C. Identifying the origin of cells. Forensic Sci Int Genet Suppl. 2008;1(1):574-576.*

RNA markers on casework, their results corresponded to those obtained through traditional testing.[86]

Flemming and Harbison[291] developed a test for saliva (two markers), semen, seminal fluid, blood, and menstrual blood, combined with three HKG. They found no cross-reaction with their markers in the samples tested, but saliva samples showed low signals from the HKG. They also tested nonhuman samples from chicken, rabbit, dog, mouse, cat, guinea pig, and pig for blood, and orangutan for saliva. The orangutan sample showed cross-reaction for the saliva markers, and cat and pig blood showed one of the HKG, but no other cross-reactions were observed. Sensitivity was also determined to be 1 μL input for blood and seminal fluid, and 0.1 μL input for semen, but other limits could not be determined because of the nature of the samples (swabs vs. liquid).[291]

A collaborative exercise was carried out in 2011 by the European DNA Profiling Group, where seven samples, plus a dilution series of blood, were sent to 16 laboratories to test three RNA blood markers: porphobilinogen deaminase, β-spectrin, and hemoglobin-β.[295] Each participating laboratory used its own methods, if established, or new methods for RNA typing, and most laboratories used different protocols than the others. Hemoglobin-β performed the best and was detected in most samples by most laboratories, but there was no participating laboratory that was able to identify all samples as blood. The report indicates the results are comparable to the use of tetramethylbenzidine (TMB) and Hexagon OBTI (see Chapter 3) and recommends the development of human-specific RNA quantification assay that would allow standard input RNA to eliminate some of the artifacts that some laboratories found (e.g., extraneous peaks, saturation, cross-reactivity).[295]

miRNA can be found as extracellular forms, which are more stable than other forms of RNA because they are complexed with proteins, thus protecting them from RNases.[296] Other work has determined for some fluids that miRNAs are encapsulated in exosomes, which also act as protection,[297] including prolonged room temperature incubation, multiple freeze–thaw cycles, RNase digestion, boiling, and variations in pH.[287,298] Early research into the use of miRNA for body fluid identification found that many miRNA markers were in all body fluids, but at different levels (differentially regulated), indicating that the proportion of each could act as an indicator for fluid type,[88] but they also identified fluid-specific miRNA for plasma, tears, breast milk, seminal fluid, and saliva.[299] Other studies have found miRNAs in blood plasma and serum,[282,286,296,300] saliva,[297,300] menstrual blood,[282] semen,[282] and breast milk.[298]

It is generally assumed that RNA has a shorter persistence than DNA and other markers within body fluids because of ribonucleases that occur naturally in cells, as well as samples having the potential to be exposed to UV light, heat, and moisture that is known to cause degradation in genetic samples. However, RNA has successfully been amplified in a 13- to 16-year-old bloodstain, although significant RNA degradation was noted.[301] The same study looked at a 6-year-old saliva stain that did not show the same level of degradation and gave good results. Another study found stability over significant time periods for mRNA in blood, semen, saliva, and vaginal secretions, as well as sensitivities ranging from 200 pg to 1912 ng, depending on the marker.[294] Degradation of RNA targets, including the HKG, has been used to attempt to provide time since deposition of various body fluids,[302] mainly blood.[303–305] Vennemann and Koppelkamm[306] advise accurate collection of samples used as biologic replicates, careful validation, normalization strategy, degradation studies, and careful and deliberate data interpretation for the use of any RNA marker.

Research into RNA typing for confirmatory body fluid identification is ongoing to find new, more suitable markers for each fluid.[292] There is also ongoing work to use multiple markers per fluid type to reduce the risk of false positives, with the idea being that cross-reactions will be less likely for multiple markers. This is a positive step, but it may still have issues when mixtures of body fluids are typed. Although it has been suggested that RNA may supplant traditional body fluid testing,[284,289] this is unlikely because of the complexity and cost of running RNA analyses. Therefore it will not be feasible to use with all body fluid samples (e.g., in mass screening at crime scenes), but all indications are that it will provide a powerful tool, especially if combined with DNA identification to attribute a donor to a particular fluid.[283]

DNA Methylation

The detection of DNA methylation is related to the study of epigenetics and is associated with changes to gene expression, and therefore is expected to differ between different fluid types. The methylation process involves the addition of a methyl group to the fifth position of the cytosine ring forming 5-methylcytosine (CpG). The methylation process is important in mammalian cellular differentiation and allows cells to maintain different characteristics by controlling and modulating gene expression.[307] Many studies have assessed the human genome for methylation and found regions that were termed tissue-specific differentially methylated regions (tDMRs),[308–310] which can be used for identification of different body fluids. There are factors that can affect methylation patterns, including environmental, diet, lifestyle (e.g., smoker or not), diseases, ethnicity, and genetic variation, so the stability of the markers between different populations is essential.[311]

There are two methods to detect methylation in a sample. The first involves digestion enzymes that cleave DNA at specific sequence locations (e.g., *HhaI*) if unmethylated, but will not digest the DNA if there is a CpG in the digestion sequence. If DNA primers are designed around this area, then the cleaved DNA will not produce a product due to broken DNA in the amplification path, but the methylated DNA will produce a product because it would remain intact. In one study by Frumkin et al.,[312] they used 15 DNA primer sets to differentiate blood, semen, saliva, and skin, with comparison to a commercial STR kit, and found their assay worked at the same level as for semen detection in a sample. The second method to detect methylation is by converting the unmethylated cytosine residues to uracil using a bisulfate conversion, which is then detected after sequencing as a thymine residue where a cytosine would normally be expected (Fig. 6.26). In this process, sodium bisulfate is used to treat the sample and converts unmethylated cytosines to uracil via deamination, whereas CpG residues are unchanged. This can be detected directly through sequencing, where the uracil is detected as a thymine, or through the use of methylation-specific PCR (MSP), where the converted DNA is amplified using modified primer sets that will only produce a product depending on the methylation state of the DNA sequence.[313] MSP is similar to the restriction-based detection in that if the sample is unmethylated, the DNA primers designed for methylated samples will not react due to sequence variation.

Lee et al.[307] used MSP and five markers to test blood, saliva, semen, menstrual blood, and vaginal fluid for methylation-based profiles. They were able to identify semen and vaginal fluid using their markers, but they recommended further body fluid–specific tDMRs. A subsequent study further developed the method to successfully identify semen

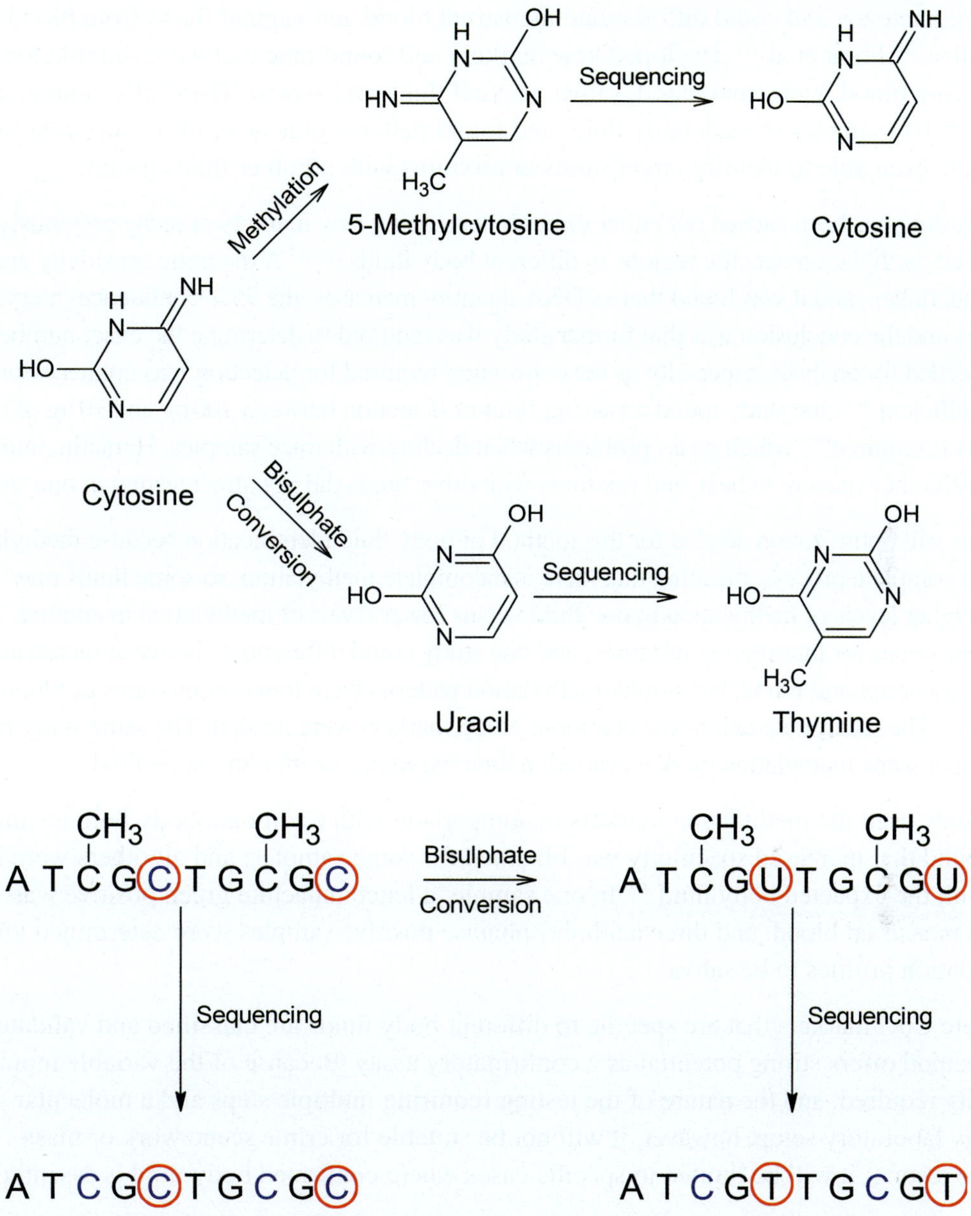

Fig. 6.26 *(Top)* DNA methylation, where cytosine is converted by DNA methyltransferase to 5-methylcytosine, which is referred to as a CpG dinucleotide. If the sample is treated with a bisulfate conversion, then the nonmethylated cytosine residues will be converted to uracil, which is then detected as thymine after sequencing. *(Bottom)* Example of the DNA sequence with two CpG residues and two C residues, treated with bisulfate conversion and the resulting sequenced products. Note the *left side* is not treated and has four C resides in the product, and the *right side* has only two C residues, the ones that were methylated, and two more T residues than the nontreated sequence. *Created using Advanced Chemistry Development Inc. ChemSketch. Toronto, Ontario; 2018.* www.acdlabs.com.

with spermatozoa and could differentiate menstrual blood and vaginal fluids from blood and saliva.[314] Forat et al.[315] developed new markers and found nine that were suitable for identifying blood, menstrual blood, saliva, vaginal fluid, and semen. They fully validated their test with 100 samples of each body fluid, and found patterns indicative of the different fluids, and were even able to identify target fluids in mixtures with all other fluids tested.

Other testing has been carried out either through developing new markers or using previously identified methylation-specific regions in different body fluids.[316,317] A theoretic sensitivity analysis was undertaken, and it was found that as DNA quantity increases, the 95% confidence interval shrinks, and the conclusion was that further study was required to determine the exact number of cells needed for analysis, especially as the conversion required for detection was not necessarily 100% efficient.[318] One study found a varying limit of detection between 100 pg and 10 ng of input DNA was required,[319] which poses problems when dealing with trace samples. Hematin, humic acid, different exposure to heat, and mixtures with other fluids did not affect testing in one study.[319]

There is still optimization needed for this method of body fluid identification because methylation is not a complete process, meaning that there is incomplete methylation, so some fluids may show higher levels of methylation in one fluid versus lower levels of methylation in another. This can pose issues for interpreting mixtures, and one study could differentiate between menstrual blood and peripheral blood, but similar methylation patterns were found in mixtures of blood and semen.[317] The recommendation was that more blood markers were needed. The same study further found that some methylation markers varied in their expression within the same fluid.

One study used the methylation markers in comparison with traditional body fluid testing and found that increased specificity was obtained for some samples, and all others were in line with the expected body fluid.[320] In one sample, a leucomalachite green positive was due to menstrual blood, and three acid phosphatase positive samples were determined via methylation profiles to be saliva.

As more CpG markers that are specific to different body fluids are classified and validated, this method offers strong potential as a confirmatory assay. Because of the variable input quantity required, and the nature of the testing requiring multiple steps and a molecular biology laboratory setup, however, it will not be suitable for crime scene work or mass sample testing; it will be limited to specific cases where confirmed body fluid is essential.

Proteomics

Proteomics is the full determination of the function and structure of proteins to understand an organism, or in the case of forensic serology, a body fluid. Proteomics uses the advances in mass spectrometry to determine the mass (m) to charge (z) ratio of intact, or parts of, proteins obtained via fragmentation. The protein content, or proteome, of different fluids is related to their function. Most of the standard testing for body fluids is based on the proteins that are present in those different fluids (e.g., hemoglobin in blood, acid phosphatase in semen, α-amylase in saliva). It is also related to the RNA found in the different fluids because the RNA codes for, and creates via translation, the proteins found in those fluids.

Proteins have been a target of forensic serology for decades (e.g., the differentiation of prostatic vs. vaginal acid phosphatase),[321] but recent advances in the technology to process and analyze proteins have resulted in rapid growth in the use of the proteome for forensic analysis. Currently, the method of choice for targeted proteomics is triple quadrupole mass spectrometer (QQQ), which is used after chromatographic separation (e.g., via HPLC, liquid chromatography, or gas chromatography). Because the proteins for specific biologic fluids will differ, those proteins that are specific can be detected for confirmatory identification of the fluid(s) present, although they have the same issues associated with them as RNA (i.e., they are differentially expressed).

For analysis, the sample is first fragmented through either a laser or enzymatically, until only small peptides are left, which are then separated by their mass and charge using one of the chromatographic separation methods. This is followed by identification of the different peptides and their original proteins using QQQ. The first quadrupole (Q1) isolates the peptides based on their m/z, the Q2 fragments them, and the Q3 selects specific fragment ions for detection.[322] There are two detection methods that can be used: parallel reaction mode (PRM) and multiple reaction monitoring (MRM) mode. PRM is more accurate and detects all product ions, so it is used for discovery and shotgun proteomics, but it is limited in terms of expensive setup and variable retention times. It is also usually performed on an Orbitrap or time-of-flight analyzer, not a QQQ. MRM mode is used for targeted proteomics, where it detects specific peptides measured against a labeled standard, then qualitatively quantifies the protein through the one-to-one correspondence between the precursor ion and standard (Fig. 6.27).

Proteomics originated in the clinical medical field,[323] but due to the nature of the field, many body fluids of forensic relevance were used to validate and test the method. Saliva,[324] semen,[325,326] vaginal fluid,[327] urine,[328–330] sweat,[331] menstrual blood,[332] breast milk,[333] and vomit[204] have all been assessed for their proteomes. Forensic studies have therefore used results from medical assessment, as well as carrying out discovery of their own markers[334–336] of relevant biologic fluids, to create targets for forensic use (Table 6.3).

Early work on forensic proteomics for body fluid identification was focused on discovering and confirming the peptide fragment markers needed for body fluid identification, but also found that the method was extremely sensitive, with detection limits at the nanoliter (10^{-9}) level for saliva and picoliter (10^{-12}) level for semen and blood.[335] The differences in the levels of sensitivity are due to the different protein concentrations in the fluids. The process can also be automated under the MRM mode as it targets only a specific, predefined set of peptide fragments.[337]

Proteomics can determine the components of a body fluid mixture using the same markers as for single fluids (see Table 6.3), but because of the differences in the protein concentration between different biologic fluids, the ratios at which each fluid can be detected will vary

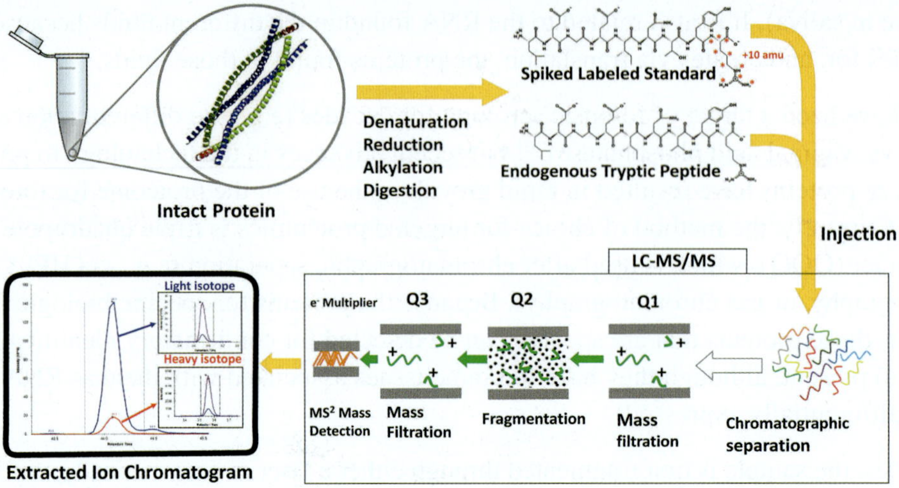

Fig. 6.27 Targeted proteomics. In targeted mass spectrometry using a triple quadrupole mass spectrometer, proteins are digested using trypsin and treated chemically with reduction and alkylation. The resulting complex peptide mixture is resolved using chromatography. As the peptides elute at known retention times, they are volatilized using electrospray ionization, and the target peptide is filtered using a precise mass window using the first quadrupole *(Q1)*, fragmented through collision-induced dissociation in a second quadrupole *(Q2)*, and two or three targeted fragments measured using the final quadrupole *(Q3)*. Peptide validation occurs through simultaneous analysis of matching stable isotope labeled synthetic target peptides. *From Parker GJ, McKiernan HE, Legg KM, et al. Forensic proteomics. Forensic Sci Int Genet. 2021;54:102529.*

Table 6.3 Proteins targeted[a] for biologic fluid identification for blood, saliva, and semen

Body Fluid	Protein Marker
Blood	Hemoglobin-α
	Hemoglobin-β
	Band 3 anion transport protein
	β-Spectrin
	α-Spectrin
Saliva	α-Amylase 1
	Cystatin SA
	Uncharacterized protein C6orf58
	Histatin-1
Semen	Semenogelin I
	Semenogelin II
	Mucin 6
	Prostate specific antigen
	Progestagen-associated endometrial protein
	Cysteine-rich secretory protein 1

[a]Note that they are some of the same targets as in other traditional and next generation (e.g., RNA) tests.
From Liu W, Butler E, Yang H, et al. Informatics approaches to forensic body fluid identification by proteomic mass spectrometry. *Applications in Forensic Proteomics: Protein Identification and Profiling*. ACS Publications; 2019:81-90.

depending on the fluids present.[337] Machine learning and other statistical approaches, including PCA, hierarchical clustering, or neural networks, can assist.

The field and use of forensic proteomics for biologic fluid identification is still being actively researched. With further development and validation, it will be a needed confirmatory assay, but even fully automated it can only process several hundred samples per week.[338] This means that it will be used on specific subsets of samples where confirmation of fluid type is required (e.g., semen or seminal fluid in sexual assaults).

References

1. Rattier JJL. Sur quelque srecherches microscopiques relatives aux taches de linge. *J Chim Méd Parm Toxicol.* 1837;3:120–122.
2. Robin C, Tardieu A. Mémoire sur quelques applications nouvelles de l'examen microscopique de diverses espèces de tache. *Ann d'Hygiène Publ Méd Légal.* 1860;13:416–442.
3. Orfila MJB. Du sperme, considéré sous le point de vue médico-légal. *J Chim Méd Parm Toxicol.* 1827;3(3):469–480.
4. Gaensslen RE. *Sourcebook in Forensic Serology, Immunology, and Biochemistry.* Washington, DC: US Government Printing Office; 1983:692.
5. Ritter B. *Ueber die Ermittelung von Blut-, Samen- und Exkrementenflecken in Kriminalfaellen: Ein spezieller Beitrag zur gerichtlichen Arzneikunde.* Stahel; 1854.
6. Berzelius JJ. *Lehrbuch der Thier-Chemie.* vol. 4. Arnold; 1831.
7. Netolitzky F. *Die Vegetabilien in den Fäces. Eine Mikroskopisch-Forensische Studie.* Perles; 1906.
8. van Ledden Hulsebosch MLQ. *Makro-und Mikroskopische Diagnostik der Menschlichen Exkremente.* Springer; 1899.
9. Moeller J. *Die Forensische Bedeutung der Exkremente. Wiener klin.* Rundschau; 1897:11.
10. Ledden-Hulsebosch V. Die mikroskopische untersuchung der exkremente. *Arch Pharm.* 1897;235(6-7): 429–435.
11. Reuter K. Naturwissenschaftliche-kriminalistische untersuchungen menschlicher ausscheidungen. In: Abderhalden E, ed. *Handbuch der Biologischen Arbeitsmthoden.* Urban & Schwarzenberg; 1932.
12. Jaffe M. *XXVII. Zur Lehre von den Eigenschaften und der Abstammung der Harnpigmente, in Band 47.* Boston, Berlin: De Gruyter; 1869:405–427.
13. Hoppe-Seyler G. *II. Heber die Ausscheidung des Urobilins in Krankheiten, in Band 124.* Boston, Berlin: De Gruyter; 1891:30–47.
14. Grimm F. *XI. Ueber Urobilin im Harne, in Band 132.* Boston, Berlin: De Gruyter; 1893:246–289.
15. Schlesinger W. Zum klinischen nachweis des urobilin. *Deutsche Med Wochenschrift.* 1903;29(32):561–563.
16. Edelmann A. Eine urobilinprobe im harn und stuhl für klinische zwecke. *Wiener Klin Wochenschrift.* 1915;28(36):978–979.
17. Lloyd JBF, Weston NT. A spectrometric study of the fluorescence detection of fecal urobilinoids. *J Forensic Sci.* 1982;27(2):352–365.
18. Nickolls LC. *The Scientific Investigation of Crime.* London: Butterworth; 1956.
19. Vanni V. A new method of personal identification through the microscopical examination of fecal matter. *Fingerpr Identific Mag.* 1949;31(4):3–8.
20. Kraft B. Neues zur kotunterscuchung in kriminalfallen. *Arch Kriminol.* 1929;84:211–215.
21. Police science legal abstracts and notes. *J Crim Law Criminol.* 1948;39:128.
22. Norris DO, Bock JH. Method for examination of fecal material from a crime scene using plant fragments. *J Forensic Identific.* 2001;51(4):367–377.
23. Norris DO, Bock JH. Use of fecal material to associate a suspect with a crime scene: report of two cases. *J Forensic Sci.* 2000;45(1):184–187.

24. Fourney RM, DesRoches AN, Buckle JL. Biological evidence and forensic DNA profiling. In: Nic Daeid N, Houck MM, eds. *Interpol's Forensic Science Review*. London: CRC Press; 2007:591–662.
25. Lewis C, Seashols-Williams SJ. Design and optimization of a 16S microbial qPCR multiplex for the presumptive identification of feces, saliva, vaginal and menstrual secretions. *J Forensic Sci*. 2022;67(4):1660–1667.
26. Nakanishi H, Shojo H, Ohmori T, et al. Identification of feces by detection of Bacteroides genes. *Forensic Sci Int Genet*. 2013;7(1):176–179.
27. Roguet A, Esen ÖC, Eren AM, et al. Forensic: an online platform for fecal source identification. *Msystems*. 2020;5(2): 00869-19.
28. Gysi M, Arora N, Sulzer A, et al. Non-invasive prenatal paternity testing with STRs: a pilot study. *Forensic Sci Int Genet Suppl*. 2015;5:e291–e292.
29. Marieb EN, Hoehn K. *Human Anatomy & Physiology*. 9th ed. London: Benjamin Cummings; 2013:1107.
30. Kaufman DP, Khattar J, Lappin SL. *Physiology, Fetal Hemoglobin*. Treasure Island, FL: StatPearls Publishing; 2023.
31. Robin C, Tardieu A. Mémoire sur l'examen microscopique des taches formées par le méconium et i'enduit foetal, pour servir a i'histoire medico-ligale de i'infanticide. *Ann d'Hygiène Publ Méd Légal*. 1857;7:350–374.
32. Grossowicz N, Aronovitch J, Rachmilewitz M, et al. Folic and folinic acid in maternal and foetal blood. *Br J Haematol*. 1960;6:296–302.
33. Culliford B. The identification of abnormal haemoglobins in bloodstains. *J Forensic Sci Soc*. 1964;4(3): 155–157.
34. Wraxall BGD. The identification of foetal haemoglobin in bloodstains. *J Forensic Sci Soc*. 1972;12(3): 457–458.
35. Weber K, Palmović V, Spasić P, et al. Die anwendung der chemiluminescenz des luminols in der gerichtlichen medizin und toxikologie II. Die wirkung des fetalen blutes auf die luminolreaktion. *Deutsche Zeitschrift Gesamte Gerichtliche Med*. 1968;64(2):158–164.
36. Fiori A. Detection and identification of bloodstains. In: Lundquist F, ed. *Methods of Forensic Science*. US Department of Justice; 1962:243–290.
37. Kohn J, Payne B. An immunological method for the detection and estimation of fetal haemoglobin. *J Clin Pathol*. 1972;25(9):830.
38. Baxter S, Rees B. The immunological identification of foetal haemoglobin in bloodstains in infanticide and associated crimes. *Med Sci Law*. 1974;14(3):163–167.
39. Wiggins KG, Wraxall BDG. The use of haemoglobin F antiserum for the detection of foetal haemoglobin (HbF). *J Forensic Sci Soc*. 1979;19(1):49–52.
40. Whitehead EM, Fredenburg ME, Lappas NT. The detection of fetal hemoglobin in bloodstains by means of thin-layer immunoassay. *J Forensic Sci*. 1983;28(4):888–893.
41. Inoue H, Takabe F, Maeno Y, et al. Identification of fetal hemoglobin in blood stains by high performance liquid chromatography. *Int J Legal Med*. 1989;102(7):437–444.
42. Inoue H, Takabe F, Iwasa M, et al. Identification of fetal hemoglobin and simultaneous estimation of bloodstain age by high-performance liquid chromatography. *Int J Legal Med*. 1991;104(3):127–131.
43. Brown TJ, Hess J, Shapiro L, et al. Pregnancy protein-SP1: identification tool in forensic bloodstains. *Can Soc Forensic Sci J*. 1993;26(2):69–80.
44. Davies A. Evaluation of results from tests performed on vaginal, anal and oral swabs received in casework. *J Forensic Sci Soc*. 1977;17(2-3):127–133.
45. Keating SM. Information from penile swabs in sexual assault cases. *Forensic Sci Int*. 1989;43(1):63–81.
46. Alkhatib S. Jail for maid who mixed her menstrual blood and other bodily fluids into family's food and water. *Straits Times*. 2020.
47. Gstalter M. Anti-vaccine protester charged after allegedly throwing menstrual blood at California lawmakers. *The Hill*. 2020.
48. Barrett KE, Barman SM, Brooks HL, et al. *Ganong's Review of Medical Physiology*. 26th ed. Sydney: McGraw-Hill; 2019.

49. Hunter J, Home E. *A Treatise on the Blood, Inflammation, and Gun-Shot Wounds*. London: John Richardson for George Nicol; 1794.
50. Casanti M. Nouvelle maniere de distinguer le sang humain de celui des autres mammiferes. *J Chim Méd Pharm Toxicol*. 1848;4(3):673–675.
51. Robin MC. Memoire sur la comparaison medico-legale des taches de sang menstruel et des autres especes de taches de sang. *Ann d'Hygiène Publ Méd Légal*. 1858;10:421–434.
52. Pouchet FA. *Théorie Positive de l'Ovulation Spontanée et de la Fécondation des Mammifères et de l'Espèce Humaine: Basée sur l'Observation de Toute la Série Animale*. vol. 1. JB Baillière; 1847.
53. Ricker C. *Anleitung zür Untersuchung Verdächtiger Flecke: Für Artze und Juristen*. St Petersburg: Jahre; 1870:64.
54. Döderlein A. *Das Scheidensekret und Seine Bedeutung für das Puerperalfieber*. Leipzig; 1892.
55. Wood ES. Examination of blood and other stains. In: Witthaus RA, Becker TC, eds. *Medical Jurisprudence, Forensic Medicine and Toxicology*. New York: William Wood & Company; 1894:3–82.
56. Wiegmann H. *Über den Glykogengehalt der Scheidenepithelien und Seine Diagnostische Bedeutung*. Verlag Nicht Ermittelbar; 1910.
57. Merkel H. Vber den glykogengehalt des scheidenepithels, seine diagnostisebe bedeutung und deren kritische bewertung. *Deutsch Zeitschrift Gesamte Gerichtliche Med*. 1924;4:1–8.
58. Popielski B. A study of menstrual blood traces. *Bull Int Acad Pol Sci Let Cl Med*. 1949;7(10):275–284.
59. Asano M, Oya M, Hayakawa M. Identification of menstrual blood stains by the electrophoretic pattern of lactate dehydrogenase isozymes. *Forensic Sci*. 1972;1(3):327–332.
60. Dixon T, Gonsowski R. A modified method of LDH isoenzyme electrophoresis in the identification of menstrual bloodstains. *J Pol Sci Admin*. 1974;2(3):263.
61. Divall GB, Ismail M. Lactate dehydrogenase isozymes in vaginal swab extracts: a problem for the identification of menstrual blood. *Forensic Sci Int*. 1983;21(2):139–147.
62. Culliford BJ. Identification of menstrual blood in dried stain form by an electrophoretic method. *J Forensic Med*. 1959;6(3):112–115.
63. Whitehead P, Divall G. Assay of "soluble fibrinogen" in bloodstain extracts as an aid to identification of menstrual blood in forensic science: preliminary findings. *Clin Chem*. 1973;19(7):762–765.
64. Whitehead P, Divall G. The identification of menstrual blood—the immunoelectrophoretic characterisation of soluble fibrinogen from menstrual bloodstain extracts. *Forensic Sci*. 1974;4:53–62.
65. Gaffney PJFDP. *Lancet*. 1972;300(7792):1422.
66. Rylatt D, Blake A, Cottis L, et al. An immunoassay for human D dimer using monoclonal antibodies. *Thromb Res*. 1983;31(6):767–778.
67. Müller-Berghaus G. *Fibrinogen and Its Derivatives. Biochemistry, Physiology, and Pathophysiology*. Proceedings of the Fibrinogen Workshop, Giseeen, FRG, 22-23 May 1986. 1986: Excerpta Medica.
68. An W. Measurement of cross linked fibrin derivatives in plasma: an immunoassay using monoclonal antibodies. *J Clin Pathol*. 1984;37:882–887.
69. Hillyard C, Blake A, Wilson K, et al. A latex agglutination assay for D dimer: evaluation and application to the diagnosis of thrombotic disease. *Clin Chem*. 1987;33(10):1837–1840.
70. Adam SS, Key NS, Greenberg CS. D-dimer antigen: current concepts and future prospects. *Blood*. 2009;113(13):2878–2887.
71. Miyaishi S, Kitao T, Yamamoto Y, et al. Identification of menstrual blood by the simultaneous determination of FDP-D dimer and myoglobin contents. *Japan J Legal Med*. 1996;50(6):400–403.
72. Baker DJ, Grimes EA, Hopwood AJ. D-dimer assays for the identification of menstrual blood. *Forensic Sci Int*. 2011;212(1-3):210–214.
73. Akutsu T, Watanabe K, Motani H, et al. Evaluation of latex agglutination tests for fibrin–fibrinogen degradation products in the forensic identification of menstrual blood. *Legal Med*. 2012;14(1):51–54.
74. Holtkötter H, Dierig L, Schürenkamp M, et al. Validation of an immunochromatographic D-dimer test to presumptively identify menstrual fluid in forensic exhibits. *Int J Legal Med*. 2015;129(1):37–41.
75. Holtkötter H, Dias Filho CR, Schwender K, et al. Forensic differentiation between peripheral and menstrual blood in cases of alleged sexual assault—validating an immunochromatographic multiplex assay for simultaneous detection of human hemoglobin and D-dimer. *Int J Legal Med*. 2018;132(3):683–690.

76. Konrad H, Hartung B, Poetsch M. Un)reliable detection of menstrual blood in forensic casework—evaluation of the Seratec PMB test with mock samples. *Int J Legal Med.* 2023:1–6.
77. Gray D, Frascione N, Daniel B. Development of an immunoassay for the differentiation of menstrual blood from peripheral blood. *Forensic Sci Int.* 2012;220(1-3):12–18.
78. Quinn AA, Elkins KM. The differentiation of menstrual from venous blood and other body fluids on various substrates using ATR FT-IR spectroscopy. *J Forensic Sci.* 2017;62(1):197–204.
79. Sharma S, Chophi R, Singh R. Forensic discrimination of menstrual blood and peripheral blood using attenuated total reflectance (ATR)-Fourier transform infrared (FT-IR) spectroscopy and chemometrics. *Int J Legal Med.* 2019.
80. Mistek-Morabito E, Lednev IK. Discrimination of menstrual and peripheral blood traces using attenuated total reflection Fourier transform-infrared (ATR FT-IR) spectroscopy and chemometrics for forensic purposes. *Analyt Bioanalyt Chem.* 2021;413:2513–2522.
81. Bauer M, Patzelt D. Evaluation of mRNA markers for the identification of menstrual blood. *J Forensic Sci.* 2002;47(6):1278–1282.
82. Bauer M, Patzelt D. Identification of menstrual blood by real time RT-PCR: technical improvements and the practical value of negative test results. *Forensic Sci Int.* 2008;174(1):55–59.
83. Richard MLL, Harper KA, Craig RL, et al. Evaluation of mRNA marker specificity for the identification of five human body fluids by capillary electrophoresis. *Forensic Sci Int Genet.* 2012;6(4):452–460.
84. He H, Ji A, Zhao Y, et al. A stepwise strategy to distinguish menstrual blood from peripheral blood by Fisher's discriminant function. *Int J Legal Med.* 2020;134:845–851.
85. Hanson EK, Mirza M, Rekab K, et al. The identification of menstrual blood in forensic samples by logistic regression modeling of miRNA expression. *Electrophoresis.* 2014;35(21-22):3087–3095.
86. Haas C, Klesser B, Maake C, et al. mRNA profiling for body fluid identification by reverse transcription endpoint PCR and realtime PCR. *Forensic Sci Int Genet.* 2009;3(2):80–88.
87. Bauer M, Polzin S, Patzelt D. Quantification of RNA degradation by semi-quantitative duplex and competitive RT-PCR: a possible indicator of the age of bloodstains? *Forensic Sci Int.* 2003;138(1-3): 94–103.
88. Hanson EK, Lubenow H, Ballantyne J. Identification of forensically relevant body fluids using a panel of differentially expressed microRNAs. *Analyt Biochem.* 2009;387(2):303–314.
89. Chen YL, Kuan WH, Liu CL. Comparative study of the composition of sweat from eccrine and apocrine sweat glands during exercise and in heat. *Int J Environ Res Publ Health.* 2020;17(10):3377.
90. Kirk PL. *Crime Investigation; Physical Evidence and the Police Laboratory.* New York: Interscience; 1953.
91. Giustic G, Panari G. Zur gerichtsmedizinischen identifizierung von urin und urinflecken. *Arch Kriminol.* 1972;150:21–30.
92. Yasuda T, Takeshita H, Sawazaki K, et al. A new individualization marker of sweat: deoxyribonuclease I (DNase I) polymorphism. *J Forensic Sci.* 1996;41(5):862–864.
93. Sagawa K, Kimura A, Saito Y, et al. Production and characterization of a monoclonal antibody for sweat-specific protein and its application for sweat identification. *Int J Legal Med.* 2003;117(2):90–95.
94. Sakurada K, Akutsu T, Fukushima H, et al. Detection of dermcidin for sweat identification by real-time RT-PCR and ELISA. *Forensic Sci Int.* 2010;194(1-3):80–84.
95. Huynh C, Brunelle E, Agudelo J, et al. Bioaffinity-based assay for the sensitive detection and discrimination of sweat aimed at forensic applications. *Talanta.* 2017;170:210–214.
96. Sterzik V, Hinderberger P, Panzer S, et al. Visualizing old biological traces on different materials without using chemicals. *Int J Legal Med.* 2018;132(1):35–41.
97. Virkler K, Lednev IK. Raman spectroscopy offers great potential for the nondestructive confirmatory identification of body fluids. *Forensic Sci Int.* 2008;181(1-3):e1–e5.
98. Sikirzhytski V, Sikirzhytskaya A, Lednev IK. Multidimensional Raman spectroscopic signature of sweat and its potential application to forensic body fluid identification. *Analyt Chim Acta.* 2012;718:78–83.
99. Hair ME, Mathis AI, Brunelle EK, et al. Metabolite biometrics for the differentiation of individuals. *Analyt Chem.* 2018;90(8):5322–5328.

100. Yudianto A, Kusuma SE. DNA isolation from sweat stain in clothes as forensic identification material. *Folia Medica Indones*. 2006;42(4):205–208.
101. Botelho SY. Tears and the lacrimal gland. *Sci Am*. 1964;211(4):78–87.
102. Josephson AS, Lockwood DW. Immunoelectrophoretic studies of the protein components of normal tears. *J Immunol*. 1964;93(4):532–539.
103. Josephson AS, Weiner RS. Studies of the proteins of lacrimal secretions. *J Immunol*. 1968;100(5): 1080–1092.
104. Bonavida B, Sapse AT, Sercarz EE. Specific tear prealbumin: a unique lachrymal protein absent from serum and other secretions. *Nature*. 1969;221(5178):375–376.
105. Aparna R, Iyer RS. Tears and eyewear in forensic investigation—a review. *Forensic Sci Int*. 2020;306 110055.
106. Aparna R, Iyer RS. Detection and visualization of human tears using alternate light sources for forensic purposes. *Sci Just*. 2021;61(6):771–778.
107. Aparna R, Iyer RS, Das T, et al. Detection, discrimination and aging of human tears stains using ATR-FTIR spectroscopy for forensic purposes. *Forensic Sci Int Rep*. 2022;6:100290.
108. Aparna R, Iyer RS, Kumar N, et al. Forensic DNA profiling of tears stains from commonly encountered substrates. *Forensic Sci Int*. 2021;328:111006.
109. Gee GN, Blackie WJ, Flemons GF, et al. Notes: the detection of urea in urine stains on carpets. *Analyst*. 1940;65(766):25–27.
110. Vandenberg N, van Oorschot RAH. The use of Polilight in the detection of seminal fluid, saliva, and bloodstains and comparison with conventional chemical-based screening tests. *J Forensic Sci*. 2006;51(2):361–370.
111. Ito T. Uber einige anwendungen ultravioletter strahlen zu gerichtlich-medizinischen zwecken. *Deutsche Zeitschrift Gesamte Gerichtliche Med*. 1927;9(1):726–727.
112. Miranda GE, Prado FB, Delwing F, et al. Analysis of the fluorescence of body fluids on different surfaces and times. *Sci Just*. 2014;54(6):427–431.
113. Rouelle HM. OBSERVATIONS Sur l'Urine humaine, & sur celles de vache & de cheval, comparées ensemble. *J de Méd.* 1773;40:451–468.
114. Fosse MR. Sur quelques principes découverts chez les végétaux grâce à de nouvelles méthodes d'analyse. *Arch Museum*. 1935;6(12).
115. Fourcroy Vauquelin. Pour servirà l'histoire naturelle chimique et médicale de Vurine humaine, dans lequelons'occupe spécialement des propriétés de la matière particulière qui la caractérise. *Ann Chim Analyt Chim Appl Rev Chim Analyt Réunies*. 1799;32:80 112.
116. Prout W. Observations sur la nature de quelques-uns des principes immédiats de l'urine, avec quelques remarques sur les moyens de prévenir les maladies qui accompagnent l'état morbifique de ce fluide. *Ann Chim Phys*. 1819;10:369–388.
117. Fose MR. Action de l'urée, de la thiourée, de l'uréthane et de quelques amiedes sur le xanthydrol. *Comp Rend Hebdomadaires Séances l'Acad Sci*. 1907;145:813–815.
118. Maiocchi G. La reazione dello xanthydrol nella ricerca dell'orina nelle macchie. *Il Cesalpino*. 1915;11: 87–96.
119. Balthazard V, Rojas N. Examen des taches d'urine. *Ann Méd Légal Criminol Pol Sci Org Congrès Méd Légal Lang Française*. 1922;2:33–37.
120. Marshall Jr EK. A rapid clinical method for the estimation of urea in urine. *J Biol Chem*. 1913;14(4): 283–290.
121. Barrett JF, Jones EB. A colorimetric method for the direct determination of urea in urine. *Biochem J*. 1932;26(4):1246.
122. Klein B. An improved method for the preparation of urease paper. *J Lab Clin Med*. 1938;23:1097.
123. Hawk PB, Bergeine O. *Practical Physiological Chemistry*. Blakiston; 1937.
124. Cook J. Test paper of urease and acid-base indicator for detection of urea. *J Assoc Off Agric Chem*. 1948;31:797–799.
125. Haury H. Urea determination with stable reagents. *Med Klin*. 1965;60:508–510.

126. Dempster W. Azostix test for blood urea level. *Br J Radiol*. 1968;41(491):878.
127. Bell S. *The Facts on File Dictionary of Forensic Science*. Infobase Publishing; 2009.
128. Petit J. Rapid estimation of urea and glucose in blood and urine of dogs and rabbits. *Rev d'Élev Méd Vét Pays Trop*. 1969;22:417–422.
129. Poon HHL. Identification of human urine by immunological techniques. *Can Soc Forensic Sci J*. 1984;17(3): 81–89.
130. Desroches AN, Buckle JL, Fourney RM. Forensic biology evidence screening past and present. *Can Soc Forensic Sci J*. 2009;42(2):101–120.
131. Kozu T, Ichinose T, Komatsu Y, et al. Identification of urine stains by a urease spray reagent. *Rep Natl Res Inst Pol Sci*. 1977;30(1):18–20.
132. Bedrosian JL, Stolorow M, Tahir M. Development of a radial gel diffusion technique for the identification of urea in urine stains. *J Forensic Sci*. 1984;29(2):601–606.
133. Zhao Y, Shi R, Bian X, et al. Ammonia detection methods in photocatalytic and electrocatalytic experiments: how to improve the reliability of NH3 production rates? *Adv Sci*. 2019;6(8): 1802109.
134. Feigl F. Zum nachweis von ammoniumsalzen mit hilfe von tüpfelreaktion. *Mikrochemie*. 1933;13(1): 129–135.
135. Ishler NH, Sloman K, Walker ME. A microchemical spot test for mammalian urine contamination on fabrics. *J Assoc Off Agri Chem*. 1947;30(4):670–672.
136. Watson D, Pratt D. Micro estimation of urea. *Nature*. 1958;181(4621): 1475-1475.
137. Goo RK, Kanai H, Inouye V, et al. Spectrophotometric determination of urea in urine stains on foods and containers. *J Assoc Off Analyt Chem*. 1980;63(5):985–987.
138. Rhodes E, Thornton J. DMAC test for urine stains. *J Pol Sci Admin*. 1976;4(1):88–89.
139. Almog J, Klein A, Tamiri T, et al. A field diagnostic test for the improvised explosive urea nitrate. *J Forensic Sci*. 2005;50(3):1–5.
140. Ong S, Wain A, Groombridge L, et al. Forensic identification of urine using the DMAC test: a method validation study. *Sci Just*. 2012;52(2):90–95.
141. Farrugia KJ, Bandey H, Dawson L, et al. A comparison of enhancement techniques for footwear impressions on dark and patterned fabrics. *J Forensic Sci*. 2013;58(6):1472–1485.
142. Jaffe M. Ueber den niederschlag, welchen pikrinsaure in normalen harn erzeugt und uber eine neue reaktion des kreatinins. *Hoppe-Seyler's Zeitschrift Physiol Chem*. 1886;10:391–400.
143. Hofmann KB. *Lehrbuch der Zoochemie*. Harvard University; 1879:761.
144. Beaunis H.É. *Nouveaux Éléments de Physiologie Humaine, Comprenant les Principes de la Physiologie Comparée et de la Physiologie Générale*. vol. 2. Paris; 1881:1484.
145. de Morais CDLM, de Lima KMG. Determination and analytical validation of creatinine content in serum using image analysis by multivariate transfer calibration procedures. *Analyt Meth*. 2015;7(16):6904–6910.
146. Barr DB, Wilder LC, Caudill SP, et al. Urinary creatinine concentrations in the US population: implications for urinary biologic monitoring measurements. *Environ Health Persp*. 2005;113(2):192–200.
147. Butler AR. The Jaffé reaction. Part II. A kinetic study of the Janovsky complexes formed from creatinine (2-imino-1-methylimazolidin-4-one) and acetone. *J Chem Soc Perkin Trans*. 1975(8):853–857.
148. Kroll M, Roach N, Poe B, et al. Mechanism of interference with the Jaffé reaction for creatinine. *Clin Chem*. 1987;33(7):1129–1132.
149. Fraser AD, Dagenais P. Oral creatine supplement use and urinary creatinine excretion. *Can Soc Forensic Sci J*. 2000;33(1):33–37.
150. Cook J. Factors influencing the assay of creatinine: prepared for the Association of Clinical Biochemists' Scientific and Technical Committee. *Ann Clin Biochem*. 1975;12(1-6):219–232.
151. Neubauer C. Uber kreatinin und kreatin. *Ann Chem Pharm*. 1866;137:288–298.
152. Weyl T. Ueber eine neue reactionen auf kreatinin und kreatin. *Berichte Deutschen Chem Gesellschaft*. 1878;11(2):2175–2177.
153. Sánchez-Viesca F, Gómez R. The chemistry of the Weyl-Salkowski test for creatinine. *Am J Chem*. 2021;11(1):18–21.
154. Tamm I, Horsfall Jr FL. Characterization and separation of an inhibitor of viral hemagglutination present in urine. *Proc Soc. Exp Biol Med*. 1950;74(1):108–114.

155. Tamm I, Horsfall Jr FL. A mucoprotein derived from human urine which reacts with influenza, mumps, and Newcastle disease viruses. *J Exp Med*. 1952;95(1):71–97.
156. Fletcher A, Neuberger A, Ratcliffe WA. Tamm-Horsfall urinary glycoprotein. The subunit structure. *Biochem J*. 1970;120(2):425–432.
157. Taylor MC, Hunt JS. Forensic identification of human urine by radioimmunoassay for Tamm-Horsfall urinary glycoprotein. *J Forensic Sci Soc*. 1983;23(1):67–72.
158. Tsutsumi H, Okajima H, Sato K, et al. Identification of human urinary stains by enzyme-linked immunosorbent assay for human uromucoid. *J Forensic Sci*. 1988;33(1):237–243.
159. Tsutsumi H, Sato K, Tamaki K, et al. Identification of human urine stains on cloth. *Int J Legal Med*. 1991;104(2):105–108.
160. Independent Forensics. *Developmental validation of RSID-Urine*. Hillside, IL.
161. Kobayashi K, Fukuoka S. Conditions for solubilization of Tamm-Horsfall protein/uromodulin in human urine and establishment of a sensitive and accurate enzyme-linked immunosorbent assay (ELISA) method. *Arch Biochem Biophys*. 2001;388(1):113–120.
162. Akutsu T, Watanabe K, Sakurada K. Specificity, sensitivity, and operability of RSID-Urine for forensic identification of urine: comparison with ELISA for Tamm-Horsfall protein. *J Forensic Sci*. 2012;57(6): 1570–1573.
163. Sato K, Tsutsumi H, Htay HH, et al. Identification of human urinary stains by the quotient uric acid/urea nitrogen. *Forensic Sci Int*. 1990;45(1):27–38.
164. Chu QC, Lin M, Geng CH, et al. Determination of uric acid in human saliva and urine using miniaturized capillary electrophoresis with amperometric detection. *Chromatographia*. 2007;65(3):179–184.
165. Nakazono T, Kashimura S, Hayashiba Y, et al. Dual examinations for identification of urine as being of human origin and for DNA-typing from small stains of human urine. *J Forensic Sci*. 2008;53(2):359–363.
166. Akutsu T, Ikegaya H, Watanabe K, et al. Evaluation of Tamm-Horsfall protein and uroplakin III for forensic identification of urine. *J Forensic Sci*. 2010;55(3):742–746.
167. Sakurai T, Irii T, Iwadate K. Simultaneous quantification of urea, uric acid, and creatinine in human urine by liquid chromatography/mass spectrometry. *Legal Med*. 2022;55:102011.
168. Nguyen JD, Duong H. *Anatomy, Abdomen and Pelvis, Female External Genitalia*. Treasure Island, FL: StatPearls Publishing; 2019.
169. Huggins GR, Preti G. Vaginal odors and secretions. *Clin Obstet Gynecol*. 1981;24(2):355–377.
170. Michael RP, Bonsall RW, Warner P. Human vaginal secretions: volatile fatty acid content. *Science*. 1974;186(4170):1217–1219.
171. Levin RJ. The ins and outs of vaginal lubrication. *Sex Relation Ther*. 2003;18(4):509–513.
172. Strassmann G. Ein beitrag zum spermanachweis. *Aerzt Sachvertaend Ztg*. 1921;27:127–129.
173. Bartholin C. *De Ovariis Mulierum et Generationis Historia Epistola Anatomica*. Amstelaedami: J. Henr Wetstenii; 1678.
174. Bora SA, Condous G. Bartholin's, vulval and perineal abscesses. *Best Pract Res Clin Obstet Gynaecol*. 2009;23(5):661–666.
175. Tamburrini S, Vascone C, Marrone V, et al. Skene's glands abscess an overlooked diagnosis in acute lower urinary symptoms. *Radiol Case Rep*. 2021;16(12):3751–3756.
176. Zaviačič M, Ablin RJ. The female prostate. *JNCI*. 1998;90(9):713.
177. Skene AJ. The anatomy and pathology of two important glands of the female urethra. *Am J Obstet Dis Women Child*. 1880;13(2):265.
178. Graaf RR. *De Mulierum Organis Generationi Inservientibus Tractatus Novus*. Lugduni Batav(orum) [Leiden]: Ex Officina Hackiana; 1672:334.
179. Streckfus CF. *Exocrine glands of the reproductive system. Exocrinology: A Textbook and Atlas of the Exocrine Cells, Glands and Organs*. Cham: Springer International Publishing; 2022:83–99.
180. Adams EG, Wraxall BG. Phosphates in body fluids: the differentiation of semen and vaginal secretion. *Forensic Sci*. 1974;3:57–62.
181. Wernert N, Albrech M, Sesterhenn I, et al. The "female prostate": location, morphology, immunohistochemical characteristics and significance. *Eur Urol*. 1992;22(1):64–69.
182. Cauvet D. Taches de sperme et taches de aang. *Ann d'Hygiène Publ Méd Légal*. 1875;44:117–126.

183. Lugol J. *Mémoire sur l'Emploi de l'Jode dans les Maladies Scrofuleuses*. Paris: JB Bailliere; 1829.
184. Jones JR, Hurxthal LM. The iodine vapor stained vaginal smear: its use in office practice. *J Clin Endocrinol*. 1951;11(4):434–444.
185. Jones JE, Leon JA. Lugol's test reexamined again: buccal cells. *J Forensic Sci*. 2004;49(1):64–67.
186. Thomas F, Van Hecke W. The demonstration of recent sexual intercourse in the male by the Lugol method. *Med Sci Law*. 1963;3(2)):169–171.
187. Rothwell TJ, Harvey KJ. The limitations of the Lugol's iodine staining technique for the identification of vaginal epithelial cells. *J Forensic Sci Soc*. 1978;18(3-4):181–184.
188. Hausmann R, Pregler C, Schellmann B. The value of the Lugol's iodine staining technique for the identification of vaginal epithelial cells. *Int J Legal Med*. 1994;106:298–301.
189. French CEV, Jensen CG, Vintiner SK, et al. A novel histological technique for distinguishing between epithelial cells in forensic casework. *Forensic Sci Int*. 2008;178(1):1–6.
190. Paterson SK, Jensen CG, Vintiner SK, et al. Immunohistochemical staining as a potential method for the identification of vaginal epithelial cells in forensic casework. *J Forensic Sci*. 2006;51(5):1138–1143.
191. de Vos J, Otto RE, Achetib N, et al. Analysis of the fluorescent properties of vaginal fluid upon ageing. *Meth Appl Fluor*. 2023;12(1):015007.
192. Fleming RI, Harbison S. The use of bacteria for the identification of vaginal secretions. *Forensic Sci Int Genet*. 2010;4(5):311–315.
193. Akutsu T, Motani H, Watanabe K, et al. Detection of bacterial 16S ribosomal RNA genes for forensic identification of vaginal fluid. *Legal Med*. 2012;14(3):160–162.
194. Giampaoli S, Berti A, Valeriani F, et al. Molecular identification of vaginal fluid by microbial signature. *Forensic Sci Int Genet*. 2012;6(5):559–564.
195. Huang H, Yao T, Wu W, et al. Specific microbes of saliva and vaginal fluid of Guangdong Han females based on 16S rDNA high-throughput sequencing. *Int J Legal Med*. 2019;133(3):699–710.
196. Juusola J, Ballantyne J. Multiplex mRNA profiling for the identification of body fluids. *Forensic Sci Int*. 2005;152(1):1–12.
197. Hanson EK, Ballantyne J. Highly specific mRNA biomarkers for the identification of vaginal secretions in sexual assault investigations. *Sci Just*. 2013;53(1):14–22.
198. Sakurada K, Motani H, Akutsu T, et al. Identification of vaginal stains by detection of 17 B-estradiol. *Can Soc Forensic Sci J*. 2008;41(1):13–19.
199. Divall GB. A new peptidase isozyme which may assist in the identification of vaginal debris. *Forensic Sci Int*. 1984;24(4):239–246.
200. Lee H, Gaensslen R, Galvin C, et al. Enzyme assays for the identification of gastric fluid. *J Forensic Sci*. 1985;30(1):97–102.
201. Yamada S, Hirata K, Tsugawa N, et al. Vomit identification by a pepsin assay using a fibrin blue-agarose gel plate. *Forensic Sci Int*. 1992;52(2):215–221.
202. Nelson WL, Ciaccio EI, Hess GP. A rapid method for the quantitative assay of proteolytic enzymes. *Analyt Biochem*. 1961;2:39–44.
203. Akutsu T, Saito H, Iwase H, et al. The applicability of ELISA detection of gastric mucosa-expressing proteins for the identification of vomit. *Int J Legal Med*. 2017;131(2):359–364.
204. Pieri M, Silvestre A, De Cicco M, et al. Mass spectrometry-based proteomics for the forensic identification of vomit traces. *J Proteom*. 2019;209 103524.
205. Hayashida K, Matsumura S, Mohri H. Forensic investigation for identification of vomit using latex agglutination turbidimetric immunoassay. *Japan J Forensic Sci Technol*. 2023;28(2):177–182.
206. Barruel M. Mémoire sur l'existence d'un principe propre à caractériser le sang de l'homme et celui des diverses espèces d'animaux. *Ann d'Hygiène Publ Méd Légal*. 1829:267–277.
207. Schmidt C. *Die Diagnostik Verdächtiger Flecke in Criminalfällen: Ein Physiologisch-Chemischer Beitrag zur Gerichtlichen Medicin*. Mitau, Leipzig: Reyher; 1848.
208. Tardieu A, Barruel JJE, Chevallier JB. Experiences sur l'odeur du sang. *Ann d'Hygiène Publ Méd Légal*. 1853;49:413–417.
209. Prevost JL, Dumas J. Examen du sang et de son action dans les divers phénomènes de la vie. *Ann Chim Phys*. 1821;18:280–296.

210. Mandl L. Recherces medico-legales sur le sang. *Gazette Méd Paris J Méd Sci Access*. 1842;10(37):561–567.
211. Fleming A. *Blood Stains in Criminal Trials*. WS Haven; 1861.
212. Gulliver G. Observations on the sizes and shapes of the red corpuscles of the blood of vertebrates, with drawings of them to a uniform scale, and extended and revised tables of measurements. *Proc Zool Soc London*. 1875:474–495.
213. Kraus R. Ueber specifische reaktionen in keimfreien filtraten aus cholera, typhus, u. pestvouillon culturen, erzeugt durch homologes serum. *Wiener Klin Wochenschrift*. 1897;32:736–738.
214. Widal MF, Sicard MA. Étude sur le sérodiagnostic et sur la réaction agglutinante chez les typhiques. *Ann Inst Pasteur*. 1897;11(5):353–432.
215. Levy E, Bruns H. Beiträge zur lehre der agglutination. *Berliner Klin Wochenschrift*. 1897;34(1):491–493.
216. Tchistovitch T. Études sur l'immunisation contre le sérum d'anguilles. *Ann Inst Pasteur*. 1899;13:406–425.
217. Nicolle C. Recherches sur la substance agglutinée. *Ann Inst Pasteur*. 1898;12(3):161–191.
218. Boyden A. Precipitin testing and classification. *Syst Zool*. 1963;12(1):1–7.
219. Bordet J. Le mécanisme de l'agglutination. *Ann Inst Pasteur*. 1899;13:225–250.
220. Wood ES. The serum test for blood. *Boston Med Surg J*. 1902;146:427–429.
221. Myers W. On immunity against proteids. *Lancet*. 1900;156(4011):98–100.
222. Nuttall GH. On the formation of specific anti-bodies in the blood, following upon treatment with the sera of different animals. *Am Natur*. 1901;35(419):927–932.
223. Uhlenhuth PT. Eine methode zur unterscheidung der verschiedenen blutarten, im besonderen zum differentialdiagnostischen nachweise des menschenblutes. *Deutsche Med Wochenschrift*. 1901;27(6):82–83.
224. Uhlenhuth P. Über die entwicklung des biologischen eiweißdifferenzierungs-verfahrens im dienste der gerichtlichen medizin unter besonderer berücksichtigung eigener forschungsergebnisse (persönliche erinnerungen). *Deutsche Zeitschrift Gesamte Gerichtliche Med*. 1949;39:309–348.
225. Thomas JC. The examination of blood and seminal stains. *Pol J*. 1937;10(4):490–503.
226. Jones FE. Massachusetts Medico-Legal Society. *Boston Med Surg J*. 1902;146:440.
227. Sutherland WD. *Blood-Stains: Their Detection and the Determination of Their Source*. London: Bailliere, Tindall and Cox; 1907.
228. Pollack OJ. Semen and seminal stains. *Arch Pathol*. 1943;35:140.
229. Gradwohl R. *Clinical Laboratory Methods and Diagnosis*. vol. 1. St. Louis, MO: CV Mosby Company; 1956:574–654.
230. Ohya I, Iwasa M, Komoriya H, et al. Identification of human saliva by antisera to alpha-amylase in human salivary glands. *Tohoku J Exp Med*. 1986;150(3):309–315.
231. Wolfe HR. The effect of injection methods on the species specificity of serum precipitins. *J Immunol*. 1935;29(1):1–11.
232. Culliford BJ. Precipitin reactions in forensic problems: a new method for precipitin reactions on forensic blood, semen and saliva stains. *Nature*. 1964;201(4924):1092–1093.
233. Ouchterlony O. In vitro method for testing the toxin-producing capacity of diphtheria bacteria. *Acta Pathol Microbiol Scand*. 1948;25(1-2):186–191.
234. Ouchterlony O. Antigen-antibody reactions in gels. *Acta Pathol Microbiol Scand*. 1949;26(4):507–515.
235. Platt SR. The effects of the argon ion laser on subsequent blood examinations. *J Forensic Sci*. 1982;27(3): 726–728.
236. Macey HL. The identification of human blood in a 166 year old stain. *Can Soc Forensic Sci J*. 1979;12(4):191–193.
237. Swander CJ, Stites JG. Evaluation of the ABAcard HemaTrace for the forensic identification of human blood. *Midwest Assoc Forensic Sci*. 1998:1–5.
238. Balitzki-Korte B, Anslinger K, Bartsch C, et al. Species identification by means of pyrosequencing the mitochondrial 12S rRNA gene. *Int J Legal Med*. 2005;119(5):291–294.
239. Parson W, Pegoraro K, Niederstatter H, et al. Species identification by means of the cytochrome b gene. *Int J Legal Med*. 2000;114(1):23–28.
240. Saferstein R. *Identification and grouping of bloodstains. Forensic Science Handbook*. Prentice Hall; 1982:267–296.
241. Allison JE. Faecal occult blood testing for colorectal cancer. *Aliment Pharmacol Ther*. 1998;12(1):1–10.

242. Spear TF, Binkley SA. The HemeSelect test: a simple and sensitive forensic species test. *J Forensic Sci Soc.* 1994;34(1):41–46.
243. Lin H, Zhang Y, Wang Q, et al. Species identification of bloodstains by ATR-FTIR spectroscopy: the effects of bloodstain age and the deposition environment. *Int J Legal Med.* 2018;132(3):667–674.
244. Goodwin C, Higgins D, Tobe SS, et al. Singleplex quantitative real-time PCR for the assessment of human mitochondrial DNA quantity and quality. *Forensic Sci Med Pathol.* 2018;14:70–75.
245. Simon C, Buckley TR, Frati F, et al. Incorporating molecular evolution into phylogenetic analysis, and a new compilation of conserved polymerase chain reaction primers for animal mitochondrial DNA. *Ann Rev Ecol Evol Syst.* 2006;37:545–579.
246. Ramón-Laca A, Linacre AM, Gleeson DM, et al. Identification multiplex assay of 19 terrestrial mammal species present in New Zealand. *Electrophoresis.* 2013;34(24):3370–3376.
247. Tobe SS, Nic Daeid N. Commentary on: comparison of presumptive blood test kits including hexagon OBTI. *J Forensic Sci.* 2009;54(1):239.
248. Cromartie RL, Wardlow A, Duncan G, et al. Development of a microfluidic device (μPADs) for forensic serological analysis. *Analyt Meth.* 2019;11(5):587–595.
249. Smith E, Dent G. *Modern Raman Spectroscopy: A Practical Approach.* John Wiley & Sons; 2019.
250. Raman CV, Krishnan KS. A new type of secondary radiation. *Nature.* 1928;121(3048):501–502.
251. Virkler K, Lednev IK. Forensic body fluid identification: the Raman spectroscopic signature of saliva. *Analyst.* 2010;135(3):512–517.
252. Shaine ML, Premasiri WR, Ingraham HM, et al. Surface enhanced Raman scattering for robust, sensitive detection and confirmatory identification of dried bloodstains. *Analyst.* 2020;145(18):6097–6110.
253. Virkler K, Lednev IK. Blood species identification for forensic purposes using Raman spectroscopy combined with advanced statistical analysis. *Analyt Chem.* 2009;81(18):7773–7777.
254. Doty KC, McLaughlin G, Lednev IK. A Raman "spectroscopic clock" for bloodstain age determination: the first week after deposition. *Analyt Bioanalyt Chem.* 2016;408(15):3993–4001.
255. Takamura A, Watanabe D, Shimada R, et al. Comprehensive modeling of bloodstain aging by multivariate Raman spectral resolution with kinetics. *Comm Chem.* 2019;2(1):1–10.
256. Menżyk A, Damin A, Martyna A, et al. Toward a novel framework for bloodstains dating by Raman spectroscopy: how to avoid sample photodamage and subsampling errors. *Talanta.* 2020;209: 120565.
257. Sikirzhytskaya A, Sikirzhytski V, Pérez-Almodóvar L, et al. Raman spectroscopy for the identification of body fluid traces: semen and vaginal fluid mixture. *Forensic Chem.* 2023;32:100468.
258. Sender R, Fuchs S, Milo R. Revised estimates for the number of human and bacteria cells in the body. *PLoS Biol.* 2016;14(8):e1002533.
259. Savage DC. Microbial ecology of the gastrointestinal tract. *Ann Rev Microbiol.* 1977;31(1):107–133.
260. Wilson M. *Bacteriology of Humans: An Ecological Perspective.* John Wiley & Sons; 2009.
261. Capone KA, et al. Diversity of the human skin microbiome early in life. *J Invest Dermatol.* 2011;131(10): 2026–2032.
262. Dominguez-Bello MG, Costello EK, Contreras M, et al. Delivery mode shapes the acquisition and structure of the initial microbiota across multiple body habitats in newborns. *Proc Nat Acad Sci.* 2010;107(26): 11971–11975.
263. Rosenthal M, Goldberg D, Aiello A, et al. Skin microbiota: microbial community structure and its potential association with health and disease. *Infect Genet Evol.* 2011;11(5):839–848.
264. Tlaskalová-Hogenová H, Štěpánková R, Hudcovic T, et al. Commensal bacteria (normal microflora), mucosal immunity and chronic inflammatory and autoimmune diseases. *Immunol Lett.* 2004;93(2):97–108.
265. Fierer N, Hamady M, Lauber CL, et al. The influence of sex, handedness, and washing on the diversity of hand surface bacteria. *Proc Nat Acad Sci.* 2008;105(46):17994–17999.
266. Fierer N, Lauber CL, Zhou N, et al. Forensic identification using skin bacterial communities. *Proc Nat Acad Sci.* 2010;107(14):6477–6481.
267. Grice EA, Segre JA. The skin microbiome. *Nat Rev Microbiol.* 2011;9(4):244–253.
268. Kong HH. Skin microbiome: genomics-based insights into the diversity and role of skin microbes. *Trends Molec Med.* 2011;17(6):320–328.

269. Dong Q, Vilo C. Evaluation of the RDP classifier accuracy using 16S rRNA gene variable regions. *Metagenomics*. 2012;2012
270. Huber JA, Mark Welch DB, Morrison HG, et al. Microbial population structures in the deep marine biosphere. *Science*. 2007;318(5847):97–100.
271. Reveillaud J, Maignien L, Eren AM, et al. Host-specificity among abundant and rare taxa in the sponge microbiome. *ISME J*. 2014
272. Kennedy DM, Stanton J-AL, García JA, et al. Microbial analysis of bite marks by sequence comparison of streptococcal DNA. *PloS One*. 2012;7(12):e51757.
273. Budowle B, Schutzer SE, Morse SA, et al. Criteria for validation of methods in microbial forensics. *Appl Environ Microbiol*. 2008;74(18):5599–5607.
274. Budowle B, Williamson PC. *Microbial Forensics*. Wiley Online Library; 2011.
275. Dembek Z, Kortepeter M, Pavlin J. Discernment between deliberate and natural infectious disease outbreaks. *Epidemiol Infect*. 2007;135(3):353–371.
276. Iturbe-Ormaetxe I, Walker T, O'Neill SL. Wolbachia and the biological control of mosquito-borne disease. *EMBO Rep*. 2011;12(6):508–518.
277. Payne D. Watching the detectives: tracking the source of Europe's latest *E coli* outbreak. *BMJ*. 2011;342: d3884.
278. Cho KT, Richardson MM, Kirkbride KP, et al. Recovery and identification of bacterial DNA from illicit drugs. *Forensic Sci Int*. 2014;235:78–85.
279. Hanssen EN, Avershina E, Rudi K, et al. Body fluid prediction from microbial patterns for forensic application. *Forensic Sci Int Genet*. 2017;30:10–17.
280. Hanssen EN, Liland KH, Gill P, et al. Optimizing body fluid recognition from microbial taxonomic profiles. *Forensic Sci Int Genet*. 2018;37:13–20.
281. Bauer M, Patzelt D. Protamine mRNA as molecular marker for spermatozoa in semen stains. *Int J Legal Med*. 2003;117(3):175–179.
282. Wang Z, Zhang J, Luo H, et al. Screening and confirmation of microRNA markers for forensic body fluid identification. *Forensic Sc Int Genet*. 2013;7(1):116–123.
283. Hanson E, Ingold S, Dorum G, et al. Assigning forensic body fluids to DNA donors in mixed samples by targeted RNA/DNA deep sequencing of coding region SNPs using ion torrent technology. *Forensic Sci Int Genet Suppl*. 2019;7(1):23–24.
284. Zubakov D, Hanekamp E, Kokshoorn M, et al. Stable RNA markers for identification of blood and saliva stains revealed from whole genome expression analysis of time-wise degraded samples. *Int J Legal Med*. 2008;122:135–142.
285. Fleming R, Harbison SA. The development of an mRNA amplification positive control for the identification of body fluids. *Can Soc Forensic Sci J*. 2014;47(2):37–45.
286. Chen X, Ba Y, Ma L, et al. Characterization of microRNAs in serum: a novel class of biomarkers for diagnosis of cancer and other diseases. *Cell Res*. 2008;18(10):997–1006.
287. Mitchell PS, Parkin RK, Kroh EM, et al. Circulating microRNAs as stable blood-based markers for cancer detection. *Proc Nat Acad Sci*. 2008;105(30):10513–10518.
288. Nussbaumer C, Gharehbaghi-Schnell E, Korschineck I. Messenger RNA profiling: a novel method for body fluid identification by real-time PCR. *Forensic Sci Int*. 2006;157(2-3):181–186.
289. Juusola J, Ballantyne J. Messenger RNA profiling: a prototype method to supplant conventional methods for body fluid identification. *Forensic Sci Int*. 2003;135(2):85–96.
290. Juusola J, Ballantyne J. mRNA profiling for body fluid identification by multiplex quantitative RT-PCR. *J Forensic Sci*. 2007;52(6):1252–1262.
291. Fleming RI, Harbison S. The development of a mRNA multiplex RT-PCR assay for the definitive identification of body fluids. *Forensic Sci Int Genet*. 2010;4(4):244–256.
292. Albani PP, Fleming R. Novel messenger RNAs for body fluid identification. *Sci Just*. 2018;58(2):145–152.
293. Patel G, Peel C. Identifying the origin of cells. *Forensic Sci Int Genet Suppl*. 2008;1(1):574–576.
294. Setzer M, Juusola J, Ballantyne J. Recovery and stability of RNA in vaginal swabs and blood, semen, and saliva stains. *J Forensic Sci*. 2008;53(2):296–305.

295. Haas C, Hanson E, Bär W, et al. mRNA profiling for the identification of blood—results of a collaborative EDNAP exercise. *Forensic Sci Int Genet*. 2011;5(1):21–26.
296. Arroyo JD, Chevillet JR, Kroh EM, et al. Argonaute2 complexes carry a population of circulating microRNAs independent of vesicles in human plasma. *Proc Nat Acad Sci*. 2011;108(12):5003–5008.
297. Gallo A, Tandon M, Alevizos I, et al. The majority of microRNAs detectable in serum and saliva is concentrated in exosomes. *PloS One*. 2012;7(3):e30679.
298. Zhou Q, Li M, Wang X, et al. Immune-related microRNAs are abundant in breast milk exosomes. *Int J Biol Sci*. 2012;8(1):118.
299. Weber JA, Baxter DH, Zhang S, et al. The microRNA spectrum in 12 body fluids. *Clin Chem*. 2010;56(11):1733–1741.
300. Courts C, Madea B. Specific micro-RNA signatures for the detection of saliva and blood in forensic body-fluid identification. *J Forensic Sci*. 2011;56(6):1464–1470.
301. Zubakov D, Kokshoorn M, Kloosterman A, et al. New markers for old stains: stable mRNA markers for blood and saliva identification from up to 16-year-old stains. *Int J Legal Med*. 2009;123(1):71–74.
302. Simard AM, DesGroseillers L, Sarafian V. Assessment of RNA stability for age determination of body fluid stains. *Can Soc Forensic Sci J*. 2012;45(4):179–194.
303. Heneghan N, Fu J, Pritchard J, et al. The effect of environmental conditions on the rate of RNA degradation in dried blood stains. *Forensic Sci Int Genet*. 2021;51 102456.
304. Fu J, Allen RW. A method to estimate the age of bloodstains using quantitative PCR. *Forensic Sci Int Genet*. 2019;39:103–108.
305. Fang C, Zhao J, Li J, et al. Massively parallel sequencing of microRNA in bloodstains and evaluation of environmental influences on miRNA candidates using realtime polymerase chain reaction. *Forensic Sci Int Genet*. 2019;38:32–38.
306. Vennemann M, Koppelkamm A. mRNA profiling in forensic genetics I: possibilities and limitations. *Forensic Sci Int*. 2010;203(1-3):71–75.
307. Lee HY, Park MJ, Choi A, et al. Potential forensic application of DNA methylation profiling to body fluid identification. *Int J Legal Med*. 2012;126:55–62.
308. Song F, Smith JF, Kimura MT, et al. Association of tissue-specific differentially methylated regions (TDMs) with differential gene expression. *Proc Nat Acad Sci*. 2005;102(9):3336–3341.
309. Illingworth R, Kerr A, DeSousa D, et al. A novel CpG island set identifies tissue-specific methylation at developmental gene loci. *PLoS Biol*. 2008;6(1):e22.
310. Doi A, Park I-H, Wen B, et al. Differential methylation of tissue-and cancer-specific CpG island shores distinguishes human induced pluripotent stem cells, embryonic stem cells and fibroblasts. *Nat Genet*. 2009;41(12):1350–1353.
311. Kader F, Ghai M, Olaniran AO. Characterization of DNA methylation-based markers for human body fluid identification in forensics: a critical review. *Int J Legal Med*. 2020;134:1–20.
312. Frumkin D, Wasserstrom A, Budowle B, et al. DNA methylation-based forensic tissue identification. *Forensic Sci Int Genet*. 2011;5(5):517–524.
313. Herman JG, Graff JR, Myöhänen S, et al. Methylation-specific PCR: a novel PCR assay for methylation status of CpG islands. *Proc Nat Acad Sci*. 1996;93(18):9821–9826.
314. An JH, Choi A, Shin K-J, et al. DNA methylation-specific multiplex assays for body fluid identification. *Int J Legal Med*. 2013;127:35–43.
315. Forat S, Huettel B, Reinhardt R, et al. Methylation markers for the identification of body fluids and tissues from forensic trace evidence. *PloS One*. 2016;11(2):e0147973.
316. Vidaki A, Giangasparo F, Syndercombe Court D. Discovery of potential DNA methylation markers for forensic tissue identification using bisulphite pyrosequencing. *Electrophoresis*. 2016;37(21):2767–2779.
317. Holtkötter H, Schwender K, Wiegand P, et al. Marker evaluation for differentiation of blood and menstrual fluid by methylation-sensitive SNaPshot analysis. *Int J Legal Med*. 2018;132(2):387–395.
318. Naue J, Hoefsloot HC, Kloosterman AD, et al. Forensic DNA methylation profiling from minimal traces: how low can we go? *Forensic Sci Int Genet*. 2018;33:17–23.

319. Silva DS, Antunes J, Balamurugan K, et al. Developmental validation studies of epigenetic DNA methylation markers for the detection of blood, semen and saliva samples. *Forensic Sci Int Genet*. 2016;23:55–63.
320. Choung CM, Lee JW, Park JH, et al. A forensic case study for body fluid identification using DNA methylation analysis. *Legal Med*. 2021;51:101872.
321. Adams EG, Wraxall BG. Phosphatases in body fluids: the differentiation of semen and vaginal secretion. *Forensic Sci*. 1974;3:57–62.
322. Parker GJ, McKiernan HE, Legg KM, et al. Forensic proteomics. *Forensic Sci Int Genet*. 2021;54 102529.
323. Al-Amrani S, Al-Jabri Z, Al-Zaabi A, et al. Proteomics: concepts and applications in human medicine. *World J Biol Chem*. 2021;12(5):57.
324. Grassl N, Kulak NA, Pichler G, et al. Ultra-deep and quantitative saliva proteome reveals dynamics of the oral microbiome. *Genome Med*. 2016;8(1):1–13.
325. Jodar M, Sendler E, Krawetz SA. The protein and transcript profiles of human semen. *Cell Tissue Res*. 2016;363:85–96.
326. Diamandis EP, Arnett WP, Foussias G, et al. Seminal plasma biochemical markers and their association with semen analysis findings. *Urology*. 1999;53(3):596–603.
327. Igoh A, Doi Y, Sakurada K. Identification and evaluation of potential forensic marker proteins in vaginal fluid by liquid chromatography/mass spectrometry. *Analyt Bioanalyt Chem*. 2015;407:7135–7144.
328. Visith T. Recent progress in urinary proteomics. *Proteomic Clin Appl*. 2007;1(8):780–791.
329. Harald M, A JB, Jan N. High-resolution proteome/peptidome analysis of peptides and low-molecular-weight proteins in urine. *Proteomic Clin Appl*. 2007;1(8):792–804.
330. Kashimura S, Hara K, Nakazono T, et al. Identification of human urine stains by HPLC analysis of 17-ketosteroid conjugates. *J Forensic Sci*. 2002;47(3):568–572.
331. Yu Y, Prassas I, Muytjens CM, et al. Proteomic and peptidomic analysis of human sweat with emphasis on proteolysis. *J Proteomic*. 2017;155:40–48.
332. Yang H, Zhou B, Prinz M, et al. Proteomic analysis of menstrual blood. *Molec Cell Proteomic*. 2012;11(10):1024–1035.
333. Ruhlen RL, Sauter ER. Proteomics of nipple aspirate fluid, breast cyst fluid, milk, and colostrum. *Proteomic Clin Appl*. 2007;1(8):845–852.
334. Van Steendam K, De Ceuleneer M, Dhaenens M, et al. Mass spectrometry-based proteomics as a tool to identify biological matrices in forensic science. *Int J Legal Med*. 2013;127:287–298.
335. Yang H, Zhou B, Deng H, et al. Body fluid identification by mass spectrometry. *Int J Legal Med*. 2013;127:1065–1077.
336. Donfack J, Wiley A. Mass spectrometry-based cDNA profiling as a potential tool for human body fluid identification. *Forensic Sci Int Genet*. 2015;16:112–120.
337. Liu W, Butler E, Yang H, et al. *Informatics approaches to forensic body fluid identification by proteomic mass spectrometry. Applications in Forensic Proteomics: Protein Identification and Profiling*. ACS Publications; 2019:81–90.
338. McKiernan HE, Brown CO, Arantes LC, et al. *NextGen serology: leveraging mass spectrometry for protein-based human body fluid identification. Applications in Forensic Proteomics: Protein Identification and Profiling*. ACS Publications; 2019:47–80.

Index

Page numbers followed by *f* indicate figures and *t* indicate tables.